117896

# The
# Renaissance
# New
# Testament

## Randolph O. Yeager

**VOLUME ELEVEN**

Acts 24:1—28:31
Romans 1:1—8:39

PELICAN PUBLISHING COMPANY

GRETNA 1983

Library of Congress Cataloging in Publication Data

Yeager, Randolph O.
    The Renaissance New Testament.

    Volumes 1-4 originally published in 1976-1978 by
Renaissance Press, Bowling Green, Ky.
    1. Bible. N.T.--Concordances, Greek.  2.  Greek
language, Biblical.  I. Title.
BS2302. Y4  1981          225.4'8'0321          79-28652
ISBN: 0-88289-758-6 (v. 11)

Manufactured in the United States of America

Published by Pelican Publishing Company, Inc.
1101 Monroe Street, Gretna, Louisiana  70053

# Creation, Science, Economics, Politics and the United States Constitution - a Potpourri

**Introduction** — Thoughtful people are those who are not emotionally inflamed by prejudice. There are thoughtless people on both sides of the current brouhaha over the question as to whether or not the Genesis account of creation can, in any constitutional way be taught in a classroom supported by tax revenues.

A story in *The Washington Post* recently said that a committee had reported favourably on the qualifications of science majors who earned Bachelor of Science degrees in a Virginia fundamentalist college to teach general science subjects - chemistry, biology, zoology, geology and physics, in Virginia High Schools. The committee is said to have recommended that the Virginia State Board of Education certify that the people in question be allowed to teach. More recently, due to statements by the President of the college in question, over a nationwide television network, another committee has reversed the recommendation of the first and, at present, the question as to whether the biblical account of creation will be taught as science in tax supported schools in Virginia is in some doubt.

If the argument is submitted to the Federal District Court for adjudication the question upon which the decision must turn seems to be this: can the Genesis account of creation be supported *solely* by an application of the scientific method, without reference to any argument that can objectively be called theology, philosophy or religion? If evidence that depends upon sense perception is available that *proves*, in the sense in which science uses that verb, that the universe was created on an *ex nihilo nihil fit* basis, in a series of flash actions that extended over six twenty-four hour days, at a time not more than ten thousand years ago, then public school teachers ought to be allowed to say so. That is, if the witness can be found who can say that he was there and saw it and heard it and smelled it and tasted it and touched it, and therefore he knows that that is how it happened, then it is true. This is what we mean by the scientific method. But if the proof for the view that the universe and all that is therein was created by God, and not by a random concatenation of material units, as the Neodarwinists insist, requires a reference to *God* or *the Bible*, as these terms are used to speak of religion, then there is clear constitutional language in the first amendment to mandate that such teaching must be confined to platforms and pulpits that are supported only by those who wish such doctrines taught and in support of which teaching no other person is compelled by law to contribute.

There is no constitutional injunction against teaching nonesense in tax supported schools. But the scientific method forbids a teacher to say that something is true before proof that it is true is at hand. A teacher who tells his students that evolution is true is not breaking the law, but he is prostituting the scientific method. For an evolutionist in a public school has no more right to say that evolution has been *proved* than the Christian has to say that science *proves* the existence of God. It was Alphonso the Learned, King of Spain from 1252 to 1284, who said, "Had I been present at the creation I would have given some useful hints for the better ordering of the universe." Dean Acheson, Secretary of State during the second Truman administration, did not really mean it when he called his book *Present at the Cretion - My Years in the State Department*, but when one listens to the Neodarwinists dogmatize about evolution, and to the preachers, speaking as scientists, dogmatize about creation, one gets the impression that they were there and are telling us what they experienced.

Fifty years ago a radio comedian listened to his friend Charlie tell a story, the acceptance of the truth of which taxed his credulity beyond endurance. In search of empirical evidence that Charlie was indeed telling the truth he asked, "Vas you dere, Sharlie?" Apparently Charlie was not present and had not spoken out of his experience, which means that his friend was free to accept or reject the story, depending upon how much faith he had in Charlie's veracity.

The Apostle John wrote, "And the angel which I saw stand upon the sea and upon the earth lifted up his hand to heaven" (Revelation 10:5). A scientist, with proper skepticism, might say, "But John it is impossible for an angel to stand with one foot upon the sea and the other upon the land!" Whereupon John replies, "But I *saw* it." The only question then is whether or not John is

iv

telling the truth. If he is the scientist must accept it.

Most Neodarwinists tell us that there is no doubt that the scientific evidence supports their story - that it is no longer hypothetical. There are a few who have retained their integrity, just as there are a few preachers who know enough about epistemology and Christianity to say that Christians accept the Bible by faith, not by science. I have not found a single evolutionist who is willing to say that he was present at the creation. Of course if such could be found, he would not use the word "creation." He would say that he was present when the random union of the first two amino acid building blocks of life united. Nor have I seen the preacher who will tell us that the reason why he can prove by science that God created the universe in six days is because he was there. This is why preachers who understand this do not say that they can prove that the Genesis account of creation is true. Indeed it is true. But Christians who understand their epistemology assert this by faith in the proposition that the Bible is the Word of God and that it speaks without error when it is speaking of those matters *which are structural to the Christian system.* And that is why they should not ask to teach their views in the public school classrooms. That is why the Supreme Court must say, if and when it reviews the decision of the lower court, that the first amendment forbids the teaching of religion at the expense of the tax payers.

But the same amendment that forbids the teaching of religion in the public schools protects the Christian's right to teach what he believes anywhere else, so long as he does not compel those who disagree with him to help pay the bills. Thus the Christian preacher can preach creation and attack evolution, in his home, at the Rotary Club (provided that he is invited to speak), on the street corner (provided that his crowd does not block the traffic and/or his voice does not constitute a public nuisance) and in his own pulpit. If the unbeliever is present and does not like what he hears, at least he is not forced to put his money in the offering plate, and he can walk out any time he wishes.

**Social Darwinism - The Logical Conclusion of Evolution.**
Neodarwinism, as taught by all except the intellectual lilliputians who teach theistic evolution, is an atheistic, materialistic, nihilistic, amoral theory of diabolical origin that spills over into the Social Sciences to justify the jungle law of the survival of the fittest, with

its doctrine that biggest is always best and that there are no natural rights as that term was understood by Rousseau, Locke, Montesquieu and Thomas Jefferson. William Graham Sumner, America's "Little Sir Echo" for Herbert Spencer, occupied the chair of Economics and Political Science at Yale from 1872 to 1909, when he became Professor Emeritus. He is famous, or if you like, infamous for his remark that "If a man cannot make his way in this world let him make his way out of it." This means, if it means anything at all, that all that the Bible says about helping the weak and feeding the poor is wrong. We live on an overcrowded planet where the escalating demand for minimal subsistence outruns possible supply. Not all can live. Someone must starve to death in order that others may survive. If it is true that survival depends upon fitness, and that the fittest are the best as evidenced by the fact that they overcame the unfit in the struggle for survival, then there should be nothing but rejoicing that the unfit perished, for if they had not, they would have lived to populate the planet with their unfit progeny. Thus Sumner gave his students at Yale their choice - "Let it be understood that we cannot go outside of this alternative: liberty, inequality, survival of the fittest: not-liberty, equality, survival of the unfittest. The former carries society forward and favors all its best members; the latter carries society downwards and favors all its worst members." (As cited in Richard Hofstadter, *Social Darwinism in American Thought,* 51). That from a preacher who was "ordained a priest of the Protestant Episcopal Church in 1869, was assistant rector of Calvary Church, New York city, and in 1870-72 was rector of the Church of the Redeemer, Morristown (N.J.)." (*Encyclopaedia Britannica*, 21, 559). If you are wondering what this genius was doing during the American Civil War, he was a student at Yale until 1863, when he went to Europe to study French and Hebrew in Geneva for a year, after which he studied divinity and history at Gottingen until 1866 (*Ibid.*). Though Sumner was not yet an evolutionist when he was drafted by the Lincoln government to fight in the Union army, he must have had some presentiment about the "survival of the fittest" and the necessity for him therefore to survive. The best way to survive when others are getting killed on a battlefield is to hire a substitute to do one's dying. This is what William Graham Sumner did. It is interesting that his most vocal opponent, Lester Ward, whose *Dynamic Sociology* opposed Sumner's *Folkways* with its Social Darwinism, served two years in the Civil War and suffered severe wounds at Chancellorsville (Hofstadter, *Social Darwinism*, 69). Although Ward accepted Darwin he rejected the view of Spencer and Sumner that survival of the fittest in the areas of natural science meant Social Darwinism. One wonders whether we might have been spared the poverty of the Great Depression (1929-1933) if the roles of Sumner and Ward had been reversed during the Civil War.

It is apparent to those who enjoy only superficial acquaintance with the writings of the Apostle Paul that he was not a Social Darwinist. For him the presence of the stranger,the naked, the hungry and thirsty, the poor, friendless and imprisoned in society offered an opportunity for the Christian, genuinely born again as a result of the theological gospel and aware of the implications of theology in the social gospel to give a cup of cold water "in my Name" and thus gain a reward.

Paul was a capitalist. He believed in the sanctity of private property rights. He believed in hard work and the profit motive. But he also believed in a redistribution of the wealth. In Ephesians 4:28 he endorsed Moses' law that had said, "Thou shalt not steal." Paul's version is "Let him that stole steal no more." He worked hard for a living. He made tents and he believed that able-bodied Christians should work hard, for he added, "but rather let him labour." Paul was not afraid to soil his hands which were probably callused as they wrought with knife, awl, needle, thread and canvas. The Christian also should be found " . . . working with his hands." Paul believed in the profit motive - ". . . the thing which is good." And the result was private ownership - ". . . that he may have. . . ." Finally what are we to do with what we have? ". . . to give to him that needeth." Thus we have the Christian conception of the capitalist system of production and distribution. Social Darwinists approve of Paul's views on production, but no evolutionist who really believes that progress in society depends upon the survival only of those who are fit can endorse the distribution of the fruits of production to the unfit. If the needy were fit and thus entitled to survive to produce the next generation they would not be needy. They would have made it on their own.

These matters are so obvious that we are amazed to note the inconsistency of the Fundamentalist political and economic right as they inveigh against evolution while they support Social

Darwinism at the polls! If Fundamentalists feel impelled to attack evolution, as indeed they ought, since the Bible describes it as heresy and true scientists can advance it only as an unproved hypothesis, how can they support with their money, their votes and their media propaganda the political and economic right that legislates the survival of the fittest? Since evolution, with its dogma that might ultimately is right and therefore that the mighty should be allowed to wage their jungle warfare against their competition in the market place with every weapon of claw and fang, then the Bible is wrong with its plea that the weak and helpless be supported. Evolution demands that they should be left to perish, since it is inevitable that they will in fact be left to perish. Indeed it is only if they are left to perish that evolution can do its glorious work of elevating the human race. But the Fundamentalists, at least those who have the attention of the media, are found in support of the party which has a long record of throwing the weight of government behind and in support of the giant multinational corporations with their wealth, while withholding societal support from those who are in need. This is why the theological conservative, who must reject evolution, not only because the evolutionists have never demonstrated that it is true, but also because his *a priori* position is on the side of the Bible, which clearly says that evolution is untrue, must be a political and economic liberal. Skepticism is the mark of the mature mind, and theologians who, though not science majors, at least know enough about science to recognize the scientific method when they see it, are magnificently and hilariously skeptical about Darwin's dream of 150 years ago that man, thanks to survival of the fittest, is a rising creature. By means of the law of claw and fang man will evolve to the point where the struggle for survival by which he left the primeval slime, grew wings and flew through the air, grew legs and climbed a tree and then grew a brain, descended from the tree and went to graduate school, will no longer be necessary!

The alternative to that is that we accept *a priori* what the Bible says about creation and the *weltanschauung* by which the Christian interprets history.

Social Darwinism is the result of Spencer's efforts to show that all social, economic, moral, ethical, political and theological theory must conform to the basic dogma - there is no God who can be known in the traditional theistic sense and there was no creation. There was an accidental union of primeval "something or other" (they do not quite know what), blessed with the good fortune of *The Three Princes of Serendip,* *which progressed by chance in a way that will blow the mind of all except mature thinkers who are by nature skeptics. This for Spencer and William Graham Sumner was the basic fact of life and they were eager to apply it in all of the Social Sciences, so that all men might rejoice in the prospect of the bright future which such truth portends. All men should awake at dawn and repeat, "Every day in every way I am getting better and better." This was to be the fitting substitute for "This is the day that the Lord hath made. I will rejoice and be glad in it." All could depend upon it. Natural law had been found to be working all things together to bring about the inevitable and happy conclusion.

If evolution is true it forms the core of reality around which all other truths must gather and with the basic tenets of which all other dogmas must conform. This is what Herbert Spencer, whose intellectual sophistication was admired far more in America than in his native Britain, where more brain power than he had is needed to leave an impression, tried to show in his *A System of Synthetic Philosophy.* Spencer tried to do for Charles Darwin what *The Renaissance New Testament* is doing for the Lord Jesus Christ. "In Him are hid all of the treasures of wisdom and knowledge" (Colossians 2:3). Spencer tried to show that in Darwin and his dogma, based as it was upon his observation of finches in the Galapagos Islands, are hid everything else that is true.

**Classical Economics and Evolution.** There have been only four great books written about economics. The science that examines and seeks to explain how society maximizes utility in a world of scarcity has risen to four great mountain peaks of literary exposition. In 1776 Adam Smith gave to the world his *Inquiry into the Nature and Causes of the Wealth of Nations.* In 1867 Karl Marx published the first volume of his *Das Kapital.* Volumes two and three of this great work, edited by Engels were published posthumously in 1885 and 1894 respectively. Alfred Marshall released for publication his *Principles of Economics* in 1890, and in 1936 John Maynard Keynes gave to the world his masterpiece *The General Theory of Employment, Interest and Money.* Thus were expounded in order Classical Economics, Communism, Neo-Classicism and Keynesian thought. Each has left its indelible mark upon our thinking. It was Alfred Marshall who said *natura non facit saltum* - "nature makes no leaps," by which he meant that

> Economic science is, and must be, one of slow and continuous growth. Some of the best work of the present generation has indeed appeared at first sight to be antagonistic to that of earlier writers; but when it has had time to settle into its proper place, and its rough edges have been worn away, it has been found to involve no real breach of continuity in the development of the science.
>
> The present treatise is an attempt to present a modern version of the old doctrines with the aid of the new work, and with reference to the new problems, of our own age.

Alfred Marshall, Principles of Economics

Thus our knowledge of the Social Sciences evolves. Each generation of economic thinkers stands upon the shoulders of its predecessors, accepting what is valid, rejecting what is false, emphasizing that which has been stressed too little and scaling down that which has been overemphasized. Each of the writers mentioned built upon his own assumption and has succeeded or failed depending upon whether his basic assumption was correct or not. Thus Adam Smith rebelled against the Mercantilism of his day because he accepted the dogma of the Age of Reason that man was a rational creature and that nature is kind to man if she is only given a chance to work her blessings upon us.

Karl Marx accepted much of the Classical thought of Adam Smith. His assumption was that there is no God and that ours is a world under the influence only of materialistic forces by which we are enslaved. Thus all of human culture is the result of the mode of the production of goods and services. This is called Economic Determinism. Marx was not glad that Classical Economics carried within it the seeds of its own destruction and must fall to the dicatatorship of the proletariat, after which the state would gradually fade away and anarchy would result. He was neither glad nor sad that such would be the case. He only predicted that since there was no God and no idealism, since man could not act, but only react to environmental forces over which he had no control, the conclusion that he predicted was certain to come to pass. Marx examined Classical Economics as he saw it in operation in England and upon the Continent and described its course and the inevitability of its demise. That his prophecy failed is due only to the fact that his materialistic *a priori* was wrong. Man can think creatively. He does have some control over his environment. You can teach a boy to ride a bicycle and you can teach a monkey to ride a bicycle. But if the chains fall off their sprocket wheels, the boy has sense enough to look at the problem, solve it mentally, put the chain back on the wheel and ride on. The monkey does not have that much sense. Thus the monkey is enslaved by an environment that he does not understand. The boy is not. Marx's mistake was his assumption that men are only evolved monkeys. It was inconceivable to him that economists, like Marshall and Keynes could look at Classical Economics, see what was wrong, modify it and go on to a better Capitalism. Yet that is what happened. Marshall improved upon the Classicists and Keynes made further improvements over the Marshallian system. Yet each school of thought has retained those elements of truth which were found in their predecessors.

Adam Smith was nothing if not an optimist. He lived during the Age of Reason as the English called it. The French called it *siecle de la lumiere*, "the century of light" and the Germans *aufklarung* - "the enlightenment." England had been treated to the empiricism of John Locke, David Hume and George Berkeley in the 17th and 18th centuries after having been introduced to the inductive method by Francis Bacon, who died in 1626, only six years before Locke was born. Locke, who died in 1704 gave systematic exposition to Bacon's scientific method in his *Essay Concerning Human Understanding*, published in 1690, in which he described the mind of man at birth a *tabula rasa* - "a blank tablet" highly impressionable but as yet wholly unimpressed and thus subject to the sensational impressions of the environment. Thus man can know only that which he senses. *Nihil est in intellectu nisi prius fuerit in sensu* - "nothing in the intellect except what was first of all in the senses."

The French who had been under the dictatorship of the *Ancien Regime*, a coalition of the royal power of the Bourbons and the ecclessiastic power of the Roman Catholic Church, since the days of Henry IV, were in the midst of a heated revolt which culminated in the French Revolution. The Physiocrats, led by the horse doctor, Francois Quesnay, who doubled in his ministrations as the medical attendant of the Queen, preached Physiocracy - "the rule of nature." They said that nature was kind and good and would, if we allowed her to do so, rescue society from the galling yoke of Bourbon and Church rule. France was also listening to Jean

Jacques Rousseau, who gave us *The Social Contract* with which our founding fathers were so enamoured when they wrote our Constitution, Voltaire, Condorcet, Diderot, the Encyclopedist, Montesquieu who taught us about the separation between legislative, judicial and executive power in his *The Spirit of the Laws,* Marat, Danton and Robespierre. As these revolutionaries wrote, preached, demonstrated in the streets of Paris, tore down the Bastille with their bare hands, beheaded the jailor and carried his head on a pike down the street, captured Louis XVI and his wife, Marie Antoinnette and gathered around the guillotine, in the *Place del Revolution* (now called *Place del Concorde!*), heads rolled, including those of the King and Queen, while Edmund Burke, across the Channel in England, while sympathetic to the need for some change in the status quo, clucked his tongue in distress at the method by which change was being made.

In Germany, the theism of the German churches, after the Peace of Westphalia in 1648, was challenged by the Idealism of Immanuel Kant, who gave a devastating rebuttal to the radical empiricism of Locke, Hume and Berkeley but only at the expense of the theology of the Lutheran churches. For Kant knowledge was possible only for those who had reasoned deductively from sense perception. Locke's dictum that there is nothing in the intellect without first of all being in the senses had been effectively answered by Leibnitz, who said, "nothing indeed except the intellect itself" and by Spinoza, who was certain that the human mind could deduce from sense perception how the laws of nature, as demonstrated in his "block universe" worked. But Kant proved to most people, except the Lutheran preachers, who named their dogs after him, that no one could be certain that Christianity was the truth except the first century Christians who had actually seen our Lord and witnessed his miracles, heard His teachings and seen Him after His resurrection. For the rest of us, there was nothing to support our faith in Christ except our faith in a Book that told about Him.

Thus Adam Smith who was not an economist, but a Professor of Moral Philosophy wrote his optimistic book which proved that nations were certain to become more wealthy, at a time when Europe was in wholesale revolt against the theological idea that man was lost in sin and doomed to blunder his miserable way through life, characterized only by irrationality and ineptitude. *Au contraire* the church was wrong. Man was neither good nor bad at birth but nature was kind and progress was possible.

The quarter century between the Peace of Paris of 1763 and the outbreak of the French Revolution in 1789 was generally one of optimism, both in Europe and in America. The Seven Years War, which was really the first World War, since it was fought in America, in Europe and in India was over. England and France had fought for control of North America for 150 years. Now it was generally agreed that North America would be British and the French seemed satisfied to have it so. The prospects for peace looked good. To be sure Great Britain lost political control over her most valuable colonies during this period, but though the lines of political control were forever broken at Yorktown in 1781 the lines of economic intercourse fell back into their old channels. The United States was worth far more to Britain, now that she was free from the controls of Mercantilism and able to exploit her vast resources on the frontier which, at that time, stretched away to the Mississippi River, with nothing to hinder except the Indians and the Spanish at the mouth of the Mississippi. Population in the United States was exploding at a time when there was plenty of cheap land on the frontier. The wagons moved westward, pushed by high land prices and low wages in the East and cheap land and high wages in the West. Land hunger was compelling and land could be had for two dollars an acre in the Ohio Valley.

Thus England's defeat in the American Revolution turned out to be a blessing in disguise for all concerned. The dark days of the French Revolution and the Napoleonic Wars were as yet unanticipated. Physiocracy dictated that the rule of nature, which was beneficent would soon replace the dictatorship of Mercantilism in the economic world and Jesuit intolerance in the world of religion. With political, economic and religious overlords out of the way, man, who had been cruelly maligned by the Church and the Bible as being lost in sin and deceived by Satan was now about to be free from all that had bound him for centuries.

It is not then until we view the additions of the Reverend Thomas Robert Malthus (1766-1834) and David Ricardo, the Jewish banker in London, to the Classical Economics of Adam Smith that we understand Thomas Carlyle's remark when he called Malthus and Ricarco "the professors of the dismal science." Until they came along economics was far from dismal. Malthus in his *Essay on the Principle of Population* (1798) showed that the sex oriented human race was predestined to breed itself into poverty, malnutrition and

xiii

starvation. But his book triggered Darwin's thought that it is only through struggle that evolution works its magic for ultimate improvement. Thus while Malthus was a short-run pessimist, he was a long-run optimist. This refinement in thought did not occur to nineteenth century social scientists however until Darwin pointed it out.

Another page in the book of Classical Economics, once regarded by Adam Smith as a rosy tinted sunrise to a better future, but a little later threatened with the Malthusian storm signals, was the "wages-fund" theory of David Ricardo. Thanks to him the future held out little hope for the masses. "Wages-fund" theory says that at any given point in time there is a fixed amount of capital investment, in terms of plant capacity, technology and unsold inventory, and that wages are paid out of that capital. Wages, therefore, could never rise higher than the quotient resulting when capital is divided by the number of workers in the labor force. Ricardo did not say that wages would be equal, but he did say that the average wage could rise no higher than the quotient thus derived. Thus as Malthus' law dictated that population would rise by geometric progression while capital increased only arithmetically, it follows that the labor force, increasing *pari passu* the population would be forced to accept smaller and smaller wages. This would be the inevitable trend until average wages fell below the subsistence level. The same phenomenon - rising population - would increase demand for food and housing, thus forcing up the price, while it would force per capita wages to fall. With lower money wages with which to buy the worker would face higher prices. Thus fewer pounds at the pay window had less purchasing power at the food counter and the standard of living plunged at a geometric rate. The result was malnutrition and exposure which in turn increased the probability that the worker and his family would fall victim to the next epidemic that swept the community. No wonder Carlyle said that economics as taught by Malthus and Ricardo was dismal.

But when Darwin read Malthus he saw a silver lining in the cloud that everyone else thought was dark indeed. "Good," said he, "because the fit can survive only as the unfit die, and that is nature's way of improving man's lot on earth."

"Good," also quoth Ricardo, "because when starvation and

disease (aided now and then by a convenient war!) reduces the labor force, wages will rise, the survivors will regain their health as more and better food, housing and medical care are available and the population will rise again! And here we go again! The essence of this set of dogmas is that if Malthus is correct (and he is) and if Ricardo had been correct (and he was not), per capita wages could only fluctuate between points slightly above and slightly below subsistence. Thus population would rise, as indeed it did in England throughout the 19th century, but there could never be any rise in the standard of living of the labor force.

Ricardo went on to say that since wages are paid out of capital, and since the number of workers, who must work or starve to death increases faster than the wages fund from which they are paid, the efforts of organized labor to raise wages are futile. One segment of the labor force might strike to enforce demands for higher wages and better working conditions, but success could come only at the expense of other unorganized workers. Thus *laissez faire*. Government cannot by taking thought ameliorate conditions in society. Thus Ricardo's thought is called "the iron law of wages." After 1859 evolutionists added, "Why should government make such attempts to interfere, since we now understand that natural law has already dictated that things will improve. Let us be patient."

David Ricardo was wrong of course. Wages are paid out of the production that capital produces, not out of capital itself. In one small sense Ricardo was correct. Depreciation reduces the wages fund as the plant wears out. Thus on a ten percent writeoff the taxable value of the capital is reduced to zero after ten years, but during those ten years the market value of production has far exceeded the profits which the entrepreneur expected to make and has any moral right to accept. Since 1935 in the United States the right of labor to organize and bargain collectively has been recognized and encouraged by law. The result has been the rise both of wages and of profits and thus the total productive capacity and performance of the economy has grown in exponential terms. Ricardo's weak, sick and starving factory workers now play golf, drive a new car, enjoy air-conditioned housing, send their children to college and eat so much and so well that they have a weight problem.

Adam Smith thought that he was giving to the world a message of cheer. The Physiocrats had shown that the rule of nature was benign. We needed only to cease our efforts to control her. When the efforts of the Mercantilists of the business community, in league with Bourbon kings and Roman Catholic prelates were abondoned all would be right.

But with the coming of Malthus and Ricardo the sunny skies of Classical Economics were darkened by the threatening clouds of poverty and misery for all but a few in a capitalistic society. However, even before Darwin, Herbert Spencer and William Graham Sumner assured us that what was inevitable was also good since it resulted in the elimination of the unfit and assured progress, Jean Baptiste Say pointed out another bit of good news. The Classical system was depression proof.

Jean Baptiste Say (1767-1832) was a French economist at the Sorbonne in Paris whose role was that of "Little Sir Echo" for Adam Smith. He added to the thought of Classical Economics with his "Law of Markets" which "proved" that there could never be a prolonged downswing of the business cycle since money not spent for consumption would accumulate until the interest rate would fall to the point where it could be spent profitably for production. Say said that if the dollar is saved it is certain to be poured back into the circular flow by new investment, either in terms of new plant, new technology or new inventories. Thus the proper policy during a recession is *laissez faire*, since the economy has a built in adjustment. To interfere in an attempt to counter the downswing is only to make it worse. Say preached this until everyone, except Thomas Carlyle forgot about the sufferings of the poverty-stricken labor force as they rejoiced in the fact that the economy would always operate at full or near full employment.

Says' error was his failure to understand that there are three, not two motives for holding money. He knew about the Transactions and the Precautionary motives. We hold money to buy what we need now (the Transactions function) and we also save some of it in order to buy what we may need in the uncertain future (the Precautionary function). Say overlooked the Speculative Motive. Money can also be used in the money market, thanks to fluctuating interest rates, not to build new plant capacity, develop new technology, provide jobs and increase the quantity of goods and services in the market, thus to enrich society, but to make more money. A United States Treasury bill that yields 15% per annum enriches the millionaire with a million dollars that he does not need to the extent of $150,000 per year, one half of which he can keep in taxes. But that is not an investment in goods and/or services. It is an investment in money and it does nothing to counter the downswing of the business cycle.

If Say had read Aristotle he would have known about the Speculative Motive for in his *Politics,* I, 10, 1258b, Aristotle distinguishes between ὁ οἰκονόμος - "one who manages a household" by which he means one who engages in the production and exchange of goods and thus increases the wealth of society, and ὁ χρηματιστής - "a money getter" or a "trafficker." The former is engaging in a natural function and that is good. The latter is pursuing an unnatural course and that is bad. In Aristotle's words

There are two sorts of wealth-getting, as I have said; one is a part of household management, the other is retail trade: the former necessary and honourable, while that which consists in exchange is justly censured; for it is unnatural, and a mode by which men gain from one another. The most hated sort, and with the greatest reason, is usury, which makes a gain out of money itself, and not from the natural object of it. For money was intended to be used in exchange, but not to increase at interest. And this term interest, which means the birth of money from money, is applied to be breeding of money because the offspring resembles the parent. Wherefore of all modes of getting wealth this is the most unnatural.

The chief reason why the rich do not invest the new wealth which they have as a result of income tax reduction, in new plant capacity, new technology and new products, thus to reduce unemployment, relieve  poverty and expand the economy to full employment, is that the money market offers interest rates which are as high, if not higher than anticipated profits. The money market offers the added advantage that it is risk proof. Thus the rich, in a position in which they have no further Transactions Motive (what could they buy more than what they already have?), and who need give no attention to the Precautionary Motive, are faced with the choices of investment in goods and services,which entails risks and offers uncertain profits or of investment in money markets which offers the same or even higher returns and no risks. Thus they are *Chrematistes* instead of *Oikonomists* - "money getters" not "profit makers." As long as interest rates are higher than expected profits plus taxes this situation will not change.

J.B.Says' "law of markets" was widely accepted on the

Continent, in England and in America throughout the 19th century, because it tended to allay the fears of business men and politicians that the business cycle might, after all, be subject to wide fluctuations of effective demand. If the economy is depression proof, as Says' law argued, then there is reason for optimism. How delighted then they were when, in 1859 they read Darwin's *Origin of Species*, which assured them that preachers, with their dreary message from the Bible about the fall of man and his ultimate confused ineptitude, were wrong and that the truth, as now made clear by Darwin, is that man has survived by virtue of the fact that every generation has been made superior to its parents and have proved this by surviving in the fierce conflict to produce the next. If man is increasingly rational as generations are born, struggle, survive, beget the next generation and then die, the future is indeed bright. And since it is the rational consumer who gives the signals to the rational producer, who then produces that which society needs most, societal utility is certain to increase.

Supply side economics with its "trickle down" theory was conceived within the philosophical womb of Physiocracy in France in the last half of the 18th century. Physiocracy is Greek for "the rule of nature." The Bible says that nature is under the curse of man's sin and therefore that nature is not kind. It is very unkind and heartless. But evolution says that the rule of nature, which upon superficial examination seems cruel, is good for those who really understand her. Of course no one understood nature until Darwin wrote his book in 1859! As the strong survive at the expense of the weak who, fortunately, perish, they produce the next generation. The development is one of progress. The evolutionary road is up. Mutation is the fortunate result. The new mutant is superior to his predecessor. He can survive in an unfriendly environment. In fact it was the inability of the previous generation to change that brought about extinction. Man will some day evolve to the point where he recognizes that war is stupid. Of course when that time comes, if he is still confined to this small planet, if he abolishes war he must find some other way to curtail population if he is to be spared the conflict that grows out of competition for food. When the man/land ratio curve becomes negative food prices will rise, the poor will get hungry, compete for food, then fight over it and we are back to war. The Reverend Malthus should take a bow! Of course future man, since he will be smarter than his predecessors, just as Darwin was smarter than Jesus, will be able to handle the overpopulation problem by aborting the unwanted fetus. His conscience need not bother him for he has no conscience, since he understands situation ethics. He need not be concerned about natural rights because Thomas Jefferson was wrong about natural rights. Natural rights do not exist in the evolutionary system, since man is not the product of divine creation but of random natural selection. If abortion does not solve the problem of overpopulation future man can resort to infanticide. The fires of Moloch can always be kindled if too many babies are born. Of course the aged must be allowed to live only so long as they are able to work and produce what the Physiocrats called the *net produit*. Did not Sumner say that if a man cannot make his way in this world he should make his way out of it. And if he refuses, someone else should show him the way.* The evolutionary Polly Anna will tell you that all of this is good, since it is necessary. It is Physiocracy - "the rule of nature."

**Laissez faire.** As we have seen the spirit of Adam Smith suffered from disquietude when he saw that the governmental regulations of Mercantilism upon industry prevented the beneficent operation of the natural law principles of the Physiocrats. Annoyed by Mercantilism and inspired by Physiocracy he wrote his *Inquiry into the Nature and Causes of the Wealth of Nations."* Published in 1776, the same year in which Thomas Jefferson wrote the *Declaration of Independence*, it is the "bible" of Classical Economics. Although the Mercantilists knew their Aristotle better than J.B.Say and recognized the Speculative Motive for holding money, which as we have seen, Say ignored, it is nevertheless true that they went too far in the direction of regulation. George III, the beloved monarch of the thirteen American colonies might have kept us under his jurisdiction if he had been willing to relax Mercantilist restriction enough to keep John Hancock happy.

The battle cry to which Adam Smith gave voice in *Wealth of Nations* was *laissez faire et laissez passer,* which is French for "hands off." Neither industry nor commerce should be regulated by government. Smith was to some extent justified in preaching

*Those who think that this is an exaggeration should remember Baby Doe,the Down's syndrome victim in the maternity ward in Bloomington, Indiana.

against Mercantilism, since government is nothing more than the creation of fallen man and can become too regulative. But by the same token government can also become too small, in which case it falls short of its proper role as set forth in the *Social Contrat* of Jean Jacque Rousseau.

Viewed in *zeitgeist* Thomas Jefferson's famous statement that "That government is best which governs least" was in the 18th century true. Jefferson lived before the rise of the giant corporation with its control of the money market. Though Mister Jefferson wrote that "all men are created equal" he did not mean that men are born with equal physical power, personal charm or native intelligence. Indeed Jefferson was abundantly aware that he was smarter than most of his peers. He did mean that government should provide that all men, however weak and stupid they might be, were to be given equal protection of the laws of the general will in court. But Jefferson hoped, argued and worked for a society composed of small entrepreneurs, agricultural, industrial, mercantile and commercial, each of whom would be able to make his greatest contribution to society through cost-effective operation, but none of whom would be big enough to affect the supply and demand curves of the free market. Thus the producer with no control over the price would adjust his output to the point where his unit cost was equal to price. A later refinement, contributed by the Marginalists, which Jefferson did not understand because he was born too soon, defines the Best Profit Point as the output where Marginal Cost equals Marginal Revenue. Of course an important component of cost is opportunity cost which the untaught call "profit." If this is done the entrepreneur, by doing the best possible for himself, automatically does the best for society. The principle that it is only when we are selfish and seek to maximize our own utility that we contribute the most to society is what Adam Smith had in mind when he spoke of "the invisible hand" that guides "the economic man." For Smith he is totally rational! But though Adam Smith may have given lip service to his faith in Holy Scripture, he understood little of what it says about fallen man.

Perfect competition by definition exists only in a market where the number of producers and consumers is so large that no one controls the market price. This was the world of Adam Smith and it was the world of Thomas Jefferson's dreams. With no control over the market price the producer had total control over his output and the consumer total control over his decision to buy or not to buy. Thus the consumer was "King" and he would exercise his royal powers in the market place by always making the rational choice between products A, B, C, D and E or V, W, X, Y and Z. By weighing with precision the pain of surrendering money against the pleasure of acquiring goods and services, he would select those purchases in the proper quantities such that the last penny spent on any item would bring him the same utility if he had spent it on any other. Thus he would achieve an Optimum Equilibrium Combination and walk from the store triumphant in the knowledge that he could not possibly have spent his money in a better way and also in the knowledge that he had rewarded the most effecient producer by buying his good and had punished the less effecient by boycotting his. Those producers whose products do not sell then get the message and leave the industry to employ their talents in another market where they can survive.

Thus the heart of the argument for Classical Economics is that man is a rational creature - a dogma that the Bible denies, although it says that God created him with adequate rational power. But now the Bible says that man is a fallen creature, rendered generally incompetent and confused by the fall. But Darwin, influenced by Malthus' observation that man was so sex oriented that he was predestined to breed the human race into mass starvation, came along eighty-three years later and said that man is the product of a struggle for survival which dictates that only rational creatures will survive. Thus if man was not rational in 1859 (and Darwin was sure that preachers who believed the Bible were not!) at least he was on his way up. All we need do is wait several million years (or is it several billion?) and man will reach the point in his intellectual improvement where he can balance utils against disutils with precision in compliance with the law of diminishing marginal utility. *Voila! Laissez faire!!* In current terms the expression is "Let us get big government off our backs." To be sure, unemployment will rise and the poor will starve, but that is evolution and therefore it is good. The poor ought to starve, since their poverty proves that they are inferior and should not be allowed to produce the next generation. As for the recession it will "bottom out" and reverse the trend as J.B.Say's law makes clear.

If all men were created equal in physical and mental power competition could never be harmful. A struggle between equals

xxi

is always profitable because each competitor is forced to exert his greatest strength and employ his best skills in order to prevail. Thus production is maximized with minimal unit input. At the same time and for the same reason neither competitor is able to inflict permanent damage on the other. In such a case competition in its productive sense could never become conflict in its unproductive sense.

But men are not equal and the result is that the strong exploit the weak. Under a *laissez faire* system of government the physically strong are forbidden by law to waylay the weak and rob them, but the industrial giants, both at the production and marketing levels are permitted to rob the poor. Robbery is the same in its sad result whether it is done with a gun, which is unlawful, or with price manipulation in a market controlled by oligopolists. Some Christian liberals saw this in 1887 as giant railroad combinations exploited farmers who had no other access to markets. The result was a departure from *laissez faire*. The Interstate Commerce Commission was created by Congress with the power to regulate railroad rates of carriers engaged in commerce across state lines. The Social Darwinists, in total consistency with their dogma that the state has no right to interfere with the Darwinian struggle for survival, and thus that a poor farmer who cannot pay the rates charged should perish and make room for someone more able to survive than he, objected. Sumner wrote that the railroad question ". . . is far wider than the scope of any proposed legislation; the railroads are interwoven with so many complex interests that legislators cannot meddle with them without doing harm to all concerned." (William Graham Sumner, *Essays,* II, 255, as cited in Hofstadter, *Social Darwinism in American Thought,* 62). Herbert Spencer was so convinced that the state had no proper police powers over the evolutionary struggle for survival that he opposed the registration of physicians with the statement that if a sick man had not the good sense to avoid submitting to the ministrations of medical quacks, he ought to die.

Let the Fundamentalist with his proper opposition to Darwinism and his inconsistent support for the political right, defend the proposition if he can that the American market is one of pure competition and therefore that it requires no regulation by the state. Is the consumer King? If so is he rational? Does he guide production with inerrant guidance to maximum utility? This one question would I ask and then feel free to rest my case - "Did you ever spend an unwise dime in your life?"

We cannot be certain who coined the phrase *laissez faire et laissez passer*. Once attributed to Colbert, finance minister for Louis XIV, it more probably came from Vincent Gournay, an early Physiocrat. Whatever the origin of the phrase the idea was clearly presented in the poem *The Fable of the Bees* by Bernard de Mandeville (1670?-1733), the Dutch philosopher, satirist and physician. His bees had organized the hive on a basis of perfect division of labor that demanded that each bee perform his appointed task or perish. There was no subsidy for the drones. The result was prosperity for the hive. Honey production was maximized; labor inputs per pound of honey were minimized. Then one sad day there came a "do gooder" into the hive with his message about the Welfare State. His concerns that natural rights for bees in the hive were being ignored were expressed and heeded. Laws were passed. Regulations were imposed. *Laissez faire* was abandoned. The bee hive went to pot; honey production plummetted and the Fundamentalist preacher bees in the hive stung the do-gooder to death!

**Neo-Classicism and the Welfare State.** In the latter half of the 19th century, the Classicism of Smith, Malthus and Ricardo, with its *laissez faire* philosophy was modified to a minor degree by the discovery of the principle of marginal analysis. Gossen, a German, Augustin Cournot and J.H. von Thunen anticipated what Stanley Jevons saw clearly and Alfred Marshall expounded in greatest detail in his *Principles of Economics*. Leon Walras in France and Carl Menger in Austria also contributed to this school. Marginal analysis, the notion that change must be measured at the margin, measures the increase/decrease of utility as each increment is added. Once understood, the concept allows us to understand that the pain which a rich man suffers when he loses a dollar is not as great as the pleasure which a poor man enjoys if he receives the dollar. This is the reasoning by which Jeremy Bentham, the founder of the Utilitarian school was able to show that a redistribution of the wealth, as the state taxes away money from the rich to distribute to the poor, results in "the greatest good for the greatest number." Thus the state as a whole can increase its utility by a judicious redistribution. This is the justification for what has come to be called The Welfare State. That it can be carried too far is obvious. The storm signal that warns the economist that what is good up to a point can be overdone is clear. When the volume of capital investment in the private sector as a ratio of gross national product declines, Keynesians will insist that the Welfare State has gone too far. This is because Keynesians believe that investment is the dynamic of a Captialist economy. As private investment goes, so goes the economy.

Of course evolutionists who know enough economics to understand the implications of their fairy story will protest that any redistribution of wealth that results in prolonging the lives of the unfit is bad. As Sumner, who based all of his Social Science on his wholesale acceptance of and boyish enthusiasm for Darwinism and the Social Darwinism of Herbert Spencer, pointed out, if we are to have liberty we must recognize that men are not equal and we must accept the conclusion that the unfit must die in order that the fit may survive. Thus liberty carries society forward and favors all its best members.

As the evolutionists speak of liberty we may well ask, "Liberty for whom?" And their answer cannot be that of Thomas Jefferson, for he predicated his "life, liberty and the pursuit of happiness" upon the assumption that God created man in His own image. Thomas Jefferson was not a Christian, but at least he was a Deist. His faith did not embrace the theistic assumption that God loves the world and has revealed Himself to man, both in the Bible and in His Son, the historic Jesus of Nazareth. He was influenced by the intellectual movements of his time. We have seen these to include the various elements in the revolt of the Age of Reason in England, of the Physiocrats and Philosophes of the Revolution in France and of Immanuel Kant in Germany. These thinkers were not kindly disposed toward Christianity and some were openly atheistic. These found what they considered solid support for their atheism in Charles Darwin. The *laissez faire* conclusions of Classicism and Neo-Classicism implied that man was rational and able to care for himself, given an equal chance, without help from the state. All of these philosophic trends tended to the conclusion that mankind was on the verge of happier days when Jefferson wrote to tell the world why the United States wished to be free from the control of George III.

**Our All-Important First Amendment.** The Western world in 1776 - in Germany and France, in Great Britain and in the United States was faced with philosophical and religious questions that divided society into three camps. Christians accepted the Bible and stood with confidence upon all that it said. For them, God created man in a special creation that made him superior to the beasts. He still retained his dignity despite the fact that he was a sinner and not always capable of clear thought and wise decisions. Deists, like Jefferson, Benjamin Franklin and Thomas Paine agreed with the theistic Christians that God created man, and thus that man possessed natural rights which ought to be protected. They also believed that it was the function of the state to secure these rights. But the Deists did not join the Christians in their worship of Jesus Christ and acceptance of the Bible as the inspired Word of God. Atheists rejected God, the Bible and the claims of the Church with reference to Jesus Christ and the Christian *weltanschauung*.

Our founding fathers had seen enough history in Europe to realize the folly of state control over the minds of free men with reference to religion. Whether it was the Roman Catholicism in France, the control of Lutheranism in Germany or the Anglican control of England, the result was the same. They determined that in America they would make a new thing. America would be a free country, not a Christian country, for if they made it Christian the question immediately would become whether it should be Christian as interpreted by Anglicans, Methodists, Presbyterians, Catholics, Baptists, Quakers or German Pietists. And if any of these or any other theistic or deistic groups were established, it would mean that America was a land where some people would be forced by law to pay taxes to support something that they did not believe. This does not mean that our founding fathers who wrote the Constitution did not want religion to be preached. Nor does it mean that they wanted atheism or deism to be suppressed. It does mean that the United States of America would, in its statement of "the supreme law of the law" make certain that all men could be free to preach or write whatever they chose. The first amendment does not forbid Christians to preach. It promises Christians that the state will never interfere with their preaching. It also says that the state will never tax money away from non-Christians to support Christians in the propagation of their message. The state will neither help nor hinder. This same freedom from state interference is promised to all other people who have something which they wish to say, which they feel that they must say and which they very much want people to hear and believe.

Christian ministers who are "set for the defence of the gospel" (Phil.1:17) must oppose evolution. And if they are adequately informed in secular areas, beyond those normally associated with the Christian faith, they will also see the need to oppose Social Darwinism in all of its forms. But let them teach and preach the Word of God at the behest and with the financial support of their own Christian brethren, and let them preach in their own pulpits. The state will never molest them nor lay a straw in their pathway to delay them. In fact, at this late date in our economic development, when Christian church property stands on land for which business concerns would pay millions of dollars, the state still allows the church to occupy the land tax free. If this were not done church real estate would be placed upon the tax rolls and tax revenues would be greater and tax burdens in consequence lighter. This amounts indirectly to a tax subsidy collected from an atheist to support a Christian church. Thus the Church is already getting more from the state than she should. Let her be content. And let her pursue the course to which God has called her. Let her fight the good fight of faith with all of her ability baptized with the supernatural power of the Holy Spirit.

If in a science class in a public school-room a Christian teaches children that God created the universe in six days, he teaches what is true, but he forces the atheistic father of one of his students to help to pay his salary while he undermines in the child that which the father wishes him to believe. This is freedom for the Christian school teacher, but not for the father and his child.

If a Christian boy or girl wishes to pray as he sits at his desk in a public class-room let him quietly bow and pray. The Supreme Court has never said that he must not. But if the prayer is a structured exercise in which all present are forced to participate, even if all they do is listen, we have that which the Constitution forbids - "the establishment of religion."

Christians who are zealous to preach the glorious gospel of Christ in a free country are to be congratulated. Christians who wish to controvert error should do so with all of their might. Let them also help to keep this country free for all those who are citizens but not Christians.

# The
# Renaissance
# New
# Testament

# The Case Against Paul

*(Acts 24:1-9)*

*Acts 24:1 - "And after five days Ananias the high priest descended with the elders, and with a certain orator named Tertullus, who informed the governor against Paul."*

Μετὰ δὲ πέντε ἡμέρας κατέβη ὁ ἀρχιερεὺς Ἀνανίας μετὰ πρεσβυτέρων τινῶν καὶ ῥήτορος Τερτύλλου τινός, οἵτινες ἐνεφάνισαν τῷ ἡγεμόνι κατὰ τοῦ Παύλου.

Μετὰ (preposition with the accusative, time extent) 50.
δὲ (continuative conjunction) 11.
πέντε (numeral) 1119.
ἡμέρας (acc.pl.fem.of ἡμέρα, time extent) 135.
κατέβη (3d.per.sing.aor.act.ind.of καταβαίνω, culminative) 324.
ὁ (nom.sing.masc.of the article in agreement with ἀρχιερεὺς) 9.
ἀρχιερεὺς (nom.sing.masc.of ἀρχιερεύς, subject of κατέβη) 151.
Ἀνανίας (nom.sing.masc.of Ἀνανίας, apposition) 3592.
μετὰ (preposition with the genitive of accompaniment) 50.
πρεσβυτέρων (gen.pl.masc.of πρεσβύτερος, accompaniment) 1141.
τινῶν (gen.pl.masc.of τις, indefinite pronoun, in agreement with πρεσβυτέρων) 486.
καὶ (adjunctive conjunction joining nouns) 14.

#3611 ῥήτορος (gen.sing.masc.of ῥήτωρ, accompaniment).

orator - Acts 24:1.

*Meaning: Cf.* ῥέω (#116). A speaker, orator. The spokesman for the high priest in the case before Fexlix - Acts 24:1.

**#3612** Τερτύλλου (gen.sing.masc.of Τέρτυλλος, apposition).

Tertellus - Acts 24:1,2.

*Meaning:* An orator who appeared against Paul in the court of Felix - Acts 24:1,2.

τινός (gen.sing.masc.of τις, indefinite pronoun, in agreement with Τερτύλλου) 486.

οἵτινες (nom.pl.masc.of ὅστις, definite relative pronoun, subject of ἐνεφάνισαν) 163.

ἐνεφάνισαν (3d.per.pl.aor.act.ind.of ἐμφανίζω, ingressive) 1666.

τῷ (dat.sing.masc.of the article in agreement with ἡγεμόνι) 9.

ἡγεμόνι (dat.sing.masc.of ἡγεμών, indirect object of ἐνεφάνισαν) 160.

κατά (preposition with the genitive of reference, opposition) 98.

τοῦ (gen.sing.masc.of the article in agreement with Παύλου) 9.

Παύλου (gen.sing.masc.of Παῦλος, reference, opposition) 3284.

*Translation - "And five days later there came down the high priest, Ananias, with some elders and some speaker, Tertullus, who (plural) filed charges with the governor against Paul."*

**Comment:** Μετά with the accusative of time extent and, in its second usage, with the genitive of accompaniment. Note that the relative pronoun οἵτινες is plural. Whether it refers only to Tertullus and Ananias, or also to the elders who also came before the court the grammar does not reveal. Knowing the temper of those who came to Caesarea (up north, but down the mountain - κατέβη) it is likely that each of them had something to say against Paul. *Cf.*#98 for κατά with the genitive. It is a genitive of reference, but the preposition κατά adds the idea of hostility or opposition. Not content to pursue Paul out of Jerusalem, Ananias made the trip to Caesarea in order to stop Paul, once and for all. He must have known, if properly advised by his lawyer, that he had no case against Paul in a Roman court. If Paul had transgressed Roman law, the prosecutor would have gone directly to the point, filed his brief and presented his evidence, with the full confidence that Felix would have found against the defendant. Instead Tertullus resorted to flattery and then charged Paul with sedition, which could only mean to a judge in a Roman court of law, sedition against the Emperor. He presented no evidence that the Christians anywhere, either in Judea or in Asia Minor, where Paul had gone, were guilty of rebelling against Rome. He was reduced to some complaints about Paul's attack upon certain Jewish "traditions." He called him a pest, but if Paul was a pest to the Jewish Establishment in Jerusalem, there is no evidence that the Romans regarded him as such.

The use of the indefinite pronouns τινῶν and τινός, adjoined to both the elders and to Tertullus would indicate some feeling of contempt on Luke's part.

*Verse 2 - "And when he was called forth, Tertullus began to accuse him saying,*

*Seeing that by thee we enjoy great quietness, and that very worthy deeds are
done unto this nation by thy providence, . . . "*

κληθέντος δὲ αὐτοῦ ἤρξατο κατηγορεῖν ὁ Τέρτυλλος λέγων, Πολλῆς
εἰρήνης τυγχάνοντες διὰ σοῦ καὶ διορθωμάτων γινομένων τῷ ἔθνει τούτῳ διὰ
τῆς σῆς προνοίας,

κληθέντος (aor.pass.part.gen.sing.masc.of καλέω, genitive absolute) 107.

δὲ (continuative conjunction) 11.

αὐτοῦ (gen.sing.masc.of αὐτός, genitive absolute) 16.

ἤρξατο (3d.per.sing.aor.mid.ind.of ἄρχω, ingressive) 383.

κατηγορεῖν (pres.act.inf.of κατηγορέω, epexegetical) 974.

ὁ (nom.sing.masc.of the article in agreement with Τέρτυλλος) 9.

Τέρτυλλος (nom.sing.masc.of Τέτυλλος, subject of ἤρξατο) 3612.

λέγων (pres.act.part.nom.sing.masc.of λέγω, recitative) 66.

Πολλῆς (gen.sing.fem.of πολύς, in agreement with εἰρήνης) 228.

εἰρήνης (gen.sing.fem.of εἰρήνη, objective genitive) 865.

τυγχάνοντες (pres.act.part.nom.pl.masc.of τυγχάνω, adverbial, causal)
2699.

διὰ (preposition with the ablative of agent) 118.

σοῦ (abl.sing.masc.of σύ, agent) 104.

καὶ (adjunctive conjunction joining participles) 14.

#3613 διορθωμάτων (gen.pl.neut.of διόρθωμα, genitive absolute).

worthy deeds - Acts 24:2.

*Meaning: Cf.* διορθόω, from διά (#118) and ὀρθός (#3314) - "to set right."
Hence, reform, amendment, correction, amelioration of social, economic and
political injustice. With reference to the alleged reforms of Felix in Palestine -
Acts 24:2.

γινομένων (pres.mid.part.gen.pl.neut. of γίνομαι, genitive absolute) 113.

τῷ (dat.sing.masc.of the article in agreement with ἔθνει) 9.

ἔθνει (dat.sing.masc.of ἔθνος, personal advantage) 376.

τούτῳ (dat.sing.masc.of οὗτος, in agreement with ἔθνει) 93.

διὰ (preposition with the ablative of agent) 118.

τῆς (abl.sing.fem.of the article in agreement with προνοίας) 9.

σῆς (abl.sing.fem.of σός, in agreement with προνοίας) 646.

#3614 προνοίας (abl.sing.fem.of πρόνοια, agency).

providence - Acts 24:2.
provision for - Romans 13:14.

*Meaning: Cf.* προνοέω (#4029). *Cf.* πρόνοος - "forethought." Hence,
providential care; social planning - Acts 24:2; planning to commit sin -
Rom.13:14.

*Translation - "And when he had been summoned, Tertullus began the*

*prosecution by saying, 'Due to the profound peace that prevails through your efforts and the reforms for this nation effected by your planning . . . ' "*

**Comment:** The main verb in Tertullus' opening statement is in verse 3. The participles are causal. The antecedent of αὐτοῦ can, from a grammatical point of view, be Τερτύλλου or Παύλου, since both are masculine gender and singular number, as is αὐτοῦ. We take it that Παύλου is the antecedent, due to κληθέντος. It was Paul who was summoned to court to face the charges to be brought. Tertullus' opening remarks are pure "eyewash" - the palaver of a lawyer who knows that he has no case and procedes to insult the intelligence of the court. There had been no peace in Palestine during Felix's administration (Acts 21:37,38), nor was he noted for administrative reforms. Sir William Ramsay has called him ". . . one of the worst of Roman officials" (*St. Paul the Traveller and the Roman Citizen*, 306).

Tertellus continues in

*Verse 3 - "We accept it always, and in all places, most noble Felix, with all thankfulness."*

πάντῃ τε καὶ πανταχοῦ ἀποδεχόμεϑα, κράτιστε Φῆλιξ, μετὰ πάσης εὐχαριστίας.

**#3615** πάντῃ (adverbial).

always - Acts 24:3.

*Meaning:* An adverb - everywhere, always, wholly, in every respect - Acts 24:3.

τε (correlative particle) 1408.
καὶ (adjunctive conjunction joining adverbs) 14.
πανταχοῦ (adverbial) 2062.
ἀποδεχόμεϑα (1st.per.pl.pres.mid.ind.of ἀποδέχομαι, progressive duration, retroactive) 2245.
κράτιστε (voc.sing.masc.of κράτιστος, in agreement with Φῆλιξ) 1712.
Φῆλιξ (voc.sing.masc.of Φῆλιξ, address) 3603.
μετὰ (preposition with the genitive, accompaniment, with things, like an instrumental) 50.
πάσης (gen.sing.fem.of πᾶς, in agreement with εὐχαριστίας) 67.

**#3616** εὐχαριστίας (gen.sing.fem.of εὐχαριστία, accompaniment).

giving of thanks - 1 Cor.14:16; Eph.5:4; 1 Tim.2:1.
thankfulness - Acts 24:3.
thanks - 1 Thess.3:9; Rev.4:9.
thanksgiving - 2 Cor.4:15; 9:11,12; Phil.4:6; Col.2:7; 4:2; 1 Tim.4:3,4; Rev. 7:12.

*Meaning: Cf.* εὐχαριστέω (#1185). Hence, the act and/or attitude of giving thanks. An expression of appreciation. In Christian worship, with reference to

thanksgiving to God - 1 Cor.14:16; Eph.5:4; 1 Tim.2:1; 1 Thess.3:9; Rev.4:9; 2 Cor.4:15; 9:11,12; Phil.4:6; Col.2:7; 4:2; 1 Tim.4:3,4; Rev.7:12. To Felix - Acts 24:3.

*Translation - "Both at all times and in all places we accept, most noble Felix, with all gratitude."*

**Comment:** It is possible to join πάντη τε καὶ πανταχοῦ to διορθωμάτων γινομένων τῷ ἔθνει τούτῳ διὰ τῆς σῆς προνοίας of verse 2, in which case we read "and reforms are being made for this nation through your planning both at all times and in all places." If so, then Tertullus adds ἀποδεχόμεθα . . . εὐχαριστίας - "we are accepting, most noble Felix, with all gratitude." It is just as possible to join πάντη τε καὶ πανταχοῦ to the sentence which follows it. Were the reforms all encompassing (the former possibility) or was Israel's praise universal (the latter). Neither was, of course, the truth. Tertullus was a typical insincere "corn field" lawyer, who had no case and knew it, and was therefore, trying to brainwash the court. It was this "foot-in-the'door" Dale Carnegie approach which, he sensed, as we gather from the next clause, was already beginning to bore Felix. The governor had heard Jewish lawyers before.

*Verse 4 - "Notwithstanding, that I be not further tedious unto thee, I pray thee that thou wouldest hear us of thy clemency a few words."*

ἵνα δὲ μὴ ἐπὶ πλεῖόν σε ἐγκόπτω, παρακαλῶ ἀκοῦσαί σε ἡμῶν συντόμως τῇ σῇ ἐπιεικείᾳ.

ἵνα (conjunction introducing the subjunctive in a negative sub-final clause) 114.

δὲ (adversative conjunction) 11.

μὴ (negative conjunction with the subjunctive in a negative sub-final clause) 87.

ἐπὶ (preposition with the accusative of extent, metaphorical) 47.

πλεῖόν (acc.sing.neut.of πλείων, adverbial) 474.

σε (acc.sing.masc.of σύ, metaphorical extent) 104.

**#3617** ἐγκόπτω (1st.per.sing.pres.act.subj.of ἐγκόπτω, negative sub-final clause).

be tedious unto - Acts 24:4.
hinder - Rom.15:22; 1 Thess.2:18; Gal.5:7; 1 Pet.3:7.

*Meaning:* A combination of ἐν (#80) and κόπτω (#929). Hence, to cut into one's path and block one's progress. To delay, detain, prevent, hinder. Paul was hindered from going to Rome - Rom.15:22; to Thessalonica - 1 Thess.2:18; in a slightly different sense, to prevent one from transacting more important business by occupying one's time with trivia - hence, to be boring or tedious - Acts 24:3; to block the progress of Christian growth by false teaching - Gal.5:7; to hinder success in prayer - 1 Pet.3:7.

παρακαλῶ (1st.per.sing.pres.act.ind.of παρακαλέω, aoristic) 230.
ἀκοῦσαι (aor.act.inf.of ἀκούω, object of παρακαλῶ) 148.
σε (acc.sing.masc.of σύ, general reference) 104.
ἡμῶν (gen.pl.masc.of ἐγώ, objective genitive) 123.

#**3618** συντόμως (adverbial).

a few words - Acts 24:4.

*Meaning:* Cf. συντέμνω (#3972). Hence, concisely. With reference to Tertullus' speech - Acts 24:4.

τῇ (instru.sing.fem.of the article in agreement with ἐπιεικείᾳ) 9.
σῇ (instru.sing.fem.of σός, in agreement with ἐπιεικείᾳ) 646.

#**3619** ἐπιεικείᾳ (instru.sing.fem.of ἐπιείκεια, cause).

clemency - Acts 24:4.
gentleness - 2 Cor.10:1.

*Meaning:* Cf. ἐπιεικής (#4584). Hence, gentleness, moderation. Used with πρᾳύτητος in 2 Cor.10:1. In Acts 24:4, Tertellus is asking Felix to be patient and give of his time to hear the lawyer's speech. The quality of mildness.

*Translation - "But lest I bore you further I ask, since you are a patient man, that you hear me. I will be brief."*

**Comment:** δὲ is adversative. The ἵνα μή clause is sub-final - a purpose to achieve a result. The infinitive is the object of παρακαλῶ. The adverb συντόμως promises brevity. Tertullus promises Felix that he will cut it short (*Cf.* συντέμνω) and hopes that the governor will be patient enough to hear him out. This, of course, is pure oratorical eyewash. It is not likely that Felix was naive enough to be favorably impressed by it.

*Verse 5 - "For we have found this man a pestilent fellow, and a mover of sedition among all the Jews throughout the world, and a ringleader of the sect of the Nazarenes."*

εὑρόντες γὰρ τὸν ἄνδρα τοῦτον λοιμὸν καὶ κινοῦντα στάσεις πᾶσιν τοῖς Ἰουδαίοις τοῖς κατὰ τὴν οἰκουμένην πρωτοστάτην τε τῆς τῶν Ναζωραίων αἱρέσεως,

εὑρόντες (aor.act.part.nom.pl.masc.of εὑρίσκω) 79.
γὰρ (causal conjunction) 105.
τὸν (acc.sing.masc.of the article in agreement with ἄνδρα) 9.
ἄνδρα (acc.sing.masc.of ἀνήρ, direct object of εὑρόντες) 63.
τοῦτον (acc.sing.masc.of οὗτος, in agreement with ἄνδρα) 93.
λοιμὸν (acc.sing.masc.of λοιμός, predicate adjective) 2720.
καὶ (adjunctive conjunction joining substantives) 14.
κινοῦντα (pres.act.part.acc.sing.masc.of κινέω, substantival, predicate nominative) 1435.

στάσεις (acc.pl.fem.of στάσις, direct object of κινοῦντα) 2836.
πᾶσιν (loc.pl.masc.of πᾶς, in agreement with Ἰουδαίοις) 67.
τοῖς (loc.pl.masc.of the article in agreement with Ἰουδαίοις) 9.
Ἰουδαίοις (loc.pl.masc.of Ἰουδαῖος, place where) 143.
τοῖς (loc.pl.masc.of the article in agreement with Ἰουδαίοις) 9.
κατὰ (preposition with the accusative, distributive use) 98.
τὴν (acc.sing.fem.of the article in agreement with οἰκουμένην) 9.
οἰκουμένην (acc.sing.fem.of οἰκουμένη, distributive use) 1491.

#3620 πρωτοστάτην (acc.sing.masc.of πρωτοστάτης, predicate accusative).

ring leader - Acts 24:5.

*Meaning:* A combination of πρῶτος (#487) and ἵστημι (#180). Hence, one who stands first; a leader; chief; champion; director. Followed by the genitive of description - Acts 24:5.

τε (adjunctive conjunction) 1408.
τῆς (gen.sing.fem.of the article in agreement with αἱρέσεως) 9.
τῶν (gen.pl.masc.of the article in agreement with Ναζωραίων) 9.
Ναζωραίων (gen.pl.masc.of Ναζωραῖος, description) 245.
αἱρέσεως (gen.sing.fem.of αἵρεσις, description) 3058.

*Translation* - *"Because having found this man a pest, both a fomenter of rebellion among all the Jews throughout the world and a leader of the Nazarene heresy."*

**Comment:** Tertullus was so prejudiced, so overwrought and so eager to mislead Felix that his Greek is very bad. We should not blame Luke who is writing direct discourse and quoting the speaker *verbatim*. "Luke cruelly reports the orator *verbatim*" says Moulton (*A Grammar of New Testament Greek*, as cited in Robertson, *Grammar*, 1135). Tertullus leaves the whole statement depending upon εὑρόντες, hanging without a main verb. This is anacoluthon. I have translated Tertullus faithfully, or to use Moulton's word "cruelly."

Psychologists have noted, researched and written about the effects of uncontrolled emotion upon public speakers. Tertullus is a good example. Andrei Yanuarievich Vishinsky, foreign minister for the U.S.S.R., was the chief Russian delegate in the United Nations. He became notorious for his speeches against the Western world. Psychologists in the United States State Department gave minute inspection to blown-up tight shots of his face as he raged against Capitalism. Careful research revealed that when Vishinsky was unsure of himself he was unable to control his salivary glands, as a result of which the reporters who sat too close were treated to a shower. American State Department psychologists developed their study of Vishinsky's speeches to the level of an exact science, the results of which proved invaluable to the West as we evaluated the Russian's speeches. We do not know how Tertullus looked in Felix's court, but we have a record of his tortured syntax, which may be evidence that he was emotionally off balance. False witnesses are always emotionally upset whether they are aware of it or not.

It may or may not be significant that Vishinsky's middle name is Russian for "two-faced." One wonders what Tertullus' middle name was?

*Verse 6 - "Who also hath gone about to profane the temple: whom we took, and would have judged according to our law."*

ὃς καὶ τὸ ἱερὸν ἐπείρασεν βεβηλῶσαι, ὃν καὶ ἐκρατήσαμεν,

ὃς (nom.sing.masc.of ὅς, relative pronoun, subject of ἐπείρασεν) 65.
καὶ (ascensive conjunction) 14.
τὸ (acc.sing.neut.of the article in agreement with ἱερὸν) 9.
ἱερὸν (acc.sing.neut.of ἱερόν, direct object of βεβηλῶσαι) 346.
ἐπείρασεν (3d.per.sing.aor.act.ind.ofd πειράζω, ingressive) 330.
βεβηλῶσαι (aor.act.inf.of βεβηλόω, epexegetical) 969.
ὃν (acc.sing.masc.of ὅς, relative pronoun, direct object of ἐκρατήσαμεν) 65.
καὶ (emphatic conjunction) 14.
ἐκρατήσαμεν (1st.per.pl.aor.act.ind.of κρατέω, constative) 828.

*Translation - ". . . who even tried to desecrate the temple, whom in fact we caught. . ."*

**Comment:** Tertullus lost his train of thought so completely that he inserted ὃν καὶ before the main verb ἐκρατήσαμεν and thus cut the participle εὑρόντες with which he started his sentence (verse 5) off from the main verb. Without ὃν καὶ it would read "But when we found this man a pest . . . a fomenter of riots . . . a leader of the Nazarenes, who also tried to profane the temple, we arrested him." That makes sense. The United Bible Societies' Committee, with a degree of certitude indicated by D (on a scale of A B C D) have omitted the following which is supported by *p 74 Sinaiticus A B P,* one numbered uncial, *049,* and *several miniscules* καὶ κατὰ τὸν ἡμέτερον νόμον ἐβουλήθημεν ἀνελεῖν. 7 παρελθὼν δὲ Λυσίας ὁ χιλίαρχος ἥρπασεν αὐτὸν ἐκ τῶν χειρῶν ἡμῶν, 8 πέμψας πρὸς σέ. Other variant readings add other details of the story. The omitted text reads, "And in keeping with our own law we want him to die, but Lysias, the colonel, came and snatched him out of our hands. Having sent to you . . . κ.τ.λ." Nestle (16th Ed.) follows Aland, as do Westcott and Hort. The King James Version contains verse 6, as *supra* and

*Verse 7 - "But the chief captain Lysias came upon us, and with great violence took him away out of our hands."*

*Verse 8 - "Commanding his accusers to come unto thee: by examining of whom thyself mayest take knowledge of all things, whereof we accuse him."*

παρ' οὖ δυνήσῃ αὐτὸς ἀνακρίνας περὶ πάντων τούτων ἐπιγνῶναι ὧν ἡμεῖς κατηγοροῦμεν αὐτοῦ.

παρ' (preposition with the ablative, with persons, "in the presence of") 154.
οὖ (abl.sing.masc.of ὅς, place where) 65.
δυνήσῃ (2d.per.sing.fut.mid.ind.of δύναμαι, predictive) 289.

αὐτὸς (nom.sing.masc.of αὐτός, intensive) 16.

ἀνακρίνας (1st.aor.act.part.nom.sing.masc.of ἀνακρίνω, adverbial, instrumental) 2837.

περὶ (preposition with the genitive of reference) 173.

πάντων (gen.pl.neut.of πᾶς, in agreement with τούτων) 67.

τούτων (gen.pl.neut.of οὗτος, reference) 93.

ἐπιγνῶναι (aor.act.inf.of ἐπιγινώσκω, epexegetical) 675.

ὧν (gen.pl.neut.ofd ὅς, reference) 65.

ἡμεῖς (nom.pl.masc.of ἐγώ, subject of κατηγοροῦμεν) 123.

κατηγοροῦμεν (1st.per.pl.pres.act.ind.of κατηγορέω, progressive duration, retroactive) 974.

αὐτοῦ (gen.sing.masc.of αὐτός, objective genitive) 16.

*Translation* - ". . . with reference to whom you yourself will be able by examination to know perfectly about these things of which we have been accusing him."

**Comment:** παρά with the ablative is used with persons to indicate "in the presence" or "by the side of." *Cf.* Mk.8:11; 12:2; John 1:40; 8:38; 16:27, etc. Paul had been brought to the side of (παρά) Felix, where the governor could personally (intensive αὐτὸς) examine him thoroughly (#2837) and come to a perfect understanding (#675) of the facts and charges involved in the case.

Thus Tertullus stated the case. We learn in verse 9 that οἵτινες of verse 1 means all of the elders who came to Caesarea with Ananias and Tertullus, as well as the priest and the prosecutor.

*Verse 9 - "And the Jews also assented, saying that these things were so."*

συνεπέθεντο δὲ καὶ οἱ Ἰουδαῖοι φάσκοντες ταῦτα οὕτως ἔχειν.

**#3621** συνεπέθεντο (3d.per.pl.2d.aor.ind.of συνεπιτίθεμαι, constative).

assent - Acts 24:9.

*Meaning:* A combination of σύν (#1542), ἐπί (#47) and τίθημι (# 455). Hence, to lay on with; to assent to the truth of testimony. With reference to the testimony of the Jews who assented to the statement of Tertullus - Acts 24:9.

δὲ (continuative conjunction) 11.

καὶ (adjunctive conjunction joining substantives) 14.

οἱ (nom.pl.masc.of the article in agreement with Ἰουδαῖοι) 9.

Ἰουδαῖοι (nom.pl.masc.of Ἰουδαῖος, subject of συνεπέθεντο) 143.

**#3622** φάσκοντες (pres.act.part.nom.pl.masc.of φάσκω, adverbial, instrumental).

affirm - Acts 25:19.
profess - Romans 1:22.
say - Acts 24:9.

*Meaning: Cf.* φημί (#354). To affirm, state, allege, insist, whether what is said is true or not. That Christ is alive - Acts 25:19; that Paul was guilty as charged - Acts 24:9; that the speaker is wise - Romans 1:22.

ταῦτα (acc.pl.neut.of οὗτος, general reference) 93.
οὕτως (demonstrative adverb) 74.
ἔχειν (pres.act.inf.of ἔχω, object of φάσκοντες) 82.

*Translation - "And the Jews also concurred, by declaring that these things were as stated."*

**Comment:** Note the meaning of συνεπιτίθημι (#3621). The Jews laid their accusations upon Paul along with those of their spokesman. They did this by affirming (instrumental φάσκοντες) that the statement of the facts (ταῦτα) possessed validity. ἔχειν can be taken as indirect discourse, or, as we have done, as an object infinitive.

Thus Tertullus testified to the court and the other Jews swore to it. From their point of view their testimony was not false. Paul and his ministry had, indeed, been a thorn in the side of the Jewish Establishment. He had not fomented riots, but they thought that he did. He was one of the leaders of the group which they looked upon an a heretical sect. Note that Tertullus did not refer to the disciples of Jesus as Christians, as they were first called in Antioch (Acts 11:26), for to have done so would be to admit that Jesus was the Messiah. The term Ναζωραῖος was a term of contempt in Jerusalem.

However much the plaintiffs in the case may have been sincere, the fact remained that they had not even alleged, much less proved that Paul had transgressed any part of the Roman code which Felix was obligated to enforce. Thus they made Paul's defence relatively simple.

## Paul Defends Himself Before Felix

*(Acts 24:10 - 23)*

*Verse 10 - "Then Paul, after the governor had beckoned unto him to speak, answered, Forasmuch as I know that thou hast been of many years a judge unto this nation, I do the more cheerfully answer for myself."*

᾽Απεκρίθη τε ὁ Παῦλος νεύσαντος αὐτῷ τοῦ ἡγεμόνος λέγειν,᾽Εκ πολλῶν ἐτῶν ὄντα σε κριτὴν τῷ ἔθνει τούτῳ ἐπιστάμενος εὐθύμως τὰ περὶ ἐμαυτοῦ ἀπολογοῦμαι,

᾽Απεκρίθη (3d.per.sing.aor.mid.ind.of ἀποκρίνομαι, ingressive) 318.
τε (continuative conjunction) 1408.
ὁ (nom.sing.masc.of the article in agreement with Παῦλος) 9.
Παῦλος (nom.sing.masc.of Παῦλος, subject of ἀπεκρίθη) 3284.
νεύσαντος (aor.act.part.gen.sing.masc.of νεύω, genitive absolute) 2765.
αὐτῷ (dat.sing.masc.of αὐτός, indirect object of νεύσαντος) 16.
τοῦ (gen.sing.masc.of the article in agreement with ἡγεμόνος) 9.

ἡγεμόνος (gen.sing.masc.of ἡγεμῶν, genitive absolute) 160.

λέγειν (pres.act.inf.of λέγω, object infinitive) 66.

ἐκ (preposition with the ablative, time separation) 19.

πολλῶν (abl.pl.neut.of πολύς, in agreement with ἐτῶν) 228.

ἐτῶν (abl.pl.neut.of ἔτος, time separation) 821.

ὄντα (pres.part.acc.sing.masc.of εἰμί, in indirect discourse, in agreement with σε) 86.

σε (acc.sing.masc.of σύ, direct object of ἐπιστάμενος) 104.

κριτὴν (acc.sing.masc.of κριτής, predicate accusative) 492.

τῷ (dat.sing.neut.of the article in agreement with ἔθνει) 9.

ἔθνει (dat.sing.neut.of ἔθνος, personal interest) 376.

τούτῳ (dat.sing.neut.of οὗτος, in agreement with ἔθνει) 93.

ἐπιστάμενος (pres.mid.part.nom.sing.masc.of ἐπίσταμαι, adverbial, causal) 2814.

#3623 εὐθύμως (adverbial).

cheerfully - Acts 24:10.

*Meaning:* Cf. εὔθυμος (#3737) and εὐθυμέω (#3726). The Textus Receptus has εὐθυμότερον - "more cheerfully" in Acts 24:10.

τὰ (acc.pl.neut.of the article, direct object of ἀπολογοῦμαι) 9.

περὶ (preposition with the genitive of reference) 173.

ἐμαυτοῦ (gen.sing.masc.of ἐμαυτοῦ, reference) 723.

ἀπολογοῦμαι (1st.per.sing.pres.mid.ind., contraction, of ἀπολογέομαι, aoristic) 2476.

*Translation - "And after the governor had motioned to him to speak, Paul replied, 'Because I know that for many years you have been judge of this nation, I cheerfully give a logical explanation of the things about myself.' "*

**Comment:** νεύσαντος αὐτῷ τοῦ ἡγεμόνος λέγειν is a genitive absolute construction with the infinitive λέγειν as the object in explantion. Paul waited for Felix to motion to him that he should speak. ἐπιστάμενος is a causal participle introducing the participle ὄντα in indirect discourse. *Cf.* Acts 15:7 for another example of ἐπίσταμαι introducing indirect discourse, although there Luke used ὅτι which is omitted in our passage. It was because Paul knew that Felix had for many years been the judge of the nation that he felt confident in making his *apologia*. The implication is that Paul thought of Felix as an objective judge of current Roman law - one not to be influenced by the sociological pressures brought to bear upon him by Jewish theological bigotry. The issue to be decided by Felix was not whether or not Paul had offended the religious convictions of the Jews, but whether or not he had violated Roman law. His theological quarrel with the Jews had nothing to do with it.

*Verse 11 - "Because that thou mayest understand that there are yet but twelve days since I went up to Jerusalem for to worship."*

δυναμένου σου ἐπιγνῶναι ὅτι οὐ πλείους εἰσίν μοι ἡμέραι δώδεκα ἀφ' ἧς ἀνέβη προσκυνήσων εἰς Ἰερουσαλήμ,

δυναμένου (pres.mid.part.gen.sing.masc.of δύναμαι, genitive absolute) 289.

σου (gen.sing.masc.of σύ, genitive absolute) 104.

ἐπιγνῶναι (aor.act.inf.of ἐπιγινώσκω, epexegetical) 675.

ὅτι (conjunction introducing an object clause in indirect discourse) 211.

πλείους (acc.pl.fem.of πλείων, time extent) 474.

εἰσίν (3d.per.pl.pres.ind.of εἰμί, progressive duration, retroactive) 86.

μοι (dat.sing.masc.of ἐγώ, person) 123.

ἡμέραι (nom.pl.fem.of ἡμέρα, subject of εἰσίν) 135.

δώδεκα (numeral) 820.

ἀφ' (preposition with the ablative of time separation) 70.

ἧς (abl.sing.fem.of ὅς, time separation) 65.

ἀνέβην (1st.per.sing.2d.aor.act.ind.of ἀναβαίνω, culminative) 323.

προσκυνήσων (fut.act.part.nom.sing.masc.of προσκυνέω, adverbial, telic) 147.

εἰς (preposition with the accusative of extent) 140.

Ἰερουσαλήμ (acc.sing.fem.of Ἰερουσαλήμ, extent) 141.

*Translation - "Because you are able to understand that no more than twelve days have passed since I went up to Jerusalem to worship."*

**Comment:** δυναμένου σου, another genitive absolute, is causal. Paul was happy to defend himself since the facts were all on his side and because Felix, a judge of long experience, was able to understand the facts. What facts? ἐπιγνῶναι introduces indirect discourse with ὅτι. Literally, "There are not more than twelve days to me (in my experience) from the time I went up to Jerusalem to worship." ἀφ' ἧς is an abbreviation of ἀφ' ἡμέρας ᾗ. Thus the locative ᾗ is attracted to the ablative ἧς. (Robertson, *Grammar*, 717). *Cf.* 2 Peter 3:4. The future participle προσκυνήσων is telic. Paul went up to Jerusalem in order to worship. The action of the future participle is subsequent to ἀνέβην, but the action was antecedent in relation to the time when Paul was speaking in Felix's court. *Cf.* ἀφ' ἧς used for "since" in Luke 7:45; Acts 24:11; 2 Pet.3:4.

Paul's first point is that the period of his life under attack in the case was only twelve days. He pursued the thought in

*Verse 12 - "And they neither found me in the temple disputing with any man, neither raising up the people, neither in the synagogues, nor in the city."*

καὶ οὔτε ἐν τῷ ἱερῷ εὗρόν με πρός τινα διαλεγόμενον ἢ ἐπίστασιν ποιοῦντα ὄχλου οὔτε ἐν ταῖς συναγωγαῖς οὔτε κατὰ τὴν πόλιν,

καὶ (continuative conjunction) 14.

οὔτε (negative copulative conjunction) 598.

ἐν (preposition with the locative of place) 80.

τῷ (loc.sing.neut.of the article in agreement with ἱερῷ) 9.

ἱερῷ (loc.sing.neut.of ἱερόν, plae where) 346.

εὑρόν (3d.per.pl.aor.act.ind.of εὑρίσκω, constative) 79.

με (acc.sing.masc.of ἐγώ, direct object of εὑρόν) 123.

πρός (preposition with the accusative of extent, with a verb of speaking) 197.

τινα (acc.sing.masc.of τις, indefinite pronoun, extent, with a verb of speaking) 486.

διαλεγόμενον (pres.mid.part.acc.sing.masc.of διαλέγομαι, adverbial, circumstantial) 2349.

ἤ (disjunctive) 465.

#3624 ἐπίστασιν (acc.sing.fem.of ἐπίστασις, direct object of ποιοῦντα).

come upon - 2 Cor.11:28.
raising up - Acts 24:12.

*Meaning:* A combination of ἐπί (#47) and στάσις. Cf. ἐφίστημι (#1877). Hence, the act of advancing toward or approaching; a pressing action against, so as to incite to mob violence. Move toward the people to incite to riot - Acts 24:12. That which arises and demands a solution - 2 Cor.11:28.

ποιοῦντα (pres.act.part.acc.sing.masc.of ποιέω, adverbial, circumstantial) 127.

ὄχλου (gen.sing.masc.of ὄχλος, description) 418.

οὔτε (disjunctive) 598.

ἐν (preposition with the locative of place) 80.

ταῖς (loc.pl.fem.of the article in agreement with συναγωγαῖς) 9.

συναγωγαῖς (loc.pl.fem.of συναγωγή, place where) 404.

οὔτε (disjunctive) 598.

κατά (preposition with the accusative, distributive) 98.

τήν (acc.sing.fem.of the article in agreement with πόλιν) 9.

πόλιν (acc.sing.fem.of πόλις, distributive) 243.

*Translation -* "And neither in the temple did they find me disputing with anyone or inciting to riot the people, either in the synagogues or throughout the city."

**Comment:** Note the οὔτε . . . ἤ . . . οὔτε . . . οὔτε . . . οὐδέ (verse 13) sequence. Tertullus had made two specific charges: (a) sedition among the Jews in Jerusalem, and (b) profanation of the temple. All that Paul did in the temple is recorded in Acts 21:26. Here he was acting in total conformity to good Judaistic usage. As for the riot - who started the riot? (Acts 21:27). It was the plaintiffs themselves, whom Tertullus was representing, who had stirred up the people to violence - against whom? Against Rome? No. Against Paul. Why? Because they did not agree with his religion.

Paul was thus very confident with his statement of

*Verse 13 -* "Neither can they prove the things whereof they now accuse me."

οὐδὲ παραστῆσαι δύνανταί σοι περὶ ὧν νυνὶ κατηγοροῦσίν μου.

οὐδὲ (disjunctive particle) 452.

παραστῆσαι (aor.act.inf.of παρίστημι, epexegetical) 1596.

δύνανταί (3d.per.pl.pres.ind.of δύναται, aoristic) 289.

σοι (dat.sing.masc.of σύ, indirect object of παραστῆσαι) 104.

περὶ (preposition with the genitive of reference) 173.

ὧν (gen.pl.neut.of ὅς, reference) 65.

νυνὶ (temporal adverb) 1497.

κατηγοροῦσιν (3d.per.pl.pres.act.ind.of κατηγορέω, progressive duration, retroactive) 974.

μου (gen.sing.masc.of ἐγώ, objective genitive) 123.

*Translation - "Neither are they able to sustain for you the charges which they have been making against me."*

**Comment:** παραστῆσαι σοι is an interesting idiom for "prove." Paul was saying that Tertullus could not produce in court (literally "stand beside you") the evidence that would sustain the charges which they had been making. Paul's statement was obviously true. There had indeed been a riot in Jerusalem, in which Paul would have been killed, but for the intervention of Claudius Lysias and his troops, but Paul did not start it. And he had not profaned the Jewish temple. κατηγοροῦσιν is an excellent example of the progressive duration present tense, with its retroactive temporal force. The Jews had been accusing Paul as they were then accusing him for the past five days.

Paul continues through verse 21 to explain his philosophy and conduct to the court, although the defense could very well have rested at the close of his statement of verse 13.

*Verse 14 - "But this I confess unto thee, that after the way which they call heresy, so worship I the God of my fathers, believing all things which are written in the law and in the prophets."*

ὁμολογῶ δὲ τοῦτό σοι ὅτι κατὰ τὴν ὁδὸν ἣν λέγουσιν αἵρεσιν οὕτως λατρεύω τῷ πατρῴῳ θεῷ, πιστεύων πᾶσι τοῖς κατὰ τὸν νόμον καὶ τοῖς ἐν τοῖς προφήταις γεγραμμένοις,

ὁμολογῶ (1st.per.sing.pres.act.ind.of ὁμολογέω, aoristic) 688.

δὲ (adversative conjunction) 11.

τοῦτο (acc.sing.neut.of οὗτος, direct object of ὁμολογῶ) 93.

σοι (dat.sing.masc.of σύ, indirect object of ὁμολογῶ) 104.

ὅτι (conjunction introducing a clause in apposition with the accusative τοῦτο) 211.

κατὰ (preposition with the accusative, standard rule) 98.

τὴν (acc.sing.fem.of the article in agreement with ὁδόν) 9.

ὁδὸν (acc.sing.fem.of ὁδός, standard rule) 199.

ἣν (acc.sing.fem.of ὅς, incorporation with ὁδόν) 65.

λέγουσιν (3d.per.pl.pres.act.ind.of λέγω, customary) 66.

αἵρεσιν (acc.sing.fem.of αἵρεσις, direct object of λέγουσιν) 3058.

οὗτως (demonstrative adverb) 74.

λατρεύω (1st.per.sing.pres.act.ind.of λατρεύω, customary) 366.

τῷ (dat.sing.masc.of the article in agreement with θεῷ) 9.

πατρῴῳ (dat.sing.masc.of πατρῷος, in agreement with θεῷ) 3576.

θεῷ (dat.sing.masc.of θεός, personal advantage) 124.

πιστεύων (pres.act.part.nom.sing.masc.of πιστεύω, adverbial, modal) 734.

πᾶσι (loc.pl.masc.of πᾶς, sphere) 67.

τοῖς (loc.pl.neut.of the article, sphere) 9.

κατὰ (preposition with the accusative, standard rule) 98.

τὸν (acc.sing.masc.of the article in agreement with νόμον) 9.

νόμον (acc.sing.masc.of νόμος, standard rule) 464.

καὶ (adjunctive conjunction joining phrases) 14.

τοῖς (loc.pl.neut.of the article in agreement with γεγραμμένοις) 9.

ἐν (preposition with the locative of place) 80.

τοῖς (loc.pl.masc.of the article in agreement with προφήταις) 9.

προφήταις (loc.pl.masc.of προφήτης, place where) 119.

γεγραμμένοις (perf.pass.part.loc.pl.neut.of γράφω, substantival, sphere) 156.

*Translation - "But I confess this to you, that in keeping with the way which they customarily call heresy, in that way I am serving the God of my fathers, by believing everything - that which is in keeping with the law and that which is written in the prophets."*

**Comment:** δὲ is adversative. "They cannot prove what they are saying about me. . . but (δὲ) I will tell you the truth . . . κ.τ.λ." Note that κατὰ τὴν ὁδὸν is also κατὰ τὸν νόμον - Christianity is a way of life that accords with the law of God (Mt.5:17). Tertullus would say that the "way" of the sect of the Nazarenes was contrary to the law of Moses. Paul says that the opposite is true, and thus, by implication, he says that the Jews were not worshipping κατὰ τὸν νόμον, although he does not push the point, since the Jews were not the defendants, and Paul had no wish to prosecute them. The early Christians insisted that their interpretation of the Old Testament was the true one and that the perversion of the law and the prophets was found in the ritualistic legalism of Judaism which rejected Jesus as Messiah. Thus the tables are turned against the religious Jewish Establishment. Saul, the bigoted Pharisee, once persecuted Christians because, in his view, they were not serving the God of their fathers. Now he says that he is preaching and practising what he formerly persecuted. But Paul, the Christian, unlike Saul, the Pharisee, though now he calls Judaism a perversion, does not persecute the Jews as he once persecuted the Christians.

Note the accusative clause introduced by ὅτι in apposition to τοῦτο. "The accusative with ὅτι we have in τοῦτο ὅτι in Romans 2:3; 6:6; Luke 10:11; Acts 24:14; 1 Cor.1:12; 15:50; 2 Cor.5:14; 10:7,11; 2 Thess.3:10; Phil.1:6,25; 1 Tim.1:9; 2 Tim.3:1; 2 Pet.1:20; 3:3,8. (Robertson, *Grammar*, 699).

Paul continues to define his position to the court in

*Verse 15 - "And have hope toward God, which they themselves also allow, that there shall be a resurrection of the dead, both of the just and unjust."*

ἐλπίδα ἔχων εἰς τὸν θεόν, ἣν καὶ αὐτοὶ οὗτοι προσδέχονται, ἀνάστασιν μέλλειν ἔσεσθαι δικαίων τε καὶ ἀδίκων.

ἐλπίδα (acc.sing.fem.of ἐλπίς, direct object of ἔχων) 2994.

ἔχων (pres.act.part.nom.sing.masc.of ἔχω, adverbial, modal) 82.

εἰς (preposition with the accusative, like a dative, attitude of mind) 140.

τὸν (acc.sing.masc.of the article in agreement with θεόν) 9.

θεόν (acc.sing.masc.of θεός, disposition or attitude of mind, like a dative) 124.

ἣν (acc.sing.fem.of ὅς, direct object of προσδέχονται) 65.

καὶ (ascensive conjunction) 14.

αὐτοὶ (nom.pl.masc.of αὐτός, intensive) 16.

οὗτοι (nom.pl.masc.of οὗτος, subject of προσδέχονται) 93.

προσδέχονται (3d.per.pl.pres.mid.ind.of προχδέχομαι, customary) 1895.

ἀνάστασιν (acc.sing.fem.of ἀνάστασις, general reference) 1423.

μέλλειν (pres.act.inf.of μέλλειν, noun use, in apposition with ἐλπίδα) 206.

ἔσεσθαι (fut.inf.of εἰμί, complementary) 86.

δικαίων (gen.pl.masc.of δίκαιος, description) 85.

τε (correlative particle) 1408.

καὶ (adjunctive conjunction joining nouns) 14.

ἀδίκων (gen.pl.masc.of ἄδικος, description) 549.

*Translation -* "... *by having faith in God, which even these themselves share, that there is going to be a resurrection, both of just and unjust."*

**Comment:** The verse continues Paul's confession which he began in verse 14. There he said that he was serving God. How? The modal participle tells us - by believing - πιστεύων. How else? We have another modal participle in verse 15. "By having hope..." ἔχων. By believing all that is written in the law and the prophets and by having hope that a resurrection will occur at some future time in which will be involved both the righteous and the wicked.

There is nothing in this confession to which the orthodox Jew could not subscribe, as Paul points out. Note ascensive καὶ and the intensive αὐτοὶ.

The infinitive μέλλειν is in apposition to ἐλπίδα. It was hope that there is going to be a resurrection, in which both the righteous and the wicked are to be involved in a judgment based upon principles of moral probity. μέλλω has the future infinitive ἔσεσθαι only three times in the N.T. - in Acts 11:28; 24:15 and 27:10. The other three times the future infinitive occurs in John 21:25; Acts 23:30 and Heb.3:18 it is involved in indirect discourse.

What then, if the difference between the confessions of Paul, the defendant and the plaintiffs in this case?

Each professes faith in the statutes of Moses and the testimony of the Old Testament Prophets. Each professes to entertain hope that the God of the Old Testament will bring to resurrection the entire human family. But Paul believed as do all Christians that the law of Moses and the prophecies of the Prophets found their fulfillment in the person and work of Jesus, the Nazarene. This the Jews in court on that day rejected. The Christian position is supported by Jesus who said to the Jews, "Search the Scriptures for they . . . testify about me" (John 5:39). Paul was later to write that the "divine righteousness had been made manifest, having been witnessed by the law and the prophets" (Romans 3:21). It was Moses, representing the law and Elijah, representing the Prophets, who appeared with our Lord upon the Mount of Transfiguration. Each had failed in his mission and they came admonishing Jesus not to fail (Luke 9:30,31).

*Verse 16 - "And herein do I exercise myself, to have always a conscience void of offence, toward God and toward men."*

ἐν τούτῳ καὶ αὐτὸς ἀσκῶ ἀπρόσκοπον συνείδησιν ἔχειν πρὸς τὸν θεὸν καὶ τοὺς ἀνθρώπους διὰ παντός.

ἐν (preposition with the locative of sphere) 80.
τούτῳ (loc.sing.neut.of οὗτος, sphere) 93.
καὶ (continuative conjunction) 14.
αὐτὸς (nom.sing.masc.of αὐτός, intensive) 16.

#3625 ἀσκῶ (1st.per.sing.pres.act.ind.of ἀσκέω, progressive duration, retroactive).

exercise - Acts 24:16.

*Meaning:* In Homer it meant to be artistic; to adorn. In later Greek it came to mean to exercise oneself with great care; to be meticulous; to labor; to strive - Followed by the infinitive in Acts 24:16.

#3626 ἀπρόσκοπον (acc.sing.fem.of ἀπρόσκοπος, predicate adjective, in agreement with συνείδησιν).

void of offence - Acts 24:16.
without offence - Phil.1:10.
give none offence - 1 Cor.10:32.

*Meaning:* α privative plus προσκόπτω (#352). Hence, the quality of behavior that causes none to stumble; to be inoffensive. With συνείδησιν - "a clear conscience" *i.e.* one that does not offend Paul - Acts 24:16. In a prohibition - 1 Cor.10:32; Phil.1:10.

συνείδησιν (acc.sing.fem.of συνείδησις, direct object of ἔχειν) 3590.
ἔχειν (pres.act.inf.of ἔχω, purpose) 82.
πρὸς (preposition with the accusative, in a general sense of fitness) 197.
τὸν (acc.sing.masc.of the article in agreement with θεὸν) 9.
θεὸν (acc.sing.masc.of θεός, fitness of personal relationship) 124.

καὶ (adjunctive conjunction joining nouns) 14.
τοὺς (acc.pl.masc.of the article in agreement with ἀνθρώπους) 9.
ἀνθρώπους (acc.pl.masc.of ἄνθρωπος, fitness of personal relationship) 341.
διὰ (preposition with the genitive in a time expression) 118.
παντός (gen.sing.masc.of πᾶς in agreement with καιρούς understood) 67.

*Translation - "And with respect to this I discipline myself at all times to have a clear conscience toward God and man."*

**Comment:** The antecedent of τούτῳ is Paul's statement of verses 14 and 15, in which he had stated his theological position with its strong insistence that it was not a perversion of true Judaism, — rather its development in full flower. Now in verse 16 Paul adds, not only that he believes his theology, but also that he has always tried to live by it. ἀσκέω (#3625) calls for discipline -self-control, painstaking attention to one's work, such as an artist demands of himself. This was how Paul always (διὰ παντός) conducted himself. *Cf.* #67 for other examples of διὰ παντός meaning "at all times." ἔχειν is a telic infinitive. Paul wanted to have a conscience unstained by offense. He considered that it was not enough to be clear with God. One must also be clear with men. The basic idea of πρός ("near to") fits here. It speaks of a general sense of fitness of relationship with others. *Cf.* 2 Cor.10:4; 2:16; John 4:35; Rom.15:17; Mt.27:4. It is in close contact that our offenses become apparent to others. So far, then, from having profaned the temple or offending the Jews, Paul avers the opposite..

*Verse 17 - "Now after many years I came to bring alms to my nation, and offerings."*

δι' ἐτῶν δὲ πλειόνων ἐλεημοσύνας ποιήσων εἰς τὸ ἔθνος μου παρεγενόμην καὶ προσφοράς,

δι' (preposition with the genitive in a time expression) 118.
ἐτῶν (gen.pl.neut.of ἔτος, time description) 821.
δὲ (continuative conjunction) 11.
πλειόνων (gen.pl.neut.of πλείων, in agreement with ἐτῶν) 474.
ἐλεημοσύνας (acc.pl.fem.of ἐλεημοσύνη, direct object of ποιήσων) 558.
ποιήσων (fut.act.part.nom.sing.masc.of ποιέω, adverbial, telic) 127.
εἰς (preposition with the accusative of extent) 140.
τὸ (acc.sing.neut.of the article in agreement with ἔθνος) 9.
ἔθνος (acc.sing.neut.of ἔθνος, extent) 376.
μου (gen.sing.masc.of ἐγώ, relationship) 123.
παρεγενόμην (lst.per.sing.aor.mid.ind.of παραγίνομαι, culminative) 139.
καὶ (adjunctive conjunction joining nouns) 14.
προσφοράς (acc.pl.fem.of προσφορά, direct object of ποιήσων) 3560.

*Translation - "Now after many years I came in order to offer alms and offerings to my nation."*

**Comment:** δὲ is continuative and explanatory. The idea in διά ("in between two") is seen in δι' ἐτων πλειόνων - "in the interval between one year when I left

Jerusalem and one of many later years when I returned." διά does not mean "after" but the context gives to it that meaning. The future participle is telic. It's time is subsequent to παρεγενόμην, of course, but antecedent to the time that Paul was speaking. Paul wished to come to Jerusalem for the purpose of delivering the money for poor relief which he had collected from the churches in Asia Minor, Macedonia and Greece. Thus the participle, being telic is also volitive.

The fact that Paul was now a Christian did not prevent him from honoring *true* Judaism, since the latter produced Jesus, Paul's personal Saviour and Israel's Messiah. Thus Paul was engaged in a sincere worship which honored the Jewish tradition more than did the views and actions of his accusers. The circumstances that led to Paul's worship in the temple and which precipitated the chain of events which resulted in his arrest, are recorded in Acts 21:17-27. If the student has forgotten he should refresh his memory by reading the passage. The motives both of James and Paul were pure and totally consistent, both with the real Judaism and with Christianity.

*Verse 18 - "Whereupon certain Jews from Asia found me purified in the temple, neither with multitude nor with tumult."*

ἐν αἷς εὗρόν με ἡγνισμένον ἐν τῷ ἱερῷ, οὐ μετὰ ὄχλου οὐδὲ μετὰ θορύβου.

ἐν (preposition with the locative of time point) 80.
αἷς (loc.pl.fem.of ὅς, relative pronoun, time point) 65.
εὗρόν (3d.per.pl.aor.act.ind.of εὑρίσκω, culminative) 79.
με (acc.sing.masc.of ἐγώ, direct object of εὗρόν) 123.
ἡγνισμένον (perf.pass.part.acc.sing.masc.of ἁγνίζω, adverbial, circumstantial, indirect discourse) 2665.
ἐν (preposition with the locative of place) 80.
τῷ (loc.sing.neut.of the article in agreement with ἱερῷ) 9.
ἱερῷ (loc.sing.neut.of ἱερόν, place where) 346.
οὐ (negative conjunction with the indicative) 130.
μετὰ (preposition with the genitive of accompaniment, metaphorical) 50.
ὄχλου (gen.sing.masc.of ὄχλος, metaphorical accompaniment) 418.
οὐδὲ (disjunctive) 452.
μετὰ (preposition with the genitive of accompaniment, metaphorical) 50.
θορύβου (gen.sing.masc.of θόρυβος, metaphorical accompaniment) 1559.

*Translation - "While I was involved in these matters they found me purified in the temple, associated neither with a mob nor with an uproar."*

**Comment:** ἐν αἷς (*cf.*Acts 10:11; 15:36) in the sense of "during" or "while." The antecedent of αἷς is ἐλεημοσύνας and προσφαράς. When they found Paul in the temple, engaged in making his offering like a good Jew, in keeping with his Nazarite vow, he had already been purified (perfect participle in ἡγνισμένον) and therefore he was ceremonially pure. Thus Paul countered the charge that he had profaned the temple. He also answered the charge of verse 5 *in re* sedition.

Paul had assembled no audience; he was engaged in no harangue, and there was no riot. Thus, according to Paul's testimony, Tertullus' charges were false, and they could be substantiated only when he could produce evidence in court. This is Paul's point in verse 19.

It is possible to construe the participle ἡγνισμένον as indirect discourse. The student must keep in mind that a participle is a cross between a verb and an adjective, and that both verbal and adjectival forces are always present, although one may be predominant. "The point to note is that even here in indirect discourse, where the participle represents the verb of the direct, the participle is still an adjective though the verbal force has become predominant" (Robertson, *Grammar*, 1123). The rumor in the streets of Jerusalem, expressed in direct discourse was, "He has been purified and he is in the temple." Thus the tense of ἡγνισμένον (perfect) is the same as it was in the direct. When Paul said that they "found" him in the temple, he does not mean that all of the Jews who were allegedly involved in a riot, were physically in the temple. They "found" him there, only in the sense that they heard that he was there.

Note that the KJV, with good grammatical justification, has translated the subject of εὑρόν, which is τινὲς ... ἀπὸ τῆς Ἀσίας, in verse 18. This is not wrong, as Luke placed the predicate ahead of the subject. Thus, in the Greek, we find the subject in

*Verse 19 - "Who ought to have been here before thee, and object, if they had ought against me."*

τινὲς δὲ ἀπὸ τῆς Ἀσίας Ἰουδαῖοι, οὓς ἔδει ἐπὶ σοῦ παρεῖναι καὶ κατηγορεῖν εἴ τι ἔχοιεν πρὸς ἐμέ —

τινὲς (nom.pl.masc.of τις, indefinite pronoun, in agreement with Ἰουδαῖοι) 486.

δὲ (adversative conjunction) 11.

ἀπὸ (preposition with the ablative of source) 70.

τῆς (abl.sing.fem.of the article in agreement with Ἀσίας) 9.

Ἀσίας (abl.sing.fem.of Ἀσία, source) 2968.

Ἰουδαῖοι (nom.pl.masc.of Ἰουδαῖος, subject of εὑρόν) 143.

οὓς (acc.pl.masc.of ὅς, general reference) 65.

ἔδει (3d.per.sing.imp.of δεῖ, progressive description) 1207.

ἐπὶ (preposition with the genitive of place description) 47.

σοῦ (gen.sing.masc.of σύ, place description) 104.

παρεῖναι (pres.inf.of πάρειμι, complementary) 1592.

καὶ (adjunctive conjunction joining infinitives) 14.

κατηγορεῖν (pres.act.inf.of κατηγορέω, complementary) 974.

εἴ (conditional particle in a mixed fourth-class condition) 337.

τι (acc.sing.neut.of τις, indefinite pronoun, direct object of ἔχοιεν) 486.

ἔχοιεν (3d.per.pl.pres.opt.of ἔχω, in a mixed fourth-class condition) 82.

πρὸς (preposition with the accusative after a verb of speaking, opposition) 197.

ἐμέ (acc.sing.masc.of ἐμός, extent after a verb of speaking, opposition) 1267.

*Translation - "But certain Jews from Asia (who) should have been here before you, and have brought charges, if they had had anything against me."*

**Comment:** The subject of εὑρόν (verse 8) is τινὲς . . .Ἰουδαῖοι (verse 9) - so that the translation should be, "But certain Jews from Asia found me while I was making my offerings in the temple, having been purified (not with a mob or with a riot) who should have been here before you and should be bringing charges, if they have anything against me." ἔδει is an imperfect tense. Robertson, (*Grammar*, 885, 886) calls this a potential imperfect and explains: "Verbs of propriety, possibility, obligation or necessity are also used in the imperfect when the obligation, etc. is not lived up to, has not been met. . . . The Greeks (and the Latins) start from the past and state the real possibility or obligation, and the reader, by comparing that with facts, notes that the obligation has not been met."

Thus Paul was saying, "The Asiatic Jews should have been here before you (but they are not) and should have brought charges (but they did not), if they have (which they have not) anything against me." Note εἴ τι ἔχοιεν, the protasis of a fourth-class "less probable future" condition. Classical Greek grammarians sometimes call this a "less vivid future" condition. Robertson describes it as having a "Remote Prospect of Determination" (*Grammar*, 1020). But the apodosis is not in keeping with the formal fourth-class condition, which calls for εἰ with the optative in the protasis and ἄν with the optative in the apodosis. "No example of this condition complete in both protasis and apodosis is to be found in the New Testament. Indeed Robertson denies that a complete example occurs in the LXX or papyri 'so far as examined.'. . . 'It is an ornament of the cultured class and was little used by the masses save in a few set phrases.' (*Grammar*, 1020) as cited in Mantey, *Manual*, 290).

But, though the fourth-class condition is incomplete, the element of extreme doubt is there in the optative ἔχοιεν. As a matter of fact, Paul had no doubts about it whatever. He knew that they had nothing against him that would stand up in court, and he expressed his doubts in the strongest terms available to him in the vernacular. Thus his statement was a challenge to Tertullus to prove his charges. He could have asked, "If the Asiastic Jews found me in the temple in an act of profanation and/or inciting to riot, why have you not brought them to this hearing to be sworn and to testify?" Paul was alluding to the Jews whose actions are described in Acts 21:27-29. Note Luke's explanation in Acts 21:29. The Jews in question were under the false impression that Paul had brought Trophimus, an Ephesian Gentile Christian, into the temple. Paul had not done so and Trophimus had not thus "profaned" the temple. *Cf*.#969 for the basic meaning of βεβηλόω "to cross the threshold" - to "rush in where angels fear to tread." Trophimus, if he came near the temple area at all, stopped before the threshold and did not enter the area which was off limits to Gentiles.

Paul seemed to imply that the Jews in question, whose false accusations started the riot that resulted in Lysias' rescue of Paul, had later learned the truth of the matter. Since it was the Asiatic Jews who started the riot, they should be in Felix's court to testify. Since Tertullus and Ananias did not have their star witnesses in court they were reduced to the necessity of establishing their case on hearsay testimony, which was wholly inadmissible in a Roman court. Ananias, Tertullus and the other elders who had come down from Jerusalem were not even present when the alleged violations occurred. If they had been, we may be sure that the prosecution would have placed them on the stand, in response to Paul's challenge of verse 20. In any case they could have testified only to the charge that Paul had fomented a riot - a charge of disturbing the Roman peace, which was hardly a felony punishable by death. Felix would hear no testimony that had substance only in contemplation of Jewish religious issues.

*Verse 20 - "Or else let these same here say, if they have found any evil doing in me, while I stood before the council."*

ἢ αὐτοὶ οὗτοι εἰπάτωσαν τί εὗρον ἀδίκημα στάντος μου ἐπὶ τοῦ συνεδρίου..

ἢ (disjunctive) 465.
αὐτοὶ (nom.pl.masc.of αὐτός, intensive) 16.
οὗτοι (nom.pl.masc.of οὗτος, subject of εἰπάτωσαν) 93.
εἰπάτωσαν (3d.per.pl.aor.impv.of εἶπον, command) 155.
τί (acc.sing.neut.of τίς, interrogative pronoun, in agreement with ἀδίκημα, indirect question) 281.
εὗρον (3d.per.pl.aor.act.ind.of εὑρίσκω, culminative) 79.
ἀδίκημα (acc.sing.neut.of ἀδίκημα, direct object of εὗρον) 3446.
στάντος (2d.aor.act.part.gen.sing.masc.of ἵστημι, genitive absolute) 180.
μου (gen.sing.masc.of ἐγώ, genitive absolute) 123.
ἐπὶ (preposition with the genitive of place description) 47.
τοῦ (gen.sing.neut.of the article in agreement with συνεδρίου) 9.
συνεδρίου (gen.sing.neut.of συνέδριον, place description) 481.

*Translation - ". . . or let these same men tell what evil they found, while I was before the San Hedrin."*

**Comment:** Having made the point that the witnesses who started the riot were not in court, Paul then suggested the only possible course for the prosecution to pursue. The men present, *i.e.* Ananias and the elders, could testify on a basis of personal knowledge only to what Paul said and did when he was arraigned before the San Hedrin (Acts 23:1-10). It was on that occasion that Ananias ordered a man standing near Paul to smite him in the mouth. Did Ananias, who, of course, would be subject to Paul's cross examination, want to tell Felix about that? What could they tell the court about the evil which Paul did or said on that occasion? The genitive absolute στάντος μου ἐπὶ τοῦ συνεδρίου is vitally important in the case. It is temporal. Paul was saying that the only testimony that Ananias and the elders could give was that which they heard during the conference in question. Any other testimony would be hearsay evidence.

Moreover, if Tertullus dared to put Ananias on the stand, Felix would learn that what Paul said on that occasion divided the council itself! Would they like the court to know about that? Paul's court-room strategy of defense was masterful. He had not studied law under Gamaliel for nothing.

*Verse 21 - "Except it be for this one voice, that I cried standing among them, Touching the resurrection of the dead, I am called in question by you this day."*

ἢ περὶ μιᾶς ταύτης φωνῆς ἧς ἐκέκραξα ἐν αὐτοῖς ἑστὼς ὅτι Περὶ ἀναστάσεω νεκρῶν ἐγὼ κρίνομαι σήμερον ἐφ' ὑμῶν.

ἢ (disjunctive) 465.

περὶ (preposition with the genitive of reference) 173.

μιᾶς (gen.sing.fem.of εἷς, in agreement with φωνῆς) 469.

ταύτης (gen.sing.fem.of οὗτος, in agreement with φωνῆς) 93.

φωνῆς (gen.sing.fem.of φωνή, reference) 222.

ἧς (gen.sing.fem.of ὅς, incorporated with φωνῆς) 65.

ἐκέκραξα (1st.per.sing.aor.act.ind.(reduplicated form) of κράζω, constative) 765.

ἐν (preposition with the locative, place, with plural pronouns) 80.

αὐτοῖς (loc.pl.masc.of αὐτός, place) 16.

ἑστὼς (perf.act.part.nom.sing.masc.of ἵστημι, adverbial, circumstantial) 180.

ὅτι (recitative) 211.

Περὶ (preposition with the genitive of reference) 173.

ἀναστάσεως (gen.sing.fem.of ἀνάστασις, reference) 1423.

νεκρῶν (gen.pl.masc.of νεκρός, description) 749.

ἐγὼ (nom.sing.masc.of ἐγώ, subject of κρίνομαι) 123.

κρίνομαι (1st.per.sing.pres.pass.ind.of κρίνω) 531.

σήμερον (temporal adverb) 579.

ἐφ' (preposition with the genitive of place description) 47.

ὑμῶν (gen.pl.masc.of σύ, place description) 104.

*Translation - ". . . except with reference to this one voice which I shouted out as I was standing among them, 'Concerning resurrection of the dead, I am being judged this day before you.' "*

**Comment:** Luke's idiom περὶ μιᾶς ταύτης φωνῆς ἧς ἐκέκραξα is unusual, though the meaning is clear. This is the only case of the attributive use of οὗτος without the article in the N.T. The idiom suggested by Blass, ἡ φωνὴ ἡ ἐγένετο ἦν μία αὕτη ". . . is, of course, the normal Greek idiom and is possibly correct" (Blass, *Grammar of New Testament Greek,* 172, as cited in Robertson, *Grammar,* 702). ὅτι is recitative with the direct quotation of Paul's previous statement in Acts 23:6, though it is not a verbatim quotation. This statement by Paul had divided the San Hedrin before, and Ananias, the high priest, who was a Pharisee who believed in the resurrection could not object to it now. Unless Tertullus was as uninformed about courtroom strategy as he was about Greek rhetoric, he had no desire to get into that with Paul, since the argument began as Pharisees and Sadducees in the San Hedrin disagreed about the resurrection. Indeed there is nothing in the text to say that Tertullus was an attorney - only that he was an orator. Perhaps Ananias could not find a lawyer who was willing to prosecute a case devoid of evidence. There was no rebuttal to Paul's devastating defense.

*Verse 22 - "And when Felix heard these things, having more perfect knowledge of that way, he deferred them, and said, When Lysias the chief captain shall come down, I will know the uttermost of your matter."*

'Ανεβάλετο δὲ αὐτοὺς ὁ Φῆλιξ, ἀκριβέστερον εἰδὼς τὰ περὶ τῆς ὁδοῦ, εἴπας, "Οταν Λυσίας ὁ χιλίαρχος καταβῇ διαγνώσομαι τὰ καθ' ὑμᾶς,

#3627 'Ανεβάλετο (3d.per.sing.aor.mid.ind.of ἀναβάλλομαι, constative).

defer - Acts 24:22.

*Meaning:* A combination of ἀνά (#1059) and βάλλω (#299). Hence, to throw up; toss up; put off; delay; defer. Felix postponed his decision in the case of the Jews *versus* Paul - Acts 24:22.

δὲ (adversative conjunction) 11.
αὐτοὺς (acc.pl.masc.of αὐτός, direct object of 'Ανεβάλετο) 16.
Φῆλιξ (nom.sing.masc.of Φῆλιξ, subject of 'Ανεβάλετο) 3603.
ἀκριβέστερον (acc.sing.neut.comp.of ἀκριβής, adverbial) 3457.
εἰδὼς (aor.part.nom.sing.masc.of ὁράω, adverbial, causal) 144b.
τὰ (acc.pl.neut.of the article, direct object of εἰδὼς) 9.
περὶ (preposition with the genitive of reference) 173.
τῆς (gen.sing.fem.of the article in agreement with ὁδοῦ) 9.
ὁδοῦ (gen.sing.fem.of ὁδός, reference) 199.
εἴπας (3d.per.sing.aor.act.ind.of εἶπον, constative) 155.
"Οταν (conjunction introducing the subjunctive in an indefinite temporal clause) 436.
Λυσίας (nom.sing.masc.of Λυσίας, subject of καταβῇ) 3604.
ὁ (nom.sing.masc.of the article in agreement with χιλίαρχος) 9.
χιλίαρχος (nom.sing.masc.of χιλίαρχος, apposition) 2258.
καταβῇ (3d.per.sing.aor.act.subj.of καταβαίνω, indefinite temporal clause) 324.
διαγνώσομαι (1st.per.sing.fut.ind.of διαγινώσκω, predictive) 3598.
τὰ (acc.pl.neut.of the article, direct object of διαγνώσομαι) 9.
καθ' (preposition with the accusative of general reference) 98.
ὑμᾶς (acc.pl.masc.of σύ, general reference) 104.

*Translation - "But Felix ordered the case continued, because he was somewhat well informed about the 'way'. He said, 'When Lysias, the colonel comes down, I will come to understand the issues between you better.' "*

**Comment:** δὲ is adversative. Both sides were disappointed. Tertullus and Ananias hoped for a conviction, although they must have known that they had not proved their case. On the other hand, Paul, with expert knowledge of the law, knew that there was only one correct decision for the court to hand down. Whether he expected Felix to dismiss the case or not, the text does not tell us. Perhaps he expected Felix, who had a reputation for corruption, to dissemble. But Felix for his own benefit (middle voice in ἀνεβάλετο) put them off. The case, which should have been dismissed, was continued. The causal participle εἰδὼς tells us why. Felix did not understand Christian theology perfectly, but better than one might expect, and he may have wanted to know more about it. The indefinite temporal clause with the subjunctive in καταβῇ indicates that Felix had some doubt that Claudius Lysias would ever come to Caesarea. As the story unfolds there is no record that he ever did, at least not for the purpose of testifying further about the case. In fact, he had said all that he knew about the case in the letter and could have added nothing substantive. Note the perfective prepositional prefix in διαγνώσομαι. Felix, with some knowledge of the issues expressed a desire to know the issues perfectly.

The governor seems, on the surface, to have been kindly disposed toward Paul, partly because of his sense of Roman justice. There was no doubt that Paul had won the legal battle in his court. His interest in Paul's theology was also stimulated, although he was soon to learn more about it than he cared to know (verse 25). His wife was Jewish and it is possible that there had been discussion with her about the relative merits of Judaism and Christianity *vis a vis* the Roman paganism. On the shabby side of the question is the fact that Felix was afflicted with the venality that was characteristic of a powerful politician in his favored position (verse 26). Felix, who was destined to face charges before Nero, because of his corrupt administration, may also have feared the consequences of treatment to a Roman citizen who had not been convicted of a crime, although this fear, if he felt it, did not prevent him from keeping Paul in jail in Caesarea until the end of his administration, two years later.

*Verse 23 - "And he commanded a centurion to keep Paul, and to let him have liberty, and that he should forbid none of his acquaintance to minister or come to him."*

διαταξάμενος τῷ ἑκατοντάρχῃ τηρεῖσθαι αὐτὸν ἔχειν τε ἄεσιν καὶ μηδένα κωλύειν τῶν ἰδίων αὐτοῦ ὑπηρετεῖν αὐτῷ.

διαταξάμενος (aor.mid.part.nom.sing.masc.of διατάσσω, adverbial, temporal) 904.

τῷ (dat.sing.masc.of the article in agreement with ἑκατοντάρχῃ) 9.

ἑκατοντάρχῃ (dat.sing.masc.of ἑκατοντάρχης, indirect object διαταξάμενος) 3210.

τηρεῖσθαι (pres.pass.inf.of τηρέω, noun use, direct object of διαταξάμενος) 1297.

αὐτὸν (acc.sing.masc.of αὐτός, general reference) 16.

ἔχειν (pres.act.inf.of ἔχω, noun use, direct object of διαταξάμενος) 82.

τε (correlative particle) 1408.

#3628 ἄνεσιν (acc.sing.fem.of ἄνεσις, direct object of ἔχειν).

liberty - Acts 24:23.
rest - 2 Cor.2:13; 7:5; 2 Thess.1:7.
be eased - 2 Cor.8:13.

*Meaning:* A combination of ἀνά (#1059), ἵημι. *Cf.*ἀνίημι (#3378). Hence, a loosening; relaxing. Relative freedom for a political prisoner - Acts 24:23;

freedom from fear - 2 Thess.1:7; freedom from poverty - 2 Cor.8:13; freedom from anxiety - 2 Cor.2:13; 7:5.

καὶ (adjunctive conjunction joining infinitives) 14.
μηδένα (acc.sing.masc.of μηδείς, direct object of κωλύειν) 713.
κωλύειν (pres.act.inf.of κωλύω, noun use, direct object of διαταξάμενος) 1296.
τῶν (gen.pl.masc.of the article in agreement with ἰδίων) 9.
ἰδίων (gen.pl.masc.of ἴδιος partitive genitive) 778.
αὐτοῦ (gen.sing.masc.of αὐτός, relationship) 16.
ὑπηρετεῖν (pres.act.inf.of ὑπηρετέω, completes κωλύειν) 3300.
αὐτῷ (dat.sing.masc.of αὐτός, personal interest) 16.

*Translation - ". . . having previously directed the centurion that he be guarded but that he be allowed some freedom and to forbid none of his own friends to minister to his needs."*

**Comment:** The participle διαταξάμενος is aorist, indicating at least simultaneous if not coincidental action with εἶπας of verse 22. Felix's decision to continue the trial was made as he ordered that Paul be kept in Caesarea, under house arrest, but with the freedoms which the infinitives indicate. He was to be guarded, perhaps against an attempt on the part of the Jews to kidnap and murder him. But he was to be given all the liberty possible consistent with house arrest. ἄνεσιν means more than physical liberty to move about. It means release from tension and worry. Paul was to be made as comfortable as possible. Nor were his friends to be forbidden to visit and minister to his needs.

Thus, even though Paul was a prisoner, he was to enjoy V.I.P. treatment, the Lord thus providing that he was to continue his ministry even though kept under house arrest. He enjoyed this same freedom to preach after he reached Rome (Acts 28:30,31). We know little of the results of Paul's ministry during his stay in Caesarea, but we may be certain that he made the most of every opportunity to preach the gospel of Christ.

## Paul Held in Custody

*(Acts 24:24 - 27)*

*Verse 24 - "And after certain days, when Felix came with his wife, Drusilla, which was a Jewess, he sent for Paul, and heard him concerning the faith in Christ."*

Μετὰ δὲ ἡμέρας τινὰς παραγενόμενος ὁ Φῆλιξ σὺν Δρουσίλλῃ τῇ ἰδίᾳ γυναικὶ οὔσῃ Ἰουδαίᾳ μετεπέμψατο τὸν Παῦλον καὶ ἤκουσεν αὐτοῦ περὶ τῆς εἰς Χριστὸν Ἰησοῦν πίστεως.

Μετὰ (preposition with the accusative of time extent) 50.
δὲ (continuative conjunction) 11.

ἡμέρας (acc.pl.fem.of ἡμέρα, time extent) 135.

τινὰς (acc.pl.fem.of τις, indefinite pronoun, in agreement with ἡμέρας) 486.

παραγενόμενος (aor.mid.part.nom.sing.masc.of παραγίνομαι, adverbial, temporal) 139.

ὁ (nom.sing.masc.of the article in agreement with Φῆλιξ) 9.

Φῆλιξ (nom.sing.masc.of Φῆλιξ, subject of μετεπέμψατο and ἤκουσεν) 3603.

σὺν (preposition with the instrumental of association) 1542.

#3629 Δρουσίλλῃ (instru.sing.fem.of Δρουσίλλα, association).

Drusilla - Acts 24:24.

*Meaning:* The daughter of Agrippa, the Elder and wife of Felix, the Governor of Judea - Acts 24:24.

τῇ (instrumental sing.fem.of the article in agreement with γυναικὶ) 9.

ἰδίᾳ (instrumental sing.fem.of ἴδιος, in agreement with γυναικὶ) 778.

γυναικὶ (instrumental sing.fem.of γυνή, apposition) 103.

οὔσῃ (pres.part.instru.sing.fem.of εἰμί, adjectival, restrictive, in agreement with γυναικὶ) 86.

Ἰουδαίᾳ (instru.sing.fem.of Ἰουδαῖος, predicate nominative) 143.

μετεπέμψατο (3d.per.sing.aor.mid.ind.of μεταπέμπω, constative) 3213.

τὸν (acc.sing.masc.of the article in agreement with Παῦλον) 9.

Παῦλον (acc.sing.masc.of Παῦλος, direct object of μετεπέμψατο) 3284.

καὶ (adjunctive conjunction joining verbs) 14.

ἤκουσεν (3d.per.sing.aor.act.ind.of ἀκούω, ingressive) 148.

αὐτοῦ (gen.sing.masc.of αὐτός, objective genitive) 16.

περὶ (preposition with the genitive of reference) 173.

τῆς (gen.sing.fem.of the article in agreement with πίστεως) 9.

εἰς (preposition with the accusative of extent, with persons, metaphorical) 140.

Χριστὸν (acc.sing.masc.of Χριστός, extent, metaphorical) 4.

Ἰησοῦν (acc.sing.masc.of Ἰησοῦς, apposition) 3.

πίστεως (gen.sing.fem.of πίστις, reference) 728.

*Translation - "And after some days Felix came with Drusilla, his own wife, who was a Jewess and sent for Paul and began to listen to him about the faith in Christ Jesus."*

**Comment:** μετὰ with the accusative of time extent, although Luke does not tell us precisely how many days elapsed before Felix and Drusilla came. There is no reason why Luke should have used ἰδίᾳ in the attributive position with γυναικὶ, except to imply that Felix often consorted with women who were not his wife. Thus the profligacy of the court is suggested. Note the ingressive aorist in ἤκουσεν and that it is followed by the genitive αὐτοῦ rather than the accusative αὐτόν, which means, if the distinction holds in this passage, that Felix heard Paul's voice as the Apostle preached but did not understand the message. The distinction between the genitive and accusative after ἀκούω cannot always be discerned from the context as an exhaustive examination of ἀκούω (#148) will reveal. Notice should be taken of the case of the object - whether genitive or accusative. In the passage before us we have the genitive after ἤκουσεν, but Felix understood at least enough of Paul's message to tremble.

*Verse 25 - "And as he reasoned of righteousness, temperance and judgment to come, Felix trembled, and answered, Go thy way for this time; when I have a convenient season I will call for thee."*

διαλεγομένου δὲ αὐτοῦ περὶ δικαιοσύνης καὶ ἐγκρατείας καὶ τοῦ κρίματος τοῦ μέλλοντος ἔμφοβος γενόμενος ὁ Φῆλιξ ἀπεκρίθη, Τὸ νῦν ἔχον πορεύου, καιρὸν δὲ μεταλαβὼν μετακαλέσομαί σε.

διαλεγομένου (pres.mid.part.gen.sing.masc.of διαλέγομαι, genitive absolute) 2349.
    δὲ (continuative conjunction) 11.
αὐτοῦ (gen.sing.masc.of αὐτός, genitive absolute) 16.
περὶ (preposition with the genitive of reference) 173.
δικαιοσύνης (gen.sing.fem.of δικαιοσύνη, reference) 322.
καὶ (adjunctive conjunction joining nouns) 14.

#3630 ἐγκρατείας (gen.sing.fem.of ἐγκράτεια, reference).

temperance - Acts 24:25; Gal.5:23; 2 Pet.1:6,6.

*Meaning:* Cf. ἐγκρατής (#4881). Self control; temperance. The virtue of one who masters and controls his appetites, often, but not exclusively, applied to sensual appetites. Not to be confused with total abstinence. Generally in Acts 24:25; the fruit of the Holy Spirit in the life of the believer - Gal.5:23; the fruit of knowledge - 2 Peter 1:6a; the source of patience - 2 Peter 1:6b.

καὶ (adjunctive conjunction joining nouns) 14.
τοῦ (gen.sing.neut.of the article in agreement with κρίματος) 9.
κρίματος (gen.sing.neut.of κρίμα, reference) 642.
τοῦ (gen.sing.neut.of the article in agreement with μέλλοντος) 9.
μέλλοντος (pres.act.part.gen.sing.neut.of μέλλω, adjectival, ascriptive, in agreement with κρίματος) 206.
ἔμφοβος (nom.sing.masc.of ἔμφοβος, predicate adjective) 2890.
γενόμενος (aor.mid.part.gen.sing.masc.of γίνομαι, adverbial, causal) 113.
ὁ (nom.sing.masc.of the article in agreement with Φῆλιξ) 9.
Φῆλιξ (nom.sing.masc.of Φῆλιξ, subject of ἀπεκρίθη) 3603.
ἀπεκρίθη (3d.per.sing.aor.mid.ind.of ἀποκρίνομαι, constative) 318.
Τὸ (acc.sing.neut.of the article in agreement with νῦν) 9.
νῦν (adverb treated as a substantive, direct object of ἔχον) 1497.
ἔχον (pres.act.part.acc.sing.neut.of ἔχω, adjectival, in agreement with νῦν, time extent) 82.
πορεύου (2d.per.sing.pres.mid.impv.of πορεύομαι, command) 170.

καιρὸν (acc.sing.masc.of καιρός, direct object of μεταλαβὼν) 767.
δὲ (continuative conjunction) 11.
μεταλαβὼν (aor.act.part.nom.sing.masc.of μεταλαμβάνω, adverbial, coincident) 3003.
μετακαλέσομαί (1st.per.sing.fut.mid.ind.of μετακαλέω, predictive) 3111.
σε (acc.sing.masc.of σύ, direct object of μετακαλέσομαί) 104.

Translation - "And as he argued about righteousness and temperance and the coming judgment, Felix, seized with fear, replied, 'For the time being, go away and when I have an opportunity, I will send for you.' "

Comment: The pagan, dissolute governor had some interest, at least from a philosophical point of view in hearing more about Paul's theology (Acts 24:22). But he got more than he asked for. Paul's remarks took an unpleasant turn for Felix. δικαιοσύνη (#322), the state of being declared righteous or right before God's moral universal law, is a great subject. It should have been of particular interest to a Roman governor whose pride was in his execution of the famous Roman justice, which demanded protection for the innocent and punishment for the guilty. To be told that there is a greater Augustus in the universe, the glorified Lord Jesus, Who is as objective in His decisions as Caesar, was to be reminded that he himself, when judged by that objective standard, was guilty. This was more than enough to disturb his emotional equilibrium.

Temperance (#3630). God is no fanatic. He demands teetotalism of no one. Everything in the universe — all the result of His creation, is good and proper in its own place and used with moderation. God expects man to exercise rational self-control, thus to make everything serve him. God forbids every man to serve any of that which He has created. But Felix, the governor, was a slave to his own unbridled passions, which led him beyond moderation to excess. Paul's thought was always opposed to the Gnosticism of those who taught, either that matter is eternal or that God erred when He created certain things that are *always* evil when taken in any amount, however small. The force of Paul's speech rested in the fact that it gave to Felix no chance to bring a reasonable rebuttal against God. Only a Gnostic will charge God with the folly of having created evil. And Paul was no Gnostic. God's righteous standard is reasonable and temperate. But no standard of excellence, however just and reasonable, is effective if it is not subject to final evaluation. A day of reckoning is inevitable in a moral universe. Judgment is coming. Paul had made this point on Mars Hill (Acts 17:31). As he made it now, Felix was seized with fear, as all of the unsaved will be (Rev.11:13). *Cf.* #'s 322, 3630 and 642 for all other uses of these three great points in Paul's argument. But, though Felix was impressed, almost to the point of being convicted, he trembled, but he also procrastinated. In such a situation Satan always suggests to the sinner that he can indulge a positive time preference. Judgment is certain, but it is also chronologically remote. The present advantage of living in sin, even when we admit that what we do is sin and merits judgment, yields greater utility than the disutility of contemplating coming judgment. Thus Felix stalled for time. He dismissed Paul with a promise to hear him at some later and more convenient time. As far as we know that time never came.

Another thought had crossed the mind of the governor. Surely Paul would be willing to be reasonable and offer to buy his way out of jail. Felix resolved to visit him often until the prisoner would be willing to make a deal that would be of mutual benefit. This is the thought of

*Verse 26 - "He hoped also that money should have been given him of Paul, that he might loose him; wherefore he sent for him the oftener, and communed with him."*

ἅμα καὶ ἐλπίζων ὅτι χρήματα δοθήσεται αὐτῷ ὑπὸ τοῦ Παύλου, διὸ καὶ πυκνότερον αὐτὸν μεταπεμπόμενος ὡμίλει αὐτῷ.

ἅμα (temporal particle) 1063.

καὶ (adjunctive conjunction, joining participles) 14.

ἐλπίζων (pres.act.part.nom.sing.masc.of ἐλπίζω, adverbial, circumstantial) 991.

ὅτι (conjunction introducing an object clause in indirect discourse) 211.

χρήματα (nom.pl.neut.of χρῆμα, subject of δοθήσεται) 2637.

δοθήσεται (3d.per.sing.fut.pass.ind.of δίδωμι, indirect discourse) 362.

αὐτῷ (dat.sing.masc.of αὐτός, indirect object of δοθήσεται) 16.

ὑπὸ (preposition with the ablative of agent) 117.

τοῦ (abl.sing.masc.of the article in agreement with Παύλου) 9.

Παύλου (abl.sing.masc.of Παῦλος, agent) 3284.

διὸ (inferential conjunction) 1622.

καὶ (continuative conjunction) 14.

πυκνότερον (acc.sing.neut.comp.of πυκνός, adverbial) 2090.

αὐτὸν (acc.sing.masc.of αὐτός, direct object of μεταπεμπόμενος) 16.

μεταπεμπόμενος (pres.mid.part.nom.sing.masc.of μεταπέμπω, adverbial, modal) 3213.

ὡμίλει (3d.per.sing.imp.act.ind.of ὁμιλέω, iterative) 2898.

αὐτῷ (instru.sing.masc.of αὐτός, association) 16.

*Translation - "... at the same time also hoping that money would be given to him by Paul, and, therefore, by sending for him more frequently he talked with him from time to time."*

**Comment:** The adverbial particle here with adjunctive καὶ and the participle ἐλπίζων sharpens the connection between the participle and the main verb ὡμίλει. *Cf.* #1063. Note the indirect discourse with ὅτι after a verb of hoping. The future passive in δοθήσεται is the same tense as in the direct. It was subsequent to ἐλπίζων in action but antecedent of course, to the time of Luke's writing. Felix was hoping that Paul would try to bribe him. διὸ καὶ - "and therefore" - ὡμίλει is an iterative imperfect, explained by the comparative πυκνότερον. More frequently than would have been Felix's policy if the governor had known that Paul had assurances from the Lord that "all things" - even house arrest in Caesarea, "work together for good to those who love the Lord and are the called according to His purpose" (Romans 8:28). With assurance like that a bribe was not only unspeakable but unnecessary.

Felix's ulterior motive was money. He possibly hoped that Paul would think that he was trying to be friendly, and that he would be receptive to Paul's offer of a bribe. The governor added deception to his other sins, all of which prevented him from listening seriously to Paul's salvation message. It is not surprizing then to see his callous disregard for Roman justice in his action of

*Verse 27 - "But after two years Porcious Festus came into Felix' room: and Felix, willing to shew the Jews a pleasure, left Paul bound."*

Διετίας δὲ πληρωθείσης ἔλαβεν διάδοχον ὁ Φῆλιξ Πόρκιον Φῆστον. θέλων τε χάριτα καταθέσθαι τοῖς Ἰουδαίοις ὁ Φῆλιξ κατέλιπε τὸν Παῦλον δεδεμένον.

**#3631** Διετίας (gen.sing.fem.of διετία, genitive absolute).

two years - Acts 24:27; 28:30.

*Meaning: Cf.* διετής (#219). The space of two years. With reference to Paul's imprisonment in Caesarea - Acts 24:27; with reference to his home imprisonment in Rome - Acts 28:30.

δὲ (continuative conjunction) 11.
πληρωθείσης (1st.aor.pass.part.gen.sing.masc.of πληρόω, genitive absolute) 115.
ἔλαβεν (3d.per.sing.aor.act.ind.of λαμβάνω, constative) 533.

**#3632** διάδοχον (acc.sing.masc.of διάδοχος, direct object of ἔλαβεν).

come into the room of - Acts 24:27.

*Meaning: Cf.* διαδέχομαι (#3143). A successor. One who succeeds to a post. With reference to Festus, the successor of Felix - Acts 24:27.

ὁ (nom.sing.masc.of the article in agreement with Φῆλιξ) 9.
Φῆλιξ (nom.sing.masc.of Φῆλιξ, subject of ἔλαβεν) 3603.

**#3633** Πόρκιον Φῆστον (acc.sing.masc. of Πόρκιος Φῆστος, apposition).

Portius Festus - Acts 24:27; 25:1,4,9,12,13,14,22,23,24; 26:24,25,32.

*Meaning:* Procurator of Judea who succeeded Felix in *c.* A.D.60 - Acts 24:27; 25:1,4,9,12,13,14,22,23,24; 26:24,25,32.

θέλων (pres.act.part.nom.sing.masc.of θέλω, adverbial, causal) 88.
τε (continuative conjunction) 1408.
χάριτα (acc.sing.masc.of χάρις, direct object of καταθέσθαι) 1700.

**#3634** καταθέσθαι (2d.aor.mid.inf.of κατατίθημι, epexegetical).

do - Acts 25:9.
show - Acts 24:27.

*Meaning:* A combination of κατά (#98) and τίθημι (#455). Hence, to lay down; deposit; to lay up for oneself some benefit. Followed by χάριν - to show a favor. With reference to Felix's action for the Jews, with the purpose of ingratiating them in order to secure some future benefit - Acts 24:27. With reference to the action of Festus under similar circumstances and for similar reasons - Acts 25:9.

τοῖς (dat.pl.masc.of the article in agreement with Ἰουδαίοις) 9.
Ἰουδαίοις (dat.pl.masc.of Ἰουδαῖος, personal advantage) 143.
ὁ (nom.sing.masc.of the article in agreement with Φῆλιξ) 9.
Φῆλιξ (nom.sing.masc.of Φῆλιξ, subject of κατέλιπε) 3603.
κατέλιπε (3d.per.sing.aor.act.ind.of καταλείπω, culminative) 369.
τὸν (acc.sing.masc.of the article in agreement with Παῦλον) 9.
Παῦλον (acc.sing.masc.of Παῦλος, direct object of κατέλιπε) 3284.
δεδεμένον (perf.pass.part.acc.sing.masc.of δέω, adverbial, circumstantial) 998.

*Translation - "And when two years had passed, Felix gave way to a successor, Portius Festus, and because he wanted to curry favor with the Jews, he left Paul in bonds."*

**Comment:** *Cf.* #533 for other examples of λαμβάνω joined with a substantive in a periphrastic idiom. In these cases the verbal idea is expressed, not by the verb but by the substantive. So Felix left office in a blaze of infamy, and a Christian suffered as a pawn in the hands of sinners devoted to the ethics of expediency. It is possible that Felix was motivated especially at this time to seek friends among his former subjects, as he was soon in need of defenders before Nero. Had it not been for the intercession of his brother, Pallas, Felix would have been fed to the lions. *Cf.*#3603.

But God, who makes the wrath of men praise Him (Psalm 76:10) and Who laughs at His opposition (Psalm 2:4) was sovereign over Paul's life and had been gracious to his Apostle by telling him in advance that, despite the hatred of the Jews and the machinations of the two-bit politicians, he would live to preach the gospel in Rome (Acts 23:11). *Cf.* Phil.1:6; Eph.2:8-10.

# Paul Appeals to Caesar

*(Acts 25: 1 - 12)*
*Acts 25:1 - "Now when Festus was come into the province, after three days he ascended from Caesarea to Jerusalem."*

Φῆστος οὖν ἐπιβὰς τῇ ἐπαρχείᾳ μετὰ τρεῖς ἡμέρας ἀνέβη εἰς Ἱεροσόλυμα ἀπὸ Καισαρείας,

Φῆστος (nom.sing.masc.of Φῆστος, subject of ἀνέβη) 3633.
οὖν (continuative conjunction) 68.
ἐπιβὰς (aor.act.part.nom.sing.masc.of ἐπιβαίνω, adverbial, temporal) 1346.
τῇ (loc.sing.fem.of the article in agreement with ἐπαρχείᾳ) 9.

ἐπαρχείᾳ (loc.sing.fem.of ἐπαρχία, place where) 3609.

μετὰ (preposition with the accusative of time extent) 50.

τρεῖς (numeral) 1010.

ἡμέρας (acc.pl.fem.of ἡμέρα, time extent) 135.

ἀνέβη (3d.per.sing.aor.act.ind.of ἀναβαίνω, culminative) 323.

εἰς (preposition with the accusative of extent) 140.

Ἱεροσόλυμα (acc.sing.masc.of Ἱεροσόλυμα, extent) 141.

ἀπὸ (preposition with the ablative of separation) 70.

Καισαρείας (abl.sing.fem.of Καισαρεία, separation) 1200.

*Translation - "Then three days after Festus had arrived in the province he went up to Jerusalem from Caesarea,"*

**Comment:** ἐπιβὰς is antecedent to ἀνέβη. Here is a case where the context tells us this, even if the tense of the participle did not. If Luke had written a present participle (ἐπιβαινῶν) we would be in trouble. Festus needed to establish good public relations with his subjects, as Felix, whom he succeeded was under attack by "the principal of the Jewish inhabitants of Caesarea (who) went up to Rome to accuse Felix; and he had certainly been brought to punishment, unless Nero had yielded to the importunate solicitations of his brother Pallas, who was at that time had in the greatest of honor by him." (Josephus, *Antiquities of the Jews*, XX, 9). Felix had left the province of Judea in shambles. The country ". . . was afflicted by the robbers, while all the villages were set on fire, and plundered by them. And then it was that the Sicarii, as they were called, who were robbers, grew numerous. They made use of small swords . . . and with these weapons they slew a great many; for they mingled themselves among the multitude at their festivals, when they were come up in crowds from all parts of the city to worship God . . . and easily slew those that they had a mind to slay. They also came frequently upon the villages belonging to their enemies, with their weapons, and plundered them, and set them on fire. So Festus sent forces, both horsemen and footmen, to fall upon those that had been seduced by a certain imposter, who promised them deliverance and freedom from the miseries they were under, if they would but follow him into the wilderness. Accordingly those forces that were sent destroyed both him that had deluded them, and those that were his followers also" (*Ibid.,* XX, 10).

Josephus' account of the social chaos which prevailed under the rule of Felix, points up the sham and pompous cant of Tertullus in his opening remarks before Felix (Acts 24:2,3).

The situation demanded Festus' immediate attention, and it is likely that it was in connection with his new law enforcement program that he made the trip up to Jerusalem. He was particularly eager to improve upon the record of his predecessor, since the Jews who were demanding punishment for Felix before Nero in Rome were from Caesarea, and Festus was anxious to show them that his administration would be different.

There is no evidence in the text that he knew about Paul's case at this time. He had been installed in the procuratorship only three days before. He was soon to learn about Paul as we see in

*Verse 2 - "Then the high priest and the chief of the Jews informed him against Paul, and besought him, . . . "*

ἐνεφάνισάν τε αυτῷ οἱ ἀρχιερεῖς καὶ οἱ πρῶτοι Ἰουδαίων κατὰ τοῦ Παύλου, καὶ παρεκάλουν αὐτὸν . . . "

ἐνεφάνισάν (3d.per.pl.aor.act.ind.of ἐμφανίζω, ingressive) 1666.

τε (continuative particle) 1408.

αυτῷ (dat.sing.masc.of αὐτός, indirect object of ἐνεφάνισάν) 16.

οἱ (nom.pl.masc.of the article in agreement with ἀρχιερεῖς) 9.

ἀρχιερεῖς (nom.pl.masc.of ἀρχιερεύς, subject of ἐνεφάνισάν) 151.

καὶ (adjunctive conjunction joining substantives) 14.

οἱ (nom.pl.masc.of the article in agreement with πρῶτοι) 9.

πρῶτοι (nom.pl.masc.of πρῶτος, subject of ἐνεφάνισάν) 487.

τῶν (gen.pl.masc.of the article in agreement with Ἰουδαίων) 9.

Ἰουδαίων (gen.pl.masc.of Ἰουδαῖος, description) 143.

κατὰ (preposition with the genitive, opposition) 98 .

τοῦ (gen.sing.masc.of the article in agreement with Παύλου) 9.

Παύλου (gen.sing.masc.of Παῦλος, opposition) 3284.

καὶ (adjunctive conjunction joining verbs) 14.

παρεκάλουν (3d.per.pl.imp.act.ind.of παρακαλέω, iterative) 230.

αὐτὸν (acc.sing.masc.of αὐτός, direct object of παρεκάλουν) 16.

*Translation - "Both the priests and the leaders of the Jews began to tell him about Paul and they were imploring him . . . "*

**Comment:** τε . . . καὶ - "both. . . and." Religious and political leaders in the Jewish community took the occasion to tell the new governor about Paul. κατὰ and the genitive means opposition. We have taken ἐνεφάνισάν as an ingressive aorist and παρεκάλοῦν as an iterative imperfect. They *began* to talk to Festus about Paul and they returned to the subject again and again.

One wonders why they were still so adamant against Paul after two years? It is reasonable to assume that during these two years Paul had not been idle, even though his audience was confined to those who chose to visit him during his period of house arrest. Did unsaved persons visit Paul, and, if so, did they accept the Lord Jesus as Saviour as a result of his witness? Though the preacher was bound, "the Word of God was not bound" (2 Tim.2:9).

Paul's enemies had decided to try again the ruse which failed before, if only because Paul's nephew discovered the plot and reported it to Claudius Lysias (Acts 23:12-21). We are reminded also of the forty men who vowed to go on a hunger strike until they had killed Paul. Were they still alive or had they fallen victim to malnutrition? It is probable that they were still alive and they may have been a part of the new plot.

*Verse 3 - "And desired favour against him, that he would send for him to Jerusalem, laying wait in the way to kill him."*

αἰτούμενοι χάριν κατ' αὐτοῦ ὅπως μεταπέμψηται αὐτὸν εἰς Ἰερουσαλήμ, ἐνέδραν ποιοῦντες ἀνελεῖν αὐτὸν κατὰ τὴν ὁδόν.

αἰτούμενοι (pres.mid.part.nom.pl.masc.of αἰτέω, adverbial, modal) 537.

χάριν (acc.sing.fem.of χάρις, direct object of αἰτούμενοι) 1700.

κατ' (preposition with the genitive, opposition) 98.

αὐτοῦ (gen.sing.masc.of αὐτός, opposition) 16.

ὅπως (conjunction introducing the subjunctive in a sub-final clause) 177.

μεταπέμψηται (3d.per.sing.aor.mid.subj.of μεταπέμπω, sub-final) 3213.

αὐτὸν (acc.sing.masc.of αὐτός, direct object of μεταπέμψηται) 16.

εἰς (preposition with the accusative of extent) 140.

Ἰερουσαλήμ (acc.sing.fem.of Ἰερουσαλήμ, extent) 141.

ἐνέδραν (acc.sing.fem.of ἐνέδρα, direct object of ποιοῦντες) 3599.

ποιοῦντες (pres.act.part.nom.pl.masc.of ποιέω, adverbial, temporal) 127.

ἀνελεῖν (aor.act.inf.of ἀναιρέω, epexegetical) 216.

αὐτὸν (acc.sing.masc.of αὐτός, direct object of ἀνελεῖν) 16.

κατὰ (preposition with the accusative, - "down along") 98.

τὴν (acc.sing.fem.of the article in agreement with ὁδόν) 9.

ὁδόν (acc.sing.fem.of ὁδός, - "down along") 199.

*Translation - ". . . asking a favor against him in order (and with the result) that he would call him to Jerusalem, as they were hiding in ambush to kill him down along the road."*

**Comment:** αἰτούμενοι, another participle, continues the sentence which began in verse 2. It is modal. The Jews continued to importune Festus by (modal αἰτούμενοι) asking him for the favor. A favor for them it would be against Paul. ὅπως introduces the sub-final clause, which is both purpose and result. They wanted Festus to send a messenger to Caesarea and order Paul to come to Jerusalem. The present participle ποιοῦντες is temporal. It indicates that as they were asking Festus to send for Paul, they were, at that same time plotting to kill him. Indeed they were already lying in wait in ambush at some point down the road. There is nothing in the text to indicate that they told Festus about the plot. In the previous plot to kill him, the Jews had told Claudius Lysias that they wanted to ask Paul some questions about his theology.

Luke's use of κατὰ τὴν ὁδόν is particularly well chosen, as κατά with the accusative, when it is used in a local sense, means "down along." This formulation fits the topography, when one is looking at the road from Caesarea to Jerusalem from the Jerusalem point of view. Somewhere "down the road" the ambush was already in place, awaiting the moment when Paul would appear on the road to the north as he walked *up* the way.

After two years the Jewish Establishment was still eager for Paul's blood. Thus is the misplaced zeal of the religious fanatic.

> "John Brown's body lies a' moulding in the grave
> But his soul goes marching on."

The same spirit was alive in Jerusalem in the first century.

*Verse 4 - "But Festus answered that Paul should be kept at Caesarea, and that he himself would depart shortly thither."*

ὁ μὲν οὖν Φῆστος ἀπεκρίθη τηρεῖσθαι τὸν Παῦλον εἰς Καισάρειαν, ἑαυτὸν δὲ μέλλειν ἐν τάχει ἐκπορεύεσθαι.

ὁ (nom.sing.masc.of the article in agreement with Φῆστος) 9.
μὲν (particle of affirmation) 300.
οὖν (continuative conjunction) 68.
Φῆστος (nom.sing.masc.of Φῆστος, subject of ἀπεκρίθη) 3633.
ἀπεκρίθη (3d.per.sing.aor.mid.ind.of ἀποκρίνομαι, constative) 318.
τηρεῖσθαι (pres.pass.inf.of τηρέω, indirect discourse) 1297.
τὸν (acc.sing.masc.of the article in agreement with Παῦλον) 9.
Παῦλον (acc.sing.masc.of Παῦλος, general reference) 3284.
εἰς (preposition with the accusative, original static use, like a locative) 140.
Καισάρειαν (acc.sing.fem.of Καισαρίας, place where) 1200.
ἑαυτὸν (acc.sing.masc.of ἑαυτός, general reference) 288.
δὲ (adjunctive conjunction joining infinitives) 11.
μέλλειν (pres.act.inf.of μέλλω, indirect discourse) 206.
ἐν (preposition with the locative of time point) 80.
τάχει (loc.sing.neut.of τάχος, time point) 2626.
ἐκπορεύεσθαι (pres.mid.inf.of ἐκπορεύομαι, complementary) 270.

*Translation - "Then Festus answered that Paul was being kept in Caesarea, and that he himself was going to leave soon."*

**Comment:** ἀπεκρίθη introduces two object infinitives in indirect discourse. Note the original static use of εἰς and the accusative. In most κοινή writing the idea would be expressed with ἐν and the locative. *Cf.* #2626 for other instances of ἐν τάχει in this sense. Thus, thanks to Festus' brusque Roman efficiency the Jewish plot to kill Paul failed again. Since Festus was not prepared to remain in Jerusalem, if the Jews wanted to press charges against Paul, they would have to come to Caesarea. There was no time to send to Caesarea and wait for Paul to come to Jerusalem. Did Festus suspect the plot? Why was he required to return to Caesarea so quickly? Why had he come to Jerusalem? Was it to put down the riots which were rampant throughout the province, and if so, had he accomplished his purpose of beginning a stricter law enforcement program? Luke does not enlighten us on these points? But Festus did not deny the Jews in Jerusalem their right to use his court if they wished to charge Paul with a law violation. But let it be done by means of the proper challenges.

*Verse 5 - "Let them, therefore, said he, which among you are able, go down with me, and accuse this man, if there be any wickedness in him."*

Οἱ οὖν ἐν ἡμῖν, φησίν, δυνατοὶ συγκαταβάντες εἴ τί ἐστιν ἐν τῷ ἀνδρὶ ἄτοπον κατηγορείτωσαν αὐτοῦ.

Οἱ (nom.pl.masc.of the article in agreement with δυνατοὶ) 9.

οὖν (inferential conjunction) 68.

ἐν (preposition with the locative, with plural pronouns) 80.

ὑμῖν (loc.pl.masc.of σύ, place where, with persons) 104.

φησίν (3d.per.sing.pres.act.ind.of φημί, historical) 354.

δυνατοί (nom.pl.masc.of δυνατός, subject of κατηγορείτωσαν) 1311.

#3635 συγκαταβάντες (2d.aor.act.part.nom.pl.masc.of συγκαταβαίνω, adverbial, temporal).

go down with - Acts 25:5.

*Meaning:* A combination of σύν (#1542), κατά (#98) and βαίνω - "to go." Hence, to go down with; to accompany someone down the way. With reference to Festus' invitation to the Jews to go with him down the road from Jerusalem to Caesarea - Acts 25:5.

εἰ (conditional particle in a first-class condition) 337.

τί (nom.sing.neut.of τι, in agreement with ἄτοπον) 486.

ἐστιν (3d.per.sing.pres.ind.of εἰμί, in a first-class condition) 86.

ἐν (preposition with the locative of place, metaphorical) 80.

τῷ (loc.sing.masc.of the article in agreement with ἀνδρὶ) 9.

ἀνδρὶ (loc.sing.masc.of ἀνήρ, place where, metaphorical) 63.

ἄτοπον (nom.sing.neut.of ἄτοπος, subject of ἐστιν) 2856.

κατηγορείτωσαν (3d.per.pl.pres.act.impv.of κατηγορέω, command) 974.

αὐτοῦ (gen.sing.masc.of αὐτός, objective genitive) 16.

*Translation - "Therefore, he said, let those of you who are able go down with me and if there is anything amiss in the man, let them file charges against him."*

**Comment:** οὖν is inferential. Since Paul was in custody in Caesarea, and since Festus' schedule demanded that he return soon, and, since the governor could not wait for Paul to be brought to Jerusalem, therefore (inferential οὖν) the trial, if such were to be held, would have to be in Caesarea. This would require the plaintiffs in the case to accompany Festus down the mountain. The first-class condition with εἰ in the protasis with the present indicative and with the aorist imperative in the apodosis, does not state that Paul was guilty, but it does say that *if there is anything amiss in the man* (with no statement from the governor one way or the other) the proper course was to file a formal complaint. But it would have to be done in Caesarea, not in Jerusalem. Festus had no choice but to permit the Jews to bring whatever charges they wished, since the Roman courts were open. It is not likely that he had any way of knowing the history of the previous hearing before Felix, since he had begun his duties as procurator only three days before.

But if Festus was in such a hurry to go down to Caesarea, why did he wait eight or ten days before he left? It is fifty miles from Jerusalem to Caesarea. The summons to Paul to come and Paul's trip to Jerusalem would have involved one hundred miles of travel time. There was plenty of time within eight days or ten days for the trial to have been conducted in Jerusalem. Festus must have known more about their murderous plot than he revealed.

*Verse 6 - "And when he had tarried among them more than ten days, he went down unto Caesarea; and the next day sitting on the judgment seat commanded Paul to be brought."*

Διατρίψας δὲ ἐν αὐτοῖς ἡμέρας οὐ πλείους ὀκτὼ ἢ δέκα, καταβὰς εἰς Καισάρειαν, τῇ ἐπαύριον καθίσας ἐπὶ τοῦ βήματος ἐκέλευσεν τὸν Παῦλον ἀχϑῆναι.

Διατρίψας (aor.act.part.nom.sing.masc.of διατρίβω, adverbial, temporal) 1991.

δὲ (adversative conjunction) 11.

ἐν (preposition with the locative of place, with plural pronouns) 80.

αὐτοῖς (loc.pl.masc.of αὐτός, with plural pronouns) 16.

ἡμέρας (acc.pl.fem.of ἡμέρα, time extent) 135.

οὐ (negative conjunction with the indicative) 130.

πλείους (acc.pl.fem.of πλείων, in agreement with ἡμέρας) 474.

ὀκτὼ (numeral) 1886.

ἢ (disjunctive) 465.

δέκα (numeral) 1330.

καταβὰς (aor.act.part.nom.sing.masc.of καταβαίνω, adverbial, temporal) 324.

εἰς (preposition with the accusative of extent) 140.

Καισάρειαν (acc.sing.fem.of Καισαρίας, extent) 1200.

τῇ (loc.sing.fem.of the article, time point) 9.

ἐπαύριον (adverbial) 1680.

καθίσας (aor.act.part.nom.sing.masc.of καθίζω, adverbial, coincident) 420.

ἐπὶ (preposition with the genitive of place description) 47.

τοῦ (gen.sing.neut.of the article in agreement with βήματος) 9.

βήματος (gen.sing.neut.of βῆμα, place description) 1628.

ἐκέλευσεν (3d.per.sing.aor.act.ind.of κελεύω, constative) 741.

τὸν (acc.sing.masc.of the article in agreement with Παῦλον) 9.

Παῦλον (acc.sing.masc.of Παῦλος, general reference) 3284.

ἀχϑῆναι (aor.pass.inf.of ἄγω, noun use, direct object of ἐκέλευσεν) 876.

*Translation - "But after he had tarried with them not more than eight or ten days, he went down to Caesarea and the next day he sat down upon the judgment seat and ordered Paul brought."*

**Comment:** The aorist participles carry the story and keep the related events in proper chronological order. The main verb is ἐκέλευσεν. Literal translation of the temporal participle, when there are several of them, becomes monotonous to the English reader. Therefore it is permissible to break the sentence into coordinate clauses, joined by the adjunctive conjunction, and/or to use temporal clauses. The literal translation is "Having tarried . . . having gone down . . . having sat down . . . he ordered. . . " The object of ἐκέλευσεν is the infinitive with τὸν Παῦλον, an accusative of general reference.

Though Festus was unwilling to bring Paul to Jerusalem for a trial among his enemies he was ready to have a speedy hearing in Caesarea and ordered proceedings the day following his return to the city.

*Verse 7 - "And when he was come, the Jews which came down from Jerusalem stood round about, and laid many and grievous complaints against Paul, which they could not prove."*

παραγενομένου δὲ αὐτοῦ περιέστησαν αὐτὸν οἱ ἀπὸ Ἱεροσολύμων καταβεβηκότες Ἰουδαῖοι, πολλὰ καὶ βαρέα αἰτιώματα καταφέροντες ἃ οὐκ ἴσχυον ἀποδεῖξαι,

παραγενομένου (aor.mid.part.gen.sing.masc.of παραγίνομαι, genitive absolute) 139.

δὲ (continuative conjunction) 11.

αὐτοῦ (gen.sing.masc.of αὐτός, genitive absolute) 16.

περιέστησαν (3d.per.pl.aor.act.ind.of περιίστημι, ingressive) 2606.

αὐτὸν (acc.sing.masc.of αὐτός, direct object of περιέστησαν) 16.

οἱ (nom.pl.masc.of the article in agreement with Ἰουδαῖοι) 9.

ἀπὸ (preposition with the ablative of source) 70.

Ἱεροσολύμων (abl.sing.fem.of Ἱεροσόλυμα, source) 141.

καταβεβηκότες (perf.act.part.nom.pl.masc.of καταβαίνω, adjectival, restrictive, in agreement with Ἰουδαῖοι) 324.

Ἰουδαῖοι (nom.pl.masc.of Ἰουδαῖος, subject of περιέστησαν) 143.

πολλὰ (acc.pl.neut.of πολύς, in agreement with αἰτιώματα) 228.

καὶ (adjunctive conjunction joining adjectives) 14.

βαρέα (acc.pl.neut.of βαρύς, in agreement with αἰτιώματα) 1432.

#3636 αἰτιώματα (acc.pl.neut.of αἰτίαμα, direct object of καταφέροντες).

complaint - Acts 25:7.

*Meaning:* For αἰτίωμα. Perhaps from αἰτέω (#537 plus μα, the result suffix. Hence, an accusation, a charge brought against one - as in the rhetorical question, "Why did you do that?" *Cf.* αἰτία (#1283). With reference to the charge brought against Paul - Acts 25:7.

καταφέροντες (pres.act.part.nom.pl.masc.of καταφέρω, adverbial, temporal) 3513.

ἃ (acc.pl.neut.of ὅς, relative pronoun, incorporation with αἰτιώματα) 65.

οὐκ (negative conjunction with the indicative) 130.

ἴσχυον (3d.per.pl.imp.ind.of ἰσχύω, progressive description) 447.

ἀποδεῖξαι (aor.inf.of ἀποδείκνυμι, complementary) 2989.

*Translation - "And when he arrived the Jews who had come down from Jerusalem surrounded him, bringing many and grievous charges which they were never able to substantiate."*

**Comment:** As soon as Paul came into the judgment hall, the Jews surrounded him, as though they feared that he would escape, an unconscious action, perhaps revealing their hatred. As they formed the circle about the defendant they were bringing against him many accusations of a serious nature. *Cf.* #3513. *Cf.* Acts 20:29; Mt.23:4. Titus 3:9 and 2 Tim.2:16 are interesting uses of #2606.

It seems that the Judaizers from Jerusalem were grievous enough, as indeed are all legalists who thus negate the work of Christ (Gal.2:21). ἴσχυον (imperfect tense) indicates a continuous inability to substantiate in court the charges that they were making. Despite this fact Festus failed the Roman test of fair play, legal justice and objectivity, because he too, as did the Jews, had a bad case of Christophobia, as do all unregenerate people.

*Verse 8 - "While he answered for himself, Neither against the law of the Jews, neither against the temple, nor yet against Caesar, have I offended anything at all."*

τοῦ Παύλου ἀπολογουμένου ὅτι Οὔτε εἰς τὸν νόμον τῶν Ἰουδαίων οὔτε εἰς τὸ ἱερὸν οὔτε εἰς Καίσαρά τι ἥμαρτον.

τοῦ (gen.sing.masc.of the article in agreement with Παύλου) 9.

Παύλου (gen.sing.masc.of Παῦλος, genitive absolute) 3284.

ἀπολογουμένου (pres.mid.part.gen.sing.masc.of ἀπολογέομαι, genitive absolute) 2476.

ὅτι (recitative) 211.

Οὔτε (negative conjunction) 598.

εἰς (preposition with the accusative, predicative) 140.

τὸν (acc.sing.masc.of the article in agreement with νόμον) 9.

νόμον (acc.sing.masc.of νόμος, opposition, predicate accusative) 464.

τῶν (gen.pl.masc.of the article in agreement with Ἰουδαίων) 9.

Ἰουδαίων (gen.pl.masc.of Ἰουδαῖος, desciption) 143.

οὔτε (negative conjunction) 598.

εἰς (preposition with the accusative, predicative use) 140.

τὸ (acc.sing.neut.of the article in agreement with ἱερὸν) 9.

ἱερὸν (acc.sing.neut.of ἱερόν, opposition, predicate accusative) 346.

οὔτε (negative conjunction) 598.

εἰς (preposition with the accusative, predicative use) 140.

Καίσαρά (acc.sing.masc.of Καίσαρι, opposition, predicate accusative) 1418.

τι (acc.sing.neut.of τις, indefinite pronoun, direct object of ἥμαρτον) 486.

ἥμαρτον (1st.per.sing.2d.aor.act.ind.of ἁμαρτάνω, culminative) 1260.

*Translation - "... while Paul was defending himself. 'Neither against the Jewish law, nor against the temple, nor against Caesar have I transgressed in any way.'"*

**Comment:** The genitive absolute τοῦ Παύλου ἀπολογουμένου belongs to the last clause of verse 8. The Jews were accusing him while Paul was defending himself. Note the οὔτε ... οὔτε ... οὔτε sequence. The Emperor to whom he referred was Nero, who succeeded Claudius in A.D.54. He ruled until his death in A.D.68. Festus had asked for this hearing - indeed had ordered it (verse 5).

The Jews had come down to Caesarea and done their best to get a conviction but had failed. Roman justice therefore demanded an acquittal and Paul's release. But just as Felix was a corrupt politician (Acts 24:27), so also was Festus, as he tried to trick Paul into consenting to a trip to Jerusalem to be put in double jeopardy in the court there and in certain jeopardy for his life along the road.

*Verse 9 - "But Festus, willing to do the Jews a pleasure, answered Paul and said, Wilt thou go up to Jerusalem, and there be judged of these things before me?"*

ὁ Φῆστος δὲ θέλων τοῖς Ἰουδαίοις χάριν καταθέσθαι ἀποκριθεὶς τῷ Παύλῳ, εἶπεν, Θέλεις εἰς Ἱεροσόλυμα ἀναβὰς ἐκεῖ περὶ τούτων κριθῆναι ἐπ' ἐμοῦ;

ὁ (nom.sing.masc.of the article in agreement with Φῆστος) 9.

Φῆστος (nom.sing.masc.of Φῆστος, subject of εἶπεν) 3633.

δὲ (adversative conjunction) 11.

θέλων (pres.act.part.nom.sing.masc.of θέλω, adverbial, causal) 88.

τοῖς (dat.pl.masc.of the article in agreement with Ἰουδαίοις) 9.

Ἰουδαίοις (dat.pl.masc.of Ἰουδαῖος, personal advantage) 143.

χάριν (acc.sing.fem.of χάρις, direct object of καταθέσθαι) 1700.

καταθέσθαι (2d.aor.mid.inf.of κατατίθημι, complementary) 3634.

ἀποκριθεὶς (aor.mid.part.nom.sing.masc.of ἀποκρίνομαι, adverbial, coincident) 318.

τῷ (dat.sing.masc.of the article in agreement with Παύλῳ) 9.

Παύλῳ (dat.sing.masc.of Παῦλος, indirect object of ἀποκριθεὶς) 3284.

εἶπεν (3d.per.sing.aor.act.ind.ofd εἶπον, constative) 155.

Θέλεις (2d.per.sing.pres.act.ind.of θέλω, direct question) 88.

εἰς (preposition with the accusative of extent) 140.

Ἱεροσόλυμα (acc.sing.masc.of Ἱεροσόλυμα, extent) 141.

ἀναβὰς (aor.act.part.nom.sing.masc.of ἀναβαίνω, adverbial, temporal) 323.

ἐκεῖ (local adverb) 204.

περὶ (preposition with the genitive of reference) 173.

τούτων (gen.pl.neut.of οὗτος, reference) 93.

κριθῆναι (aor.pass.inf.of κρίνω, complementary) 531.

ἐπ' (preposition with the genitive of place description) 47.

ἐμοῦ (gen.sing.masc.of ἐμός, place description) 1267.

*Translation - "But because Festus wanted to ingratiate himself with the Jews, he said to Paul, 'Are you willing to go up to Jerusalem there to be judged before me with reference to these things?' "*

**Comment:** What a whore! An honest judge would have ruled for Paul and released him, perhaps with a lecture to the prosecutor for taking up the court's valuable time. But (adversative δὲ) Festus had received the same nefarious proposition that Claudius Lysias did (Acts 25:3) and, like Felix (Acts 24:27) saw a chance to use a despised Christian as a political football. Festus was as naive as he was corrupt. Did he think that Paul, a lawyer trained in Gamaliel's school, would be stupid enough to agree to such a proposition? What further evidence could the Jews present than had been offered at the hearing just concluded? Furthermore, even if they had new evidence to present which was not heard in the hearing before Felix, the principle of double jeopardy dictates that a defendant cannot be tried twice for the same crime. Paul had already been tried before Felix (Acts 24:1-22) and now the second time before Festus (Acts 25:7,8). Does the phrase ἐπ' ἐμοῦ imply that Festus would guarantee to Paul a safe passage in and out of Jerusalem, and protective custody while he was there? Could Paul trust the word of a Roman lawyer who had already demonstrated his lack of concern for elemental justice?

Whatever the answers to these questions are, Paul was not taken in by Festus' suggestion.

*Verse 10 - "Then said Paul, I stand at Caesar's judgment seat, where I ought to be judged: to the Jews have I done no wrong, as thou very well knowest."*

εἶπεν δὲ ὁ Παῦλος, Ἑστὼς ἐπὶ τοῦ βήματος Καίσαρός εἰμι, οὗ με δεῖ κρίνεσθαι. Ἰουδαίους οὐδὲν ἠδίκησα, ὡς καὶ σὺ κάλλιον ἐπιγινώσκεις.

εἶπεν (3d.per.sing.aor.act.ind.of εἶπον, constative) 166.

δὲ (adversative conjunction) 11.

ὁ (nom.sing.masc.of the article in agreement with Παῦλος) 9.

Παῦλος (nom.sing.masc.of Παῦλος, subject of εἶπεν) 3284.

Ἑστὼς (perf.act.part.nom.sing.masc.of ἵστημι, periphrastic present) 180.

ἐπὶ (preposition with the genitive of place description) 47.

τοῦ (gen.sing.neut.of the article in agreement with βήματος) 9.

βήματος (gen.sing.neut.of βῆμα, place description) 1628.

Καίσαρός (gen.sing.masc.of Καίσαρι, description) 1418.

εἰμί (1st.per.sing.pres.ind.of εἰμί, periphrastic present) 86.

οὗ (gen.sing.neut.of ὅς, relative pronoun, place description) 65.

με (acc.sing.masc.of ἐγώ, general reference) 123.

δεῖ (3d.per.sing.pres.ind.of δεῖ) 1207.

κρίνεσθαι (pres.pass.inf.of κρίνω, complementary) 531.

Ἰουδαίους (acc.pl.masc.of Ἰουδαῖος, direct object of ἠδίκησα) 143.

οὐδὲν (acc.sing.neut.of οὐδείς, double accusative, object of ἠδίκησα) 446.

ἠδίκησα (1st.per.sing.aor.act.ind.of ἀδικέω, culminative) 1327.

ὡς (particle introducing a comparative clause) 128.

καὶ (adjunctive conjunction) 14.

σὺ (nom.sing.masc.of σύ, subject of ἐπιγινώσκεις) 104.

#3637 κάλλιον (comp.neut.sing.of καλός).

very well - Acts 25:10.

*Meaning:* The comparative neuter of καλλίων (*cf.* καλός #296), used adverbially. "Better than your question would indicate that you know." Acts 25:10.

ἐπιγινώσκεις (2d.per.sing.pres.act.ind.of ἐπιγινώσκω, static) 675.

*Translation -* "*But Paul said, 'I have been (and still am) standing before the judgment throne of the Emperor, where it is proper for me to be tried. I have not inflicted a single wrong upon the Jews, as also you are very well aware.'* "

**Comment:** δὲ is adversative as Paul rejects the sly suggestion of Festus. The discourse is direct as Luke wants us to know exactly what Paul said to this corrupt judge. "I have been standing before the Emperor's court." It was not the court of Festus ultimately, since his decisions were subject to judicial review in the appelate jurisdictions. Paul brought this home to Festus with some force. "This court is the court of Imperial Rome, of which I am a citizen. I belong in this court - not in a kangeroo court in the temple in Jerusalem. Whatever this court decides should be decided in contemplation of the fact that its decision will be reviewed by Nero." Thus Paul implied a threat that Festus would be reversed and that such reversal might prove deleterious to his position as procurator. δεῖ is to be construed as necessity due to the nature of the case. *Cf.*#1207, 1,b. This was due to the fact that Paul was a Roman citizen. To interpret καὶ as ascensive is to indicate the asperity that Paul no doubt felt but that he did not express. "As *even* you know very well" would be too snide. Paul was probably more diplomatic and said, "as *also* you know very well," *i.e.* "much better than you seem to wish to admit." There is a veiled threat in all that Paul was saying to Festus. "Remember, your Honor, I am going to appeal your decision to Nero. Do you want him to know how prejudiced and duplicit you are?" Note ἐπιγινώσκεις (#675), the more highly perceptive word than γινώσκω (#131). That Festus got Paul's point seems clear from his desire to share responsibility in the case with Agrippa (Acts 25:14-27), and that he did not forward any sort of report to Rome about Paul (Acts 28:17-21). The crafty little Judean puppet decided to allow discretion to be the better part of valor and to walk softly before the long arm of justice of which Imperial Rome was traditionally proud. As events developed, however, when Paul arrived in Rome, he found a tyrant in control, even more corrupt than Felix and Festus.

When a comparative is used absolutely, as κάλλιον is in our passage and there is no object of comparison expressed in the text, it should not be taken as a substitute for the positive. Clyde (*Greek Syntax*, 41) was wrong when he said that an absolute comparative form is used "through politeness for the positive." Robertson (*Grammar*, 664,665) says that "It is not used for the positive. It is true that no object of comparison is expressed, but that is because the context makes the point perfectly clear. In rapid familiar conversation this would often be true." Blass (*Grammar of New Testament Greek*, 142) agrees that sometimes the comparative is no more than a positive, but Winer (*Winer-Thayer, A Grammar of the Idiom of the New Testament*, 242) supports Robertson by saying that the point of comparison may "ordinarily be gathered from the context." Moulton's translation of Winer has him saying, "In most cases this may easily be perceived from the context." (*Moulton translation*, 303). The point of course "is always in the context." (Robertson, *Ibid*, 664). "One does not need to deny the 'elative' comparative sense of 'very' here and elsewhere," in answer to Moulton who speaks of "elative comparisons." (Moulton, *Prolegomena*, 236). "The elative is still comparative." To deny the elative comparative in some examples, Robertson charges "is to a certain extent to surrender to translation the true interpretation of the Greek idiom" (*Ibid.*, 665). In the case of Acts 25:10 "Paul hints that Festus knows his innocence better than he is willing to admit." (*Ibid.*).

*Verse 11 - "For if I be an offender, or have committed anything worthy of death, I refuse not to die: but if there be none of these things whereof they accuse me, no man may deliver me unto them. I appeal unto Caesar."*

εἰ μὲν οὖν ἀδικῶ καὶ ἄξιον θανάτου πέπραχά τι, οὐ παραιτοῦμαι τὸ ἀποθανεῖν, εἰ δὲ οὐδέν ἐστιν ὧν οὗτοι κατηγοροῦσίν μου, οὐδείς με δύναται αὐτοῖς χαρίσασθαι. Καίσαρα ἐπικαλοῦμαι.

εἰ (conditional particle in a first-class condition) 337.

μὲν (affirmative particle) 300.

οὖν (inferential conjunction) 68.

ἀδικῶ (1st.per.sing.pres.act.ind.of ἀδικέω, first-class condition) 1327.

καὶ (adjunctive conjunction joining verbs) 14.

ἄξιον (acc.sing.neut.of ἄξιος, predicate adjective) 285.

θανάτου (abl.sing.masc.of θάνατος, comparison) 381.

πέπραχά (1st.per.sing.perf.act.ind.of πράσσω, intensive) 1943.

τι (acc.sing.neut.of τις, indefinite, direct object of πέπραχά) 486.

οὐ (negative conjunction with the indicative) 130.

παραιτοῦμαι (1st.per.sing.pres.mid.ind.of παραιτέομαι, progressive duration, retroactive) 2530.

τὸ (acc.sing.neut.of the article in agreement with ἀποθανεῖν) 9.

ἀποθανεῖν (2d.aor.act.inf.of ἀποθνήσκω, noun use, object of παραιτοῦμαι) 774.

εἰ (conditional particle, in a first-class condition) 337.

δὲ (adversative conjunction) 11.

οὐδέν (acc.sing.neut.of οὐδείς, predicate nominative) 446.

ἐστιν (3d.per.sing.pres.ind.of εἰμί, aoristic) 86.

ὧν (gen.pl.neut.of ὅς, relative pronoun, reference) 65.

οὗτοι (nom.pl.masc.of οὗτος, subject of κατηγοροῦσίν) 93.

κατηγοροῦσίν (3d.per.pl.pres.act.ind. of κατηγορέω, progressive duration, retroactive) 974.

μου (gen.sing.masc.of ἐγώ, objective genitive) 123.

οὐδείς (nom.sing.masc.of οὐδείς, subject of δύναται) 446.

με (acc.sing.masc.ofd ἐγώ, direct object of χαρίσασθαι) 123.

δύναται (3d.per.sing.pres.mid.ind.of δύναμαι, static) 289.

αὐτοῖς (dat.pl.masc.of αὐτός, indirect object of χαρίσασθαι) 16.

χαρίσασθαι (1st.aor.inf.of χαρίζομαι, complementary) 2158.

Καίσαρα (acc.sing.masc.of Καισαρί, extent, after a verb of speaking) 1418.

ἐπικαλοῦμαι (1st.per.sing.pres.mid.ind.of ἐπικαλέω, aoristic) 884.

*Translation - "If therefore in fact I am guilty and if I have been doing anything worthy of death, I do not refuse to die. But since not one thing with reference to which these men have been accusing me (is true), no one is able to deliver me to to them. I appeal to the Emperor."*

**Comment:** Here the context allows us to interpret the protases of the two first-class conditions differently. Both are first-class conditions, with εἰ and any tense in the indicative in the protasis and no fixed form for the apodosis. In the first we have the present and perfect indicatives in the protasis (if clause) and the present indicative in the apodosis (result clause). In the second, we have the present indicative in both protasis and apodosis. In the first Paul, for the sake of the argument, is temporarily assuming the truth of the facts, although he denies both that he is guilty or has done anything in the past worthy of death. But if he is guilty (which he is not) then he truthfully says that he is not trying to escape the death penalty. In the second case, Paul is saying that he is not guilty and that *since* he is not, there is no man who has the legal authority to betray him to the Jews, who were planning to kill him. The context has already provided us with the information that Paul was not legally guilty of the crimes of which he was accused. He was not only not guilty in a legal sense, but he also implies in the first condition that he had not actually ever committed a felony for which the death penalty was required.

Thus Paul challenged Festus. "Either condemn me to death here and now on the basis of evidence presented in this court or turn me over to these cut-throats at your peril." Paul meant that there was no legal way that Festus could remand the case back to a kangeroo court in the Jerusalem San Hedrin. Paul's appeal to Nero imposed upon Festus the necessity to handle the case with the utmost legal probity. Festus should have declared Paul not guilty and released him forthwith.

Instead he conferred with the prosecution!

*Verse 12 - "Then Festus, when he had conferred with the council, answered, Hast thou appealed unto Caesar? Unto Caesar shalt thou go."*

τότε ὁ Φῆστος συλλαλήσας μετὰ τοῦ συμβουλίου ἀπεκρίθη, Καίσαρα ἐπικέκλησαι, ἐπὶ Καίσαρα πορεύσῃ.

τότε (temporal conjunction) 166.

ὁ (nom.sing.masc.of the article in agreement with Φῆστος) 9.

Φῆστος (nom.sing.masc.of Φῆστος, subject of ἀπεκρίθη) 3633.

συλλαλήσας (aor.act.part.nom.sing.masc.of συλλαλέω, adverbial, temporal) 1223.

μετὰ (preposition with the genitive, accompaniment, conversation) 50.

τοῦ (gen.sing.neut.of the article in agreement with συμβουλίου) 9.

συμβουλίου (gen.sing.neut.of συμβούλιον, conversation) 980.

ἀπεκρίθη (3d.per.sing.aor.mid.ind.of ἀποκρίνομαι. constative) 318.

Καίσαρα (acc.sing.masc.of Καίσαρι, extent, after a verb of speaking) 1418.

ἐπικέκλησαι (2d.per.sing.perf.mid.ind.of ἐπικαλέω, intensive) 884.

ἐπὶ (preposition with the accusative of extent) 47.

Καίσαρα (acc.sing.masc.of Καίσαρι, extent) 1418.

πορεύσῃ (2d.per.sing.fut.mid.ind.of πορεύομαι, predictive) 170.

*Translation - "Then, after Festus had conferred with the council, he replied, 'Have you appealed to the Emperor? To the Emperor you shall go!' "*

**Comment:** Paul meant that he would appeal to Nero only if he needed to do so in order to secure his rights. The text is not clear as to what council is meant - whether with Ananias and the Jews who had come down from Jerusalem or with one of his own advisory bodies. Just why he should have sought advice from anyone is not clear, since his legal duty was clear. His statement to King Agrippa (Acts 25:24-27) is neither explanatory nor exculpatory.

## Paul Brought Before Agrippa and Bernice

*(Acts 25:13 - 27)*

*Verse 13 - "And after certain days king Agrippa and Bernice came unto Caesarea to salute Festus."*

Ἡμερῶν δὲ διαγενομένων τινῶν Ἀγρίππας ὁ βασιλεὺς καὶ Βερνίκη κατήντησαν εἰς Καισάρειαν ἀσπασάμενοι τὸν Φῆστον.

Ἡμερῶν (gen.pl.fem.of ἡμέρα, genitive absolute) 135.
δὲ (continuative conjunction) 11.
διαγενομένων (aor.mid.part.gen.pl.fem.of διαγίνομαι, genitive absolute) 2887.
τινῶν (gen.pl.fem.of τις, indefinite pronoun, in agreement with Ἡμερῶν) 486.
Ἀγρίππας (nom.sing.masc.of Ἀγρίππας, subject of κατήντησαν) 136C.
ὁ (nom.sing.masc.of the article in agreement with βασιλεὺς) 9.
βασιλεὺς (nom.sing.masc.of βασιλεύς, apposition) 31.
καὶ (adjunctive conjunction joining nouns) 14.

#3638 Βερνίκη (nom.sing.fem.of Βερενίκα (Macedonian form), subject of κατήντησαν).

Bernice - Acts 25:13,23; 26:30.

*Meaning:* The daughter of Herod Agrippa the Elder. First she married her uncle Herod, King of Chalcis. After his death she married Polemon, King of Cilicia. She deserted him soon and returned to Agrippa, her brother, with whom she had previously lived incestuously. She finally became the mistress of Titus, the Emperor. She heard Paul preach - Acts 25:13,23; 26:30.

κατήντησαν (3d.per.pl.aor.act.ind.of καταντάω, culminative) 3353.
εἰς (preposition with the accusative of extent) 140.
Καισάρειαν (acc.sing.fem.of Καισαρίας, extent) 1200.
ἀσπασάμενοι (aor.mid.part.nom.pl.masc.of ἀσπάζω, adverbial, coincident) 551.
τὸν (acc.sing.masc.of the article in agreement with Φῆστον) 9.
Φῆστον (acc.sing.masc.of Φῆστος, direct object of ἀσπασάμενοι) 3633.

*Translation - "And a short time later Agrippa, the king and Bernice came to Caesarea greeting Festus."*

**Comment:** διά is composition in διαγενομένων indicates the duality which is inherent in the preposition. Some days passed "in between" (διά) the time of verse 12 and that of Agrippa's state visit. Agrippa II and his full sister, Bernice, both children of Agrippa I (#136B) were living incestuously. Due to the regal status of the parties involved we may regard it as a state visit. Some MSS read the future participle of purpose ἀσπασόμενοι instead of the aorist ἀσπασάμεν-οι. Here is another one of those controversial instances of an anarthrous aorist participle following the main verb which is alleged to show subsequent action. Since such is not good Greek grammar, some grammarians, including Burton, Ramsay and Rackham have attributed the error to the influence of the Hebrew. The passages cited are Acts 16:23; 22:24; 23:35; 24:23 and 25:13. Ramsay adds Acts 16:6 and Rackham adds Acts 12:25 and Acts 21:14. Note our exegesis of each of these passages. There are no Hebraisms. The aorist participles in question show either simultaneity or antecedence. In Acts 25:13, we need not resort to the variant reading and read ἀσπασάμενοι, a future participle of purpose, in which case we would translate "they came to Caesarea in order to salute Festus." They came to Caesarea and greeted Festus on arrival - a simultaneous action. Robertson (*Grammar*, 863) points to the fact that κατά is composition in κατήντησαν is perfective - thus that the aorist is effective and accents the end of the journey, reinforced by κατά. What Robertson calls "effective" aorist is also called "culminative." In such contexts, the emphasis is upon the result of the action. The monarchs came to Caesarea and when they arrived, quite naturally they greeted Festus (ἀσπασάμενοι). This is simultaneity. It is possible to construe the participle as a letter, written previously and announcing their arrival. It is used in this sense 17 times in Romans 16. *Cf. #551).*

*Verse 14 - "And when they had been there many days, Festus declared Paul's cause unto the king, saying, There is a certain man left in bonds by Felix."*

ὡς δὲ πλείους ἡμέρας διέτριβον ἐκεῖ, ὁ Φῆστος τῷ βασιλεῖ ἀνέθετο τὰ κατὰ τὸν Παῦλον λέγων, Ἀνήρ τίς ἐστιν καταλελειμμένος ὑπὸ Φήλικος δέσμιος,

ὡς (particle introducing a definite temporal clause) 128.
δὲ (continuative conjunction) 11.
πλείους (acc.pl.masc.of πλείων, in agreement with ἡμέρας) 474.
ἡμέρας (acc.pl.fem.of ἡμέρα, time extent) 135.
διέτριβον (3d.per.pl.2d.aor.act.ind.of διατρίβω, culminative) 1991.
ἐκεῖ (local adverb) 204.
ὁ (nom.sing.masc.of the article in agreement with Φῆστος) 9.
Φῆστος (nom.sing.masc.of Φῆστος, subject of ἀνέθετο) 3633.
τῷ (dat.sing.masc.of the article in agreement with βασιλεῖ) 9.
βασιλεῖ (dat.sing.masc.of βασιλεύς, indirect object of ἀνέθετο) 31.

**#3639** ἀνέθετο (3d.per.sing.2d.aor.mid.ind.of ἀνατίθημι, culminative).

communicate - Gal.2:2.
declare - Acts 25:14.

*Meaning:* A combination of ἀνά (#1059) and τίθημι (#455). To set forth a thing; expound; explain. With reference to Festus to Agrippa - Acts 25:14; Paul to the brethren in the Jerusalem church - Gal.2:2.

τά (acc.pl.neut.of the article, direct object of ἀνέθετο) 9.
κατά (preposition with the accusative, periphrasis for the genitive of reference) 98.
τὸν (acc.sing.masc.of the article in agreement with Παῦλον) 9.
Παῦλον (acc.sing.masc.of Παῦλος, for the genitive of reference) 3284.
λέγων (pres.act.part.nom.sing.masc.of λέγω, recitative) 66.
'Ανήρ (nom.sing.masc.of ἀνήρ, subject of ἐστιν) 63.
τίς (nom.sing.masc.of τις, indefinite pronoun, in agreement with ἀνήρ) 486.
ἐστιν (3d.per.sing.pres.ind.of εἰμί, perfect periphrastic) 86.
καταλελειμμένος (perf.pass.part.nom.sing.masc.of καταλείπω, perfect periphrastic) 369.
ὑπὸ (preposition with the ablative of agent) 117.
Φήλικος (abl.sing.masc.of Φῆλιξ, agent) 3603.
δέσμιος (nom.sing.masc.of δέσμιος, predicate adjective) 1624.

*Translation - "And after they had been there several days, Festus laid Paul's case before the king, saying, 'A certain man is here, having been left a prisoner by Felix.'"*

**Comment:** δὲ is continuative. ὡς introduces the temporal clause. *Cf.* #128. Note κατὰ τὸν Παῦλον as a periphrasis for the genitive of reference. But "it is more than a mere circumlocution for the genitive" (Blass, *Grammar of New Testament Greek*, 133, as cited in Robertson, *Grammar,*608). *Cf.* Eph.1:15; Rom.1:15; 9:5; Eph.6:21; Acts 25:14,23. Festus not only told Agrippa about Paul but he also directed his attention to Paul. Thus the idea of extent, with κατὰ and the accusative is there. The perfect periphrastic has intensive force. Paul had been in Caesarea in bonds for more than two years.

*Verse 15 - "About whom, when I was at Jerusalem, the chief priests and the elders of the Jews informed me, desiring to have judgment against him."*

περὶ οὗ γενομένου μου εἰς Ἱεροσόλυμα ἐνεφάνισαν οἱ ἀρχιερεῖς καὶ οἱ πρεσβύτεροι τῶν Ἰουδαίων, αἰτούμενοι κατ' αὐτοῦ καταδίκην.

περὶ (preposition with the genitive of reference) 173.
οὗ (gen.sing.masc.of ὅς, relative pronoun, reference) 65.
γενομένου (aor.mid.part.gen.sing.masc.of γίνομαι, genitive absolute) 113.
μου (gen.sing.masc.of ἐγώ, genitive absolute) 123.
εἰς (preposition with the accusative, like a locative of place) 140.

Ἱεροσόλυμα (acc.sing.fem.of Ἱεροσόλυμα, original static use, like a locative) 141.

ἐνεφάνισαν (3d.per.pl.aor.act.ind.of ἐμφανίζω, culminative) 1666.

οἱ (nom.pl.masc.of the article in agreement with ἀρχιερεῖς) 9.

ἀρχιερεῖς (nom.pl.masc.of ἀρχιερεύς, subject of ἐνεφάνισαν) 151.

καὶ (adjunctive conjunction joining nouns) 14.

οἱ (nom.pl.masc.of the article in agreement with πρεσβύτεροι) 9.

πρεσβύτεροι (nom.pl.masc.of πρεσβύτερος, subject of ἐνεφάνισαν) 1141.

τῶν (gen.pl.masc.of the article in agreement with Ἰουδαίων) 9.

Ἰουδαίων (gen.pl.masc.of Ἰουδαῖος, description) 143.

αἰτούμενοι (pres.mid.part.nom.pl.masc.of αἰτέω, adverbial, complementary) 537.

κατ' (preposition with the genitive, opposition) 98.

αὐτοῦ (gen.sing.masc.of αὐτός, opposition) 16.

#3640 καταδίκην (acc.sing.fem.of καταδική, direct object of αἰτούμενοι).

judgment - Acts 25:15.

*Meaning:* A combination of κατά (#98) and δίκη - "judgment" - hence a condemnatory legal decision - Acts 25:15.

*Translation - "While I was in Jerusalem the priests and the elders of the Jews told me about him and requested a judgment against him."*

**Comment:** The antecedent of οὗ is ἀνήρ of verse 14. The genitive absolute tells us when Festus heard about Paul. It was while he was in Jerusalem (Acts 25:1-3).

εἰς with the accusative in its original static use, like the locative of place. κατ' αὐτοῦ means opposition. *Cf.* #98.

*Verse 16 - "To whom I answered, It is not the manner of the Romans to deliver any man to die, before that he which is accused have the accusers face to face, and have license to answer for himself concerning the crime laid against him."*

πρὸς οὓς ἀπεκρίθην ὅτι οὐκ ἔστιν ἔθος Ῥωμαίοις χαρίζεσθαί τινα ἄνθρωπον πρὶν ἢ ὁ κατηγορούμενος κατὰ πρόσωπον ἔχοι τοὺς κατηγόρους τόπον τε ἀπολογίας λάβοι περὶ τοῦ ἐγκλήματος.

πρὸς (preposition with the accusative of extent, with a verb of speaking) 197.

οὓς (acc.pl.masc.of ὅς, relative pronoun, extent with a verb of speaking) 65.

ἀπεκρίθην 1st.per.sing.aor.mid.ind.of ἀποκρίνομαι, constative) 318.

ὅτι (conjunction introducing an object clause in indirect discourse) 211.

οὐκ (negative conjunction with the indicative) 130.

ἔστιν (3d.per.sing.pres.ind.of εἰμί, customary, indirect discourse) 86.

ἔθος (nom.sing.neut.of ἔθος, predicate nominative) 1788.

Ῥωμαίοις (dat.pl.masc.of Ῥωμαῖος, possession) 2610.

χαρίζεσθαι (pres.pass.inf.of χαρίζομαι, noun use, subject of ἔστιν) 2158.

τινα (acc.sing.masc.of τις, indefinite pronoun, in agreement with ἄνθρωπον) 486.

ἄνθρωπον (acc.sing.masc.of ἄνθρωπος, general reference) 341.

πρὶν (conjunction introducing the optative in a temporal clause) 77.

ἤ (disjunctive) 465.

ὁ (nom.sing.masc.of the article in agreement with κατηγορούμενος) 9.

κατηγορούμενος (pres.pass.part.nom.sing.masc.of κατηγορέω, substantival, subject of ἔχοι) 974.

κατὰ (preposition with the accusative, adverbial) 98.

πρόσωπον (acc.sing.neut.of πρόσωπον, adverbial) 588.

ἔχοι (3d.per.sing.pres.act.opt.of ἔχω, indirect discourse)

τοὺς (acc.pl.masc.of the article in agreement with κατηγόρους) 9.

κατηγόρους (acc.pl.masc.of κατήγορος, direct object of ἔχοι) 3606.

τόπον (acc.sing.masc.of τόπος, direct object of λάβοι) 1019.

τε (adjunctive particle) 1408.

ἀπολογίας (gen.sing.fem.of ἀπολογία, description) 3573.

λάβοι (3d.per.sing.2d.aor.act.opt.of λαμβάνω, indirect discourse) 533.

περὶ (preposition with the genitive of reference) 173.

τοῦ (gen.sing.neut.of the article in agreement with ἐγκλήματος) 9.

ἐγκλήματος (gen.sing.neut.of ἔγκλημα, reference) 3605.

*Translation - "To whom I replied that it was not the custom of the Romans that any man be delivered before the accused meets the accusers to their face and he have a chance to give an explanation with reference to the accusation."*

**Comment:** Indirect discourse after ἀπεκρίθην has ὅτι and the optative mode (ἔχοι and λάβοι) in a temporal clause. The only example in the New Testament of the optative in a temporal clause is here; however the optative us due, not to the temporal clause, but to the indirect discourse. Normally the subjunctive with ἄν would occur in indirect discourse, where the less vivid future fulfillment is in view. The change from subjunctive to optative, which is permissible in indirect discourse is "a neat classic idiom found in Luke alone in the New Testament" (Robertson, *Grammar*, 977). The element of doubt is found in the fact there might be a case in which the accused had no chance to reply to his accusers in open court on a face to face basis. If such opportunity is not found, there can be no judgment.

The subject of ἔστιν is the infinitive χαρίζεσθαί with τινα ἄνθρωπον adjoined in general reference, while the predicate is ἔθος. "For any man to be delivered . . is not customary for the Romans." Two things must happen before a trial can be held: The accused must have the accuser face to face (if ever it is possible) and he must have his chance to answer the charges.

If Festus really said all of this to the Jews in Jerusalem, Luke does not record it (Acts 25:4,5), though he did say something like it. Of course, before Agrippa, Festus would seek to make himself appear in the best possible light.

He should have added that once Paul had the chance to face his accusers in open court, hear their accusations against him, and reply to them, as he did on at least three occasions, and the prosecution has failed to make its point, it is the custom of the Romans to declare the defendant not guilty and to inform him that he is free to go.

*Verse 17 - "Therefore, when they were come hither, without any delay on the morrow I sat on the judgment seat, and commanded the man to be brought forth."*

συνελθόντων οὖν ἐνθάδε ἀναβολὴν μηδεμίαν ποιησάμενος τῇ ἐξῆς καθίσας ἐπὶ τοῦ βήματος ἐκέλευσα ἀχθῆναι τὸν ἄνδρα,

συνελθόντων (aor.mid.part.gen.pl.masc.of συνέρχομαι, adverbial, temporal) 78.

οὖν (inferential conjunction) 68.

ἐνθάδε (adverbial) 2010.

**#3641** ἀναβολὴν (acc.sing.fem.of ἀναβολή, direct object of ποιησάμενος).

delay - Acts 25:17.

*Meaning: Cf.* ἀναβάλλομαι (#3627). Hence, a putting off; deferment; delay; postponement - Acts 25:17.

μηδεμίαν (acc.sing.fem.of μηδείς, in agreement with ἀναβολὴν) 713.

ποιησάμενος (aor.mid.part.nom.sing.masc.of ποιέω, adverbial, coincident) 127.

τῇ (loc.sing.fem.of the article, time point) 9.

ἐξῆς (adverb of succession) 2152.

καθίσας (aor.act.part.nom.sing.masc.of καθίζω, adverbial, coincident) 420.

ἐπὶ (preposition with the genitive of place description) 47.

τοῦ (gen.sing.neut.of the article in agreement with βήματος) 9.

βήματος (gen.sing.neut.ofd βῆμα, place description) 1628.

ἐκέλευσα (1st.per.sing.aor.act.ind.ofd κελεύω,constative) 741.

ἀχθῆναι (aor.pass.inf.of ἄγω, noun use, direct object of ἐκέλευσα) 876.

τὸν (acc.sing.masc.of the article in agreement with ἄνδρα) 9.

ἄνδρα (acc.sing.masc.of ἀνήρ, general reference) 63.

*Translation - "So when they came here I did not delay. The next day I sat upon the judgment throne and ordered the man to be brought."*

**Comment:** If we supply αὐτῶν with συνελθόντων we have a genitive absolute. We can take the participle as a temporal adverb - "When they arrived . . ." *i.e.* in Caesarea from Jerusalem. The "they" are those referred to in Acts 25:7. Festus did not delay. ἀναβολὴν μηδεμίαν ποιησάμενος tells us that and τῇ ἐξῆς gives the time point. It was the day following that when Festus, accompanied by the Jews arrived in Caesarea, which may suggest that they arrived in the city at an hour too late to conduct the hearing, and also that they were too tired from the trip. This statement squares with Acts 25:6. Note ἐπὶ τοῦ βήματος in Acts 25:10 where it means "before the judgment seat" while here the same phrase means "on the judgment seat." ἐπί with the genitive indicates place where, and depends, as always upon the context to sharpen the idea. Both the judge (Festus) and the defendant (Paul) are ἐπὶ τοῦ βήματος - either "before" or "upon" the throne.

Only the uninitiated will suppose that because the same prepositional phrase is used for both men, Paul was sitting *upon* the judgment seat with Festus. The locative idea is present in both cases, but in different senses. Note the object passive infinitive in ἀχϑῆναι after ἐκέλευσα with τὸν ἄνδρα in general reference.

Verse 18 reveals that Festus was surprized to hear the nature of the charges brought against Paul. One wonders if he was being totally truthful about this since the governor had been briefed on the case by the Jews when he was in Jerusalem, at which time they asked him to summon Paul to Jerusalem for trial (Acts 25:2,3). Luke did not divulge the nature of the charges which Festus heard at that time. If Festus was truly surprized to learn that the charges concerned only matters of theological interest to the Jewish community and not infractions of Roman civil and/or criminal law, we must conclude that the Jews in Jerusalem had misinformed him on the earlier occasion.

*Verse 18 - "Against whom when the accusers stood up, they brought none accusation of such things as I supposed."*

περὶ οὗ σταϑέντες οἱ κατήγοροι οὐδεμίαν αἰτίαν ἔφερον ὧν ἐγὼ ὑπενόουν πονηρῶν,

περὶ (preposition with the genitive of reference) 173.
οὗ (gen.sing.masc.of ὅς, relative pronoun, reference) 65.
σταϑέντες (aor.mid.part.nom.pl.masc.of ἵστημι, adverbial, temporal) 180.
οἱ (nom.pl.masc.of the article in agreement with κατήγοροι) 9.
κατήγοροι (nom.pl.masc.of κατήγορος, subject of ἔφερον) 3606.
οὐδεμίαν (acc.sing.fem.of οὐδείς, in agreement with αἰτίαν) 446.
αἰτίαν (acc.sing.fem.of αἰτία, direct object of ἔφερον) 1283.
ἔφερον (3d.per.pl.imp.act.ind.of φέρω, progressive description) 683.
ὧν (gen.pl.neut.of ὅς, relative pronoun, reference) 65.
ἐγὼ (nom.sing.masc.of ἐγώ, subject of ὑπερνόουν) 123.

**#3642** ὑπερνόουν (1st.per.sing.imp.act.ind.of ὑπερνοέω, customary).

suppose - Acts 25:18.

*Meaning:* A combination of ὑπέρ (#545) and νοέω (#1160). Therefore, to think on a different or higher level. To assume something different (and more lofty - ὑπέρ) - from reality. Festus' view of the Jewish charges against Paul - Acts 25:18.

πονηρῶν (gen.pl.neut.of πονηρός, in agreement with ὧν) 438.

*Translation - "Against whom, when they stood up, the accusers brought not one charge concerning such evil deeds as I had been led to expect."*

**Comment:** *Cf.* Mt.20:24 for περί with the genitive in the sense of hostility or opposition. ὑπερνόουν speaks of a higher, more sophisticated view of the situation, entertained by Festus, than that held by the Jews. He was expecting something worthy of the attention of a Roman court. On the contrary the case dealt with matters which Festus considered beneath his dignity.

*Verse 19 - "But had certain questions against him of their own superstition, and of one Jesus, which was dead, whom Paul affirmed to be alive."*

ζητήματα δέ τινα περὶ τῆς ἰδίας δεισιδαιμονίας εἶχον πρὸς αὐτὸν καὶ περί τινος Ἰησοῦ τεθνηκότος, ὃν ἔφασκεν ὁ Παῦλος ζῆν.

ζητήματα (acc.pl.neut.of ζήτημα, direct object of εἶχον) 3334.
δὲ (adversative conjunction) 11.
τινα (acc.pl.neut.of τις, indefinite pronoun, in agreement with ζητήματα) 486.
περὶ (preposition with the genitive of reference) 173.
τῆς (gen.sing.fem.of the article in agreement with δεισιδαιμονίας) 9.
ἰδίας (gen.sing.fem.of ἴδιος, in agreement with δεισιδαιμονίας) 778.

#3643 δεισιδαιμονίας (gen.sing.fem.of δεισιδαιμονία, reference).

superstition - Acts 25:19.

*Meaning:* Cf. δεισιδαίμων (#3409). Hence, fear of the supernatural. Festus is using the word as one who is a thoroughgoing antisupernaturalist, and, from his point of view, applying it to Judaism as taught by the Jerusalem establishment - Acts 25:19.

εἶχον (3d.per.pl.imp.act.ind.of ἔχω, progressive description) 82.
πρὸς (preposition with the accusative of extent, opposition) 197.
αὐτὸν (acc.sing.masc.of αὐτός, opposition) 16.
καὶ (adjunctive conjunction joining prepositional phrases) 14.
περὶ (preposition with the genitive of reference) 173.
τινος (gen.sing.masc.of τις, indefinite pronoun, in agreement with Ἰησοῦ) 486.
Ἰησοῦ (gen.sing.masc.of Ἰησοῦς, reference) 3.
θεθνηκότος (perf.part.gen.sing.masc.of θνήσκω, adjectival, restrictive, in agreement with Ἰησοῦ) 232.
ὃν (acc.sing.masc.of ὅς, relative pronoun, direct object of ἔφασκεν) 65.
ἔφασκεν (3d.per.sing.aor.act.ind.of φάσκω, constative) 3622.
ὁ (nom.sing.masc.of the article in agreement with Παῦλος) 9.
Παῦλος (nom.sing.masc.of Παῦλος, subject of ἔφασκεν) 3284.
ζῆν (pres.act.inf.ofd ζάω, object infinitive in indirect discourse) 340.

*Translation - "But they were raising some issues against him with reference to their religion, and about some Jesus, now dead, whom Paul insisted was alive."*

**Comment:** δὲ is adversative. The issues which were raised in court were not what Festus expected. They were concerned with theological differences between the Jews and Paul. Festus was treating the entire affair in a cavalier manner, as one who considered himself far superior both to the accusers and the accused. In view of his attitude we might translate δεισιδαιμονίας as "superstition," but only if we regard "religion" as a synonym for Christianity. For those of us who disdain both religion and superstition, with little more respect for the former than for the latter, and who, in no case regard either as synonymous with Christianity, the word "religion" expresses what Festus felt. Superstition is based upon that which is totally without reality, while religion binds, whereas Christianity liberates.

Festus' attitude may be discerned by the fact that he had no doubt that Jesus was dead, and also by his use of the indefinite pronouns τινα and τινος, which I take as expressions of contempt - "some questions" and "some Jesus" - while neither their questions nor this Jesus is of any importance. Whether Jesus was alive or dead, the entire matter was beneath the dignity of the Roman court in Festus' view.

Current deists, some of whom occupy pulpits formerly dedicated to Christianty, join Festus in his contempt for the view that Jesus is alive, while Paul, with his stout affirmation that Jesus, once dead, was then and shall ever be alive has his co-witnesses still, albeit regarded with disdain by modern deists, just as Festus disdained both Paul and the Jews who wanted him dead.

*Verse 20 - "And because I doubted of such manner of questions, I asked him whether he would go to Jerusalem, and there be judged of these matters."*

ἀπορούμενος δὲ ἐγὼ τὴν περὶ τούτων ζήτησιν ἔλεγον εἰ βούλοιτο πορεύεσθαι εἰς Ἱεροσόλυμα κἀκεῖ κρίνεσθαι περὶ τούτων.

ἀπορούμενος (pres.mid.part.nom.sing.masc.of ἀπορέομαι, adverbial, causal) 2254.
δὲ (continuative conjunction) 11.
ἐγὼ (nom.sing.masc.of ἐγώ, subject of ἔλεγον) 123.
τὴν (acc.sing.fem.of the article in agreement with ζήτησιν) 9.
περὶ (preposition with the genitive of reference) 173.
τούτων (gen.pl.neut.of οὗτος, reference) 93.
ζήτησιν (acc.sing.fem.of ζήτησις, direct object of ἀπορούμενος) 1994.
ἔλεγον (1st.per.sing.imp.act.ind.of λέγω, inchoative) 66.
εἰ (conditional particle in an elliptical fourth-class condition, in indirect question) 337.
βούλοιτο (3d.per.sing.pres.ind.opt.of βούλομαι, indirect question, in an elliptical fourth-class condition) 953.
πορεύεσθαι (pres.mid.inf.of πορεύομαι, complementary) 170.
εἰς (preposition with the accusative of extent) 140.
Ἱεροσόλυμα (acc.sing.fem.of Ἱεροσόλυμα, extent) 141.
κἀκεῖ (adjunctive conjunction and local adverb, crasis) 204.
κρίνεσθαι (pres.pass.inf.of κρίνω, complementary) 531.
περὶ (preposition with the genitive of reference) 173.
τούτων (gen.pl.neut.of οὗτος, reference) 93.

*Translation - "And since I was in doubt about how to delve into these matters, I raised the question if he might be willing to go to Jerusalem and there be placed in jeopardy with reference to them."*

**Comment:** *Cf.*#2254 and note the figure of speech. In terms of the parlance of the 1970's Festus was saying to Agrippa and Bernice, "No way!" He found himself, as it were, in the position of a traveller who wished to cross a stream but had no ford, bridge or boat. Festus could not deal with the problem of investigating these matters (περὶ τούτων), and thus felt himself incompetent to reach the proper judicial decision. Who was he, he asks Agrippa incredulously, to judge matters between the Jews and Paul about which he was totally ignorant? So, according to his story, he asked Paul the question. But let us note carefully how he says he asked it and then compare with the way in which he did, in fact, ask it (Acts 25:9). He told Agrippa that his question to Paul was in the form of an elliptical fourth-class condition, with εἰ and the optative mode in βούλοιτο in the protasis. Thus he was asking, "Surely you do not wish to go to Jerusalem and there be judged concerning these matters, do you?" The fourth-class condition, with the optative indicates a "Remote Prospect of Determination" (Robertson, *Grammar*, 1020). It is indirect question, but the direct, while using the same tenses, would have used the negative conjunction μή, not οὐκ with the verb in the optative, which indicates a rhetorical question the reply to which is expected to be "Of course not." The direct question in Acts 25:9 translates to "Do you want to go up to Jerusalem there to be judged concerning these matters *before me?*" There is nothing in this direct question with the indicative to hint to Paul that Festus was suggesting to him that he should reply in the negative. The question which he really asked Paul is an open question, with no hint of pressure from Festus, one way or the other. Paul's ready reply in the negative was the result of his own mature understanding of the legal situation, and was in no way influenced by the manner in which the question was asked.

Note further that Festus said that the trial in Jerusalem, if Paul wished to defend himself there, was to be before the governor. And yet he had just told Agrippa that he felt incompetent to reach an objective decision in the case. If Festus wanted to swear himself off the bench in Caesarea, why did he want to preside on the bench in Jerusalem? Would he understand the issues of the case better in Jerusalem when he admitted in Caesarea that he knew little about them?

The real reason that Festus asked Paul the question was that he hoped by arranging another trip to Jerusalem for Paul, and thus making it possible for the Jews to ambush and kill him, he would ingratiate himself with the troublesome Jewish leadership in Palestine. But this is not the version that he gave to Agrippa. The real reason why he related it to the king as he did was that he wished to represent himself as an honest judge. The essence of the question, as reported in verse 20 may be stated as follows: "Are you willing by any remote chance (I do not see why you should be!) to go to Jerusalem for trial?" If he had really asked the question like that he would have been suggesting to Paul that he (Paul) ought to get the point and say, "No."

*Verse 21 - "But when Paul had appealed to be reserved unto the hearing of Augustus, I commanded him to be kept till I might send him to Caesar."*

τοῦ δε Παύλου ἐπικαλεσαμένου τηρηθῆναι αὐτὸν εἰς τὴν τοῦ Σεβαστοῦ διάγνωσιν, ἐκέλευσα τηρεῖσθαι αὐτὸν ἕως οὗ ἀναπέμψω αὐτὸν πρὸς Καίσαρα.

τοῦ (gen.sing.masc.of the article in agreement with Παύλου) 9.

δὲ (adversative conjunction) 11.

Παύλου (gen.sing.masc.of Παῦλος, genitive absolute) 3284.

ἐπικαλεσαμένου (aor.mid.part.gen.sing.masc.of ἐπικαλέω, genitive absolute, adverbial, temporal/causal) 884.

τηρηθῆναι (aor.pass.inf.of τηρέω, noun use, object of ἐπικαλεσαμένου) 1297.

αὐτὸν (acc.sing.masc.of αὐτός, general reference) 16.

εἰς (preposition with the accusative of extent) 140.

τὴν (acc.sing.fem.of the article in agreement with διάγνωσιν) 9.

τοῦ (gen.sing.masc.of the article in agreement with Σεβαστοῦ) 9.

#3644 Σεβαστοῦ (gen.sing.masc.of Σεβαστός, description).

Augustus - Acts 25:21,25; 27:1.

*Meaning:* Augustus; the title given to the Roman Emperor - Acts 25:21,25. A title of honor given to a Roman legion for valor in battle - Acts 27:1. Highly decorated; a cohort of heros - "The Augustan band."

#3645 διάγνωσιν (acc.sing.fem.of διάγνωσις, time extent).

hearing - Acts 25:21.

*Meaning:* A combination of διά (#118) and γινώσκω (#131). Hence, diagnosis; a thorough review of facts. With reference to a regal review - Acts 25:21.

ἐκέλευσα (1st.per.sing.aor.act.ind.of κελεύω, constative) 741.

τηρεῖσθαι (pres.pass.inf.of τηρέω, object infinitive in indirect discourse) 1297.

αὐτὸν (acc.sing.masc.of αὐτός, general reference) 16.

ἕως (preposition with the genitive of time description) 71.

οὗ (gen.sing.neut.of ὅς, relative pronoun, time description) 65.

ἀναπέμψω (1st.per.sing.fut.act.ind.of ἀναπέμπω, in a temporal clause) 2829.

αὐτὸν (acc.sing.masc.of αὐτός, direct object of ἀναπέμψω) 16.

πρὸς (preposition with the accusative of extent) 197.

Καίσαρα (acc.sing.masc.of Καίσαρι, extent) 1418.

*Translation* - "*But because Paul asked that he be kept until a review by Augustus, I ordered him to be kept in custody until I can send him to the Emperor.*"

**Comment:** The genitive absolute aorist participle ἐπικαλεσαμένου is causal and temporal. Because of Paul's appeal to Caesar - *i.e.* that he be detained, pending a review by Augustus, Festus ordered that he be kept in custody. There are two temporal constructions: εἰς τὴν ... διάγνωσιν - an accusative of time extent, and ἕως οὗ ἀναπέμφω - "until such time as I send him up. . . " - a genitive of time description.

It is idle to speculate about what might have happened in other circumstances, but one cannot help wondering what Festus would have done with Paul if the Apostle had not taken an appeal to the higher jurisdiction. In view of the governor's desire to curry favor with the Jews in Jerusalem, would he have kept Paul in prison until he died, or would he have delivered him to the Jews? It was Paul's demand for a fair trial before the Emperor that the Lord foresaw when He promised Paul that he would witness for Him in Rome (Acts 23:11).

Festus' account of the case elicited from Agrippa a desire to hear Paul preach.

*Verse 22 - "Then Agrippa said unto Festus, I would also hear the man myself. Tomorrow, said he, thou shalt hear him."*

Ἀγρίππας δὲ πρὸς τὸν Φῆστον, Ἐβουλόμην καὶ αὐτὸς τοῦ ἀνθρώπου ἀκοῦσαι. Αὔριον, φησίν, ἀκούσῃ αὐτοῦ.

Ἀγρίππας (nom.sing.masc.of Ἀγρίππας, subject of εἶπεν, understood) 136C.

δὲ (continuative conjunction) 11.

πρὸς (preposition with the accusative of extent, after a verb of speaking) 197.

τὸν (acc.sing.masc.of the article in agreement with Φῆστον) 9.

Φῆστον (acc.sing.masc.of Φῆστος, extent, after a verb of speaking) 3633.

Ἐβουλόμην (1st.per.sing.imp.mid.ind.of βούλομαι, voluntative) 953.

καὶ (emphatic conjunction) 14.

αὐτὸς (nom.sing.masc.of αὐτός, intensive) 16.

τοῦ (gen.sing.masc.of the article in agreement with ἀνθρώπου) 9.

ἀνθρώπου (gen.sing.masc.of ἄνθρωπος, objective genitive) 341.

ἀκοῦσαι (aor.act.inf.of ἀκούω, complementary) 148.

Αὔριον (temporal adverb) 633.

φησίν (3d.per.sing.pres.act.ind.of φημί, historical) 354.

ἀκούσῃ (2d.per.sing.fut.act.ind.of ἀκούω, predictive) 148.

αὐτοῦ (gen.sing.masc.of αὐτός objective genitive) 16.

*Translation - "And Agrippa said to Festus, 'I myself in fact have been rather wanting to hear the man.' 'Tomorrow,' he said, 'you shall hear him.' "*

**Comment:** Note ἐβουλόμην as a good example of the voluntative imperfect. "The want of attainment in the imperfect prepares it to submit quite easily to the expression of a desire or disposition, since the statement of a wish itself implies the lack of realization. There are but a few instances of this usage in the New Testament, but adequate grammatical treatment requires that they be recognized as a distinct class." (Mantey, *Manual*, 190). Rom.9:3; Gal.4:20; Philemon 13 are other examples. Robertson (*Grammar*, 885,886) calls ἐβουλόμην a potential imperfect and quites Gildersleeve (*Syntax of Classical Greek*, 95) as calling it "modal." Robertson translates, "I was just on the point of wishing." Freely rendered we have "I could wish" or "I should wish." "I have been wishing" translates the iterative actions of the past in an instensive sense - "I have wished again and again to hear the man and now again I express my desire."

Paul's influence is evident in that the King had heard of him and the impact of his preaching upon the people. Christianity had now survived for thirty years and its fruits could not be denied. The movement had long since disproved any notion that it was only a "flash in the pan" explosion that would soon pass. King Agrippa seems to have sensed some of this.

*Verse 23 - "And on the morrow, when Agrippa was come, and Bernice, with great pomp,   and was entered into the place of hearing, with the chief captains, and principal men of the city, at Festus commandment Paul was brought forth."*

Τῇ οὖν ἐπαύριον ἐλθόντος τοῦ Ἀγρίππα καὶ τῆς Βερνίκης μετὰ πολλῆς φαντασίας καὶ εἰσελθόντων εἰς τὸ ἀκροατήριον σύν τε χιλιάρχοις καὶ ἀνδράσιν τοῖς κατ᾽ ἐξοχὴν τῆς πόλεως, καὶ κελεύσαντος τοῦ Φήστου ἤχθη ὁ Παῦλος.

Τῇ (loc.sing.fem.of the article, time point) 9.

οὖν (inferential conjunction) 68.

ἐπαύριον (temporal adverb) 1680.

ἐλθόντος (aor.mid.part.gen.sing.masc.of ἔρχομαι, genitive absolute) 146.

τοῦ (gen.sing.masc.of the article in agreement with Ἀγρίππα) 9.

Ἀγρίππα (gen.sing.masc.of Ἀγρίππος, genitive absolute) 136C.

καὶ (adjunctive conjunction joining nouns) 14.

τῆς (gen.sing.fem.of the article in agreement with Βερνίκης) 9.

Βερνίκης (gen.sing.fem.of Βερνίκη, genitive absolute) 3638.

μετὰ (preposition with the genitive of physical accompaniment) 50.

πολλῆς (gen.sing.fem.of πολύς, in agreement with φαντασίας) 228.

#3645 φαντασίας (gen.sing.fem.of φαντασία, physical accompaniment).

pomp - Acts 25:23.

*Meaning:* Cf. φαντάζω (#5078) and φάντασμα (#1130). Spectacular appearance; pomp; ostentatious display. With reference to the appearance of Agrippa and Bernice - Acts 25:23.

καὶ (adjunctive conjunction joining participles) 14.

εἰσελθόντων (aor.mid.part.gen.pl.masc.of εἰσέρχομαι, genitive absolute) 234.

εἰς (preposition with the accusative of extent) 140.

τὸ (acc.sing.neut.of the article in agreement with ἀκροατήριον) 9.

#3646 ἀκροατήριον (acc.sing.neut.of ἀκροατήριον, extent).

place of hearing - Acts 25:23.

*Meaning:* Cf. ἀκροάομαι - "to hold a hearing." Hence, a place set aside for hearing. Auditorium. In Caesarea, a public assembly hall for general use. The place where Agrippa heard Paul preach - Acts 25:23.

σύν (preposition with the instrumental of association) 1542.
τε (correlative conjunction) 1408.
χιλιάρχοις (instru.pl.masc.of χιλίαρχος, association) 2258.
καὶ (adjunctive conjunction joining nouns) 14.
ἀνδράσιν (instru.pl.masc.of ἀνήρ, association) 63.
τοῖς (instru.pl.masc.of the article in agreement with ἀνδράσιν) 9.
κατ' (preposition with the accusative, standard rule) 98.

#3647 ἐξοχήν (acc.sing.fem.of ἐξοχή, standard rule).

principal - Acts 25:23.

*Meaning:* Cf. ἐξέχω - "to stand out." Hence, prominent. κατ' ἐξοχήν - "measured according to the standard rule of prominence." - Acts 25:23.

τῆς (gen.sing.fem.of the article in agreement with πόλεως) 9.
πόλεως (gen.sing.fem.of πόλις, description) 243.
καὶ (adjunctive conjunction joining participles) 14.
κελεύσαντος (aor.act.part.gen.sing.masc.of κελεύω, genitive absolute) 741.
τοῦ (gen.sing.masc.of the article in agreement with Φήστου) 9.
Φήστου (gen.sing.masc.of Φῆστος, genitive absolute) 3633.
ἤχθη (3d.per.sing.aor.pass.ind.of ἄγω, culminative) 876.
ὁ (nom.sing.masc.of the article in agreement with Παῦλος) 9.
Παῦλος (nom.sing.masc.of Παῦλος, subject of ἤχθη) 3284.

*Translation -* "Therefore the next day when Agrippa and Bernice had come with great fanfare and entered into the auditorium with the colonels and men of the city who were prominent, at Festus' command Paul was brought in."

**Comment:** οὖν is inferential. Agrippa expressed a desire to hear Paul and Festus gave his promise. "Therefore. . . " The sentence, stripped of the three genitive absolutes, is "Therefore the next day Paul was brought in." But not before the King and his consort came in accompanied by the military and political officials of the city, after which Festus ordered that he be brought. The city fathers came "according to prominence." How typical this is. A politician comes to town. There is a motorcade, replete with banners floating on the breeze and horns blaring. The parade makes its way from the airport to the city hall. The mayor and the city council sit on the platform. But there is a seating order in keeping with the pecking order. The dog and pony show has not changed in two thousand years. Festus ordered Paul brought in. One wonders if Paul had a sense of humor that equipped him to smile at all of this. He had a big audience and he made the most of his opportunity.

Only the Holy Spirit can tell what the people were thinking as they took their places in the auditorium. Were there hungry hearts? Were there minds still struggling with Pilate's question? What, in fact, is truth, if, indeed, any man can tell? Perhaps some came out of curiosity. They had heard of this preacher and now there was opportunity to see him. Some were prepared to scoff. Others may honestly have hoped for light on the great eternal questions - From whence? Why? Whither? Perhaps Paul could tell them.

*Verse 24 - "And Festus said, King Agrippa, and all men which are here present with us, ye see this man about whom all the multitude of the Jews have dealt with me, both at Jerusalem, and also here, crying that he ought not to live any longer."*

καί φησιν ὁ Φῆστος, Ἀγρίππα βασιλεῦ καὶ πάντες οἱ συμπαρόντες ἡμῖν ἄνδρες, θεωρεῖτε τοῦτον περὶ οὗ ἅπαν τὸ πλῆθος τῶν Ἰουδαίων ἐνέτυχόν μοι ἕν τε Ἱεροσολύμοις καὶ ἐνθάδε, βοῶντες μὴ δεῖν αὐτὸν ζῆν μηκέτι.

καὶ (continuative conjunction) 14.
φησιν (3d.per.sing.pres.act.ind.ofd φημί, historical) 354.
ὁ (nom.sing.masc.of the article in agreement with Φῆστος) 9.
Φῆστος (nom.sing.masc.of Φῆστος, subject of φησιν) 3633.
Ἀγρίππα (voc.sing.masc.of Ἀγρίππος, address) 136C.
βασιλεῦ (voc.sing.masc.of βασιλεύς, apposition) 31.
καὶ (adjunctive conjunction joining nouns) 14.
πάντες (voc.pl.masc.of πᾶς, in agreement with ἄνδρες) 67.
οἱ (voc.pl.masc.of the article in agreement with συμπαρόντες) 9.

#3648 συμπαρόντες (pres.act.part.voc.pl.masc.of συμπάρειμι, adjectival, ascriptive, in agreement with ἄνδρες).

be here present with - Acts 25:24.

*Meaning:* A combination of σύν (#1542), παρά (#154) and εἰμί (#86). Hence, to be present with, or alongside. As an adjective modifying men - "the men here assembled with us." - Acts 25:24.

ἡμῖν (instru.pl.masc.of ἐγώ, association) 123.
ἄνδρες (voc.pl.masc.of ἀνήρ, address) 63.
θεωρεῖτε (2d.per.pl.pres.act.ind.of θεωρέω, aoristic) 1667.
τοῦτον (acc.sing.masc.of οὗτος, direct object of θεωρεῖτε) 93.
περὶ (preposition with the genitive of reference) 173.
οὗ (gen.sing.masc.of ὅς, relative pronoun, reference) 65.
ἅπαν (nom.sing.neut.of ἅπας, in agreement with πλῆθος) 639.
τὸ (nom.sing.neut.of the article in agreement with πλῆθος) 9.
πλῆθος (nom.sing.neut.of πλῆθος, subject of ἐνέτυχόν) 1792.
τῶν (gen.pl.masc.of the article in agreement with Ἰουδαίων) 9.
Ἰυδαίων (gen.pl.masc.of Ἰουδαῖος, description) 143.

#3649 ἐνέτυχόν (3d.per.pl.2d.aor.act.ind.of ἐντυγχάνω, culminative).

deal with - Acts 25:24.
make intercession - Rom.8:27,34; 11:2; Heb.7:25.

*Meaning:* A combination of ἐν (#80) and τυγχάνω (#2699). Hence, to come upon, or hit upon a person or thing. Thus often in Greek. To go to a person for conference or supplication. Hence, to entreat; to insist that something be done - that Paul be executed - Acts 25:24; with reference to the Holy Spirit's intercession for the saints - Rom.8:27; of Christ's intercession for us - Rom.8:34; Heb.7:25; of Elias' prayer about Israel - Rom.11:2.

μοι (dat.sing.masc.of ἐγώ, indirect object of ἐνέτυχόν) 123.

ἐν (preposition with the locative of place) 80.

τε (correlative particle) 1408.

Ἱεροσολύμοις (loc.sing.masc.of Ἱεροσόλυμα, place where) 141.

καὶ (adjunctive conjunction joining a prepositional phrase and an adverb) 14.

ἐνθάδε (local adverb) 2010.

βοῶντες (pres.act.part.nom.pl.masc.of βοάω, adverbial, modal) 256.

μὴ (negative conjunction with the infinitive in indirect discourse) 87.

δεῖν (pres.inf.of δεῖ, object infinitive in indirect discourse) 1207.

αὐτὸν (acc.sing.masc.of αὐτός, general reference) 16.

ζῆν (pres.act.inf.of ζάω, complementary) 340.

μηκέτι (temporal adverb) 1368.

*Translation - "And Festus said, 'King Agrippa, and all the men assembled with us, you see this fellow about whom all of the multitude of the Jews remonstrated with me, both in Jerusalem and here, crying out that he ought not to live any longer.' "*

**Comment:** Here is a typical speech of a small-time politician who is having his big moment, as he shows off before the King and Queen, all of the notables from City Hall and the brass from the Pentagon. Note his contemptuous use of τοῦτον, with ἄνθρωπον omitted. If Festus had known or cared anything about good taste and class, he would have introduced Paul as a prominent evangelist and leader of the new movement called Christianity. But he seemd to be more interested in pointing out that Paul was the object of a widespread attack from the Jews. Note the exaggeration in ἄπαν τὸ πλῆθος τῶν Ἰουδαίων. The statement is not true. ἄπας (#639) is α intensive and means literally all of the Jews. The Hebrew Christians did not want Paul dead, nor could Festus have proved that even all of the unregenerate Jews were against him. Note the indirect discourse following the modal participle βοῶντες, with the infinitive δεῖν complemented by the infinitive ζῆν. Note also the intensive negation of μηδεῖν αὐτόν ζῆν μηκέτι. It is true that some Jews, both in Jerusalem and in Caesarea had demanded Paul's death. But Festus implies that he is the sole protector of the defendant from the hatred of religious fanaticism, when, in fact, had Paul not threatened him with an appeal to Caesar, Festus, for reasons of political expediency, would have delivered him to his murderers.

It is only when we pay strict attention to diction, grammar and syntax in the context, on the one hand and to *zeitgeist* on the other that we can discern what lies between the lines. This is true in the exegesis of any document, particularly of one which was written long before our examination of it.

*Verse 25 - "But when I found that he had committed nothing worthy of death and that he himself had appealed to Augustus, I have determined to send him."*

ἐγὼ δὲ κατελαβόμην μηδὲν ἄξιον αὐτὸν θανάτου πεπραχέναι, αὐτοῦ δὲ τούτου ἐπικαλεσαμένου τὸν Σεβαστὸν ἔκρινα πέμπειν.

ἐγὼ (nom.sing.masc.of ἐγώ, subject of κατελαβόμην) 123.

δὲ (adversative conjunction) 11.

κατελαβόμην (1st.per.sing.aor.mid.ind.of καταλαμβάνω, culminative) 1694.

μηδὲν (acc.sing.neut.of μηδείς, direct object of πεπραχέναι) 713.

ἄξιον (acc.sing.neut.of ἄξιος, predicate adjective) 285.

αὐτὸν (acc.sing.masc.of αὐτός, general reference) 16.

θανάτου (abl.sing.masc.of θάνατος, comparison) 381.

πεπραχέναι (perf.act.inf.of πράσσω, object infinitive in indirect discourse) 1943.

αὐτοῦ (gen.sing.masc.of αὐτός, intensive, genitive absolute) 16.

δὲ (adversative conjunction) 11.

τούτου (gen.sing.masc.of οὗτος, genitive absolute) 93.

ἐπικαλεσαμένου (aor.mid.part.gen.sing.masc.of ἐπικαλέω, genitive absolute, adverbial, causal) 884.

τὸν (acc.sing.masc.of the article in agreement with Σεβαστὸν) 9.

Σεβαστὸν (acc.sing.masc.of Σεαστός, direct object of ἐπικαλεσαμένου) 3644.

ἔκρινα (1st.per.sing.aor.act.ind.of κρίνω, constative) 531.

πέμπειν (pres.act.inf.of πέμπω, complementary) 169.

*Translation -* "*But I ascertained that he had done nothing worthy of death: but, because he himself appealed to Augustus, I decided to send him.*"

**Comment:** δὲ is adversative. Despite popular clamor for Paul's death, at least according to Festus' story, his investigation found nothing. Note the ablative of comparison - a capital crime is one the punishment for which is equal to the pain of death. The ablative of comparison properly follows ἄξιος - "equal to." *Cf.* Mt.3:8 - "fruit equal to repentance" *i.e.* behavior of such quality that it convinces John the Baptist that the Pharisees have repented.

The intensive perfect infinitive is indirect discourse after κατελαβόμην. Moulton (*Prolegomena*, 146, as cited by Robertson, *Grammar*, 908) calls it "the vivid present of story telling." Festus should have been asked at this point why then, since he had ruled that Paul was not guilty, had he not dismissed the case and ordered Paul freed? The governor added lamely that since Paul (causal participle in the genitive absolute ἐπικαλεσαμένου) had appealed to Nero, he had decided to send him to Rome for a further review of the case, even though there were no proper charges against him! As a result Festus is faced with the dilemma of sending a prisoner to Nero in Rome, but without an indictment, except those which had failed of substantiation in his own court. No appeal was necessary and none was proper. Paul had nothing to appeal. Yet he is still a prisoner.

Festus was getting more and more upset as his remarks prove in

*Verse 26 -* "*Of whom I have no certain thing to write unto my lord, Wherefore I*

*have brought him forth before you, and specially before thee, O King Agrippa,*
*that, after examination had, I might have somewhat to write."*

περὶ οὗ ἀσφαλές τι γράψαι τῷ κυρίῳ οὐκ ἔχω, διὸ προήγαγον αὐτὸν ἐφ'
ὑμῶν καὶ μάλιστα ἐπὶ σοῦ, βασιλεῦ 'Αγρίππα, ὅπως τῆς ἀνακρίσεως
γενομένης σχῶ τί γράψω, . . .

περὶ (preposition with the genitive of reference) 173.

οὗ (gen.sing.masc.of ὅς, relative pronoun, reference) 65.

ἀσφαλές (acc.sing.neut.of ἀσφαλής, in agreement with τι) 3565.

τι (acc.sing.neut.of τις, indefinite pronoun, direct object of ἔχω) 486.

γράψαι (aor.act.inf.of γράφω, completes ἔχω) 156.

τῷ (dat.sing.masc.of the article in agreement with κυρίῳ) 9.

κυρίῳ (dat.sing.masc.of κύριος, indirect object of γράψαι) 97.

οὐκ (negative conjunction with the indicative) 130.

ἔχω (1st.per.sing.pres.act.ind.of ἔχω, progressive duration, retroactive) 82.

διὸ (inferential particle) 1622.

προήγαγον (1st.per.sing.aor.act.ind.of προάγω, culminative) 179.

αὐτὸν (acc.sing.masc.of αὐτος, direct object of προήγαγον) 16.

ἐφ' (preposition with the genitive of place description) 47.

ὑμῶν (gen.pl.masc.of σύ, place description) 104.

καὶ (adjunctive conjunction joining prepositional phrases) 14.

μάλιστα (adverbial) 3536.

ἐπὶ (preposition with the genitive of place description) 47.

σοῦ (gen.sing.masc.of σύ, place description) 104.

βασιλεῦ (voc.sing.masc.of βασιλεύς, address) 31.

'Αγρίππα (voc.sing.masc.of'Αγρίππας, address) 136C.

ὅπως (conjunction with the subjunctive in a purpose clause) 177.

τῆς (gen.sing.fem.of the article in agreement with ἀνακρίσεως) 9.

#3650 ἀνακρίσεως (gen.sing.fem.of ἀνάκρισις, genitive absolute).

examination - Acts 25:26.

*Meaning:* A combination of ἀνά (#1059) and κρίσις (#478). Hence, a
preliminary hearing, similar to a grand jury investigation for the purpose of
gathering evidence to present to a judge - Acts 25:26.

γενομένης (aor.mid.part.gen.sing.fem.of γίνομαι, genitive absolute) 113.

σχῶ (1st.per.sing.2d.aor.act.subj.of ἔχω, purpose) 82.

τί (acc.sing.neut.of τις, indefinite pronoun, direct object of σχῶ) 486.

γράψω (1st.per.sing.fut.act.ind.or 1st.per.sing.aor.act.subj.of γράφω,
deliberative) 156.

*Translation* - "*Concerning whom I have nothing certain to write to my superior;*
*therefore I have brought him out before you, and especially before you, King*
*Agrippa, so that after the hearing I will have something to write."*

**Comment:** Cf.#3565. Festus had nothing to write to Nero that would justify his
action in sending Paul to Rome. Nothing that he could say to Nero now would
"stand up in court" (ἀσφαλές) διό introduces the inferential clause. That is why
Festus had brought Paul before Agrippa in the hope, either that Agrippa would
find something in what Paul had already said which was illegal or that Paul

in an unguarded moment would make some derogatory statement about the Romans that would justify the charge of sedition. Paul had contempt for the courts, both of Festus and of Felix, and with ample justification, but he had not expressed it. He had moved for a mistrial and had warned Festus that his decision was subject to the consideration of the appelate jurisdiction in Rome, but that is not what is meant by contempt of court. Paul had not yet broken the Roman law, either in the hearing of Claudius Lysias, or of Felix or of Festus. Perhaps he would do so now. ὅπως and the subjunctive in σχῶ indicate his purpose and the result for which he so ardently wished.

We cannot tell whether γράφω is future indicative or aorist subjunctive, since the two forms have the same spelling, but the context allows either. "The Future Indicative is sometimes used in questions of deliberation, asking not what will happen, but what can or ought to be done. Such questions may be real questions asking information, or rhetorical questions taking the place of a direct assertion." (Burton, *New Testament Moods and Tenses,* 36). "Questions may be classified as questions of fact and questions of deliberation. In the question of fact the speaker asks what is (*or* was *or* will be). In the question of deliberation, the speaker asks what he is to do, or what is to be done; it concerns not fact but possibility, desirability, or necessity." (*Ibid.,*76). These two types of questions to which Burton has alluded ". . . employ the moods and tenses as other simple declarative sentences in both direct and indirect discourse. But deliberative questions ask not for the facts, but about the 'possibility, desirability or necessity' of a proposed course of action. The subjunctive as the mood of doubtful assertion is perfectly natural here. The future is also doubtful from the nature of the case. So deliberative questions use either the subjunctive of the future indicative." (Robertson, *Grammar*, 875). Thus whether we take γράφω as future indicative or aorist subjunctive we have Festus' deliberation about the future. There is uncertainty, not only in the question as to what he will write to Nero, but also in the question as to whether or not he will have anything at all to write, as the subjunctive σχῶ tells us. Festus was not certain that when Paul had finished speaking he would have any legal basis at all for sending him to Rome to face Nero, or that, if he had, what it would be.

Festus stated the dilemma very well in verse 27. He had painted himself into a corner because of his willingness to throw Paul, a Roman citizen to the Jewish wolves in Jerusalem, because the governor felt that he had to live with the Jews, but not with the Christians. He did not reckon with the fact that Paul was not only a good Christian but also a good lawyer.

*Verse 27 - "For it seemeth to me unreasonable to send a prisoner and not withal to signify the crimes laid against him."*

ἄλογον γὰρ μοι δοκεῖ πέμποντα δέσμιον μὴ καὶ τὰς κατ' αὐτοῦ αἰτίας σημᾶναι.

#3651 ἄλογον (acc.sing.masc.of ἄλογος, predicate adjective).

brute - 2 Peter 2:12; Jude 10.
unreasonable - Acts 25:27.

*Meaning:* α privative and λόγος (#510). Hence, illogical. With no more rational power than that possessed by beasts - 2 Peter 2:12; Jude 10. Illogical - Acts 25:27, in a statement by Festus about his own policies.

γὰρ (causal conjunction) 105.

μοι (dat.sing.masc.of ἐγώ, person) 123.

δοκεῖ (3d.per.sing.pres.act.ind.of δοκέω, static) 287.

πέμποντα (pres.act.part.nom.sing.masc.of πέμπω, substantival, subject of δοκεῖ) 169

δέσμιον (acc.sing.masc.of δέσμιος, direct object of πέμποντα) 1624.

μὴ (negative conjunction with the infinitive) 87.

καὶ (adjunctive conjunction joining infinitives) 14.

τὰς (acc.pl.fem.of the article in agreement with αἰτίας) 9.

κατ' (preposition with the genitive, opposition) 98.

αὐτοῦ (gen.sing.masc.of αὐτός, opposition) 16.

αἰτίας (acc.pl.fem.of αἰτία, direct object of σημᾶναι) 1283.

σημᾶναι (1st.aor.act.inf.of σημαίνω, noun use, subject of δοκεῖ) 2708.

*Translation - "Because to send a prisoner and not to specify the charges against him seems to me illogical."*

**Comment:** No! One is amazed at the clarity of the perception of proper legal procedure manifested by the governor. We can imagine the scene if Festus were present in Nero's court when Paul is brought before the Emperor. The dialogue might go something like this:

Nero: "Who is this man?"
Festus: "Paul of Tarsus of Cilicia."
Nero: "Is he a slave?"
Festus: "He is a Roman citizen."
Nero: "What is his profession?"
Festus: "He is a lawyer."
Nero: "What has he done?"
Festus: "Nothing."
Nero: "What are the charges against him?"
Festus: "There are none."
Nero: "Then why is he here?"
Festus: "I do not know."

It is scant wonder that Festus was worried.

We have a double subject of the verb δοκεῖ - one a participle in its substantival use and the other an infinitive with its noun use predominant. Thus we see the versatility of the verbal adjective and the verbal noun. Each can be the subject of a verb. "To send and not to specify . . . seems absurd."

There was only one way out of Festus' dilemma. He could set Paul free. In that case Paul's appeal to the Emperor would be moot.

Back of all of the foolishness, foibles, flaws and frailties of the flesh of sinful men, was the sovereign will of God Who had already told Paul that he was gong to Rome, there to witness and ultimately to die.

## Paul Defends Himself Before Agrippa

*(Acts 26:1 - 11)*

*Acts 26:1 - "Then Agrippa said unto Paul, Thou art permitted to speak for thyself. Then Paul stretched forth the hand, and answered for himself."*

Ἀγρίππας δὲ πρὸς τὸν Παῦλον ἔφη, Ἐπιτρέπεταί σοι περὶ σεαυτοῦ λέγειν. τότε ὁ Παῦλος ἐκτείνας τὴν χεῖρα ἀπελογεῖτο

Ἀγρίππας (nom.sing.masc.of Ἀγρίππας, subject of ἔφη) 136C.
δὲ (continuative conjunction) 11.
πρὸς (preposition with the accusative of extent with a verb of speaking) 197.
τὸν (acc.sing.masc.of the article in agreement with Παῦλον) 9.
Παῦλον (acc.sing.masc.of Παῦλος, extent, with a verb of speaking) 3284.
ἔφη (3d.per.sing.aor.act.ind.of φημί, constative) 354.
Ἐπιτρέπεταί (3d.per.sing.pres.pass.ind.of ἐπιτρέπω, aoristic) 747.
σοι (dat.sing.masc.of σύ, personal interest) 104.
περὶ (preposition with the genitive of reference) 173.
σεαυτοῦ (gen.sing.masc.of σεαυτός, reflexive personal pronoun, reference) 347.
λέγειν (pres.act.inf.of λέγω, noun use, subject of ἐπιτρέπεταί) 66.
τότε (continuative conjunction) 166.
ὁ (nom.sing.masc.of the article in agreement with Παῦλος) 9.
Παῦλος (nom.sing.masc.of Παῦλος, subject of ἀπελογεῖτο) 3284.
ἐκτείνας (aor.act.part.nom.sing.masc.of ἐκτείνω, adverbial, coincident) 710.
τὴν (acc.sing.fem.of the article in agreement with χεῖρα) 9.
χεῖρα (acc.sing.fem.of χείρ, direct object of ἐκτείνας) 308.
ἀπελογεῖτο (3d.per.sing.imp.mid.ind.of ἀπολογέομαι, inchoative) 2476.

*Translation - "And Agrippa said to Paul, 'You have permission to speak for yourself.' Then Paul stretched out his hand and began his defense."*

**Comment:** ἀπελογεῖτο is an inchoative imperfect. Paul began his defense.

*Verse 2 - "I think myself happy, King Agrippa, because I shall answer for myself this day before thee touching all the things whereof I am accused of the Jews."*

Περὶ πάντων ὧν ἐγκαλοῦμαι ὑπὸ Ἰουδαίων, βασιλεῦ Ἀγρίππα, ἥγημαι ἐμαυτὸν μακάριον ἐπὶ σοῦ μέλλων σήμερον ἀπολογεῖσθαι,

Περὶ (preposition with the genitive of reference) 173.
πάντων (gen.pl.neut.of πᾶς, reference) 67.
ὧν (gen.pl.neut.of ὅς, relative pronoun, reference) 65.
ἐγκαλοῦμαι (1st.per.sing.pres.pass.ind.of ἐγκαλέω, progressive duration, retroactive) 3495.

ὑπό (preposition with the ablative of agent) 117.

'Ιουδαίων (abl.pl.masc.of 'Ιουδαῖος, agent) 143.

βασιλεῦ (voc.sing.masc.of βασιλεύς, address) 31.

'Αγρίππα (voc.sing.masc.of 'Αγρίππας, address) 136C.

ἥγημαι (1st.per.sing.perf.mid.ind.of ἡγέομαι, intensive) 162.

ἐμαυτὸν (acc.sing.masc.of ἑαυτός, reflexive personal pronoun, direct object of ἥγημαι) 723.

μακάριον (acc.sing.masc.of μακάριος, predicate adjective) 422.

ἐπὶ (preposition with the genitive of place description) 47.

σοῦ (gen.sing.masc.of σύ, place description) 104.

μέλλων (pres.act.part.nom.sing.masc.of μέλλω, adverbial, causal) 206.

σήμερον (temporal adverb) 579.

ἀπολογεῖσθαι (pres.mid.inf.of ἀπολογέομαι,complementary) 2476.

*Translation - "With reference to all these things of which I have been accused by the Jews, King Agrippa, I have considered myself fortunate, since my defense is about to begin before you."*

**Comment:** Paul here accents the result ahead of the cause. The result of the accusations is that he considers himself to be fortunate - ἥγημαι ἐμαυτὸν μακάριον. The cause for this good fortune is that his defense was about to begin. When? σήμερον. Where? ἐπὶ σοῦ. About what? περὶ πάντων ὧν ἐγκαλοῦμαι. By whom is he accused? ὑπὸ'Ιουδαίων. It is easy to push the perfect tense too far - "I have considered myself (and I still do) happy." How long before the time did Paul know that he was going to have the privilege of speaking before the King? The text does not tell us, but the implication is that it was not long. Luke's time points are seldom precise. It was "several days" after Agrippa arrived that Festus told him about Paul, at which time Agrippa expressed a wish to hear him. (Acts 25:14). The hearing took place the next day (Acts 25:23). Paul may have been told the day before that he would speak before Agrippa. In any case the perfect tense, with its intensive force applies. As soon as Paul got the news he rejoiced and as he arose to speak he was still happy about it.

ἥγημαι is a redundant middle voice, as is evident from the fact that the reflexive ἐμουτόν is added, but ἡγέομαι (#162) is a weak middle to begin with.

Paul flatters the King. It was a special privilege for him to state his case before royalty, but he was especially happy to speak before Agrippa. The reason is in

*Verse 3 - "Especially because I know thee to be expert in all customs and questions which are among the Jews: wherefore I beseech thee to hear me patiently."*

μάλιστα γνώστην ὄντα σε πάντων τῶν κατὰ 'Ιουδαίους ἐθῶν τε καὶ ζητημάτων. διὸ δέομαι μακροθύμως ἀκοῦσαί μου.

μάλιστα (adverbial) 3536.

#3652 γνώστην (acc.sing.masc.of γνώστης, predicate adjective).

expert - Acts 26:3. 1

*Meaning: Cf.* γινώσκω (#131). Hence, knowledgeable; an expert; a connoisseur. Followed by a genitive of reference in Acts 26:3.

ὄντα (pres.act.part.of εἰμί, adverbial, causal, accusative absolute) 86.

σε (acc.sing.masc.of σύ, accusative absolute) 104.

πάντων (gen.pl.neut.of πᾶς, in agreement with ἐθῶν and ζητημάτων) 67.

τῶν (gen.pl.neut.of the article in agreement with ἐθῶν and ζητημάτων) 9.

κατὰ (preposition with the accusative, standard rule) 98.

Ἰουδαίους (acc.pl.masc.of Ἰουδαῖος, standard rule) 143.

ἐθῶν (gen.pl.neut.of ἔθος, reference) 1788.

τε (correlative particle) 1408.

καὶ (adjunctive conjunction joining nouns) 14.

ζητημάτων (gen.pl.neut.of ζήτημα, reference) 3334.

διὸ (inferential particle) 1622.

δέομαι (1st.per.sing.pres.mid.ind.of δέομαι, aorist) 841.

#3653 μακροθύμως (adverbial).

patiently - Acts 26:3.

*Meaning: Cf.* μακροθυμέω (#1274); μακροθυμέω #5832); μακρός (#2546) plus θυμός (#2034). To behave with a long spirit; *i.e.* with patience; patiently. To resist the urge (θυμός) to act for a long time (μακρός) - Acts 26:3.

ἀκοῦσαί (aor.act.inf.of ἀκούω, direct object of δέομαι) 148.

μου (gen.sing.masc. of ἐγώ, objective genitive) 123.

*Translation - "Especially in view of the fact that you are knowledgeable about everything Jewish - both its folkways and mores. So I am asking you to listen to me with patience."*

**Comment:** In ὄντα σε we have an accusative absolute - a rare construction. Generally the genitive occurs with a participle and a substantive in an absolute construction. We can supply γινώσκω and take ὄντα σε as its object, but such addition is not necessary, since the accusative absolute is good Greek. ὄντα is causal. It was because Agrippa was an expert in the fields that Paul wished to discuss that the speaker was happy. It is much easier to develop a logical case if the audience is already acquainted with the subject matter. King Agrippa was well qualified to listen to Paul and make a judgment. κατά with the accusative means up and down horizontally - *i.e.* "you are expert in regard to the entire range of Jewish customs and questions that relate to their theology.

Paul asks the king to listen with patience, because he felt that there would be a tendency for the king to resist the view which he was about to present, that Christianity is the only logical fulfillment of Judaism. To one steeped in Jewish tradition this is hard to grasp at first, but the manner in which the early Christians tied the Old Testament law and prophets together with the facts of the Christian gospel accounts is ultimately convincing to one who begins with some background in Judaism, as King Agrippa had, and then listens with patience.

The Pulpit Commentary (*Acts and Romans*, II, Vol.2., 269) notes the contrast ". . . between the conduct of our Lord when he stood before the bar of Caiaphas and of Pontus Pilate, and that of St. Paul when he was brought before Festus and Agrippa." Jesus "held His peace" before Caiaphas and when He was accused before Pilate he said nothing. "Even when Pilate himself appealed to him, he gave him no answer, not even to one word; but, like a lamb dumb before the shearer, opened not his mouth. St. Paul, on the contrary, when his enemies launched vehement accusations against him, stood boldly on his defence. . . . Both before the Sanhedrin and before Felix, as well as before Festus and Agrippa, he maintained his own cause with consummate skill and dignity; not cowed by their violence, nor losing his temper in meeting their attack; but confronting them with the boldness of a pure conscience, and with the energy of an invincible courage."

Why the contrast?

It was because "Christ must suffer. According to the determinate counsel and foreknowledge of God, Jesus was to lay down His life as a sacrifice for sin. And He was willing to do so. His own will was one with the Father's will, that thus it should be. As, therefore, he would not pray to his Father to send him twelve legions of angels, to free him from his enemies, so neither would he resist his condemnation by assertions or proofs of his sinless purity. He was silent before his unjust judges, as he bore his cross, as he stretched out his hands upon it, as finally he bowed the head and gave up the ghost. It was otherwise with St. Paul. He had no life to give for the world's sins, nor was he yet to die at all. He had more years to run in the Lord's service, nor did he know when his time would come. He must live and work awhile for the souls of Jews and Gentiles, and must leave no stone unturned to exhibit his integrity before mankind."

Paul and all other Christians must live for the world for the same reason that Jesus died for it. Jesus knew His hour. We do not know ours, but we need not know it, since He does. Our obligation is to stay alive as long as possible to witness to the truth of the gospel until He knows that we have done all that He had planned for us to do. Then it will be time for us to go home to glory (2 Timothy 4:6-8).

That Paul was going to put a different interpretation upon Jewish customs and questions was obvious. So he congratulates Agrippa for his knowledge of the field of battle and issues a warning. The king had a wide knowledge of Jewish culture to which Paul could appeal. Congratulations! But beware that you do not reject my theology since it is not the conventional wisdom. This was his advice. In effect he was saying, "Hear me out."

*Verse 4 - "My manner of life from my youth which was at the first among mine own nation at Jerusalem, know all the Jews."*

Τὴν μέν οὖν βίωσίν μου ἐκ νεότητος τὴν ἀπὸ ἀρχῆς γενομένην ἐν τῷ ἔθνει μου ἐν τε Ἱεροσολύμοις ἴσασι πάντες Ἰουδαῖοι,

Τὴν (acc.sing.fem.of the article in agreement with βίωσίν) 9.
μὲν (particle of affirmation) 300.

οὖν (continuative conjunction) 68.

**#3654** βίωσίν (acc.sing.fem.of βίωσις, direct object of ἴσασι).

manner of life - Acts 26:4.

*Meaning:* Cf. βιόω (#5205); βιός (#2202); βιωτικός (#2736). Manner of life; way of living; life style - Acts 26:4.

μου (gen.sing.masc.of ἐγώ, possession) 123.

ἐκ (preposition with the ablative of time separation, point of departure) 19.

νεότητος (abl.sing.fem.of νεότης, in a time expression) 2635.

τὴν (acc.sing.fem.of the article in agreement with γενομένην) 9.

ἀπ' (preposition with the ablative of time separation) 70.

ἀρχῆς (abl.sing.fem.of ἀρχή, time separation) 1285.

γενομένην (aor.mid.part.acc.sing.fem.of γίνομαι, adjectival, restrictive, in agreement with βίωσίν) 113.

ἐν (preposition with the locative, with plural nouns and pronouns) 80.

τῷ (loc.sing.neut.of the article in agreement with ἔθνει) 9.

ἔθνει (loc.sing.neut.of ἔθνος, place where) 376.

μου (gen.sing.masc.of ἐγώ, relationship) 123.

ἐν (preposition with the locative of place where) 80.

τε (adjunctive particle) 1408.

Ἱεροσολύμοις (loc.sing.masc.of Ἱεροσόλυμα, place where) 141.

ἴσασι (οἴδασι) - (3d.per.pl.pres.ind.of ὁράω, static) 144b.

πάντες (nom.pl.masc.of πᾶς, in agreement with Ἰουδαῖοι) 67.

Ἰουδαῖοι (nom.pl.masc.of Ἰουδαῖος, subject of ἴσασι) 143.

*Translation - "My life style from my youth, in fact, at the beginning among my nation and in Jerusalem is well known by all the Jews, . . . "*

**Comment:** Paul began by saying that he had nothing to hide. His life style was well known. His history was an open book for all to read. And he added that the Jews had read it. ἀπ' ἀρχῆς means from the day of his birth. He had spent his early years in Jerusalem and later moved to Tarus in Cilicia.

*Verse 5 - "Which knew me from the beginning, if they would testify, that after the most straitest sect of our religion, I lived a Pharisee."*

προγινώσκοντές με ἄνωθεν ἐὰν θέλωσι μαρτυρεῖν, ὅτι κατὰ τὴν ἀκριβεστάτην αἵρεσιν τῆς ἡμετέρας θρησκείας ἔζησα Φαρισαῖος.

**#3655** προγινώσκοντες (pres.act.part.nom.pl.masc.of προγινώσκω, adjectival, restrictive, in agreement with Ἰουδαῖοι).

foreknow - Rom.8:29; 11:2.
foreordain - 1 Peter 1:20.
know - Acts 26:5.
know before - 2 Pet.3:17.

*Meaning:* A combination of πρό (#442) and γινώσκω (#131). Hence, to know previously; to be prescient. The Jews knew Paul at a time prior to the time when he spoke to Agrippa - Acts 26:5; to be told in advance; forewarned - 2 Pet.3:17. Christ, the Lamb of God was foreknown before the foundation of the world - 1 Pet.1:20; with reference to God's foreknowledge of the elect - Rom.8:29; of Israel - Rom.11:2. Distinct from προορίζω (#3042) as in Rom.8:29,30.

με (acc.sing.masc.of ἐγώ, direct object of προγινώσκοντες) 123.

ἄνωθεν (adverbial) 1663.

ἐὰν (conditional particle in a third-class condition) 363.

θέλωσι (3d.per.pl.pres.act.subj.of θέλω, third-class condition) 88.

μαρτυρεῖν (pres.act.inf.of μαρτυρέω, complementary) 1471.

ὅτι (conjunction introducing an object clause in indirect discourse) 211.

κατὰ (preposition with the accusative, standard rule) 98.

τὴν (acc.sing.fem.of the article in agreement with αἵρεσιν) 9.

ἀκριβεστάτην (acc.sing.fem.of ἀκριβής, superlative in agreement with αἵρεσιν) 3457.

αἵρεσιν (acc.sing.fem.of αἵρεσις, standard rule) 3058.

τῆς (gen.sing.fem.of the article in agreement with θρησκείας) 9.

ἡμετέρας (gen.sing.fem.of ἡμέτερος, in agreement with θρησκείας) 2571.

#3656 θρησκείας (gen.sing.fem.of θρησκεία, description).

religion - Acts 26:5; Jam.1:26,27.
worshipping - Col.2:18.

*Meaning: Cf.* θρῆσκος (#5112); θρησκεύω - "to fear the gods," "to be reverent." A later word - external, formal, ritualistic ceremony of a religious nature. Phariseeism - Acts 26:5; any formal religion, with outward ceremony but lacking ethical content - Jam.1:26; true religion - Jam.1:27; false religious ceremony - Col.2:18.

ἔξησα (1st.per.sing.aor.act.ind.of ζάω, constative) 340.

Φαρισαῖος (nom.sing.masc.of Φαρισαῖος, predicate nominative) 276.

*Translation - "... because they knew me before, from the beginning, if they were willing to say so - that in keeping with the strictest interpretation of their religion I lived a Pharisee."*

**Comment:** προγινώσκοντες, the causal participle continues the sentence after ἴσασι of verse 4. The reason why the Jews knew Paul's life style (verse 4) was because (causal προγινώσκοντες) they had known him from the day he was born (ἄνωθεν). This adverb does not mean "from birth" but "from the beginning" or, as musicians says, "from the top." It is the context that gives it this meaning here. Paul was telling Agrippa that there were Jews who knew him and his parents when he was born. What, specifically, did they know about him? He specifies only one thing, although they knew other things about him as well. ὅτι introduces the indirect discourse. They knew that his earliest religious affiliation was with the Pharisees. That the Pharisees were divided in their religious doctrine and practice is clear from Paul's use of the superlative adjective ἀκριβεστάτην. Some Pharisees were lax in their religious observances and existential in their dogma, but not Paul. He observed the Pharisaic rule to the letter. He alluded to this later (Phil.3:5,6). Note ἐὰν and the subjunctive in θέλωσι. It is a third-class condition. Paul doubted that the Jews would be willing to testify in court. Hence the subjunctive, contrary-to-fact "were" in our translation - "If they *were* willing to testify (which I doubt) they would say . . . κ.τ.λ."

Paul was being accused by the Jews for his refusal now to live as a strict Pharisee should. He had done so before he met the Lord Jesus on the road to Damascus. As a Pharisee he should be persecuting the Christians, as he had done before (Phil.3:6). But "he which persecuted us in times past now preacheth the faith which once he destroyed" (Gal.1:23). But Paul was still a good Pharisee, because in his view true Phariseeism, so far from being the false religion (θρησκείας) of the current practices of the Pharisees, was Christianity. "The hope of the promise made of God unto our fathers" was not the Jewish version of Phariseeism as then practiced in Jerusalem, but the gospel of Jesus Christ. This is the thought in

*Verse 6 - "And now I stand and am judged for the hope of the promise made of God unto our fathers."*

καὶ νῦν ἐπ' ἐλπίδι τῆς εἰς τοὺς πατέρας ἡμῶν ἐπαγγελίας γενομένης ὑπὸ τοῦ θεοῦ ἕστηκα κρινόμενος,

καὶ (adversative conjunction) 14.

νῦν (temporal adverb) 1497.

ἐπ' (preposition with the locative, sphere) 47.

ἐλπίδι (loc.sing.fem.of ἐλπίς, sphere) 2994.

τῆς (gen.sing.fem.of the article in agreement with ἐπαγγελίας) 9.

εἰς (preposition with the accusative of extent, after a verb of speaking) 140.

τοὺς (acc.pl.masc.of the article in agreement with πατέρας) 9.

πατέρας (acc.pl.masc.of πατήρ, extent, after a verb of speaking) 238.

ἡμῶν (gen.pl.masc.of ἐγώ, relationship) 123.

ἐπαγγελίας (abl.sing.fem.of ἐπαγγελία, source) 2929.

γενομένης (aor.mid.part.abl.sing.fem.of γίνομαι, adjectival, restrictive in agreement with ἐπαγγελίας) 113.

ὑπὸ (preposition with the ablative of agent) 117.

τοῦ (abl.sing.masc.of the article in agreement with θεοῦ) 9.

θεοῦ (abl.sing.masc.of θεός, agent) 124.

ἕστηκα (1st.per.sing.perf.ind.of ἵστημι, intensive) 180.

κρινόμενος (pres.pass.part.nom.sing.masc.of κρίνω, telic) 531.

*Translation - "But now I am standing here for the purpose of being examined about the hope that stems from the promise made by God unto our fathers."*

**Comment:** I have taken καὶ as adversative. It was ironical that Paul should be in court defending himself against charges made by Pharisees, when, in fact, he was the only good Pharisee among them. He had been an orthodox Pharisee in the past, as they would have been forced to admit under oath. The difference between them now lay in their differing interpretation of what Phariseeism was, or should have been. Pure Phariseeism, in Paul's view, leads to faith in Jesus as the Messiah. It was the corrupt "religion of the Pharisees" which Jesus had attacked with such vigor (Matthew 23) that rejected Jesus and now sought to kill Paul, His messenger.

Why was Paul in court? It was in order to be judged (telic κρινόμενος). In what area of his life would the examination be concentrated? What in Paul's life did the prosecution object to? It was in the area of his hope (locative of sphere in ἐπ' ἐλπίδι. What was the source of Paul's hope? It was the promise (ablative of source in ἐπαγγελίας). Who made this promise? God (ablative of agent in τοῦ θεοῦ). To whom did God make this promise which was the source of Paul's hope? To the fathers (accusative of extent in εἰς τοὺς πατέρας). Whose fathers? The common ancestry both of Paul and the Jews who were in court against him - the defendant and his accusers. Paul was saying that the promise which God made to him personally and to his ancestors, was made also to the Jews, because they came from the same ancestral stock as did Paul. Thus the issue was this: who is the true Pharisee? And which branch of Phariseeism had missed the turn on the road of divine revelation? Those who had recognized in Jesus of Nazareth the fulfillment of all of God's promises to the fathers, and had accepted Him as Messiah and Saviour were the true Pharisees. This number included Paul. Those who failed to recognize Jesus as Messiah had missed the turn. All they had left was an empty religion which produced bigotry, hatred and the misplaced zeal of fanaticism. Paul thus emphasizes the fanatical zeal of the Pharisees who were pursuing him relentlessly for being a consistent Pharisee!

He was glad to have the opportunity to discuss all of this with Agrippa, because the king had sufficient background in Judaism to follow his reasoning.

The point is the promise of God and the hope which it engenders. The promise is the subject of the next verse.

*Verse 7 - "Unto which promise our twelve tribes, instantly serving God day and night, hope to come. For which hope's sake, king Agrippa, I am accused of the Jews."*

εἰς ἣν τὸ δωδεκάφυλον ἡμῶν ἐν ἐκτενείᾳ νύκτα καὶ ἡμέραν λατρεῦον ἐλπίζει καταντῆσαι. περὶ ἧς ἐλπίδος ἐγκαλοῦμαι ὑπὸ Ἰουδαίων, βασιλεῦ.

εἰς (preposition with the accusative of extent, aim or purpose) 140.
ἣν (acc.sing.fem.of ὅς, extent, aim or purpose) 65.
τὸ (nom.sing.neut.of the article in agreement with δωδεκάφυλον) 9.

#3657 δωδεκάφυλον (nom.sing.neut.of δωδεκάφυλον, subject of ἐλπίζει).

twelve tribes - Acts 26:7.

*Meaning:* A combination of δώδεκα (#820) andφυλή (#1313). Twelve tribes - Acts 26:7.

ἡμῶν (gen.pl.masc.of ἐγώ, relationship) 123.
ἐν (preposition with the locative, accompanying circumstance) 80.

**#3658** ἐκτενείᾳ (loc.sing.fem.of ἐκτεινία, accompanying circumstance).

*Meaning: Cf.* ἐκτείνω (#710); ἐκτενής (#5209) ἐκτενέστερον (#2795) and ἐκτενῶς (#3245). Hence, with intent earnestness; devoted application; constant effort. In description of the zeal of the Jews for nationalism - Acts 26:7.

νύκτα (acc.sing.fem.of νύξ, distributive) 209.
καὶ (adjunctive conjunction joining nouns) 14.
ἡμέραν (acc.sing.fem.of ἡμέρα, distributive) 135.
λατρεῦον (pres.act.part.nom.pl.neut.of λατρεύω, adverbial, modal) 366.
ἐλπίζει (3d.per.sing.pres.act.ind.of ἐλπίζω, progressive duration, retroactive) 991.
καταντῆσαι (aor.act.inf.of καταντάω, complementary) 3353.
περὶ (preposition with the genitive of reference) 173.
ἧς (gen.sing.fem.of ὅς, relative pronoun, reference) 65.
ἐλπίδος (gen.sing.fem.of ἐλπίς, reference) 2994.
ἐγκαλοῦμαι (1st.per.sing.pres.pass.ind.of ἐγκαλέω, progressive duration, retroactive) 3495.
ὑπὸ (preposition with the ablative of agent) 117.
Ἰουδαίων (abl.pl.masc.of Ἰουδαῖος, agent) 143.
βασιλεῦ (voc.sing.masc.of βασιλεύς, address) 31.

*Translation - ". . . for the realization of which our twelve tribes by the service which they have been giving day and night with constant effort have been hoping. It is with reference to this hope that I have been accused by the Jews, your Majesty."*

**Comment:** The antecedent of ἥν is ἐλπίδι of verse 6. ἐν ἐκτενείᾳ - a locative of accompanying circumstance - "with constant and consistent application." It speaks of the fanatical attention to detail which characterized the Pharisaic tradition. The idea of consistency is fortified by νύκτα καὶ ἡμέραν - "night after night and day after day." They were always extending themselves in constant service around the clock. They had always hoped as they yet hoped (progressive duration in ἐλπίζει) to achieve the realization of their hope - the implementation of God's promise to Abraham, Isaac, Jacob, Judah and David that Israel at last would enjoy a national identity as the leader of all nations. That is the same hope that Paul had and that all Christians have. Yet Paul is being condemned for possessing the same hope for which they longed, prayed and worked. If Paul, as a Christian, had broken Jewish tradition, why did all the Jews (the twelve tribes) long for the same event in Israel's future?

The Jewish rebuttal to Paul's argument, however, was running like this: that they did indeed share Paul's hope that God would redeem His promises to the forefathers and would send Messiah. But Paul believed that Jesus of Nazareth was the fulfillment of that divine promise - the unconditional covenant which God gave to Abraham and his posterity, whereas the Jews denied it because Jesus was dead. This last, Paul rejected. Jesus was not dead, although, in fact, He had died, in expiation for Israel's sins as well as for the sins of the elect who were scattered among the Gentile nations as well, but He had risen from the dead on the third day. We have at last arrived at the basic issue which divided Paul from his accusers. All of them believed in the same God. They agreed that God had promised Abraham and his posterity an everlasting national existence. Each expected this rise to prominence for the nation to be effected by the Messiah when He came. Jesus represented Himself as that Messiah, but He was now dead. This the Pharisees believed. Paul did not. As a good Pharisee he knew that the resurrection of the dead was to be expected. Did not all Pharisees believe in the resurrection? Indeed they did (Acts 23:6-8), but they did not believe in the resurrection of Jesus of Nazareth.

It is quite logical therefore for Paul to express feigned surprize before the king that the Jews who were accusing him of having profaned their religion, did not believe in the resurrection of the dead.

*Verse 8 — "Why should it be thought a thing incredible with you, that God should raise the dead?"*

τί ἄπιστον κρίνεται παρ' ὑμῖν εἰ ὁ θεὸς νεκροὺς ἐγείρει;

τί (acc.sing.neut.of τίς, interrogative pronoun, cause) 281.

ἄπιστον (acc.sing.neut.of ἄπιστος, predicate adjective) 1231.

κρίνεται (3d.per.sing.pres.pass.ind.of κρίνω, direct question) 531.

παρ' (preposition with the locative, with persons, "among you.") 154.

ὑμῖν (loc.pl.masc.of σύ, place where) 104.

εἰ (conditional particle in a first-class condition) 337.

ὁ (nom.sing.masc.of the article in agreement with θεὸς) 9.

θεὸς (nom.sing.masc.of θεός, subject of ἐγείρει, first-class condition) 124.

νεκροὺς (acc.pl.masc.of νεκρός, direct object of ἐγείρει) 749.

ἐγείρει (3d.per.sing.pres.act.ind.of ἐγείρω, first-class condition) 125.

*Translation - "Why would it be considered incredible in your intellectual circles, if God should raise the dead?"*

**Comment:** We supply διά with τί - "on account of what?" εἰ introduces the first-class condition. "If God should raise the dead . . . why . . . ?" Paul has not said that God raises the dead, but he is asking a hypothetical question. "If God should raise the dead, why would some say that it was untrue because impossible?" The Pharisees believed in the resurrection. Paul had believed in it as a Pharisee. Apparently Agrippa believed in it. Why then, should they reject it, when Paul applied it to the case of Jesus of Nazareth?

Now Paul tells Agrippa that he did not believe that Jesus had risen either, but that Jesus convinced him that it was true.

*Verse 9 - "I verily thought with myself that I ought to do many things contrary to the name of Jesus of Nazareth."*

ἐγὼ μὲν οὖν ἔδοξα ἐμαυτῷ πρὸς τὸ ὄνομα Ἰησοῦ τοῦ Ναζωραίου δεῖν πολλὰ ἐναντία πρᾶξαι,

ἐγὼ (nom.sing.masc.of ἐγώ, subject of ἔδοξα) 123.
μὲν (particle of affirmation) 300.
οὖν (continuative conjunction) 68.
ἔδοξα (1st.per.sing.aor.act.ind.of δοκέω, constative) 287.
ἐμαυτῷ (dat.sing.masc.of ἐμαυτοῦ, personal interest) 723.
πρὸς (preposition with the accusative of extent, hostility) 197.
τὸ (acc.sing.neut.of the article in agreement with ὄνομα) 9.
ὄνομα (acc.sing.neut.of ὄνομα, hostility) 108.
Ἰησοῦ (gen.sing.masc.of Ἰησοῦς, possession) 3.
τοῦ (gen.sing.masc.of the article in agreement with Ναζωραίου) 9.
Ναζωραίου (gen.sing.masc.of Ναζωραῖος, apposition) 245.
δεῖν (pres.inf.of δεῖ, object of ἔδοξα) 1207.
πολλὰ (acc.pl.neut.of πολύς, direct object of πρᾶξαι) 228.
ἐναντία (acc.pl.neut.of ἐναστίος, in agreement with πολλὰ) 1128.
πρᾶξαι (aor.act.inf.of πράσσω, complementary) 1943.

*Translation -* "*Indeed I thought that I myself should do many contrary things against the name of Jesus of Nazareth."*

**Comment:** Note μὲν οὖν (#68) for the idiom which means "Indeed" or "Truthfully." δεῖν, completed by πρᾶξαι is indirect discourse after ἔδοξα. Opposition to the person and work of Jesus of Nazareth was a consistent policy for Saul, the Pharisee, before he became Paul, the Christian. He had interpreted his duty exactly as his critics were still interpreting theirs. Their zeal to kill Paul was matched by Paul's zeal in his former unregenerate days to kill Stephen.

Saul of Tarsus, the unsaved Pharisee was nothing if not consistent (Phil.3:6). What he thought he ought to do he did, as he tells the king in

*Verse 10 -* "*. . . which things I also did in Jerusalem: and many of the saints did I shup up in prison, having received authority from the chief priests: and when they were put to death I gave my voice against them."*

ὃ καὶ ἐποίησα ἐν Ἱεροσολύμοις, καὶ πολλούς τε τῶν ἁγίων ἐγὼ ἐν φυλακαῖς κατέκλεισα τὴν παρὰ τῶν ἀρχιερέων ἐξουσίαν λαβών, ἀναιρουμένων τε αὐτῶν κατήνεγκα ψῆφον,

ὃ (acc.sing.neut.of ὅς, relative pronoun, direct object of ἐποίσα) 65.
καὶ (emphatic conjunction) 14.
ἐποίησα (1st.per.sing.aor.act.ind.ofd ποιέω, constative) 127.
ἐν (preposition with the locative of place) 80.
Ἱεροσολύμοις (loc.sing.neut.of Ἱεροσόλυμα, place) 141.
καὶ (continuative conjunction) 14.
πολλούς (acc.pl.masc.of πολύς, direct object of κατέκλεισα) 228.

τε (correlative particle) 1408.

τῶν (gen.pl.masc.of the article in agreement with ἁγίων) 9.

ἁγίων (gen.pl.masc.of ἅγιος, partitive genitive) 84.

ἐγώ (nom.sing.masc.of ἐγώ, subject of κατέκλεισα) 123.

ἐν (preposition with the locative of place) 80.

φυλακαῖς (loc.pl.fem.of φυλακή, place where) 494.

κατέκλεισα (1st.per.sing.aor.act.ind.of κατακλείω, constative) 1948.

τὴν (acc.sing.fem.of the article in agreement with ἐξουσίαν) 9.

παρὰ (preposition with the ablative of source) 154.

τῶν (abl.pl.masc.of the article in agreement with ἀρχιερέων) 9.

ἀρχιερέων (abl.pl. masc.of ἀρχιερεύς, source) 151.

ἐξουσίαν (acc.sing.fem.of ἀξουσία, direct object of λαβών) 707.

λαβών (aor.act.part.nom.sing.masc.of λαμβάνω, adverbial, temporal) 533.

ἀναιρουμένων (pres.pass.part.gen.pl.masc.of ἀναιρέω, genitive absolute) 216.

τε (correlative particle) 1408.

αὐτῶν (gen.pl.masc.of αὐτός, genitive absolute) 16.

κατήνεγκα (1st.per.sing.1st.aor.act.ind.of καταφέρω, constative) 3513.

#3659 φῆφον (acc.sing.masc.of φῆφος, direct object of κατήνεγκα).

    stone - Rev.2:17,17.
    voice - Acts 26:10.

*Meaning:* A small worn smooth pebble, such as was used in voting or in casting lots. Paul brought a black stone of condemnation against the early Christians - Acts 26:10. Jesus will give the white stone of approval to the overcomers - Rev.2:17,17. Paul voted against Stephen; Jesus voted for him!

*Translation - ". . . which also I did in Jerusalem, and many of the saints also I incarcerated in prisons, after I had received authority from the priests, and as they were being killed I cast the condemning stone against them."*

**Comment:** ὅ refers to Paul's statement in verse 9 which revealed his former attitude toward Christianity. As a Pharisee he thought his proper course of action was to persecute the Christians (verse 9). Verse 10 says that he implemented this policy. "This also I did . . . κ.τ.λ." Then he spelled it out in detail, in terms of imprisonment for many of the saints and death for others. All of this he did with the full authority which he received from the priests. λαβών, the aorist participle, indicates that he received the official authority for what he did from the Jewish leadership *before* he shut up the saints in prison. Hence, if Roman justice was sought against the Jews who murdered the Christians, who had broken no Roman law, Festus would be compelled to indict the members of the San Hedrin as *particeps criminis*, since it was they who issued the order upon which Saul acted. Thus Paul turned the tables upon his persecutors by charging them with judicial murder - a felony under Roman law, since the San Hedrin did not have jurisdiction in cases involving capital crimes.

But Paul's main thrust is not to implicate the San Hedrin in murder. It is to show that his previous actions as a Pharisee were precisely what current Pharisees were still doing. All of this was in preparation for what follows in his testimony (verses 12-18).

*Verse 11 - "And I punished them oft in every synagogue and compelled them to blaspheme; and being exceedingly mad against them, I persecuted them even unto strange cities."*

καὶ κατὰ πάσας τὰς συναγωγὰς πολλάκις τιμωρῶν αὐτοὺς ἠνάγκαζον βλασφημεῖν, περισσῶς τε ἐμμαινόμενος αὐτοῖς ἐδίωκον ἕως καὶ εἰς τὰς ἔξω πόλεις.

καὶ (continuative conjunction) 14.
κατὰ (preposition with the accusative, distributive) 98.
πάσας (acc.pl.fem.of πᾶς, in agreement with συναγωγὰς) 67.
τὰς (acc.pl.fem.of the article in agreement with συναγωγὰς) 9.
συναγωγὰς (acc.pl.fem.of συναγωγή, distributive) 404.
πολλάκις (adverbial) 1230.
τιμωρῶν (pres.act.part.nom.sing.masc.of τιμωρέω, adverbial, modal) 3577.
αὐτοὺς (acc.pl.masc.of αὐτός, direct object of ἠνάγλαζπμ)
ἠνάγκαζον (1st.per.sing.imp.act.ind.of ἀναγκάζω conative) 1126.
βλασφημεῖν (pres.act.inf.of βλασφημέω, completes ἠνάγκαζον) 781.
περισσῶς (adverbial) 1630.
τε (correlative particle) 1408.

#3660 ἐμμαινόμενος (pres.pass.part.nom.sing.masc.of ἐμμαίνομαι, adverbial, causal).

be mad against - Acts 26:11.

*Meaning:* A combination of ἐμ and μαίνομαι (#2407). Hence, to rage against; to be totally consumed with anger against something or someone. With reference to Saul's attitude toward the early Christians - Acts 26:11.
αὐτοῖς (dat.pl.masc.of αὐτός, personal disadvantage) 16.
ἐδίωκον (1st.per.sing.imp.act.ind.of διώκω, inchoative) 434.
ἕως (preposition with a time expression) 71.
καὶ (ascensive conjunction) 14.
εἰς (preposition with the accusative of extent) 140.
τὰς (acc.pl.fem.of the article in agreement with πόλεις) 9.
ἔξω (adverbial) 449.
πόλεις (acc.pl.fem.of πόλις, extent) 243.

*Translation - "And throughout all the synagogues tortured them as I tried to make them say blasphemous things, and because I was utterly consumed with rage against them, I began to pursue them until they even fled to foreign cities."*

**Comment:** κατὰ πάσας τὰς συναγωγὰς is distributive. Paul went from one synaggogue to another until he had visited them all. *Cf.* #3577. He was visiting retributive vengeance upon the Christians in order to avenge what he thought was an insult to the offended honor of the God of the Hebrews. The torture (modal τιμωρῶν) was his method of trying to make the Christians say something impious about the Lord Jesus Christ. ἠνάγκαζον is a conative imperfect. The action involved was begun but interrupted. We can translate it only by the word "tried." Paul tried (and failed) to compel the Christians to indulge in impieties. They had supernatural help (Mt.10:16-20). The causal participle ἐμμαινόμενος tells us why he acted so irrationally. It was because he was consumed with rage, as a result of which he began a policy of pursuit (inchoative imperfect in ἐδίωκον) that continued until the Christians had been driven out of Palestine to find refuge in foreign cities.

Thus Paul made it clear that before he was saved he was a good Pharisee, in terms of the way he interpreted Phariseeism at that time, and, as such, was doing to the Christians precisely what the Pharisees were now trying to do to him. It was illegal then, a fact which becomes more startling when we remember that the San Hedrin was involved, and his attitude was improper, and it was still illegal. What was proper for a Pharisee to do in the name of his religion was illegal under Roman law. Claudius Lysias, Felix, Festus and Agrippa were responsible for the enforcement of Roman law, and had only slight interest in the traditions of Judaism, whether interpreted by Pharisees, Sadducees or Zealots.

But insofar as Saul of Tarsus was concerned, all of that was about to change.

## Paul Tells of His Conversion
### (Acts 9:1-19; 22:6-16; 26:12-18)

*Verse 12 - "Whereupon as I went to Damascus with authority and commission from the chief priests, . . . "*

Ἐν οἷς πορευόμενος εἰς τὴν Δαμασκὸν μετ᾽ ἐξουσίας καὶ ἐπιτροπῆς τῆς τῶν ἀρχιερέων . . .

Ἐν (preposition with the locative of time point) 80.

οἷς (loc.pl.neut.of ὅς, relative pronoun, time point) 65.

πορευόμενος (pres.mid.part.nom.sing.masc.ofd πορεύομαι, adverbial, temporal) 170.

εἰς (preposition with the accusative of extent) 140.

τὴν (acc.sing.fem.of the article in agreement with Δαμασκὸν) 9.

Δαμασκὸν (acc.sing.fem.of Δαμασκός, extent) 3181.

μετ᾽ (preposition with the genitive of accompaniment) 50.

ἐξουσίας (gen.sing.fem.of ἐξουσία, accompaniment) 707.

καὶ (adjunctive conjunction joining nouns) 14.

#3661 ἐπιτροπῆς (gen.sing.fem.of ἐπιτροπή, accompaniment).

commission - Acts 26:12.

*Meaning:* A combination of ἐπί (#47) and τροπή (#5106). Cf. ἐπιτρέπω (#747).

Hence, authority, power, permission, commission. With reference to the John Doe warrants which Paul had from the San Hedrin - Acts 26:12.

τῆς (gen.sing.fem.of the article in agreement with ἐπιτροπῆς) 9.
τῶν (abl.pl.masc.of the article in agreement with ἀρχιερέων) 9.
ἀρχιερέων (abl.pl.masc.of ἀρχιερεύς, source) 151.

*Translation - "... at which time, as I was going to Damascus with police powers and warrants from the high priest..."*

**Comment:** ἐν οἷς refers to the time point involved in the last clause of verse 11. Paul was in pursuit of the Christians. He had already pursued them out of Palestine and was enroute to Damascus, apparently on a tip that there were Christians there. While he was engaged in this business, and as he was going (present middle temporal participle in πορευόμενος) to Damascus, something happened. We will learn about it in verse 13. He was in pursuit of the heretics. Where? To Damascus. Armed with what? Police power and the piece of paper to prove it. Note the article τῆς in the predicate position, joined with ἐπιτροπῆς and followed by τῶν ἀρχιερέων - in definition. The document which Paul carried was "from the high priest." The paper was a John Doe warrant, not legally binding in modern law, but Paul was using it indiscriminately on any Christian he could find, although there could be no specification of identity (Acts 9:2). Once again Paul reminded Festus and Agrippa that the San Hedrin was involved in this nefarious business. All of this, of course, was illegal under Roman law.

Luke has already told us about Paul's emotional state as he prepared to make the trip to Damascus. He was ἐμπνέων ἀπειλῆς καὶ φόνου εἰς τοὺς μαθητὰς τοῦ κυρίου (Acts 9:1). This mood was characteristic of the Jews in Jerusalem as they struggled with the problem of the Christians (Acts 4:29; Heb.11:37).

*Verse 13 - "At midday, O King, I saw in the way a light from heaven, above the brightness of the sun shining round about me and them which journeyed with me."*

ἡμέρας μέσης κατὰ τὴν ὁδὸν εἶδον, βασιλεῦ, οὐρανόθεν ὑπὲρ τὴν λαμπρότητα τοῦ ἡλίου περιλάμψαν με φῶς καὶ τοὺς σὺν ἐμοὶ πορευομένους,

ἡμέρας (gen.sing.fem.of ἡμέρα, time description) 135.
μέσης (gen.sing.fem.of μέσος, in agreement with ἡμέρας) 873.
κατὰ (preposition with the accusative, "down along") 98.
τὴν (acc.sing.fem.of the article in agreement with ὁδὸν) 9.
ὁδὸν (acc.sing.fem.of ὁδός, "down along" ) 199.
εἶδον (1st.per.sing.aor.act.ind.of ὁράω, ingressive) 144.
βασιλεῦ (voc.sing.masc.of βασιλεύς, address) 31.
οὐρανόθεν (adverbial) 3326.
ὑπὲρ (preposition with the accusative, comparative degree) 545.
τὴν (acc.sing.fem.of the article in agreement with λαμπρότητα) 9.

#3662A λαμπρότητα (acc.sing.fem.of λαμπρότης, comparison).

brightness - Acts 26:13.

*Meaning:* brightness; brilliance. Followed by a genitive of description, τοῦ ἡλίου - Acts 26:13.

τοῦ (gen.sing.masc.of the article in agreement with ἡλίου) 9.
ἡλίου (gen.sing.masc.of ἥλιος, description) 546.
περιλάμψαν (aor.act.part.acc.sing.neut.of περιλάμπω, adjectival, ascriptive, in agreement with φῶς) 1878.
με (acc.sing.masc.of ἐγώ, object of περιλάμψαν) 123.
φῶς (acc.sing.neut.of φῶς, direct object of εἶδον) 379.
καὶ (adjunctive conjunction joining substantives) 14.
τοὺς (acc.pl.masc.of the article in agreement with πορευομένους) 9.
σὺν (preposition with the instrumental of association) 1542.
ἐμοὶ (instru.sing.masc.of ἐμός, association) 1267.
πορευομένους (pres.mid.part.acc.pl.masc.of πορεύομαι, substantival, direct object of περιλάμψαν) 170.

*Translation - "At noon down the road, your Majesty, I saw a light from heaven, greater than the brightness of the sun, surrounding me and those who were travelling with me."*

**Comment:** In ἡμέρας μέσης we have a genitive of time description. κατά with the accusative means "down along" and it gives us a clear picture of Paul's experience. We use the term which I have incorporated into the translation in the same sense, *viz.* "on the road ahead." The light which Paul saw was not following him. It met him. The participle περιλάμψαν is adjectival in the attributive position. It is thus ascriptive. Paul saw the "surrounding me light." There is special point in the fact that the Lord came to Paul at noon, when the sun was brightest, thus making the superiority of the heavenly light over that of the sun more remarkable. The light of the sun on its brightest day cannot compare with the Light of the Son (John 1:4; 8:12).

*Verse 14 - "And when we were all fallen to the earth, I heard a voice speaking unto me, and saying in the Hebrew tongue, Saul, Saul, why persecutest thou me? It is hard for thee to kick against the pricks."*

πάντων τε καταπεσόντων ἡμῶν εἰς τὴν γῆν ἤκουσα φωνὴν λέγουσαν πρός με τῇ Ἑβραΐδι διαλέκτῳ, Σαοὺλ Σαούλ, τί με διώκεις; σκληρόν σοι πρὸς κέντρα λακτίζειν.

πάντων (gen.pl.masc.of πᾶς, in agreement with ἡμῶν) 67.
τε (continuative particle) 1408.
καταπεσόντων (aor.act.part.gen.pl.masc.of καταπίπτω, genitive absolute, adverbial, temporal) 2196.
ἡμῶν (gen.pl.masc.of ἐγώ, genitive absolute) 123.
εἰς (preposition with the accusative of extent) 140.
τὴν (acc.sing.fem.of the article in agreement with γῆν) 9.

γῆν (acc.sing.fem.of γῆ, extent) 157.

ἤκουσα (1st.per.sing.aor.act.ind.of ἀκούω, constative) 148.

φωνὴν (acc.sing.fem.of φωνή, direct object of ἤκουσα) 222.

λέγουσαν (pres.act.part.acc.sing.fem.of λέγω, adjectival, restrictive, in agreement with φωνὴν) 66.

πρός (preposition with the accusative of extent, after a verb of speaking) 197.

με (acc.sing.masc.of ἐγώ, extent, after a verb of speaking) 123.

τῇ (instru.sing.fem.of the article in agreement with διαλέκτῳ) 9.

Ἑβραΐδι (instru.sing.fem.of Ἑβραΐς, in agreement with διαλέκτῳ) 3572.

διαλέκτῳ (instru.sing.fem.of διάλεκτος, manner) 2946.

Σαούλ (voc.sing.masc.of Σαῦλος, address) 3155.

Σαούλ (voc.sing.masc.of Σαῦλος, address) 3155.

τί (acc.sing.neut.of τίς, interrogative pronoun, direct question, cause) 281.

με (acc.sing.masc.of ἐγώ, direct object of διώκεις) 123.

διώκεις (2d.per.sing.pres.act.ind.of διώκω, progressive duration, retroactive) 434.

σκληρόν (acc.sing.neut.of σκληρός, predicate adjective) 1537.

σοι (dat.sing.masc.of σύ, personal disadvantage) 104.

πρὸς (preposition with the accusative of extent) 197.

#3662B κέντρα (acc.pl.neut.of κέντρον, extent).

prick - Acts 26:14.
sting - 1 Cor.15:;55,56; Rev.9:10.

*Meaning: Cf.* κεντέω - "to prick, stab, sting, spur on with a painful penetration." Hence, a goad used to spur on animals at labor. "To kick against the goads" is to offer vain and perilous resistance - Acts 26:14. Since bees and **scorpions** sometimes have lethal stings in their tails (Rev.9:10), sin is said to be the "sting" of death, since sin brings spiritual and physical death - 1 Cor.15:55,56.

#3663 λακτίζειν (pres.act.inf.of λακτίζω, noun use, subject of ἐστίν, understood).

kick - Acts 26:14.

*Meaning: Cf.* λάξ - an adverb, meaning "with the heel." Hence, to strike out with the heel; to kick backward. Metaphorically of Paul's resistance to God's will - Acts 26:14.

*Translation - "And after all of us had fallen to the ground I heard a voice saying to me in the Hebrew dialect, 'Saul, Saul, why have you been pursuing me? It is hard for you to kick back against the goads.' "*

**Comment:** There is a valuable spiritual truth hidden in the fact that the genitive absolute participle καταπεσόντων, is in the aorist tense, and that it indicates antecedent action to that of the main verb ἤκουσα, though, from a strict grammatical point of view, it can be taken as coincident. Saul of Tarsus fell to the ground *before* he heard our Lord's voice - an item which may help us to understand the effectual call of the Holy Spirit in His exercise of irresistible grace. Is the grace of God that brings salvation (Titus 2:11) irresistible? Is the grace of God in the sound of His voice or in the strength of His fist? Or in both,and, if so, how is it first applied? The Holy Spirit began to speak to Saul, at least as early as the moment when he heard Stephen preach (Acts 7). But Saul could not hear the Lord until he had fallen to the ground. It is likely that the intense madness of the zeal which characterized Saul's attack upon the Christians, to which he alluded (verse 11) was his reaction to the conviction of the Holy Spirit. How else do we explain the fact that other Pharisees in Jerusalem who shared Saul's disdain for Christianity did not go to the lengths to which he went in an attempt to destroy it. If they had, since the numerical superiority of unbelievers over Christians was overwhelming, Christianity would have been wiped out. The difference was that Saul of Tarsus was "elect according to the foreknowledge of God through sanctification of the Spirit. . . " (1 Peter 1:2), "a called apostle and set apart unto the good news of God" (Romans 1:1) and he had been God's property from the day he was born (Galatians 1:15), whereas other Pharisees did not share in the election of grace (Romans 11:5). The more Saul felt the sting of the goad of God the more ferociously he kicked. It is a totally irrational procedure, normal for a mule and an unsaved sinner under conviction. We neither expect dumb beasts nor sinners to behave rationally. How futile to resist the will of the sovereign God! There are many examples of this principle in Scripture. Zacchaeus accepted Christ at the foot of the tree, not from the vantage point of his perch upon a limb, as he sat looking down on Jesus (Luke 19:6). Isaiah was not ready to preach until he saw the Lord "high and lifted up." Only then did we hear him say, "Woe is me! For I am undone." (Isaiah 6:1-5). Job was more interested in defending himself against false charges than in listening to the voice of God until he had listened to the lecture of Job 38:1 - 41:34, after, and as a result of which he said, "I abhor myself and repent in dust and ashes" (Job.42:6). Nebuchadnezzar, who tried to burn Shadrach, Meshach and Abednego in the fiery furnace was reduced to eating grass before he came to realize that "the most High ruleth in the kingdom of men, and giveth it to whomsoever He will" (Daniel 4:25-37).

Irresistible grace in some cases must first employ irresistible power. If Saul of Tarsus had listened to the voice of the Holy Spirit when he first heard Him, instead of mistaking it for the voice of fanatical Phariseeism telling him that he would save the Christians even if he had to kill them (!), and if he had stopped kicking against the goad of God, the Lord would have stopped using it. But God had to knock him down in order to talk to him.

The author remembers a man in Jersey Shore, Pennsylvania who attended the revival services. He had just visited his dentist and had a new gold tooth installed. During the invitation at the close of the service he reacted to the call of the Holy Spirit to repent and trust Christ with such anger that he bit off his new tooth. He removed the broken gold tooth from his mouth, and as he continued to grind the teeth which were left, he stormed out of the service and went out to the banks of the Susquehanna River where he intended to spend the rest of the night fishing. But the fish did not bite. As he sat thinking about the gospel message against which he reacted with such vigor, the Holy Spirit reminded him of what it would cost to get the tooth replaced. That, in his experience was the same point in Saul's experience when he fell to the ground. The fisherman repented and trusted Christ and came back to town to tell his wife that he was saved.

The Holy Spirit is the supreme diplimat. He considers our prejudices and does not unduly arouse or ignite them. Saul was a sophisticated scholar, at ease with the κοινή Greek of the day as much as with his native Hebrew. But at that particular moment he was very much a Jew and a fanatical Pharisee at that. So the Lord spoke to him in Hebrew.

The proverb σκληρόν σοι πρὸς κέντρα λακτίζειν was original, of course with Jesus, since He is the originator of all that is good, but He had given it to some one long before, and it had been copied by later writers. It "is found in Pindar, Aeschylus, Euripedes, Plautus, Terence, etc. . . " (The Pulpit Commentary, *The Acts of the Apostles*, 18. II. 266)."The passage in Eurip., Bacch., ' l. 793, 794 (750, 751), brings out the force of the proverb, viz. fruitless resistance to a superior power, most distinctly: 'Better to sacrifice to him, than, being mortal, by vainly raging against God, to kick against the goads.' " (*Ibid.*).

We have no way of knowing whether Saul recognized our Lord's quotation of the proverb as having come from the Greek classics. It is interesting that Jesus should have alluded to this secular reference. In the sense that all truth is divine in its origin we can say that truth is never secular. The reason why it is hard (σκληρὸν) to kick against the goads is because it is stupid. "The way of the transgressor is (always) hard" (Prov.13:15). Ask Nebuchadnezzar, Job, Saul of Tarsus, or my friend in Pennsylvania.

Could Saul have resisted Jesus and ultimately have gone to hell? This is the theological question that has divided the Calvinists from the Arminians for centuries. However loquaciously we may have argued the point, the fact, to which we must all agree is that he did not.

In His high priestly prayer of John 17, Jesus identified Himself so intimately with the members of His body (John 17:21), both those then present and all others who would believe upon Him, that he spoke of Saul's persecution of the saints as His own. Jesus did not say, "Why are you persecuting the Christians?" He said, "Why are you persecuting me?"

*Verse 15 - "And I said, Who art thou Lord? And he said, I am Jesus whom thou persecutest."*

ἐγὼ δὲ εἶπα, Τίς εἶ, κύριε; ὁ δὲ κύριος εἶπεν, Ἐγώ εἰμι Ἰησοῦ ὃν σὺ διώκεις.

ἐγὼ (nom.sing.masc.of ἐγω, subject of εἶπα) 123.

δὲ (continuative conjunction) 11.

εἶπα (1st.per.sing.aor.act.ind.of εἶπον, constative) 155.

Τίς (nom.sing.masc.of τίς, interrogative pronoun, predicate nominative, in direct question) 281.

εἶ (2d.per.sing.pres.ind.of εἰμί, aoristic, direct question) 86.

κύριε (voc.sing.masc.of κύριος, address) 97.

ὁ (nom.sing.masc.of the article in agreement with κύριος) 9.

δὲ (continuative conjunction) 11.

κύριος (nom.sing.masc.of κύριος, subject of εἶπεν) 97.

εἶπεν (3d.per.sing.aor.act.ind.of εἶπον,constative) 155.

Ἐγώ (nom.sing.masc.of ἐγώ, subject of εἰμι) 123.

εἰμι (1st.per.sing.pres.ind.of εἰμί, static) 86.

Ἰησοῦς (nom.sing.masc.of Ἰησοῦς, apposition) 3.

ὅν (acc.sing.masc.of ὅς, relative pronoun, direct object of διώκεις) 65.

σὺ (nom.sing.masc.of σύ, subject of διώκεις, emphatic) 104.

διώκεις (2d.per.sing.pres.act.ind.of διώκω, progressive duration, retroactive) 434.

*Translation - "And I said, 'Who are you, Sir?' And the Lord said, 'I AM, Jesus, whom you have been pursuing.' "*

**Comment:** Κύριος is a term of high respect, and can mean either "Sir" or "Lord" depending upon the context. In the mouth of Saul of Tarsus under the conditions of this context, it probably means only "Sir." There is no doubt that Saul was impressed. The brilliant light from heaven was enough to make him realize that he was dealing with something supernatural. If indeed Saul called him "Sir" on this occasion it was the last time he ever used the word in this sense, for on that day Jesus became the Lord of his life (Phil.2:9-11; Eph.1:20-23; Acts 10:36; Rom.10:12; 14:9; 1 Tim.6:15; Rev.17:14).

Note that when Jesus was asked a direct question about His identity, He replied in the same terms that He used when He answered the same question for Moses (Exodus 3:13,14; John 4:26).

Again, as in the verse before, Jesus identifies the persecution of the Christians as being directed against Him personally. But all of that was over, insofar as Saul of Tarsus was to be concerned, as the strong adversative, ἀλλά, which is the next word indicates.

*Verse 16 - "But rise, and stand upon thy feet: for I have appeared unto thee for this purpose, to make thee a minister and a witness both of these things which thou hast seen, and of those things in the which I will apppear unto thee."*

ἀλλὰ ἀνάστηθι καὶ στῆθι ἐπὶ τοὺς πόδας σου, εἰς τοῦτο γὰρ ὤφθην σοι, προχειρίσασθαί σε ὑπηρέτην καὶ μάρτυρα ὧν τε εἶδές με ὧν τε ὀφθήσομαί σοι,

ἀλλὰ (adversative conjunction) 342.

ἀνάστηθι (2d.per.sing.2d.aor.act.impv.of ἀνίστημι, command) 789.

καὶ (adjunctive conjunction joining verbs) 14.

στῆθι (2d.per.sing.2d.aor.act.impv.of ἵστημι, command) 180.

ἐπὶ (preposition with the accusative, place) 47.

τοὺς (acc.pl.masc.of the article in agreement with πόδας) 9.

πόδας (acc.pl.masc.of πούς, place) 353.

σου (gen.sing.masc.of σύ, possession) 104.

εἰς (preposition with the accusative, purpose) 140.

τοῦτο (acc.sing.neut.of οὗτος, purpose) 93.

γὰρ (causal conjunction) 105.

ὤφθην (1st.per.sing.1st.aor.pass.ind.of ὁράω, culminative) 144a.

σοι (dat.sing.masc.of σύ, indirect object of ὤφθην) 104.

προχειρίσασθαί (pres.pass.inf.acc.sing.neut. of προχειρίζομαι, purpose) 3579.

σε (acc.sing.masc.of σύ, general reference) 104.

ὑπηρέτην (acc.sing.masc.of ὑπηρέτης, predicate accusative) 493.

καὶ (adjunctive conjunction joining nouns) 14.

μάρτυρα (acc.sing.masc.of μάρτυς, predicate accusative) 1263.

ὧν (gen.pl.neut.of ὅς, relative pronoun, reference) 65.

τε (correlative particle) 1408.

εἶδες (2d.per.sing.aor.act.ind.of ὁράω, culminative) 144a.

με (acc.sing.masc.of ἐγώ) 123.

ὧν (gen.pl.neut.of ὅς, relative pronoun, reference) 65.

τε (correlative particle) 1408.

ὀφθήσομαί (1st.per.sing.fut.pass.ind.of ὁράω, predictive) 144a.

σοι (dat.sing.masc.of σύ, indirect object of ὀφθήσομαί) 104.

*Translation - "But rise and stand on your feet, because it is for this purpose that I have been introduced to you - that you are appointed a servant and a witness with reference to the fact that you have seen me and to that which I will reveal to you."*

**Comment:** It is singular that Jesus should have said to Saul essentially what He said to Job under similar circumstances (Job 38:1-3). γὰρ is causal. The reason Jesus wanted Paul to stop groveling in the dust and stand up was that He had work for him to do. It is false humility and a facade behind which we conceal our sloth when we fall before our Lord on our face. We are to stand on our feet and "go and disciple all nations" (Mt.28:19). One cannot do that when he is lying in the dust on the Damascus road.

εἰς τοῦτο is a purpose construction. *Cf.* #140. The infinitive προχειρίσασθαί σε is in the accusative, since it is in apposition with τοῦτο. "for this purpose . . . namely, that you are now being appointed a servant and a witness. . . . κ. τ. λ. " *Cf.* #493 for the basic meaning, which emphasizes Paul's subordination (as well as ours) to Christ. P74 A C2 E P Φ and Sinaiticus and several miscules and numbered uncials omit με, though Aland *et al* have opted to leave it in the text, but only with a C degree of certitude. "In order to represent the balance between external evidence and transcriptional probability, a majority of the Committee preferred to include με in the text, but to enclose it within square brackets" (Metzger, *A Textual Commentary on the Greek New Testament*, 495). There are compelling grammatical reasons to conclude that it does not belong, since it is next to impossible to associate it with the rest of the sentence. The sentence translates smoothly without it.

Paul was to witness both what he had seen and what was still to be revealed to him. *Cf.* Acts 9:17; 2 Cor.12:1-4; Gal.1:17; 2:6-9. Thus our Lord predicted Paul's graduate education in theology in the third heavens. His theological education was to be quite complete, not less so than that of the other Apostles who had spent three years with Jesus on earth. Paul was to spend some time with Him in Paradise - an experience to which he alluded in defense of his apostleship. Jesus' charge to Paul to witness what he had seen and what he was yet to see reminds us of Revelation 1:19 and Jesus' similar instructions to John. Just as Jesus took John to the throne of God in heaven (Rev.4:1) to complete his theological education so that he might write the Book of the Revelation, so also he took Paul to the throne of God to reveal to him that part of the Christian gospel which Paul was later to call the "mystery" (Eph.3:1-11). It was because of his faithful preaching to the Gentile, thus to carry out the mysterious purpose of God in the church age, that Paul was in trouble with the Jews. If they had been with him in Paradise (2 Cor.12:1-4) they would have understood.

*Verse 17 - "Delivering thee from the people, and from the Gentiles, unto whom now I send thee."*

ἐξαιρούμενός σε ἐκ τοῦ λαοῦ καὶ ἐκ τῶν ἐθνῶν, εἰς οὓς ἐγὼ ἀποστέλλω σε.

ἐξαιρούμενος (pres.mid.part.nom.sing.masc.of ἐξαιρέω, adverbial, circumstantial) 504.
σε (acc.sing.masc.of σύ, direct object of ἐξαιρούμενος0 104.
ἐκ (preposition with the ablative of separation) 19.
τοῦ (abl.sing.masc.of the article in agreement with λαοῦ) 9.
λαοῦ (abl.sing.masc.of λαός, separation) 110.
καὶ (adjunctive conjunction joining prepositional phrases) 14.
ἐκ (preposition with the ablative of separation) 19.
τῶν (abl.pl.neut.of the article in agreement with ἐθνῶν) 9.
ἐθνῶν (abl.pl.neut.of ἔθνος, separation) 376.
εἰς (preposition with the accusative of extent) 140.
οὓς (acc.pl.masc.of ὅς, relative pronoun, extent) 65.
ἐγὼ (nom.sing.masc.of ἐγώ, subject of ἀποστέλλω) 123.
ἀποστέλλω (1st.per.sing.pres.act.ind.ofd ἀποστέλλω, predictive) 215.
σε (acc.sing.masc.of σύ, direct object ofd ἀποστέλλω) 104.

*Translation - " . . . delivering you from the people and from the Gentiles unto whom I am going to send you."*

**Comment:** The long sentence begins in verse 16 and continues through verse 18. Jesus revealed Himself to Paul for the purpose expressed in the infinitive προχειρίσασθαί in verse 16. If Paul is to be Christ's witness he must be rescued both from the Jews who are trying to kill him and also from the Romans who have him in custody.The deliverance therefore is both from death and from imprisonment. Thus we can consider ἐξαιρούμενος as either modal or circumstantial, for if the Lord had not delivered Paul from his enemies, both Jew and Gentile, he could not have finished his work to which Jesus had appointed him. Thus Paul was hinting, at least, to Festus and Agrippa, as well as to the Jews, that he was not worried about the dispostion of his case before the court now pending. The sovereign Lord of the universe, whose presence creates a brightness greater than that of the sun at noon, had promised him at their first meeting that He would deliver his witness from his enemies.

If some object that at this point in Paul's career he had already gone to the Gentiles in three missionary journeys and had established Christian churches all over Asia Minor, in Macedonia and in Greece, and therefore that his work may have been finished, it must be said that he had not yet been to Rome, and that he had our Lord's promise that he was soon to go to the capital city of the empire (Acts 23:11). Thus Paul spoke with the confidence that banishes fear. He did not know when or how he would go to Rome, nor did he know how long he would preach there, and he certainly did not know that he would die there, but he knew with a certitude that grew out of his faith in the sovereignty of God that he was not going to be killed by the Jews or kept in jail by the Romans - at least, not this time. Jesus had assured him from the first that neither Jew nor Gentile could harm him until his divinely appointed work was finished. Paul often expressed this concept of immunity from death for the Christian until his work is done. *Cf.* Phil.1:6; Eph.2:10; 2 Tim.4:6,7; Rev.3:2.

Having made his point before the gala assemblage, Paul could not be sure that Festus or Agrippa understood it. Thus he was not necessarily taunting them, as if to dare them to act in such a way as to frustrate the will of God. He did not know whether they got the point or not, but it really made no essential difference. Paul knew that he was going to walk out of Caesarea alive and still able to go to Rome and preach the "unsearchable riches of Christ" (Eph.3:8).

The long sentence concludes in verse 18 with a brief outline of the work of an evangelist.

*Verse 18 - "To open their eyes, and to turn them from darkness to light, and from the power of Satan unto God, that they may receive forgiveness of sins, and inheritance among them which are sanctified by faith that is in me."*

ἀνοῖξαι ὀφθαλμοὺς αὐτῶν, τοῦ ἐπιστρέψαι ἀπὸ σκότους εἰς φῶς καὶ τῆς ἐξουσίας τοῦ Σατανᾶ ἐπὶ τὸν θεόν, τοῦ λαβεῖν αὐτοὺς ἄφεσιν ἁμαρτιῶν καὶ κλῆρον ἐν τοῖς ἡγιασμένοις πίστει τῇ εἰς ἐμέ.

ἀνοῖξαι (aor.act.inf.of ἀνοίγω, purpose) 188.
ὀφθαλμοὺς (acc.pl.masc.of ὀφθαλμος, direct object of ἀνοῖξαι) 501.
αὐτῶν (gen.pl.masc.of αὐτός, possession) 16.
τοῦ (gen.sing.neut.of the article, purpose) 9.
ἐπιστρέψαι (aor.act.inf.of ἐπιστρέφω, purpose) 866.
ἀπὸ (preposition with the ablative of separation) 70.
σκότους (abl.sing.masc.of σκότος, separation) 602.
εἰς (preposition with the accusative of extent) 140.
φῶς (acc.sing.neut.of φῶς, extent) 379.
καὶ (adjunctive conjunction joining prepositional phrases) 14.
ἐξουσίας (abl.sing.fem.of ἐξουσία, separation) 707.

τοῦ (gen.sing.masc.of the article in agreement with Σατανᾶ) 9.

Σατανᾶ (gen.sing.masc.of Σατανᾶ, description) 365.

ἐπὶ (preposition with the accusative of extent, metaphorical) 47.

τὸν (acc.sing.masc.of the article in agreement with θεόν) 9.

θεόν (acc.sing.masc.of θεός, extent, metaphorical) 124.

τοῦ (gen.sing.neut.of the article, purpose) 9.

λαβεῖν (2d.aor.act.inf.of λαμβάνω, purpose) 533.

αὐτοὺς (acc.pl.masc.of αὐτός, general reference) 16.

ἄφεσιν (acc.sing.fem.of ἄφεσις, direct object of λαβεῖν) 1576.

ἁμαρτιῶν (gen.pl.fem.of ἁμαρτία, description) 111.

καὶ (adjunctive conjunction joining nouns) 14.

κλῆρον (acc.sing.masc.of κλῆρος, direct object of λαβεῖν) 1648.

ἐν (preposition with the locative, with plural substantives) 80.

τοῖς (loc.pl.masc.of the article in agreement with ἡγιασμένοις) 9.

ἡγιασμένοις (perf.pass.part.loc.pl.masc.of ἁγιάζω, substantival, with plural persons) 576.

πίστει (instru.sing.fem.of πίστις, means) 728.

τῇ (instru.sing.fem.of the article in agreement with πίστει) 9.

εἰς (preposition with the accusative, like a locative) 140.

ἐμέ (acc.sing.masc.of ἐμός, static use, like a locative) 1267.

*Translation - ". . . to open their eyes so as to turn them from darkness to light, and from the authority of Satan to God, in order that they might receive forgiveness of sins and an inheritance along with those who have been set apart by means of faith in me."*

**Comment:** There are three purpose clauses, each one introducing the next. Jesus was sending Paul to the Gentiles in order that he might open their eyes. Why? In order that they might turn. Why? In order that they might receive . . ." How? By faith. What faith? Not faith in Paul, but the faith which they found manifest in Paul's life.

Festus and the other Gentiles present may have resented Paul's inference that Gentile eyes were closed - that they were walking in darkness and would have no light until they turned toward it. He further implied that they were under the power of Satan and would continue to be enslaved by him until they turned to God. Further they were sinners and needed forgiveness, and they were wretched and poverty-stricken with no inheritance that would stand the test of eternity. Finally he had implied that the Gentiles, who were blind, in the dark, under Satan's power and unforgiven had not been selected by God and set apart for anything specific. On the contrary they were adrift without a compass and without the means of locomotion to avoid the helpless slavery to natural law in a world and upon a sea that they did not understand.

The verse has a wealth of adverbial prepositional phrases. The student should study in depth #'s 188, 501, 866, 602, 379, 707, 365, 1576, 111, 1648, 576 and 728. This requires painstaking effort but it is highly rewarding and cost effective, as it uncovers the results in the realm of the spirit of the gospel of Christ which Paul preached.

Paul seems to be saying that his converts would be given the gift of faith by which they would be set apart to God's service, by observing his own faith - the faith which dictated his life style and gave him the assurance of the truth of what he preached. The preacher whose life style does not reveal anything supernatural to his audience and who does not indicate great faith in the truth of his message will not be used of God to inspire faith in others. This is not to say that the source of the faith that saves the sinner is his confidence in the man who has told him about Christ. Confidence in another Christian, however dedicated he may be, is not the same as faith in Jesus Christ. The former is induced by sociology. The latter is the gift of God, not either of works or of social research. Faith is not self generating. Some have said that if there had been no America, Columbus' faith would have created one. But faith is not creative. It flows from the existence of that in which it believes. Columbus believed in the land which he sought because it was there. Faith does not create Christ. Christ inspires and generates faith. When Paul's converts saw the evidences of his faith in his life and preaching, they came to believe in the Christ who had given him his faith. John 3:16, properly translated does not say, "that whosoever believeth in Him." ὁ πιστεύων εἰς αὐτόν - means "the one believing upon Him" and so in all similar passages.

Note that ἡγιασμένοις, the substantival participle is in the the perfect tense. This indicates a current condition as a result of a past completed action. The new converts receive forgiveness of sin and their new inheritance in association with others who have already been set apart by the same faith that saved the newcomers. Paul was told that day on the Damascus that he was to go at some future time, after he had received proper theological education to the Gentiles in order to open eyes (now closed) in order that they might turn (not yet turned) and that they might receive (not yet received) an inheritance among a group of people who had already been set apart, but who at the time when Jesus said this to Paul, had not yet actually experienced the things which were prepared for them. *Cf.* Acts 20:32 where we have the same construction.

Sacerdotalists, who have a vested interest in their view that they, by their action, upon earth and in historic time, sanctify, set apart, redeem, bind and loose (Mt.16:19) or remit and retain sins (John 20:23), thus to make Heaven's decision contingent upon man's ritual, resist these perfect tense constructions and read future time into them. This is unblushing eisegesis. Who has given any of us the right to put a future tense interpretation upon a perfect tense verb or participle? Sacerdotalism reduces the body of Christ to a network of social institutions attempting to make cultural impacts upon society, through the dynamics of human effort. When Constantine ordered the baptism of an entire Roman army he thought that by so doing he would make society Christian. Our sovereign Lord will carry on His work of taking out from the Gentiles a people for His name (Acts 15:14) by sending out preachers like Paul, with his faith and his theology, and the word which is preached will "accomplish that which (He pleases) and it shall prosper in the thing whereto (He) sent it" (Isaiah 55:11).

Neither Felix, Festus or Agrippa, nor Ananias or Tertullus can stop it.

# Paul's Testimony to Jews and Gentiles

*(Acts 26:19 - 23)*

*Verse 19 - "Whereupon, O King Agrippa, I was not disobedient unto the heavenly vision."*

Ὅθεν, βασιλεῦ Ἀγρίππα, οὐκ ἐγενόμην ἀπειθὴς τῇ οὐρανίῳ ὀπτασίᾳ,

Ὅθεν (continuative conjunction) 1020.

βασιλεῦ (voc.sing.masc.of βασιλεύς, address) 31.

Ἀγρίππα (voc.sing.masc.of Ἀγρίππας, address) 136C.

οὐκ (negative conjunction with the indicative) 130.

ἐγενόμην (1st.per.sing.aor.ind.of γίνομαι, progressive duration) 113.

ἀπειθὴς (nom.sing.masc.of ἀπειθής, predicate adjective) 1800.

τῇ (loc.sing.fem.of the article in agreement with ὀπτασίᾳ) 9.

οὐρανίῳ (loc.sing.fem.of οὐράνιος in agreement with ὀπτασίᾳ) 554.

ὀπτασίᾳ (loc.sing.fem.of ὀπτασία, sphere) 1804.

*Translation - "And, King Agrippa, I have not been disobedient to the heavenly vision."*

**Comment:** Ὅθεν is continuative with an element of cause in it. "Phrases like ἀνθ᾽ ὧν (Lu.12:2), διό (Mt.27:8), διόπερ (1 Cor.8:13), ὅθεν (Ac.26:19), δι᾽ ἣν αἰτίαν (2 Tim.1:6,12), οὗ χάριν (Lu.7:47) are not always regarded as formally causal. The construction is sometimes paratactic. Indeed, the subordination of the ὅτι and διότι clauses is often rather loose." (Blass, *Grammar of New Testament Greek,* 274, as cited in Robertson, *Grammar,* 962). Burton (*New Testament Moods and Tenses,* 98) says it a little more clearly - "From the nature of the causal clause as making an assertion, it results that it is easily disjoined from the clause which states the fact of which it gives the cause of reason, and becomes an independent sentence." Thus we can take verse 19 as an independent sentence, in which case Ὅθεν is paratactic. The context indicates of course that Paul's obedience was the result of the encounter which he had with Jesus on the road to Damascus.

Just as Paul had not been disobedient to his previous theological views in his preregenerate days, so he was not disobedient to his new views, now that he was saved. Paul's life illustrates the fact that he was aware of the connection between epistemology and ethics. What one believes should affect what one does.

*Verse 20 - "But shewed first unto them of Damascus, and at Jerusalem, and throughout all the coasts of Judea, and then to the Gentiles, that they should repent and turn to God, and do works meet for repentance."*

ἀλλὰ τοῖς ἐν Δαμασκῷ πρῶτόν τε καὶ Ἱεροσολύμοις, πᾶσάν τε τὴν χώραν τῆς Ἰουδαίας καὶ τοῖς ἔθνεσιν ἀπήγγελλον μετανοεῖν καὶ ἐπιστρέφειν ἐπὶ τὸν θεόν, ἄξαι τῆς μετανοίας ἔργα πράσσοντας.

ἀλλὰ (alternative conjunction) 342.
τοῖς (dat.pl.masc.of the article, indirect object of ἀπήγελλον) 9.
ἐν (preposition with the locative of place) 80.
Δαμασκῷ (loc.sing.masc.of Δαμασκός, place) 3181.
πρῶτόν (acc.sing.neut.of πρῶτος, temporal adverb) 487.
τε (correlative particle) 1408.
καὶ (adjunctive conjunction joining nouns) 14.
Ἱεροσολύμοις (loc.sing.neut.of Ἱεροσόλυμα, place) 141.
πασάν (acc.sing.fem.of πᾶς in agreement with χώραν, extent) 67.
τε (adjunctive particle) 1408.
τὴν (acc.sing.fem.of the article in agreement with χώραν) 9.
χώραν (acc.sing.fem.of χώρα, extent) 201.
τῆς (gen.sing.fem.of the article in agreement with Ἰουδαίας) 9.
Ἰουδαίας (gen.sing.fem.of Ἰουδαία, description) 134.
καὶ (adjunctive conjunction joining nouns) 14.
τοῖς (dat.pl.neut.of the article in agreement with ἔθνεσιν) 9.
ἔθνεσιν (dat.pl.neut.of ἔθνος, indirect object of ἀπήγελλον) 376.
ἀπήγγελλον (1st.per.sing.imp.act.ind.of ἀπαγγέλλω, inchoative) 176.
μετανοεῖν (pres.act.inf.of μετανοέω, object infinitive in indirect discourse) 251.
καὶ (adjunctive conjunction joining infinitives) 14.
ἐπιστρέφειν (pres.act.inf.of ἐπιστρέφω, object infinitive in indirect discourse) 866.
ἐπὶ (preposition with the accusative of extent) 47.
τὸν (acc.sing.masc.of the article in agreement with θεόν) 9.
θεόν (acc.sing.masc.of θεός, extent) 124.
ἄξια (acc.pl.neut.of ἄξιος, in agreement with ἔργα, predicate adjective) 285.
τῆς (abl.sing.fem.of the article in agreement with μετανοίας) 9.
μετανοίας (abl.sing.fem.of μετάνοι,comparison) 286.
ἔργα (acc.pl.neut.of ἔργον, direct object of πράσσοντας) 460.
πράσσοντας (pres.act.part.acc.pl.masc.of πράσσω, adverbial, complementary) 1943.

*Translation* - *"But first, both to those in Damascus and also in Jerusalem, and throughout the entire Judean country, and to the Gentiles, I began to preach that they repent and turn to God as they performed deeds consistent with repentance."*

**Comment:** Note the τε . . . καὶ . . . τε sequence, the first such in the New Testament. *Cf.* #1408 for the various combinations. First, Paul preached in Damascus, by virtue of the geographical circumstances. That was where he was when his eyes were opened and he received his call to preach. Paul began immediately (Acts 9:19,20). We have noted with some amazement that many Christians announce a call to preach, either as pastors, evangelists or missionaries and then plan to go somewhere else to begin! Not Paul, although he was forced to flee for his life from Damascus (Acts 9:23-26) and come to Jerusalem , where he continued to preach (Acts 9:28-29). Paul's ministry also reached the outlying areas of Judea, and finally, pursuant to the direction of the Holy Spirit (Acts 13:2) he went to the Gentiles. His message? Repentance, faith and holy living. Note that the participle πράσσοντας, joins the two infinitives in direct discourse, the objects of ἀπήγγελλον, which is inchoative, although after Paul began to preach (inchoative) he continued to preach (progressive duration). *Cf.* Mt.3:8 where John the Baptist used the same ablative of comparison construction.

Paul's complete evangelistic theology which was given to all men everywhere, whether they be Jews or Gentiles, ties together faith and practice. The order is: repent, believe and adopt a new ethical life style. Turn away from (μετανοέω) because of the change of mind set, turn toward (because of faith) and live a consistent ethical pattern that is capable of such an influence as to convince the world that the repentance was genuine. There is no room for antinomianism here. *Cf.* 1 Thess.1:3 in comparsion with verse 9, where Paul defines the "work of faith" as both the turn from idols and the turn to God. *Cf.* comment *en loc.*

Having described in brief detail the sweep and scope of his ministry and its theological content, he then said that it was for that reason that the Jews were trying to kill him.

*Verse 21 - "For these causes the Jews caught me in the temple, and went about to kill me."*

ἕνεκα τούτων με ᾿Ιουδαῖοι συλλαβόμενοι (ὄντα) ἐν τῳς ἱερῷ ἐπειρῶντο διαχειρίσασθαι.

ἕνεκα (improper preposition with the genitive, cause) 435.

τούτων (gen.pl.neut.of οὗτος, cause) 93.

με (acc.sing.masc.of ἐγώ, direct object of συλλαβόμενοι and διαχειρίσασθαι) 123.

᾿Ιουδαῖοι (nom.pl.masc.of ᾿Ιουδαῖος, subject of ἐπειρῶντο) 143.

συλλαβόμενοι (2d.aor.mid.part.nom.pl.masc.of συλλαμβάνω, adjectival, restrictive, in agreement with ᾿Ιουδαῖοι) 1598.

ὄντα (pres.part., acc.sing.masc.of εἰμί, adverbial, temporal) 86.

ἐν (preposition with the locative of place) 80.

τῷ (loc.sing.neut.of the article in agreement with ἱερῷ) 9.

ἱερῷ (loc.sing.neut.of ἱερόν, place) 346.

#3664 ἐπειρῶντο (3d.per.pl.imp.mid.ind.of πειράω, voluntative).

go about - Acts 26:21.

*Meaning:* To make an effort; to attempt - followed by the infinitive - with reference to the attempt of the Jews to kill Paul - Acts 26:21.

διαχειρίσασθαι (1st.aor.mid.inf.of διαχειρίζομαι, complementary) 3067.

*Translation - "It is because of these things that the Jews who seized me when I was in the temple have made repeated attempts to beat me to death."*

**Comment:** The improper preposition ἕνεκα (#435) is followed here, as always, by the genitive. τούτων refers to the material in verses 19,20. The participle συλλαβόμενοι is adjectival, in the predicate position, and thus restrictive. Paul was not talking about all of the Jews - only those who seized him in the temple. ὄντα is temporal. It tells us when the Jews arrested Paul. The point of time represented by ὄντα is simultaneous with συλλαβόμενοι, but, of course, antecedent to the time when Paul was telling Agrippa about it. ἐπειρῶντο is voluntative (they tried to kill him, but failed) and iterative (they made repeated attempts). The Jews failed because the sovereign God had other plans for Paul. No Jew, nor any Gentile, however deadly his attempt, could kill Paul until God permitted it. (Isaiah 54:17).

This is Paul's point in

*Verse 22 - "Having therefore obtained help of God, I continue unto this day, witnessing both to small and great, saying none other things than those which the prophets and Moses did say should come."*

ἐπικουρίας οὖν τυχὼν τῆς ἀπὸ τοῦ θεοῦ ἄχρι τῆς ἡμέρας ταύτης ἕστηκα μαρτυρόμενος μικρῷ τε καὶ μεγάλῳ, οὐδὲν ἐκτὸς λέγων ὧν τε οἱ προφῆται ἐλάλησαν μελλόντων γίνεσθαι καὶ Μωϋσῆς,

**#3665** ἐπικουρίας (gen.sing.fem.of ἐπικουρία, objective genitive).

help - Acts 26:22.

*Meaning:* A combination of ἐπί (#47) and κουρέω - "to give aid." ἐπί is perfective. Hence, to give total help; assistance. With reference to God's help given to Paul to preserve his life amid the attempts of enemies to kill him - Acts 26:22.

οὖν (inferential conjunction) 68.
τυχὼν (2d.aor.act.part.of τυγχάνω, adverbial, causal) 2699.
τῆς (gen.sing.fem.of the article in agreement with ἐπικουρίας) 9.
ἀπὸ (preposition with the ablative of source) 70.
τοῦ (abl.sing.masc.of the article in agreement with θεοῦ) 9.
θεοῦ (abl.sing.masc.of θεός, source) 124.
ἄχρι (preposition with the genitive in a time expression) 1517.
τῆς (gen.sing.fem.of the article in agreement with ἡμέρας) 9.
ἡμέρας (gen.sing.fem.of ἡμέρα, time description) 135.
ταύτης (gen.sing.fem.of οὗτος, in agreement with ἡμέρας) 93.
ἕστηκα (1st.per.sing.perf.act.ind.of ἵστημι, iterative) 180.
μαρτυρόμενος (pres.mid.part.nom.sing.masc.of μαρτυρέω, adverbial, complementary) 1471.
μικρῷ (dat.sing.masc.of μικρός, indirect object of μαρτυρόμενος) 901.
τε (correlative particle) 1408.

καὶ (adjunctive conjunction joining substantives) 14.

μεγάλῳ (dat.sing.masc.of μέγας, indirect object of μαρτυρόμενος) 184.

οὐδὲν (acc.sing.neut.of οὐδείς, direct object of λέγων) 446.

ἐκτὸς (adverbial) 1461.

λέγων (pres.act.part.nom.sing.masc.of λέγω, adverbial, modal) 66.

ὧν ( abl.sing.neut.of ὅς, with ἐκτός) 65.

τε (correlative particle) 1408.

οἱ (nom.pl.masc.of the article in agreement with προφῆται) 9.

προφῆται (nom.pl.masc.of προφήτης, subject of ἐλάλησαν) 119.

ἐλάλησαν (3d.per.pl.aor.act.ind.of λαλέω, culminative) 815.

μελλόντων (pres.act.part.gen.pl.masc.of μέλλω, indirect discourse) 206.

γίνεσθαι (pres.mid.inf.of γίνομαι, completes μελλόντων in indirect discourse) 113.

καὶ (adjunctive conjunction joining nouns) 14.

Μωϋσῆς (nom.sing.masc.of Μωϋσῆς, subject of ἐλάλησαν) 715.

*Translation - "Therefore, since I have had protection from God unto this day I have stood witnessing, again and again, both to small and great, saying nothing except that which both the Prophets and Moses have said would happen."*

**Comment:** οὖν is inferential. Because the Jews made repeated attempts upon Paul's life, he enjoyed protection from God, from the day when he first needed it until the moment of our story. Just as οὖν is inferential, τυχὼν is causal. The perfect tense in ἕτηκα is iterative, rather than consummative. Obviously Paul did not witness continuously (*i.e.* without intervals) but he did witness repeatedly. Again and again Paul "took his stand" - in synagogues, on the street, on Mars Hill, in the ἀγορά in Athens, on board ship, from house to house in Ephesus, in the Philippian jail. To whom did he tell the gospel story? To small and great, for the Commission was to "teach all nations" and that without discrimination. What did he say? Nothing except what was written, both in the law of Moses and in the Prophets. Thus again Paul makes the point, which he had developed earlier in his remarks that a good Pharisee must always be true to all that is written in the Law and the Prophets. Thus Paul continued after his conversion as a Pharisee, but with a new and enlightened concept of what is involved in the Pharisaic tradition. By contrast he was implying that his enemies among the Jews, who professed to be good Pharisees did not understand their position.

This passage teaches the continuity of the Judeo-Christian revelation from the Law to the Prophets to Christ and His Apostles. There is no break between the message of the Old Testament and that of the New.

The New is in the Old contained<br>
The Old is in the New explained

*Verse 23 - ". . . that Christ should suffer and that he should be the first that should rise from the dead, and should shew light unto the people, and to the Gentiles."*

εἰ παθητὸς ὁ Χριστός, εἰ πρῶτος ἐξ ἀναστάσεως νεκρῶν φῶς μέλλει καταγγέλλειν τῖ τε λαῷ καὶ τοῖς ἔθνεσιν.

εἰ (conditional particle in an elliptical condition, in indirect discourse) 337.

**#3666** παθητὸς (nom.sing.masc.of παθητός, predicate adjective).

should suffer - Acts 26:23.

*Meaning:* subject to and capable of suffering - Acts 26:23.
ὁ (nom.sing.masc.of the article in agreement with Χριστός) 9.
Χριστός (nom.sing.masc.of Χριστός, subject of ἐστιν, understood) 4.
εἰ (conditional particle in an elliptical condition) 337.
πρῶτος (nom.sing.masc.of πρῶτος, predicate adjective) 487.
ἐξ (preposition with the ablative of separation) 19.
ἀναστάσεως (abl.sing.fem.of ἀνάστασις, separation) 1423.
νεκρῶν (gen.pl.masc.of νεκρός, description) 749.
φῶς (acc.sing.neut.of φῶς, direct object of καταγγέλλειν) 379.
μέλλει (3d.per.sing.pres.act.ind.of μέλλω, aoristic) 206.
καταγγέλλειν (pres.act.inf.of καταγγέλλω, completes μέλλει) 3023.
τῷ (dat.sing.masc.of the article in agreement with λαῷ) 9.
τε (correlative particle) 1408.
λαῷ (dat.sing.masc.of λαός, indirect object of καταγγέλλειν) 110.
καὶ (adjunctive conjunction joining nouns) 14.
τοῖς (dat.pl.neut.of the article in agreement with ἔθνεσιν) 9.
ἔθνεσιν (dat.pl.neut.of ἔθνος, indirect object of καταγγέλλειν) 376.

*Translation - ". . . if the Messiah suffers and by being the first to rise from the dead proclaims light to the people and to the Gentiles."*

**Comment:** εἰ in the sense of ὅτι in introduction of indirect discourse. Paul's message was concerned with what Moses and the Prophets had said would happen if Messiah died and rose again from the dead, and if, after His resurrection, He ordered the great commission to His church to preach the gospel which would promise the light of salvation, not only to His own nation, the Jews, but also to the Gentiles. That Messiah was to be the Suffering Saviour before He could be the King was made clear in the Old Testament. But this could happen only if Messiah arose from the dead and only if, in the age to follow His resurrection the gospel was made available to all the world. Paul was insisting that everything he had preached was in the Jewish Scriptures and that his gospel is the only answer to the dilemma, posed by two conflicting pictures of Messiah. Was He to suffer or to reign? He was to do both. Thus, the resurrection is an essential part of the story. But why should the Pharisees object to the resurrection? Did they not believe in the resurrection? He is the Light of the World (John 8:12). *Cf.* Mt.4:16; Isa.9:1,2; 60:1-3; Lk.2:32.
    This kind of logic was more than Festus could endure.

# Paul Appeals to Agrippa to Believe

*(Acts 26: 24 - 32)*

*Verse 24 - "And as he thus spake for himself, Festus said with a loud voice, Paul, thou art beside thyself; much learning doth make thee mad."*

Ταῦτα δὲ αὐτοῦ ἀπολογουμένου ὁ Φῆστος μεγάλη τῇ φωνῇ φησιν, Μαίνη, Παῦλε. τὰ πολλά σε γράμματα εἰς μανίαν περιτρέπει.

Ταῦτα (acc.pl.neut.of οὗτος, direct object of ἀπολογουμένου) 93.

δὲ (adversative conjunction) 11.

αὐτοῦ (gen.sing.masc.of αὐτός, genitive absolute) 16.

ἀπολογουμένου (pres.mid.part.gen.sing.masc.of ἀπολογέομαι, genitive absolute) 2476.

ὁ (nom.sing.masc.of the article in agreement with Φῆστος) 9.

Φῆστος (nom.sing.masc.of Φῆστος, subject of φησιν) 3633.

μεγάλη (instru.sing.fem.of μέγας, in agreement with φωνῇ) 184.

τῇ (instru.sing.fem.of the article in agreement with φωνῇ) 9.

φωνῇ (instru.sing.fem.of φωνή, manner) 222.

φησιν (3d.per.sing.pres.act.ind.of φημί, historical) 354.

Μαίνη (2d.per.sing.pres.mid.ind.of μαίνομαι, progressive duration, retroactive) 2408.

Παῦλε (voc.sing.masc.of Παῦλος, address) 3284.

τὰ (nom.pl.neut.of the article in agreement with γράμματα) 9.

πολλὰ (nom.pl.neut.of πολύς, in agreement with γράμματα) 228.

γράμματα (nom.pl.neut.of γράμμα, subject of περιτρέπει) 2100.

εἰς (preposition with the accusative of extent, metaphorical) 140.

**#3667** μανίαν (acc.sing.fem.of μανία, extent, metaphorical).

make mad - Acts 26:24.

*Meaning:* Cf. μαίνομαι (#2408). Hence, madness, frenzy, insanity. With reference to Festus' evaluation of Paul - Acts 26:24.

**#3668** περιτρέπει (3d.per.sing.pres.act.ind.of περιτρέπω, progressive duration, retroactive).

make mad - ACts 26:24.

*Meaning:* A combination of περί (#173) and τρέπω - "to turn." Hence, to turn around; to reverse direction. Joined with εἰς μανίαν in Acts 26:24. Transitively - i.e. - "is turning you to madness" - "is driving you insane."

*Translation - "But as he was saying these things in his own defense, Festus raised his voice and said, 'You are out of your mind, Paul. Your great learning has driven you insane.' "*

**Comment:** δὲ is adversative. As Paul was trying to win Agrippa, Festus was working against him. When the article is joined to the substantive but not with the adjective as in μεγάλη τῇ φωνῇ, "the result is the equivalent of a relative clause." (Robertson, *Grammar*, 789). Thus the translation is "with the voice which is raised." Why did Festus shout? Perhaps in order that what he said could be heard throughout τὸ ἀκροατήριον, though that was necessary only if he wanted all to hear his observation that Paul had lost his mind. If he intended only for Paul to hear, he need not have shouted. It is likely that Festus himself was overwrought. Felix became agitated and trembled as he heard Paul preach (Acts 24:25). Festus himself may have lost his emotional equilibirum as he shouted at Paul that he had lost his. One defense mechanism for the sinner under the convicting power of the gospel is to assert that the preacher is crazy.

*Verse 25 - "But he said, I am not mad , most noble Festus, but speak forth the words of truth and soberness."*

ὁ δὲ Παῦλος, Οὐ μαίνομαι, φησίν, κράτιστε Φῆστε, ἀλλὰ ἀληθείας καὶ σωφροσύνης ῥήματα ἀποφθέγγομαι.

ὁ (nom.sing.masc.of the article in agreement with Παῦλος) 9.
δὲ (adversative conjunction) 11.
Παῦλος (nom.sing.masc.of Παῦλος, subject of φησίν) 3284.
Οὐ (negative conjunction with the indicative) 130.
μαίνομαι (1st.per.sing.pres.mid.ind.of μαίνομαι, aoristic) 2408.
φησίν (3d.per.sing.pres.act.ind.of φημί, historical) 354.
κράτιστε (voc.sing.masc.of κράτιστος, in agreement with Φῆστε) 1712.
Φῆστε (voc.sing.masc.of Φῆστος, address) 3633.
ἀλλὰ (alternative conjunction) 342.
ἀληθείας (gen.sing.fem.of ἀλήθεια, description) 1416.
καὶ (adjunctive conjunction joining nouns) 14.

**#3669** σωφροσύνης (gen.sing.fem.of σωφροσύνη, description).

soberness - Acts 26:25.
sobriety - 1 Tim.2:9,15.

*Meaning:* Cf. σώφρων (#4729), σωφρονέω (#2224), σωφρονισμός (#4807), σωφρονίζω (#4891) and σωφρόνως (#4898). Soundness of mind. The opposite of μανία (#3667) - Acts 26:25; self control, sobriety - 1 Tim.2:9,15.

ῥήματα (acc.pl.neut.of ῥῆμα, direct object of ἀποφθέγγομαι) 343.
ἀποφθέγγομαι (1st.per.sing.pres.mid.ind.of ἀποφθέγγομαι, progressive duration, retroactive) 2960.

*Translation - "But Paul said, 'I am not insane, most noble Festus; rather I have been speaking words of sober truth.' "*

**Comment:** Paul countered Festus' adverse comment with his own adverse reply. Contrary to Festus' opinion of what he had to say his words had the dignity of truth and of the highest academic sophistication. *Cf*.#2960 - lofty speech of great scholarly content. *Cf.* Acts 2:4,14; 2 Pet.2:16,18. So far from being the ravings of a frenetic maniac, Paul's remarks revealed a sophistication that few could command.

The expository preacher, who follows the arguments of the inspired text, as Paul did, has a built- in advantage over the secular orator. His logic is not his own, but that of the Word of God itself. His task is to grace it with proper rhetoric and commanding delivery. The Right Reverend Monsignor Fulton John Sheen, the preacher on the widely known "Catholic Hour" from 1930 to 1945, was famous for his skillful exposition of the Bible. When congratulated for the success of his radio program he said that his success "is due to my writers." What greater writers does any preacher need than Moses, Isaiah, Jeremiah, Hosea, Malachi, David and Daniel? The conviction which Felix and Festus felt and to which Agrippa may almost have yielded was not due to Paul's eloquence, but to the faithfulness with which he expounded the Word and showed its relevance to the current scene.

Paul made no further appeal to Festus, but concentrated the remainder of his attention upon King Agrippa.

*Verse 26 - "For the king knoweth of these things, before whom also I speak freely: for I am persuaded that none of these things are hidden from him, for this thing was not done in a corner."*

ἐπίσταται γὰρ περὶ τούτων ὁ βασιλεύς, πρὸς ὃν καὶ παρρησιαζόμενος λαλῶ. λανθάνειν γὰρ αὐτὸν τούτων οὐ πείθομαι οὐθέν, οὐ γὰρ ἐστιν ἐν γωνίᾳ πεπραγμένον τοῦτο.

ἐπίσταται (3d.per.sing.pres.mid.ind.of ἐπίσταμαι, progressive duration, retroactive) 2814.

γὰρ (causal conjunction) 105.

περὶ (preposition with the genitive of reference) 173.

τούτων (gen.pl.neut.of οὗτος, reference) 93.

ὁ (nom.sing.masc.of the article in agreement with βασιλεύς) 9.

βασιλεύς, (nom.sing.masc.of βασιλεύς, subject of ἐπίσταται) 31.

πρὸς (preposition with the accusative of extent, with a verb of speaking) 197.

ὃν (acc.sing.masc.of ὅς, relative pronoun, extent with a verb of speaking) 65.

καὶ (emphatic conjunction) 14.

παρρησιαζόμενος (pres.mi.part.nom.sing.masc.of παρρησιάομαι, adverbial, modal) 3197.

λαλῶ (1st.per.sing.pres.act.ind.of λαλέω, progressive duration) 815.

λανθάνειν (pres.act.inf.of λανθάνω, object of πείθομαι in indirect discourse) 2247.

γὰρ (causal conjunction) 105.

αὐτὸν (acc.sing.masc.of αὐτός, general reference) 16.

τούτων (gen.pl.neut.of οὗτος, partitive genitive) 93.

οὐ (negative conjunction with the infinitive) 130.

πείθομαι (1st.per.sing.pres.mid.ind.of πείθω, aoristic) 1629.

οὐϑέν (acc.sing.neut.of οὐδείς, direct object of λανϑάνειν) 446.

οὐ (negative conjunction with the indicative) 130.

γὰρ (causal conjunction) 105.

ἐστιν (3d.per.sing.pres.ind.of εἰμί, perfect periphrastic) 86.

ἐν (preposition with the locative of place) 80.

γωνίᾳ (loc.sing.fem.of γωνία, place) 567.

πεπραγμένον (perf.pass.part.nom.sing.neut.of πράσσω, perfect periphrastic) 1943.

τοῦτο (nom.sing.neut.of οὗτος, subject of ἐστίν) 93.

*Translation - "Because the king before whom I am in fact speaking freely is aware of these things, for I am convinced that not one of these things has escaped him, because this has not happened in a corner."*

**Comment:** If Paul was insane, then so, in fact was Agrippa. This is the force of Paul's inference with the first γὰρ. If Paul had, in fact, been speaking incoherently, Agrippa could not have followed his thought. But perhaps he had not understood what Paul was saying. Paul was certain that this was not the case. The reason why Paul spoke with such boldness was that he felt the rapport that existed between him and the king. From the beginning of the gospel (ἐστιν . . . πεπραγμένον) the death, burial and resurrection of Jesus was preached with such force that the church became very well known. King Agrippa could not have been unaware of it.

Paul's point was that in recent history in Palestine, only sixty years before, the birth of Messiah had taken place - a birth that had been foretold by the Prophets and anticipated by Moses (Deut.18:15). And in the next thirty years the Person and Work of Jesus of Nazareth had been revealed. His claim to Messiahship was supported by His miracles. He spoke of a coming kingdom of universal peace that can result only from universal righteousness. He was opposed by the Jewish Establishment, but He promised that if they killed Him He would rise again from the dead. Before His death He prophesied the fall of Jerusalem and looked ahead to the close of the church age to the fall of Antichrist and His own ascent to the throne of David. By the time Paul spoke to Agrippa, Mark, Matthew and Luke had written of these things. In the thirty years since Jesus death and resurrection the Christian community had grown beyond the confines of Palestine. Paul had taken it to the Aegean and Peter and others had taken it to North Africa and east to the Euphrates.

There was no question that King Agrippa knew about it. The question remained - did the birth, life, death, burial and resurrection of Jesus fulfill the prophecies of the Old Testament. If so, then Paul's point was established and Christianity was here to stay.

It was time for Paul to ask what salesmen call "the closing question."

*Verse 27 - "King Agrippa, believest thou the prophets? I know that thou belivest."*

πιστεύεις, βασιλεῦ Ἀγρίππα, τοῖς προφήταις; οἶδα ὅτι πιστεύεις.

πιστεύεις (2d.per.sing.pres.act.ind.of πιστεύω, progressive duration, retroactive, direct question) 734.

βασιλεῦ (voc.sing.masc.of βασιλεύς, address) 31.

'Αγρίππα (voc.sing.masc.of 'Αγρίππα, address) 136C.

τοῖς (dat.pl.masc.of the article in agreement with προφήταις) 9.

προφήταις (dat.pl.masc.of προφήτης, person) 119.

οἶδα (1st.per.sing.pres.act.ind.ofd ὁράω, aoristic) 144b.

ὅτι (conjunction introducing an object clause in indirect discourse) 211.

πιστεύεις (2d.per.sing.pres.act.ind.of πιστεύω, progressive duration, retroactive, indirect discourse) 734.

*Translation -* "*King Agrippa, do you believe the prophets? I know that you believe.*"

**Comment:** The only logical "closing question" for Paul to ask the king after his masterful logical development. The answer was so obviously positive that Paul hastens to provide the answer himself, and challenge the king to deny it.

*Verse 28 -* "*Then Agrippa said unto Paul, Almost thou persuadest me to be a Christian.*"

ὁ δὲ 'Αγρίππας πρὸς τὸν Παῦλον, Ἐν ὀλίγῳ με πείθεις Χριστιανὸν ποιῆσαι.

ὁ (nom.sing.masc.of the article in agreement with 'Αγρίππας) 9.

δὲ (continuative conjunction) 11.

'Αγρίππας (nom.sing.masc.of 'Αγρίππας, subject of εἶπεν, understood) 136C.

πρὸς (preposition with the accusative of extent, with a verb of speaking) 197.

τὸν (acc.sing.masc.of the article in agreement with Παῦλον) 9.

Παῦλον (acc.sing.masc.of Παῦλος, extent, with a verb of speaking) 3284.

Ἐν (preposition with the locative, instrumental means) 80.

ὀλίγῳ (loc.sing.neut.of ὀλίγος, means) 669.

με (acc.sing.masc.of ἐγώ, general reference) 123.

πείθεις (2d.per.sing.pres.act.ind.of πείθω, direct question) 1629.

Χριστιανὸν (acc.sing.masc.of Χριστιανός, predicate accusative) 3240.

ποιῆσαι (aor.act.inf.of ποιέω, object of πείθεις) 127.

*Translation -* "*And Agrippa (said) to Paul, 'Do you think that by these few words you can make a Christian out of me?'*"

**Comment:** It is a difficult passage. Was Agrippa being sarcastic? Paul's reply in verse 29 helps a little. Does ἐν ὀλίγῳ mean "in a short time" or "with little effort"?

"The difficulty of capturing the nuances intended in this verse is notorious. . . . the reading that is supported by *p* 74 vid *Sinaiticus B 33 81 syr* h mg *cop*bo *al* seems to account best for the other readings, which appear to be attempts at smoothing the meaning. Thus, instead of πείθεις codex Alexandrinus reads πείθη ("you *trust* (or *think*) that you can make me a Christian"), which is adopted by

Lachmann, Alford, A. C. Clark, though the verb seems to have been suggested by πείθομαι of ver. 26. The reading γενέσθαι of the Byzantine text (E P Φ 049 most minuscules, followed by the Textus Receptus) appears to have come from the following verse. Hort, who suspected some primitive corruption in the text, suggested that possibly πέποιθας should be read for με πείθεις." (Metzger, *A Textual Commentary on the Greek New Testament*, 496).

In Rev. 17:10 ὀλίγον means "a short time." In Mark 6:31 it means "a short time" and also "a little bit," - also in 1 Peter 5:10, while in 1 Peter 5:12 it means "a few words." In James 4:14 it means "a short time." In Acts 14:28 ὀλίγον is adjoined to χρόνον. A cost effective research project, which will require some painstaking effort can determine whether we have either ἐν ὀλίγῳ or ἐν μεγάλῳ elsewhere in the New Testament except in Acts 26:29, and, if so, what the context may reveal about the meaning of these two prepositional phrases which Paul used in reply to Agrippa. It is this precise research which provides the objectivity which is so important in exegesis. The phrase must always be interpreted in the light of the context.

Whether Agrippa was being sarcastic or admitting that the Holy Spirit had used Paul's message to convict him, it seems safe to assert that he was uncomfortable. If sarcastic it may have been a defense mechanism - an attempt to laugh it off. If honest, it indicates "an awakened conscience." (The Pulpit Commentary, *The Acts of the Apostles*, II, 276). "Paul recognizes in him the stirrings of faith, and boldly aims a blow at his conscience. . . . But Agrippa fences. What he feels he will not avow. He would lead a double life - representing one thing to the world, thinking another himself. He is the type of a numerous class, who would gladly be blessed, were it not for the strait door and the narrow path, which they will not tread (Luke xiii.24). How near we may be to bliss, yet how far from it! The heart may be touched, the intellect illuminated, the will aroused, the hour acceptable, and yet — some deep stream of passion runs at our feet, which we will not ford; some "cunning bosom sin" keeps out the good angels of repentance and faith that would enter. The reply of Paul to Agrippa's light words again brings out a sharp contrast. Better be the "prisoner of Jesus Christ" than the prisoner of passion! Better the regal freedom of the redeemed man's soul, in poverty and chains, than the splendour of the potentate enslaved by lust and by the fear of men! . . . Agrippa was convinced but not converted . . . Festus hardened in indifferent cynicism. Some wanting little, others much, to make them Christians." (*Ibid.*)

Festus ". . . represents the cynic or indifferentist is matters of religion, or the worldly view of the unspiritual man. Character is "spiritually discerned" only by inward and outward sympathy. The best in Paul was misunderstood, as his worst had been. Says Luther, "The world esteems others as prudent so long as they are mad, and as mad when they cease to be mad and become wise." Saul passed for a wise and able man in the days of his persecuting fury. When he "came to himself," and was clothed in a right mind, he was reckoned mad. One day the tables will be turned, and the children of this world will say, "We fools held his life to be senseless, and now he is numbered among the children of God." (Wisd. v.5)." (*Ibid.*)

The unsaved find it profitable to excuse their unbelief by saying that the

Christian is insane. In an ill-disguised attempt to be gracious Festus handed Paul a left-handed compliment by saying that his insanity was due to his superior intellect and comprehensive education. The football jock who displays his I.Q. on his uniform likes to say that there is only a fine line between genius and lunacy. It is a popular line with the mentally deficient. Thus it has always been. When Jesus spoke words over the heads of his enemies they said, "He hath a devil and is mad" (John 10:20). At Pentecost scoffers said, "These men are full of new wine" (Acts 2:13). As long as Paul left out the heart of the gospel message, as he did on Mars Hill, he was afforded high respect among his academic peers. They even invited him to speak. But when he went to Corinth, determined to know nothing among the Corinthians "save Jesus Christ and him crucified" (1 Cor.2:1) they called him a fool (1 Cor.4:10).

The Christian Renaissance Man should not fret because of this. Such reaction is to be expected. It is standard procedure for the unregenerate to react as Festus reacted to Paul. The most expeditious way to put an end to an argument is to opine that one's opponent is crazy. It has the added advantage that it is not illegal. Another way to win an argument is to murder your opponent, as the Jews in Jerusalem were trying to do - a method which Hitler, the Ayatollah Khomeini, the Ku Klux Klan and the White Citizens' Council have employed, but that is against the law.

We hear no more in Scripture of Festus or Agrippa. Did the gospel seed which Paul planted that day germinate? Or did "the fowls come and devour" it? (Mt.13:4). If there was germination, in whom did growth result? Whatever the result we may be sure that it was in accord to the will of Him Who sent it (Isaiah 55:11).

Paul's response to Agrippa is classic.

*Verse 29 - "And Paul said, I would to God that not only thou, but also all that hear me this day, were both almost, and altogether such as I am, except these bonds."*

ὁ δὲ Παῦλος, Εὐξαίμην ἂν τῷ θεῷ καὶ ἐν ὀλίγῳ καὶ ἐν μεγάλῳ οὐ μόνον σὲ ἀλλὰ καὶ πάντας τοὺς ἀκούοντάς μου σήμερον γενέσθαι τοιούτους ὁποῖος καὶ ἐγώ εἰμι, παρεκτὸς τῶν δεσμῶν τούτων.

ὁ (nom.sing.masc.of the article in agreement with Παῦλος) 9.

δὲ (continuative conjunction) 11.

Παῦλος (nom.sing.masc.of Παῦλος, subject of εἶπεν, understood) 3284.

#3670 Εὐξαίμην (1st.per.sing.1st.aor.mid.optative, potential).

can wish - Rom.9:3.
pray - 2 Cor.13:7; James 5:16.
wish - Acts 27:29; 2 Cor.13:9; 3 John 2.

*Meaning:* To wish for something. Followed by the infinitive - Rom.9:3; To pray to God for something - followed by the accusative of direct object - 2 Cor.13:9; by the infinitive - 2 Cor.13:7; by ὑπέρ and the ablative - James 5:16; by the infinitive in indirect discourse in 3 John 2; Acts 26:29.

ἄν (contingent particle with the potential optative) 205.
τῷ (dat.sing.masc.of the article in agreement with θεῷ) 9.
θεῷ (dat.sing.masc.of θεός, indirect object of εὐξαίμην) 124.
καὶ (adjunctive conjunction joining prepositional phrases) 14.
ἐν (preposition with the locative of sphere) 80.
ὀλίγῳ (loc.sing.neut.of ὀλίγος, sphere) 669.
καὶ (adjunctive conjunction joining prepositional phrases) 14.
ἐν (preposition with the locative of sphere) 80.
μεγάλῳ (loc.sing.neut.of μέγας, sphere) 184.
οὐ (negative conjunction with the infinitive) 130.
μόνον (acc.sing.neut.of μόνος, adverbial) 339.
σὲ (acc.sing.masc.of σύ, general reference) 104.
ἀλλὰ (alternative conjunction) 342.
καὶ (adjunctive conjunction joining substantives) 14.
πάντας (acc.pl.masc.of πᾶς, in agreement with ἀκούοντας) 67.
τοὺς (acc.pl.masc.of the article in agreement with ἀκούοντας) 9.
ἀκούοντας (pres.act.part.acc.pl.masc.of ἀκούω, substantival, general
reference) 148.
μου (gen.sing.masc.of ἐγώ, objective genitive) 123.
σήμερον (temporal adverb) 579.
γενέσθαι (aor.mid.inf.of γίνομαι, object of εὐξαίμην, indirect discourse)
113.
τοιούτους (acc.pl.masc.of τοιοῦτος, predicate accusative) 785.

#3671 ὁποῖος (nom.sing.masc.of ὁποῖος, in agreement with ἐγώ, correlative).

of what sort - 1 Cor.3:13.
such as - Acts 26:29.
what manner of - 1 Thess.1:9; James 1:24.
whatsoever - Gal.2:6.

*Meaning:* The relative ὅ (#65) and ποῖος (#1298). Of what sort, type, quality -
- whether gold, silver, precious stones, wood, hay or stubble - 1 Cor.3:13; as Paul
was, *i.e.* regenerated - Acts 26:29; with reference to ethical quality - 1 Thess.1:9;
of what level of prestige - Gal.2:6; of what character - James 1:24.

καὶ (adjunctive conjunction, joining substantives) 14.
ἐγώ (nom.sing.masc.of ἐγώ, subject of εἰμι) 123.
εἰμι (1st.per.sing.pres.ind.of εἰμί, aoristic) 86.
παρεκτὸς (improper preposition with the ablative of comparison) 509.
τῶν (abl.pl.masc.of the article in agreement with δεσμῶν) 9.
δεσμῶν (abl.pl.masc.of δεσμός, comparison) 2229.
τούτων (abl.pl.masc.of οὗτος, in agreement with δεσμῶν) 93.

*Translation -* "*And Paul said, 'I could only ask God that whether by a small or
great effort, not only you but also all those listening to me today might be exactly*

*like I am, except for these chains.' "*

**Comment:** *Cf.*Luke 16:10 where we have ἐν ἐλαχίστῳ . . . ἐν πολλῷ. In our passage ἐν ὀλίγῳ καὶ ἐν μεγάλῳ - we have "one way or another" -"by small of great effort" or "with few or many words." The thought is that the means by which the end is accomplished is not important. "The result that I am seeking is that you may be as I am except for these chains." παρεκτός with the ablative of separation. (#509). Whatever Agrippa may have meant by ἐν ὀλίγῳ ("almost" *i.e.* "you came close to succeeding" or in sarcasm) Paul replied in kind.

The potential optative in εὐξαίμην ἄν has the protasis suppressed as always in this idiom. That is εὐξαίμην ἄν is the apodosis of an unexpressed protasis. "The optative is the ideal mood of the Greek language, the mood of the fancy" (Gildersleeve, *Syntax*, Part I, 153, as cited in Robertson, *Grammar*, 937). Moulton says, "It was used to express a future in a milder form, and to express a request in deferential style." (*Prolegomena*, 197, as cited in *Ibid.*) He adds that ἄν joined to εὐξαίμην gives the verb a "contingent meaning" and turns our thoughts to the unexpressed protasis of a fourth-class (less vivid future) condition. (Moulton, *Ibid.*, 166, as cited in Robertson, *Grammar*, 937). It is a "softened assertion." Luke has it only here in Acts 26:29, except in questions. Paul was being fanciful. "Would it not be wonderful if you and all of the rest were saved as I am!" He did not say that he thought that his wish would be granted . The potential optative differs from the potential (voluntative) imperfect of Acts 25:22, in that there Agrippa had often wished in the past (iterative imperfect) that he might hear Paul speak, without having his wish granted, although now at last, as he indulged the wish for the last time, it was to be granted. We have no way of knowing whether Paul's wish, not specifically having been indulged in the past, but now being expressed (constative aorist) for only one time, was ever granted. This is the force of the contingent particle ἄν.

In the potential (voluntative) imperfect in Rom.9:3 we have ηὐχόμην "where Paul almost expressed a moral wrong. He holds himself back from the abyss by the tense. He does not say εὔχομαι (cf.2 Cor.13:7), nor εὐξαίμην ἄν (Ac.26:29)." (Robertson, *Grammar*, 886).

With his usual display of class, Paul added the last clause. There was only one way in which he was less fortunate than his audience. He was in chains; they were not. But he was free and they were in bondage to sin. Thus his position was infinitely superior to theirs and he wished fervently and yet, realistically, with great doubt, that they might all be saved. It is the same thought that Jesus expressed to the women in Jerusalem (Luke 23:27-31).

The interview was over. Agrippa and his party rose to leave. What momentous issues had been decided? Would Agrippa, Bernice, Festus and the others ever be the same again? One thing was unchanged. Paul future was secure in the hands of our sovereign Lord. No one could change that. He would indeed go to Rome, there to preach for two years and then go to his reward.

*Verse 30 - "And when he had thus spoken, the king rose up, and the governor, and Bernice, and they that sat with them, . . . "*

'Ανέστη τε ὁ βασιλεὺς καὶ ὁ ἡγεμὼν ἥ τε Βερνίκη καὶ οἱ συνκαθήμενοι αὐτοῖς,

'Ανέστη (3d.per.sing.2d.aor.act.ind.of ἀνίστημι, constative) 789.
τε (correlative particle) 1408.
ὁ (nom.sing.masc.of the article in agreement with βασιλεὺς) 9.
βασιλεὺς (nom.sing.masc.of βασιλεύς, subject of'Ανέστη) 31.
καὶ (adjunctive conjunction joining nouns) 14.
ὁ (nom.sing.masc.of the article in agreement with ἡγεμὼν) 9.
ἡγεμὼν (nom.sing.masc.of ἡγεμών, subject of'Ανέστη) 160.
ἥ (nom.sing.fem.of the article in agreement with Βερνίκη) 9.
τε (correlative particle) 1408.
Βερνίκη (nom.sing.fem.of Βερνίκη, subject of'Ανέστη) 3638.
καὶ (adjunctive conjunction joining substantives) 14.
οἱ (nom.pl.masc.of the article in agreement with συγκαθήμενοι) 9.
συγκαθήμενοι (pres.mid.part.nom.pl.masc.of συγκάθημαι, substantival, subject of'Ανέστη) 2812.
αὐτοῖς (instru.pl.masc.of αὐτός, association after σύν in composition) 16.

*Translation -* "And both the king and the governor and Bernice and those sitting with them arose, . . . "

**Comment:** Note the τε. . . καὶ . . . τε . . . καὶ sequence. Agrippa, Festus, Bernice and the distinguished city officials (Acts 25:23) arose to leave.

*Verse 31 -* "And when they were gone aside, they talked with themselves, saying, This man doeth nothing worthy of death, or of bonds."

καὶ ἀναχωρήσαντες ἐλάλουν πρὸς ἀλλήλους λέγοντες ὅτι Οὐδὲν θανάτου ἥ δεσμῶν ἄξιον πράσσει ὁ ἄνθρωπος οὗτος.

καὶ (adjunctive conjunction joining verbs) 14.
ἀναχωρήσαντες (aor.act.part.nom.pl.masc.of ἀναχωρέω, adverbial, temporal) 200.
ἐλάλουν (3d.per.pl.imp.act.ind.of λαλέω, inchoative) 815.
πρὸς (preposition with the accusative of extent, after a verb of speaking) 197.
ἀλλήλους (acc.pl.masc.of ἀλλήλων, extent, after a verb of speaking) 1487.
λέγοντες (pres.act.part.nom.pl.masc.of λέγω, adverbial, coincident) 66.
ὅτι (recitative) 211.
Οὐδὲν (acc.sing.neut.of οὐδείς, direct object of πράσσει) 446.
θανάτου (abl.sing.masc.of θάνατος, comparison) 381.
ἥ (disjunctive) 465.
δεσμῶν (abl.pl.masc.of δεσμός, comparison) 2229.
ἄξιον (acc.sing.neut.of ἄξιος, pred.adjective , in agreement with Οὐδὲν) 285.
πράσσει (3d.per.sing.pres.act.ind.of πράσσω, progressive duration, retroactive) 1943.

ὁ (nom.sing.masc.of the article in agreement with ἄνθρωπος) 9.
ἄνθρωπος (nom.sing.masc.of ἄνθρωπος, subject of πράσσει) 341.
οὗτος (nom.sing.masc.of οὗτος, in agreement with ἄνθρωπος) 93.

*Translation - "And when they had stepped aside they began to confer with one another, saying, 'This man has been doing nothing worthy of death or imprisonment.' "*

**Comment:** The king, Festus and their party withdrew to some spot where they could confer without being interrupted and began (inchoative ἐλάλουν) to discuss what Paul had said. It would be interesting to know how Festus and Agrippa conducted themselves in this conversation. Festus may have still been upset and the king may have been pondering Paul's logic. At any rate they reached the conclusion of the text. However much Paul may have offended the Jews on theological grounds, he had broken no Roman law, and could not be held. However, King Agrippa imagined some legal technicality that stood in the way of Paul's release. One wonders what? Neither Felix nor Festus had handed down a final decision. Festus had not yet written to Nero. He did not know what to write. That was the reason for the hearing before Agrippa (Acts 25:24-27). Nobody in Rome was aware of the events in Palestine, at least not in any official capacity. There seems to have been no legal reason why Paul could not have been released at the close of the hearing to go his way.

One thing worked in Paul's favor, as a blessing in disguise. He got a free trip to Rome, the city which he had long desired to visit and to the church he had long desired to meet (Romans 1:10-13). He had often planned to visit Rome, but always before he had been hindered. Now, in God's good time he was to go - and preach - and die.

Pentecost fell on May 28 in the year A.D.57. The events from the day that Paul and his party reached Jerusalem (Acts 21:17) to the hearing before Felix in Caesarea (Acts 24:23) required twelve days. Two years later Festus became the procurator (Acts 24:27). Paul spent some time under house arrest in Caesarea before he was brought before Agrippa, after which he began his voyage to Rome. The time from the accession of Festus to the shipwreck on Malta was about five months. Thus they landed on Malta in November, in the year 59. They remained on the island three months (Acts 28:11) and embarked for Rome in February in the year 60. Paul lived in his own hired house in Rome for two years (Acts 28:30), which brings us to the year 62. The remainder of his days were spent in a Roman prison. (Sir William Ramsay, *St. Paul the Traveller and the Roman Citizen*, 289-303, *et passim*). There is a two year discrepancy between Ramsay's figures and those of the Scofield Reference Bible, which add to years to Ramsay's dates.

*Verse 32 - "Then said Agrippa unto Festus, This man might have been set at liberty, if he had not appealed unto Caesar."*

Ἀγρίππας δὲ τῷ Φήστῳ ἔφη, Ἀπολελύσθαι ἐδύνατο ὁ ἄνθρωπος οὗτος εἰ μὴ ἐπεκέκλητο Καίσαρα.

'Αγρίππας (nom.sing.masc.of 'Αγρίππας, subject of ἔφη) 136C.

δὲ (adversative conjunction) 11.

τῷ (dat.sing.masc.of the article in agreement with Φήστῳ) 9.

Φήστῳ (dat.sing.masc.of Φῆστος, indirect object of ἔφη) 3633.

ἔφη (3d.per.sing.aor.act.ind.of φημί, constative) 354.

ἀπολελύσθαι (perf.pass.inf.of ἀπολύω, completes ἐδύνατο) 92.

ἐδύνατο (3d.per.sing.imp.mid.ind.of δύναμαι, customary) 289.

ὁ (nom.sing.masc.of the article in agreement with ἄνθρωπος) 9.

ἄνθρωπος (nom.sing.masc.of ἄνθρωπος, subject of ἐδύνατο) 341.

οὗτος (nom.sing.masc.of οὗτος, in agreement with ἄνθρωπος) 93.

εἰ (conditional particle in a second-class condition) 337.

μὴ (negative conjunction with the indicative) 87.

ἐπεκέκλητο (3d.per.sing.pluperf.mid.ind.of ἐπικαλέω, in a second-class condition) 884.

Καίσαρα (dat.sing.masc.of Καισαρί, indirect object of ἐπεκέκλητο) 1418.

*Translation - "But Agrippa said to Festus, 'This man might have been released if he had not appealed to Caesar.' "*

**Comment:** The implication in Agrippa's statement is that Paul might have been set free by Festus on the previous occasion (Acts 25:9-11) if he had not appealed to Caesar. There is implied antecedence in the perfect infinitive which has extensive force. Thus Agrippa was criticizing Festus for not releasing Paul then, for Paul made no appeal to Nero until Festus asked him if he was willing to go back to Jerusalem. The second-class condition has the pluperfect in the protasis. "If he had not, at that former time, appealed to Caesar, he could have, at that time, been released." It is evident that Festus failed in his attempt to find in Paul some legal ground for sending him on appeal to Rome. If it was illogical to send a prisoner to Rome without preferring charges against him (Acts 25:27) before Paul's speech before Agrippa, was it more logical, now that the speech was over and Paul was still without guilt (Acts 26:31)? But Festus sent him to Rome anyway, because God had already decreed and announced to Paul that Paul would visit Rome to preach the gospel in the capital city of the Empire (Acts 23:11).

# Paul Sails for Rome

*(Acts 27:1-12)*

*Acts 27:1 - "And when it was determined that we should sail into Italy, they delivered Paul and certain other prisoners unto one named Julius, a centurion of Augustus' band."*

Ὡς δὲ ἐκρίθη τοῦ ἀποπλεῖν ἡμᾶς εἰς τὴν Ἰταλίαν παρεδίδουν τόν τε Παῦλον καὶ τινας ἑτέρους δεσμώτας ἑκατοντάρχῃ ὀνόματι Ἰουλίῳ σπείρης Σεβαστῆς.

Ὡς (conjunction introducing a definite temporal clause) 128.
δὲ (continuative conjunction) 11.
ἐκρίθη (3d.per.sing.aor.pass.ind.of κρίνω, culminative) 531.
τοῦ (gen.sing.neut.of the article in agreement with ἀποπλεῖν) 9.
ἀποπλεῖν (pres.act.inf.of ἀποπλέω, noun use, subject of ἐκρίθη) 3275.

ἡμᾶς (acc.pl.masc.of ἐγώ, general reference) 123.
εἰς (preposition with the accusative of extent) 140.
τὴν (acc.sing.fem.of the article in agreement with Ἰταλίαν) 9.
Ἰταλίαν (acc.sing.fem.of Ἰταλία, extent) 3432.
παραδίδουν (3d.per.pl.imp.act.ind.of παραδίδωμι) 368.
τὸν (acc.sing.masc.of the article in agreement with Παῦλον) 9.
τε (correlative particle) 1408.
Παῦλον (acc.sing.masc.of Παῦλος, direct object of παρεδίδουν) 3284.
καὶ (adjunctive conjunction joining nouns) 14.
τινας (acc.pl.masc.of τις, indefinite pronoun, in agreement with δεσμώτας) 486.
ἐτέρους (acc.pl.masc.of ἕτερος, in agreement with δεσμώτας) 605.

#3672 δεσμώτας (acc.pl.masc.of δεσμώτης, direct object of παρεδίδουν).

prisoner - Acts 27:1,42.

*Meaning: Cf.* δεσμεύω (#1431), δέσμιος (#1624), δεσμοφύλαξ (#3375), δεσμός (#2229), δεσμωτήριον (#905). Hence, one who is bound. A prisoner. Paul and his companions on the ship to Rome - Acts 27:1,42.

ἑκατοντάρχῃ (dat.sing.masc.of ἑκατόνταρχος, indirect object of παρεδίδουν) 3210.
ὀνόματι (dat.sing.neut.of ὄνομα, possession) 108.

#3673 Ἰουλίῳ (dat.sing.masc.of Ἰούλιος, possession).

Julius - Acts 27:1,3.

*Meaning:* A Roman centurion - Acts 27:1,3.

σπείρης (gen.sing.fem.of σπεῖρα, description) 1635.
Σεβαστῆς (gen.sing.fem.of Σεβαστός, description) 3644.

*Translation - "And when it was decided that we should sail to Italy, they delivered both Paul and some other prisoners to a centurion named Julius of the Imperial regiment."*

**Comment:** Ὡς introduces the definite temporal clause. Note ἡμᾶς, the first personal pronoun, which indicates that Luke sailed with Paul. The articular infinitive, though genitive in case (τοῦ) is nevertheless the subject of the verb ἐκρίθη. Though the normal use of τοῦ with the infinitive in the New Testament is final, not all examples are purpose or result. Only Luke and Paul use τοῦ with the infinitive frequently. Robertson counts 24 in the Gospel of Luke, 24 in Acts and 13 in the Pauline epistles. This is five-sixths of the examples in the N.T.

of which Luke has produced two-thirds of the total. Matthew has seven. There are none in John's writings. Robertson calls it "a curious construction" and cites Luke 17:1; Acts 10:25 and Acts 27:1. (Robertson, *Grammar,* 1067, 1068).

Paul and the other prisoners were committed to the safe keeping of Julius, a captain in the Imperial Regiment, which was noted for its efficiency and bravery. Paul's journey to Rome, one that he had long desired, was about to begin (Romans 1:10,11).

*Verse 2 - "And entering into a ship of Adramyttium, we launched, meaning to sail by the coasts of Asia, one Aristarchus, a Macedonian of Thessalonica, being with us."*

ἐπιβάντες δὲ πλοίῳ Ἀδραμυττηνῷ μέλλοντι πλεῖν εἰς τοὺς κατὰ τὴν Ἀσίαν τόπους ἀνήχθημεν, ὄντος σὺν ἡμῖν Ἀριστάρχου Μακεδόνος Θεσσαλονικέως.

ἐπιβάντες (aor.act.part.nom.pl.masc.of ἐπιβαίνω, adverbial, temporal) 1346.

δὲ (continuative conjunction) 11.

πλοίῳ (loc.sing.neut.of πλοῖον, place) 400.

#3674 Ἀδραμυττηνῷ (loc.sing.neut.of Ἀδραμυττηνός, apposition).

Adramyttiym - Acts 27:2.

*Meaning:* The ship in which Paul sailed to Rome - Acts 27:2.

μέλλοντι (pres.act.part.dat.sing.masc.of μέλλω, adjectival, restrictive, in agreement with πλοίῳ) 206.

πλεῖν (pres.act.inf.of πλέω, complementary) 2209.

εἰς (preposition with the accusative of extent) 140.

τοὺς (acc.pl.masc.of the article in agreement with τόπους) 9.

κατὰ (preposition with the accusative, distributive) 98.

τὴν (acc.sing.fem.of the article in agreement with Ἀσίαν) 9.

Ἀσίαν (acc.sing.fem.of Ἀσία, in agreement with τόπους) 2968

τόπους (acc.pl.masc.of τόπος, distributive) 1019.

ἀνήχθημεν (1st.per.pl.1st.aor.pass.ind.of ἀνάγω, ingressive) 329.

ὄντος (pres.part.gen.sing.masc.of εἰμί, genitive absolute) 86.

σὺν (preposition with the instrumental of association) 1542.

ἡμῖν (instru.pl.masc.of ἐγώ, association) 123.

Ἀριστάρχου (gen.sing.masc.of Ἀρίσταρχος, genitive absolute) 3485.

Μακεδόνος (gen.sing.masc.of Μακεδών, apposition) 3359.

Θεσσαλονικέως (abl.sing.masc.of θεσσαλονικεύς, source) 3504.

*Translation - "And when we had boarded an Adramyttian ship bound for the ports along the Asian coast, we put to sea, with Aristarchus, the Macedonian from Thessalonica with us."*

**Comment:** The participle μέλλοντι defines the ship. She was bound for ports along the coast of Asia Minor to her home port. Adramyttium is a port city on the northeastern coast of the Aegean Sea, near Troas, a short distance south of the point where the Hellespont pours into the Aegean. Thus the ship was to sail north along the Palestinian and Syrian coasts, perhaps to Antioch and westward along the southern coast of Cilicia, and Pamphylia to Myra, a coastal town of Lycia. From that point the course would be to the northwest, threading the sinuosities of the coast line, beyond Hallicarnassis to Ephesus and beyond.

"In the harbour o Caesareia there was no convenient ship about to sail for Rome. . . . Communication direct with Rome might be found in some of the great Asian harbours, or, failing any suitable ship in the late season, the prisoners might be taken (like Ignatius half a century later) by Troas and Philippi and the land road to Dyrrachium, and thence to Brundisium and Rome.

"The direct run from Lycia to the Syrian coast was often made, but it is hardly possible that a direct run from Syria back to Myra was ever attempted by ancient ships. They never ventured on such a run except when a steady wind was blowing which could be trusted to last. But westerly breezes blow with great steadiness through the summer months in the Levant; and it is certain that ancient ships westward bound sailed east of Cyprus, as the Adramyttian ship now did. Luke explains that they sailed on this side of Cyprus; and he must, therefore, have expected to take the other side. Now, a sailor or a person accustomed to these seas would not have thought of making any explanation, for the course of the ship was the normal one. But Luke had come to Sidon from Myra by the west side of Cyprus, and he, therefore, was impressed with the difference and (contrary to his usual custom) he gives a formal explanation; and his explanation stamps him as a stranger to these seas." (Sir William Ramsay, *St. Paul the Traveller and the Roman Citizen*, 316,317).

Aristarchus, Paul's old friend from Thessalonica (#3485) who had been involved in the Ephesian riot and was also with Paul in Athens was on board, as also was Luke as is indicated by the first person in ἀνήχθημεν.

*Verse 3 - "And the next day we touched at Sidon and Julius courteously entreated Paul, and gave him liberty to go unto his friends to refresh himself."*

τῇ τε ἑτέρᾳ κατήχθημεν εἰς Σιδῶνα, φιλανθρώπως τε ὁ Ἰούλιος τῷ Παύλῳ χρησάμενος ἐπέτρεφεν πρὸς τοὺς φίλους πορευθέντι ἐπιμελείας τυχεῖν.

τῇ (loc.sing.fem.of the article in agreement with ἑτέρᾳ) 9.
τε (continuative particle) 1408.
ἑτέρᾳ (loc.sing.fem.of ἕτερος, time point) 605.
κατήχθημεν (1st.per.pl.aor.pass.ind.of κατάγω, constative) 2056.
εἰς (preposition with the accusative of extent) 140.
Σιδῶνα (acc.sing.masc.of Σιδῶν, extent) 940.

#3675 φιλανθρώπως (adverbial).

courteously - Acts 27:3.

*Meaning:* Cf. φίλος (#932) and ἄνθρωπος (#341). Hence, in a friendly way to man; an adverb. Courteously. With reference to Julius' treatment of Paul - Acts 27:3.

τε (continuative particle) 1408.

ὁ (nom.sing.masc.of the article in agreement with Ἰούλιος) 9.

Ἰούλιος (nom.sing.masc.of Ἰούλιος, subject of ἐπέτρεφεν) 3673.

τῷ (dat.sing.masc.of the article in agreement with Παύλῳ) 9.

Παύλῳ (dat.sing.masc.of Παῦλος, personal advantage) 3284.

χρησάμενος (aor.mid.part.nom.sing.masc.of χράω, adverbial, causal) 2447.

ἐπέτρεφεν (3d.per.sing.aor.act.ind.of ἐπιτρέπω, constative) 747.

πρὸς (preposition with the accusative of extent) 197.

τοὺς (acc.pl.masc.of the article in agreement with φίλους) 9.

φίλους (acc.pl.masc.of φίλος, extent) 932.

πορευθέντι (aor.mid.part.dat.sing.masc.of πορεύομαι, in agreement with Παύλῳ, adverbial, temporal) 170.

#3676 ἐπιμελείας (gen.sing.fem.of ἐπιμέλεια, objective genitive).

refresh self - Acts 27:3.

*Meaning:* Cf.**ἐπιμελέομαι** (#2432); ἐπιμελῶς (#2541). Hence, care, attention. With reference to personal help, perhaps physical as well as psychological, which Paul received at Sidon - Acts 27:3.

τυχεῖν (2d.aor.inf.of τυγχάνω, complementary) 2699.

*Translation - "And the next day we put in at Sidon and because Julius was friendly with Paul he allowed him to go to his friends to receive treatment."*

**Comment:** Paul had been in prison for more than two years since his arrest by Claudius Lysias. His personal grooming needed attention as well as his personal health. A victim of ophthalmia he may have needed medical attention for his eyes. On their first day out of Caesarea they reached Sidon, 75 miles up the coast. Thanks to Julius Paul was permitted to go to shore.

*Verse 4 - "And when we had launched from thence we sailed under Cyprus, because the winds were contrary."*

κἀκεῖθεν ἀναχθέντες ὑπεπλεύσαμεν τὴν Κύπρον διὰ τὸ τοὺς ἀνέμους εἶναι ἐναντίους,

κἀκεῖθεν (local and temporal adverb) 2348.

ἀναχθέντες (aor.pass.part.nom.pl.masc.of ἀνάγω, adverbial, temporal) 329.

#3677 ὑπεπλεύσαμεν (1st.per.pl.aor.act.ind.of ὑποπλέω, ingressive).

sail under - Acts 27:4,7.

*Meaning:* A combination of ὑπό (#117) and πλέω (#2209). Hence, to sail under. In nautical language to sail to the side of - followed by the accusative, τὴν

Κύπρον - Acts 27:4; τὴν Κρήτην - Acts 27:7.

τὴν (acc.sing.fem.of the article in agreement with Κύπρον) 9.
Κύπρον (acc.sing.fem.of Κύπρος, extent) 3238.
διά (preposition with the accusative, cause) 118.
τὸ (acc.sing.neut.of the article, in agreement with εἶναι, cause) 9.
τοὺς (acc.pl.masc.of the article in agreement with ἀνέμους) 9.
ἀνέμους (acc.pl.masc.of ἄνεμος, general reference) 698.
εἶναι (pres.inf.of εἰμί, acc.sing.neut., cause) 86.
ἐναντίους (acc.pl.masc.of ἐναντίος, in agreement with ἀνέμους) 1128.

*Translation - "And from there, we put to sea and sailed. east of Cyprus because
the winds were against us."*

**Comment:** The course which the ship captain took out of Sidon for ports along
the coast of Asia Minor to the west was the normal one for the last fall months,
as strong westerly winds are common. As Ramsay points out (p.111) it is strange
that Luke should have mentioned the fact, except for the fact that he was
unfamiliar with the sailing conditions in that part of the Mediterranean at that
season. They could not have taken a direct course to the west from Sidon, due to
the winds which were blowing dead against them. Thus they turned to the north
and skirted Cyprus on the east (lee) side, thus to take advantage of the protection
which the Cyprian land mass provided. This explains why they came to Cilician
and Pamphylian waters.

*Verse 5 - "And when we had sailed over the sea of Cilicia and Pamphylia, we
came to Myra, a city of Lycia."*

τό τε πέλαγος τὸ κατὰ τὴν Κιλικίαν καὶ Παμφυλίαν διαπλεύσαντες
κατήλθομεν εἰς Μύρα τῆς Λυκίας.

τό (acc.sing.neut.of the article in agreement with πέλαγος) 9.
τε (continuative particle) 1408.
πέλαγος (acc.sing.neut.of πέλαγος, direct object of διαπλεύσαντες) 1253.
τὸ (acc.sing.neut.of the article in agreement with πέλαγος) 9.
κατά (preposition with the accusative, "down along" ) 98.
τὴν (acc.sing.fem.of the article in agreement with Κιλικίαν) 9.
Κιλικίαν (acc.sing.fem.of Κιλικία, "down along") 3092.
καὶ (adjunctive conjunction joining nouns) 14.
Παμφυλίαν (acc.sing.fem.of Παμφυλία, "down along" ) 2972.

#3678 διαπλεύσαντες (aor.act.part.nom.pl.masc.of διαπλέω, adverbial,
temporal).

sail over - Acts 27:5.

*Meaning:* A combination of διά (#118) and πλέω (#2209). Hence, to sail
through or across - Acts 27:5.

κατῆλθομεν (1st.per.pl.aor.mid.ind.of κατέρχομαι, constative) 2037.
εἰς (preposition with the accusative of extent) 140.

**#3679** Μύρα (acc.sing.neut.of Μύρα, extent).

Myra - Acts 27:5.

*Meaning:* A city, two and one half miles    inland, in the maritime region of Asia
Minor of Lycia - Acts 27:5.

τῆς (gen.sing.fem.of the article in agreement with Λυκίας) 9.

**#3680** Λυκίας (gen.sing.fem.of Λυκία, description).

Lycia - Acts 27:5.

*Meaning:* A maritime region of Asia Minor, west of Pamphylia; southeast of
Karia, on the coast - Acts 27:5.

*Translation - "And after we had sailed across the sea down along the coasts of
Cilicia and Pamphylia we arrived at Myra of Lycia."*

**Comment:** Rounding Cyprus on the northeast corner of the island they sailed
north and west into the deep water (πέλαγος) off the coasts of Cilicia and
Pamphylia. The distance from the northwest tip of Cyprus to Myra, as the crow
flies is about one hundred seventy-five miles. They probably sailed further than
that since they did not venture far from the coast line, as they tacked against the
westerly winds. The Pamphylian coast line veers slightly to the northwest, and,
at the Lycian border turns sharply south before turning west again to Myra.
Consult the map. Ancient Myra was near the modern Turkish city, Kas.
    Since the Adramyttian ship was bound for her home port in the northeastern
Aegean Sea it was necessary for Julius to find another ship for the remainder of
the voyage to Italy.

*Verse 6 - "And there the centurion found a ship of Alexandria sailing into Italy;
and he put us therein."*

κἀκεῖ εὑρὼν ὁ ἑκατοντάρχης πλοῖον Ἀλεξανδρῖνον πλέον εἰς τὴν Ἰταλίαν
ἐνεβίβασεν ἡμᾶς εἰς αὐτό.

κἀκεῖ (continuative conjunction and local adverb, crasis) 204.
εὑρὼν (aor.act.part.nom.sing.masc.of εὑρίσκω, adverbial, temporal/causal)
79.
ὁ (nom.sing.masc.of the article in agreement with ἑκατοντάρχης) 9.
ἑκατοντάρχης (nom.sing.masc.of ἑκατοντάρχης, subject of ἐνεβίβασεν)
3210.
πλοῖον (acc.sing.neut.of πλοῖον, direct object of εὑρὼν) 400.

**#3681** 'Αλεξανδρῖνον (acc.sing.neut.of 'Αλεξανδρινός, in agreement with πλοῖον).

Alexandrian - Acts 27:6; 28:11.

*Meaning:* Alexandrian; pertaining to Alexandria - Acts 27:6; 28:11.

πλέον (pres.act.part.acc.sing.neut.of πλέω, adjectival, restrictive, in agreement with πλοῖον) 2209.
εἰς (preposition with the accusative of extent) 140.
τὴν (acc.sing.fem.of the article in agreement with 'Ιταλίαν) 9.
'Ιταλίαν (acc.sing.fem.of 'Ιταλία, extent) 3432.

**#3682** ἐνεβίβασεν (3d.per.sing.aor.act.ind.of ἐμβιβάζω, constative).

put - Acts 27:6.

*Meaning:* A combination of ἐν (#80) and βιβάζω - "cause to go." Hence, cause to go in; put in or on. Followed by a direct object and εἰς with the accusative of extent - Acts 27:6.

ἡμᾶς (acc.pl.masc.of ἐγώ, direct object of ἐνεβίβασεν) 123.
εἰς (preposition with the accusative of extent) 140.
αὐτό (acc.sing.neut.of αὐτός, extent) 16.

*Translation - "And there when the centurion had found an Alexandrian ship bound for Italy he put us aboard her."*

**Comment:** εὑρων is causal and temporal. The participle πλέον is adjectival. There may have been other ships with an Alexandrian registry, but the ship of our verse was the one that was bound for Italy. She carried a cargo of wheat (Acts 27:38). Apparently she was a larger vessel, able to navigate amid the storms of the open sea. The voyage from Myra to the western end of the island of Crete covered a distance of 330 nautical miles. An additional 450 miles, in the waters of the southern Adriatic and Mediterranean Seas, lay between Crete and Sicily. This leg of the voyage would be made without the protection of a friendly coastline to which they might turn in the event of stormy weather and unmanageable seas. They sailed much further than that, since they sailed westward on the south side of Crete and were driven aimlessly about in the Adriatic before being wrecked in the surf on Malta, sixty miles south of Sicily.

*Verse 7 - "And when we had sailed slowly many days, and scarce were come over against Cnidus, the wind not suffering us, we sailed under Crete, over against Salmone."*

ἐν ἱκαναῖς δὲ ἡμέραις βραδυπλοοῦντες καὶ μόλις γενόμενοι κατὰ τὴν Κνίδον, μὴ προσεῶντος ἡμᾶς τοῦ ἀνέμου, ὑπεπλεύσαμεν τὴν Κρήτην κατὰ Σαλμώνην,

ἐν (preposition with the locative, in a time expression) 80.

ἱκαναῖς (loc.pl.fem.of ἱκανός, in agreement with ἡμέραις) 304.
δὲ (adversative conjunction) 11.
ἡμέραις (loc.pl.fem.of ἡμέρα, time expression) 135.

#3683 βραδυπλοοῦντες (pres.act.part.nom.pl.masc.of βραδυλπλοέω, adverbial, temporal).

sail slowly - Acts 27:7.

*Meaning:* A combination of βραδύς (#2905) and πλέω (#2209). Hence, to sail slowly - Acts 27:7.

καὶ (adversative conjunction) 14.
μόλις (adverbial) 2342.
γενόμενοι (aor.part.nom.pl.masc.of γίνομαι, adverbial, causal) 113.
κατὰ (preposition with the accusative, "down along.") 98.
τὴν (acc.sing.fem.of the article in agreement with Κνίδον) 9.

#3684 κνίδον (acc.sing.fem.of Κνίδος, distributive).

Cnidus - Acts 27:7.

*Meaning:* Cnidus or Gnidus (now called Cape Crio). Also a city of the same name, on the coast of Caria - Acts 27:7. It is located at the point of a narrow peninsula directly south of Halicarnassus.

μὴ (negative conjunction with the participle) 87.

#3685 προσεῶντος (pres.part.gen.sing.masc.of προσεάω, adverbial, causal).

suffer - Acts 27:7.

*Meaning:* A combination of πρός (#197) and ἐάω (#1521). Hence, to allow; permit. That which is permitted is supplied by the context in Acts 27:7.

ἡμᾶς (acc.pl.masc.of ἐγώ, direct object of προσεῶντος) 123.
τοῦ (gen.sing.masc.of the article in agreement with ἀνέμου) 9.
ἀνέμου (gen.sing.masc.of ἄνεμος, genitive absolute) 698.
ὑπεπλεύσαμεν (1st.per.pl.aor.act.ind.of ὑποπλέω, ingressive) 3677.
τὴν (acc.sing.fem.of the article in agreement with Κρήτην) 9.

#3686 Κρήτην (acc.sing.fem.of Κρήτη, place after ὑπό in composition).

Crete - Acts 27:7,12,13,21; Titus 1:5.

*Meaning:* The largest and most fertile island in the Mediterranean and Aegean Seas. Now called both Crete and Candia - Acts 27:7,12,13,21; Titus 1:5.

κατὰ (preposition with the accusative - "down along") 98.

#3687 Σαλμώνην (acc.sing.fem.of Σαλμώνη, place).

Salmone - Acts 27:7.

*Meaning:* An eastern (partly northern) promontory of Crete, opposite Cnidus and Rhodes - Acts 27:7.

*Translation - "But because for many days we sailed slowly and scarcely reached Cnidus, because the wind was against us, we sailed under Crete off Cape Salmone.*

**Comment:** The participles are causal. Adverse westerly winds, which are characteristic of the fall season in those waters meant very slow progress. Luke, the careful historian, apparently had not kept a record of the time, and did not know precisely how many days were spent in the trip from Myra to Cnidus, but he remembered that it was too long. The captain chose the protection of the lee side of Crete with its friendly southern coast line. ὑποπλέω (#3677) means "under" in nautical language; *i.e.* in the shelter of a body of land, where the winds and the tides sweep in toward the land. It should not be interpreted as the south side necessarily, although in this case it was. The distance from Cnidus to Cape Salmone is about 100 nautical miles.

*Verse 8 - "And hardly passing it, came unto a place which is called The Fair Havens; nigh whereunto was the city of Lasea."*

μόλις τε παραλεγόμενοι αὐτὴν ἤλθομεν εἰς τόπον τινὰ καλούμενον Καλοὺς Λιμένας, ᾧ ἐγγὺς πόλις ἦν Λασαία.

μόλις (adverbial) 2342.
τε (continuative particle) 1408.

**#3688** παραλεγόμενοι (pres.mid.part.nom.pl.masc.of παραλέγω, adverbial, temporal).

pass - Acts 27:8.
sail by - Acts 27:13.

*Meaning:* A combination of παρά (#154) and λέγω - "to lay" hence, to lie alongside; coast along; to pass or sail by - Acts 27:8,13.

αὐτὴν (acc.sing.fem.of αὐτός, direct object of παραλεγόμενοι) 16.
ἤλθομεν (1st.per.pl.aor.mid.ind.of ἔρχομαι, ingressive) 146.
εἰς (preposition with the accusative of extent) 140.
τόπον (acc.sing.masc.of τόπος, extent) 1019.
τινὰ (acc.sing.masc.of τις, indefinite pronoun, in agreement with τόπον) 486.
καλούμενον (pres.pass.part.acc.sing.masc.of καλέω, adjectival, restrictive, in agreement with τόπον) 107.
Καλοὺς (acc.pl.masc.of καλός, in agreement with Λιμένας) 296.

**#3689** Λιμένας (acc.pl.masc.of λιμήν, predicate accusative).

haven - Acts 27:8,12.

*Meaning: Cf.* λίμην (#2041). A placid body of water; a harbor; a haven - Acts 27:8,12.

ᾧ (dat.sing.masc.of ὅς, relative pronoun, reference) 65.

ἐγγὺς (nom.sing.fem.of ἐγγύς, predicate adjective) 1512.

πόλις (nom.sing.fem.of πόλις, subject of ἦν) 243.

ἦν (3d.per.sing.imp.ind.of εἰμί, progressive description) 86.

**#3690** Λασαία (nom.sing.fem.of Λασαία, apposition).

Lasea - Acts 27:8.

*Meaning:* A city on the island of Crete, the site of which was discovered five miles east of Fair Havens, in 1856. Not mentioned by ancient geographers but mentioned by Luke in Acts 27:8.

*Translation - "And after passing it by with difficulty we came to a certain place called Fair Havens, near to which was the city of Lasea."*

**Comment:** ἐγγύς here with the dative in ᾧ. *Cf.* Acts 9:38; 27:8; Luke 19:11; Acts 1:12. (Robertson, *Grammar*, 640).

As winter approached with weather conditions becoming more uncertain the odds for a continued safe passage to Italy were smaller, as we see as the story continues in

*Verse 9 - "Now when much time was spent, and when sailing was now dangerous, because the fast was now already past, Paul admonished them, . . . "*

Ἱκανοῦ δὲ χρόνου διαγενομένου καὶ ὄντος ἤδη ἐπισφαλοῦς τοῦ πλοὸς διὰ τὸ καὶ τὴν νηστείαν ἤδη παρεληλυθέναι, παρῄνει ὁ Παῦλος

Ἱκανοῦ (gen.sing.masc.of ἱκανός, in agreement with χρόνου) 304.

δὲ (adversative conjunction) 11.

χρόνου (gen.sing.masc.of χρόνος, genitive absolute) 168.

διαγενομένου (aor.part.gen.sing.masc.of διαγίνομαι, genitive absolute) 2887.

καὶ (adjunctive conjunction joining genitive absolutes) 14.

ὄντος (pres.part.gen.sing.masc.of εἰμί, genitive absolute) 86.

ἤδη (temporal adverb) 291.

**#3691** ἐπισφαλοῦς (gen.sing.masc.of ἐπισφαλής, predicate adjective).

dangerous - Acts 27:9.

*Meaning:* ἐπί (#47) and σφάλλω - "to cause to fall." Hence, dangerous; prone to fall. With πλοός - Acts 27:9.

τοῦ (gen.sing.masc.of the article in agreement with πλοὸς) 9.

πλοὸς (gen.sing.masc.of πλοός, genitive absolute) 3545.

διὰ (preposition with the accusative, cause) 118.

καὶ (adjunctive conjunction) 14.

τὴν (acc.sing.fem.of the article in agreement with νηστείαν) 9.

νηστείαν (acc.sing.fem.of νηστεία, general reference) 1239.

ἤδη (temporal adverb) 291.

παρεληλυθέναι (2d.perf.mid.inf.of παρέρχομαι, noun use, in a causal clause) 467.

#3692 παρῄνει (3d.per.sing.imp.act.ind.of παραινέω, inchoative).

admonish - Acts 27:9.
exhort - Acts 27:22.

*Meaning:* A combination of παρά (#154) and αἰνέω (#1881). To admonish; to exhort. Followed by the object infinitive in indirect discourse in Acts 27:22; followed by λέγων and direct discourse in Acts 27:9.

ὁ (nom.sing.masc.of the article in agreement with Παῦλος) 9.
Παῦλος (nom.sing.masc.of Παῦλος, subject of παρῄνει) 3284.

*Translation - "But since much time had elapsed and they already faced a dangerous voyage and because the fast had been completed, Paul began to warn them, . . . "*

**Comment:** Two genitive absolutes, both of which are causal, the first antecedent and the second coincident to the main verb, παρῄνει reveal the order of events. (1) Much time had elapsed; it was late in the fall season. (2) The voyage westward into the Mediterranean toward Sicily was before them, and it was dangerous, since the season for storms at sea was upon them. (3) Paul began to warn them. The autumn fast was over. διά with the articular infinitive in the 2d.perfect tense. "Because the fast was over." Meyer thinks that the fast was a Jewish custom in connection with the great day of atonement which occurred on the 10th day of Tisri. *Cf.* Lev.16:29ff; 23:26ff. If so, the date was after October 17th. The year was A.D.60.

*Verse 10 - "And said to them, Sirs, I perceive that this voyage will be with hurt and much damage, not only to the lading and ship, but also of our lives."*

λέγων αὐτοῖς, Ἄνδρες, θεωρῶ ὅτι μετὰ ὕβρεως καὶ πολλῆς ζημίας οὐ μόνον τοῦ φορτίου καὶ τοῦ πλοίου ἀλλὰ καὶ τῶν ψυχῶν ἡμῶν μέλλειν ἔσεσθαι τὸν πλοῦν.

λέγων (pres.act.part.nom.sing.masc.of λέγω, recitative) 66.
αὐτοῖς (dat.pl.masc.of αὐτός, indirect object of λέγων) 16.
Ἄνδρες (voc.pl.masc.of ἀνήρ, address) 63.
θεωρῶ (1st.per.sing.pres.act.ind.of θεωρέω, aoristic) 1667.
ὅτι (conjunction introducing an object infinitive in indirect discourse) 211.
μετὰ (preposition with the genitive of accompaniment) 50.

#3693 ὕβρεως (gen.sing.fem.of ὕβρις, accompaniment).

harm - Acts 27:2.
hurt - Acts 27:10.

reproach - 2 Cor.12:10.

*Meaning: Cf.* ὑπέρ (#545). Hence, properly an injury of a psychological nature caused by insolence, pride, impudence, haughty attitude. Therefore, an affront; an insult - 2 Cor.12:10. trop.injury suffered as a result of a storm at sea - Acts 27:10,21.

καὶ (adjunctive conjunction joining nouns) 14.
πολλῆς (gen.sing.fem.of πολύς, in agreement with ζημίας) 228.

**#3694** ζημίας (gen.sing.fem.of ζημία, accompaniment).

damage - Acts 27:10.
loss - Acts 27:21; Phil.3:7,8.

*Meaning:* loss. Physical loss of a ship and/or its cargo and of human life - Acts 27:10,21. Religious accomplishments and prestige as a result thereof are counted ζημίαν, *i.e.* as a liability - Phil.3:7. All things of earth - physical, mental, etc are loss, in contrast to Christ - Phil.3:8.

οὐ (negative conjunction with the infinitive) 130.
μόνον (acc.sing.neut.of μόνος, adverbial) 339.
τοῦ (gen.sing.masc.of the article in agreement with φορτίου) 9.

**#3695** φορτίου (gen.sing.masc.of φόρτος, description).

lading - Acts 27:10.

*Meaning: Cf.* φέρω (#354). Hence, that which is being carried. Cargo, lading - Acts 27:10.

καὶ (adjunctive conjunction joining nouns) 14.
τοῦ (gen.sing.neut.of the article in agreement with πλοίου) 9.
πλοίου (gen.sing.neut.of πλοῖον, description) 400.
ἀλλὰ (alternative conjunction) 342.
καὶ (adjunctive conjunction joining nouns) 14.
τῶν (gen.pl.fem.of the article in agreement with ψυχῶν) 9.
ψυχῶν (gen.pl.fem.of ψυχή, description) 233.
ἡμῶν (gen.pl.masc.of ἐγώ, possession) 123.
μέλλειν (pres.act.inf.of μέλλω, object infinitive in indirect discourse) 206.
ἔσεσθαι (fut.inf.of εἰμί, completes μέλλειν) 86.
τὸν (acc.sing.masc.of the article, in agreement with πλοῦν) 9.
πλοῦν (acc.sing.masc.of πλοός, general reference) 3545.

*Translation -* "... *saying to them, 'Gentlemen, I foresee that the voyage is going to result in harm and much loss, not only to the cargo and the ship but also to our lives.'* "

**Comment:** θεωρῶ (#1667) here in a slightly different sense than in most usages, where it means physical rather than mental perception. There is nothing to suggest that Paul was speaking from any greater wisdom than that of his own experience as a sea voyager. The stormy season was at hand. Paul had seen the Mediterranean on a rampage before (2 Cor.11:25).

ὅτι here introduces indirect assertion with the infinitive. Blass (*Grammar of New Testament Greek*, 233, as cited in Robertson, *Grammar*, 1036) says that this is "quite irregularly" done but Robertson adds ". . . it is just the classic mingling of two constructions seen in the more usual form in Acts 14:22, where a change is made from the infinitive to ὅτι and δεῖ." It is a mixture of the ὅτι construction in indirect assertion and the infinitive construction (Robertson, *Ibid.*, 1047). Note the genitive after μετά. οὐ μόνον . . . ἀλλὰ καί is regular - "not only . . . but also."

That Paul felt free to offer his advice to the captain indicates that, though technically he was a prisoner, he had a certain degree of prestige among those on board.

However, Paul's advice was rejected as we see in

*Verse 11 - "Nevertheless the centurion believed the master and the owner of the ship, more than these things which were spoken by Paul."*

ὁ δὲ ἑκατοντάρχης τῷ κυβερνήτῃ καὶ τῷ ναυκλήρῳ μᾶλλον ἐπείθετο ἢ τοῖς ὑπὸ Παύλου λεγομένοις.

ὁ (nom.sing.masc.of the article in agreement with ἑκατοντάρχης) 9.
δὲ (adversative conjunction) 11.
ἑκατοντάρχης (nom.sing.masc.of ἑκατοντάρχης, subject of ἐπείθετο) 3210.
τῷ (instru.sing.masc.of the article in agreement with κυβερνήτῃ) 9.

**#3696** κυβερνήτῃ (instru.sing.masc.of κυβερνήτης, means).

master - Acts 27:11.
ship master - Rev.18:17.

*Meaning:* Cf. κυβερνάω - "to steer." Hence, the pilot of a ship - Acts 27:11; Rev.18:17.

καὶ (adjunctive conjunction joining nouns) 14.
τῷ (instru.sing.masc.of the article in agreement with ναυκλήρῳ).

**#3697** ναυκλήρῳ (dat.sing.masc.of ναύκληρος, means).

owner of the ship - Acts 27:11.

*Meaning:* A combination of ναῦς (#3745) and κλῆρος (#1648). Hence, ship owner who has hired out his ship to carry cargo - Acts 27:11.

μᾶλλον (adverbial) 619.
ἐπείθετο (3d.per.sing.imp.mid.ind.of πείθω, inchoative) 1629.
ἢ (disjunctive) 465.
τοῖς (instru.pl.neut. of the article in agreement with λεγομένοις)9.
ὑπὸ (preposition with the ablative of agent) 117.
Παύλου (abl.sing.masc.of Παῦλος, agent) 3284.

λεγομένοις (pres.pass.part.instru.pl.neut.of λέγω, substantival, means) 66.

*Translation - "But the centurion came to be more influenced by the pilot and the owner of the ship than by the things being said by Paul."*

**Comment:** δέ is adversative. Paul, the prisoner, was not rebuked for offering his opinion but his advice was less influential with Julius than that of the pilot and the captain. Note the instrumental of means in the two nouns and the participial substantive λεγομένοις. *Cf.* #465 for other instances of μᾶλλον in the sense of "more than."

The rationale by which the decision to procede was made is explained in

*Verse 12 - "And because the haven was not commodious to winter in, the more part advised to depart thence also, if by any means they might attain to Phenice, and there to winter; which is an haven of Crete, and lieth toward the southwest and northwest."*

ἀνευθέτου δὲ τοῦ λιμένος ὑπάρχοντος πρὸς παραχειμασίαν οἱ πλείονες ἔθεντο βουλὴν ἀναχθῆναι ἐκεῖθεν, εἴ πως δύναιντο καταντήσαντες εἰς Φοίνικα παραχειμάσαι, λιμένα τῆς Κρήτης βλέποντα κατὰ λίβα καὶ κατὰ χῶρον.

**#3698** ἀνευθέτου (gen.sing.masc.of ἀνεύθετος, genitive absolute, predicate adjective).

not commodious - Acts 27:12.

*Meaning:* A combination of ἀνά (#1059), εὖ (#1536) and θέτος, from τίθημι (#455). Not well situated; unfit - Acts 27:12.

δέ (continuative conjunction) 11.
τοῦ (gen.sing.masc.of the article in agreement with λιμένος) 9.
λιμένος (gen.sing.masc.of λιμήν, genitive absolute) 3689.
ὑπάρχοντος (pres.act.part.gen.sing.masc.of ὑπάρχω, genitive absolute) 1303.
πρὸς (preposition with the accusative, purpose) 197.

**#3699** παραχειμασίαν (acc.sing.fem.of παραχειμασία, purpose).

to winter in - Acts 27:12.

*Meaning: Cf.* παραχειμάζω (#3702). For spending the winter; for wintering - Acts 27:12.

οἱ (nom.pl.masc.of the article in agreement with πλείονες) 9.
πλείονες (nom.pl.masc.of πλείων, subject of ἔθεντο) 474.
ἔθεντο (3d.per.pl.2d.aor.mid.ind.of τίθημι, ingressive) 455.
βουλὴν (acc.sing.fem.of βουλή, direct object of ἔθεντο) 2163.
ἀναχθῆναι (1st.aor.mid.inf.of ἀνάγω, object infinitive in indirect discourse) 329.

ἐκεῖθεν (adverbial) 396.

εἰ (conditional particle with the optative in a fourth-class condition) 337.

**#3700** πῶς (indefinite adverb).

by any means - Acts 27:12; Rom.1:10; 11:14; 1 Cor.8:9; 9:27; 2 Cor.11:3;
Gal.2:2; Phil.3:11; 1 Thess.3:5.
haply - 2 Cor.9:4.
perhaps - 2 Cor.2:y.
lest - Gal.4:11.
(not translated) - Acts 27:29; 2 Cor.12:20,20.

*Meaning:* An indefinite adverb. With εἰ in a fourth-class condition with the
optative, where the proposition of the protasis is in great doubt - Acts 27;12; with
the future with ποτε Rom.1:10; with the aorist - Rom.11:14; Phil.3:11; With μή
- "lest" or "for fear that" Acts 27:29; 1 Cor.8:9; 9:27; 2 Cor.11:3; Gal.2:2; 4:11; 1
Thess.3:5; 2 Cor.2:7; 12:20,20; μήπως ἐὰν ἔλθωσιν - 2 Cor.9:4; μὴ πως and μὴ
ποτε are practically the same thing. *cf.* #2399 for a list of μή with ποτε.

δύναιντο (3d.per.pl.pres.mid.opt.of δύναμαι, fourth-class condition) 289.
καταντήσαντες (aor.act.part.nom.pl.masc. of καταντάω, adverbial,
temporal) 3353.
εἰς (preposition with the accusative of extent) 140.

**#3701** Φοίνικα (acc.sing.masc.of Φοίνιξ, extent).

Phenice - Acts 27:12.

*Meaning:* A port on the extreme northwest tip of Crete. Not to be confused with
#3237. It was for this port that the ship that carried Paul was bound when she
was blown off course and wrecked - Acts 27:12.

**#3702** παραχειμάσαι (aor.act.inf.of παραχειμάζω, complementary).

winter - Acts 27:12; 28:11; 1 Cor.16:6; Titus 3:12.

*Meaning:* A combination of παρά (#154) and χειμάζω - "to spend the winter." -
Acts 27:12; 28:11; 1 Cor.16:6; Titus 3:12.

λιμένα (acc.sing.fem.of λίμην, in apposition with Φοίνικα) 3689.
τῆς (gen.sing.fem.of the article in agreement with Κρήτης) 9.
Κρήτης (gen.sing.fem.of Κρήτη, description) 3686.
βλέποντα (pres.act.part.acc.sing.masc.of βλέπω, adjectival, restrictive,
in agreement with Φοίνικα) 499.
κατὰ (preposition with the accusative, "down along") 98.

**#3703** λίβα (acc.sing.neut.of λίψ, adverbial).

southwest - Acts 27:12.

*Meaning: Cf.* λείβω - "to pour forth." Hence, southwest, the direction in the Greek world from which the rains came. *Cf.* "norther" - the direction from which cold waves come in the northern United States - Acts 27:12.

καὶ (adjunctive conjunction joining prepositional phrases) 14.
κατὰ (preposition with accusative, "down along") 98.

#3704 χῶρον (acc.sing.neut.of χῶρος, adverbial).

northwest - Acts 27:12.

*Meaning:* That quarter of the heavens from which the northwest wind blows - Acts 27:12.

**Comment:** ἀνευθέτου . . . παραχειρασίαν is a genitive absolute with a causal participle. It was the fact that the Fair Haven port was not conisdered a proper place in which to spend the winter months that the decision was made to make the attempt to reach Phenice. Indirect assertion after ἔθεντο βουλήν with the infinitive ἀναχθῆναι. εἰ with the optative and the indefinite adverb πως is a fourth-class condition combining purpose and the implication of indirect discourse. There was great doubt that they would be able to make it to Phenice, a more suitable harbor in which to await the better sailing conditions in the spring. Note βλέποντα in a nautical sense. Lasea is on the southern shore of Crete about midway between the two ends of the island. Their trip to Phenice, if they had made it, would have taken them down the coast to the southwest a short distance and then up the coast to the northwest. Consult the map. Luke's navigation notes are accurate.

## The Storm at Sea

*(Acts 27:13-38)*

*Verse 13 - "And when the south wind blew softly, supposing that they had obtained their purpose, loosing thence, they sailed close by Crete."*

Ὑποπνεύσαντος δὲ νότου δόξαντες τῆς προθέσεως κεκρατηκέναι, ἄραντες ἆσσον παρελέγοντο τὴν Κρήτην.

#3705 Ὑποπνεύσαντος (aor.act.part.gen.sing.masc.of ὑποπνέω, genitive absolute, temporal/causal).

blow softly - Acts 27:13.

*Meaning:* A combination of ὑπό (#117) and πνέω (#697). To blow beneath; to blow with less than major intensity; hence, to blow softly. ὑπό here in the sense of low degree - Acts 27:13.

δὲ (continuative conjunction) 11.

νότου (gen.sing.masc.of νότος; genitive absolute) 1015.

δόξαντες (aor.act.part.nom.pl.masc.of δοκέω, adverbial, causal) 287.

τῆς (gen.sing.fem.of the article in agreement with προθέσεως) 9.

προθέσεως (gen.sing.fem.of πρόθεσις, objective genitive) 968.

κεκρατηκέναι (perf.act.inf.of κρατέω, object infinitive in indirect assertion) 828.

ἄραντες (aor.act.part.nom.pl.masc.of αἴρω, adverbial, temporal, coincident) 350.

#3706 ἆσσον (adverbial).

close by - Acts 27:13.

*Meaning:* The comparative of ἄγχι - "near" hence, "nearer." In Acts 27:13 it is joined to παρελέγοντο.

παρελέγοντο (3d.per.pl.imp.mid.ind.of παραλέγω, inchoative) 3688.

τὴν (acc.sing.fem.of the article in agreement with κρήτην) 9.

κρήτην (acc.sing.fem.of κρήτη, place after παρά in composition) 3686.

*Translation - "And when the south wind blew gently, because they supposed that they had obtained their purpose, they hoisted anchor and began to sail very close to the coast."*

**Comment:** The aorist participle in the genitive absolute is causal and temporal. As the wind arose they concluded that their goal was within reach. Since ἆσσον is the comparative of ἄγχι, but there is nothing with which to compare, it means that they were sailing closer to the coast line than they would have under circumstances of better weather. It was dangerous to venture too far out into the southern Mediterranean at that season. Thus they began (inchoative imperfect in παρελέγοντο) to sail with great caution down the coast, to the southwest, until they reached the point, not far distant from Lasea where the coast line turned to the northwest. With a gentle south breeze, they hoped to make it safely to Phenice, where they would remain for the remainder of the winter season. They never reached Phenice. Two weeks later they were wrecked on the island of Malta.

*Verse 14 - "But not long after there arose against it a tempestuous wind, called Euroclydon."*

μετ' οὐ πολὺ δὲ ἔβαλον κατ' αὐτῆς ἄνεμος τυφωνικὸς ὁ καλούμενος Εὐρακύλων.

μετ' (preposition with the accusative, time extent) 50.

οὐ (negative conjunction with the indicative) 130.

πολὺ (acc.sing.neut.of πολύς, time extent) 228.

δὲ (adversative conjunction) 11.

ἔβαλον (3d.per.sing.aor.act.ind.of βάλλω, ingressive) 299.

κατ' (preposition with the ablative of separation) 98.

αὐτῆς (abl.sing.fem.of αὐτός, separation) 16.

ἄνεμος (nom.sing.masc.of ἄνεμος, subject of ἔβαλον) 698.

#3708 τυφωνικὸς (nom.sing.masc.of τυφωνικός, in agreement with ἄνεμος).

tempestuous - Acts 27:14.

*Meaning: Cf.* τυφῶν - "typhoon." Whirlwind. Tempestuous storm. Typhoon, represented by Hesiod as the son of Typhoeus and father of the Winds in *Theogonia*, 307 with 869. (Liddell & Scott). - Acts 27:14.

ὁ (nom.sing.masc.of the article in agreement with καλούμενος) 9.

καλούμενος (pres.pass.part.nom.sing.masc.of καλέω, substantival, apposition) 107.

#3709 Ἐυρακύλων (nom.sing.masc.of Ἐυρακύλων, appellation).

Euroclydon - Acts 27:14.

*Meaning:* fr. εὖρος - "Europe" and the Latin *aquilo. cf.*εὐρόνοτος and euroauster. The Euroaquilo - "the Greek east wind combined with the Latin north-east (more exactly east-north-east) wind." (Moulton & Milligan).

*Translation - "But not long after a typhoon like wind, the one called Euroclydon (euroauster) beat down from Crete."*

**Comment:** δὲ is adversative. Despite their care to cling closely to the shore line, they were in jeopardy. The aorist ἔβαλον is culminative. The antecedent of αὐτῆς is Κρήτην of verse 13. Note the ablative of source or separation. The sudden storm beat upon them from the island. The wind came from the northeast, thus driving them away from the shore and out to sea. In their attempt to select the lesser of two evils, the centurion, captain and pilot, had disregarded Paul's good advice, and now fell into desperate straits.

The crew tried unsuccessfully to "bear up into the wind" - *i.e.* turn the bow directly in the face of the oncoming wind.

*Verse 15 - "And when the ship was caught, and could not bear up into the wind, we let her drive."*

συναρπασθέντος δὲ τοῦ πλοίου καὶ μὴ δυναμένου ἀντοφθαλμεῖν τῷ ἀνέμῳ ἐπιδόντες ἐφερόμεθα.

συναρπασθέντος (1st.aor.pass.part.gen.sing.neut.of συναρπάζω, genitive absolute) 2228.

δὲ (adversative conjunction) 11.

τοῦ (gen.sing.neut.of the article in agreement with πλοίου) 9.

πλοίου (gen.sing.neut.of πλοῖον, genitive absolute) 400.

καὶ (adjunctive conjunction joining participles) 14.

μὴ (negative conjunction with the participle) 87.

δυναμένου (pres.mid.part.gen.sing.neut.of δύναμαι, genitive absolute) 289.

#3710 ἀντοφθαλμεῖν (pres.act.inf.of ἀντοφθαλμέω, complementary).

bear up - Acts 27:15.

*Meaning:* Cf. ἀντόφθαλμος, from ἀντί and ὀφθαλμος - "a looking in the eye." Figuratively, of a ship sailing straight into the wind. To tack - Acts 27:15.

τῷ (dat.sing.masc.of the article in agreement with ἀνέμῳ) 9.

ἀνέμῳ (dat.sing.masc.of ἄνεμος, reference) 698.

ἐπιδόντες (2d.aor.act.part.nom.pl.masc.of ἐπιδίδωμι, adverbial, causal) 656.

ἐφερόμεθα (1st.per.pl.imp.pass.ind.of φέρω, inchoative) 683.

*Translation - "But when the ship was caught and we were unable to tack into the wind, we surrendered to the wind and were driven before it."*

**Comment:** As they were being driven out to sea, away from the shelter of the coast line, they tried to face into the wind and, by tacking go forward. Unable to do this, they had no choice but to surrender to the tempest, turn the ship around and let her be driven into the seething waters. They did not escape for two weeks.

*Verse 16 - "And running under a certain island which is called Clauda, we had much work to come by the boat."*

νησίον δέ τι ὑποδραμόντες καλούμενον Καῦδα ἰσχύσαμεν μόλις περικρατεῖς γενέσθαι τῆς σκάφης,

#3711 νησίον (acc.sing.neut.of νησίον, extent, after ὑπό in composition).

island - Acts 27:16.

*Meaning:* Cf. νῆσος (#3277) of which νησίον is the diminutive - Acts 27:16.

δέ (continuative conjunction) 11.

τι (acc.sing.neut.of τις, indefinite pronoun in agreement with νησίον) 486.

#3712 ὑποδραμόντες (2d.aor.act.part.nom.pl.masc.of ὑποτρέχω, adverbial, temporal).

run under - Acts 27:16.

*Meaning:* A combination of ὑπό (#117) and τρέχω (#1655). Hence, to sail/run under (on the lee side of) an island - Acts 27:16.

καλούμενον (pres.pass.part.acc.sing.neut.of καλέω, substantival, apposition with νησίον) 107.

#3713 Καῦδα (nom.sing.fem.of Καῦδα,(κλαῦδα) appellation).

Clauda - Acts 27:16.

*Meaning:* A small island off the southwestern coast of Crete - Acts 27:16.

ἰσχύσαμεν (1st.per.pl.aor.act.ind.of ἰσχύω, constative) 447.
μόλις (adverbial) 2342.

**#3714** περικρατεῖς (acc.sing.masc.of περικρατής, general reference).

come by - Acts 27:16.

*Meaning:* A combination of περί (#173) and κράτος (#1828). Hence, the act of exercising complete control over something. With a genitive of reference, τῆς σκάφης - Acts 27:16.

γενέσθαι (aor.mid.inf.of γίνομαι, complementary) 113.
τῆς (gen.sing.fem.of the article in agreement with σκάφης) 9.

**#3715** σκάφης (gen.sing.fem.of σκάφη, reference).

*Meaning: Cf.* σκάπτω (#2141). Hence, anything dug or hollowed out. A hollow vessel - trough, tray, tub. A ship made like a pirogue, *i.e.* a hollow, canoe-type vessel. The cockboat of a ship - Acts 27:16,30,32.

*Translation - "And when we had run under a certain island called Kauda, we were scarecely able to secure the cockboat."*

**Comment:** The storm drove them under the lee side (south side) of Cauda. They were in danger of losing the cockboat, a small boat which serves as a tender to the larger ship. περικρατεῖς γενέσθαι - "to exercise control." They took steps to prevent its being torn loose from the lines which attached it to the stern of the ship. In the event that the ship was driven aground in stormy seas the boat would be essential in the rescue of men and materials. It was with great difficulty that they prevented the loss of the boat at this time. They hauled it on board, but abandoned it two weeks later as we learn in vss.17,30,32.

*Verse 17 - "Which when they had taken up, they used helps, undergirding the ship; and fearing lest they should fall into the quicksands, strake sail, and so were driven."*

ἣν ἄραντες βοηθείαις ἐχρῶντο ὑποζωννύντες τὸ πλοῖον. φοβούμενοί τε μὴ εἰς τὴν Σύρτιν ἐκπέσωσιν, χαλάσαντες τὸ σκεῦος, οὕτως ἐφέροντο.

ἣν (acc.sing.fem.of ὅς, relative pronoun, direct object of ἄραντες) 65.
ἄραντες (aor.act.part.nom.pl.masc.of αἴρω, adverbial, temporal) 350.

**#3716** βοηθείαις (instru.pl.fem.of βοήθεια, means).

help - Acts 27:17.
to help - Heb.4:16.
succour - 2 Cor.6:2.

*Meaning: Cf.* βοηθέω (#1173), βοή (#5157), βοηθός (#5085). From βοή - "to cry" and θέω - "to run." Hence, help in an emergency. Something pressed into service when there is no time to find a better tool, *e.g.* a stone used to drive a nail when there is no hammer. A check of all of the words listed in this article reveals the thought of help asked and/or granted in an emergency - Acts 27:17; Heb.4:16; 2 Cor.6:2.

ἐχρῶντο (3d.per.pl.imp.mid.ind.of χράομαι, inchoative) 2447.

#3717 ὑποζωννύντες (pres.act.part.nom.pl.masc.of ὑποζώννυμι, adverbial, telic).

undergird - Acts 27:17.

*Meaning:* A combination of ὑπό (#117) and ζώννυμι (#2924). Hence, to undergird, *i.e.* to bind together with laterally placed ropes, wires or other binding devices the underportion (hull) of a ship, endangered in a storm at sea, to prevent her from breaking up - Acts 27:17.

τό (acc.sing.neut.of the article in agreement with πλοῖον) 9.
πλοῖον (acc.sing.neut.of πλοῖον, direct object of ὑποζωννύντες) 400.
φοβούμενοί (pres.mid.part.nom.pl.masc.of φοβέομαι, adverbial, causal) 101.
τε (continuative particle) 1408.
μή (negative conjunction with the subjunctive in a negative sub-final clause) 87.
εἰς (preposition with the accusative of extent) 140.
τήν (acc.sing.fem.of the article in agreement with Σύρτιν) 9.

#3718 Σύρτιν (acc.sing.fem.of σύρτις, extent).

*Meaning: Cf.* σύρω (#2922). Hence, quicksand areas in shallow spots in the Mediterranean. Two such areas are marked on the map: (1) ἡ μεγάλη Σύρτις, just north of the North African coast line between Tripoli and Libya, the center of which is about 400 nautical miles southwest of Cauda. (2) ἡ μικρά Σύρτις is off the coast, about 200 miles south of Carthage and 800 miles southwest of Cauda. The former is the one that the sailors feared, though it is doubtful that their knowledge of oceanography included a familiarity with depth charts. The text does not say that they were in immediate danger of being driven aground in quicksand, only that the wind was driving them in that direction and that they feared that they would - Acts 27:17.

ἐκπέσωσιν (3d.per.pl.2d.aor.act.subj.of ἐκπίπτω, negative sub-final clause) 3247.
χαλάσαντες (aor.act.part.nom.pl.masc.of χαλάω, adverbial, temporal) 2045.
τό (acc.sing.neut.of the article in agreement with σκεῦος) 9.
σκεῦος (acc.sing.neut.of σκεῦος, direct object of χαλάσαντες) 997.
οὕτως (demonstrative adverb) 74.
ἐφέροντο (3d.per.pl.imp.pass.ind.of φέρω, inchoative) 683.

*Translation - "We raised it up and began to employ every possible makeshift device in order to undergird the ship. And because they were afraid that they would fall into the Minor Surtis, they lowered the sail and began to be carried at the mercy of the winds."*

**Comment:** ἦν, the relative pronoun refers to τῆς σκάφης, of verse 16 which they almost lost in the storm. They hauled it over the side and then, in desperation began (inchoative ἐχρῶντο) to press into service whatever ropes were available to lash around the hull of the ship to prevent her from breaking up in the waves. *Cf.* #3716. The ship having been safeguarded as best they could, the sailors faced a new danger. They were being borne southward toward the Surtis. To be driven upon the quicksand banks would mean the destruction of the ship and the loss of life of all on board. It is not likely that they knew the Mediterranean well enough to know precisely where these two danger spots were (#3718), but they knew the general locations and they knew that they were being driven relentlessly in that direction. They were also not certain of their exact location, since the stars were not visible. Because of their fear (causal φοβούμενοί) they took no chances. They reduced sail cover and were thus committed to the mercy of wind and wave. The ship began to be totally out of human control.

However, although the pilot, the captain and the centurion did not know it, they were safe, because they had on board at least two passengers who were in the service of the sovereign God - Paul, a preacher whose work on earth would not be complete until he had preached the gospel in Rome, and Luke, a physician with the divinely appointed privilege of writing about it. They had already been told by the Lord Jesus that they would reach Rome safely (Acts 23:11). It is possible that all others on board owed the rescue to the fact that they were fellow passengers with two of God's elect servants.

Note μή with the aorist subjunctive in a negative sub-final clause after φοβούμενοί, a verb of fearing which uses only μή instead of the usual ἵνα μή.

*Verse 18 - "And we being exceedingly tossed with a tempest, the next day they lightened the ship."*

σφοδρῶς δὲ χειμαζομένων ἡμῶν τῇ ἑξῆς ἐκβολὴν ἐποιοῦντο,

#3719 σφοδρῶς (comparative adverb).

exceedingly - Acts 27:18.

*Meaning: Cf.* σφόδρα (#185). Exceedingly - Acts 27:18.

δὲ (adversative conjunction) 11.

#3720 χειραζομένων (pres.pass.part.gen.pl.masc.of χειράζω, genitive absolute, causal).

toss with a tempest - Acts 27:18.

*Meaning: Cf.* χειμών (#1193). Hence to afflict with a tempest; to toss about by waves - Acts 27:18.

ἡμῶν (gen.pl.masc.of ἐγώ, genitive absolute) 123.

τῇ (loc.sing.fem.of the article in agreement with ἑξῆς) 9.

ἑξῆς (loc.sing.fem.of ἑξῆς, time point) 2152.

#3721 ἐκβολὴν (acc.sing.fem.of ἐκβολή, direct object of ἐποιοῦντο).

lighten the ship - Acts 27:18.

*Meaning:* Cf. ἐκβάλλω (#649). Hence, a casting out. An act of throwing out, of throwing overboard, in a context where a ship is involved - Acts 27:18.

ἐποιοῦντο (3d.per.pl.imp.act.ind.of ποιέω, inchoative) 127.

*Translation - "But since we were being violently tossed about, the next day they began to throw the cargo overboard."*

**Comment:** δὲ is adversative; χειμαζομένων is causal. τῇ is a locative of time point. They began (inchoative ἐποιοῦντο) to throw overboard various items which were least needed in order to lighten the ship. The items chosen were on a reverse priority basis, as the blocks, tackles and ropes were not thrown overboard until the third day (verse 19) and the commercial cargo of the ship, the wheat, was the last to be sacrificed (verse 38).

The sailors were good seamen. When trouble came, first they rescued the cockboat, albeit with difficulty (verse 16). Then they undergirded the ship (verse 17). The next day they sacrificed items which were least valuable and/or essential (verse 18); next they threw over the side the tackle, ropes, sails and other nautical gear (verse 19).

*Verse 19 - "And the third day we cast out with out own hands the tackling of the ship."*

καὶ τῇ τρίτῃ αὐτόχειρες τὴν σκευὴν τοῦ πλοίου ἔρριφαν.

καὶ (continuative conjunction) 14.

τῇ (loc.sing.fem.of the article in agreement with ἡμέρα understood) 9.

τρίτῃ (loc.sing.fem.of τρίτος, in agreement with ἡμέρα understood) 1209.

#3722 αὐτόχειρες (nom.pl.masc.of αὐτόχειρ, subject of ἔρριφαν).

with one's own hand - Acts 27:19.

*Meaning:* A combination of αὐτός (#16) and χείρ (#308). Hence, one's own hand - Acts 27:19.

τὴν (acc.sing.fem.of the article in agreement with σκευὴν) 9.

#3723 σκευὴν (acc.sing.fem.of σκευή, direct object of ἔρριφαν).

tackling - Acts 27:19.

*Meaning:* Cf. σκεῦος (#997). Hence, equiptment; apparatus; furniture. In context with a ship - tackle equipment - Acts 27:19.

ἔρριψαν (3d.per.pl.aor.act.ind.of ῥίπτω, constative) 837.

*Translation* - "*And the third day with their own hands they threw the tackle overboard.*"

**Comment:** τῇ τρίτῃ - it was now the 3rd day since the storm hit the Mediterranean. The ship had now been rid of all impedimenta except the wheat down in the hold (verse 38).

*Verse 20* - "*And when neither sun nor stars in many days appeared, and no small tempest lay on us, all hope that we should be saved was then taken away.*"

μήτε δὲ ἡλίου μήτε ἄστρων ἐπιφαινόντων ἐπὶ πλείονας ἡμέρας, χειμῶνός τε οὐκ ὀλίγου ἐπικειμένου, λοιπὸν περιῃρεῖτο ἐλπὶς πᾶσα τοῦ σῴζεσθαι ἡμᾶς.

μήτε (disjunctive) 518.
δὲ (adversative conjunction) 11.
ἡλίου (gen.sing.masc.of ἥλιος, genitive absolute) 546.
μήτε (disjunctive) 518.
ἄστρων (gen.pl.masc.of ἀστήρ, genitive absolute) 145.
ἐπιφαινόντων (pres.act.part.gen.pl.masc.of ἐπιφαίνω, genitive absolute, temporal/causal) 1859.
ἐπὶ (preposition with the accusative, time extent) 47.
πλείονας (acc.pl.fem.of πλείων, in agreement with ἡμέρας) 474.
ἡμέρας (acc.pl.fem.of ἡμέρα, time extent) 135.
χειμῶνός (gen.sing.masc.of χειμών, genitive absolute) 1193.
τε (continuative particle) 1408.
οὐκ (negative conjunction with the participle, litotes) 130.
ὀλίγου (gen.sing.masc.of ὀλίγος, genitive absolute, litotes) 669.
ἐπικειμένου (pres.act.part.gen.sing.masc.of ἐπίκειμαι, genitive absolute) 2040.
λοιπὸν (acc.sing.neut.of λοιπός, adverbial) 1402.

#3724 περιῃρεῖτο (3d.per.sing.imp.pass.ind.of περιαιρέω, inchoative).

take away - Acts 27:20; 2 Cor.3:16.
take up - Acts 27:40; Heb.10:11.
fetch a compass - Acts 28:13.

*Meaning:* A combination of περί (#173) and αἱρέομαι (#350). Hence, to be taken from; to remove that which surrounds (περί). Psychologically - ἐλπίς - Acts 27:20; τὸ κάλυμμα - *i.e.* misunderstanding - 2 Cor.3;16; ritualistically - ἁμαρτίας - Heb.10:11. physically - ἀγκύρας - Acts 27:40; 28:13.

ἐλπὶς (nom.sing.fem.of ἐλπίς, subject of περιῃρεῖτο) 2994.
πᾶσα (nom.sing.fem.of πᾶς, in agreement with ἐλπὶς) 67.
τοῦ (gen.sing.neut.of the article, description) 9.

σώζεσθαι (pres.pass.inf.of σώζω, description) 109.
ἡμᾶς (acc.pl.masc.of ἐγώ, general reference) 123.

*Translation - "But after neither sun nor stars appeared for many days and with no small tempest raging about us what little hope we had that we would be saved began to be taken away."*

**Comment:** δέ is adversative. Despite the further efforts of the sailors (verse 19) to avert disaster, the elements raged on against them. Two situations combined to contribute to their frustration and drain away the last hope that ship and passengers could survive: (1) Clouds and mist by day and darkness at night made it impossible to navigate by sun or stars. Thus they had no sense of direction and continued to fear that they were being driven aground on ἡ Σύρτις. (2) The tempest still continued to drive the ship here and there. It was totally out of their control and at the mercy of the storm. Thus the last hope that they could be saved began to be eroded (inchoative imperfect in περιῃρεῖτο). Note the articular infinitive in the genitive to describe ἐλπίς.

Though Luke uses the editiorial first person (ἡμᾶς) he was speaking of the despair of all others on board. He, Paul and Aristarchus did not share this fear. It was time for Paul to reassure them. His speech follows in verses 21 - 26.

*Verse 21 - "But after long abstinence Paul stood forth in the midst of them and said, Sirs, ye should have hearkened unto me, and not have loosed from Crete, and to have gained this harm and loss."*

Πολλῆς τε ἀσιτίας ὑπαρχούσης τότε σταθεὶς ὁ Παῦλος ἐν μέσῳ αὐτῶν εἶπεν, Ἔδει μέν, ὦ ἄνδρες, πειθαρχήσαντάς μοι μὴ ἀνάγεσθαι ἀπὸ τῆς Κρήτης κερδῆσαί τε τὴν ὕβριν ταύτην καὶ τὴν ζημίαν.

Πολλῆς (gen.sing.fem.of πολύς, in agreement with ἀσιτίας) 228.
τε (continuative particle) 1408.

**#3725** ἀσιτίας (gen.sing.fem.of ἀσιτία, genitive absolute).

abstinence - Acts 27:21.

*Meaning:* Cf. ἄσιτος (#3735). From α privative and σῖτος (#311). ἀσιτία also means abstinence. Restraint from speech - Acts 27:21.

ὑπαρχούσης (pres.part.gen.sing.fem.of ὑπάρχω, genitive absolute, adverbial, temporal) 1303.
τότε (temporal adverb) 166.
σταθεὶς (aor.mid.part.nom.sing.masc.of ἵστημι, adverbial, coincident) 180.
ὁ (nom.sing.masc.of the article in agreement with Παῦλος) 9.
Παῦλος (nom.sing.masc.of Παῦλος, subject of εἶπεν) 3284.
ἐν (preposition with the locative of place) 80.
μέσῳ (loc.sing.neut.of μέσος, place) 873.
αὐτῶν (gen.pl.masc.of αὐτός, place description) 16.
εἶπεν (3d.per.sing.aor.act.ind.of εἶπον, constative) 155.
Ἔδει (3d.per.sing.imp.act.ind.of δέω, progressive description) 1207.

μέν (particle of affirmation) 300.

ὤ (exclamation) 1177.

ἄνδρες (voc.pl.masc.of ἀνήρ, address) 63.

πειθαρχήσαντάς (1st.aor.act.part.acc.pl.masc.of πειθαρχέω, adverbial, temporal) 3060.

μοι (dat.sing.masc.of ἐγώ, personal interest) 123.

μὴ (negative conjunction with the infinitive) 87.

ἀνάγεσθαι (pres.mid.inf.of ἀνάγω, noun use, subject of ἔδει) 329.

ἀπό (preposition with the ablative of separation) 70.

τῆς (abl.sing.fem.of the article in agreement with Κρήτης) 9.

Κρήτης (abl.sing.fem.of Κρήτη, separation) 3686.

κερδῆσαι (aor.act.inf.of κερδαίνω, noun use, subject of ἔδει) 1214.

τε (adjunctive particle) 1408.

τὴν (acc.sing.fem.of the article in agreement with ὕβριν) 9.

ὕβριν (acc.sing.fem.of ὕβρις, direct object of κερδῆσαι) 3693.

ταύτην (acc.sing.fem.of οὗτος, in agreement with ὕβριν) 93.

καὶ (adjunctive conjunction joining nouns) 14.

τὴν (acc.sing.fem.of the article in agreement with ζημίαν) 9.

ζημίαν (acc.sing.fem.of ζημία, direct object of κερδῆσαι) 3694.

*Translation - "And after remaining silent for a long time Paul stood up among them and said, 'O Sirs, When you heard my suggestion you should not have sailed from Crete and brought about this disaster and loss.' "*

**Comment:** The context must decide whether the long fast, was abstinence from food or from speech. The word, in its primary meaning, means "no food" (#3725). Paul may have wanted to speak before he did, since events after they left Fair Haven abundantly supported the soundness of his advice that they should have remained there for the winter. It would not have been diplomatic for him to have spoken too soon, in the sense of "I told you so." But, after some time, he felt that what he had to say was not improper in view of the fact that he added his assurance that lives would not be lost.

ἔδει, a verb of oligation or propriety, introduces a second-class condition, with the condition determined as unfilfilled. Such verbs are in the imperfect tense when the obligation, at the time of writing or speaking, has not been met. Winer (Winer, Th.,282, as cited in Robertson, *Grammar*, 886) says that the Greeks and Latins start from the past and state the real possibility of obligation, and the reader, by comparing that with facts, notes that the obligation has not been met. So Paul is saying, "In the past, when I warned you to stay at Lasea (Acts 27:9-11) you were then under the obligation, after you listened to me, not to sail from Crete (which they did) and thus we would not have sustained the loss of cargo and damage to the ship (which they also did)."

Having rebuked them, Paul then consoled them.

*Verse 22 - "And now I exhort you to be of good cheer: for there shall be no loss of any man's life among you, but of the ship."*

καὶ τὰ νῦν παραινῶ ὑμᾶς εὐθυμεῖν, ἀποβολὴ γὰρ φυχῆς οὐδεμία ἔσται ἐξ
ὑμῶν πλὴν τοῦ πλοίου.

καὶ (adversative conjunction) 14.
τὰ (acc.pl.neut.of the article, joined with νῦν) 9.
νῦν (temporal adverb) 1497.
παραινῶ (1st.pers.sing.pres.act.ind.of παραινέω, aoristic) 3692.
ὑμᾶς (acc.pl.masc.of σύ, general reference) 104.

#3726 εὐθυμεῖν (pres.act.inf.of εὐθυμέω, object infinitive, indirect command).

be merry - James 5:13.
be of good cheer - Acts 27:22,25.

*Meaning:* εὐ (#1536) plus θυμέω - "to emote." Hence, to be happy. *Cf.* εὔθυμος
(#3737), εὐθύμως (#3623). With reference to Paul's encouragement to his
shipmates in the storm - Acts 27:22,25.

*Cf.* also James 5:13.

#3727 ἀποβολή (nom.sing.fem.of ἀποβολή, subject of ἔσται).

casting away - Romans 11:15.
loss - Acts 27:22.

*Meaning:* A combination of ἀπό (#70) and βάλλω (#299). Hence that which is
cast away or lost. Followed by a genitive of description - φυχῆς in Acts 27:22.
The loss of Israel - Romans 11:15.

γὰρ (causal conjunction) 105.
φυχῆς (gen.sing.fem.of φυχή, description) 233.
οὐδεμία (nom.sing.fem.of οὐδείς, in agreement with ἀποβολή) 446.
ἔσται (3d.per.sing.fut.ind.of εἰμί, predictive) 86.
ἐξ (preposition with the partitive genitive) 19.
ὑμῶν (gen.pl.masc.of σύ, partitive genitive) 104.
πλὴν (adversative conjunction) 944.
τοῦ (gen.sing.neut.of the article in agreement with πλοίου) 9.
πλοίου (gen.sing.neut.of πλοῖον, description) 400.

*Translation - "But now I am exhorting you to cheer up, because not a single one
of you will lose his life - only the ship."*

**Comment:** *Cf.*#1497 for the list of passages where we have the articles τὰ or τοῦ
with νῦν. Note Luke's use of the accusative after παραινῶ instead of the dative.
Note the brachylogy in πλὴν τοῦ πλοίου.

It was already clear to Paul that his own life would be spared (Acts 23:11).
Now God's grace which was to save Paul's life is seen to extend to all of those on
board, of whom there were 276 people (verse 37).

*Verse 23 - "For there stood by me this night the angel of God, whose I am, and whom I serve."*

παρέστη γάρ μοι ταύτῃ τῇ νυκτὶ τοῦ θεοῦ οὗ εἰμι (εἰμι) ᾧ καὶ λατρεύω, ἄγγελος. . .

παρέστη (3d.per.sing.2d.aor.act.ind.of παρίστημι, constative) 1596.
γάρ (causal conjunction) 105.
μοι (loc.sing.masc.of ἐγώ, place, after παρά in composition) 123.
ταύτῃ (loc.sing.fem.of οὗτος, in agreement with νυκτὶ) 93.
τῇ (loc.sing.fem.of the article in agreement with νυκτὶ) 9.
νυκτὶ (loc.sing.fem.of νύξ, time point) 209.
τοῦ (gen.sing.masc.of the article in agreement with θεοῦ) 9.
θεοῦ (gen.sing.masc.of θεός, description) 124.
οὗ (gen.sing.masc.of ὅς, relative pronoun, relationship) 65.
εἰμι (1st.per.sing.pres.ind.of εἰμί, progressive duration, retroactive) 86.
(ἐγώ) (nom.sing.masc.of ἐγώ, subject of εἰμι) 123.
ᾧ (dat.sing.masc.of ὅς, relative pronoun, personal advantage) 65.
καὶ (continuative conjunction) 14.
λατρεύω (1st.per.sing.pres.act.ind.of λατρεύω, progressive duration, retroactive) 366.
ἄγγελος (nom.sing.masc.of ἄγγελος, subject of παρέστη) 96.

*Translation - "Because there stood by me this night a messenger of God Whose I am and Whom I serve . . . "*

**Comment:** γὰρ is causal. Paul's reason for optimism is the heavenly message which he is about to describe. Note the emphasis of τοῦ θεοῦ ahead of ἄγγελος, the subject of the verb, which is the last word in the clause. The fact that the message came from a messenger is not important. It is important that this messenger was sent from God, not from one of the pagan deities which were being worshipped by some of Paul's companions on board. They had been fasting and importuning their gods with their liturgical rubrics and litanies. There is no evidence that Paul had even been praying, except perhaps to thank the Lord for the safety which he already knew was his. He was not afraid as Μὴ φοβοῦ of verse 24 indicates. παρέστη reminds us of the promise of our Lord in His Great Commission - "καὶ ἰδοὺ ἐγὼ μεθ' ὑμῶν εἰμι πάσας τὰς ἡμέρας . . . κ.τ.λ." (Μτ.?).

*Verse 24 - "Saying, Fear not, Paul; thou must be brought before Caesar: and, lo, God hath given thee all them that sail with thee."*

λέγων, Μὴ φοβοῦ, Παῦλε. Καίσαρί σε δεῖ παραστῆναι, καὶ ἰδοὺ κεχάρισταί σοι ὁ θεὸς πάντας τοὺς πλέοντας μετὰ σοῦ.

λέγων (pres.act.part.nom.sing.masc.of λέγω, recitative) 66.
Μὴ (negative conjunction with the imperative) 87.
φοβοῦ (2d.per.sing.aor.mid.impv.of φοβέομαι, ingressive) 101.

Παῦλε (voc.sing.masc.of Παῦλος, address) 3284.

Καίσαρί (loc.sing.masc.ofd Καίσαρι, place, with παρά in composition) 1418.

σε (acc.sing.masc.ofd σύ, general reference) 104.

δεῖ (3d.per.sing.pres.ind.of δέω, introducing the infinitive in indirect assertion) 1207.

παραστῆναι (aor.act.inf.of παρίστημι, noun use, subject of δεῖ)

καὶ (continuative conjunction) 14.

ἰδοὺ (exclamation) 95.

κεχάρισταί (3d.per.sing.perf.mid.ind.of χαρίζομαι, intensive) 2158.

σοι (dat.sing.masc.of σύ, indirect object of κεχάρισταί) 104.

ὁ (nom.sing.masc.of the article in agreement with θεὸς) 9.

θεὸς (nom.sing.masc.of θεός, subject of κεχάρισταί) 124.

πάντας (acc.pl.masc.of πᾶς, in agreement with πλέοντας) 67.

τοὺς (acc.pl.masc.of the article in agreement with πλέοντας) 9.

πλέοντας (pres.act.part.acc.pl.masc.of πλέω, substantival, direct object of κεχάρισταί) 2209.

μετὰ (preposition with the genitive of accompaniment) 50.

σοῦ (gen.sing.masc.of σύ, accompaniment) 104.

*Translation - ". . . saying, 'Do not begin to fear, Paul. It has been decreed that you will stand before Nero. And, Look! God has given to you all those who are sailing with you.' "*

**Comment:** Μὴ φοβοῦ - μή with the ingressive aorist imperative. "Do not fear even once" or "Do not begin to fear" which is proof that Paul had not yet feared. δεῖ has as its subject the infinitive παραστῆναι. "That you should stand before Nero has already been established as a part of God's plan for your life. *Cf.* #1207. That was enough to prove that Paul was not going to drown in the Mediterranean Sea. It does not secure his fellow passengers. But the angel adds the next sentence. Note the perfect tense - the tense that "looks at both ends of the action." God, in what men call the "past" had decreed that all on board should be safe. That is the past fact. The present result is that all are therefore safe. Note the substantive participle τοὺς πλέοντας, the object of κεχάρισταί.

This common grace - that God should save lost sinners from drowning solely because they happened to be fellow passengers with Paul, who is the recipient of saving and guiding grace is often seen in history. The Christians on the Mayflower who were ordained of God to found Plymouth in the American wilderness were brought safely across the Atlantic on a ship which also carried some unsaved persons. A corn field belonging to an atheist which lies across the fence from one owned by a Christian gets rain on his crop in answer to the Christian's prayer for rain.

*Verse 25 - "Wherefore, sirs, be of good cheer: for I believe God, that it shall be even as it was told me."*

διὸ εὐθυμεῖτε, ἄνδρες πιστεύω γὰρ τῷ θεῷ ὅτι οὕτως ἔσται καθ' ὃν τρόπον λελάληταί μοι.

διό (inferential conjunction) 1622.

εὐθυμεῖτε (2d.per.pl.pres.act.impv.of εὐθυμέω, entreaty) 3726.

ἄνδρες (voc.pl.masc.of ἀνήρ, address) 63.

πιστεύω (1st.per.sing.pres.act.ind.of πιστεύω, progressive duration, retroactive) 734.

γάρ (causal conjunction) 105.

τῷ (dat.sing.masc.of the article in agreement with θεῷ) 9.

θεῷ (dat.sing.masc.of θεός, person) 124.

ὅτι (conjunction introducing an object clause in indirect discourse) 211.

οὕτως (demonstrative adverb) 74.

ἔσται (3d.per.sing.fut.ind.of εἰμί, predictive) 86.

καθ᾽ (preposition with the accusative, in a comparative clause) 98.

ὅν (acc.sing.masc.of ὅς, in agreement with πρόπον) 65.

τρόπον (acc.sing.masc.of τρόπος, in a comparative clause) 1477.

λελάληταί (3d.per.sing.perf.pass.ind.of λαλέω, intensive) 815.

μοι (dat.sing.masc.of ἐγώ, indirect object of λελάληταί) 123.

*Translation - "Therefore, cheer up, Gentlemen! Because I believe that it is going to be exactly as it has been told to me."*

**Comment:** διό is inferential. Paul's conclusion was based upon the information he received from the Lord in verse 24. γάρ is causal as Paul explains why he thinks there is ground for optimism. "I believe God." Paul's faith in what God said and his faith in God is because of *who* God is. Hence, "I believe *because* of God" is not too farfetched. Note the idiom καθ᾽ ὅν τρόπον also in Acts 15:11. What God told Paul is exactly how it was going to be.

*Verse 26 - "Howbeit we must be cast upon a certain island."*

εἰς νῆσον δέ τινα δεῖ ἡμᾶς ἐκπεσεῖν.

εἰς (preposition with the accusative of extent) 140.

νῆσον (acc.sing.masc.of νῆσος, extent) 3277.

δέ (adversative conjunction) 11.

τινα (acc.sing.masc.of τις, indefinite pronoun, in agreement with νῆσον) 486.

δεῖ (3d.per.sing.pres.ind.of δέω, static) 1207.

ἡμᾶς (acc.pl.masc.of ἐγώ, general reference) 123.

ἐκπεσεῖν (aor.act.inf.of ἐκπίπτω, noun use, subject of δεῖ) 3247.

*Translation - "However we must be cast upon some island."*

**Comment:** Paul did not know what island, but that detailed information was not necessary. *Cf.* #1207 for other passages where we have the necessity of divine appointment.

*Verse 27 - "But when the fourteenth night was come, as we were driven up and down in Adria, about midnight the shipmen deemed that they drew near to some country."*

'Ως δὲ τεσσαρεσκαιδεκάτη νὺξ ἐγένετο διαφερομένων ἡμῶν ἐν τῷ 'Αδρίᾳ, κατὰ μέσον τῆς νυκτὸς ὑπενόουν οἱ ναῦται προσάγειν τινὰ αὐτοῖς χώραν.

'Ως (particle introducing a definite temporal clause) 128.
δὲ (continuative conjunction) 11.

#3728 τεσσαρεσκαιδεκάτη (nom.sing.fem.of τεσσαρεσκαιδέκατος, in agreement with νὺξ).

fourteenth - Acts 27:27,33.

*Meaning:* A combination of τέσσαρες (#1508), καί (#14) and δέκα (#1330). Hence, fourteenth - Acts 27:27,33.

νὺξ (nom.sing.fem.of νύξ, subject of ἐγένετο) 209.
ἐγένετο (3d.per.sing.aor.ind.of γίνομαι, culminative) 113.
διαφερομένων (pres.pass.part.gen.pl.masc.of διαφέρω, genitive absolute) 620.
ἡμῶν (gen.pl.masc.of ἐγώ, genitive absolute) 123.
ἐν (preposition with the locative of place) 80.
τῷ (loc.sing.masc.of the article in agreement with 'Αδρίᾳ) 9.

#3729 'Αδρίᾳ (loc.sing.masc.of 'Αδρίας, place).

Adria - Acts 27:27.

*Meaning:* The southern portion of what is now called the Adriatic Sea, which reaches north to Venice between Italy and the Dalmatian coast. The Sea of Adria lies between Sicily and the southern portion of the Greek peninusla. At the point farthest north in their helpless drift before the storm they were probably 175 nautical miles off the coast of Syracuse, Sicily, east and slightly north - Acts 27:27.

κατὰ (preposition with the accusative in a time expression) 98.
μέσον (acc.sing.masc.ofd μέσος, time expression) 873.
τῆς (gen.sing.fem.of the article in agreement with νυκτὸς) 9.
νυκτὸς (gen.sing.fem.of νύξ, description) 209.
ὑπενόουν (3d.per.pl.imp.act.ind.of ὑπονοέω, inchoative) 3298.
οἱ (nom.pl.masc.of the article in agreement with ναῦται) 9.

#3730 ναῦται (nom.pl.masc.of ναύτης, subject of ὑπενόουν).

sailor - Rev.18:17.
shipman - Acts 27:27,30.

*Meaning:* Cf. ναῦς (#3745). A mariner; sailor; seaman - Acts 27:27,30; Rev.18:17.

προσάγειν (pres.act.inf.of προσάγω, noun use, object ofd ὑπενόουν) 2343.
τινὰ (acc.sing.fem.of τις, indefinite pronoun, in agreement with χώραν) 486.
αὐτοῖς (dat.pl.masc.of αὐτός, reference) 16.

χώραν (acc.sing.fem.of χώρα, extent) 201.

*Translation - "And on the fourteenth night as we were being carried here and there in the Adriatic, about midnight the sailors began to suspect that they were approaching some land."*

**Comment:**Ὡς introduces the temporal clause, in terms of days, and κατὰ μέσον τῆς νυκτὸς tells us the approximate hour. The genitive absolute in the present tense adds that it was as they were being carried through the Adriatic Sea. The inchoative imperfect in ὑπονόουν is proper. Luke does not tell us how the sailors began to suspect that there was land ahead. It may have been the sound of the waves upon the shore.

*Verse 28 - "And sounded, and found it twenty fathoms: and when they had gone a little further, they sounded again, and found it fifteen fathoms."*

καὶ βολίσαντες εὗρον ὀργυιὰς εἴκοσι, βραχὺ δὲ διαστήσαντες καὶ πάλιν βολίσαντες εὗρον ὀργυιὰς δεκαπέντε.

καὶ (inferential conjunction) 14.

#3731 βολίσαντες (aor.act.part.nom.pl.masc.of βολίζω, adverbial, instrumental).

   sound - Acts 27:28,28.

*Meaning: Cf.* βολίς - "a dart." Hence, to suspend a heavy sounding line into the water to determine depth - Acts 27:28,28.

εὗρον (3d.per.pl.2d.aor.act.ind.of εὑρίσκω, constative) 79.

#3732 ὀργυιὰς (acc.pl.fem.of ὀργυιά, direct object of εὗρον).

   fathom - Acts 27:28,28.

*Meaning: Cf.* ὀργέω - "to stretch out." Hence, a fathom is the distance between the two middle fingerstips when the arms are stretched out laterally as far as possible. About six feet - Acts 27:28,28.

   εἴκοσι (numeral) 2283.
   βραχὺ (acc.sing.neut.of βραχύς, adverbial) 2274.
   δὲ (continuative conjunction) 11.
   διαστήσαντες (1st.aor.act.part.nom.pl.masc.of διΐστημι, adverbial, temporal) 2818.
   καὶ (adjunctive conjunction joining participles) 14.
   πάλιν (adverbial) 355.
   βολίσαντες (aor.act.part.nom.pl.masc.of βολίζω, adverbial, instrumental) 3731.
   εὗρον (3d.per.pl.2d.aor.act.ind.of εὑρίσκω, constative) 79.
   ὀργυιὰς (acc.pl.fem.of ὀργυιά, direct object of εὗρον) 3732.

δεκαπέντε (numeral) 2601.

*Translation* - *"Therefore by sounding they found one hundred and twenty feet, and after having navigated the ship a little closer, they sounded again and found ninety feet."*

**Comment:** εὗρον is a second aorist, while διαστήσαντες is a first aorist. When the two are found together the 1st aorist is transitive (takes an object) and the 2d.aorist is intransitive. Here διαστήσαντες is indeed a transitive verb, though the object is not in the text. We supply τὴν ναῦν. The two soundings not far apart revealed that the ship was entering an area of shallow water, which supported their view that land was lying somewhere ahead in the darkness. Expert seamanship dictated caution as we see in

*Verse 29* - *"Then fearing lest we should have fallen upon rocks, they cast four anchors out of the stern, and wished for the day."*

φοβούμενοί τε μὴ που κατὰ τραχεῖς τόπους ἐκπέσωμεν, ἐκ πρύμνης ῥίψαντες ἀγκύρας τέσσαρας ηὔχοντο ἡμέραν γενέσθαι.

φοβούμενοι (pres.mid.part.nom.pl.masc.of φοβέομαι, adverbial, causal) 101.
τε (continuative particle) 1408.
μὴ (negative conjunction with the subjunctive) 87.
που (for πως) - (final conjunction) 3700.
κατὰ (preposition with the accusative, extent) 98.
τραχεῖς (acc.pl.masc.of τραχύς, in agreement with τόπους) 1940.
τόπους (acc.pl.masc.of τόπος, extent, after κατὰ) 1019.
ἐκπέσωμεν (1st.per.pl.2d.aor.act.subj.of ἐκπίπτω, negative purpose) 3247.
ἐκ (preposition with the ablative of separation) 19.
πρύμνης (abl.sing.fem.of πρύμνα, separation) 2206.
ῥίψαντες (aor.act.part.nom.pl.masc.of ῥίπτω, adverbial, temporal) 837.

#3733 ἀγκύρας (acc.pl.fem.of ἄγκυρα, direct object of ῥίψαν̣τες).

anchor - Acts 27:29,30,40; Heb.6:19.

*Meaning:* Cf. ἀγκάλαι (#1899). The ancient anchor was not greatly different in design from the modern anchor. Used literally in Acts 27:29,30,40; figuratively in Heb.6:19.

τέσσαρας (acc.pl.fem.of τέσσαρες, in agreement with ἀγκύρας) 1508.
ηὔχοντο (3d.per.pl.imp.mid.ind.of εὔχομαι, inchoative) 3670.
ἡμέραν (acc.sing.fem.of ἡμέρα, general reference) 135.
γενέσθαι (aor.mid.inf.of γίνομαι, object of ηὔχοντο) 113.

*Translation* - *"And due to the fear that they would fall upon rocky places they cast four anchors out of the stern and began anxiously to wish for daylight."*

**Comment:** φοβούμενοι is causal. Their fear dictated their action. Normally we would have ἵνα μὴ in a negative sub-final clause, but φοβέομαι is one of the verbs that uses μή as the conjunction. μή που is for μή πως and differs little from μήποτε (#351). They feared lest by some chance, since they were without control of the ship, due to the storm of the past two weeks, and also due to the darkness, that they might (subjunctive in ἐκπέσωμεν) fall upon the rocky ledge of the shoreline. Hence the action of casting the anchors out of the stern and the beginning (inchoative imperfect in ηὔχοντο) of a long and anxious wait for daylight. In November and in that latitude they waited perhaps six or seven hours.

*Verse 30 - "And as the shipmen were about to flee out of the ship, when they had let down the boat into the sea, under colour as though they would have cast anchors out of the foreship, . . . "*

τῶν δὲ ναυτῶν ζητούντων φυγεῖν ἐκ τοῦ πλοίου καὶ χαλασάντων τὴν σκάφην εἰς τὴν θάλασσαν προφάσει ὡς ἐκ πρῴρης ἀγκύρας μελλόντων ἐκτείνειν,

τῶν (gen.pl.masc.of the article in agreement with ναυτῶν) 9.
δὲ (continuative conjunction) 11.
ναυτῶν (gen.pl.masc.of ναύτης, genitive absolute) 3730.
ζητούντων (pres.act.part.gen.pl.masc.of ζητέω, genitive absolute) 207.
φυγεῖν (aor.act.inf.of φεύγω, complementary) 202.
ἐκ (preposition with the ablative of separation) 19.
τοῦ (abl.sing.neut.of the article in agreement with πλοίου) 9.
πλοίπυ (abl.sing.neut.of πλοῖον, separation) 400.
καὶ (adjunctive conjunction joining participles) 14.
χαλασάντων (aor.act.part.gen.pl.masc.of χαλάω, genitive absolute) 2045.
τὴν (acc.sing.fem.of the article in agreement with σκάφην) 9.
σκάφην (acc.sing.fem.of σκάφη, direct object of χαλασάντων) 3715.
εἰς (preposition with the accusative of extent) 140.
τὴν (acc.sing.fem.of the article in agreement with θάλασσαν) 9.
θάλασσαν (acc.sing.fem.of θάλασσα, extent) 374.
προφάσει (instru.sing.fem.of πρόφασις, means) 2704.
ὡς (particle introducing a comparative clause) 128.
ἐκ (preposition with the ablative of separation) 19.

#3734 πρῴρης (abl.sing.fem.of πρῶρα, separation).

forepart - Acts 27:41.
foreship - Acts 27:30.

*Meaning:* The bow of a ship. Distinct from πρύμα in verse 41 - Acts 27:30.

ἀγκύρας (acc.pl.fem.of ἄγκυρα, direct object of ἐκτείνειν) 3733.
μελλόντων {pres.act.part.gen.pl.masc.of μέλλω,) 206.
ἐκτείνειν (pres.act.inf.of ἐκτείνω, completes μελλόντων) 710.

*Translation - "And when the sailors tried to flee out of the ship and had lowered the lifeboat into the sea on the pretext that they were going to cast anchors out of the bow. . . "*

**Comment:** The genitive absolutes prepare for the main verb εἶπεν in verse 31. The sailors were trying to flee from the ship. They lowered the boat which they had rescued from the sea two weeks before (verses 16,17) into the sea, as if they were going to anchor the bow of the ship as well as the stern.

Apparently Paul thought that the sailors would be needed on board when morning light made it possible to effect some means of bringing the ship safely to shore.

*Verse 31 - "Paul said to the centurion and to the soldiers, Except these abide in the ship, ye cannot be saved."*

εἶπεν ὁ Παῦλος τῷ ἑκατοντάρχῃ καὶ τοῖς στρατιώταις, Ἐὰν μὴ οὗτοι μείνωσιν ἐν τῷ πλοίῳ, ὑμεῖς σωθῆναι οὐ δύνασθε.

εἶπεν (3d.per.sing.aor.act.ind.of εἶπον, constative) 155.
ὁ (nom.sing.masc.of the article in agreement with Παῦλος) 9.
Παῦλος (nom.sing.masc.of Παῦλος, subject of εἶπεν) 3284.
τῷ (dat.sing.masc.of the article in agreement with ἑκατοντάρχῃ) 9.
ἑκατοντάρχῃ (dat.sing.masc.of ἑκατοντάρχης, indirect object of εἶπεν) 3210.
καὶ (adjunctive conjunction joining nouns) 14.
τοῖς (dat.pl.masc.of the article in agreement with στρατιώταις) 9.
στρατιώταις (dat.pl.masc.of στρατιώτης, indirect object of εἶπεν) 724.
Ἐὰν (conditional particle in a third-class condition) 363.
μὴ (negative conjunction with the subjunctive) 87.
οὗτοι (nom.pl.masc.of οὗτος, subject of μείνωσιν) 93.
μείνωσιν (3d.per.pl.aor.act.subj.of μένω, third-class condition) 864.
ἐν (preposition with the locative of place) 80.
τῷ (loc.sing.neut.of the article in agreement with πλοίῳ) 9.
πλοίῳ (loc.sing.neut.of πλοῖον, place where) 400.
ὑμεῖς (nom.pl.masc.of σύ, subject of δύνασθε) 104.
σωθῆναι (1st.aor.pass.inf.of σώζω, complementary) 109.
οὐ (negative conjunction with the indicative) 130.
δύνασθε (2d.per.pl.pres.ind.of δύναμαι, futuristic) 289.

*Translation - ". . . Paul said to the centurion and to the soldiers, 'If these men do not remain on the ship, you are not going to be able to be saved.' "*

**Comment:** A third-class condition with ἐάν and the subjunctive in μείνωσιν in the protasis and a present indicative in the apodosis. The condition is undetermined but with a prospect of determination. Paul did not know whether the fleeing sailors could be kept on board or not, but there was a chance that they could. One thing was certain - if they escaped the rest of the people on board except the Christians would be lost. They had been granted rescue from the sea solely because they were fellow passengers with Paul (verses 22-24). Paul apparently was saying that God's promise to them was null if they tried to escape. The centurion, Julius, believed what Paul said, and took immediate steps to prevent their escape.

*Verse 32 - "Then the soldiers cut off the ropes of the boat, and let her fall off."*

τότε ἀπέκοφαν οἱ στρατιῶται τὰ σχοινία τῆς σκάφης καὶ εἴασαν αὐτὴν ἐκπεσεῖν.

τότε (continuative conjunction) 166.
ἀπέκοφαν (3d.per.pl.aor.act.ind.of ἀποκόπτω, constative) 2352.
οἱ (nom.pl.masc.of the article in agreement with στρατιῶται) 9.
στρατιῶται (nom.pl.masc.of στρατιώτης, subject of ἀπέκοφαν and εἴασαν) 724.
τὰ (acc.pl.neut.of the article in agreement with σχοινία) 9.
σχοινία (acc.pl.neut.of σχοίνιον, direct object of ἀπέκοφαν) 1981.
τῆς (gen.sing.fem.of the article in agreement with σκάφης) 9.
σκάφας (gen.sing.fem.of σκάφη, description) 3715.
καὶ (adjunctive conjunction joining verbs) 14.
εἴασαν (3d.per.pl.aor.act.ind.of ἐάω, constative) 1521.
αὐτὴν (acc.sing.fem.of αὐτός, general reference) 16.
ἐκπεσεῖν (aor.act.inf.of ἐκπίπτω, object of εἴασαν) 3247.

*Translation - "Then the soldiers cut away the ropes of the lifeboat and allowed her to fall off."*

**Comment:** εἴασαν has ἐκπεσεῖν as its object with αὐτὴν in general reference. The little cockboat which was saved with such difficulty from the storm (verses 16,17) was now sacrificed in order to meet Paul's demand that no one leave the ship until they all left it.

*Verse 33 - "And while the day was coming on, Paul besought them all to take meat, saying, This day is the fourteenth day that ye have tarried and continued fasting, having taken nothing."*

Ἄχρι δὲ οὗ ἡμέρα ἤμελλεν γίνεσθαι παρεκάλει ὁ Παῦλος ἅπαντας μεταλαβεῖν τροφῆς λέγων, Τεσσαρεσκαιδεκάτην σήμερον ἡμέραν προσδοκῶντες ἄσιτοι διατελεῖτε, μηδὲν προσλαβόμενοι.

Ἄχρι (preposition introducing a relative temporal clause) 1517.
δὲ (continuative conjunction) 11.
οὗ (gen.sing.neut.of ὅς, relative pronoun, in a temporal clause) 65.
ἡμέρα (nom.sing.fem.of ἡμέρα, subject of ἤμελλεν) 135.
ἤμελλεν (3d.per.sing.imp.act.ind.of μέλλω, inchoative) 206.
γίνεσθαι (pres.mid.inf.of γίνομαι, complementary) 113.
παρεκάλει (3d.per.sing.imp.act.ind.of παρακαλέω, inchoative) 230.
ὁ (nom.sing.masc.of the article in agreement with Παῦλος) 9.
Παῦλος (nom.sing.masc.of Παῦλος, subject of πατεκάλει) 3284.
ἅπαντας (acc.pl.masc.of ἅπας, direct object of παρεκάλει) 639.
μεταλαβεῖν (2d.aor.act.inf.of μεταλαμβάνω, purpose) 3003.

τροφῆς (gen.sing.fem.of τροφή, objective genitive) 266.

λέγων (pres.act.part.nom.sing.masc.of λέγω, recitative) 66.

Τεσσαρεσκαιδεκάτην (acc.sing.fem.of τεσσαρεσκαιδέκατος, in agreement with ἡμέραν) 3728.

σήμερον (temporal adverb) 579.

ἡμέραν (acc.sing.fem.of ἡμέρα, time extent) 135.

προσδοκῶντες (pres.act.part.nom.pl.masc.of προσδοκέω, adverbial, complementary) 906.

#3735 ἄσιτοι (nom.pl.masc.of ἄσιτος, adverbial).

fasting - Acts 27:33.

*Meaning:* A combination of α privative and σῖτος (#311). Hence, fasting, abstaining from food - Acts 27:33.

#3736 διατελεῖτε (2d.per.pl.pres.act.ind.of διατελέω, progressive duration, retroactive).

continue - Acts 27:33.

*Meaning:* A combination of διά (#118) and τελέω (#704). Hence, to continue thoroughly to the end; to persist. In profane Greek, joined with participles or infinitives. In Acts 27:33 joined with ἄσιτοι - "you continue in a state of fasting" or "you have been fasting consistently."

μηθὲν (acc.sing.neut.of μηδείς, direct object of προσλαβόμενοι) 713.

προσλαβόμενοι (aor.mid.part.nom.pl.masc.of προσλαμβάνω, adverbial, modal) 1210.

*Translation - "And just before dawn Paul began to urge everyone to eat. He said, 'Today is the fourteenth day that you have continued to watch without food, taking nothing.' "*

**Comment:** ἄχρι οὗ - cf.#1517, 2, a,b,bb, for ἄχρι with the relative and ἄν. Sometime between μέσον τῆς νυκτός (verse 27) and ἡμέραν ἤμελλεν γίνεσθαι - "midnight and dawn."

Paul knew that no one was going to drown. He also knew that as soon as the morning light came they would be able to see the land. He also knew that the ship was going to break up and be lost. It was time for the crew and the passengers to rejoice. So he began (inchoative imperfect in παρεκάλει) to urge them to eat. It was the fourteenth day that they had spent. Doing what? Watching and expecting deliverance from the storm (προσδοκῶντες). During this period of watch they had been fasting (ἄσιτοι διατελεῖτε with ὄντος supplied) - *i.e.* continuing, being foodless." How did they accomplish this? The modal participle says that they did it by "taking nothing." Having reminded them of the long fast, Paul adds the inferential clause in

*Verse 34 - "Wherefore I pray you to take some meat: for this is for your health:*

*for there shall not an hair fall from the head of any of you."*

διὸ παρακαλῶ ὑμᾶς μεταλαβεῖν τροφῆς, τοῦτο γὰρ πρὸς τῆς ὑμετέρας
σωτηρίας ὑπάρχει, οὐδενὸς γὰρ ὑμῶν θρὶξ ἀπὸ τῆς κεφαλῆς ἀπολεῖται.

διὸ (inferential conjunction) 1622.

παρακαλῶ (1st.per.sing.pres.act.ind.of παρακαλέω, aoristic) 230.

ὑμᾶς (acc.pl.masc.of σύ, direct object of παρακαλῶ) 104.

μεταλαβεῖν (aor.act.inf.of μεταλαμβάνω, epexegetical) 3003.

τροφῆς (gen.sing.fem.of τροφή, object genitive) 266.

τοῦτο (nom.sing.neut.of οὗτος, subject of ὑπάρχει) 93.

γὰρ (causal conjunction) 105.

πρὸς (preposition with the ablative) 197.

ὑμετέρας (abl.sing.fem.of ὑμέτερος, in agreement with σωτηρίας) 2127.

σωτηρίας (abl.sing.fem.of σωτηρία, point of view) 1852.

σωτηρίας (acc.sing.fem.of σωτηρία, purpose) 1852.

ὑπάρχει (3d.per.sing.pres.act.ind.of ὑπάρχω, static) 1303.

οὐδενὸς (gen.sing.masc.of οὐδείς, possession) 446.

γὰρ (causal conjunction) 105.

ὑμῶν (gen.pl.masc.of σύ, partitive genitive) 104.

θρὶξ (nom.sing.fem.of θρίξ, subject of ἀπολεῖται) 261.

ἀπὸ (preposition with the ablative of separation) 70.

τῆς (abl.sing.fem.of the article in agreement with κεφαλῆς) 9.

κεφαλῆς (abl.sing.fem.of κεφαλή, separation) 521.

ἀπολεῖται (3d.per.sing.2d.fut.mid.ind.of ἀπόλλυμι, predictive) 208.

*Translation - "Therefore I am urging you to eat, for this will be good for you, because a hair will not fall from the head of a single one of you."*

**Comment:** διὸ is inferential. We can either say that παρακαλῶ has the object infinitive μεταλαβεῖν in indirect discourse with ὑμᾶς in general reference, or we can say that ὑμᾶς is the direct object of παρακαλῶ and that the infinitive is epexegetical. He was urging that "you take food." Or he was urging "you to take food." The idea is the same in either case.

Literary influence on the κοινή uses πρὸς with the ablative in σωτηρίας - the only ablative with πρὸς in the New Testament. As an ablative, it means "from the point of view of your advantage." (Robertson, *Grammar*, 623), although it can also be construed as a genitive - "on the side of." In either case it expresses purpose. Paul was saying, "Eat or your health will suffer." The last sentence is an interesting cluster of genitives (description, possession, partitive) and an ablative of separation. For two weeks the pagans had been fasting to save their lives. How needless! God had already told Paul that not one of them would perish.

*Cf.* our comment on verse 21. The text does not say that Paul fasted. Others did. Does ἀσιτίας in verse 21 mean abstinence from food or abstinence from speech? If from food only, then does it apply to Paul or only to the unsaved seamen? Why should Paul, Luke and Aristarchus have fasted? The 35th verse says that he began to eat, but this does not say that this was the first food he had eaten in two weeks.

*Verse 35 - "And when he had thus spoken, he took bread and gave thanks to God in presence of them all; and when he had broken it, he began to eat."*

εἴπας δὲ ταῦτα καὶ λαβὼν ἄρτον εὐχαρίστησεν τῷ θεῷ ἐνώπιον πάντων καὶ κλάσας ἤρξατο ἐσθίειν.

εἴπας (aor.act.part.nom.sing.masc.of εἶπον) 155.

δὲ (continuative conjunction) 11.

ταῦτα (acc.pl.neut.of οὗτος, direct object of εἴπας) 93.

καὶ (adjunctive conjunction joining participles) 14.

λαβὼν (aor.act.part.nom.sing.masc.of λαμβάνω, adverbial, coincident) 533.

ἄρτον (acc.sing.masc.of ἄρτος, direct object of λαβὼν) 338.

εὐχαρίστησεν (3d.per.sing.aor.act.ind.of εὐχαριστέω, constative) 1185.

τῷ (dat.sing.masc.of the article in agreement with θεῷ) 9.

θεῷ (dat.sing.masc.of θεός, indirect object of εὐχαρίστησεν) 124.

ἐνώπιον (improper preposition with the genitive of place description) 1798.

πάντων (gen.pl.masc.of πᾶς, place description) 67.

καὶ (adjunctive conjunction joining verbs) 14.

κλάσας (aor.act.part.nom.sing.masc.of κλάω, adverbial, coincident) 1121.

ἤρξατο (3d.per.sing.aor.mid.ind.of ἄρχω, ingressive) 383.

ἐσθίειν (pres.act.inf.of ἐσθίω, complementary) 610.

*Translation - "And having said these things he took bread, gave thanks to God before them all and when he had broken it he began to eat."*

**Comment:** The aorist participles make the order of events clear. They are good examples of the aorist participle in its temporal relation to the main verb. The actions of εἴπας and λαβὼν are antecedent to εὐχαρίστησεν, to be sure (in no case is the action of the aorist participle subsequent to that of the main verb), but the amount of time between Paul's speech and when he picked up the bread and gave thanks is insignificant. The same is true of the passage of time between κλάσας and ἤρξατο. Paul finished his speech, recorded in verses 33, 34, took the bread, prayed his prayer of thanksgiving to God, broke the bread into pieces and began to eat - all of this in a matter of only a minute or two. Thus we are justified in calling the participles coincident, although in strict application they are temporally antecedent. No damage is done to exegesis when we view the grammar and syntax in the light of the event being described, and, with the help of a little imagination as to how the scene was enacted, make our translation and comment. Great damage occurs, however, when we construe the action of an aorist participle as having taken place *after* the time of the action of the main verb. I mention it here in order to give the student practice in examining the construction and relating it to the facts as they occurred. If a long period of time had elapsed between the times indicated by these participles and the main verbs we would refer to them as adverbially temporal (and thus antecedent), instead of adverbially coincident.

Paul's example inspired good cheer among them. If Paul's God had given him such assurance that he could break the fast, calling God's attention to the fact by praying a prayer of thanksgiving, not only for the bread, but, no doubt for deliverance from the storm, then that was good enough for them.

It is not difficult to imagine the gusto with which Julius, the pilot, the captain, the crew and the other passengers fell upon the viands. They had not eaten for two weeks. Paul, Luke and Aristarchus could give heartfelt thanks to God that their religion allowed them to eat every day. What sacrifices pagans make to pagan gods in the name of pagan religion! I repeat that there is no hard evidence in any of the texts that mention the fast to prove that Paul and his Christian friends participated in it. A victorious Christian, who has already been assured by the Lord that he was not going to die in a shipwreck, does not go without food for two weeks in an attempt to persuade the Lord not to forget His promise. Our God is not likely to forget what He has promised and Paul was not likely to think that He needed to be reminded. The asceticism of Medieval and modern Gnostics reminds us of the fast of a shipload of pagans caught on a small wheat ship in the midst of a Mediterranean Euroclydon. Those famished people might very well have enjoyed their food on every day of those two weeks. They had three Christians on board. The writer ate little for ten days while enroute to Europe, but the difficulty was not lack of faith in God. It was *mal de mer*. I was

> like a missionary's daughter
> casting bread upon the water
> in a way I hadn't orter.

Verse 36 tells us with what enthusiasm the people fell upon the cuisine.

*Verse 36 - "Then were they all of good cheer, and they also took some meat."*

εὔθυμοι δὲ γενόμενοι πάντες καὶ αὐτοὶ προσελάβοντο τροφῆς.

#3737 εὔθυμοι (nom.pl.masc.of εὔθυμος, pred. adjective).

be of good cheer - Acts 27:36.

*Meaning:* A combination of εὐ (#1536) and θυμός (#2034). Hence, well disposed; happy; of good cheer - Acts 27:36.

δὲ (inferential conjunction) 11.
γενόμενοι (aor.mid.part.nom.pl.masc.of γίνομαι, adverbial, causal) 113.
πάντες (nom.pl.masc.of πᾶς, subject of προσελάβοντο) 67.
καὶ (adjunctive conjunction joining substantives) 14.
αὐτοὶ (nom.pl.masc.of αὐτός, intensive) 16.
προσελάβοντο (3d.per.pl.aor.act.ind.of προσλαμβάνω, ingressive) 1210.
τροφῆς (abl.sing.fem.of τροφή, source) 266.

*Translation - "So because they all began to feel better, they themselves also began to take some of the food."*

**Comment:** Paul's optimism was infectious. Everybody cheered up. Even to the point that they themselves (intensive αὐτοὶ) began to take some of the food. A little imagination will reconstruct the scene. Two hundred seventy three people on a small ship that has been through two weeks of frightful storm at sea. For days they had been fasting and praying to whatever gods may be. Now they were near land, and a preacher, a Hebrew Christian, in irons, has announced that all will be safe. The wave of relief spreads throughout the crowd. Smiles appear, shouts of happiness are heard and eager hands stuff food into famished mouths. For the first time in two weeks there is laughter on pagan lips. Of course Paul, Luke and Aristarchus have been relaxed for two weeks, except perhaps for seasickness! One wonders if Doctor Luke carried a remedy in his bag, and, if so, was it effective?

*Verse 37 - "And we were in all in the ship two hundred threescore and sixteen souls."*

ἤμεθα δὲ αἱ πᾶσαι ψυχαὶ ἐν τῷ πλοίῳ διακόσιαι ἑβδομήκοντα ἕξ.

ἤμεθα (1st.per.pl.imp.ind.of εἰμί) 86.
δὲ (explanatory conjunction) 11.
αἱ (nom.pl.fem.of the article in agreement with ψυχαὶ) 9.
πᾶσαι (nom.pl.fem.of πᾶς, in agreement with ψυχαὶ) 67.
ψυχαὶ (nom.pl.fem.of ψυχή, subject of ἤμεθα) 233.
ἐν (preposition with the locative of place) 80.
τῷ (loc.sing.neut.of the article in agreement with πλοίῳ) 9.
πλοίῳ (loc.sing.neut.of πλοῖον, place) 400.
διακόσιαι (nom.pl.fem.of διακόσιος, numeral, in agreement with ψυχαὶ) 2265.
ἑβδομήκοντα (numeral) 2410.
ἕξ (numeral) 1220.

*Translation - "And we, the total number of souls on board the ship were two hundred, seventy six."*

**Comment:** Variant readings have 275, 76,70 and 270. πᾶσαι in the attributive position - "the total number of souls." Vaticanus has ὡς ἑβδομήκοντα ἕξ. "In any case ὡς with an exact statement of number is inappropriate (despite Luke's penchant for qualifying numbers by using ὡς or ὡσεί. cf. Luke 3:23 Ac.2:41; 4.4; 5.7,36; 10.3; 13.18,20; 19.7,34)." (Metzger, *A Textual Commentary on the Greek New Testament*, 499,500).

*Verse 38 - "And when they had eaten enough, they lightened the ship, and cast out the wheat into the sea."*

κορεσθέντες δὲ τροφῆς ἐκούφιζον τὸ πλοῖον ἐκβαλλόμενοι τόν σῖτον εἰς τὴν θάλασσαν.

#3738 κορεσθέντες (1st.aor.pass.part.nom.pl.masc.of κορέννυμι, adverbial, temporal).

eat enough - Acts 27:38.
full - 1 Cor.4:8.

*Meaning: Cf.* κόρος (#2567) to satisfy, sate, fill full. With reference to food - Acts 27:38; of spiritual utility (sarcasm) - 1 Cor.4:8.

δὲ (continuative conjunction) 11.
τροφῆς (abl.sing.fem.of τροφή, source) 266.

#3739 ἐκούφιζον (3d.per.pl.imp.act.ind.of κουφίζω, inchoative).

lighten - Acts 27:38.

*Meaning: Cf.* κοῦφος - "light." Intrans. "to be light" in weight. transitively - "to lighten." With reference to a ship, by throwing cargo overboard - Acts 27:38.

τὸ (acc.sing.neut.of the article in agreement with πλοῖον) 9.
πλοῖον (acc.sing.neut.of πλοῖον, direct object of ἐκούφιζον) 400.
ἐκβαλλόμενοι (pres.mid.part.nom.pl.masc.of ἐκβάλλω, adverbial, modal) 649.
τὸν (acc.sing.masc.of the article in agreement with σῖτον) 9.
σῖτον (acc.sing.masc.of σῖτος, direct object of ἐκβαλλόμενοι) 311.
εἰς (preposition with the accusative of extent) 140.
τὴν (acc.sing.fem.of the article in agreement with θάλασσαν) 9.
θάλασσαν (acc.sing.fem.of θάλασσα, extent) 374.

*Translation - "And when they had gorged themselves on food, they began to lighten the ship by throwing the wheat out into the sea."*

**Comment:** Perhaps "gorge" is a little extreme, but κορέννυμι (#3738) means "to be fully satisfied." In view of the fact that they had been fourteen days without food, one can estimate with reasonable accuracy the intensity of their desire to eat. It is not likely that many were temperate. One wonders whether, in view of their experiences of the next hour, many retained that which they had eaten. It is enough to know that all reached the shore alive.

When they had eaten they began to lighten the ship (inchoative imperfect in ἐκούφιζον). Their method (modal participle in ἐκβαλλόμενοι) was to throw the wheat overboard. All else - deck cargo, tackle, life boat, and now the wheat in the hold was sacrificed. It is interesting to note that this decision to sacrifice the wheat, which had great commercial value to the owners, was made before the morning light enabled them to see what prospects existed for a safe approach to the beach. Apparently the officials on board had total confidence in Paul's prediction that, although no lives would be lost, the ship and its cargo would be destroyed, despite repeated efforts to save her (verses 18,19,22,32,38).

# The Shipwreck

*(Acts 27:39 - 44)*

*Verse 39 - "And when it was day, they knew not the land: but they discovered a*

*certain crrek with a shore into the which they were minded, if it were possible, to*
*thrust in the ship."*

Ὅτε δὲ ἡμέρα ἐγένετο, τὴν γῆν οὐκ ἐπεγίνωσκον, κόλπον δέ τινα κατενόουν
ἔχοντα αἰγιαλὸν εἰς ὃν ἐβουλεύοντο εἰ δύναιντο ἐξῶσαι τὸ πλοῖον.

Ὅτε (conjunction introducing the indicative in a definite temporal clause) 703.

δὲ (continuative conjunction) 11.

ἡμέρα (nom.sing.fem.of ἡμέρα, subject of ἐγένετο) 135.

ἐγένετο (3d.per.sing.aor.ind.of γίνομαι, culminative, definite temporal
clause) 113.

τὴν (acc.sing.fem.of the article in agreement with γῆν) 9.

γῆν (acc.sing.fem.of γῆ, direct object of ἐπεγίωσκον) 157.

οὐκ (negative conjunction with the indicative) 130.

ἐπεγίνωσκον (3d.per.pl.imp.act.ind.of ἐπιγινώσκω, progressive description)
675.

κόλπον (acc.sing.masc.of κόλπος, direct object of κατενόουν) 1702.

δὲ (adversative conjunction) 11.

τινα (acc.sing.masc.of τις, indefinite pronoun, in agreement with κόλπον)
486.

κατενόουν (3d.per.pl.imp.act.ind.of κατανοέω, inchoative) 648.

ἔχοντα (pres.act.part.acc.sing.masc.of ἔχω, adjectival, restrictive, in
agreement with κόλπον) 82.

αἰγιαλὸν (acc.sing.masc.of αἰγιαλός, direct object of ἔχοντα) 1026.

εἰς (preposition with the accusative of extent) 140.

ὃν (acc.sing.masc.of ὅς, relative pronoun, extent) 65.

ἐβουλούοντο (3d.per.pl.imp.mid.ind.of βούλομαι, voluntative) 90.

εἰ (conditional particle in a fourth-class condition, with the optative of
indirect question) 337.

δύναιντο (3d.per.pl.pres.mid.opt.of δύναμαι, fourth-class condition, indirect
question) 289.

ἐξῶσαι (aor.act.inf.of ἐξωθέω, complementary) 3144.

τὸ (acc.sing.neut.of the article in agreement with πλοῖον) 9.

πλοῖον (acc.sing.neut.of πλοῖον, general reference) 400.

*Translation - "And when the day dawned, they were unable to recognize the*
*land, but they began to make out some stream having a shore line into which*
*they had rather been wishing if they were only able to put the ship."*

**Comment:** Ὅτε and the temporal clause is a welcome relief from Luke's usual
temporal participle. Since we have οὐκ with ἐπεγίνωσκον, we need not think of
the verb as a conative imperfect - one which denotes unsuccessful effort. Rather
it is a progressive description. No one on board recognized the island.
Apparently no one on board had been in that part of the Mediterranean before,
at least not in the immediate vicinity of the island. But they began to make out in
the growing morning light the valley between two hills (κόλπον, #1702), through
which there flowed a stream down to the coast. Its shore line looked inviting. In

ἐβουλεύοντο we have a voluntative imperfect tense. "The want of attainment in the imperfect prepares it to submit quite easily to the expression of a desire or disposition, since the statement of a wish itself implies the lack of realization" (Mantey, *Manual*, 190). *Cf.* Rom.9:3; Acts 25:22; Gal.4:20; Philemon 13. The sailors, the captain and the pilot entertained a fleeting wish that they could save the ship. There was no great confidence that they could have done so, as is clear from εἰ and the optative mode in the fourth-class condition with its indirect question. It is the deliberative optative. ". . . the context shows doubt and perplexity in the indirect questions which have ἄν and the optative in the N.T. (Lu.1:62; 6:11; 9:46; 15:26; Ac.5:24; 10:17). . . See indirect question εἰ βούλοιτο in Ac.25:20. . . " (Robertson, *Grammar*, 940). ". . . in ἔλεγον εἰ βούλοιτο πορεύεσθαι (Ac.25:20) we have the opt.of ind.discourse. The direct was εἰ βούλῃ. The same thing is true of 27:39, ἐβουλεύοντο εἰ δύναιντο ἐκσῶσαι τὸ πλοῖον." (*Ibid.*, 1021). ". . . the indirect questions with εἰ and the optative (Ac.25:20; 27:39) are instances where the indicative would be used in the direct." (*Ibid.*, 1031). The possibility occurred to them that it might be possible to navigate the ship into the mouth of the stream that flowed down from the hills and beach it upon the shore. But there was great doubt that they could do so. Note the meaning of ἐξῶσαι (#3144). The attempt would be made to push the bow of the ship through the surf and up into the quieter water of the steam and upon the shore. At the least they were willing to try.

Their thoughts indicate that, although they had sacrificed the cargo, with great financial loss to the owner, they hoped at least to save the ship, Paul's statement about its destruction to the contrary notwithstanding. It was a question of the force and direction of the shifting winds upon the mainsail which they hoisted and the strength and skill of the pilot at the wheel. The attempt failed as verses 40 and 41 tell us.

*Verse 40 - "And when they had taken up the anchors, they committed themselves unto the sea, and loosed the rudder bands, and hoisted up the mainsail to the wind, and made toward the shore."*

καὶ τὰς ἀγκύρας περιελόντες εἴων εἰς τὴν θάλασσαν, ἅμα ἀνέντες τὰς ζευκτηρίας τῶν πηδαλίων, καὶ ἐπάραντες τὸν ἀρτέμωνα τῇ πνεούσῃ κατεῖχον εἰς τὸν αἰγιαλόν.

καὶ (inferential conjunction) 14.

τὰς (acc.pl.fem.of the article in agreement with ἀγκύρας) 9.

ἀγκύρας (acc.pl.fem.of ἄγκυρα, direct object of περιελόντες) 3733.

περιελόντες (2d.aor.act.part.nom.pl.masc.of περαιρέω, adverbial, coincident) 3724.

εἴων (3d.per.pl.imp.act.of ἐάω, inchoative) 1521.

εἰς (preposition with the accusative of extent) 140.

τὴν (acc.sing.fem.of the article in agreement with θάλασσαν) 9.

θάλασσαν (acc.sing.fem.of θάλασσα, extent) 374.

ἅμα (temporal adverb) 1063.

ἀνέντες (2d.aor.act.part.nom.pl.masc.of ἀνίημι, adverbial, coincident) 3378.

τὰς (acc.pl.fem.of the article in agreement with ζευκτηρίας) 9.

**#3740** ζευκτηρίας (acc.pl.fem.of ζευκτηρία, direct object of ἀνέντες).

band - Acts 27:40.

*Meaning:* from the adjective ζευκτήριος - suitable for joining or binding together. Hence, ropes or bands. With the genitive of description τῶν πηδαλίων in Acts 27:40.

τῶν (gen.pl.neut.of the article in agreement with πηδαλίων) 9.

**#3741** πηδαλίων (gen.pl.neut.of πηδάλιον, description).

helm - James 3:4.
rudder - Acts 27:40.

*Meaning:* from πηδόν - "the blade of an oar" - hence, a ship's rudder; steering device - Acts 27:40; James 3:4.

καὶ (adjunctive conjunction joining participles) 14.
ἐπάραντες (aor.act.part.nom.pl.masc.of ἐπαίρω, adverbial, modal) 1227.
τὸν (acc.sing.masc.of the article in agreement with ἀρτέμωνα) 9.

**#3742** ἀρτέμωνα (acc.sing.masc.of ἀρτέμων, direct object of ἐπάραντες).

mainsail - Acts 27:40.

*Meaning:* The top-sail or fore-sail of a ship - Acts 27:40.

τῇ (loc.sing.fem.of the article in agreement with πνεούσῃ) 9.
πνεούσῃ (pres.act.part.loc.sing.fem.of πνέω, substantival, place) 697.
κατεῖχον (3d.per.pl.imp.act.ind.of κατέχω, inchoative) 2071.
εἰς (preposition with the accusative of extent) 140.
τὸν (acc.sing.masc.of the article in agreement with αἰγιαλόν) 9.
αἰγιαλόν (acc.sing.masc.of ἀγιαλός, extent) 1026.

*Translation -* "*Accordingly they cut the anchor ropes and left them in the sea while they untied the ropes on the rudders and hoisted the foresail to the breeze and began making for the shore.*"

**Comment:** On the basis of the plan to make the attempt to navigate the ship safely to shore - a plan in which they had scant confidence, the crew did what was necessary to get under way. They cut the lines to the four anchors and left them in the sea. At the same time (ἅμα) they untied the lines with which they had lashed the rudder to the ship. During the time that they were at the mercy of the storm, they had tied down the rudder to prevent it from weaving about out of control. Now they needed it. Freed now from the four anchors and with a free rudder which could now respond to the pilot at the wheel, they needed power. So they hoisted the mainsail. πλεούσῃ is a substantival participle - "to the blowing wind." κατεῖχον is inchoative. They began the attempt to make it safely to the beach.

In view of the fact that Paul had told them that the ship would be lost, it is interesting to speculate about their thinking as they sought to bring the ship in safely. No one should be blamed for doing all within human power to avert the loss of the ship, despite Paul's prediction. But why did they cut away the anchors? Was it impossible under the existing conditions to raise them? Were there other anchors on board to replace those that were consigned to the sea? Did they aniticipate that, if they were able to save the ship, other anchors could be obtained on the island? The text offers no answers to these questions.

*Verse 41 - "And falling into a place where two seas met, they ran the ship aground; and the forepart stuck fast, and remained unmoveable, but the hinder part was broken with the violence of the waves."*

περιπεσόντες δὲ εἰς τόπον διθάλασσον ἐπέκειλαν τὴν ναῦν, καὶ ἡ μὲν πρῷρα ἐρείσασα ἔμεινεν ἀσάλευτος, ἡ δὲ πρύμα ἐλύετο ὑπὸ τῆς βίας (τῶν κυμάτων).

περιπεσόντες (2d.aor.act.part.nom.pl.masc.of περιπίπτω, adverbial, coincident) 2420.
  δὲ (adversative conjunction) 11.
  εἰς (preposition with the accusative of extent) 140.
  τόπον (acc.sing.masc.of τόπος, extent) 1019.

#3743 διθάλασσον (acc.sing.masc.of διθάλασσος, in agreement with τόπον).

where two seas meet - Acts 27:41.

*Meaning:* A combination of δίς (#2630) and θάλασσα (#374). Lying between two seas; washed by the sea on both sides. τόπος διθάλασσος - an isthmus or tongue of land, the end of which is covered by waves and hence hidden from view of a pilot. A projecting reef or bar against which the waves wash on both sides - Acts 27:41.

#3744 ἐπέκειλαν (3d.per.pl.aor.act.ind.of ἐπικέλλω, constative).

run aground - Acts 27:41.

*Meaning:* A combination of ἐπί (#47) and κέλλω - "to drive on" "to propel." Followed by a direct object - τὴν ναῦν - "to drive a ship upon the land" "to run aground." ' Acts 27:41.

τὴν (acc.sing.fem.of the article in agreement with ναῦν) 9.

#3745 ναῦν (acc.sing.fem.of ναῦς, direct object of ἐπεκειλαν).

ship - Acts 27:41.

*Meaning:* Cf. νάω or νέω - "to float." Hence a ship; a sea going vessel of considerable size. Distinct from πλοῖον (#400) - Acts 27:41.

καὶ (continuative conjunction) 14.
ἡ (nom.sing.fem.of the article in agreement with πρῷρα) 9.
μὲν (particle of affirmation) 300.
πρῷρα (nom.sing.fem.of πρῷα, subject of ἔμεινεν) 3734.

#3746 ἐρείσασα (aor.act.part.nom.sing.fem.of ἐρείδω, adverbial, causal).

stick fast - Acts 27:41.

*Meaning:* To fix; stick fast; intransitive - to be stuck. With reference to the ship on the sand bar - Acts 27:41.

ἔμεινεν (3d.per.sing.aor.act.ind.of μένω, progressive description) 864.

#3747 ἀσάλευτος (nom.sing.fem.of ἀσάλευτος, predicate adjective).

unmoveable - Acts 27:41.
which cannot be moved - Heb.12:28.

*Meaning:* α privaitve plus σαλεύω (#911); Hence, unshaken; unmoveable; firm. With reference to a ship aground - Acts 27:41; metaphorically - a kingdom whose future is secure - Heb.12:28.

ἡ (nom.sing.fem.of the article in agreement with πρύμνα) 9.
δὲ (adversative conjunction) 11.
πρύμνα (nom.sing.fem.of πρύμνα, subject of ἐλύετο) 2206.
ἐλύετο (3d.per.sing.imp.pass.ind.of λύω, inchoative) 471.
ὑπὸ (preposition with the ablative of agent) 117.
τῆς (abl.sing.fem.of the article in agreement with βίας) 9.
βίας (abl.sing.fem.of βία, agent) 3063.
(τῶν) (gen.pl.fem.of the article in agreement with κυμάτων) 9.
(κυμάτων) (gen.pl.fem.of κῦμα, description) 754.

*Translation - "But they fell into a place between two seas and ran the ship aground, and the bow stuck fast and remained unmoveable, but the stern began to be broken up by the violence of the waves."*

**Comment:** Inchoative imperfect in ἐλύετο. Variant readings have "by the violence," or "by the waves." One reading omits ὑπό. The dual nature of διά (#118) is clear in διθάλασσον - "in between two seas." Thus Paul's prediction that everything, including the ship, nautical equipment and cargo would be lost and only the 276 passengers would be saved was fulfilled.

*Verse 42 - "And the soldier's counsel was to kill the prisoners, lest any of them should swim out and escape."*

τῶν δὲ στρατιωτῶν βουλὴ ἐγένετο ἵνα τοὺς δεσμώτας ἀποκτείνωσιν, μή τις ἐκκολυμβήσας διαφύγῃ.

τῶν (gen.pl.masc.of the article in agreement with στρατιωτῶν) 9.
δὲ (explanatory conjunction) 11.
στρατιωτῶν (gen.pl.masc.of στρατιώτης, possession) 724.
βουλὴ (nom.sing.fem.of βουλή, subject of ἐγένετο) 2163.
ἐγένετο (3d.per.sing.aor.ind.of γίνομαι, constative) 113.
ἵνα (conjunction with the subjunctive in a purpose clause) 114.
τοὺς (acc.pl.masc.of the article in agreement with δεσμώτας) 9.
δεσμώτας (acc.pl.masc.of δεσμώτης, direct object of ἀποκτείνωσιν) 3672.
ἀποκτείνωσιν (3d.per.pl.pres.act.subj.of ἀποκτείνω, purpose) 889.
μὴ (negative conjunction with the subjunctive in a negative purpose clause) 87.
τις (nom.sing.masc.of τις, indefinite pronoun, subject of διαφύγῃ) 486.

#3748 ἐκκολυμβήσας (aor.act.part.nom.pl.masc.of ἐκκολυμβάω, adverbial, modal).

swim out - Acts 27:42.

*Meaning:* A combination of ἐκ (#19) and κολυμβάω (#3751). Hence, to swim out - Acts 27:42.

#3749 διαφύγῃ (3d.per.sing.aor.act.subj.of διαφεύγω, negative purpose clause).

escape - Acts 27:42.

*Meaning:* A combination of διά (#118) and φεύγω (#202). Hence, to flee so as to put distance between two; to flee utterly; to escape - Acts 27:42.

*Translation - "Now the advice of the soldiers was to the effect that the prisoners should be killed, lest any by swimming out should escape."*

**Comment:** The ἵνα clause with the subjunctive is purpose. μὴ with the subjunctive in negative purpose. The pagan Roman soldiers, charged with the responsibility of delivering their prisoners and totally insensitive to the sovereign will of God, were thinking only of the practical course to follow. They may have feared punishment if their prisoners escaped. *Cf.* Acts 16:27.
Note the modal participle in ἐκκολυμβήσας.

*Verse 43 - "But the centurion, willing to save Paul, kept them from their purpose; and commanded that they which could swim should cast themselves first into the sea, and get to land."*

ὁ δὲ ἑκατοντάρχης βουλόμενος διασῶσαι τὸν Παῦλον ἐκώλυσεν αὐτοὺς τοῦ βουλήματος, ἐκέλευσέν τε τοὺς δυναμένους κολυμβᾶν ἀπορίψαντας πρώτους ἐπὶ τὴν γῆν ἐξιέναι,

ὁ (nom.sing.masc.of the article in agreement with ἑκατοντάρχης) 9.
δὲ (adversative conjunction) 11.
ἑκατοντάρχης (nom.sing.masc.of ἑκατοντάρχης, subject of ἐκώλυσεν and ἐκέλευσεν) 3210.

βουλόμενος (pres.mid.part.nom.sing.masc.of βούλομαι, adverbial, causal) 953.

διασῶσαι (aor.act.inf.of διασώζω, epexegetical) 1138.

τὸν (acc.sing.masc.of the article in agreement with Παῦλον) 9.

Παῦλον (acc.sing.masc.of Παῦλος, direct object of διασῶσαι) 3284.

ἐκώλυσεν (3d.per.sing.aor.act.ind.of κωλύω, constative) 1296.

αὐτοὺς (acc.pl.masc.of αὐτός, direct object of ἐκώλυσεν) 16.

τοῦ (gen.sing.neut.of the article in agreement with βουλήματος) 9.

**#3750** βουλήματος (gen.sing.neut.of βούλημα, reference).

purpose - Acts 27:43.
will - Romans 9:19; 1 Peter 4:3.

*Meaning:* Cf. βούλομαι (#953); βουλή (#2163). Hence, will, purpose. A plan to kill the prisoners - Acts 27:43; the purpose of God - Romans 9:19; of the unregenerate Gentiles - 1 Peter 4:3.

ἐκέλευσεν (3d.per.sing.aor.act.ind.of κελεύω, constative) 741.

τε (adjunctive particle, joining verbs) 1408.

τοὺς (acc.pl.masc.of the article in agreement with δυναμένους) 9.

δυναμένους (pres.mid.part.acc.pl.masc.of δύναμαι, substantival, direct object of ἐκέλευσεν) 289.

**#3751** κολυμβᾶν (pres.act.inf.of κολυμβάω, epexegetical).

swim - Acts 27:43.

*Meaning:* Cf. κολυμβήθρα (#2092). To swim - Acts 27:43.

**#3752** ἀπορίψαντας (aor.act.part.nom.pl.masc.of ἀπορρίπτω, adverbial, coincident).

cast one's self - Acts 27:43.

*Meaning:* A combination of ἀπό (#70) and ρίπτω (#837). Hence, to cast away from - in this context, to leap from the ship - to leap overboard - Acts 27:43.

πρώτους (acc.pl.masc.of πρῶτος, adverbial, in agreement with δυναμένους) 487.

ἐπὶ (preposition with the accusative of extent) 47.

τὴν (acc.sing.fem.of the article in agreement with γῆν) 9.

γῆν (acc.sing.fem.of γῆ, extent) 157.

ἐξιέναι (pres.inf.of ἐξεῖμι, epexegetical) 3303.

*Translation* - "But because the centurion wanted to save Paul he put a stop to their plan (frustrated them with reference to their plan) and he ordered those who were able to swim to jump overboard first and swim to shore."

**Comment:** δὲ is adversative. The soldiers' plan to kill the prisoners is opposed and frustrated by the centurion. We are told why. βουλόμενος is a causal participle. The centurion wanted to save Paul's life. Thus we have the sovereign God using a pagan Roman army officer, in the exercise of the superior authority of his rank, fulfilling the divine purpose. This is the penultimate reference to Julius, the centurion. In Acts 28:16 he is reported as having delivered the prisoners to the captain of the guard in Rome. Luke tells us nothing about his spiritual experience, if indeed, he had one. We may be sure that Paul, and perhaps Luke and Aristarchus as well, witnessed to him of the grace of God and the gospel of Christ by which it is available. He could not have failed to be impressed with the dignity of Paul's behavior since he met him in Caesarea at the beginning of the voyage, especially during the preceding two weeks. While others fasted and intoned their heathen supplications to their gods, Paul calmly announced that his God had assured him that no lives would be lost. His prediction about the ship and its cargo had been fulfilled. Did the Holy Spirit use all of these things to draw Julius to Christ? What was his reaction to the two incidents on Malta - the serpent bite and the healing of Publius' father? We must respect the divine reticency to inform us about these matters. I shall not be surprized to find Julius at the rapture. If the Holy Spirit had chosen to tell us the story of the conversion of every member of the Body of Christ, the world indeed would not hold the books that would have been written.

πρώτους is adverbial, but note that it agrees in case and number with δυναμένους, thus indicating that the order was that those who could swim were ordered into the water first. Thus the timbers and boards which were floating beside the wreck would be available for those who could not swim.

The plan also provided that the soldiers who could swim would be ready at the shore line to assist the others as they came and to prevent the escape of the prisoners.

The escape of all those on board who could not swim is described in

*Verse 44 - "And the rest, some on boards, and some on broken pieces of the ship. And so it came to pass, that they escaped all safe to land."*

καὶ τοὺς λοιποὺς οὓς μὲν ἐπὶ σανίσιν οὓς δὲ ἐπί τινων τῶν ἀπὸ τοῦ πλοίου, καὶ οὕτως ἐγένετο πάντας διασωθῆναι ἐπὶ τὴν γῆν.

καὶ (continuative conjunction) 14.
τοὺς (acc.pl.masc.of the article in agreement with λοιποὺς) 9.
λοιποὺς (acc.pl.masc.of λοιπός, direct object of ἐκέλευσεν) 1402.
οὓς (acc.pl.masc.of οὗς, relative pronoun, attracted to λοιποὺς) 65.
μὲν (particle of affirmation) 300.
ἐπὶ (preposition with the locative of place) 47.

#3753 σανίσιν (loc.pl.fem.of σανίς, place).

board - Acts 27:44.

*Meaning:* Cf. σανδάλιον (#2249), which is probably a Persian word - "a board under the foot" - hence, a sandal, with which σανίς may have an etymological connection. A board or plant. A piece of lumber - Acts 27:44.

οὕς (acc.pl.masc.of ὅς, relative pronoun, attracted to λοιπούς) 65.

δὲ (adjunctive conjunction joining relative pronouns) 11.

ἐπὶ (preposition with the genitive of place description) 47.

τινων (gen.pl.neut.of τις, indefinite pronoun, place description) 486.

τῶν (gen.pl.neut.of the article, partitive genitive) 9.

ἀπὸ (preposition with the ablative of source) 70.

τοῦ (abl.sing.neut.of the article in agreement with πλοίου) 9.

πλοίου (abl.sing.neut.of πλοῖον, source) 400.

καὶ (continuative conjunction) 14.

οὕτως (demonstrative adverb) 74.

ἐγένετο (3d.per.sing.aor.ind.of γίνομαι, constative) 113.

πάντας (acc.pl.masc.of πᾶς, general reference) 67.

διασωθῆναι (aor.pass.inf.of διασῴζω, noun use, subject of ἐγένετο) 1138.

ἐπὶ (preposition with the accusative of extent) 47.

τὴν (acc.sing.fem.of the article in agreement with γῆν) 9.

γῆν (acc.sing.fem.of γῆ, extent) 157.

*Translation - ". . . and the rest, some on boards and some on various (pieces) from the ship. And that is how it happened. All were brought safely to shore."*

**Comment:** τοὺς λοιποὺς is also the object of ἐκέλευσεν in verse 43. Julius ordered the swimmers to swim out and leave the buoys for those who could not swim. He also ordered the rest to escape on plants and/or pieces of the ship that was breaking up in the waves. The relative pronouns are attracted in case to their antecedent τοὺς λοιπούς. Note the μὲν . . . δὲ sequence, which is common. "Some one way . . . others another."

Note ἐπὶ here, both with the locative of place where and with the genitive of place description. One could even construe σανίσαν as an instrumental of means, since the form can be either locative, instrumental or dative. The student may wish to examine all of the contexts in which ἐπί is used with the oblique case forms, to determine whether there is a context in which ἐπί is used clearly with the instrumental of manner or means. We can find it with the dative. But note ἐπί with the genitive of place description - ἐπὶ τινων. Robertson warns against overrefinement. The ground meaning of ἐπί is "upon" - "on top of" as opposed to ὑπό - "beneath" or "under." It differs from ὑπέρ in that it means "resting upon" not merely "over." (Kuhner-Gerth, *Ausf. Gramm. d. griech. Spr.*, I, 495, as cited in Robertson, *Grammar,* 600). "The only safety consists in holding on to the root-idea and working out from that in each special context." (*Ibid.*). "It would be overrefinement to insist on too much distinction. . . " in many cases (*Ibid.,* 601).

The Greek is facile and the student should not strain to find over-refined distinctions. The thing that we are after is the point of the passage, with as much clarity as the prepositions and cases can provide. Here the thought is clear. The non-swimmers escaped from the wreck and came safely to shore, by means of and resting upon (not floating above) whatever they could find that would float and bear their weight in the water. Thus the genitive of place description and the locative of place where both fill the bill and Luke uses both to express the same idea.

The infinitive διασωθῆναι is the subject of ἐγένετο, with πάντας, as always in such a construction, an accusative of general reference. Thus God's promise to Paul and Paul's promise to his fellow passengers was fulfilled (verses 21-26).

## Paul on the Island of Malta

*(Acts 28:1 - 10).*

*Acts 28:1 - "And when they were escaped, then they knew that the island was called Melita."*

Καὶ διασωθέντες τότε ἐπέγνωμεν ὅτι Μελίτη ἡ νῆσος καλεῖται.

Καὶ (continuative conjunction) 14.

διασωθέντες (aor.pass.part.nom.pl.masc.of διασώζω, adverbial, temporal) 1138.

τότε (temporal adverb) 166.

ἐπέγνωμεν (1st.per.pl.2d.aor.act.ind.of ἐπιγινώσκω, constative) 675.

ὅτι (conjunction introducing an object clause in indirect discourse) 211.

#3754 Μελίτη (nom.sing.fem.of Μελίτη, appellation).

Melita - Acts 28:1.

*Meaning:* A large island lying between North Africa and Sicily. Now called Malta. *Sicula Melita* must not be confused with *Melita Illyrica*, now known as Meleda in the Adriatic. Malta is about 52 nautical miles (60 statute miles) directly south of the island of Sicily - Acts 28:1.

ἡ (nom.sing.fem.of the article in agreement with νῆσος) 9.

νῆσος (nom.sing.fem.of νῆσος, subject of καλεῖται) 3277.

καλεῖται (3d.per.sing.pres.pass.ind.of καλέω, static) 107.

*Translation - "And after we had been rescued we learned that the island was called Malta."*

**Comment:** The participle is temporal, not necessarily coincident. We do not know how long after the rescue that they learned the name of the island. Note the indirect discourse in the object clause after ὅτι, with the static present tense in καλεῖται.

The time was mid-November. The shipwrecked people were miserable - cold, wet, tired, frightened - some of them seasick. They needed comfort. They found it.

*Verse 2 - "And the barbarous people shewed us no little kindness: for they kindled a fire, and received us every one, because of the present rain, and because of the cold."*

οἵ τε βάρβαροι παρεῖχον οὐ τὴν τυχοῦσαν φιλανθρωπίαν ἡμῖν, ἅφαντες γὰρ πυρὰν προσελάβοντο πάντας ἡμᾶς διὰ τὸν ὑετὸν τὸν ἐφεστῶτα καὶ διὰ τὸ φῦχος.

οἱ (nom.pl.masc.of the article in agreement with βάρβαροι) 9.
τε (continuative particle) 1408.

#3755 βάρβαροι (nom.pl.masc.of βάρβαρος, subject of παρεῖχον).

barbarian - Acts 28:4; Rom.1:14; 1 Cor.14:11,11; Col.3:11.
barbarous - Acts 28:2.

*Meaning:* One whose speech marks him of inferior cultural attainment. The stutterer who says βαρβαρβάρ - thus onomatopoeia. The word is not used by Luke disrespectfully in Acts 28:2,4 of the Maltese who were of Phoenician and / or Punic origin. In Romans 1:14 it seems to designate all persons not Greek. Used properly in 1 Cor.14:11,11 of one whose speech cannot be understood. In Col.3:11, of an inhabitant of a land that had some refinement but had not had the opportunity to become Christian.

παρεῖχον (3d.per.pl.imp.act.ind.of παρέχω, inchoative) 1566.
οὐ (negative conjunction with the indicative, litotes) 130.
τὴν (acc.sing.fem.of the article in agreement with φιλανθρωπίαν) 9.
τυχοῦσαν (2d.aor.act.part.acc.sing.fem.of τυγχάνω, adjectival, ascriptive, in agreement with φιλανθρωπίαν) 2699.

#3756 φιλανθρωπίαν (acc.sing.fem.of φιλανθρωπία, direct object of παρεῖχον).

kindness - Acts 28:2.
love toward men - Titus 3:4.

*Meaning:* A combination of φίλος (#932) and ἄνθρωπος (#341). Hence philanthropy; kindness; gracious and helpful behavior toward and service to others. Benevolence. With reference to the kindness of the Maltese natives to the shipwreck victims - Acts 28:2; God's kindness to man - Titus 3:4. *Cf.* φιλανθρώπως (#3675).

ἡμῖν (dat.pl.masc.of ἐγώ, indirect object of παρεῖχον) 123.
ἅφαντες (aor.act.part.nom.pl.masc.of ἅπτω, adverbial, temporal) 711.
γὰρ (inferential conjunction) 105.

#3757 πυρὰν (acc.sing.fem.of πυρά, direct object of ἅφαντες).

fire - Acts 28:2,3.

*Meaning: Cf.* πῦρ (#298). A fire; a pile of burning fuel - on Malta - Acts 28:2,3. The one obvious difference between πυρά and πῦρ is that πῦρα refers to a bonfire.

προσελάβοντο (3d.per.pl.aor.mid.ind.of προσλαμβάνω, ingressive) 1210.
πάντας (acc.pl.masc.of πᾶς, in agreement with ἡμᾶς) 67.
ἡμᾶς (acc.pl.masc.of ἐγώ, direct object of προσελάβοντο) 123.
διὰ (preposition with the accusative, cause) 118.
τὸν (acc.sing.masc.of the article in agreement with ὑετὸν) 9.
ὑετὸν (acc.sing.masc.of ὑετός, cause) 3327.
τὸν (acc.sing.masc.of the article in agreement with ἐφεσθῶτα) 9.
ἐφεστῶτα (perf.act.part.acc.sing.masc.of ἐφίστημι, adjectival, ascriptive, in agreement with ὑετὸν, in the emphatic attributive position) 1877.
καὶ (adjunctive conjunction joining prepositional phrases) 14.
διὰ (preposition with the accusative, cause) 118.
τὸ (acc.sing.neut.of the article in agreement with φῦχος) 9.
φῦχος (acc.sing.neut.of φύχος, cause) 2821.

*Translation -* "*And the barbarians began to go out of their way to be kind to us, as they built a fire and began to care for us because of the rain which was continuing to fall and because of the cold.*"

**Comment:** The litotes οὐ τὴν τυχοῦσαν φιλανθρωπίαν - translates literally to "not by chance kindness." The participle τυχοῦσαν is an adjective in the attributive position and is therefore ascriptive. The kindness which they showed was not accidental. Thus our translation. The Maltese did more for their uninvited guests than normally they would have done, because the need was greater - the trauma of the shipwreck and the narrow escape of the victims from the pounding surf was made worse by the rain which continued to fall and the cold. The kindled fire was only the beginning of their ministrations. No doubt there was food, dry clothing and shelter from the cold rainstorm.

The Apostle Paul was nothing if not useful. As he helped to gather fuel for the fire the first of two supernatural episodes took place.

*Verse 3 -* "*And when Paul had gathered a bundle of sticks, and laid them on the fire, there came a viper out of the heat, and fastened on his hand.*"

συστρέψαντος· δὲ τοῦ Παύλου φρυγάνων τι πλῆθος καὶ ἐπιθέντος ἐπὶ τὴν πυράν, ἔχιδνα ἀπὸ τῆς θέρμης ἐξελθοῦσα καθῆψεν τῆς χειρὸς αὐτοῦ.

συστρέψαντος (aor.act.part.gen.sing.masc.of συστρέφω, genitive absolute) 1240.
δὲ (continuative conjunction) 11.
τοῦ (gen.sing.masc.of the article in agreement with Παύλου) 9.
Παύλου (gen.sing.masc.of Παῦλος, genitive absolute) 3284.

#3758 φρυγάνων (gen.pl.neut.of φρύγανον, partitive genitive).

stick - Acts 28:3.

*Meaning:* Cf. φρύγω, φρύσσω, φρύπτω - "to dry or parch." Hence, φρύγανον is a dry stick; a piece of firewood. Generally in the plural; hence, firewood - Acts 28:3.

τι (acc.sing.neut.of τις, indefinite pronoun, in agreement with πλῆθος) 486.
πλῆθος (acc.sing.neut.of πλῆθος, direct object of συστρέφαντος) 1792.
καὶ (adjunctive conjunction joining participles) 14.
ἐπιθέντος (aor.act.part.gen.sing.masc.of ἐπιτίθημι, genitive absolute) 818.
ἐπὶ (preposition with the accusative of extent) 47.
τὴν (acc.sing.fem.of the article in agreement with πυράν) 9.
πυράν (acc.sing.fem.of πυρά extent) 3757.
ἔχιδνα (nom.sing.fem.of ἔχιδνα, subject of καθῆφεν) 280.
ἀπὸ (preposition with the ablative of separation) 70.
τῆς (abl.sing.fem.of the article in agreement with θέρμης) 9.

#3759 θέρμης (abl.sing.fem.of θέρμη, separation).

heat - Acts 28:3.

*Meaning:* Cf. θερμαίνω (#2813); θέρος (#1513). Heat. From the bonfire of Acts 28:3.

ἐξελθοῦσα (aor.mid.part.nom.sing.fem.of ἐξέρχομαι, adverbial, coincident) 161.

#3760 καθῆφεν (3d.per.sing.aor.act.ind.of καθάπτω, constative).

fasten on - Acts 28:3.

*Meaning:* A combination of κατά (#98) and ἄπτω (#711). Hence, to fasten down upon; to bite down upon. With reference to the serpent that bit Paul, followed by an objective genitive in Acts 28:3.

τῆς (gen.sing.fem.of the article in agreement with χειρὸς) 9.
χειρὸς (gen.sing.fem.of χείρ, objective genitive) 308.
αὐτοῦ (gen.sing.masc.of αὐτός, possession) 16.

*Translation -* "*And when Paul had gathered a bundle of dry sticks and laid them upon the fire, a snake emerged from the heat and sunk its fangs into his hand.*"

**Comment:** Two genitive absolutes, both in the aorist tense, introduce the main verb. Paul, always mindful of the comforts of others, had joined the natives in gathering firewood. When he laid his bundle of sticks upon the bonfire the snake, driven out by the heat, bit him. I have translated καθῆφεν freely - "Fasten down upon" (literally). This could be done by a snake only by sinking the fangs into his hand. *Cf.* our comments on Mark 16:9-20. It is significant that one of the powers attributed by the writer to the saints is the power to withstand snakebite (Mk.16:18). It is an interesting conjecture that the writer had Paul's experience in mind and included it in this totally spurious passage. Perhaps many of the 276 shipwrecked people helped to gather firewood but Luke mentions only Paul.

The snake is associated in Scripture with Satan (Genesis 3:1; Rev.12:9; 20:2). Whenever a preacher of the gospel of Christ, like Paul starts a fire, the snake can be expected to come out of the fire and try to bite the hand that builds it. A genuine Holy Spirit motivated revival will bring the snakes out, but Christians, like Paul on Malta, need not fear. We only shake off the snake and feel no harm.

*Verse 4 - "And when the barbarians saw the venomous beast hang on his hand, they said among themselves, No doubt this man is a murderer, whom, though he hath escaped the sea, yet vengeance suffereth not to live."*

ὡς δὲ εἶδον οἱ βάρβαροι κρεμάμενον τὸ θηρίον ἐκ τῆς χειρὸς αὐτοῦ, πρὸς ἀλλήλους ἔλεγον, Πάντως φονεύς ἐστιν ὁ ἄνθρωπος οὗτος ὃν διασωθέντα ἐκ τῆς θαλάσσης ἡ δίκη ζῆν οὐκ εἴασεν.

ὡς (conjunction introducing the indicative in a definite temporal clause) 128.
δὲ (continuative conjunction) 11.
εἶδον (3d.per.pl.aor.act.ind.of ὁράω, constative) 144a.
οἱ (nom.pl.masc.of the article in agreement with βάρβαροι) 9.
βάρβαροι (nom.pl.masc.of βάρβαρος, subject of εἶδον and ἔλεγον) 3755.
κρεμάμενον (pres.mid.part.acc.sing.neut.of κρεμάννυμι, adjectival, restrictive, in agreement with θηρίον, predicate position) 1249.
τὸ (acc.sing.neut.of the article in agreement with θηρίον) 9.
θηρίον (acc.sing.neut.of θηρίον, direct object of εἶδον) 1951.
ἐκ (preposition with the ablative of separation) 19.
τῆς (abl.sing.fem.of the article in agreement with χειρὸς) 9.
αὐτοῦ (gen.sing.masc.of αὐτός, possession) 16.
πρὸς (preposition with the accusative of extent with a verb of speaking) 197.
ἀλλήλους (acc.pl.masc.of ἀλλήλων, extent, with a verb of speaking) 1487.
ἔλεγον (3d.per.pl.imp.act.ind.of λέγω, iterative) 66.
Πάντως - (adverbial) 2029.
φονεύς (nom.sing.masc.of φονεύς, predicate nominative) 1405.
ἐστιν (3d.per.sing.pres.ind.of εἰμί, aoristic) 86.
ὁ (nom.sing.masc.of the article in agreement with ἄνθρωπος) 9.
ἄνθρωπος (nom.sing.masc.of ἄνθρωπος, subject of ἐστιν) 341.
οὗτος (nom.sing.masc.of οὗτος, in agreement with ἄνθρωπος) 93.
ὃν (acc.sing.masc.of ὅς, relative pronoun, general reference) 65.
διασωθέντα (aor.pass.part.acc.sing.masc.of διασώζω, adverbial, concessive) 1138.
ἐκ (preposition with the ablative of source) 19.
τῆς (abl.sing.fem.of the article in agreement with θαλάσσης) 9.
θαλάσσης (abl.sing.fem.of θάλασσα, source) 374.
ἡ (nom.sing.fem.of the article in agreement with δίκη) 9.

#3761 δίκη (nom.sing.fem.of δίκη, subject of εἴασεν).

vengeance - Acts 28:4; Jude 7.
punished - 2 Thess.1:9.

*Meaning:* Cf. δικαιοκρισία (#3835), δικαίωμα (#1781), δικαιόω (#933), ιδίκαιος (#85), δικαίως (#2855), δικαίωσις (#3895), δικαιοσύνη (#322), δικαστής (#3127). Thayer thinks also that it is related to δείκνυμι (#359). That which is right, just, that which ought to be done; a just sentence of condemnation as in a court of law. Personified as the goddess Justice. Avenging justice - Acts 28:4; the execution of the sentence - Jude 7; 2 Thess.1:9.

ζῆν (pres.act.inf.of ζάω, object infinitive in indirect assertion) 340.
οὐκ (negative conjunction with the infinitive in indirect assertion) 130.
εἴασεν (3d.per.sing.aor.act.ind.of ἐάω, culminative) 1521.

*Translation - "And when the natives saw the beast hanging out of his hand, they began to say to one another, 'Doubtless this man is a murderer whom, though he was rescued from the sea, justice has not permitted to live.' "*

**Comment:** ὡς introduces the definite temporal clause. The use of ἐκ and the ablative gives us a good picture of the scene. The snake, with fangs imbedded in Paul's flesh was hanging down "out of his hand" (ἐκ τῆς χειρὸς αὐτοῦ). This picture supports our translation of καθῆψεν in verse 3.

Another serpent (ὄφις #658) was also hanged (John 3:14) as a type of Christ, the uplifted curse (Gal.3:13) Who too was hanged (Acts 5:30; 10:39; Gal.3:13, cf.#1249) upon a tree. ἔλεγον is iterative. One can imagine the rumor that passed among the people, as it was repeated again and again. Note that φονεύς is emphasized. Note also the contemptuous use of οὗτος. Cf. Mt.26:61,71; Lk.22:56; Mk.2:7; Lk.15:2; John 6:42; 9:24; 12:34; Acts 7:40; 19:26; Lk.15:30; 18:11; Acts 5:28. There are many other examples in the New Testament. Watch for them. The participle διασωθέντα is concessive - "Despite the fact that he was saved . . . κ.τ.λ."

It is clear that the people on the island had a highly developed ethical sense and a strong faith in some sort of universal justice which was active in human affairs.

*Verse 5 - "And he shook off the beast into the fire and felt no harm."*

ὁ μὲν οὖν ἀποτινάξας τὸ θηρίον εἰς τὸ πῦρ ἔπαθεν οὐδὲν κακόν.

ὁ (nom.sing.masc.of the article, subject of ἔπαθεν) 9.
μὲν (particle of affirmation) 300.
οὖν (continuative conjunction) 68.
ἀποτινάξας (aor.act.part.nom.sing.masc.of ἀποτινάσσω, adverbial, coincident) 2252.
τὸ (acc.sing.neut.of the article in agreement with θηρίον) 9.
θηρίον (acc.sing.neut.of θηρίον, direct object of ἀποτινάξας) 1951.
εἰς (preposition with the accusative of extent) 140.
τὸ (acc.sing.neut.of the article in agreement with πῦρ) 9.
πῦρ (acc.sing.neut.of πῦρ, extent) 298.
ἔπαθεν (3d.per.sing.2d.aor.act.ind.of πάσχω, culminative) 1208.

οὐδὲν (acc.sing.neut.of οὐδείς, in agreement with κακόν) 446.

κακόν (acc.sing.neut.of κακός, direct object of ἔπαθεν) 1388.

*Translation - "Then he shook the snake off into the fire and suffered no pain."*

**Comment:** μὲν here as it frequently does, sharpens the outlines of its adjuncts. Paul shook off the beast. εἰς τὸ πῦρ is a predicate use of the preposition with the usual accusative of extent. The fate of the serpent suggests the fate of another serpent (Rev.20:10). Paul suffered no pain or other physical ill. But this does not justify the snake handlers for many reasons. First, Mark 16:18 is not a part of the Holy Spirit inspired text of the Gospel of Mark. Mark did not write it. Second, the snake handlers are not the Apostle Paul. Third, even Paul did not pick up the snake and fondle it for the amusement and amazement of the congregation, nor to prove that he was a good Christian. He was busy building a fire. The snake bite was an accident. Fourth, the snake handlers do not necessarily have the assurance from the Lord, as Paul did, that they still have work to do for him. Paul was not poisoned by the snake because he could not go to Rome to witness for Christ, if he died of snake bite on the island of Malta.

*Verse 6 - "Howbeit they looked when he should have swollen, or fallen down dead suddenly: but after they had looked a great while, and saw no harm come to him, they changed their minds, and said that he was a god."*

οἱ δὲ προσεδόκων αὐτὸν μέλλειν πίμπρασθαι ἢ καταπίπτειν ἄφνω νεκρόν. ἐπὶ πολὺ δὲ αὐτῶν προσδοκώντων καὶ θεωρούντων μηδὲν ἄτοπον εἰς αὐτὸν γινόμενον, μεταβαλόμενοι ἔλεγον αὐτὸν εἶναι θεόν.

οἱ (nom.pl.masc.of the article, subject of προσεδόκων) 9.

δὲ (adversative conjunction) 11.

προσεδόκων (3d.per.pl.imp.act.ind.of προσδοκάω, concessive) 906.

αὐτὸν (acc.sing.masc.of αὐτός, general reference) 16.

μέλλειν (pres.act.inf.of μέλλω, object infinitive in indirect assertion) 206.

#3762 πίμπρασθαι (pres.pass.inf.of πίμπρημι, epexegetical).

swell - Acts 28:6.

*Meaning:* Cf. πρήθω - "to blow" or "to burn." Hence, to swell; to become inflamed and infected. LXX, Numbers 5:21,22,27. The normal result of snakebite - Acts 28:6.

ἢ (disjunctive) 465.

καταπίπτειν (pres.act.inf.of καταπίπτω, epexegetical) 2196.

ἄφνω (adverbial) 2957.

νεκρόν (acc.sing.masc.of νεκρός, predicate accusative) 749.

ἐπὶ (preposition with the accusative of time extent) 47.

πολὺ (acc.sing.neut.of πολύς, in agreement with χρόνον, understood) 228.

δὲ (adversative conjunction) 11.

αὐτῶν (gen.pl.masc.of αὐτός, genitive absolute) 16.

προσδοκώντων (pres.act.part.gen.pl.masc.of προσδοκάω, genitive absolute, adverbial, causal) 906.

καὶ (adjunctive conjunction joining participles) 14.

θεωρούντων (pres.act.part.gen.pl.masc.of θεωρέω, adverbial, causal) 1667.

μηδὲν (acc.sing.neut.of μηδείς, direct object of θεωρούντων) 713.

ἄτοπον (acc.sing.neut.of ἄτοπος, in agreement with μηδὲν) 2856.

εἰς (preposition with the accusative of extent) 140.

αὐτὸν (acc.sing.masc.of αὐτός, extent) 16.

γινόμενον (pres.mid.part.acc.sing.neut.of γίνομαι, adjectival, restrictive, in agreement with μηδὲν) 113.

#3763 μεταβαλόμενοι (aor.mid.part.nom.pl.masc.of μεταβάλλω, adverbial, causal).

change one's mind - Acts 28:6.

*Meaning:* A combination of μετά (#50) and βάλλω (#299). Hence, to turn around; in the middle voice, to turn one's self around. Hence, to change the mind. Reverse a previous opinion. With reference to the natives on Malta *in re* Paul - Acts 28:6.

ἔλεγον (3d.per.pl.imp.act.ind.of λέγω, inchoative)l 66.

αὐτὸν (acc.sing.masc.of αὐτός, general reference) 16.

εἶναι (pres.inf.of εἰμί, object of ἔλεγον in indirect discourse) 86.

θεόν (acc.sing.masc.of θεός, predicate accusative) 124.

*Translation - "And they began to look for him to become swollen or suddenly to fall down dead; but after a long time, though they were expecting it, because they saw nothing unusual happen to him, they changed their minds and began to say that he was a god."*

**Comment:** προσεδόκων is inchoative. The natives had seen Paul shake off the snake. It was natural that they would begin to watch for and expect the evil results. μέλλειν, the object infinitive of προσεδόκων is explained by the two infinitives πίμπρασθαι and καταπίπτειν Note ἐπὶ πολύ with χρόνον supplied in a temporal phrase. *Cf.* Acts 4:17; 18:20; 20:9,11 for other temporal uses of ἐπί with other adjuncts. προσδοκώντων is concessive. Despite the fact that they expected to see Paul fall down deal, they saw nothing amiss. εἰς αὐτὸν is a predicate usage of εἰς. *Cf.* #140. μεταβαλόμενοι is causal and temporal and ἔλεγον is both inchoative and iterative. They began and continued to offer their opinion that Paul was a god.

This reaction of the natives is natural. Apparently they recognized the snake as deadly. With a strong tradition of ethical justice, their first reaction that Paul was a murderer (or some sort of sinner) was logical. When, however, he did not suffer it was likewise logical to assume that he was supernatural. Only a god could survive the bite of a snake so deadly. If we assume that the natives were correct that the snake was a deadly poisonous variety, Paul's healing was a miracle, since Paul had some preaching to do in Rome. But his healing was not due to his own supernatural powers. If the natives had said, "He is God's yielded servant" they would have been correct. One can imagine the excitement as they ran here and there repeating, "He is a god! He is a god!" Did Publius believe that Paul was a god?

*Verse 7 - "In the same quarters were possessions of the chief man of the island, whose name was Publius; who received us, and lodged us three days courteously."*

Ἐν δὲ τοῖς περὶ τὸν τόπον ἐκεῖνον ὑπῆρχεν χωρία τῷ πρώτῳ τῆς νήσου ὀνόματι Ποπλίῳ, ὃς ἀναδεξάμενος ὑμᾶς τρεῖς ἡμέρας φιλοφρόνως ἐξένισεν.

Ἐν (preposition with the locative of place) 80.
δὲ (explanatory conjunction) 11.
τοῖς (loc.pl.neut.of the article in agreement with χωρίοις, understood) 9.
περὶ (preposition with the accusative of place description) 173.
τὸν (acc.sing.masc.of the article in agreement with τόπον) 9.
τόπον (acc.sing.masc.of τόπος, place description) 1019.
ἐκεῖνον (acc.sing.masc.of ἐκεῖνος, in agreement with τόπον) 246.
ὑπῆρχεν (3d.per.sing.imp.act.ind.of ὑπάρχω, progressive description) 1303.
χωρία (nom.pl.neut.of χωρίον, subject of ὑπῆρχεν) 1583.
τῷ (dat.sing.masc.of the article in agreement with πρώτῳ) 9.
πρώτῳ (dat.sing.masc.of πρῶτος, possession) 487.
τῆς (gen.sing.fem.of the article in agreement with νήσου) 9.
νήσου (gen.sing.fem.of νῆσος, description) 3277.
ὀνόματι (dat.sing.neut.of ὄνομα, possession) 108.

#3764 Ποπλίῳ (dat.sing.masc.of Πόπλιος, in agreement with ὀνόματι).

Publius - Acts 28:7,8.

*Meaning:* Publius (a Roman name). The chief magistrate of the island of Malta - Acts 28:7,8.

ὃς (nom.sing.masc.of ὅς, relative pronoun, subject of ἐξένισεν) 65.

#3765 ἀναδεξάμενος (aor.mid.part.nom.sing.masc.of ἀναδέχομαι, adverbial, coincident).

receive - Acts 28:7; Heb.11:17.

*Meaning:* A combination of ἀνά (#1059) and δέχομαι (#867). Hence, to take up; take to one's self; receive. In the middle voice, to rescue for one's self. To entertain guests - Acts 28:7. Psychologically, to believe in and accept assurances from God - Heb.11:17.

ἡμᾶς (acc.pl.masc.of ἐγώ, direct object of ἀναδεξάμενος and ἐξένισεν) 123.
τρεῖς (acc.pl.fem.of τρεῖς, in agreement with ἡμέρας) 1010.
ἡμέρας (acc.pl.fem.of ἡμέρα, time extent) 135.

#3766 φιλοφρόνως (adverbial).

courteously - Acts 28:7.

*Meaning:* A combination of φίλος (#932) and φρήν (#4235). Hence, courteously; with friendly understanding and compassion - Acts 28:7.

ἐξένισεν (3d.per.sing.aor.act.ind.of ἐξένισεν, constative) 3214.

*Translation - "Now in the immediate area were the country estates of the chief of the island - a man named Publius, who took us in and entertained us courteously for three days."*

**Comment:** δὲ is explanatory. We supply χωρίοις with τοῖς. περὶ with the accusative, in much the same sense as the genitive of place description. *Cf.* also Luke 13:8; Acts 13:13. "In the large area that extended around the spot where the refugees came ashore. χωρία in a diminutive sense - plots of land, belonging to the governor. τρεῖς ἡμέρας, the accusative of time extent belongs with ἐξένισεν. Publius, the Roman governor of the island, had a kind, understanding and compassionate heart (*cf.*#3766).

It was "bread on the water" for the governor, as we see in

verse 8. It may be inferred from his name as well as from his position that Publius was a Roman. The fact that Paul also was a Roman citizen (Acts 22:27) plus the fact that he clearly stood out as an unusual individual in comparison with most of those on board, may have influenced Publius. There is also the possibility that Julius and Publius had a talk about Paul.

*Verse 8 - "And it came to pass, that the father of Publius lay sick of a fever and of a bloody flux, to whom Paul entered in, and prayed, and laid his hands on him, and healed him."*

ἐγένετο δὲ τὸν πατέρα τοῦ Ποπλίου πυρετοῖς καὶ δυσεντερίῳ συνεχόμενον κατακεῖσθαι, πρὸς ὃν ὁ Παῦλος εἰσελθὼν καὶ προσευξάμενος ἐπιθεὶς τὰς χεῖρας αὐτῷ ἰάσατο αὐόν.

ἐγένετο (3d.per.sing.aor.ind.of γίνομαι, constative) 113.
δὲ (continuative conjunction) 11
τὸν (acc.sing.masc.of the article in agreement with πατέρα) 9.
πατέρα (acc.sing.masc.of πατήρ, general reference) 238.
τοῦ (gen.sing.masc.of the article in agreement with Ποπλίου) 9.
Ποπλίου (gen.sing.masc.of Πόπλιος, relationship) 3764.
πυρετοῖς (instru.pl.masc.of πυρετός, means) 738.
καὶ (adjunctive conjunction joining nouns) 14.

#3767 δυσεντερίῳ (instru.sing.neut.of δυσεντέριον, means).

bloody flux - Acts 28:8.

*Meaning:* A combination of δυς ("an inseparable prefix conveying the idea of difficulty, opposition, injuriousness or the like, and corresponding to our *mis-*, *un-* . . . opp.to εὖ" (Thayer, *Lexicon,* 160) ) and ἔντερον - "intestine." Hence, intestinal difficulty; inflamation of the bowel - with reference to the illness of the father of Publius - Acts 28:8.

συνεχόμενον (pres.pass.part.acc.sing.masc.of συνέχω, adverbial, causal) 414.

κατακεῖσθαι (pres.pass.inf.of κατάκειμαι, subject of ἐγένετο) 2065.

πρὸς (preposition with the accusative of extent) 197.

ὅν (acc.sing.masc.of ὅς, relative pronoun, extent) 65.

ὁ (nom.sing.masc.of the article in agreement with Παῦλος) 9.

Παῦλος (nom.sing.masc.of Παῦλος, subject of ἰάσατο) 3284.

εἰσελθὼν (aor.part.nom.sing.masc.of εἰσέρχομαι, adverbial, coincident) 234.

καὶ (adjunctive conjunction joining participles) 14.

προσευξάμενος (aor.mid.part.nom.sing.masc.of προσεύχομαι, adverbial, coincident) 544.

ἐπιθεὶς (aor.mid.part.nom.sing.masc.of ἐπιτίθημι, adverbial, coincident) 818.

τὰς (acc.pl.fem.of the article in agreement with χεῖρας) 9.

χεῖρας (acc.pl.fem.of χείρ, direct object of ἐπιθεὶς) 308.

αὐτῷ (loc.sing.masc.of αὐτός, place) 16.

ἰάσατο (3d.per.sing.aor.mid.ind.of ἰάομαι, constative) 721.

αὐτόν (acc.sing.masc.of αὐτός, direct object of ἰάσατο) 16.

*Translation - "And it happened that the father of Publius had come down with remittent fever and dysentery and Paul went in to him, prayed and laid hands on him and healed him."*

**Comment:** The subject of ἐγένετο is the infinitive κατακεῖσθαι. That was what had happened. The man was laid low. The participle συνεχόμενον gives the reason. Remittent fever (plural instrumental in πυρετοῖς) and δυσεντερίῳ - an inflamation of the intestinal tract. A remittent fever is characterized by alternating periods of abatement and increase of symptoms.

In 1603 - 1611 in England, where and when the King James Version was translated enteritis was so severe that the patient usually passed blood. Hence, the KJV "bloody flux." The Greek does not say that the patient was passing blood. Luke, a physician, probably would have said so if he were. πρὸς ὅν - an accusative of extent with εἰσελθὼν. The participles tell the story. Paul walked in, prayed for the man, laid his hands upon him and healed him. Luke modestly omits any part he may have had in this episode. Did he examine the patient and offer a diagnosis? The healing was a miracle. Thus Paul repaid Publius for his kindness to them. The patient had a febrile intestinal infection.

The kindness of Publius reminds us of the mature attitude and conduct of other Roman officers and politicians, Julius the centurion , Sergius Paulus, of Paphos (Acts 13:7) and the officials in Ephesus (Acts 19:31) being cases in point.

The murderer, turned god, has lived up to his reputation as a miracle worker, and his services came to be in great demand.

*Verse 9 - "So when this was done, others also which had diseases in the island, came, and were healed."*

τούτου δὲ γενομένου καὶ οἱ λοιποὶ οἱ ἐν τῇ νήσῳ ἔχοντες ἀσθενείας προσήρχοντο καὶ ἐθεραπεύοντο,

τούτου (gen.sing.neut.of οὗτος, genitive absolute) 93.

δὲ (inferential conjunction) 11.

γενομένου (aor.part.gen.sing.neut.of γίνομαι, adverbial, causal) 113.

καὶ (adjunctive conjunction joining substantives) 14.

οἱ (nom.pl.masc.of the article in agreement with λοιποὶ) 9.

λοιποὶ (nom.pl.masc.of λοιπός, subject of προσήρχοντο and ἐθεραπεύοντο) 1402.

οἱ (nom.pl.masc.of the article in agreement with ἔχοντες) 9.

ἐν (preposition with the locative of place) 80.

τῇ (loc.sing.fem.of the article in agreement with νήσῳ) 9.

νήσῳ (loc.sing.fem.of νῆσος, place) 3277.

ἔχοντες (pres.act.part.nom.pl.masc.of ἔχω, adjectival, restrictive, in agreement with λοιποὶ) 82.

ἀσθενείας (acc.pl.fem.of ἀσθένια, direct object of ἔχοντες) 740.

προσήρχοντο (3d.per.pl.imp.mid.ind.of προσέρχομαι, iterative) 336.

καὶ (adjunctive conjunction joining verbs) 14.

ἐθεραπεύοντο (3d.per.pl.imp.pass.ind.of θεραπεύω, iterative) 406.

*Translation* - *"So, because of this, the other people on the island who were sick also came and were healed."*

**Comment:** δὲ is inferential, since the genitive absolute τοῦ γενομένου is both temporal and causal. οἱ λοιποὶ is modified both by the participle ἔχοντες, a restrictive adjective and by the prepositional phrase ἐν τῇ νήσῳ. Those on the island who were sick came and were healed. Since οἱ λοιποὶ refers to the group as a whole, we can take προσήρχοντο and ἐθεραπεύοντο as iterative imperfects. No single individual came again and again to be healed, but the group, as represented by individuals continued to come to Paul for help. It provides an interesting picture. Paul, Luke and Aristarchus administer the program, receiving the long line of patients who arrive ill and go away cured.

The Maltese people were grateful as we see in

*Verse 10 - "Who also honored us with many honors; and when we departed, they laded us with such things as were necessary."*

οἱ καὶ πολλαῖς τιμαῖς ἐτίμησαν ἡμᾶς καὶ ἀναγομένοις ἐπέθεντο τὰ πρὸς τὰς χρείας.

οἱ (nom.pl.masc.of the article, subject of ἐτίμησαν) 9.

καὶ (continuative conjunction) 14.

πολλαῖς (instru.pl.fem.of πολύς, in agreement with τιμαῖς) 228.

τιμαῖς (instru.pl.fem.of τιμή, manner) 1619.

ἐτίμησαν (3d.per.pl.aor.act.ind.of τιμάω, constative) 1142.

ἡμᾶς (acc.pl.masc.of ἐγώ, direct object of ἐτίμησαν) 123.

καὶ (adjunctive conjunction joining verbs) 14.

ἀναγομένοις (pres.mid.part.dat.pl.masc.of ἀνάγω, substantival, indirect object of ἐπέθεντο) 329.

ἐπέθεντο (3d.per.pl.2d.aor.mid.ind.of ἐπιτίθημι, constative) 818.

τὰ (acc.pl.neut.of the article, direct object of ἐπέθεντο) 9.

πρὸς (preposition with the accusative, purpose) 197.

τὰς (acc.pl.fem.of the article in agreement with χρείας) 9.

χρείας (acc.pl.fem.of χρεία, purpose) 317.

*Translation - "And they rewarded us with many gifts, and they placed on board for those who sailed the things we needed."*

**Comment:** *Cf.* #'s 1142 and 1619, where the thought is always "honor" but expressed in a tangible way. They placed on board (ἐπέθεντο #818) as a gift for those who sailed away (#329), the things that were needed - πρὸς τὰς χρείας - "for the purpose of meeting our need."

It may be significant that Malta is the only place where Paul did not encounter opposition. The text does not mention any witnessing that was done except through prayer and healing. Paul and his Christian companions received nothing but kindness on Malta.

# Paul Arrives at Rome

*(Acts 28:11-16)*

*Verse 11 - "And after three months we departed in a ship of Alexandria which had wintered in the isle, whose sign was Castor and Pollux."*

Μετὰ δὲ τρεῖς μῆνας ἀνήχθημεν ἐν πλοίῳ παρακεχειμακότι ἐν τῇ νήσῳ Ἀλεξανδρίνῳ, παρασήμῳ Διοσκούροις.

Μετὰ (preposition with the accusative of time extent) 50.

δὲ (continuative conjunction) 11.

τρεῖς (acc.pl.fem.of τρεῖς, in agreement with μῆνας) 1010.

μῆνας (acc.pl.fem.of μήν, time extent) 1809.

ἀνήχθημεν (1st.per.pl.aor.pass.ind.of ἀνάγω, ingressive) 329.

ἐν (preposition with the locative of place) 80.

πλοίῳ (loc.sing.neut.of πλοῖον, place) 400.

παρακεχειμακότι (perf.mid.part.loc.sing.neut.of παραχειμάζω, adjectival, restrictive, in agreement with πλοίῳ) 3702.

ἐν (preposition with the locative of place) 80.

τῇ (loc.sing.fem.of the article in agreement with νήσῳ) 9.

νήσῳ (loc.sing.fem.of νῆσος, place where) 3277.

Ἀλεξανδρίνῳ (loc.sing.neut.of Ἀλεχάνδρινος, in agreement with πλοίῳ) 3681.

**#3768** παρασήμῳ (loc.sing.neut.of παράσημος, in agreement with πλοίῳ).

whose sign was - Acts 28:11.

*Meaning:* A combination of παρά (#154) and σῆμα - "sign." Hence, designated by a sign; identified by some distinguishing mark. In modern times we name ships and paint the name on the side - Acts 28:11.

**#3769** Διοσκούροις (loc.pl.masc.of Διόσκουροι, appellation).

Castor and Pollux - Acts 28:12.

*Meaning:* from Διός - "Zeus" and κοῦρος - "children" or κόρος - "boy" and κόρη - "girl." Hence, Dioscuri, the name given to Castor and Pollux, the twin children of Zeus and Leda, the titelary deities of sailors. The designation of the ship which took Paul from Malta to Syracuse - Acts 28:11.

*Translation - "And after three months we sailed in a ship which had spent the winter in the island. She had an Alexandrian registry, designated Dioscuri."*

**Comment:** μετά with the accusative of time extent - "after." They left Fair Haven in October (Acts 27:9) and spent two weeks in the storm. It was near February 1, 61 when they left Malta and sailed north to Syracuse. The ship that was wrecked was also of Alexandrian registry (Acts 27:6) - a fact which may suggest the volume of commerce between Alexandria and Rome. Note the perfect participle παρακεχειμακότι which emphasizes both the duration of the stay on the island and the fact of current residence.

*Verse 12 - "And landing at Syracuse, we tarried there three days."*

καὶ καταχθέντες εἰς Συρακούσας ἐπεμείναμεν ἡμέρας τρεῖς,

καὶ (continuative conjunction) 14.

καταχθέντες (aor.pass.part.nom.pl.masc.of κατάγω, adverbial, temporal) 2056.

εἰς (preposition with the accusative of extent) 140.

**#3770** Συρακούσας (acc.sing.fem.of Συράκουσαι, extent).

Syracuse - Acts 28:12.

*Meaning:* A large maritime city of Sicily, now called Siragosa. Excellent harbor. Surrounded by a wall 180 stadia in length, according to Strabo (*Strabo 6, 270*), but Leake says that Strabo exaggerated. The wall is 122 stadia or 14 English miles in length. Paul visited here three days on his way to Rome (Acts 28:12). Syracuse is the birthplace of Archimedes (*c.*287 B.C.), who said, δός μοι ποῦ στῶ καὶ κινῶ τὴν γῆν, and ran naked through the streets crying εὕρηκα, εὕρηκα. Also the city of Plato's philosophical studies, where he founded the Academy of philosophical and scientific research *c.* 388 B.C. Paul was familiar with Plato's writing. *Cf.* note on Romans 8:28.

ἐπεμείναμεν (1st.per.pl.aor.act.ind.of ἐπιμένω, constative) 2379.
ἡμέρας (acc.pl.fem.of ἡμέρα, time extent) 135.
τρεῖς (numeral) 1010.

*Translation - "And we put in at Syracuse and stayed three days."*

**Comment:** One wonders what Paul did at Syracuse 348 years after Archimedes, who discovered the principle of displacement, was born and 450 years after Plato established his Academy. Was he allowed to leave the ship? If so, did he walk on or near the spot where Archimedes was killed bv a Roman soldier who found him drawing a mathematical diagram in the sand? "It is said that Archimedes was so absorbed in calculation that his only remark to the intruder was, "Do not disturb my diagrams." (Funk and Wagnalls, *New Encyclopedia*, II, 212,213). The famous scientist was not more dedicated to his work than the Apostle Paul was dedicated to the propagation of the Gospel of Jesus Christ. He could well have said to the Roman soldier in Rome who killed him, "Do not distort my gospel."

*Verse 13 - "And from thence we fetched a compass, and came to Rhegium: and after one day the south wind blew, and we came the next day to Puteoli."*

ὅθεν περιελόντες κατηντήσαμεν εἰς Ῥήγιον. καὶ μετὰ μίαν ἡμέραν ἐπιγενομένου νότου δευτεραῖοι ἤλθομεν εἰς Ποτιόλους,

ὅθεν (local adverb) 1020.
περιελόντες (2d.aor.act.part.nom.pl.masc.of περιαιρέω, adverbial, temporal) 3724.
κατηντήσαμεν (1st.per.pl.aor.act.ind.of καταντάω, culminative) 3353.
εἰς (preposition with the accusative of extent) 140.

#3771 Ῥήγιον (acc.sing.neut.of Ῥήγιον, extent).

Rhegium - Acts 28:13.

*Meaning:* Cf. ῥήγνυμι (#654). Modern Reggio is on the Italian mainland opposite Messina, Sicily. Pliny (*Natural History*, 3,8,((14)) ) believed that the area got its name from the belief that at one time Sicily was joined to Italy at that point and had since broken away - Acts 28:13.

καὶ (continuative conjunction) 14.
μετὰ (preposition with the accusative of time extent) 50.
μίαν (acc.sing.fem.of εἶς, in agreement with ἡμέραν) 469.
ἡμέραν (acc.sing.fem.of ἡμέρα, time extent) 135.

#3772 ἐπιγενομένου (aor.mid.part.gen.sing.masc.of ἐπιγίνομαι, genitive absolute, causal).

blow - Acts 28:13.

*Meaning:* A combination of ἐπί (#47) and γίνομαι (#113). Hence, to happen upon; to come upon. In a context with νότου - "to spring up" - Acts 28:13.

νότου (gen.sing.masc.of νότος, genitive absolute) 1015.

#3773 δευτεραῖοι (nom.pl.masc.of δευτεραῖος, adverbial).

the next day - Acts 28:13.

*Meaning:* Cf. δεύτερος (#1371). Pertaining to the second. With ἡμέρα, implied - Acts 28:13.

ἤλθομεν (1st.per.pl.aor.ind.of ἔρχομαι, culminative) 146.
εἰς (preposition with the accusative of extent) 140.

#3774 Ποτιόλους (acc.sing.masc.of Ποτίολοι, extent).

Puteoli - Acts 28;13.

*Meaning:* A city of Campania, Italy on the bay of Naples. Now called Pozzuoli - Acts 28:13.

*Translation - "Then we weighed anchor and came to Rhegium and after one day because a south wind sprang up we came the next day to Puteoli."*

**Comment:** Cf. #3724. The KJV "fetch a compass" is a farfetched translation. Montgomery's "touching around" is little better. Cf. Goodpseed and mine. The course to Rhegium ran through the treacherous straits of Messina between Scylla and Charybdis. The participle ἐπιγενομένου is causal. They needed a wind from the south to carry them up the western coast of Italy to the Bay of Naples and Puteoli.

*Verse 14 - "Where we found brethren, and were desired to tarry with them seven days: and so we went toward Rome."*

οὗ εὑρόντες ἀδελφοὺς παρεκλήθημεν παρ' αὐτοῖς ἐπιμεῖναι ἡμέρας ἐπτά, καὶ οὕτως εἰς τὴν Ῥώμην ἤλθαμεν.

οὗ (gen.sing.neut.of ὅς, the relative pronoun, place description) 65.
εὑρόντες (aor.act.part.nom.pl.masc.of εὑρίσκω, adverbial, temporal/causal) 79.
ἀδελφοὺς (acc.pl.masc.of ἀδελφός, direct object of εὑρόντες) 15.
παρεκλήθημεν (1st.per.pl.aor.pass.ind.of παρακελέω, constative) 230.
παρ' (preposition with the instrumental of association) 154.
αὐτοῖς (instru.pl.masc.of αὐτός, association) 16.
ἐπιμεῖναι (aor.act.inf.of ἐπιμένω, epexegetical) 2379.
ἡμέρας (acc.pl.fem.of ἡμέρα, time extent) 135.
ἐπτά (numeral) 1024.
καὶ (continuative conjunction) 14.
οὕτως (demonstrative adverb) 74.
εἰς (preposition with the accusative of extent) 140.

'Ρώμην (acc.sing.fem.of 'Ρώμη, extent) 3434.

ἤλθαμεν (1st.per.pl.aor.mid.ind.of ἔρχομαι, culminative) 146.

*Translation - "Where, because we found brethren, we were implored to remain with them seven days; and thus we came to Rome."*

**Comment:** οὖ, the relative pronoun, has Ποτιόλους as its antecedent, but derives its genitive case from its use in its own clause. There Paul, Luke and Aristarchus found Christians who begged them to stay for a week. The record does not say that Paul was able to grant their request. He was in the custody of Julius, the centurion, who was, in turn obligated to the ship captain not to delay the voyage more than necessary. It is doubtful that they did remain in Puteoli long, since Luke would have described for us what they did there. The remainder of the trip to Rome was made by land, as they walked up the Appian Way. The distance from Naples to Rome is a little more than 100 miles.

*Verse 15 - "And from thence when the brethren heard of us, they came to meet us as far as Appii forum and The three taverns; whom when Paul saw, he thanked God, and took courage."*

κἀκεῖθεν οἱ ἀδελφοὶ ἀκούσαντες τὰ περὶ ἡμῶν ἦλθαν εἰς ἀπάντησιν ἡμῖν ἄχρι 'Αππίου Φόρου καὶ Τριῶν Ταβερνῶν, οὓς ἰδὼν ὁ Παῦλος εὐχαριστήσας τῷ θεῷ ἔλαβε θάρσος.

κἀκεῖθεν (local adverb) 2348.

οἱ (nom.pl.masc.of the article in agreement with ἀδελφοὶ) 9.

ἀδελφοὶ (nom.pl.masc.of ἀδελφός, subject of ἦλθαν) 15.

ἀκούσαντες (aor.act.part.nom.pl.masc.of ἀκούω, adverbial, temporal/causal) 148.

τὰ (acc.pl.neut.of the article, direct object of ἀκούσαντες) 9.

περὶ (preposition with the genitive of reference) 173.

ἡμῶν (gen.pl.masc.of ἐγώ, reference) 123.

ἦλθαν (3d.per.pl.aor.mid.ind.of ἔρχομαι, ingressive) 146.

εἰς (preposition with the accusative, purpose) 140.

ἀπάντησιν (acc.sing.fem.of ἀπάντησις, purpose) 1533.

ἡμῖν (instru.pl.masc.of ἐγώ, association) 123.

ἄχρι (preposition with the genitive of place description) 1517.

#3775 'Αππίου (gen.sing.masc.of 'Αππιος, place description).

Appii - Acts 28:15.

*Meaning:* Appius, a Roman praenomen. In Appii Forum - "The Market of Appius." A town in Italy, 43 Roman miles south of Rome on the Appian Way, the famous road which was paved by Appius Claudius Caecus in 312 B.C. It led through the *porta Capena* to Capua and south to Brundisium, the modern city of Brindis. The paving stones, still in place after 2200 years are polygonal. Christian tourists who travel this highway between Rome and Naples have the assurance that on these same stones once walked the feet of the Apostle Paul.

**#3776** Φόρου (gen.sing.neut.of Φόρον, place description).

Forum - Acts 28:15.

*Meaning:* Forum. *Cf.* #3775 - Acts 28:15.

καὶ (adjunctive conjunction joining nouns) 14.
Τριῶν (gen.pl.fem.of τρεῖς, in agreement with Ταβερνῶν) 1010.

**#3777** Ταβερνῶν (gen.pl.fem.of Ταβέρναι, description).

Taverns - Acts 28:15.

*Meaning:* Three Taverns. The name of an inn on the Appian Way. Ten miles north of the Appii Forum, and thus 33 Roman miles south of Rome - Acts 28:15.

οὓς (acc.pl.masc.of ὅς, relative pronoun, direct object of ἰδών) 65.
ἰδών (aor.act.part.nom.sing.masc.of ὁράω, adverbial, temporal/causal) 144a.
ὁ (nom.sing.masc.of the article in agreement with Παῦλος) 9.
Παῦλος (nom.sing.masc.of Παῦλος, subject of ἔλαβε) 3284.
εὐχαριστήσας (aor.act.part.nom.sing.masc.of εὐχαριστέω, adverbial, coincident) 1185.
τῷ (dat.sing.masc.of the article in agreement with θεῷ) 9.
θεῷ (dat.sing.masc.of θεός, indirect object of εὐχαριστήσας) 124.
ἔλαβε (3d.per.sing.aor.act.ind.of λαμβάνω, constative) 533.

**#3778** θάρσος (acc.sing.neut.of θάρσος, direct object of ἔλαβε).

courage - Acts 28:15.

*Meaning: Cf.* θαρσέω (#780); θαῤῥέω (#4307). Hence, courage, confidence - Acts 28:15.

*Translation - "When the brethren heard the news about us they came from Rome as far as Appii Forum and the Three Taverns in order to meet us. When Paul saw them he gave thanks to God and took courage."*

**Comment:** κἀκεῖθεν is joined to οἱ ἀδελφοὶ like an adjective - "The brethren from Rome." ἀκούσαντες is both temporal and causal. When and because the Roman Christians heard the news, they started south. Note τὰ περὶ ἡμῶν as the object of ἀκούσας - "the things about us." We are not told how the news reached Rome to the effect that Paul and his party had landed at Puteoli and were enroute to the city. Not all of the traffic northward was on foot. Perhaps some horseman or chariot driver reached the city ahead of those who were walking.

The purpose for the trip to the south is set forth in the phrase εἰς ἀπάντησιν - "for the purpose of meeting." *Cf.* #1533, for the other two passages where this word occurs, and in what connection. This word tells us nothing about how long Paul and his new Christian friends from Rome tarried at the spot of meeting before all they returned and Paul advanced to the city. How long did the virgins tarry at the spot where they met the Bridegroom, if indeed they tarried at all? Or did the Bridegroom, hastening to his wedding dinner, tarry at all? The raptured and resurrected saints will meet the Lord in the air as He descends from heaven (1 Thess.4:13-18). The same word is used for the meeting. Will there be a seven year delay in our Lord's descent to earth at the time of the meeting? Posttribulationists (who, to be sure, are premillenial) are advised not to be too exultant about this as an argument from silence is not conclusive. The case for a premillenial posttribulational rapture of the church rests on scriptural ground that is very solid. *Cf.* Luke 14:14; 1 Cor.15:52; Rev.3:10; 11:15-18; 1 Thess.4:16 in comparison with Psalm 110:1 *et al.* Nonetheless it is interesting to note that the Holy Spirit chose this word (ἀπάντησιν) for the meeting of two groups, headed in opposite directions, after which one group turned around and retraced its steps and the other continued in the same direction as before the meeting. The virgins met the Bridegroom. Who turned around? Who continued on His way? The Roman Christians met Paul on the Appian Way. Who turned around? Who continued on his way? The saints will meet the Lord in the air. Who will turn around? And who will continue on His way? The Bridegroom did not sit down with the wise virgins and have a party before he went on to his wedding. Nor did Paul tarry long with the Christians on the road to Rome. Though there is nothing in ἀπάντησιν to indicate how long Paul paused on the road before proceding with his friends to Rome, there is also nothing to indicate that they stayed out there at the Appii Forum for seven years! We are reminded in verse 16 that Julius, the centurion was still in the group. He had a military obligation to deliver his prisoner to the captain of the guard in Rome.

*Verse 16 - "And when we came to Rome the centurion delivered the prisoners to the captain of the guard: but Paul was suffered to dwell by himself with a soldier that kept him."*

Ὅτε δὲ εἰσήλθομεν εἰς Ῥώμην, ἐπετράπη τῷ Παύλῳ μένειν καθ᾽ ἑαυτὸν σὺν τῷ φυλάσσοντι αὐτὸν στρατιώτῃ.

Ὅτε (conjunction introducing the indicative in a definite temporal clause) 703.
δὲ (explanatory conjunction) 11.
εἰσήλθομεν (1st.per.pl.aor.mid.ind.of εἰσέρχομαι, definite temporal clause, culminative) 234.
εἰς (preposition with the accusative of extent) 140.
Ῥώμην (acc.sing.fem.of Ῥώμη, extent) 3434.
ἐπετράπη (3d.per.sing.1st.aor.pass.ind.of ἐπιτρέπω, constative) 747.
τῷ (dat.sing.masc.of the article in agreement with Παύλῳ) 9.
Παύλῳ (dat.sing.masc.of Παῦλος, personal advantage) 3284.
μένειν (pres.act.inf.of μένω, epexegetical) 864.
καθ᾽ (preposition with the accusative, distributive) 98.
ἑαυτὸν (acc.sing.masc.of ἑαυτοῦ, distributive) 288.
σὺν (preposition with the instrumental of association) 1542.
τῷ (instru.sing.masc.of the article in agreement with στρατιώτῃ) 9.
φυλάσσοντι (pres.act.part.instru.sing.masc.of φυλάσσω, in agreement with στρατιώτῃ) 1301.
αὐτὸν (acc.sing.masc.of αὐτός, direct object of φυλάσσοντι) 16.

στρατιώτῃ (instru.sing.masc.of στρατιώτης, association) 724.

*Translation - "And when we got to Rome permission was granted to Paul to live by himself with the soldier guarding him."*

**Comment:** Again Luke treats us to a definite temporal clause with Ὅτε instead of his more common adverbial temporal participle. *Cf.* Acts 27:39. The participle φυλάσσοντι is a good example of the adjectival use in the attributive position (between the article and the noun). Permission was given to Paul to stay alone with "the guarding him soldier." As though Paul would try to escape! It is interesting to conjecture about the spiritual influence that Paul may have had with certain of the Roman political and military officials with whom he was in contact. Did he lead this soldier to Christ? Did Julius become a Christian? How did Claudius Lysias react to Paul's message? We know that he led the Philippian jailor to Christ (Acts 16:31-33). Sergius Paulus also believed (Acts 13:7-12). The material about the centurion delivering the other prisoners to the captain of the guard is an expansion of the Western text which "passed into the Byzantine text and lies behind the A.V." (Metzger, *A Textual Commentary on the Greek New Testament*, 501).

Paul, the prisoner, had been granted special privileges before (Acts 24:23) and would be again (Acts 28:30).

## Paul Preaches in Rome

*(Acts 28:17 - 31)*

*Verse 17 - "And it came to pass, that after three days Paul called the chief of the Jews together: and when they were come together, he said unto them, Men and brethren, though I have committed nothing against the people or customs of our fathers, yet was I delivered prisoner from Jerusalem into the hands of the Romans."*

Ἐγένετο δὲ μετὰ ἡμέρας τρεῖς συγκαλέσασθαι αὐτὸν τοὺς ὄντας τῶν Ἰουδαίων πρώτους. συνελθόντων δὲ αὐτῶν ἔλεγεν πρὸς αὐτούς, Ἐγώ, ἄνδρες ἀδελφοί, οὐδὲν ἐναντίον ποιήσας τῷ λαῷ ἢ τοῖς ἔθεσι τοῖς πατρῴοις δέσμιος ἐξ Ἱεροσολύμων παρεδόθην εἰς τὰς χεῖρας τῶν Ῥωμαίων,

Ἐγένετο (3d.per.sing.aor.ind.of γίνομαι, constative) 113.
δὲ (explanatory conjunction) 11.
μετὰ (preposition with the accusative of time extent) 50.
ἡμέρας (acc.pl.fem.of ἡμέρα, time extent) 135.
τρεῖς (numeral) 1010.
συγκαλέσασθαι (aor.mid.inf.of συγκαλέω, noun use, subject of ἐγένετο) 2251.
αὐτὸν (acc.sing.masc.of αὐτός, general reference) 16.
τοὺς (acc.pl.masc.of the article in agreement with ὄντας) 9.

ὄντας (pres.part.acc.pl.masc.of εἰμί, substantival, direct object of συγκαλέσασθαι) 86.

τῶν (gen.pl.masc.of the article in agreement with Ἰουδαίων) 9.

Ἰουδαίων (gen.pl.masc.of Ἰουδαῖος, partitive genitive) 143.

πρώτους (acc.pl.masc.of πρῶτος, predicate adjective) 487.

συνελθόντων (aor.mid.part.gen.pl.masc.of συνέρχομαι, genitive absolute) 78.

δὲ (continuative conjunction) 11.

αὐτῶν (gen.pl.masc.of αὐτός, genitive absolute) 16.

ἔλεγεν (3d.per.sing.imp.act.ind.of λέγω, inchoative) 66.

πρὸς (preposition with the accusative of extent, after a verb of speaking) 197.

αὐτούς (acc.pl.masc.of αὐτός, extent, after a verb of speaking) 16.

Ἐγώ (nom.sing.masc.of ἐγώ, subject of παρεδόθην) 123.

ἄνδρες (voc.pl.masc.of ἀνήρ, address) 63.

ἀδελφοί (voc.pl.masc.of ἀδελφός, address) 15.

οὐδὲν (acc.sing.neut.of οὐδείς, direct object of ποιήσας) 446.

ἐναντίον (acc.sing.neut.of ἐναντίος, adverbial) 1128.

ποιήσας (aor.act.part.nom.sing.masc.of ποιέω, adverbial, concessive) 127.

τῷ (dat.sing.masc.of the article in agreement with λαῷ) 9.

λαῷ (dat.sing.masc.of λαός, personal disadvantage) 110.

ἢ (disjunctive) 465.

τοῖς (dat.pl.neut.of the article in agreement with ἔθεσι) 9.

ἔθεσι (dat.pl.neut.of ἔθος, disadvantage) 1788.

τοῖς (dat.pl.masc.of the article in agreement with πατρῴοις) 9.

πατρῴοις (dat.pl.masc.of πατρῷος, in agreement with ἔθεσι) 3576.

δέσμιος (nom.sing.masc.of δέσμιος, predicate nominative) 1624.

ἐξ (preposition with the ablative of separation) 19.

Ἱεροσολύμων (abl.sing.masc.of Ἱεροσόλυμα, separation) 141.

παρεδόθην (1st.per.sing.aor.pass.ind.of παραδίδωμι, culminative) 368.

εἰς (preposition with the accusative of extent) 140.

τὰς (acc.pl.fem.of the article in agreement with χεῖρας) 9.

χεῖρας (acc.pl.fem.of χείρ, extent) 308.

τῶν (gen.pl.masc.of the article in agreement with Ῥωμαίων) 9.

Ῥωμαίων (gen.pl.masc.of Ῥωμαῖος, description) 2610.

*Translation - "Now after three days he called together those who were leaders among the Jews. And when they had assembled he said to them, 'I, men, brethren, despite the fact that I have done nothing against the people or the customs of our fathers, have been delivered into the hands of the Romans from Jerusalem as a prisoner."*

**Comment:** The infinitive in its noun use is the subject of ἐγένετο with αὐτὸν joined as an accusative of general reference. The object of συγκαλέσασθαι is the substantival participle ὄντας with its adjuncts τῶν Ἰουδαίων πρώτους. The leading men among the Jews (partitive genitive). The translation follows the word order in the Greek despite the fact that it does not make for smooth reading. Paul's emphasis is upon his innocence, not upon the fact that he is a prisoner of the Romans.

This was Paul's first visit to Rome. In keeping with the directive of the Great Commission he made it a point that his first contact in the city should be with the Jews (Acts 1:8; Rom.1:16). Paul was especially interested to find out if the Jews in Jerusalem had written to the Jews in Rome and voiced their opposition to him. He also wanted to make the point that the Roman judiciary had found him innocent of every charge for which he could be punished under Roman law.

Paul had already written to the church at Rome, a congregation that he had never seen, when he was in Corinth sometime during the winter months of 57-58. It was now the spring of the year 61. The last chapter of his epistle to the Romans lists several members of the church with whom he was acquainted, including Priscilla and Aquila (Romans 16:3), Epaenetus, his first convert in Greece (verse 5), two of his relatives, Andronicus and Junia (verse 7), another relative, Herodian (verse 11) and Rufus, "whose father, as it is supposed, carried our Saviour's cross, Mark xv.21" (Translator, *Calvin's Commentaries, Romans,* Grand Rapids: Eerdman's, xi). It is quite likely that some or all of those mentioned in Romans 16 came to meet Paul as he approached the city. So, although he had already met many or all of his old friends and perhaps had made new acquaintances among the Roman Christians, his first official functions in Rome related to the Jews in the city.

*Verse 18 - "Who, when they had examined me, would have let me go, because there was no cause of death in me."*

οἵτινες ἀνακρίναντές με ἐβούλοντο ἀπολῦσαι διὰ τὸ μηδεμίαν αἰτίαν θανάτου ὑπάρχειν ἐν ἐμοί.

οἵτινες (nom.pl.masc.of ὅστις, relative pronoun, subject of ἐβούλοντο) 163.

ἀνακρίναντές (aor.act.part.nom.pl.masc.of ἀνακρίων, adverbial, temporal) 2837.

με (acc.sing.masc.of ἐγώ, direct object of ἀνακρίναντές) 123

ἐβούλοντο (3d.per.pl.imp.mid.ind.of βούλομαι, voluntative) 953.

ἀπολῦσαι (aor.act.inf.of ἀπολύω, object of ἐβούλοντο) 92.

διὰ (preposition with the accusative of cause) 118.

τὸ (acc.sing.neut.of the article in agreement with ὑπάρχειν) 9.

μηδεμίαν (acc.sing.fem.of μηδείς, in agreement with αἰτίαν) 713.

αἰτίαν (acc.sing.fem.of αἰτία, general reference) 1283.

θανάτου (gen.sing.masc.of θάνατος, description) 381.

ὑπάρχειν (pres.act.inf.of ὑπάρχω, accusative of cause) 1303.

ἐν (preposition with the locative of place) 80.

ἐμοί (loc.sing.masc.of ἐμός, place) 1267.

*Translation - "Who, after they had tried me, had rather wished to set me free, because there was no reason why I should be put to death."*

**Comment:** The definite relative in οἵτινες. The Romans - Claudius Lysias, Felix and Festus, each had held hearings, heard accusations against Paul and after hearing his defense, wished to dismiss the case. The voluntative imperfect in ἐβούλετο indicates the desire or disposition of the court but not the realization. In each case the court found nothing in Paul's record that demanded the death penalty. This is expressed by the causal clause with διὰ and the accusative in τὸ . . . ὑπάρχειν. The reason why the Roman courts in Judea had not released Paul, even though they found no reason to hold him is stated in

*Verse 19 - "But when the Jews spake against it, I was constrained to appeal unto Caesar; not that I had ought to accuse my nation of."*

ἀντιλεγόντων δὲ τῶν Ἰουδαίων ἠναγκάσθην ἐπικαλέσασθαι Καίσαρα, οὐχ ὡς τοῦ ἔθνους μου ἔχων τι κατηγορεῖν.

ἀντιλεγόντων (pres.act.part.gen.pl.masc.of ἀντιλέγω, genitive absolute, causal) 1903.
δὲ (adversative conjunction) 11.
τῶν (gen.pl.masc.of the article in agreement with Ἰουδαίων) 9.
Ἰουδαίων (gen.pl.masc.of Ἰουδαῖος, genitive absolute) 143.
ἠναγκάσθην (1st.per.sing.aor.pass.ind.of ἀναγκάζω, ingressive) 1126.
ἐπικαλέσασθαι (aor.mid.inf.of ἐπικαλέω, epexegetical) 884.
Καίσαρα (acc.sing.masc.of Καίσαρα, direct object of ἐπικαλέσασθαι) 1418.
οὐχ (negative conjunction with the concessive participle) 130.
ὡς (conditional particle) 128.
τοῦ (gen.sing.neut.of the article in agreement with ἔθνους) 9.
ἔθνους (gen.sing.neut.of ἔθνος, objective genitive) 376.
μου (gen.sing.masc.of ἐγώ, relationship) 123.
ἔχων (pres.act.part.nom.sing.masc.of ἔχων, adverbial, concessive) 82.
τι (acc.sing.neut.of τις, indefinite pronoun, direct object of ἔχων) 486.
κατηγορεῖν (pres.act.inf.of κατηγορέω, object of ἔχων) 974.

*Translation - "But because the Jews spoke against it, I felt compelled to file an appeal for myself to Caesar, not as though I had anything to say against my nation."*

**Comment:** δὲ is adversative. Felix, Festus and Agrippa agreed (at the same and at different times) that Paul should be released, but the Jews opposed it. ἀντιλεγόντων is causal and temporal - "When and because they did . . . " ἠναγκάσθην is an ingressive aorist. The compulsion to appeal to Caesar presented itself to the defendant. Most verbs of emotion or decision yield to the ingressive idea. Paul had no thought of the necessity for an appeal to Caesar until it became clear that the lower courts, for political reasons, might yield to the importunities of the prosecution. He was seized with the compulsion (ingressive aorist) to appeal. οὐχ ὡς - "not as if" - brings out the force of the concessive participle ἔχων.

The disclaimer is an example of Paul's diplomacy. An appeal from a lower Roman court to Caesar in a case in which the Jewish people were involved as litigants could be construed as an attempt to bring reproach upon the Jewish nation as a whole. The Jews, because of their religious nationalism, had a record of fractiousness which had often worn the Roman patience thin. No patriotic Jew who cherished the Hope of Israel would bring the actions of the nation to the attention of the Emperor unnecessarily. Paul's appeal to Caesar would not call in question the views of the nation as a whole. Indeed, he had demonstrated in his speech before Agrippa that he was and had always been a better Pharisee than the Pharisees who were demanding his death. He was only asking for an opportunity to show the Emperor that a few misguided fanatics in Jerusalem had misunderstood his motives and misjudged his actions with reference to a silly vow which he had been induced to take as a public relations measure.

It was important that Paul avoid leaving the impression with the local Jewish community in Rome that he was engaged in an attack all up and down the line against the Jewish tradition. Far from it! His theology as a Christian was in line completely with the Jewish tradition as seen in its best, because most completely understood light.

He makes this point to his guests in

*Verse 20 - "For this cause therefore have I called for you, to see you, and to speak with you: because that for the hope of Israel I am bound with this chain."*

διὰ ταύτην οὖν τὴν αἰτίαν παρεκάλεσα ὑμᾶς ἰδεῖν καὶ προσλαλῆσαι ἕνεκεν γὰρ τῆς ἐλπίδος τοῦ Ἰσραὴλ τὴν ἅλυσιν ταύτην περίκειμαι.

διὰ (preposition with the accusative, cause) 118.

ταύτην (acc.sing.fem.of οὗτος, in agreement with αἰτίαν) 93.

οὖν (inferential conjunction) 68.

αἰτίαν (acc.sing.fem.of αἰτία, cause) 1283.

παρεκάλεσα (1st.per.sing.aor.act.ind.of παρακαλέω, constative) 230.

ὑμᾶς (acc.pl.masc.of σύ, direct object of παρεκάλεσα) 104.

ἰδεῖν (aor.act.inf.of ὁράω, purpose) 144a.

καὶ (adjunctive conjunction joining infinitives) 14.

προσλαλῆσαι (aor.act.inf.of προσλαλέω, purpose) 3304.

ἕνεκεν (for ἕνεκα) - (improper preposition with the genitive, cause) 435.

γὰρ (causal conjunction) 105.

τῆς (gen.sing.fem.of the article in agreement with ἐλπίδος) 9.

ἐλπίδος (gen.sing.fem.of ἐλπίς, cause) 2994.

τοῦ (gen.sing.masc.of the article in agreement with Ἰσραὴλ) 9.

Ἰσραὴλ (gen.sing.masc.of Ἰσραὴλ, description) 165.

τὴν (acc.sing.fem.of the article in agreement with ἅλυσιν) 9.

ἅλυσιν (acc.sing.fem.of ἅλυσις, direct object of περίκειμαι) 2216.

ταύτην (acc.sing.fem.of οὗτος, in agreement with ἅλυσιν) 93.

περίκειμαι (1st.per.sing.pres.pass.ind.of περίκειμαι, progressive duration, retroactive) 2351.

*Translation - "Therefore it is for this reason that I have called to see and talk with you, for it is because of the hope of Israel that I have been compelled to carry around this chain."*

**Comment:** διά with the accusative ταύτην αἰτίαν is causal. Often in the New Testament. *Cf.* #118. The use of ἔνεκεν with the genitive to show cause and γάρ the causal conjunction need not disturb us. The first causal clause refers to the reason Paul had asked for the conference with the Roman Jewish leaders. He had been attacked by a group of Jerusalem Jews who demanded his death, and, although he had been declared guiltless by two lower Roman courts, he had found it necessary to appeal to Caesar in order to save his life. But, although he would speak to the Emperor against the group that had attacked him, his remarks would not be properly construed as an attack upon the nation. Then he added "Because (causal γάρ) it is because of (ἔνεκεν with the genitive) the hope of Israel. . . . κ.τ.λ." Note that though πεoίκειμαι in the passive is intransitive, it has the accusative here and is transitive. "The passive is usually intransitive but it is not necessarily so. . . . Transitive passives are usually verbs that in the active have two accusatives or an accusative of the thing with the person in the dative or ablative. This accusative of the thing is retained in the passive." (Robertson, *Grammar,* 485, 815,816). περιτίθημι with ἅλυσιν means "to wrap a chain around" - hence the accusative. περιτίθημι also is followed by an accusative of nerson - "I tied up (wrapped a chain around) the prisoner."

Paul's amillenialism is conspicuous for its absence. Apparently he did not believe that national Israel had forfeited forever her hope of fulfillment of the Davidic covenant (2 Sam.7:12-20). If he had he would not have identified Christianity with τῆς ἐλπίδος τοῦ Ἰσραήλ. That Christianity offers national salvation to a remnant in Israel (Revelation 7:1-8), as well as personal salvation to the Jewish believer, is a fact clearly taught in Scripture, but unfortunately understood only by premillenialists. Paul would have been guilty of deception if he had spoken of the "hope of Israel" to Jews when he knew that there was no such hope. Otherwise we must conclude that Paul did not know what he was talking about. If Paul is to be corrected on this point the amillenialists will have to do it. The premillenialists are as confused as he is.

*Verse 21 - "And they said unto him, We neither received letters out of Judea concerning thee , neither any of the brethren that came shewed or spake any harm of thee."*

οἱ δὲ πρὸς αὐτὸν εἶπαν,Ἡμεῖς οὔτε γράμματα περὶ σοῦ ἐδεξάμεθα ἀπὸ τῆς Ἰουδαίας, οὔτε παραγενόμενός τις τῶν ἀδελφῶν ἀπήγγειλεν ἢ ἐλάλησέν τι περὶ σοῦ πονηρόν.

οἱ (nom.pl.masc.of the article, subject of εἶπαν) 9.

δὲ (continuative conjunction) 11.

πρὸς (preposition with the accusative of extent with a verb of speaking) 197.

αὐτὸν (acc.sing.masc.of αὐτός, extent, with a verb of speaking) 16.

εἶπαν (3d.per.pl.aor.act.ind.of εἶπον, constative) 155.

Ἡμεῖς (nom.pl.masc.of ἐγώ, subject of ἐδεξάμεθα) 123.

οὔτε (negative copulative conjunction) 598.

γράμματα (acc.pl.neut.of γράμμα, direct object of ἐδεξάμεθα) 2100.

περὶ (preposition with the genitive of reference) 173.

σοῦ (gen.sing.masc.of σύ, reference) 104.

ἐδεξάμεθα (1st.per.pl.aor.mid.ind.of δέχομαι, culminative) 867.

ἀπό (preposition with the ablative of source) 70.

τῆς (abl.sing.fem.of the article in agreement with Ἰουδαίας) 9.

Ἰουδαίας (abl.sing.fem.of Ἰουδαία, source) 134.

οὔτε (negative copulative conjunction) 598.

παραγενόμενός (aor.mid.part.nom.sing.masc.of παραγίνομαι, adjectival, restrictive in agreement with τις) 139.

τις (nom.sing.masc.of τις, indefinite pronoun, subject of ἀπήγγειλεν and ἐλάλησέν) 486.

τῶν (gen.pl.masc.of the article in agreement with ἀδελφῶν) 9.

ἀδελφῶν (gen.pl.masc.of ἀδελφός, partitive genitive) 15.

ἀπήγγειλεν (3d.per.sing.aor.act.ind.of ἀπαγγέλλω, culminative) 176.

ἤ (disjunctive) 465.

ἐλάλησέν (3d.per.sing.aor.act.ind.of λαλέω, culminative) 815.

τι (acc.sing.neut.of τις, indefinite pronoun, direct object of ἐλάλησέν) 486.

περί (preposition with the genitive of reference) 173.

σοῦ (gen.sing.masc.of σύ, reference) 104.

πονηρόν (acc.sing.neut.of πονηρός, predicate adjective) 438.

*Translation -* "*And they said to him, 'We have neither received letters about you from Judea, nor have any of the brethren who came here reported or said anything about you that was evil.'* "

**Comment:** The negative copulative particles οὔτε . . . οὔτε unite the paratactic clauses and οὔτε . . . τις intensifies the force of their statement. There had been neither a letter nor a personal messenger. Not one had had a single evil thing to say about Paul. This sounds like a surprisingly favourable reception for Paul in Rome, as God had prepared the hearts of the Jews so that Paul would be given the opportunity to witness, in accord with God's promise to him (Acts 23:11).

*Verse 22 -* "*But we desire to hear of thee what thou thinkest: for as concerning this sect, we know that everywhere it is spoken against.*"

ἀξιοῦμεν δὲ παρὰ σοῦ ἀκοῦσαι ἃ φρονεῖς, περὶ μὲν γὰρ τῆς αἱρέσεως ταύτης γνωστὸν ἡμῖν ἐστιν ὅτι πανταχοῦ ἀντιλέγεται.

ἀξιοῦμεν (1st.per.pl.pres.act.ind.of ἀξιόω, progressive duration, retroactive) 2151.

δὲ (intensive) 11.

παρὰ (preposition with the ablative of source) 154.

σοῦ (abl.sing.masc.of σύ, source) 104.

ἀκοῦσαι (aor.act.inf.of ἀκούω, epexegetical) 148.

ἃ (acc.pl.neut.of ὅς, relative pronoun, direct object of φρονεῖς) 65.

φρονεῖς (2d.per.sing.pres.act.ind.of φρονέω, progressive duration, retroactive) 1212.

περὶ (preposition with the genitive of reference) 173.

μὲν (particle of affirmation) 300.
γὰρ (causal conjunction) 105.
τῆς (gen.sing.fem.of the article in agreement with αἱρέσεως) 9.
αἱρέσεως (gen.sing.fem.of αἵρεσις, reference) 3058.
ταύτης (gen.sing.fem.of οὗτος, in agreement with αἱρέσεως) 93.
γνωστὸν (acc.sing.neut.of γνωστός, predicate adjective) 1917.
ἡμῖν (dat.pl.masc.of ἐγώ, personal interest) 123.
ἐστιν (3d.per.sing.pres.ind.of εἰμί, progressive duration, retroactive) 86.
ὅτι (conjunction introducing an object clause in indirect discourse) 211.
πανταχοῦ (adverbial) 2062.
ἀντιλέγεται (3d.per.sing.pres.pass.ind.of ἀντιλέγω, progressive duration, retroactive) 1903.

*Translation - "As a matter of fact we have been wanting to hear from you what you have been thinking, because the fact is that with reference to this heresy, we have understood that everywhere it has been criticized."*

**Comment:** The Jews had heard nothing bad about Paul. On the contrary, they knew that he had become a Christian and that he was the foremost evangelist of the gospel of Christ to the Gentiles, despite the fact that he had never before come to Rome. It is very likely that Paul's friends, some of whom were his converts, who were members of the church in Rome, and who are mentioned in Romans 16, had spoken of him. His fame had preceded him to the city and the local Jewish community wanted to meet him and hear what he had been thinking and saying. Their interest in his opinion was heightened by the fact which they ruefully admitted to him that it was their understanding that the gospel which Paul preached was regarded everywhere in Rome as a dangerous heresy. It is easy to see the retroactive force of progressive duration in these present tense verbs. Everyone in Rome except the Christians were denouncing Christianity. Nero had ascended the throne in 54 and the reign of the first five years had been peaceful. But in 59, perhaps eighteen months before Paul reached the city, the Emperor had engaged in a reign of terror, although the city was not burned, a tragedy for which the Christians were blamed, until July of 64, after Paul had left town. Nevertheless Christianity was not popular in Rome and Paul got to the city in time to get involved.

It is thus easy to understand why the Jews in the city were glad to meet Paul and to listen to his exposition of the new religion.

*Verse 23 - "And when they had appointed him a day, there came many to him into his lodging: to whom he expounded and testified of the kingdom of God, persuading them concerning Jesus, both out of the law of Moses and out of the prophets, from morning till evening."*

Ταξάμενοι δὲ αὐτῷ ἡμέραν ἦλθον πρὸς αὐτὸν εἰς τὴν ξενίαν πλείονες, οἷς ἐξετίθετο διαμαρτυρόμενος τὴν βασιλείαν τοῦ θεοῦ πείθων τε αὐτοὺς περὶ τοῦ Ἰησοῦ ἀπό τε τοῦ νόμου Μωϋσέως καὶ τῶν προφητῶν ἀπὸ πρωῒ ἕως ἑσπέρας.

Ταξάμενοι (aor.mid.part.nom.pl.masc.of τάσσω, adverbial, temporal) 722.
δὲ (continuative conjunction) 11.
αὐτῷ (dat.sing.masc.of αὐτός, indirect object of ταξάμενοι) 16.
ἡμέραν (acc.sing.fem.of ἡμέρα, direct object of ταξάμενοι) 135.
ἦλθον (3d.per.pl.aor.ind.of ἔρχομαι, constative) 146.
πρὸς (preposition with the accusative of extent) 197.
αὐτὸν (acc.sing.masc.of αὐτός, extent) 16.
εἰς (preposition with the accusative of extent) 140.
τὴν (acc.sing.fem.of the article in agreement with ξενίαν) 9.

#3779 ξενίαν (acc.sing.fem.of ξενία, extent).

lodging - Acts 28:23.

*Meaning:* Cf. ξένος (#1547), ξενίζω (#3214). Hence, lodging place; dwelling place - Acts 28:23; Philemon 22. Differing from οἶκος (#784) as a motel differs from a home.

πλείονες (nom.pl.masc.of πλείων, subject of ἦλθον) 474.
οἷς (dat.pl.masc.of ὅς, relative pronoun, indirect object of ἐξετίθετο) 65.
ἐξετίθετο (3d.per.sing.imp.mid.ind.of ἐκτίθημι, iterative) 3120.
διαμαρτυρόμενος (pres.mid.part.nom.sing.masc.of διαμαρτυρέω, adverbial, modal) 2589.
τὴν (acc.sing.fem.of the article in agreement with βασιλείαν) 9.
βασιλείαν (acc.sing.fem.of βασιλεία, direct object of διαμαρτυρόμενος) 253.
τοῦ (gen.sing.masc.of the article in agreement with θεοῦ) 9.
θεοῦ (gen.sing.masc.of θεός, description) 124.
πείθων (pres.act.part.nom.sing.masc.of πείθω, adverbial, modal, conative) 1629.
τε (continuative particle) 1408.
αὐτοὺς (acc.pl.masc.of αὐτός, direct object of πείθων) 16.
περὶ (preposition with the genitive of reference) 173.
τοῦ (gen.sing.masc.of the article in agreement with Ἰησοῦ) 9.
Ἰησοῦ (gen.sing.masc.of Ἰησοῦς, reference) 3.
ἀπὸ (preposition with the ablative of source) 70.
τε (correlative particle) 1408.
τοῦ (abl.sing.masc.of the article in agreement with νόμου) 9.
νόμου (abl.sing.masc.of νόμος, source) 464.
Μωϋσέως (gen.sing.masc.of Μωϋσῆς, description) 715.
καὶ (adjunctive conjunction joining nouns) 14.
τῶν (abl.pl.masc.of the article in agreement with προφητῶν) 9.
προφητῶν (abl.pl.masc.of προφήτης, source) 119.
ἀπὸ (preposition with the ablative of time separation) 70.
πρωΐ (adverbial) 1192.
ἕως (improper preposition with the genitive of time description) 71.
ἑσπέρας (gen.sing.fem.of ἑσπέρα, time description) 2909.

*Translation* - "*And when they had arranged a day with him many came to him at his lodging, to whom he lectured from time to time by explaining thoroughly the kingdom of God and seeking to persuade them with reference to Jesus, both from the law of Moses and from the prophets, from early morning until twilight.*"

**Comment:** ταξάμενοι is antecedent to ἦλθον. The Jews and Paul agreed upon the day when it would be convenient both for him and for them to visit him in his dwelling. ἐξετίθετο is iterative. It suggests that there were many such days. The sessions went on from early morning to the twilight hours. Note the participle θείθων, due to the meaning of the word. Paul continued to persuade (present tense in πείθων) but he did not succeed in all cases as we learn in verse 24.

His sources - Moses and the Prophets - are the same ones that he always used, and that Jesus Himself also used (Luke 24:27). A careful study of the preaching of all of the Apostles reveals that they always presented the New Testament theology of the gospel of Christ as a logical extension of the message of the Old Testament. Jesus Christ was the fulfillment of the ethical and moral standards of the Mosaic law (Mt.5:17), and, in His person and work, He was the historic implementation of all of the predictions of the Prophets. Thus the gospel, by Scriptural definition, is that Christ died for our sins and rose again, "according to the Scriptures" (1 Cor.15:3,4). This was Paul's point in the hearing before Festus and Agrippa, as he demonstrated that, far from departing from the traditions of the Pharisees, as he was being accused, he was the only good Pharisee present, since the keystone of his argument was the resurrection of Jesus in the same body in which He suffered. This was something that the Pharisees were supposed to believe (Acts 23:8).

Now in Rome, Paul continued to argue that the only logical conclusion to which one could come if he believed Moses and the Prophets was that Jesus of Nazareth was the Messiah and that salvation, both individually and nationally could be found only in Him. With only brief pauses for recuperation and refreshment (iterative imperfect in ἐξετίθετο) he was everlastingly at it, from dawn to dusk. Thus he finished his course and kept the faith (2 Tim.4:7).

The obligation to preach the gospel always rested heavily upon Paul (1 Cor.9:16), perhaps especially so in Rome, now that he was delivered both from shipwreck and snakebite. Paul never worried about the future, because, though he did not know what was in the future, he knew Who was in the future. He was concerned that he should be always faithful to his calling in the present.

*Verse 24 - "And some believed the things which were spoken and some believed not."*

καὶ οἱ μὲν ἐπείθοντο τοῖς λεγομένοις, οἱ δὲ ἠπίστουν.

καὶ (continuative conjunction) 14.
οἱ (nom.pl.masc.of the article, subject of ἐπείθοντο) 9.
μὲν (affirmative particle) 300.
ἐπείθοντο (3d.per.pl.imp.pass.ind.of πείθω, inchoative) 1629.

τοῖς (loc.pl.masc.of the article in agreement with λεγομένοις) 9.

λεγομένοις (pres.pass.part.loc.pl.masc.of λέγω, substantival, sphere) 66.

οἱ (nom.pl.masc.of the article, subject of ἠπίστουν) 9.

δὲ (adversative conjunction) 11.

ἠπίστουν (3d.per.pl.imp.act.ind.of ἀπιστεύω, progressive description) 2893.

*Translation - "And there were those who began to be convinced of the things which were said, but others continued to disbelieve."*

**Comment:** Since τοῖς λεγομένοις can be either locative, instrumental or dative, we can translate as a locative of sphere ("they began to believe *in the sphere of the matters* under discussion), or we can translate as an instrumental of means ("they began to be convinced by what was said" ) or we can call it a dative ("they began to believe *with reference to* what was said.") In each case we get the same result. We can take καὶ also as inferential, since "faith cometh by hearing and hearing by the Word of God" (Rom.10:13-17). God sent Paul; being sent, he went; having gone he preached; when he preached they heard; when they heard some began to believe. The sequence in Romans 10 suggests that when they believed they called and when they called they were saved.

Why not all? (Acts 13:48). Paul was binding and loosing on earth that which had already been bound or loosed in heaven. (Mt.16:19; 18:18; John 20:23). *Cf.* our discussion of these passages, *en loc.*

Paul's ministry was adequate to secure the results on earth of that which had been ordered in the eternal council of the Godhead. The gospel of Christ smells like life to some and like death to others (2 Cor.2:15-17). Unregenerates of course reject this theology (Mt.11:25) and even some born again children of God have difficulty with it (John 6:66). Calvinists often lose their crowds, just as Jesus did. But when the sinner is breathed upon by the Spirit of God (John 3:8) then he becomes a "fool for Christ" (1 Cor.3:18; 4:10).

It is not likely that Paul ever preached the gospel to an audience and saw all present receive Christ as Saviour. It is also highly unlikely that his preaching was ultimately unfruitful in the lives of all in the audience. The gospel of Christ is the great divider. However there are always times when the preacher of the gospel contributes to the seed sowing and/or the watering, while some other preacher reaps the harvest. Thus we enter into the labors of one another (1 Cor.3:6-9).

*Verse 25 - "And when they agreed not among themselves, they departed, after that Paul had spoken one word, Well spake the Holy Ghost by Esaias the prophet unto our fathers."*

ἀσύμφωνοι δὲ ὄντες πρὸς ἀλλήλους ἀπελύοντο, εἰπόντος τοῦ Παύλου ῥῆμα ἓν ὅτι Καλῶς τὸ πνεῦμα τὸ ἅγιον ἐλάλησεν διὰ Ἠσαΐου τοῦ προφήτου πρὸς τοὺς πατέρας ὑμῶν

**#3780** ἀσύμφωνοι (nom.pl.masc.of ἀσύμφωνος, predicate adjective).

agree not - Acts 28:25.

*Meaning:* A combination of α privative, σύν (#1542) and φωνή (#222). Hence, the state of being in disagreement; in a musical context, the adjective means dissonant. At variance philosophically and theologically - Acts 28:25. *Cf.* συμφωνέω (#1265), συμφώνησις (#4320), συμφωνία (#2557) and σύμφωνος (#4153).

δὲ (adversative conjunction) 11.
ὄντες (pres.part.nom.pl.masc.of εἰμί, adverbial, causal) 86.
πρὸς (preposition with the accusative of extent, in a context of speaking) 197.
ἀλλήλους (acc.pl.masc.of ἀλλήλων, extent, in a context of speaking) 1487.
ἀπελύοντο (3d.per.pl.imp.mid.ind.of ἀπολύω, inchoative) 92.
εἰπόντος (aor.act.part.gen.sing.masc.of εἶπον, adverbial, temporal, genitive absolute) 155.
τοῦ (gen.sing.masc.of the article in agreement with Παύλου) 9.
Παύλου (gen.sing.masc.of Παῦλος, genitive absolute) 3284.
ῥῆμα (acc.sing.neut.of ῥῆμα, direct object of εἰπόντος) 343.
ἓν (acc.sing.neut.of εἷς, in agreement with ῥῆμα) 469.
ὅτι (recitative) 211.
Καλῶς (adverbial) 977.
τὸ (nom.sing.neut.of the article in agreement with πνεῦμα) 9.
πνεῦμα (nom.sing.neut.of πνεῦμα, subject of ἐλάλησεν) 83.
τὸ (nom.sing.neut.of the article in agreement with ἅγιον) 9.
ἅγιον (nom.sing.neut.of ἅγιος, in agreement with πνεῦμα) 84.
ἐλάλησεν (3d.per.sing.aor.act.ind.of λαλέω, constative) 815.
διὰ (preposition with the ablative of agent) 118.
'Ησαΐου (abl.sing.masc.of 'Ησαΐας, agent) 255.
τοῦ (abl.sing.masc.of the article in agreement with προφήτου) 9.
προφήτου (abl.sing.masc.of προφήτης, apposition) 119.
πρὸς (preposition with the accusative of extent after a verb of speaking) 197.
τοὺς (acc.pl.masc.of the article in agreement with πατέρας) 9.
πατέρας (acc.pl.masc.of πατήρ, extent, after a verb of speaking) 238.
ὑμῶν (gen.pl.masc.of ἐγώ, relationship) 123.

*Translation - "But because they were at odds among themselves they began to leave, after Paul had made one observation, 'Well did the Holy Spirit speak through Isaiah, the prophet, to our fathers. . . "*

**Comment:** ὄντες is causal. Because the Jews got involved in an argument over the truth and meaning of what Paul had preached, he was led to make one more observation (#3780). When the gospel of Christ is presented to a random audience social harmony ends (Mt.10:34,35). The same sun that melts wax hardens clay, though this analogy fails (as most analogies do), because it puts the difference in the various members of the audience, whereas the difference lies in the depths of the wise council of an inscrutable Deity.

The Jews came to Paul's room in harmony. They left in disagreement. Some were saved; others were not. They did not begin to leave (inchoative imperfect in ἀπελύοντο) until Paul, who listened to their argument, made one last observation - a quotation from Isaiah 6:9,10.

*Verse 26* - *"Saying, Go unto this people, and say, Hearing ye shall hear, and shall not understand; and seeing ye shall see, and not perceive."*

λέγων, Πορεύθητι πρὸς τὸν λαὸν τοῦτον καὶ εἶπον,'Ακοῇ ἀκούετε καὶ οὐ μὴ συνῆτε, καὶ βλέποντες βλέφετε καὶ οὐ μὴ ἴδητε,

λέγων (pres.act.part.nom.sing.masc.of λέγω, recitatitve) 66.

Πορεύθητι (2d.per.sing.aor.mid.impv.of πορεύομαι, command) 170.

πρὸς (preposition with the accusative of extent) 197.

τὸν (acc.sing.masc.of the article in agreement with λαὸν) 9.

λαὸν (acc.sing.masc.of λαός, extent) 110.

τοῦτον (acc.sing.masc.of οὗτος, in agreement with λαὸν) 93.

καὶ (adjunctive conjunction joining verbs) 14.

εἶπον (2d.per.sing.aor.act.impv.of εἶπον, command) 155.

ἀκοῇ (instru.sing.fem.of ἀκοή, means) 409.

ἀκούσετε (2d.per.pl.fut.act.ind.of ἀκούω, predictive) 148.

καὶ (adversative conjunction) 14.

οὐ (negative conjunction with μὴ and the subjunctive) 130.

μὴ (negative conjunction with the subjunctive) 87.

συνῆτε (2d.per.pl.2d.aor.subj.of συνίημι, emphatic negation) 1039.

καὶ (continuative conjunction) 14.

βλέποντες (pres.act.part.nom.pl.masc.of βλέπω, adverbial, concessive) 499.

βλέφετε (2d.per.pl.fut.act.ind.of βλέπω, predictive) 499.

καὶ (adversative conjunction) 14.

οὐ (negative conjunction with μὴ and the subjunctive) 130.

μὴ (negative conjunction with the subjunctive) 87.

ἴδητε (2d.per.pl.aor.act.subj.of ὁράω, emphatic negation) 144b.

*Translation* - *". . . saying, 'Go to this people and say, 'With your ears you will listen and listen, but you will never understand and although you will look and will see, but you will never perceive .' ' "*

**Comment:** The durative nature of ἀκούετε, βλέποντες and βλέφετε is the point. Sinners hear and see again and again, but for all of their empirical experience, both auditory and optical, as sensory perceptions occur repeatedly, at no time do unregenerate men grasp the eternal significance of the sensory world about them. The contrast is between ἀκούω (#148) - "sense perception" and συνίημι (#1039) - "intellectual grasp" and between βλέπω (#499) - "sense perception" and ὁράω (#144b), which also is intellectual grasp.

Sinners who worship sense perceptions and reject logical systems that assume by faith revealed concepts as "givens" are "ever learning" ( ἀκούετε and βλέφετε) "and never able to come to a knowledge of the truth" (συνῆτε and ἴδητε) (2 Tim.3:7). Isaiah's statement (Isa.6:9,10) has its counterpart in 1 Cor.2:9,10. This is what Jesus told the Jews thirty years before. *Cf.* Mt.13:14,15. He spoke in parable and they did not understand. Paul rejected the parabolic approach and laid it out logically from dawn to dusk, as he correlated the Mosaic code and the prophetic predictions of the Old Testament with the empirical facts of history, but they still did not understand. *Cf.* comment on Mt.13:14,15; 1 Cor.2:9,10.

*Verse 27 - "For the heart of this people is waxed gross, and their ears are dull of hearing, and their eyes have they closed; lest they should see with their eyes, and hear with their ears, and understand with their heart, and should be converted and I should heal them."*

ἐπαχύνθη γὰρ ἡ καρδία τοῦ λαοῦ τούτου, καὶ τοῖς ὠσὶν βαρέως ἤκουσαν, καὶ τοὺς ὀφθαλμοὺς αὐτῶν ἐκάμμυσαν, μήποτε ἴδωσιν τοῖς ὀφθαλμοῖς καὶ τοῖς ὠσὶν ἀκούσωσιν καὶ τῇ καρδίᾳ συνῶσιν καί ἐπιστρέφωσιν, καὶ ἰάσομαι αὐτούς.

ἐπαχύνθη (3d.per.sing.aor.pass.ind.of παχύνω, culminative) 1042.
γὰρ (causal conjunction) 105.
ἡ (nom.sing.fem.of the article in agreement with καρδία) 9.
καρδία (nom.sing.fem.of καρδία, subject of ἐπαχύνθη) 432.
τοῦ (gen.sing.masc.of the article in agreement with λαοῦ) 9.
λαοῦ (gen.sing.masc.of λαός, possession) 110.
τούτου (gen.sing.masc.of οὗτος, in agreement with λαοῦ) 93.
καὶ (continuative conjunction) 14.
τοῖς (instru.pl.neut.of the article in agreement with ὠσὶν) 9.
ὠσὶν (instru.pl.neut.of οὖς, means) 887.
βαρέως (adverbial) 1043.
ἤκουσαν (3d.per.pl.aor.act.ind.of ἀκούω, culminative) 148.
καὶ (adversative conjunction) 14.
τοὺς (acc.pl.masc.of the article in agreement with ὀφθαλμοὺς) 9.
ὀφθαλμοὺς (acc.pl.masc.of ὀφθαλμός, direct object of ἐκάμμυσαν) 501.
αὐτῶν (gen.pl.masc.of αὐτός, possession) 16.
ἐκάμμυσαν (3d.per.pl.aor.act.ind.of καμμύω, culminative) 1044.
μήποτε ( prohibitory conjunctive particle introducing a negative final clause) 351.
ἴδωσιν (3d.per.pl.aor.act.subj.of ὁράω, negative purpose) 144b.
τοῖς (instru.pl.masc.of the article in agreement with ὀφθαλμοῖς) 9.
ὀφθαλμοῖς (instru.pl.masc.of ὀφθαλμός, means) 501.
καὶ (adjunctive conjunction joining verbs) 14.
τοῖς (instru.pl.neut.of the article in agreement with ὠσὶν) 9.
ὠσὶν (instru.pl.neut.of οὖς, means) 887.
ἀκούσωσιν (3d.per.pl.aor.act.subj.of ἀκούω, negative purpose) 148.
καὶ (adjunctive conjunction joining verbs) 14.
τῇ (instru.sing.fem.of the article in agreement with καρδίᾳ) 9.
καρδίᾳ (instru.sing.fem.of καρδία, means) 432.
συνῶσιν (3d.per.pl.aor.act.ind.of συνίημι, negative purpose) 1039.
καὶ (adjunctive conjunction joining verbs) 14.
ἐπιστρέφωσιν (3d.per.pl.aor.act.subj.of ἐπιστρέφω, negative purpose) 866.

καὶ (adjunctive conjunction joining verbs) 14.
ἰάσομαι (1st.per.sing.fut.mid.ind.of ἰάομαι, negative purpose) 721.
αὐτούς (acc.pl.masc.of αὐτός, direct object of ἰάσομαι) 16.

*Translation* - *"Because the heart of this people has been atrophied and they heard dully with their years and they closed their eyes, lest they perceive with their eyes and hear with their ears and understand with their heart and turn around and I heal them."*

**Comment:** The blame for the sad state of the unregenerate is laid squarely on their own doorstep by the causal γὰρ of verse 27. Why do the radical empiricists never understand what they see and hear? Because that is the way they want it. Why is their heart obtuse and their ears dull of hearing? Because they closed their eyes and turned away their ears. The negative purpose, with μήποτε and the subjunctives in ἴδωσιν ἀκούσωσιν συνῶσιν and ἐπιστρέφωσιν and the future indicative in ἰάσομαι, all tell us the motivation for deliberately rejecting the truth. They did so to prevent their perceiving, hearing, meaningfully understanding, repenting or being healed by divine grace.

ποτε loses the time element in μήποτε - "lest at any time" and carries instead the idea of contingency - "lest perchance," or "in the fear that." *Cf.* John 3:19,20. where the negative purpose is expressed by ἵνα μὴ and the subjunctive.

Paul's quotation from Isaiah explains why the Jews who rejected his message did not believe, but it leaves unexplained those who believed. The only answer is divine grace - Acts 13:48.

*Verse 28 - "Be it known therefore unto you, that the salvation of God is sent unto the Gentiles, and that they will hear it."*

γνωστὸν οὖν ἔστω ὑμῖν ὅτι τοῖς ἔθνεσιν ἀπεστάλη τοῦτο τὸ σωτήριον τοῦ θεοῦ, αὐτοὶ καὶ ἀκούσονται.

γνωστὸν (acc.sing.neut.of γνωστός, predicate adjective) 1917.
οὖν (inferential conjunction) 68.
ἔστω (3d.per.sing.pres.impv.of εἰμί, command) 86.
ὑμῖν (dat.pl.masc.of σύ, personal interest) 104.
ὅτι (conjunction introducing an object clause in indirect discourse) 211.
τοῖς (dat.pl.neut.of the article in agreement with ἔθνεσιν) 9.
ἔθνεσιν (dat.pl.neut.of ἔθνος, indirect object of ἀπεστάλη) 376.
ἀπεστάλη (3d.per.sing.2d.aor.pass.ind.of ἀποστέλλω, culminative) 215.
τοῦτο (nom.sing.neut.of οὗτος, in agreement with σωτήριον) 93.
τὸ (nom.sing.neut.of the article in agreement with σωτήριον) 9.
σωτήριον (nom.sing.neut.of σωτήριον, subject of ἀπεστάλη) 1901.
τοῦ (gen.sing.masc.of the article in agreement with θεοῦ) 9.
θεοῦ (gen.sing.masc.of θεός, description) 124.
αὐτοὶ (nom.pl.masc.of αὐτός, subject of ἀκούσονται) 16.
καὶ (continuative conjunction) 14.
ἀκούσονται (3d.per.pl.fut.mid.ind.of ἀκούω, predictive) 148.

*Translation - "So I want you to know that this salvation of God has been sent unto the Gentiles, and that they will hear it."*

**Comment:** Indirect discourse after ὅτι. Note the preterite force of the culminative aorist in ἀπεστάλη. God had already sent His gospel to the Gentiles in Rome (Acts 1:8; 9:15; 15:13-18; John 10:16; Rom.1:16). Paul's reason for seeking out the Jews first was his obedience to Christ's commission. Paul was certain that the gospel which some of the Jews accepted and that others rejected would be accepted also by some of the Gentiles (Eph.3:1-7; Rev.10:7). Note the demonstrative αὐτοί.

*Verse 29 - "And when he had said these words the Jews departed, and had great reasoning among themselves."*

*(Note: p74 vid, Sinaiticus A B E Φ 048 33 81 181 629, et al* omit verse 29. The United Bible Societies' Committee has therefore omitted it with a B degree of certitude). "The Western expansion . . . was probably made because of the abrupt transition from ver.28 to ver.30." (Metzger, *A Textual Commentary on the Greek New Testament,* 502).

*Verse 30 - "And Paul dwelt two whole years in his own hired house, and received all that came in unto him."*

Ἐνέμεινεν δὲ διετίαν ὅλην ἐν ἰδίῳ μισθώματι, καὶ ἀπεδέχετο πάντας τοὺς εἰσπορευομένους πρὸς αὐτόν,

Ἐνέμεινεν (3d.per.sing.aor.act.ind.of ἐμμένω, constative) 3331.
δὲ (continuative conjunction) 11.
διετίαν (acc.sing.fem.of διετία, time extent) 3631.
ὅλην (acc.sing.fem.of ὅλος, in agreement with διετίαν) 112.
ἐν (preposition with the locative of place) 80.
ἰδίῳ (loc.sing.neut.of ἴδιος, in agreement with μισθώματι) 778.

#3781 μισθώματι (loc.sing.neut.of μίσθωμα, place).

hired house - Acts 28:30.

*Meaning:* The price of something. In the LXX - Hosea 2:12; Deut.23:18; Mic.1:7; Prov.19:13; Ezek.16:31-34. In the New Testament, that which is rented or bought - a dwelling house, or a rented room - Acts 28:30.

καὶ (adjunctive conjunction joining verbs) 14.
ἀπεδέχετο (3d.per.sing.imp.mid.ind.of ἀποδέχομαι, iterative) 2245.
πάντας (acc.pl.masc.of πᾶς, in agreement with εἰσπορευομένους) 67.
τοὺς (acc.pl.masc.of the article in agreement with εἰσπορευομένους) 9.
εἰσπορευομένους (pres.mid.part.acc.pl.masc.of εἰσπορεύομαι, substantival, direct object of ἀπεδέχετο) 1161.
πρὸς (preposition with the accusative of extent) 197.
αὐτόν (acc.sing.masc.of αὐτός, extent) 16.

*Translation* - *"And he lived for two whole years in his own rented quarters and he received everyone who came to see him."*

**Comment:** Unlike πᾶς, ὅλην is indefinite. Luke is not being precise - "for the greater part of, or a little more than two years." ἐνέμεινεν, a verb of duration is here, nevertheless a constative aorist. Thus Luke is regarding this two year period as a time point in Paul's life. It is nonetheless a literal two year period. Other constative aorists of similar nature are found in Heb.11:23,27; Rom.5:14; Rev.20:4; 1 Thess.5:10; John 7:9; 10:40; Acts 11:26; 14:3; 18:11. Gildersleeve (*Syntax*, 105, as cited in Robertson, *Grammar*, 833) calls the constative an "aorist of long duration." Let the student be warned that the constative aorist does not negate the idea that the time period involved is literal. Amillenialists make this mistake with reference to Rev.20:4. It is only that the writer is emphasizing the *fact* of the action rather than the *time duration*.

ἀπεδέχετο is iterative, as is clear when we look at the durative nature of the present participle εἰσπορευομένους. Thus the fact that Paul was in chains and under house arrest with a soldier on duty to guard him, did not in any way hinder his preaching and teaching ministry in Rome. Not many preachers have the privilege of sitting at home to receive a constant stream of visitors who come to hear him preach the gospel. It may often have been heard in Rome - "Let us go down to Paul's house and hear him preach."

*Verse 31* - *"Preaching the kingdom of God and teaching those things which concern the Lord Jesus Christ, with all confidence, no man forbidding him."*

κηρύσσων τὴν βασιλείαν τοῦ θεοῦ καὶ διδάσκων τὰ περὶ τοῦ κυρίου Ἰησοῦ Χριστοῦ μετὰ πάσης παρρησίας ἀκωλύτως.

κηρύσσων (pres.act.part.nom.sing.masc.of κηρύσσω, adverbial, complementary) 249.
τὴν (acc.sing.fem.of the article in agreement with βασιλείαν) 9.
βασιλείαν (acc.sing.fem.of βασιλεία, direct object of κηρύσσων) 253.
τοῦ (gen.sing.masc.of the article in agreement with θεοῦ) 9.
θεοῦ (gen.sing.masc.of θεός, description) 124.
καὶ (adjunctive conjunction joining participles) 14.
διδάσκων (pres.act.part.nom.sing.masc.of διδάσκω, adverbial, complementary) 403.
τὰ (acc.pl.neut.of the article, direct object of διδάσκων) 9.
περὶ (preposition with the genitive of reference) 173.
τοῦ (gen.sing.masc.of the article in agreement with κυρίου) 9.
κυρίου (gen.sing.masc.of κύριος, reference) 97.
Ἰησοῦ (gen.sing.masc.of Ἰησοῦς, apposition) 3.
Χριστοῦ (gen.sing.masc.of Χριστός, apposition) 4.
μετὰ (preposition with the genitive, in an instrumental sense) 50.
πάσης (gen.sing.fem.of πᾶς, in agreement with παρρησίας) 67.
παρρησίας (gen.sing.fem.of παρρησία, manner) 2319.

**#3782** ἀκωλύτως (adverbial).

no man forbidding - Acts 28:31.

*Meaning:* A combination of α privative and κωλύω (#1296). Hence, without restraint or opposition - Acts 28:13.

*Translation - ". . . always preaching the kingdom of God and continuing to teach the message about the Lord Jesus Christ, openly and without restraint."*

**Comment:** Again we have the iterative force of the present participles κηρύσσων and διδάσκων. Again and again during those two years, as his guests came to listen, he preached and taught the gospel. The message of the Kingdom of God cannot be separated from the material relating to the Lord Jesus Christ, whose life, death, resurrection and second coming are the basis upon which God's kingdom will at last be extended throughout all creation.

Paul had the courage of his convictions and he spoke without fear. This is the force of μετὰ πάσης παρρησίας. There were no reservations. He declared the whole counsel of God. The adverb indicates that there were no restrictions placed upon Paul's freedom to preach and teach.

Luke closes his story of Paul without relating the events surrounding his death. The last picture that Doctor Luke gives is a vignette of an old man, a Roman citizen, a distinguished Jewish lawyer, the Apostle to the Gentiles, sitting in his own house, bound with a chain, with a Roman soldier on guard, but with a voice ringing out with the verve, vivacity and vitality born of the indwelling Holy Spirit and with the scholarly comprehension of which he alone was capable, to an audience of first century Romans - preaching the good news of the gospel of Jesus Christ.

It will now be our privilege to study in depth the contribution of the Apostle Paul to the literature of the New Testament.

# Paul's Epistle to the Church at Rome

## Salutation

*(Romans 1:1-7)*

*Romans 1:1 - "Paul, a servant of Jesus Christ, called to be an apostle, separated unto the gospel of God."*

Παῦλος δοῦλος Χριστοῦ Ἰησοῦ, κλητὸς ἀπόστολος, ἀφωρισμένος εἰς εὐαγγέλιον θεοῦ,

Παῦλος (nom.sing.masc.of Παῦλος, nominative absolute) 3284.
δοῦλος (nom.sing.masc.of δοῦλος, apposition) 725.
Χριστοῦ (gen.sing.masc.of Χριστός, relationship) 4.
Ἰησοῦ (gen.sing.masc.of Ἰησοῦς, apposition) 3.
κλητὸς (nom.sing.masc.of κλητός, predicate adjective, in agreement with Παῦλος) 1411.
ἀπόστολος (nom.sing.masc.of ἀπόστολος, apposition) 844.
ἀφωρισμένος (perf.pass.part.nom.sing.masc.of ἀφορίζω, adjectival, restrictive, in agreement with Παῦλος) 1093.
εἰς (preposition with the accusative, purpose) 140.
εὐαγγέλιον (acc.sing.neut.of εὐαγγέλιον, purpose) 405.
θεοῦ (gen.sing.masc.of θεός, description) 124.

*Translation - "Paul, a slave of Christ Jesus, a called apostle, set apart for the divine good news, . . ."*

**Comment:** It is a high honor to be one of the twelve Apostles. But Paul's first designation of himself was as a slave - δοῦλος Χριστοῦ'Ιησοῦ - *Cf.*#725. He was later to write (Romans 6:16) his definition of a slave - he is a slave (δοῦλος) who obeys, without regard to the source of the command. Our Lord Jesus became a slave (Phil.2:7). Thus Christ Jesus, the slave of God in incarnation, earned to right to command His slaves, of whom Paul was one.

He was a "called apostle." *Cf.* Rom.8:30. *Cf.* comment on Acts 1:15-26. Paul, not Matthias was selected by God to take Judas' place. He will have a place in the kingdom in a judiciary capacity with jurisdiction over one of the tribes of Israel (Mt.19:28).

To Paul and to the other Apostles were given the sign gifts. He and they were entrusted by the Holy Spirit with the knowledge and wisdom to provide the early church with direction in matters of faith and practice, in the period before the New Testament was written. Some of these gifts were *ad hoc* as Paul pointed out in 1 Cor.13:8. When the perfect revelation of the will of God for His church was completed with the completion of the New Testament literature and the establishment of the canon, these apostolic gifts were no longer needed and were phased out. Since the Holy Spirit has already taken that which pertains to Christ, which things include all that the Father has, and has revealed it unto us in the New Testament, there is nothing further to be added, the current charismatic interest in ecstasy to the contrary notwithstanding. John 16:13-15.

Paul's authorship of thirteen of the epistles of the New Testament is beyond dispute and he may have written the epistle to the Hebrews. The matter is not clear, though one can find dogmatists on both sides of the question. Romans ". . . was written at Corinth . . . about the end of the year 57, or at the beginning of the year 58. . . it is the fifth Epistle in order of time; the two Epistles to the Thessalonians, the Epistle to the Galatians, and the first to the Corinthians, having been previously written. Then followed the second Epistle to the Corinthians, the Epistles to the Ephesians, Philippians, Colossians, Philemon, and the Hebrews, the first to Timothy, the Epistle to Titus, and the second to Timothy." (Calvin's Commentaries, *Romans,*Translator's Preface, x, xi).

Most scholars agree that Paul was converted in 35. He wrote his first letter, to the Thessalonians, seventeen years later, in 52. Thirteen years later, in 65, he wrote his second letter to Timothy and thus completed his contribution to the New Testament literature. It is not likely that he lived long after dictating 2 Timothy 4:6,7. "Tradition says, (*sic*) that he was beheaded at Rome, June 29, A.D.66" (*Ibid.,* x, xi *et passim*).

Since Paul remained in Rome for only two years at the time of his first visit, and since he came to Rome for the first time in the spring of 61, we are left with the problem of where he spent and what he did during the last three years of his life. When he was released from house arrest in 63, ". . . most writers are of the opinion, that he returned early in 63 to Judea, in company with Timothy, and left Titus at Crete; that he visited the Churches in Asia Minor, then the Churches in Macedonia; that he wintered at Nicopolis, a city of Epirus, in 64; that afterwards he proceeded to Crete and also to Corinth; and that early in 65 he again visited Rome, was taken prisoner, and beheaded in the following year. . . .

It is generally supposed that he wrote his Epistle to the Ephesians, Philippians,

Colossians, Philemon and perhaps Hebrews (if indeed he wrote Hebrews) during his first visit to Rome.(*Ibid*, xi). There is no evidence that Paul realized his ambition to visit Spain.

That Paul wrote to the Romans while in Corinth during the winter of 57/58 seems evident from the following evidence offered by Coneybeare & Howson: "The date of this Epistle is very precisely fixed by the following statements contained in it: (1) St.Paul had never yet been to Rome (1:11,13,15). (2) He was intending to go to Rome after first visiting Jerusalem (15:23-28). This was exactly his purpose during his three months' residence at Corinth. See Acts 19:21. (3). He was going to bear a collection of alms from Macedonia and Achaia to Jerusalem (15:26,31). This he did carry from Corinth to Jerusalem at the close of this three months' visit. See Acts 24:17. (4). When he wrote the Epistle, Timotheus, Sosipater, Gaius and Erastus were with him (16:21,23); of these, the first three are explressly mentioned in Acts, as having been with him at Corinth during the three months' visit (see Acts 20:4), and the last, Erastus, was himself a Corinthian, and had been sent shortly before from Ephesus (Acts 19:22) with Timotheus on the way to Corinth. Compare 1 Cor.16:10,11. (5) Phoebe, a deaconess of the Corinthian port of Cenchrea was the bearer of the Epistle (16:1) to Rome." (*The Life and Epistles of St.Paul*, II, 156,157).

Called to his apostleship from before the foundation of the earth, he was also separated unto the gospel which has its source in God. We can take $\vartheta\epsilon o\hat{v}$ either as a genitive of description or an ablative of source. Both ideas are true. Since it is without the article we have translated it as an adjective. $\epsilon\dot{v}\alpha\gamma\gamma\dot{\epsilon}\lambda\iota o\nu$ $\tauo\hat{v}$ $\vartheta\epsilon o\hat{v}$ would translate as "the good news of God" (possession or description) or "the good news from God" (ablative of source). As it stands it is "the divine ("godly") good news." $\dot{\alpha}\phi\omega\rho\iota\sigma\mu\dot{\epsilon}\nu o\varsigma$ is a perfect passive participle. It indicates a present (at the time of writing) condition which is durative, as a result of a past completed action which is punctiliar. God's complete act in the past resulted in Paul's current state and position as being separated unto the gospel. It can also be inferred that he would continue to be so separated until his death (2 Tim.4:6-8). *Cf.* also Phil.1:6; Eph.2:10; Rev.3:10. Thus this perfect tense has preterite and durative present force, which elements are implicit in the perfect tense, and, because of the cross-fertilization of Scripture, it is also proleptical, though the proleptical (future) aspect is not derived from the perfect tense. The perfect tense is never proleptic *per se*. That Paul was, at the time when he wrote this, separated and that he would remain separated to the gospel is clear from other Scriptures.

To be separated is to be set apart. The student should study with care the word in all of its contexts, as listed under #1093. The purpose of this separation is found in the $\epsilon i\varsigma$ $\epsilon\dot{v}\alpha\gamma\gamma\dot{\epsilon}\lambda\iota o\nu$ phrase. $\epsilon i\varsigma$ with the accusative expressed purpose. Why does God separate a preacher $\epsilon i\varsigma$ $\epsilon\dot{v}\alpha\gamma\gamma\dot{\epsilon}\lambda\iota o\nu$ $\vartheta\epsilon o\hat{v}$? In order that he may preach the good news. This does not mean that Paul did not engage in other activities, for indeed he did, nor does it mean that when he did, God was displeased. He made tents for a living and once gathered firewood for a fire. He engaged in a great many activities as he was "made all things to all men, that I might by all means save some. And this I do for the gospel's sake. . . " (1 Cor.9:22,23). Thus everything he did v'as designed for the purpose of furthering the gospel.

In Philemon 1:1 Paul calls himself a "prisoner" (δέσμιος #1624) of Christ in a reference to the fact that he was in jail. In that sense he was a prisoner of Nero, but he was there by the will of his Sovereign Lord, Who is greater than Nero.

Although God's call to Paul was in eternity, it was implemented in historic time. *Cf.* Acts 9:1-20; 22:6-21; 26:12-19. His separation unto the gospel was also a divinely ordered commission. *Cf.* Eph.3:7. God, Who calls, also brings about the fulfillment of His purpose. *Cf.* Gal.1:15,16.

The Epistle to the Romans is Paul's most scientific and closely reasoned statement of the plan of salvation. Here we have the lawyer at his best as he stands before the bar of reason. Salvation must be by grace if man is to be saved at all, since he is incapable of pleasing God. Divine justice demands payment for transgression, but this payment cannot be made by the defendant. If it is made at all it must be made by one who owes no sin debt to God. Only thus can the court of heaven acquiesce in man's plea for mercy and only thus can divine love express itself to the full. It was the Judge of all the earth (Gen.18:25) who came to earth to pay the debt (John 5:22). In Romans we learn what is meant by words like "right" and "righteousness." *Cf.* the list of related words, built upon the same root (δικ), (*The Renaissance New Testament*, I, 54), and the discussion of #85. Romans answers the question so often posed by the skeptic: if sin is so deadly and God is so holy, how can He forgive a sinner and save him, without compromising His holiness?

The argument in Romans is devastating in its attack upon the notion that salvation can be earned by works produced by man. It also shows that while no amount of good works can bring the sinner into right relationships with God, once the sinner has that right relationship, by grace through faith, no amoung of evil can separate Him from God, nor terminate his standing as God's child. However low, miserable and degrading our state may be, children of God never suffer any diminution of our standing.

In Romans as in all of his epistles Paul protrays New Testament Christianity, with its central emphasis upon the person and work of Jesus the Messiah, as no more, and certainly no less, than the inevitable fulfillment of the predictions of the Old Testament prophecies and the satisfaction of all of the moral demands of the Mosaic law. Christianity is something new only in the sense that the ear of ripened corn is a later development of the seed corn and that the flower is the inevitable development of the bud. Even the "mystery" of which Paul was the custodian, that the Gentiles also were included in the eternal plan of redemption, was not totally unrevealed in the Old Testament. Paul did not say that the mystery was not revealed at all to Israel before the incarnation of our Lord. He said that it was not revealed "as it is now revealed unto his holy apostles and prophets by the Spirit" (Eph.3:5). The "mystery" was partial in the Old Testament. It became complete in the New Testament.

The dispensational question which deals with the difference between the manner in which God deals with the Church, as the Body of Christ, and the way he will deal with Israel as His chosen political unit is discussed in Romans 9,10,11.

Finally the Apostle Paul never divorces the assurance of salvation from the Christian's obligation to live a holy life. The theological gospel and the social gospel can never be disassociated. The notion that we ought to live in sin in order that grace may abound is a violation of the very nature of the believer's relation to God. The theoretical, if it is true, always yields the practical. There is no place for antinomianism in Paul's thinking. Orthodox doctrine demands the separated life. Thus, after four chapters of distinction between law and grace in Galatians, in which Paul exults because of the freedom which we have in Christ, he begins chapter 5 with an inferential clause - "Stand fast *therefore* in the liberty wherewith Christ hath made us free" (Gal.5:1). In Ephesians he takes three chapters to set forth the doctrine of salvation by grace, and opens in chapter four with "I *therefore*, the prisoner of the Lord, beseech you that you walk worthy of the vocation wherewith ye are called." (Eph.4:1). In Philippians he devotes three chapters to doctrine and then adds, "*Therefore*, my brethren dearly beloved and longed for my joy and crown, so stand fast in the Lord. . . " (Phil.4:1). The Colossian epistle is divided about equally. Two chapters teach doctrine and the last two are filled with ethical admonitions. Again Paul uses the inferential - "If ye *then* be risen with Christ, seek those things which are above." The writer of Hebrews devotes almost the entire book to the superiority of Jesus Christ over the Old Testament prophets, the angels, Moses and Aaron, and closes with the 13th chapter, the theme of which is holy living.

We need not be surprized therefore to find in Romans, eight chapters which are doctrinal and three chapters which are dispensational, followed by five chapters which begin, "I beseech you *therefore* brethren, by the mercies of God, that ye present your bodies a living sacrifice, holy, acceptable unto God, which is your reasonable service. And be not conformed to this world, but be ye transformed, *by the renewing of your mind*. . . " (Rom.12:1,2).

The accusation that Calvinists are antinomians is a foul canard.

*Verse 2 - ". . . which he had promised afore by his prophets in the holy scriptures."*

ὃ προεπηγγείλατο διὰ τῶν προφητῶν αὐτοῦ ἐν γραφαῖς ἁγίαις,

ὃ (acc.sing.neut.of ὅς, relative pronoun, direct object of προεπηγγείλατο) 65.

#3783 προεπηγγείλατο (3d.per.sing.1st.aor.mid.ind.of προεπαγγέλλομαι, culminative).

promise before - Rom.1:2.
bounty - 2 Cor.9:5.

*Meaning:* A combination of πρό (#442) and ἐπαγγέλλομαι (#2752). Hence, to announce before in a chronological sense; in the middle, to make a promise - with reference to the divine gospel which was promised by God through the Old Testament prophets - Rom.1:2; of the financial pledges for poor relief in Jerusalem made by the Corinthians - 2 Cor.9:5.

διὰ (preposition with the ablative of agent) 118.

τῶν (abl.pl.masc.of the article in agreement with προφητῶν) 9.

προφητῶν (abl.pl.masc.of προφήτης, agent) 119.

αὐτοῦ (gen.sing.masc.of αὐτός, possession) 16.

ἐν (preposition with the locative of place) 80.

γραφαῖς (loc.pl.fem.of γραφή, place) 1389.

ἁγίαις (loc.pl.fem.of ἅγιος, in agreement with γραφαῖς) 84.

*Translation* - ". . . *which he promised before through His prophets in Holy Scriptures.*"

**Comment:** The antecedent of δ is εὐαγγέλιον of verse 1. *Cf.* Gal.3:8; 1 Pet.1:9-12; Lk.24:27; Acts 28:23. The gospel unto which, and for purposes of propagation of which, Paul had been set apart, was not something new. It had been promised before in Old Testament times by God who used the Old Testament prophets as His agents. They preserved their messages in the writings of the Old Testament. Both Peter, Stephen, Philip and Paul, as well as other preachers, insofar as their teachings are recorded in Acts, made constant appeals to Moses and the Prophets to show that Jesus was the Messiah in Whose person and work the "Hope of Israel" as set forth in the Old Testament was to be realized, and that this was the gospel of salvation which they preached. *Cf.* Acts 28:20. *Cf.* Acts 7:2-53 for Stephen's remarks; Acts 2:14-36; 3:12-26; 4:8-12, 24-30; 5:29-32; 10:34-43 for Peter; Philip in Acts 8:30-35 and Paul in Acts 13:16-41, etc.etc.

The so-called "Revolt against Paul" which stirred theological circles to controversy at the turn of the twentieth century, charged that there is no connection between Paul's theology and that of Jesus as recorded in the Gospel - that Paul misinterpreted, twisted, distorted and misrepresented the message of Jesus. The battle cry of the Modernists was "Let's go back to Jesus" as though to go back to Jesus was to desert and repudiate Paul. On the contrary Paul here says that the good news that came from God is firmly rooted in the Judaic tradition.

What was God's promise to Abraham? That He would give to Abraham and to his seed the land of Palestine which would be shown to him, for an everlasting possession and that in him all the nations of the earth would be blessed. Here is a heavenly promise to do what the United Nations cannot do. The hope of mankind on this planet is tied to the sanctity of God's promise to Abraham. Paul pointed out (Gal.3:16) that when God told Abraham that the promise would be redeemed, not to him personally, but "to thy seed", that Abraham's *seed* was singular, not plural. "He saith not, And to seeds, as of many; but as of one, And to thy seed, which is Christ." Now it is easy to see that if God had not narrowed the line of posterity which descended from Abraham, to a single individual, there could be no resolute hope that the promise would ever be redeemed. For every generation of Abraham's family produced a succeeding generation. Meanwhile Israel wandered, homeless, desolate and despised, in and out of Egypt, off to Babylon and back and finally to the ends of the earth as they fled from the

Romans in A.D.70. Even today, though they are in political control of a very small part of the original grant, they are surrounded on three sides by powerful states under the control of the sons of Ishmael, deserted by many powerful Gentiles nations and supported with an alliance with the United States that gives only halfhearted support. A promise, even if it comes from God, that does not designate by whom it will be redeemed, is no source of comfort and hope. All that could be said is that God will give to some generation of the children of Abraham the throne that will rule the world in righteousness. Thus each generation would live, hope and die with only the unfulfilled dream that perhaps the next generation will see the promise fulfilled. Or if not the next generation, then, perhaps the next, or the next or the nex . . . ne    n. ....!

But God did not say "seeds." He said, "To thy seed." But Abraham had two sons. Was the King to be Ishamael or Isaac? It was Isaac's line, not Ishmael's that would produce Him, because the world got from Ishmael only Mohammed, the Arab League, the Palestine Liberation Organization and Yasir Arafat, who wishes only to push Israel into the Mediterranean Sea. But Isaac also had two sons - Jacob and Esau. God had already made the choice. "The elder will serve the younger." (Gen.25:23; Rom.9:12). Esau was a "porno" (Greek - πόρνος - Heb.12:16), who thought so little of the "hope of Israel" that he traded it for a bowl of soup. He gave the world the Edomites, slated for destruction for their hatred for Israel (Obadiah 1-21). But Jacob had twelve sons and one daughter. He need not look to the descendants of any for deliverance except from the tribe of Judah (Gen.49:10). The King when He came to reign in righteousness, would come from the tribe of Judah. Judah committed adultery with his daughter-in-law (Genesis 38) and though he did not forfeit his privilege to head the tribe that would produce the Messiah, he forfeited his own right to sit on the throne and also the right to reign of the next nine generations (Deut.23:2). But David was not banned, since he was the eleventh generation, and it was to whom that God reiterated His promise which He had made to Abraham, and confirmed to Isaac and Jacob (2 Samuel 7:10-17). Thus the seed of Abraham, who descended from the patriarch through Isaac, not Ishmael, through Jacob not Esau, through Judah not through one of the other eleven sons of Jacob and through the family of David, the Messiah would come. But David had many sons, the first of whom were rejected because their mother, Michal, was a Benjamite. Solomon and Nathan were David's sons by Bathsheba. From which branch of the Davidic family, the Solomonic or the Nathanic, would the Messiah emerge? Solomon was the favorite and we have the story of the court intrigue that placed him upon the throne when David was too senile to resist. But God did not favor it. He allowed the Solomonic line to reign over the nation until the Babylonian captivity when he ordered Jeremiah the Prophet to record it in the register of the kings of Judah that Jeconiah, the last of the Solomonic line to be king, had died without issue. Actually he had several sons, but by God's order, officially he had none, as the record was to show that that dynasty ended when the last king died without recognized issue (Jer.22:30). But the family of Nathan had produced the line that gave the world Mary, the virgin daughter of Heli (Luke 3:23-31). But Mary was a woman and she could not reign over the nation. But, though disqualified on the grounds of sex, she had not forfeited her legal right to convey the throne rights to her firstborn son, Jesus. However, there was a caveat. The law provided that a Jewish woman could inherit her father's estate in cases where there were no sons (Numbers 27) only if she married within her own tribe (Numbers 36). She was free to marry outside her tribe if she chose, but the penalty was the forfeiture of her inheritance. This is why the Matthew genealogy is given. Joseph, the carpenter, to whom Mary was engaged, was descended from David through Solomon. Mary was descended from the same Davidic family through the Nathanic line. Thus we have the evidence that when Mary promised her hand in marriage to the carpenter, she did not violate the law of Numbers 36. She married within her own tribe, the tribe of Judah and even within the same Davidic family of that tribe. Thus her right to sit upon the throne of David was not in jeopardy by reason of her engagement to Joseph and she conveyed it to Jesus.

We conclude from all of this that before Jesus was born, the only person in all of the nation of Israel who had the legal right to David's throne was Mary, and that, although she could not exercise that right, she could and did pass it down to Jesus her firstborn son. Now, Jesus did not marry and died without issue. Under the law the dynasty ended in Jesus. Thus when Israel demanded that Pilate crucify her king she was asking for the death of the only man in the nation who could claim the promises that God had made to Abraham, Isaac, Jacob and David. The question can then be asked: If Jesus of Nazareth is not the Jewish Messiah, who is?

This, in part, is what Paul meant when he wrote that the gospel of God had been previously promised by the Old Testament prophets in the Holy Scriptures. They focused the foregleams of prophetic truth upon a manger in the City of David and as the shepherds and the cattle looked at the tiny bundle of incarnate deity they were looking at the only hope of the world.

The Apostles in the early church, beginning with Peter at Pentecost and ending with Paul in Rome held forth to the Jew first and later to the Gentile the truth that God would deal in grace with the human race and bring divine order out of human chaos only through the One of Whom He spoke when he told Abraham that His blessing would come "not to seeds, as of many, but to thy seed, which is Christ" (Gal.3:16).

*Verse 3 - ". . . concerning his Son Jesus Christ our Lord, which was made of the seed of David, according to the flesh, . . ."*

περὶ τοῦ υἱοῦ αὐτοῦ τοῦ γενομένου ἐκ σπέρματος Δαυὶδ κατὰ σάρκα,

περὶ (preposition with the genitive of reference) 173.
τοῦ (gen.sing.masc.of the article in agreement with υἱοῦ) 9.
υἱοῦ (gen.sing.masc.of υἱός, reference) 5.
αὐτοῦ (gen.sing.masc.of αὐτός, relationship) 16.
τοῦ (gen.sing.masc.of the article in agreement with γενομένου) 9.
γενομένου (aor.pass.part.gen.sing.masc.of γίνομαι, adjectival, ascriptive, emphatic attributive position, in agreement with υἱοῦ) 113.
ἐκ (preposition with the ablative of source) 19.

σπέρματος (abl.sing.neut.of σπέρμα, source) 1056.

Δαυὶδ (gen.sing.masc.of Δαυίδ, description) 6.

κατὰ (preposition with the accusative, reference) 98.

σάρκα (acc.sing.fem.of σάρξ, reference) 1202.

*Translation -* "*. . . about His Son, who was born from the seed of David as far as his physical nature is concerned,* : *. . .*"

**Comment:** περὶ τοῦ υἱοῦ αὐτοῦ is joined to εὐαγγέλιον of verse 1. The good news is "about His Son." No one is preaching the gospel if he is not talking about God's Son. The gospel is Christo-centric. All that can be said about man is bad news. There is no good news except in Jesus Christ. It is good news because it has God as its source (ablative of source in θεοῦ in verse 1) and God's Son as its subject matter (genitive of reference in τοῦ υἱοῦ in verse 3). The participial adjective τοῦ γενομένου defines τοῦ υἱοῦ. God's good news will be of no help to man until and unless it is made available.

God's Son in heaven is not good news. A resource is not a resource unless it is known, available usable and used. God's Son in heaven before the incarnation was unknown, unavailable, unusable and unused. This is why He had to become τοῦ γενομένου ἐκ σπέρματος Δαυὶδ κατὰ σάρκα. With reference to His physical body (κατὰ σάρκα) its source was said to be David. His mother, Mary, was bone of David's bone and flesh of David's flesh, and she gave her physical nature to her Son Jesus. Jesus was born in a genealogical line that descended from David (Luke 323-31). *Cf.* Gal.4:4; 1 Tim.2:5; Heb.2:14; John 1:14; 1 John 1:1,2. Thus God's Son had a human fleshly nature.

The verse contradicts the Docetic heresy. Jesus not only looked and therefore seemed (δοκέω #287) like a man. He was a man. If He needed only to be human in order to be our Saviour He could have derived this by His birth from any woman. Mary was not indispensable as a source for His humanity. But when God's Son became a man He had to become David's man, else God's promise to David (2 Samuel 7:10-17) would have failed. When God said to David, speaking of the king's descendant who would sit forever on David's throne, "I will be his father and he shall be my son" He was talking about Jesus Christ (Heb.1:5b). *Cf.* John 7:42; 2 Tim.2:8 (where Paul associates the fact with the gospel which he preaches). *Cf.*#1056 and note that Jesus was also sired, physically speaking by Isaac and Abraham. Thus He fulfills the Abrahamic Covenant, which was repeated to Isaac and Jacob, as well as the Davidic Covenant. *Cf.* also Acts 2:30 where the same thought (ἐκ σπέρματος Δαυὶδ) is expressed with ἐκ καρποῦ τῆς ὀσφύος αὐτοῦ - "out of the fruit of his loins." Thus the gospel, preannounced in Old Testament Scripture, concerns His Son, Who is human and Who thus fulfills the Davidic Covenant.

Paul's mind was so full of theology as he began this epistle that the great elements of Christology and Soteriology come tumbling out in glorious profusion as the Greek staggers beneath its weight. He uses only one sentence in the entire Salutation which comprises the first seven verses.

So far Paul has presented Jesus as the only legal heir to David's eternal throne. But he has left Him dead. Verse 4 corrects that.

*Verse 4 - "... and declared to be the Son of God with power, according to the spirit of holiness, by the resurrection from the dead."*

τοῦ ὁρισθέντος υἱοῦ θεοῦ ἐν δυνάμει κατὰ πνεῦμα ἁγιωσύνης ἐξ ἀναστάσεως νεκρῶν, Ἰησοῦ Χριστοῦ τοῦ κυρίου ἡμῶν,

τοῦ (gen.sing.masc.of the article in agreement with ὁρισθέντος) 9.

ὁρισθέντος (1st.aor.pass.part.gen.sing.masc.of ὁρίζω, adjectival, ascriptive, in agreement with υἱοῦ of verse 3) 2764.

υἱοῦ (gen.sing.masc.of υἱός, objective genitive) 5.

θεοῦ (gen.sing.masc.of θεός, relationship) 124.

ἐν (preposition with the locative, instrumental use) 80.

δυνάμει (loc.sing.fem.of δύναμις, instrumental use) 687.

κατὰ (preposition with the accuative, standard rule) 98.

πνεῦμα (acc.sing.neut.of πνεῦμα, standard rule) 83.

#3784 ἁγιωσύνης (gen.sing.fem.of ἁγιωσύνω, description).

holiness - Rom.1:4; 1 Thess.3:13; 2 Cor.7:1.

*Meaning:* The word is unknown to profane Greek authors. *Cf.* Ps.96:6; 145:5 (LXX). The phrase πνεῦμα ἁγιωσύνης does not mean "the Holy Spirit," *i.e.* the third Person of the Godhead. It refers rather to the human spirit of Jesus, as distinct from his flesh which spirit is embued with holiness. *cf.* comment *infra.* - Rom.1:4. In 1 Thess.3:13; 2 Cor.7:1 it means holiness in a gestalt closure sense - the quality of lacking nothing. The function of "putting it all together" which is the goal of every Christian.

ἐξ (preposition the ablative of means) 19.

ἀναστάσεως (abl.sing.fem.of ἀνάστασις, means) 1423.

νεκρῶν (gen.pl.masc.of νεκρός, description) 749.

Ἰησοῦ (gen.sing.masc.of Ἰησοῦς, apposition with υἱοῦ of verse 3) 3.

Χριστοῦ (gen.sing.masc.of Χριστός, apposition) 4.

τοῦ (gen.sing.masc.of the article in agreement with κυρίου) 9.

κυρίου (gen.sing.masc.of κύριος, apposition) 97.

ἡμῶν (gen.pl.masc.of ἐγώ, relationship) 123.

*Translation - "Who was endorsed as God's Son with power, in keeping with the holiness of His spirit, by resurrection from the dead, Jesus Christ our Lord."*

**Comment:** The gospel (verse 1), preannounced (verse 2) is about God's Son (verse 3), Who was born a man (verse 3) and overwhelmingly demonstrated to be God's Son (verse,4). And this human/divine Son of God, born of David, but thoroughly established as God's Son by virtue of His powerful resurrection which, because of the total holiness of His human spirit, He fully expected (verse 4) is none other than the historic Jesus Christ, whom Paul worships by calling Him τοῦ κυρίου ἡμῶν.

Just as τοῦ γενομένου (verse 3) defines τοῦ υἱοῦ αὐτοῦ, so also does τοῦ ὁρισθέντος in verse 4. Paul is saying two distinct things about God's Son: (1) He was human, born of David's seed and hence identified with the human race insofar as his physical nature was concerned, and (2) this human Jesus nevertheless was supernaturally supported in His claim to be the Eternal Son of God. The participle ὁρισθέντος here means ratified, demonstrated or overwhelmingly declared to be God's Son.

Though He had the human flesh of David it was not the *sinful* flesh of David, since His spirit was complete (κατὰ πνεῦμα ἁγιωσύνης). Note the two κατά - accusative phrases - κατὰ σάρκα - "as it relates to his flesh" and κατὰ πνεῦμα ἁγιωσύνης - "as it relates to His human spirit" which is defined further as complete (fulfilled, perfected). Jesus' human spirit had achieved closure. There was nothing human that Jesus had not experienced when He stood before Pilate. This does not mean that He had experienced sin, but sin is not an essential part of humanity *per se.* It is characteristic of depraved human nature. Jesus was Adam's son, but not Adam's seed, for His father was the Holy Spirit, not Joseph the carpenter. As Adam's son He was a total human being, but He was not a totally depraved human being. Thus the writer of Hebrews could say that "He was tested in all points as we are, *except sin*" (Heb.4:15). Our Lord's "testing points" by which He was able to identify with us as a human being included every human emotion and impulse except the inducement to evil. He knew what it was to be tired, sad, discouraged, lonely, disillusioned, disgusted, even enraged, and all of the others except any that would have involved Him in the transgression of His holy law. There was one, however, which He had never known until He came to the Garden of Gethsemane. He had never until that moment feared anything. One searches the gospel records in vain for an instance when Jesus experienced mortal terror, until, in the Garden, He suddenly realized how dreadful was the ordeal of the cross which faced Him. And it was precisely *because* He feared and thus achieved closure in His round of human experience that He qualified to be our "merciful and faithful high priest" (Heb.2:17). Despite the fact that He was the Son of God (John 1:1; Mt.3:17), ". . . yet learned he obedience by the things which he suffered, and being made perfect, he became the author of eternal salvation unto all them that obey him" (Heb.5:8,9). The perfection mentioned here is not moral perfection, for He always had that. It refers rather to the fact that when Jesus feared the cross, He was then, at last, perfectly qualifiied to be our High Priest, for only after that could He sympathize with the members of His body who come to Him in prayer and confess that we fear.

*Cf.* our fuller discussion of this wonderful truth in Hebrews 4:14 - 5:10.

Jesus had spoken with confidence of His coming resurrection from the dead on many occasions, as in John 1:51; 2:19; Mt.16:21; 24:30,31 *et al.*

Thus Jesus went through his earthly period of incarnation with the human (though not sinful) frailties of human flesh, knowing that He was the eternal Son of God, Creator, Sovereign - the One Who was scheduled in the divine plan to die for the redemption of the elect, but due also to rise again, ascend to heaven and come again to claim His inherited right to sit forever on David's throne. But it was only in the hour of His arrest in the Garden that He had the one human experience which He lacked - without which He would not have qualified as our "merciful and faithful high priest" (Heb.2:17). Now, fully qualified as a human being He died the supernatural death described in John 10:18, and the Father said, "Thou art my Son; this day have I begotten thee" (Psalm 2:7; Acts 13:30-33).

That Jesus is both God and man is paradoxical. The Son of Man, due to be lifted up on a cross, nevertheless Eternal and Sovereign Deity, is the stumbling block over which the unregenerate so-called High Critics stumble into total confusion. That it does not commend itself to unaided human reason is obvious. And since the Higher Critics reject all supernatural assistance to their perceptive faculties, they gag over this paradox. It all depends upon one's assumptions. The Critics accept nothing by faith. That which is not clear to the unaided human mind must be rejected out of hand as tender-minded and naive. Yet it is precisely the naivete that is the key that unlocks the conundrum (Mt.11:25,26; 18:3; 1 Cor.2:9-16). Whenever in Scripture the human and the divine are juxtaposed this paradox appears. Unfortunately some trade away a place of heavenly glory for the privilege of a superficial appearance of what they consider erudition as they read a "scholary paper" (!) at a national meeting of the pundits. Whatever glory may result from an appearance on the program of one of these meetings is not worth five minutes of a stroll down Hallelujah Avenue in the New Jerusalem.

*Cf.*#2764 for other uses of ὁρίζω. Note the power (δυνάμει # 687) of God's ratification of Jesus' sonship in resurrection (Ps.2:16; Acts 13:30-37; Heb.5:1-10)

Only in the incarnation, as God and Man meet in one dual-natured personality, can be found the solution to soul sorrow. For reasons sufficient unto Himself, but which He has not been willing to divulge, it pleased the Sovereign God to permit evil in His universe. He could have ruled otherwise, if He had chosen. Christians are not Gnostics. We do not know the origin of evil. But we do know that when it appeared in heaven it was not tolerated (Isaiah 14:12-20; Ezekiel 28:11-16; Luke 10:18). There is no problem of evil in heaven. When it appeared there it was exported to earth. Thus the problem is here on earth, not in heaven. What social scientist will deny that we have a problem of evil on earth? If Katharine Lee Bates had not died in 1929, but survived to 1982, and if she had visited the Bronx, or Hough Avenue, or Watts or the Anacostia area of our nation's capitol, she might not have written

> Thine alabaster cities gleam,
> Undimmed by human tears!

Today we must write not about America the beautiful, but about the plastic presumption of overcrowded slums where rats challenge little children for first place in the density of population per square mile figures and if these wretched, drug and crime ridden ghettos are no longer dimmed by human tears it is only because there are no more to shed. Silent grief and despair is far more poignant than the raucus and sloppy variety.

But God's steadfast love has not allowed Him to forget that when He threw Satan and his evil out of heaven, He unloaded him and his misery upon the earth.

Love demands that redemption must go where sin and its degradation exists. The Good Samaritan could not help the poor traveller who had fallen among the thieves until he "came where he was." (Luke 10:33). Nor could even God help us by remote control. If Ὁ ΛΟΓΟΣ is the resource that must be known, available, usable and used, He must become incarnate. If He wants to tell us all about God He must come to us for we cannot go to Him. This is why "the Word became flesh and tabernacled among us" for a period in history long enough for Him to know from experience how it fells to be human and then to take our place on the cross that He did not deserve, pay the debt that we could not pay, manifest His sovereignty by rising from the dead and then, after ordering His disciples to carry the good news to the ends of the earth, go back to heaven to sit at the Father's right hand until His enemies have been made His footstool (Psalm 110:1).

Every basic element of Christian theology is found in Romans 1:1-4 - Salvation, Service, Conciliation, Prophecy, Incarnation, Kingdom truth, Jesus' humanity, His deity, Resurrection, the Lordship of Christ and Holistic completion. The remainder of the epistle expounds in depth the elements in this concentrated capsule of the first four verses.

*Verse 5 - ". . . by whom we have received grace and apostleship for obedience to the faith among all nations, for his name, . . . "*

δι' οὗ ἐλάβομεν χάριν καὶ ἀποστολὴν εἰς ὑπακοὴν πίστεως ἐν πᾶσιν τοῖς ἔθνεσιν ὑπὲρ τοῦ ὀνόματος αὐτοῦ,

δι' (preposition with the ablative of agent) 118.
οὗ (abl.sing.masc.of ὅς, relative pronoun, agent) 65.
ἐλάβομεν (1st.per.pl.aor.act.ind.of λαμβάνω, culminative) 533.
χάριν (acc.sing.fem.of χάρις, direct object of ἐλάβομεν) 1700.
καὶ (adjunctive conjunction joining nouns) 14.
ἀποστολὴν (acc.sing.fem.of ἀποστολή, direct object of ἐλάβομεν) 2954.
εἰς (preposition with the accusative, purpose) 140.

**#3785** ὑπακοὴν (acc.sing.fem.of ὑπακοή, purpose).

obedience - Rom.1:5; 6:16; 16:19; 2 Cor.7:15; 10:6; Philemon 21; Rom.16:26; 2 Cor.10:5; 1 Peter 1:2; Heb.5:8; Rom.5:19.
obedient - Rom.15:18; 1 Pet.1:14.
obey - Rom.6:16.
obeying - 1 Pet.1:22.

*Meaning:* Cf. ὑπακούω (#760). Opposed to παρακοή (#3905). Obedience, compliance, submission to higher authority. Followed by an ablative of source - Rom.1:5; 16:26; with εἰς - I Pet.1:2; Rom.5:19; followed by εἰς and the accusative - Rom.6:16,16; 16:19; 2 Cor.10:5 (with the genitive of reference); 1 Pet.1:22. As a direct object - 2 Cor.7:15; Heb.5:8; as the subject of a clause (opposed to παρακοή) - 2 Cor.10:6; dative of reference - Philemon 21; with εἰς in a purpose construction followed by the genitive of description - Rom.16:26; with εἰς (purpose) followed by a genitive of description - Rom.15:18; in a genitive of description - 1 Pet.1:14.

πίστεως (abl.sing.fem.of πίστις, source) 728.
ἐν (preposition with the locative with plural nouns) 80.
πᾶσιν (loc.pl.neut.of πᾶς, in agreement with ἔθνεσιν) 67.
τοῖς (loc.pl.neut.of the article in agreement with ἔθνεσιν) 9.
ἔθνεσιν (loc.pl.neut.of ἔθνος, place) 376.
ὑπέρ (preposition with the ablative, - "in behalf of") 545.
τοῦ (abl.sing.neut.of the article in agreement with ὀνόματος) 9.
ὀνόματος (abl.sing.neut.of ὄνομα, "in behalf of") 108.
αὐτοῦ (gen.sing.masc.of αὐτός, possession) 16.

*Translation - "Under whose management we have received grace and the appointment as an apostle, for the purpose of obedience that comes from faith, in order to minister among all nations in behalf of His name."*

**Comment:** The antecedent of οὗ is Ἰησοῦ Χριστοῦ τοῦ κυρίου of verse 4. Christ is the source and the administrative agent, through whose management Paul had received the grace of salvation and the call to be an apostle. Note the editorial "we" as Paul was thinking also of other apostles. Note that Paul emphasizes χάριν ahead of ἀποστολήν. It is better to be saved than it is to be an Apostle. Apostles must first be saved, but not all saints are Apostles. Matthias (Acts 1:25) was not an Apostle. He was only the result of a misguided business meeting that Peter, in one of his many compulsive moments, called. Paul was an Apostle (Rom.1:5; 1 Cor.9:2), as was Peter (Gal.2:8).

The εἰς clause is purpose. Obedience is one of the purposes for which God saves us. There is no antinomianism here. This obedience man cannot generate from his own resources. It flows from his God-given faith (ablative of source). Cf.Heb.11:6; James 2:14-26. The antinomian contention that what one believes has no connection with how one behaves, and that salvation is on the basis of faith alone, cannot be maintained. Faith alone can save, to be sure, but it is the kind of faith that works. Saving faith is the source of obedience. Unsaved people cannot obey God, for to obey Him is to please Him (Heb.11:6). God's gift to us is for the purpose of enabling us to obey Him and the obedience is the fruit of faith. Grace gives faith; faith generates obedience; obedience glorifies God. The twisted logic of the antinomians - that we ought to continue in sin in order that God may have the opportunity to be more gracious and thus add to His glory is dealt with sternly later in the epistle (Romans 6).

Disobedience to God is the height of irrationality in His moral universe, in which He is determined to uphold His righteous standards. Viewed from the human viewpoint God's commands may seem, even to the Christian, irrational, but faith tells us that we are irrational if we flaunt His authority, not God for laying down His rule.

Calvinists have sometimes stressed the objective side of salvation to the exclusion of the subjective side, while Arminians have reversed the emphasis. If and when this is done both sides are wrong. The resolution comes when we see

with Paul that faith produces obedience just as the seed produces the corn and
the bud the rose. Paul could not separate faith from works any more than root
and fruit, cause and result and foundation and superstructure can be separated.

Paul's obedience was to the Commission (Mt.28:18-20; Acts 1:8) and to the
specific orders of his own apostleship (Acts 26:17-19). What was his motivation
as he spent the rest of his life travelling among the Gentiles, enduring great
hardships but always preaching the gospel? He did it in behalf of ($\dot{v}\pi\acute{e}\rho$) the name
of Christ. Goodspeed and Montgomery join $\dot{v}\pi\alpha\kappa o\grave{\eta}\nu$ $\pi\iota\sigma\tau\acute{e}\omega\varsigma$ to $\tau o\hat{\iota}\varsigma$ $\acute{e}\vartheta\nu\epsilon\sigma\iota\nu$
and translate that Paul's apostleship was commissioned so that all nations would
yield to God the obedience of their faith. This, of course, is true, but such a
translation leaves $\dot{e}\nu$ $\pi\hat{\alpha}\sigma\iota\varsigma$ dangling.

*Verse 6 - ". . . among whom are ye also the called of Jesus Christ, . . . "*

$\dot{e}\nu$ $o\hat{\iota}\varsigma$ $\dot{e}\sigma\tau\epsilon$ $\kappa\alpha\grave{\iota}$ $\dot{v}\mu\epsilon\hat{\iota}\varsigma$ $\kappa\lambda\eta\tau o\grave{\iota}$ $\mathrm{'}I\eta\sigma o\hat{v}$ $X\rho\iota\sigma\tau o\hat{v},$

$\dot{e}\nu$ (preposition with the locative with a plural pronoun) 80.
$o\hat{\iota}\varsigma$ (loc.pl.neut.of $\ddot{o}\varsigma$, relative pronoun, place where) 65.
$\dot{e}\sigma\tau\epsilon$ (2d.per.pl.pres.ind.of $\epsilon\dot{\iota}\mu\acute{\iota}$, progressive duration, retroactive) 86.
$\kappa\alpha\grave{\iota}$ (adjunctive conjunction joining substantives) 14.
$\dot{v}\mu\epsilon\hat{\iota}\varsigma$ (nom.pl.masc.of $\sigma\acute{v}$, subject of $\dot{e}\sigma\tau\epsilon$) 104.
$\kappa\lambda\eta\tau o\grave{\iota}$ (nom.pl.masc.of $\kappa\lambda\eta\tau\acute{o}\varsigma$, predicate nominative) 1411.
$\mathrm{'}I\eta\sigma o\hat{v}$ (gen.sing.masc.of $\mathrm{'}I\eta\sigma o\hat{v}\varsigma$, relationship) 3.
$X\rho\iota\sigma\tau o\hat{v}$ (gen.sing.masc.of $X\rho\iota\sigma\tau\acute{o}\varsigma$, apposition) 4.

*Translation - ". . . among whom you also are the called ones of Jesus Christ."*

**Comment:** The antecedent of $o\hat{\iota}\varsigma$ is $\acute{e}\vartheta\nu\epsilon\sigma\iota\nu$ of verse 5. The Roman Christians
were among those Gentiles scattered throughout the earth whom Jesus Christ
had called to salvation. Note the progressive duration with its retroactive force
in the verb $\dot{e}\sigma\tau\epsilon$. The Christians in Rome had been included in that category
from the point in eternity when God decreed to call them, although His decree
had waited for its implementation in historic time. Until what point? We cannot
be sure, when the first Christian in Rome felt the call of the Holy Spirit to come
to Christ, nor do we know who preached the sermon that brought salvation to
the first convert in Rome. It is likely that it happened at Pentecost when
"strangers of Rome" heard Peter's sermon in Jerusalem (Acts 2:10) and then
heard the gospel again, for those who could not understand Peter's $\kappa o\iota\nu\acute{\eta}$ Greek,
if indeed there were any present who could not, in their native tongue. There is
no evidence that Peter visited Rome during the years when the Roman church
was being established. There is much evidence that he spent much of that time in
Judea.

Paul's commission mandated his missionary journeys to as many Gentile
nations as he could reach in his lifetime. And this he had done at the time when
he wrote this epistle (57/58) and this he would continue to do until he lost his life
in Rome, according to tradition on 29 June 66. Those whom he could not reach
personally he has reached through his writings.

Not all the individuals in all of the nations will hear. If they did we would have universalism, which would be all right with me, to be sure, but the Word of God teaches otherwise and it is the will of the Sovereign God, not mine, that is the deciding factor. Some who hear the gospel will accept; others will reject. Those who are called (κλητοί #1411) will hear. To them the gospel smells like life and they like it. To others it smells like death and they are revolted by it (2 Cor.2:14-17). To them that perish the gospel sounds like nonesense (1 Cor.1:18). Just as Paul was κλητὸς ἀπόστολος - "called to be an Apostle" - so the Roman saints were κλητοί to salvation (*cf.* verse 7). Through whose agency?'Ἰησοῦ Χριστοῦ. The grammar permits us to take Ἰησοῦ Χριστοῦ as a genitive of relationship, joined to κλητοὶ. It also permits us to take Ἰησοῦ Χριστοῦ as an ablative of agency. Both ideas are true. The "called" have a relationship with Jesus Christ. They also were called to that relationship through the agency of Jesus Christ. The same Sovereign risen Lord Who is Head over all things to His church (Eph.1:22), Who called the Apostles, also calls all of His elect saints. Many are called (Mt.22:14) and therefore many are justified (Romans 8:3), but of the many who are called and justified, only a few are the "choice ones." The vast majority of the human family has been "called" by death in infancy. And, since at the time of their death, they "had not sinned after the similitude of Adam's transgression" (Romans 5:14, although they were not *saved*, since they had never been *lost*, they were *safe*. Sinners become lost sinners when they transgress the law of God as Adam did - *i.e.* with intellectual eyes wide open. It is deliberate transgression of the law that makes us guilty before the bar of Eternal justice. Infants have not reached the age of discretion, and though they are sinners by nature, they are not sinners by choice, until they are able to tell the difference between right and wrong. It is not for any of us, however adept in child psychology, to set arbitrarily an age when the child becomes legally responsible before God for his choices. That is God's business.

But even if all who have grown to the age of discretion went to hell, heaven would still have the greater population, due to the high infant mortality rates. Thanks be to God, the Holy Spirit has also called upon some of us who did not die in infancy and it was to some of this group that Paul is directing his letter.

In verse 7 Paul finally finishes the sentence of salutation, with which he began his letter in verse one.

*Verse 7 - ". . . to all that be in Rome, beloved of God, called to be saints: Grace to you and peace from God our Father, and the Lord Jesus Christ."*

πᾶσιν τοῖς οὖσιν ἐν Ῥώμῃ ἀγαπητοῖς θεοῦ, κλητοῖς ἁγίοις. χάρις ὑμῖν καὶ εἰρήνη ἀπὸ θεοῦ πατρὸς ἡμῶν καὶ κυρίου Ἰησοῦ Χριστοῦ.

πᾶσιν (dat.pl.masc.of πᾶς, in agreement with οὖσιν) 67.

τοῖς (dat.pl.masc.of the article in agreement with οὖσιν) 9.

οὖσιν (pres. part.dat.pl.masc.of εἰμί, substantival, indirect object) 86.

ἐν (preposition with the locative of place) 80.

Ῥώμῃ (loc.sing.fem.of Ῥώμη, place where) 3434.

ἀγαπητοῖς (dat.pl.masc.of ἀγαπητός, predicate adjective, in agreement with θεοῦ (abl.sing.masc.of θεός, agent) 124.

κλητοῖς (dat.pl.masc.of κλητός, in apposition with οὖσιν) 1411.

ἁγίοις (dat.pl.masc.of ἅγιος predicate dative) 84.

χάρις (nom.sing.fem.of χάρις, subject of εἴη, understood) 1700.

ὑμῖν (dat.pl.masc.of σύ, personal advantage) 104.

καὶ (adjunctive conjunction joining nouns) 14.

εἰρήνη (nom.sing.fem.of εἰρήνη, subject of εἴη, understood) 865.

ἀπὸ (preposition with the ablative of source) 70.

θεοῦ (abl.sing.masc.of θεός, source) 124.

πατρὸς (abl.sing.masc.of πατήρ, apposition) 238.

ἡμῶν (gen.pl.masc.of ἐγώ, relationship) 123.

καὶ (adjunctive conjunction joining nouns) 14.

κυρίου (abl.sing.masc.of κύριος, source) 97.

Ἰησοῦ (abl.sing.masc.of Ἰησοῦς, apposition) 3.

Χριστοῦ (abl.sing.masc.of Χριστός, apposition) 4.

*Translation - "To all those in Rome, beloved of God, called saints: grace unto you and peace from God, our Father and the Lord Jesus Christ."*

**Comment:** The epistle is not directed to everyone who lived in Rome. πᾶσιν is modified by ἀγαπητοῖς θεοῦ and κλητοῖς ἁγίοις - "those beloved of God" and "those who have been called by God and thus are now saints." Thus Paul was addressing every Christian in Rome, with the presumption that they all belonged to the same local church! With χάρις and εἰρήνη the optative εἴη is understood. "The optative εἴη more frequently drops out in wishes" (Robertson, *Grammar*, 395, 396). *Cf.* also Romans 15:33; Mt.16:22.

Note that Paul puts God the Father and the Lord Jesus Christ on the same level as sources of grace and peace. Thus the salutation is ended. It is one long, perfectly constructed Greek sentence of seven verses length. It begins with Παῦλος (verse 1) and ends with ἁγίοις (verse 7), after which Paul then adds the benediction χάρις . . . Ἰησοῦ Χριστοῦ.

The theology which Paul teaches in the next eleven chapters and the ethical admonitions of the last five were his by revelation at the feet of the glorified Lord Jesus. Paul shared with the other eleven Apostles the experience of having met personally and been instructed by our Lord, even though, as the last of the Apostles to be called, he was "born out of due time" (1 Cor.15:8). Called to salvation and to the service of the cross of Christ, but only after the resurrection and ascension of Jesus, Paul found it necessary to make a special trip to heaven in order to go to school to Jesus. Just as he had been brought up at the feet of Gamaliel in Jerusalem for his education in jurisprudence (Acts 22:3), so he had been brought up at the feet of Jesus for his education in theology (2 Cor.12:1-4). His education was in no sense inferior, either in its sweep or scope to that of the other Apostles who had the advantage of three years of personal association with Jesus before He died (Gal.2:6).

For purposes of rapport as we explore with our readers the writings of Paul I introduce what Calvinist theologians have chosen to call the "Tulip." The word is an acrostic which forms the word as the initial letters of five phrases are arranged vertically -

Total depravity
Unconditional election
Limited atonement
Irresistible grace
Perseverance of the saints

Not all theologians accept this theology as being an objective analysis of that taught in the New Testament by Jesus and the Apostles. Not all agree with the Calvinists that logic demands that if any one of the five points are accepted, all of the others must be. This system was that of Augustine and of John Calvin and is still taught by the modern school known as the Reformed Theologians. It is the system to which the writer subscribes. We believe that it is impossible in any logical way for one to accept one or more, but not all five of the elements in the Tulip. There are no logical one, two, three or four point Calvinists. It was this that Oliver Wendell Holmes, Sr. attacked with such charm and humor in his famous "The Deacon's Masterpiece" in which he described "The Wonderful One Horse Shay," a vehicle so uniformly strong in all of its parts that, since it could not break down in any one part first, it would run forever. However, the deacon who built it, forgot the possibility that although it could not break down anywhere first, it could break down everywhere at once. And thus it happened, to the Calvinistic deacon's surprize and dismay.

Now small boys get out of the way,
Here comes the wonderful one horse shay.

Exactly one hundred years from the day that it was built, with its predicted eternal longevity, it collapsed, simultaneously, in all of its parts, and left the deacon sitting upon a rock. Thus Holmes correctly represented the Calvinistic theology which was popular in Boston in the nineteenth century. If the Tulip is Biblical theology it is true and therefore indestructible in each of its five points and as such will survive for all time and eternity. If it is false in any one of its five points it cannot be true in any of the others.

The Apostle Paul in faithful representation of the theology of Jesus as reported by the Gospel writers, especially but not exclusively John, taught all of the five points of the Tulip, though he is not responsible for the formulation of the phrases that form the Tulip. Paul was neither an Augustinian nor a Calvinist since he lived three centuries before the former and thirteen before the latter. However it is convenient for purposes of communication to refer to the Tulip as Calvinism, though it is better called the theology of Jesus, Pauline, Petrine of New Testament theology. Paul in Romans, as in all of his epistles has supported each of the five points in the Tulip.

# Paul's Desire to Visit Rome
### (Romans 1:8-15)

*Verse 8 - "First, I thank my God through Jesus Christ for you all, that your faith is spoken of throughout the whole world."*

Πρῶτον μὲν εὐχαριστῶ τῷ θεῷ μου διὰ Ἰησοῦ Χριστοῦ περὶ πάντων ὑμῶν, ὅτι ἡ πίστις ὑμῶν καταγγέλλεται ἐν ὅλῳ τῷ κόσμῳ.

Πρῶτον (acc.sing.neut.of πρῶτος, adverbial) 487.

μὲν (particle of affirmation) 300.

εὐχαριστῶ (1st.per.sing.pres.act.ind.of εὐχαριστέω, present duration, retroactive) 1185.

τῷ (dat.sing.masc.of the article in agreement with θεῷ) 9.

θεῷ (dat.sing.masc.of θεός, indirect object of εὐχαριστῶ) 124.

μου (gen.sing.masc.of ἐγώ, relationship) 123.

διὰ (preposition with the ablative of agent) 118.

Ἰησοῦ (abl.sing.masc.of Ἰησοῦς, agent) 3.

Χριστοῦ (abl.sing.masc.of Χριστός, apposition) 4.

περὶ (preposition with the genitive of reference) 173.

πάντων (gen.pl.masc.of πᾶς, reference) 67.

ὑμῶν (gen.pl.masc.of σύ, description) 104.

ὅτι (conjunction introducing a subordinate causal clause) 211.

ἡ (nom.sing.fem.of the article in agreement with πίστις) 9.

πίστις (nom.sing.fem.of πίστις, subject of καταγγέλλεται) 728.

ὑμῶν (gen.pl.masc.of σύ, possession) 104.

καταγγέλλεται (3d.per.sing.pres.pass.ind.of καταγγέλλω, progressive duration, retroactive) 3023.

ἐν (preposition with the locative of place) 80.

ὅλῳ (loc.sing.masc.of ὅλος, in agreement with κόσμῳ) 112.

τῷ (loc.sing.masc.of the article in agreement with κόσμῳ) 9.

κόσμῳ (loc.sing.masc.of κόσμος, place where) 360.

*Translation - "First of all, in truth I have been giving thanks to my God through Jesus Christ for all of you, because your faith has been the subject of discussion throughout the entire civilized world."*

**Comment:** πρῶτον μὲν - this is μέν *solitarium*, "the original use of μέν, meaning 'first of all in truth' " (Robertson, *Grammar*, 1152). διὰ with the ablative of agent, because Christ is the agent between the believer and God the Father. ὅτι is causal, in introduction of the subordinate clause. Paul was grateful to God because in his travels he had heard the faith of the Roman Christians discussed wherever he had gone throughout the civilized Mediterranean world. We cannot push ὅλῳ too far. Paul had not heard the Pawnee Indians in Kansas discuss the faith of the Romans.

This does not mean that the Romans were better Christians than those from Ephesus or Philippi, necessarily. Rome, the center of the commercial and political world was in a better position to communicate her thoughts than other more sequestered cities. The traders could not visit Rome without coming in contact with the vigorous testimony of the Roman saints. In a day of Emperor worship the lot of the Christians was hard, perhaps harder in the capitol than in other cities where law enforcement may not have been so thorough and so vigorous. The Christians obeyed Caesar, but they worshipped only Jesus Christ. For another possible view *cf.* comment on verse 9. *Cf.* Romans 16:19.

*Verse 9 - "For God is my witness, whom I serve with my spirit in the gospel of His Son, that without ceasing I make mention of you always in my prayers."*

μάρτυς γάρ μού ἐστιν ὁ θεός, ᾧ λατρεύω ἐν τῷ πνεύματί μου ἐν τῷ εὐαγγελίῳ τοῦ υἱοῦ αὐτοῦ, ὡς ἀδιαλείπτως μνείαν ὑμῶν ποιοῦμαι . . .

μάρτυς (nom.sing.masc.of μάρτυς, predicate nominative) 1263.
γάρ (causal conjunction) 105.
μού (gen.sing.masc.of ἐγώ, possession) 123.
ἐστιν (3d.per.sing.pres.ind.of εἰμί, aoristic) 86.
ὁ (nom.sing.masc.of the article in agreement with θεός) 9.
θεός (nom.sing.masc.of θεός, subject of ἐστιν) 124.
ᾧ (dat.sing.masc.of ὅς, relative pronoun, indirect object of λατρεύω) 65.
λατρεύω (1st.per.sing.pres.act.ind.of λατρεύω. customarv) 366.
ἐν (preposition with the locative of sphere) 80.
τῷ (loc.sing.neut.of the article in agreement with πνεύματί) 9.
πνεύματί (loc.sing.neut.of πνεῦμα, sphere) 83.
μου (gen.sing.masc.of ἐγώ, possession) 123.
ἐν (preposition with the locative of sphere) 80.
τῷ (loc.sing.neut.of the article in agreement with εὐαγγελίῳ) 9.
εὐαγγελίῳ (loc.sing.neut.of εὐαγγέλιον, sphere) 405.
τοῦ (gen.sing.masc.of the article in agreement with υἱοῦ) 9.
υἱοῦ (gen.sing.masc.of υἱός, description) 5.
αὐτοῦ (gen.sing.masc.of αὐτός, relationship) 16.
ὡς (declarative conjunction) 128.

#3786 ἀδιαλείπτως (adverbial).

without ceasing - Romans 1:9; 1 Thess.1:2; 2:13; 5:17.

*Meaning:* α privative and διαλείπω (#2176). Hence, without long intermission; assiduously; continually (not continuously, which means no interruptions); iteratively - with reference to Paul's mention of the faith of the Roman Christians - Romans 1:9; prayers for the Thessalonians - 1 Thess.1:2; 2:13; in Paul's admonition - 1 Thess.5:17.

#3787 μνείαν (acc.sing.fem.of μνεία, direct object of ποιοῦμαι).

remembrance - Phil.1:3; 1 Thess.3:6; 2 Tim.1:3.
mention - Romans 1:9; Eph.1:16; 1 Thess.1:2; Philemon 4.

*Meaning: Cf.* μιμνήσκομαι, #485. Mention, remembrance, memory. Followed by a genitive of description - Phil.1:3; Romans 1:9; Philemon 4; 1 Thess.3:6; 2 Tim.1:3; without an adjunct - Eph.1:16; 1 Thess.1:2. Paul uses the word in all places except 1 Thess.3:6 and Romans 1:9 (debateable) in connection with prayer.

ὑμῶν (gen.pl.masc.of σύ, reference) 104.

ποιοῦμαι (1st.per.sing.pres.act.ind.of ποιέω, progressive duration, retroactive) 127.

*Translation - "Because God is my witness, Whom I am serving in my spirit as I preach the gospel of His Son, that I am always speaking about you."*

**Comment:** γάρ is causal, as Paul goes on to support his contention of verse 8. Perhaps Paul means that wherever he has gone throughout his travels, he has been speaking of the faith of the Roman Christians (verse 8) and now (verse 9) calls God to corroborate his statement that, in his work as an evangelist (locative of sphere in ἐν τῷ εὐαγγελίῳ) he has always spoken of them to his audience. He also prayed for them (verse 10). It is a matter of editing. Verse 10 cannot stand alone and clarifies the time when and manner in which Paul mentioned them.

ὡς is declarative, though the κοινή normally uses ὅτι to introduce indirect assertions. Thayer says, "ὅτι expresses the thing itself and ὡς the mode or quality of the thing." (Thayer, *Lexicon*, 681). Robertson adds, "With this explanation it is possible to consider it declarative, though really meaning 'how.'" (Grammar, 1032. See also Lk.24:6; 8:47; 23:55; Acts 10:38; 20:20; Rom.1:9; Phil.1:8; 1 Thess.2:10; Acts 17:22.

*Verse 10 - "Making request, if by any means now at length I might have a prosperous journey by the will of God to come unto you."*

πάντοτε ἐπὶ τῶν προσευχῶν μου, δεόμενος εἴ πως ἤδη ποτὲ εὐοδωθήσομαι ἐν τῷ θελήματι τοῦ θεοῦ ἐλθεῖν πρὸς ὑμᾶς.

πάντοτε (adverbial) 1567.
ἐπὶ (preposition with the genitive in a time expression) 47.
τῶν (gen.pl.fem.of the article in agreement with προσευχῶν) 9.
προσευχῶν (gen.pl.fem.of προσευχή, time description) 1238.
μου (gen.sing.masc.of ἐγώ, possession) 123.
δεόμενος (pres.mid.part.nom.sing.masc.of δέομαι, adverbial, modal) 841.
εἴ (conditional particle in an elliptical condition) 337.
πως (indefinite adverb in an elliptical condition) 3700
ἤδη (temporal adverb) 291.
ποτὲ (temporal particle) 2399.

**#3788** εὐοδωθήσομαι (1st.per.sing.1st.fut.pass.ind.of εὐοδόω, in an elliptical condition).

have a prosperous journey - Romans 1:10.
prosper - 1 Cor.16:2; 3 John 2.

*Meaning:* A combination of εὐ (#1536) and ὁδόω - "to lead by the right way." Hence, to have a happy and prosperous trip of a right sort. In Romans 1:10 ἐν τῷ θελήματι τοῦ θεοῦ is really pleonastic since the thought is implicit in the verb. In an economic sense in 1 Cor.16;12. In everything - 3 John 2a; in a spiritual sense in 3 John 2b.

ἐν (preposition with the locative of sphere) 80.
τῷ (loc.sing.neut.of the article in agreement with θελήματι) 9.
θελήματι (loc.sing.neut.of θέλημα, sphere) 577.
τοῦ (gen.sing.masc.of the article in agreement with θεοῦ) 9.
θεοῦ (gen.sing.masc.of θεός, description) 124.
ἐλθεῖν (aor.inf.of ἔρχομαι, result) 146.
πρὸς (preposition with the accusative of extent) 197.
ὑμᾶς (acc.pl.masc.of σύ, extent) 104.

*Translation - "Always in my prayers if in some way now at last I may be given a prosperous journey, in accord with the will of God to come to you."*

**Comment:** ἐπί with the genitive of time description to indicate "when I pray." εἰ here introduces an elliptical condition, where the apodosis is missing, though implied in the protasis. Here the protasis is one of a first-class condition, with εἰ and the future indicative. The idea is clear from δεόμενος, which precedes the protasis - "Praying to see if . . . κ.τ.λ." Robertson says that the apodosis "is virtually contained in the protasis." (*Grammar*, 1024). We know what the apodosis would say, if it were present, from what is in the protasis - "Praying to see if I may come to you, in which case, I will come." Note the free use of particles to express in written form all that Paul felt, which could possibly have been read from his facial expression, tone of voice or bodily gesture, had we been present. One look at a Frenchman in animated converstion reveals the advantage that the spoken vernacular has over the written. Paul and Jesus, among others, were far more charming to hear than to read. The κοινή vernacular sometimes uses the particles to give us the total impression, which otherwise we would miss. How does one translate into written form the rising inflection of the voice, the crisp tone of sarcasm or the raised eyebrow or shrug of the shoulder? εἰ πως ἤδη τοτε - "if in some way or other, now, after so long a wait . . . the result will be that I may be given a safe trip to come to you, if the Lord is willing."

Paul was never sure when he prayed about it that he would ever visit Rome, since at the time he wrote the epistle (57/58) his appeal to Caesar in Festus' court (Acts 25:11) was still future to him. God answered Paul's prayers in this matter with the assurance of Acts 23:11.

*Verse 11 - "For I long to see you, that I may impart unto you some spiritual gift, to the end ye may be established."*

ἐπιποθῶ γὰρ ἰδεῖν ὑμᾶς, ἵνα τι μεταδῶ χάρισμα ὑμῖν πνευματικὸν εἰς τὸ στηριχθῆναι ὑμᾶς,

#3789 ἐπιποθῶ (1st.pers.sing.pres.act.ind.of ἐπιποθέω, progressive duration, retroactive).

long - Romans 1:11; Phil.2:26.
long after - 2 Cor.9:14; Phil.1:8.
earnestly desire - 2 Cor.5:2.
desire greatly - 1 Thess.3:6; 2 Tim.1:4.
desire - 1 Pet.2:2.
lust - James 4:5.

*Meaning:* A combination of ἐπί (#47) which is perfective and ποθέω - "to long for." Hence a heightened form of ποθέω. To desire with intensity; to crave; to yearn after. In an evil sense, to lust. Followed by an infinitive in 2 Cor.5:2; Romans 1:11; 1 Thess.3:6; 2 Tim.1:4; by a direct object - Phil.2:26; 1 Pet.2:2; 2 Cor.9:14; Phil.1:8. Followed by πρὸς φθόνον - James 4:5. For our glorified bodies - 2 Cor.5:2; to see the Roman Christians - Romans 1:11; to see Paul - 1 Thess.3:6; to see Timothy - 2 Tim.1:4; to see the Philippians - Phil.1:8; 2:26; for the Word of God - 1 Pet.2:2; for the spiritual growth of the Corinthians - 2 Cor.9:14. In an evil sense - envy - James 4:5.

γὰρ (causal conjunction) 105.
ἰδεῖν (aor.act.inf.of ὁράω, epexegetical) 144a.
ὑμᾶς (acc.pl.masc.of σύ, direct object of ἰδεῖν) 104.
ἵνα (conjunction introducing the subjunctive in a final clause) 114.
τι (acc.sing.neut.of τις, indefinite pronoun, in agreement with χάρισμα) 486.
μεταδῶ (1st.per.sing.aor.act.subj.of μεταδίδωμι, final clause) 1942.

**#3790** χάρισμα (acc.sing.neut.of χάρισμα, direct object of μεταδῶ).

free gift - Romans 5:15,16.
gift - Romans 1:11; 6:23; 11:29; 12:6; 1 Cor.1:7; 7:7; 12:4,9,28,30,31 2 Cor.1:11; 1 Tim.4:14; 2 Tim.1:6; 1 Pet.4:10.

*Meaning:* χάρις (#1700) plus μα the result suffix. Hence, the result of grace - a gift. Eternal life - Romans 5:15,16; 6:23; 11:29; money gifts - 2 Cor.1:11; spiritual gifts, *i.e.* special abilities given by the Holy Spirit to the Christian for enrichment in service, generally, or as specified - Rom.1:11; 12:6; 1 Cor.1:7; 7:7; 12:4, 9 (healing), 28 (healing, helps, governments, language ability), 30,31; 1 Tim.4:14; 2 Tim.1:6; 1 Pet.4:10.

ὑμῖν (dat.pl.masc.of σύ, indirect object of μεταδῶ) 104.

**#3791** πνευματικὸν (acc.sing.neut.of πνευματικός, in agreement with χάρισμα).

spiritual - 1 Cor.15:44,44,46,46; Eph.5:19; 6:12; Romans 1:11; Eph.1:3; Col.1:9; 3:16; Rom.7:14; 1 Pet.2:5; 1 Cor.10:3,4,4,; 2:13,13; 12:1; 14:1; Rom.15:27; 1 Cor.2:15; 14:37; Gal.6:1; 1 Pet.2:5; 1 Cor.3:1; 9:11; 15:46.

*Meaning:* spiritual. With reference to evil spirits - Eph.6:12. Dominated and motivated by and in keeping with the ethical principles of the Holy Spirit. Resurrection bodies - 1 Cor.15:46,46; gifts - Romans 1:11; 1 Cor.12:1; 14:1;

blessings - Eph.1:3; Romans 15:27; understanding - Col.1:9; songs - Eph.5:19; Col.3:16; ethics - Romans 7;14; in a metaphorical sense - home - 1 Peter 2:5a; meat - 1 Cor.10:3; drink - 1 Cor.10:4,4; saints - 1 Cor.2:15; 3:1; 14:37; Gal.6:1; sacrifices - 1 Peter 2:5b. *Cf.* also 1 Cor.2:13,13 - "discussing spiritual matters in spiritual terms." With reference to blessings generally flowing from the preaching of the gospel - 1 Cor.9:11. With reference to the spiritual body in resurrection - 1 Cor.15:44,44,46,46.

εἰς (preposition with the accusative in a purpose construction) 140.
τὸ (acc.sing.neut.of the article in agreement with στηριχϑῆναι) 9.
στηριχϑῆναι (acc.pass.inf.acc.sing.neut.of στηρίζω, purpose) 2359.
ὑμᾶς (acc.pl.masc.of σύ general reference) 104.

*Translation - "Because I am very eager to see you in order that I may share with you some spiritual gift so that you may be grounded."*

Comment: γάρ is causal. *Cf.* #3789 - a very strong deisre is indicated. ἰδεῖν, the epexegetical infinitive indicates purpose, and is followed by a final clause of purpose with ἵνα and the aorist subjunctive in μεταδῶ. *Cf.*#1942 for other instances of this "social gospel" verb. Paul wanted to minister to the Roman Christians so that they might be enriched in some way. Note τι, the indefinite pronoun, since the enrichment by the bestowing of gifts is the prerogative of the Holy Spirit (1 Cor.12:11) and Paul did not presume to know what gifts the Christians in Rome might receive. But he was certain that they would receive some gifts as they grew in grace. *Cf.* 2 Thess.3:3; Jam.5:8; 1 Peter 5:10; Luke 22:32; Rev.3:2 for στηρίζω (#2359) in this sense.

This statement would sound egotistical if it were not for what Paul adds in

*Verse 12 - "That is, that I may be comforted together with you by the mutual faith both of you and me."*

τοῦτο δέ ἐστιν συμπαρακληϑῆναι ἐν ὑμῖν διὰ τῆς ἐν ἀλλήλοις πίστεως ὑμῶν τε καὶ ἐμοῦ.

τοῦτο (nom.sing.neut.of οὗτος, subject of ἐστιν) 93.
δέ (explanatory conjunction) 11.
ἐστιν (3d.per.sing.pres.ind.of εἰμί, aoristic) 86.

#3792 συμπαρακληϑῆναι (aor.pass.inf.of συμπαρακαλέω, predicate nominative).

be comforted together - Romans 1:12.

*Meaning:* A combination of σύν (#1542), παρά (#154) and καλέω (#107). Hence, literally "to be called alongside with" - to be comforted; to be brought into a close mutual relationship and fellowship, with a result of comfort - Romans 1:12.

ἐν (preposition with the locative with plural pronouns) 80.
ὑμῖν (loc.pl.masc.of σύ, association) 104.

Romans 1:12    *The Renaissance New Testament*    221

διὰ (preposition with the ablative of means) 118.

τῆς (abl.sing.fem.of the article in agreement with πίστεως) 9.

ἐν (preposition with the locative with plural pronouns) 80.

ἀλλήλοις (loc.pl.masc.of ἀλλήλων, place) 1487.

πίστεως (abl.sing.fem.of πίστις, means) 728.

ὑμῶν (gen.pl.masc.of σύ, possession) 104.

τε (correlative particle) 1408.

καὶ (adjunctive conjunction joining pronouns) 14.

ἐμοῦ (gen.sing.masc.of ἐμός, possession) 1267.

*Translation - "Now what I mean is that I may be comforted along with you by means of the faith, both yours and mine, which interplays between us."*

**Comment:** Paul hastens to explain his remark of verse 11, lest he appear conceited, as though he was personally a fount of blessing for the Romans who could do nothing in return for him. Hence, δὲ is explanatory. Paul expected to derive comfort and encouragement in association with them, by means of (διὰ and the ablative) a mutual faith (ἐν ἀλλήλοις) - theirs and his. Each, by being a blessing would bestow a blessing upon the other. This is the true basis for κοινωνία (#3001). The Church of Jesus Christ is like a building. The Apostles and Prophets of the Old Testament provide the foundation. Jesus Christ Himself is the chief corner stone, with Whose lines and angles all other parts must conform. This building is being built and will not be complete until the "days of the seventh angel when he shall begin to sound" (Rev.10:7). As each new piece is added, the building grows unto an holy temple in the Lord. It will be the habitation of God throughout eternity. All of this is done through the ministry of the Holy Spirit (Eph.2:20-22).

The Church of Jesus Christ is also His Body. Christ is the head (Eph.1:22,23). Every organ of the body is connected with the Head by the ministry of the Holy Spirit (1 Cor.6:19). As the Body approaches completion (Rev.10:7) it becomes stronger and stronger, since it is made more compact by the contribution that each joint in the body supplies. Thus the Body of Christ edifies itself. It does this because the members of the Body of Christ love each other (Eph.4:16). Thus Paul later developed the thought which he conveyed to the Romans in Romans 1:11,12. Paul loved the Roman Christians even before he saw them. It was love before first sight. That is how they had fallen in love with Jesus (1 Peter 1:8). This is the true ecumenicity. This is the unity of the *organism* of the Body of Christ, and there need be no universal *organization*, particularly in view of the fact that the architects of the organization would include as members of the body those who have no supernatural connection with the Head, since they have repudiated His claim to deity and all else supernatural. Why should a deist, an agnostic, an atheist or a secular humanist wish to be associated in the same body with theists? "Can two walk together, except they be agreed?" Amos asked incredulously (Amos 3:3) and Paul replied with another incredulous question - "What fellowship hath righteousness with unrighteousness? What communion hath light with darkness? What concord hath Christ with Belial? What part hath he that believeth with an infidel?" (2 Cor.6:14,15). Nobody is in the Body of Christ, nor, to change the figure, is he a part of the Building of God, until and unless he has been born from above (John 3:3,8). The Body and the Building are not held together by human standards of morals and ethics, nor by philosophical systems, nor by social programs, nor by economic power. They are held together and given life and health by the Holy Spirit. His part in the program was to call with an effectual call through God's irresistible grace, convince of sin, righteousness and judgment, regenerate and indwell. The Holy Spirit has done this for everyone who has called with faith upon the name of the Son of God (Romans 10:13). We share mutually in the resurrection life and victory of Christ, Who has already demonstrated that He is bigger than sin and death, both spiritual and physical. But, unfortunately, since we are not yet glorified, and since some of us are not too intelligent and/or well educated, and since most of us are subject to sociological influences and peer pressure, and also, since most of us are too intellectually lazy to study the Word of God for ourselves, since it is easier to go to church once a week and accept, like little children, taking medicine what is offered from the pulpit, we have differing opinions on minor and even some major points of faith and practice. We agree at least on one point - the point of Peter's confession of Matthew 16:16. Jesus is the Messiah, the Son of the living God. That is enough to assure that we are at least a little finger in the Body of Christ and/or a two-by-four in the Building of God. That is enough to assure that we shall spend eternity with Him. But the minor points of difference are irritating and often cause, not a break in the structure of the Body/Building, but a break in the fellowship that otherwise would be enjoyed by all. Thus some call baptism immersion in water, while other sprinkle babies. Some drink grape juice at the Lord's table, officially declared Christian by the Women's Christian Temperance Union (!). Others drink wine. Some sing hymns at church while another plays the piano or organ. Others sing only *a capella*. Still others sing *a capella*, but only after they have got the right pitch from a tuning fork. Some think that if the devil is in a piano, he is also in a tuning fork. Others think that the devil is in one but not the other . Still others think that he is in neither the piano nor the tuning fork. All of us respect Mary the virgin, but some pay her more homage than the Scripture warrants. Some hold up their hands when they sing hymns. Others, like Presbyterians are less emotionally responsive. Some of us have the gift of some capacity to deal with foreign languages. Others cannot even speak their mother tongue properly, while others think of "tongues" in terms of incomprehensible gibberish uttered under the influence of ectasy.

The point to remember is that everyone who has accepted Jesus Christ as His Lord and Saviour is a member of His Body and a component part in His Building, regardless of how mistaken or correct he may be in his views of what the Bible teaches. Being correct in matters of faith and practice does not improve the Christian's position in Christ. His position was already secure. Being wrong does not threaten his position. His state (condition) may be poor, but his standing (position) can never change, for he is in Christ.

All of this explains why Paul wanted to go to Rome. The fellowship which would be his with the Roman Christians would help each of them. He could do things for them that they could not do for themselves and receive from them only that which they could give. No two Christians ever met in the name of Christ without His divine presence (Mt.18:20) and without enjoying mutual edification. This is one of the reasons why failure to attend the worship services is an offense to God and an insult to fellow Christians (Heb.10:25). We grow in grace and in the knowledge of Christ (2 Peter 3:18) as we fellowship with others who love and wish to know Him better. The child of God who does not recognize his need to grow is poor indeed. Let him remember the pit from which divine grace has rescued him (Psalm 40:2). Let him feel the Rock of Ages under his feet; let him sing the new song that God has put into his mouth. Then many will see it, and fear and trust in the Lord (Psalm 40:3) and he will have become a soul winner. Few Christians realize what threats we are to society on earth and to God's universal economy, apart from His grace. Few of us realize how many other people we have hurt and how deeply they have been wounded because, though we were God's children, we drifted from the protection of His care. Every child of God, this side of glorification is a tragic accident going somewhere to happen - a threat to the innocent bystander. The flesh which we must carry with us until the rapture (Romans 7:24; 1 Cor.15:52-54) is no better now than it was before we were saved. It is still the flesh - the source of all human tragedy - the loaded gun that we did not know was loaded - the Rube Goldberg invention that can only work one way - the wrong way. Its works are listed in Galatians 5:19-21. Not one crime in the list is beyond the scope of possibility or even probability of the child of God who temporarily forgets that it is only when we "walk in the Spirit (that we do not) fulfill the lusts of the flesh" (Gal.5:16).

Instead of remembering how much we love other Christians and how much we need to see and talk with them, we spend our days congratulating ourselves that we know our Bibles better than they do and that we do not harbor the heresies that they preach. A baby-sprinkling Presbyterian who humbly walks with his Lord, despite the fact that he does not know the meaning of a Greek verb, is good for a backslidden Baptist, who happens to have one small point correct. Arminians and Calvinists who struggle with perhaps the greatest theological problem and amillenialists and premillenialists, who read each other's literature in search of error, should remember that each is an essential organ in the Body of Christ and an important part of the Building of God.

Thus, though we need not concern ourselves with the ecumenicity that God has already created in His Body and Building, we very much need to improve the quality of the interchange of fellowship within it.

Most Christians who want to go to Rome will spend their time visiting the Forum, the Circus Maximus, the Sistine Chapel and St.Peter's Basilica, not visiting with other Christians. Paul spent his time in Rome preaching the gospel and fellowshipping with other Christians. If Paul went to southern California he would find the Christians there, hold a prayer meeting, sing hymns of praise and conduct a Bible study. That is why he wanted to go to Rome. It is not likely that he would spend much time at Disneyland.

*Verse 13 - "Now I would not have you ignorant, brethren, that oftentimes I purposed to come unto you (but was let hitherto,) that I might have some fruit among you also, even as among other Gentiles."*

οὐ θέλω δὲ ὑμᾶς ἀγνοεῖν, ἀδελφοί, ὅτι πολλάκις προεθέμην ἐλθεῖν πρὸς ὑμᾶς, καὶ ἐκωλύθην ἄχρι τοῦ δεῦρο, ἵνα τινὰ καρπὸν σχῶ καὶ ἐν ὑμῖν καθὼς καὶ ἐν τοῖς λοιποῖς ἔθνεσιν.

οὐ (negative conjunction with the indicative) 130.

θέλω (1st.per.sing.pres.act.ind.of θέλω, aoristic) 88.

δὲ (explanatory conjunction) 11.

ὑμᾶς (acc.pl.masc.of σύ, general reference) 104.

ἀγνοεῖν (pres.inf.of ἀγνοέω, direct object of θέλω) 2345.

ἀδελφοί (voc.pl.masc.of ἀδελφός, address) 15.

ὅτι (conjunction introducing an object clause in indirect assertion) 211.

πολλάκις (adverbial) 1230.

#3793 προεθέμην (1st.per.sing.2d.aor.mid.ind.of προτίθημι, constative).

purpose - Romans 1:13; Ephesians 1:9.
set forth - Romans 3:25.

*Meaning:* A combination of πρό (#442) and τίθημι (#455). To plan ahead - Romans 1:13. To ordain or establish before the fact. To decree that something will occur. In contexts where God's decrees are in view - His redemptive purpose - Eph.1:9; Rom.3:25; with reference to human plans which often fail of fulfillment - Romans 1:13.

ἐλθεῖν (aor.inf.of ἔρχομαι, epexegetical) 146.

πρὸς (preposition with the accusative of extent) 197.

ὑμᾶς (acc.pl.masc.of σύ, extent) 104.

καὶ (adversative conjunction) 14.

ἐκλύθην (1st.per.sing.aor.pass.ind.of κωλύω, culminative) 1296.

ἄχρι (preposition with the genitive in a time expression) 1517.

τοῦ (gen.sing.neut.of the article in a time expression) 9.

δεῦρο (temporal adverb) 1304.

ἵνα (conjunction introducing the subjunctive in a purpose clause) 114.

τινὰ (acc.sing.masc.of τις, indefinite pronoun, in agreement with καρπὸν) 486.

καρπὸν (acc.sing.masc.of καρπός, direct object of σχῶ) 284.

σχῶ (1st.per.sing.2d.aor.act.subj.of ἔχω, purpose clause) 82.

καὶ (adjunctive conjunction) 14.

ἐν (preposition with the locative with plural pronouns) 80.

ὑμῖν (loc.pl.masc.of σύ, place where) 104.

καθὼς (correlative adverb) 1348.

καὶ (adjunctive conjunction joining substantives) 14.

ἐν (preposition with the locative with plural substantives) 80.

λοιποῖς (loc.pl.masc.of λοιπός, in agreement with ἔθνεσιν, place) 1402.

ἔθνεσιν (loc.pl.masc.ofd ἔθνος, place) 376.

*Translation - "Now I do not want you to be unaware, brethren, that I have often made plans to come to you, (although I have been hindered so far) in order that I might have some fruit also among you just as I have also had among other Gentiles."*

**Comment:** δὲ I take to be explanatory, although it can be adversative. He had just said (verse 11) that at the time of writing he was eager to see them, but he added that his present desire was not a sudden new impulse. He had often had the same desire in the past (Acts 19:21). καὶ in the parenthesis is adversative - "I planned to come, but I was hindered." When man plans (προεθέμην #3793) a trip that counters God's plans (Eph.1:9), God hinders him. προτίθημι does not guarantee inevitability *per se*, unless it is God who is purposing. His purposes are certain, but, God be thanked, our plans are subject to divine cancellation. How many ill-advised plans we make when we are out of fellowship with the Holy Spirit and our Lord, particularly when we are suffering from an inferiority complex! How many preachers have been "led of the Lord" to go on the radio or television, when in reality they were subconsciously trying to prove something to themselves! How many preachers who cannot write a good English sentence have started a church paper, with hopes of circulating it around the nation! Little children make plans every day and discuss them with enthusiasm and parents smile with love and indulgence. Our Lord may also smile when we try to plan the future. It is important to learn what Paul had - that what backsliders call disappointments are really "His Appointments." It is not wise for those who do not know the road ahead to drive. We fulfill His will for our lives (Eph.2:10) best when the nail-pierced hands are on the controls and we are riding in the back seat in silence.

The idiom ἄχρι τοῦ δεῦρο uses the adverb δεῦρο with the genitive article of time designation, τοῦ, like a substantive - "Until the time to which I have now come." *Cf.* τὰ νῦν (Acts 5:38), ἕως τοῦ νῦν (Mark 13:19), ἀπὸ τοῦ νῦν (Lk.1:48). The Greek article, adjoined to an adverb to convey a substantive idea, gives the Greek a great advantage over the Latin. ἵνα and the subjunctive in σχῶ is a final clause. Paul had a legitimate purpose in wishing to visit Rome. He had preached to many Gentiles in many places in Asia Minor, Macedonia and Greece, and he had led many to Christ. He wished also to go to Rome, and even to Spain (Romans 15:28). This latter plan was one which God vetoed.

*Verse 14 - "I am debtor both to the Greeks, and to the Barbarians; both to the wise, and to the unwise."*

Ἕλλησίν τε καὶ βαρβάροις, σοφοῖς τε καὶ ἀνοήτοις ὀφειλέτης εἰμί, . . .

Ἕλλησίν (dat.pl.masc.of Ἕλλην, personal advantage) 2373.
τε (correlative particle) 1408.
καὶ (adjunctive conjunction joining nouns) 14.
βαρβάροις (dat.pl.masc.of βάρβαρος, personal advantage) 3755.
σοφοῖς (dat.pl.masc.of σοφός, personal advantage) 949.
τε (correlative particle) 1408.

καὶ (adjunctive conjunction joining substantives) 14.

ἀνοήτοις (dat.pl.masc.of ἀνόητος, personal advantage) 2904.

'φειλέτης (nom.sing.masc.of ὀφειλέτης, predicate nominative) 581.

εἰμί (1st.per.sing.pres.ind.of εἰμί, progressive duration, retroactive) 86.

*Translation - "Both to Greeks and to barbarians, both to sophisticates and the gullible I am a debtor."*

**Comment:** The difference between Greeks and barbarians is one of the quality of acculturation. All men are acculturated, but "Greeks" have grown up in a society of thinkers who have, therefore, become skeptics and that is good, whereas barbarians have been conditioned by the demagogues of society who have brainwashed them with oratorical nostrums, panaceas and snake oil. Most people today are barbarians. Witness the manner in which Madison Avenue leads the country around by the nose. Witness also the techniques of some (not all) electronic evangelists. Whether one is a highly educated skeptic who understands everybody except himself and thus trusts no one but himself or a naive dolt who will pay ten dollars for the Brooklyn bridge, he is a lost sinner without Christ, and Paul acknowledges his obligation to God which can be discharged only by reaching both the skeptic and the fool, both the good man and the knave with the gospel of Christ.

The Greeks thought of themselves as culturally superior to all non-Greeks - and with good reason. They were the greatest thinkers of the ancient world. Because precise thought demands precise language for expression, the Greeks developed the most facile language of all time - the one which the Holy Spirit chose as the medium for His highest revelation of truth. σοφός (#949) refers to philosophers - people who have developed great skill in rational activity, whereas ἀνοῆτος (#2904) refers, not to those who cannot think, but to those who do not.

Paul's commission (Mt.28:18-20; Acts 1:8) put him under the moral obligation to preach to everyone without regard to race, national origin, sex, color or previous educational attainment. A philosopher must come to Christ as a little child just as much as an unlearned barbarian. There are not many plans of salvation - each geared to the cultural level of the prospect. A preacher in Washington, D.C. welcomed at the altar of repentance and faith, a United States Senator and a poor rag picker - a poverty stricken woman of the streets, with the observation that it was obvious that "the ground at the foot of the cross of Christ is level." Thus we must preach the gospel to everyone. The uncouth find no advantage in the fact that they are boors and the couth are not penalized because they know which fork to use and who wrote the *Moonlight Sonata*. A Ph.D. can be saved, and he needs to be saved, as well and as much as a moron. The point is that all must achieve the poverty of spirit (Mt.5:4) of a little child (Mt.18:3) to be saved, since God is pleased to reveal His truth only to babes (Mt.11:25). People on both ends of the continuum and all others in between are lost, and Paul felt the obligation to reach them with the gospel of Christ.

*Verse 15 - "So, as much as in me is, I am ready to preach the gospel to you that are at Rome also."*

οὕτως τὸ κατ' ἐμὲ πρόθυμον καὶ ὑμῖν τοῖς ἐν Ῥώμῃ εὐαγγελίσασθαι.

ὅτως (inferential conjunction) 74.

τὸ (acc.sing.neut.of the article in agreement with ἐμὲ) 9.

κατ' (preposition with the accusative of extent) 98.

ἐμὲ (acc.sing.masc.of ἐμός, extent) 1267.

πρόθυμον (acc.sing.neut.of πρόθυμος, predicate adjective, in the κατ' phrase) 1588.

καὶ (adjunctive conjunction joining substantives) 14.

ὑμῖν (dat.pl.masc.of σύ, indirect object of εὐαγγελίσασθαι) 104.

τοῖς (dat.pl.masc.of the article in agreement with ὑμῖν) 9.

ἐν (preposition with the locative of place)80.

Ῥώμῃ (loc.sing.fem.of Ῥώμη, place) 3434.

εὐαγγελίσασθαι (1st.aor.mid.inf.of εὐαγγελίζω, epexegetical) 909.

*Translation - "Therefore, insofar as I am able, I am eager to preach also to you in Rome."*

**Comment:** οὕτως here like an inferential conjunction, more than like a demonstrative adverb. Paul felt the obligation to preach (verse 14). Therefore (inferential οὕτως) he was eager to preach. τὸ κατ' ἐμὲ "is more than a mere circumlocution for the genitive" (Blass, *Grammar of New Testament Greek*, 133 as cited in Robertson, *Grammar*, 608). *Cf.* other examples in Phil.1:12; Eph.1:15; Rom.9:5; Eph.6:21; Acts 25:23, *et al.*τὸ in the prepositional phrase can be nominative as well as accusative with the reflexive pronoun with κατά. "In accordance with that which is in me" or "insofar as I am able." πρόθυμον (#1588) means more than "ready." It means "eager." Note the middle voice in the infinitive εὐαγγελίσασθαι. Paul's call to the ministry, as every God-called preacher knows, means more than that he wanted the gospel to be preached. It means that *he* wanted to preach it - not that others had not nor could not preach it as well, or even better, but he wanted to preach it *for himself.* Some MSS omit ἐν Ῥώμῃ.

In verse 14 Paul said, "I am debtor."
In verse 15 he said, "I am eager."
In verse 16 he said, "I am not ashamed."

# The Power of the Gospel

*(Romans 1:16-17)*

*Verse 16 - "For I am not ashamed of the gospel of Christ: for it is the power of God unto salvation to everyone that believeth; to the Jew first, and also to the Greek."*

Οὐ γὰρ ἐπαισχύνομαι τὸ εὐαγγέλιον, δύναμις γὰρ θεοῦ ἐστιν εἰς σωτηρίαν παντὶ τῷ πιστεύοντι, Ἰουδαίῳ τε πρῶτον καὶ Ἕλληνι.

Οὐ (negative conjunction with the indicative) 130.

γὰρ (causal conjunction) 105.

ἐπαισχύνομαι (1st.per.sing.pres.mid.ind.of ἐπαισχύνομαι, progressive duration, retroactive) 2318.

τὸ (acc.sing.neut.of the article in agreement with εὐαγγέλιον, general reference) 405.

εὐαγγέλιον (acc.sing.neut.of εὐαγγέλιον, general reference) 405.

δύναμις (nom.sing.fem.of δύναμις, predicate nominative) 687.

γὰρ (causal conjunction) 105.

θεοῦ (gen.sing.masc.of θεός, description) 124.

ἐστιν (3d.per.sing.pres.ind.of εἰμί, progressive duration, retroactive) 86.

εἰς (preposition with the accusative, purpose) 140.

σωτηρίαν (acc.sing.fem.of σωτηρία, purpose) 1852.

παντὶ (dat.sing.masc.of πᾶς, in agreement with πιστεύοντι) 67.

τῷ (dat.sing.masc.of the article in agreement with πιστεύοντι) 9.

πιστεύοντι (pres.act.part.dat.sing.masc.of πιστεύω, substantival, personal advantage) 734.

Ἰουδαίῳ (dat.sing.masc.of Ἰουδαῖος, personal advantage) 143.

τε (correlative particle) 1408.

πρῶτον (acc.sing.neut.of πρῶτος, adverbial) 487.

καὶ (adjunctive conjunction joining verbs) 14.

Ἕλληνι (dat.sing.masc.of Ἕλλην, personal advantage) 2373.

*Translation - "Because I am not ashamed with reference to the gospel, because it is divine power for salvation, for every believer, for both the Jew, first and also for the Greek."*

**Comment:** γὰρ in both places is causal. Paul was eager to preach the gospel in Rome because (γὰρ) he was not ashamed of it. Why not? Because (γὰρ) it is God's dynamite. *Cf.*#'s 2318 and 2563. Our verb here is an intensified form of αἰσχύνομαι. Study both verbs for other occasions for shame. Note, especially Mark 8:38; Lk.9:26; 2 Tim.1:8,12,16; Heb.2:11; 11:16. This matter of offence is reciprocal. God's shame is not in direct ratio to that of the believer. Since God is not ashamed of me (Heb.2:11; 11:16) how vicious for me to be ashamed of Him.

Paul is proud of the good news because of what it is and what it can do. "God's power" or "divine power" is unlimited (1 John 4:4; John 1:5; Mt.28:18, but the word here is ἐξουσία, not δύναμις, Eph.1:19-23). But God's power, insofar as it relates to salvation, is totally potential and becomes kinetic only when released through the gospel and then only for the advantage of the believer. God's power (δύναμις) as it relates to the unbeliever, is exercised, not in salvation but in judgment (John 3:18; 2 Thess.1:7-9).

Divine omnipotence does not mean that God is not limited. It does mean that He is not limited by any force outside Himself. He is under restraint by the limitations of His own perfect nature, one of which is His holiness. Since He is holy (complete, fulfilled, total, holistic, lacks nothing) He is also righteous, for righteousness (a legal term which means the quality of one who always does the right thing) is a safeguard of God's holiness. He must always do right (Gen.18:25). This means that He must always reward good and punish evil. Now it happens that in all of human history there is not a single instance of an unbeliever doing good. Believers do good, but cannot take the credit for it, since it is "God who works in (them) both to will and to do of His good pleasure" (Phil.2:13). The unsaved sinner cannot do anything that the court of heaven calls good (John 6:63; 9:4). Everything he does is evil (Psalm 21:4; 7:11). Thus divine rejection and punishment of the lost is not vindictive - it is righteous.

But God found in one man that which pleased Him and was therefore bound by His righteousness to reward Him for it. "The man Christ Jesus" (1 Tim.2:5) did "always those things that please Him" (John 8:29; Mt.3:17). Especially at the cross where the Man, Christ Jesus, Whose hour had come surrendered His own will in order that He might do the will of the Father (Mt.26:42), and with much crying and many tears  (Heb.5:7) He "endured the cross" and "despised the shame" (Heb.12:2). That was good. And God the Father rewarded Him for it. Forty-three days later he sat down "at the right hand of God" (Heb.12:2) there to remain in perfect rest and glory until God makes His enemies His footstool (Psalm 110:1). Since His resurrection Jesus has the name which is above all others, at the mention of which every knee shall bow (Phil.2:7-11) and He sits "far above" all other inferior powers in the universe, as "head over all things to the church, which is His body" (Eph.1:21-23). In view of the "travail of His soul" He will be satisifed (Isa.53:11). Our Lord will see the complete answer to His prayer of John 17:9-21 and enjoy the fellowship of His saints, for whom He died. He will not be ashamed to call us His brothers and sisters (Heb.2:11). Thus a righteous God will reward all of the good He sees. What matters it if it happens to be true that only that which He observed in Jesus Christ His Son was good?

It is therefore clear that God's omnipotence does not mean that He can save those who reject His Son, for to do so would involve a repudiation of His righteousness and a compromise of His holiness. Just as God cannot indulge in philosophical nonesense, and thus cannot create a rock too heavy for Him to lift (!) nor a stick that has no ends (!), so He cannot be unholy or unrighteous, for if He were He would not be God. One cannot deny His own existence, nor change His own nature.

But God can in perfect righteousness save the believer, for He has already punished the believer's transgressions of His moral law at the expense of His Son at the cross. Every believer then is saved eternally, but only because he has been given the faith to believe the gospel.

The gospel offer is universal in the sense that it is offered both to Jews and to all other national groups who are not Jewish, whom Paul calls Greeks.

Paul said that he was not ashamed of the good news. The magnitude of a compliment is properly measured in terms of him who offers it. Paul was a great scholar. His learning was thorough, not only in the Jewish, but also in the Classical tradition. He had spent twenty-three years at the time of writing to the Romans, arguing the philosophical and theological claims of the gospel with the best minds that the opposition afforded. If there had been weak spots in the gospel armor, they would have been revealed by this time. It was Oliver Wendell Holmes, Jr., Associate Justice on the United States Supreme Court who said that the acid test of the truth of a proposition was its ability to get accepted in the competition of a free market of ideas. No one has ever shown that, given the *a priori* assumptions of the Christian faith, the good news of the Gospel is unreasonable. If it be objected that a system that depends upon an *a priori* assumption must be rejected, then we must reject all philosophical and scientific systems for there are none that do not begin with certain "givens." Christians assume that God exists and that the Bible is true. We build from there. Atheists assume that God does not exist and therefore they assume that matter has always existed. Both propositions are assumptions. The "faith" of the materialist in his assumption brings him down to pessimism. The "faith" of the Christian in his assumption brings him up to an optimistic view of the world and a hope for the future. Why should not the Christian be given the opportunity to play the epistemological game by the same rules that govern the atheist? If Paul should properly have been ashamed of the gospel, then it follows, and for the same reason that his enemies should have been ashamed of theirs.

Paul was confident that, despite the fact that some had offered a great deal of sophisticated opposition to Christianity, he had nothing to fear, in the ongoing debate. If the Athenians could not disprove the gospel, the Romans certainly could not. Of course, the superior intellectual worth of Christianity, as Paul appreciated it, is apparent to the prospect only after he has become a Christian. Before he is saved it is "foolishness unto him" (1 Cor.1:18a), but unto the believer, who is saved, "it is the power of God" (1 Cor.1:18b).

The entire matter depends upon one's point of view. Archimedes, who discovered the principle of the lever said δός μοι ποῦ στῶ καὶ κινῶ τὴν γῆν - "give me a place to stand and I will move the earth." Logicians since have borrowed his term and his philosophy and announced their *pou sto* - their *a priori* assumption and asked that, for the sake of the discussion, it be accepted. Then they have asked to be judged on the basis of the logic with which they have built their system upon their *pou sto* (the place where they have asked to stand). All the Christian apologist need do is to force the unbeliever to build his system logically upon his *a priori* assumption, his *pou sto* and then, once the superstructure has been built, challenge him to conduct his life in keeping with it. It is not likely that a Christian with this approach will ever be found to be ashamed of the gospel of Christ.

*Verse 17 - "For therein is the righteousness of God revealed from faith to faith: as it is written, The just shall live by faith."*

δικαιοσύνη γὰρ θεοῦ ἐν αὐτῷ ἀποκαλύπτεται ἐκ πίστεως εἰς πίστιν, καθὼς γέγραπται, Ὁ δὲ δίκαιος ἐκ πίστεως ζήσεται.

δικαιοσύνη (nom.sing.fem.of δικαιοσύνη, subject of ἀποκαλύπτεται) 322.
γὰρ (causal conjunction) 105.
θεοῦ (gen.sing.masc.of θεός, description) 124.

ἐν (preposition with the locative of place/means) 80.

αὐτῷ (loc.sing.masc.of αὐτός, place/means) 16.

ἀποκαλύπτεται (3d.per.sing.pres.pass.ind.of ἀποκαλύπτω, progressive duration, retroactive) 886.

ἐκ (preposition with the ablative of source 19.

πίστεως (abl.sing.fem.of πίστις, source) 728.

εἰς (preposition with the accusative, extent) 140.

καθὼς (adverbial) 1348.

γέγραπται (3d.per.sing.perf.pass.ind.of γράφω, intensive) 156.

ὁ (nom.sing.masc.of the article in agreement with δίκαιος) 9.

δὲ (adversative conjunction) 11.

δίκαιος (nom.sing.masc.of δίκαιος, subject of ζήσεται) 85.

ἐκ (preposition with the ablative of means) 19.

πίστεως (abl.sing.fem.of πίστις, means)

ζώσεται (3d.per.sing.fut.mid.ind.of ζάω, predictive) 340.

*Translation - "Because divine righteousness has been (and is) revealed in it, from faith to faith, just as it stands written, 'But the just shall live by faith.' "*

**Comment:** γάρ is causal. Paul's reason why he is not ashamed of the gospel is that in, and by means of it (ἐν with the locative of place and also in its instrumental use) a righteousness which is divine in nature, because it has God as its source, and which is characterized as being consistent with God's nature has been revealed to man. ἀποκαλύπτεται is a good example of the progressive duration, with its retroactive thrust. Paul saw the righteousness of God in the gospel more than twenty years before he wrote to the Romans. "For more than twenty years I have seen revealed in the gospel divine righteousness and I still see it revealed."

Note that θεοῦ is anarthrous. It is therefore descriptive, not possessive. The righteousness belongs to God, to be sure, Paul would have written ἡ δικαιοσύνη τοῦ θεοῦ if he had meant that. Without the article we read "divine (godly) righteousness." It is also possible to think of θεοῦ as an ablative of source, because certainly there is no other source of righteousness except God.

The gospel of Christ reveals the power (δύναμις) of God because it reveals the righteousness (δικαιοσύνη) of God. The Deity is powerless to act unrighteously. If He cannot act righteously He cannot act at all. δικαιοσύνη (#322) is the quality of thinking, acting upon and approving only that which is right (just). Abraham asks in rhetorical question "Shall not the Judge of all the earth do right?" (Gen.18:25). God's power can move to save the believer (verse 16), be he Jew or Greek, because when God saves the believer He is doing the right thing in the ethical and legal sense. If God could save the believer only by compromising His righteousness, His nature would render Him powerless to save. Whatever God does in relation to the sinner who believes must be in perfect alignment with the legal standards of Heaven's holy court. Where can man go to see the righteousness of God in action and evaluate it? To the gospel of Christ where God's power is exerted to save the sinner who believes. When God does this He acts with complete legal and ethical probity. Thus God's power in kinetic action to save the believer is also revelatory of God's righteousness.

That is why Paul was not ashamed of it. Because Paul was a lawyer and he would have been ashamed to preach a message which promised that God would indeed save the sinner, but that in order to do so, He would find it necessary to act on a level *below* the highest principles and ideals. The gospel on the contrary, teaches that the highest principles of righteousness, which govern the court decisions of heaven, demand that God save the believer, since his debt, charged to his account because of his transgressions of the law, has been fully paid at Calvary. There can be no double jeopardy in a court with a standard of complete righteousness. When a defendant, charged with a crime, and convicted in open court is sentenced, he must pay the penalty. Once he has paid it, he cannot be tried for that crime the second time. The believer's sin debt was paid by his substitute, Who had to become a man in order to qualify to pay it. When Jesus on the cross suffered the agonies of hell as He was separated from God, without knowing why - ("My God, my God, Why have you forsaken me?"), and when the three hours of hell on a cross was over, He said "It is finished" - Τετέλεστια - "It has been finished, and therefore it is now finished, and will remain finished forever." The debt was paid.

That is why the gospel of Christ is "good news" - "the result of a good message" and therefore "good news." Why should anyone be ashamed of good news? If it were bad news we should be reluctant to tell it.

> I love to tell the story of unseen things above,
> Of Jesus and His glory, of Jesus and His love.
> I love to tell the story, because I know 'tis true;
> It satisfies my longings as nothing else can do.
>
> I love to tell the story; more wonderful it seems
> Than all the golden fancies of all our golden dreams.
> I love to tell the story; it did so much for me
> And that is just the reason I tell it now to thee.

The lyrics of this old gospel song, written by Katherine Hankey, are wonderful and good and true, but her reasons for being proud of the gospel of Christ are all said to be subjective. To be sure we are glad that the gospel does so much for us, and that is good reason that we are not ashamed of it, but Paul was looking at the gospel from the standpoint of a lawyer. He "loved to tell the story" because it is such a perfect example of what the righteousness of God is like. How the power of God can be released to save, without violation of His righteousness, is a story that could thrill to its depths only the soul of a lawyer who sees it, not only from the subjective side of the coin, as Hankey did, but also from the objective side.

What produces this action to save and this revelation of God's righteousness? It is God's gift of faith to men. ἐκ πίστεως is an ablative of source. The believer's faith in Christ is the result of God's gift of faith to him. The faith which has its source in God is the cause and its result is the believer's faith which extends to the promises of God - From the faith which God gives to the faith which man exercises.

In Romans 1:5 we noted that faith is the source of obedience (ὑπακοὴν πίστεως, where we have the ablative of source). Now, in verse 17 we note that faith is also the source of divine righteousness (indeed, has there ever been any other kind?) - δικαιοσύνη . . . θεοῦ . . . ἐκ πίστεως, where we have another ablative of source. Now as we note Heb.11:6 that "without faith it is impossible to please God," we swing full circle. God is the source of faith, faith is the source of obedience and obedience is practical divine righteousness, which pleases God.

Ephesians 2:8,9 does not say that faith is the gift of God. *Cf.* our grammatical analysis of the passage *en loc.* What it says is that the fact that we are saved by grace through faith is the gift of God. Thus, indirectly, faith is the gift of God, since faith and grace are the two elements in the salvation equation, neither of which are produced by man. The antecedent of τοῦτο in Eph.2:8 can be neither χάριτί nor πίστεως, since there is no agreement in gender, but τοῦτο being neuter gender, whereas χάριτί and πίστεως are both feminine, has as its antecedent the statement as a whole that "by grace are you saved through faith." That fact is said to have come not from the sinner. That is what is said to be the gift of God, not of works, lest the Christian should boast. More on this *en loc.*

"The just shall live by faith" is not exclusively a New Testament revelation. It is Paul's citation of Habakkuk 2:4. The entire passage says, "Behold, his soul which is lifted up is not upright in him" (man is a sinner by nature and cannot be saved by his own efforts) "but the just shall live by his faith." Salvation is not achieved by the uplift of human moral reformation, but by faith. Since the conjunction is adversative in Hab.2:4 it is adversative also in the quotation in Romans 1:17. The man designated as "just" (δίκαιος #85) is declared by the court of heaven to be righteous, not only as though he had never sinned, but also as though in a positive way, he had fulfilled all of the positive demands of God's holy law. This is the just man. We did not say "totally righteous" because he who is not *totally* righteous is not righteous at all. We must remember that there is no difference between the claims of righteousness and holiness. Since holiness basicly means completeness (wholeness) partial holiness and partial righteousness are contradictions in terms. Thus we eschew redundancy.

The just man lives by faith - the faith which has its source in God; the faith which he exercises in his commitment to Jesus Christ. Thus the cause is adequate to the result. This is irresistible grace, the fourth point in the Tulip. (*Cf.* page 214, *supra*). Thus it is ἐκ πίστεως εἰς πίστιν.

Habakkuk 2:4 is quoted three times in the New Testament. In Romans 1:17 the emphasis is upon the first two words - "*The just* shall live by faith." In Galatians 3:11 the emphasis is upon the middle couplet - "The just *shall live* by faith." In Hebrews 10:38 the emphasis is upon the last two words - "The just shall live *by faith.*" The spotlight of emphasis shifts from "The just" in Romans, to "shall live" in Galatians and finally to "by faith" in Hebrews. Romans defines a just man; Galatians assures us that he shall live; he shall not die; and Hebrews tells us how this just man shall live - he shall live by faith - the kind of faith that changed the lives of all those heros and heroines of faith who are named in Hebrews 11. Let the Arminians note that Calvinists also believe in the holy living of the supernaturally regenerated child of God. The difference is that we also believe that "The steps of a good man are ordered by the Lord: and he delighteth in his way, . . . " and further that "though he fall, he shall not be utterly cast down: for the Lord upholdeth him with his hand" (Psalm 37:23,24).

Paul has stated his thesis. He is proud of his gospel of good news and he is eager to preach it to all men because, as a Jewish Rabbinical scholar of the law, one who grew up in Gamaliel's school, he is prepared to show that only in the gospel is there a demonstration of God's power to save a sinner and, at the same time, be consistent with His divine righteousness and holiness. If Paul can show us how this is done he will have succeeded in the Epistle to the Romans.

A lawyer in western Indiana said, "I want to be saved but I am lawyer enough not to ask God to do for me what is not right." After he understood Paul's argument in Romans, he accepted Christ. A prosecuting attorney in Ohio heard an exposition of Paul's argument in Romans and accepted Christ with the comment, "No lawyer could reject that."

If Paul is going to show how the human race can be justified, he must first prove that the human race is lost. This he sets out to do, first, by indicting the uncivilized Gentile nations in Romans 1:18-32, then by indicting the civilized Gentile world in Romans 2:1-16. Finally he indicts the Jews in Romans 2:17-29. His conclusion is found in Romans 3:1-20. Here the prosecutor terminates his universal indictment and in Romans 3:21 he begins to reveal God's righteousness in Christ.

Since man is a sinner and a transgressor of God's moral law, without the enforcement of which the universe is not viable, he can become a "just" man only by faith.

If Habakkuk had said, "The just shall live by reason" his statement would have been internally contradictory, since a just man who is also a reasonable man would be forced to take into account the fact that he is a transgressor, and then he would be forced justly to concede that he could not live. The equation Justice plus Transgression, if it is rationally solved must equal death, not life. We cannot say, "The just man must die" because if he must die, it is only because he is a sinner, and if he is a sinner he is not a just man. Man's reason cannot lead him to conclude that a law breaker can, in simple, elemental justice, escape the penalty for sin, which is death (Romans 3:23). The only way that a just man concludes that he is going to live forever is by abandoning human reason and accepting, like a child, the faith from God and exercising it in his humble acceptance of and commitment to God. That God should save a sinner, since God hates sin, is not reasonable to the unaided intellect of the natural man.

Economists know that the TANSTAAFL principle in an economy where supply lags behind demand, and where the rule is scarcity, must always be true. "There ain't no such thing as a free lunch." There is no such thing as sinning and escaping the penalty. Everything has its price. Nothing is without cost. This is man's reasoning. To believe the gospel promise is to accept it by faith. Thus the preaching of the cross is foolishness to all those who accept the norms of human reason, but to us who are saved it is the power ($\delta \acute{v} \nu \alpha \mu \iota \varsigma$) of God, because we are applying the norms of faith. Faith and reason blend into the same thing only in the rarified and sophisticated atmosphere of revelation, which comes to the believer, only after he is regenerated. Not before. We approach God by faith and walk through the door of salvation like babes. We are convinced of only one thing - that we are hopelessly lost except for the intervention of the grace of God. Like babes we trust in and believe that which does not commend itself to our reason. Once inside the door of salvation, with new and expanded mental perceptivity we grasp the divine logic of the gospel. But the transgressor who is as proud of his intellect as he is blind to his lost condition is not willing to abandon his faith in his own highly touted IQ, and who refuses the role of the little child, will never have faith. And it is only by faith that he gets through the door (Mt.11:25; 5:44; 18:3; 1 Cor.1:18).

Christian faith is not irrational. It only appears to be so to those who are irrational. It is superrational. Calvinists are not Thomists. They believe that the intellect of man was influenced by the fall of Adam as much as were his will and emotion. In the Garden of Eden, Satan, with an unintended assist from Eve and a deliberate assist from Adam (1 Tim.2:14; Gen.3:1-6) "blinded the minds of them which believe not" as well as corrupting their emotions and subverting their wills (2 Cor.3:14; 4:4; 1 John 2:11). Thus the unregenerate cannot think his way to God, and the foundation for Medieval Scholasticism is revealed as shifting sand.

This is what we mean by the T in the Tulip. Man is totally depraved. This does not mean that he is so evil that he cannot get worse. His depravity is extensive, not intensive. It extends to the total man - to his will, his intellect and his emotion. Only in his physical body is he alive, and even there he carries the seeds of ultimate biodegradibility, which normally takes place after seventy years. The psychic man is "dead I in trespasses and sins" (Eph.2:1), and he is helpless until the Holy Spirit rescues him and gives him the kind of life that is so completely qualitative that it is eternally quantitative.

In the first seventeen verses of the epistle to the Romans Paul has introduced the argument. The remainder of the book is devoted to a fuller expostion of all of that to which he points in his introduction. Only those who are lost need to be saved. Thus, the first order of business is to prove that the human race is lost. Paul begins with the Gentile world in its more uncivilized development.

## The Guilt of Mankind

*(Romans 1:18-31)*

*Verse 18 - "For the wrath of God is revealed from heaven against all ungodliness and unrighteousness of men, who hold the truth in unrighteousness."*

Ἀποκαλύπτεται γὰρ ὀργὴ θεοῦ ἀπ' οὐρανοῦ ἐπὶ πᾶσαν ἀσέβειαν καὶ ἀδικίαν ἀνθρώπων τῶν τὴν ἀλήθειαν ἐν ἀδικίᾳ κατεχόντων,

Ἀποκαλύπτεται (3d.per.sing.pres.pass.ind.of ἀποκαλύπτω, progressive duration, retroactive) 886.

γὰρ (causal conjunction) 105.

ὀργὴ (nom.sing.fem.of ὀργή, subject of ἀποκαλύπτεται) 283.

θεοῦ (gen.sing.masc.of θεοῦ, description) 124.

ἀπ' (preposition with the ablative of source) 70.

οὐρανοῦ (abl.sing.masc.of οὐρανός, source) 254.

ἐπὶ (preposition with the accusative, opposition) 47.

πᾶσαν (acc.sing.fem.of πᾶς, in agreement with ἀσέβειαν) 67.

#3794 ἀσέβειαν (acc.sing.fem.of ἀσέβεια, opposition).

ungodliness - Rom.1:18; 11:26; 2 Tim.2:16; Tit.2:12.
ungodly - Jude 15,18.

*Meaning:* Cf. ἀσεβής (#3882), ἀσεβέω (#5313). α privative plus σέβω - "to revere." Hence, a want of reverence toward God. It is the attitude of contempt which leads to the transgression of the law of God. ἀσέβεια is human pride and contempt for higher power. It is a psychological sin. The opposite of poverty of spirit (Mt.5:4).

καὶ (adjunctive conjunction joining nouns) 14.

ἀδικίαν (acc.sing.fem.of ἀδικία, opposition) 2367.

ἀνθρώπων (gen.pl.masc.of ἄνθρωπος, definition) 341.

τῶν (gen.pl.masc.of the article in agreement with κατεχόντων) 9.

τὴν (acc.sing.fem.of the article in agreement with ἀλήθειαν) 9.

ἀλήθειαν (acc.sing.fem.of ἀλήθεια, direct object of κατεχόντων) 1416.

ἐν (preposition with the locative of sphere) 80.

ἀδικίᾳ (loc.sing.fem.of ἀδικία, sphere) 2367.

κατεχόντων (pres.act.part.gen.pl.masc.of κατέχω, adjectival, restrictive, in agreement with ἀνθρώπων) 2071.

*Translation - "Because divine wrath has always been revealed from heaven against all human irreverence and unrighteousness of those who suppress the truth that relates to unrighteousness."*

**Comment:** Divine power is revealed in the gospel (verse 16). Divine righteousness is also revealed (verse 17). And now we learn that divine wrath is revealed (verse 18). In other passages it is also clear that divine love and grace are revealed in the gospel, but that is not Paul's point here. Where sin is an empirical fact divine righteousness always involves divine wrath, for God can take no other attitude toward sin, as long as the sinner is irreverent and disrespectful. If the sinner abandons his irreverence and asks for mercy then divine love is revealed and the grace that brings salvation. Righteousness rewards good where it is found and punishes evils. Thus the same God can with righteousness bestow salvation upon the believer and with the same righteousness visit His wrath upon the unbeliever.

The wrath of God comes from heaven (ablative of source in ἀπ' οὐρανου). Note the similarity of language in 2 Thess.1:7-9. God's wrath is always burning. He "... is angry with the wicked every day. If he (*i.e.* the wicked) turn not, he (*i.e.* God) will whet His sword; He hath bent His bow and made it ready" (Psalm

7:11,12). God's wrath is always burning against sin, but judgment awaits the Second Coming. Meanwhile God is whetting His sword and tightening the string on his bow. This figurative language means only that the judgment is held in abeyance and the divine warfare will be called off if the enemy "turns" (repents).

Why God's wrath? And against whom displayed? ἀσέβειαν (#3794) is the sin of the unrepentant attitude - the lack of reverence. This attitude precedes the overt transgression involved in ἀδικίαν. This irreverence and lawless behavior is characteristic of men who constantly suppress the truth of God, which they clearly understand, in the areas that involve the moral law of the universe. They do not necessarily suppress the truth in other spheres. ἐν ἀδικίᾳ is a locative of sphere construction. The unsaved can be totally open to the areas of truth which do not demand from them obedience to the moral law. Thus research scientists, in all areas - the social, physical and natural sciences, as well as the humanities are sincerely in search of truth and delighted when they find it, but when their research leads them to conclusions that demand from them compliance with the moral laws of God, - these are the spheres in which they suppress the truth. It is man's moral nature, not his lack of intellect that leads to his rejection of God's law. Hell will be full of intellectual giants who were moral infants. Why would any man wish to suppress or restrain truth? He does not, except when the truth he understands forbids the sins which he wishes to commit. It is because of his addiction to sin. He does not sin in ignorance of the truth, but in the presence of the truth, which he understands better than he would like. His choice is to accept the truth and deny himself indulgence in the sin which he desires, or indulge himself in sin and suppress the truth. God's truth and man's sin cannot both be enthroned in the heart of a rational man. One or the other must yield its place.

These men whom Paul described were not benighted. They understood and recognized the conflict between the truth and its claims upon their lives and their temptations and the imperious demand they made upon their actions. They knew that they could not entertain both. So they opted for sin and against truth. With full knowledge that theirs was a short-run analysis and that in the long-run they were asking for divine wrath, they nevertheless chose the temporary benefits of sinful indulgence and accepted the eternal punishment which would be theirs in the long-run. Thus they sinned "after the similitude of Adam's transgression" (Romans 5:14), for that is how he sinned. He was not deceived (1 Tim.2:14). He deliberately disobeyed God with the eyes of his understanding with reference to the consequences, wide open.

The question now becomes this: how much truth did these men have? The answer is found in verses 19,20. When they sinned against the light, how much light did they have?

*Verse 19 - "Because that which may be known of God is manifest in them: for God hath showed it unto them."*

διότι τὸ γνωστὸν τοῦ θεοῦ φανερόν ἐστιν ἐν αὐτοῖς, ὁ θεὸς γὰρ αὐτοῖς ἐφανέρωσεν.

διότι (particle introducing a causal clause) 1795.

τό (nom.sing.neut.of the article in agreement with γνωστὸν) 9.

γνωστὸν (nom.sing.neut.of γνωστός, subject of ἐστιν) 1917.

τοῦ (gen.sing.masc.of the article in agreement with θεοῦ) 9.

θεοῦ (gen.sing.masc.of θεός, reference) 124.

φανερόν (nom.sing.neut.of φανερός, predicate adjective, in agreement with γνωστὸν) 981.

ἐστιν (3d.per.sing.pres.ind.of εἰμί, static) 86.

ἐν (preposition with the locative with plural pronouns) 80.

αὐτοῖς (loc.pl.masc.of αὐτός, place) 16.

ὁ (nom.sing.masc.of the article in agreement with θεὸς) 9.

θεὸς (nom.sing.masc.of θεός, subject of ἐφανέρωσεν) 124.

γὰρ (causal conjunction) 105.

αὐτοῖς (dat.pl.masc.of αὐτός, indirect object of ἐφανέρωσεν) 16.

ἐφανέρωσεν (3d.per.sing.aor.act.ind.of φανερόω, culminative) 1960.

*Translation - "Because that which is obvious about God is known to them, for God has shown it to them."*

**Comment:** The heathen, against whom God's wrath is being readied (verse 18) are those who had some truth, but who suppressed it because they were unwilling to commit themselves to the moral and philosophical course which it, in all logic demanded. They chose rather to ignore and even repudicate it in order to indulge in sin. What was this truth that was so obvious to them? Was it the story of the virgin birth, life, teachings, death, burial, bodily resurrection, ascension, advocacy and second coming of Jesus Christ? Were they visited by missionaries with Bible in hand? No, because Paul is talking about those, some of whom were born, lived and died before even the Old Testament was written, others who lived in sequestered parts of the earth where the gospel story had never been told, and all of whom knew nothing of the Old Testament prophets or the New Testament history of Jesus.

But some facts about God are known to all, whether they have been formally evangelized or not. That they had some revelation of God is proved by the telltale evidences present in their culture. For example, Homer's story about a great national hero, Achilles, who was invincible until wounded in the heel, faintly recalls Genesis 3:15. Did the Hebrews spread the story of the promises of the Abrahamic Covenant, that salvation would come to the human family through the death of the Seed of the woman who would die in heel-bruising death? Was this story circulated among the Gentiles? If so, they rejected it out of hand, but retained the faint traces of the details of the story in their own cultural traditions. All the families of the earth go back to the flood, as descendants of either Ham, Shem or Japeth, the sons of Noah, and anthropologists report that most of them had their own version of a flood.

These views are possible - even probable, but Paul's argument does not depend upon them. He tells us more specifically what he means by τὸ γνωστὸν τοῦ θεοῦ (verse 19) in verse 20. Most of the heathen religions in the Middle East during the Hellenistic period (323 B.C. — A.D.325) had stories about a virgin birth which are corruptions of the true gospel expectations revealed to Old Testament saints by the "holy men of God (who) spake as they were moved by the Holy Spirit" (2 Peter 1:21).

Verse 20 tells us what these bits and pieces of truth are, how well they were understood, how they came to be understood and the result that followed from the fact that they were understood.

*Verse 20 - "For the invisible things of him from the creation of the world are clearly seen, being understood by the things that are made, even his eternal power and Godhead; so that they are without excuse."*

τὰ γὰρ ἀόρατα αὐτοῦ ἀπὸ κτίσεως κόσμου τοῖς ποιήμασιν νοούμενα καθορᾶται, ἥ τε ἀΐδιος αὐτοῦ δύναμις καὶ θειότης, εἰς τὸ εἶναι αὐτοὺς ἀναπολογήτους.

τὰ (nom.pl.neut.of the article in agreement with ἀόρατα) 9.
γὰρ (causal conjunction) 105.

#3795 ἀόρατα (nom.pl.neut.of ἀόρατος, subject of καθορᾶται).

invisible - Rom.1:20; Col.1:15,16; 1 Tim.1:17; Heb.11:27.

*Meaning:* α privative plus ὁράω (#144a). Hence, either unseen or incapable of being seen; invisible - Rom.1:20; Col.1:15; 1 Tim.1:17; Heb.11:27. Opposed to ὁρατά in Col.1:16. The contexts in which the word occurs demand, not that which cannot be understood, but that which cannot be seen in the physically optical sense.

αὐτοῦ (gen.sing.masc.of αὐτός, reference) 16.
ἀπὸ (preposition with the ablative of time separation) 70.
κτίσεως (abl.sing.fem.of κτίσις, in a time expression) 2633.
κόσμου (gen.sing.masc.of κόσμος, description) 360.
τοῖς (instru.neut.pl.of the article in agreement with ποιήμασιν) 9.

#3796 ποιήμασιν (instru.pl.neut.of ποιήμα, means).

thing that is made - Rom.1:20.
workmanship - Eph.2:10.

*Meaning:* ποιέω (#127) and μα, the result suffix. Hence, the result of the act of making or creating. In the New Testament, the result of creation - The physical universe - stars, planets, moons, plants, animals, man - Rom.1:20; the regenerated Christian - Eph.2:10.

νοούμενα (pres.pass.part.nom.pl.neut.of νοέω, adverbial, causal) 1160.

#3797 καθορᾶται (3d.per.sing.pres.pass.ind.of καθοράω, progressive duration, retroactive).

see clearly - Rom.1:20.

*Meaning:* A combination of κατά (#98) and ὁράω (#144a), in which combination κατά is perfective. Hence, to understand clearly - Romans 1:20.

ἥ (nom.sing.fem.of the article in agreement with δύναμις) 9.
τε (correlative particle) 1408.

**#3798** ἀΐδιος (nom.sing.fem.of ἀΐδιος, in agreement with δύναμις).

eternal - Romans 1:20.
everlasting - Jude 6.

*Meaning:* for ἀείδιος, from ἀεί - eternal, everlasting. God's power - Romans 1:20; with reference to chains of punishment - Jude 6.

αὐτοῦ (gen.sing.masc.of αὐτός, possession) 16.
δύναμις (nom.sing.fem.of δύναμις, apposition) 687.
καί (adjunctive conjunction joining nouns) 14.

**#3799** θειότης (nom.sing.masc.of θειότης, apposition).

Godhead - Romans 1:20.

*Meaning: Cf.* θεότης (#4615). θειότης means the quality or attributes of deity, whereas θεότης means deity itself. The Deity (θεότης) possesses the attributes of God (θειότης). - Romans 1:20.

εἰς (preposition with the articular infinitive in the accusative, purpose) 140.
τό (acc.sing.neut.of the article in agreement with εἶναι) 9.
εἶναι (pres.inf.of εἰμί, verb use, accusative case, purpose) 86.
αὐτούς (acc.pl.masc.of αὐτός, general reference) 16.

**#3800** ἀναπολογήτους (acc.pl.masc.of ἀναπολόγητος, predicate adjective, in agreement with αὐτούς).

inexcuseable - Romans 2:1.
without excuse - Romans 1:20.

*Meaning:* α privative plus ἀπολογέομαι (#2476). Hence, without excuse or defense. Having no grounds for explanation, extenuation or justification - Romans 1:20; 2:1.

*Translation - "Because the attributes of God which are not subject to sense perception have been understood perfectly ever since the creation, because they have come to be known by the things which were made, - namely His eternal power and attributes of deity, so that they are without excuse."*

**Comment:** How do we know that God showed to the heathen some of the things that can be known about Himself? Because (causal γάρ) they had come to understand some things about God. Concepts of truth that cannot be known through sense perception - that cannot be seen physically, smelled, heard, touched or tasted, but which can be known - these things have been understood by the heathen. Vital to a correct interpretation of this passage and to a complete appreciation of Paul's argument is the fact that they *did know God*. Verse 18 says that they suppressed truth. Verse 19 says some knowledge about God had been revealed to them and that their culture and life style proves that this is so. Verse 20 says that some things about God were perfectly well understood. Paul even tells us what these things were - eternal power and the qualities of deity, and he adds that their perception of these things about God was so complete that they were without excuse, if and when they did not live up to their light.

It is wrong to say that if we do not know all of truth about anything, whether it be truth about God or truth about nature, we do not know truth at all. If that were true it would follow that Christians know nothing either, since no Christian at this point (short of glorification) knows all that there is to know about God and His total truth. Complete knowledge and wisdom is hid in Christ (Col.2:3). Since, then, the heathen knew enough truth to make him morally responsible for it, so that he merited favourable consideration if he followed it, and unfavorable consideration if he did not, the question becomes the degree to which he knew the truth and the manner in which he arrived at what he knows.

Science knows of only one approach to truth. Truth can be known only by experience. There is nothing in the intellect without first of all being in the senses. All knowledge is grounded in sensation. If the scientist cannot see it or hear it or taste it or smell it or feel it, then he concludes that he cannot know it.

Philosophy says that the road to truth is reason. Plato tried to think his way to the formula for the ideal man by developing a mind construct about the ideal state. For him the state (πόλις, by which he meant Athens, or any other self-contained political entity) was only the individual writ large. Plato spent little time in observation of things. He spent his time thinking. And his ideal man was the Philosopher-King.

*Until philosophers are kings, or the kings and princes of this world have the spirit and power of philosophy, and political greatness and wisdom meet in one, and those commoner natures who pursue either to the exclusion of the other are compelled to stand aside, cities will never have rest from their evils, - no, nor the human race, as I believe, - and then only will this our State have a possibility of life and behold the light of day.*
Plato, *Republic*, V, 473, D.

Plato thus wrote the formula for the perfect Statesman, into whose hands the people could safely place all policy making responsibility, judicial decision and implemental power. The Philosopher-King thus would be too intelligent to make a mistake, too kind to inflict an injury, even if he were stupid enough to make a mistake, and powerful enough to enforce his will upon society. Only if those three qualities were present could the state "have a possibility of life and behold the light of day."

Plato thought so much and observed so little that he lost all touch with reality. His system had consistency and coherence, but it lacked correspondance with reality. Thus it was flawed. The human race could never produce such an intellectual, moral and administrative genius. *Charles Louis de Secondat, Baron de la Brede et de Montesquieu* (1689-1755) realized this and wrote *De L' Esprit des Lois,* a notable work in political science, in which he examined the relative merits of republic, monarchical and despotic forms of government. He concluded that since the human race could never produce Plato's Philosopher-King, if a nation wished to remain viable the legislative, judicial and executive functions of the government must be placed in different hands. It was Montesquieu who influenced our founding fathers who separated the three powers of government in the United States Constitution and provided a careful balance between them. The theory is that the blunders of any one or two of the branches would be corrected by the wisdom of the other two or three. If the legislature mandates unwisely, either the court will declare the law unconstitutional or the executive will veto it. Powers are also nicely balanced between the federal and the state and local governments. When these balances have been maintained the republican form of government works as well as could be expected from a system that bases its policies upon the collective wisdom of the people. When any of the three branches gains ascendàncy over the other two, Montesquieu's balance of powers is upset and the state suffers an unnecessary loss of freedom.

Plato's student, the great Aristotle, who loved Plato dearly but philosophy more than he loved his teacher, insisted that although reason was important in our quest for reality it needed experience as a supplement. One might reason forever about the ideal oak leaf in heaven, but one should also look carefully at the oak leaves on earth, even though they were not ideal - *i.e.* not perfect copies of the one in heaven. Thus Aristotle gave us his "Golden Mean" philosophy - a philosophy with which the Apostle Paul agreed. Witness Paul's admonition that we are to let our moderation be known to all men (Phil.4:5), which in Aristotelian terms means to settle for the "Golden Mean" and that the fruit of the Spirit is temperance (Gal.5:23).

Unfortunately "the god of this world has blinded the minds of them which believe not. . . " (2 Cor.4:4) and the philosophical fanatics have lined up against each other at opposite extremes. Those who wished only to think repudiated experience and those who wished only to experience renounced discursive logic. The idealists said,"No matter" and the materialists countered with, "Never mind." Thus Locke, Hume and Berkeley, the radical empiricists opposed DesCartes, Leibniz and Spinoza, the logicians. "Locke was wrong when he said, 'There is nothing in the intellect except what was first in the senses'; Leibniz was right when he added, '. . . nothing, except the intellect itself.'" (Will Durant, *The Story of Philosophy*, 296). Thus he opened the way for Immanuel Kant who conceded that knowledge begins with sense perceptions, but that without reason, that which is seen, heard, tasted, smelled or touched is nothing more than unorganized stimulus - as such worthless. Reason turns the stimulus to organized sensation which he called perception. Organized perception becomes conception, which then becomes organized knowledge, which is what we call science. Armed with this we have the wisdom needed for organized life. Thus the sequence is sensation, perception, conception, knowledge, science, wisdom and the good life. In order to experience this development both experience and reason, both matter and mind, are necessry. But Kant disappointed the hopes of those Christian theologians who, with Thomas Aquinas, have built their apologetics upon reason and experience instead of building it, as they should have done, upon faith. The Jesuits and their Protestant brethren who are making the same mistake, were devastated when they read Kant's *Critique of Pure Reason, Critique of Practical Reason* and *Metaphysics of Ethics.*

Why should this be so? Because Kant destroyed Christianity for everyone except the first century Christians who knew Jesus personally. They saw Him, heard His voice and felt His touch. He was a part of their sensory stimulii. With those sensory experiences they could use reason (discursive logic) to organize stimulus and thus transform it to perception, conception, knowledge, wisdom and the good life. Empiricism says that there is no knowledge except in sense perception. Reason says there is no knowledge beyond a reasonable evaluation of experience. Science (Locke, Hume, Berkeley) says that knowledge (certitude) begins and ends with experience. Reason (DesCartes, Leibniz, Spinoza, Kant) says that certitude is found when experience, with which it must begin, has been subjected to reason. Thomas Aquinas and the Medieval Scholastics, from whom the Jesuits and many Protestant theologians, are descended, would not have found Kant objectionable, because St. Thomas taught that the intellect of Adam was not affected by the fall. Thus reason is adequate to lead us to God, salvation and heaven. But this can be true only for those who personally experienced Jesus Christ of Nazareth in the sensory sense. The rest of us have never seen, heard or touched Him. We have no starting point, except a book, which we must accept by faith. Kant did not belief in faith as a guide to certitude, although he may have recommedned it for those naive, intellectually inferior people who needed a crutch to maintain psychic balance. Kant would say that first century Christians *knew the Lord* and were sure of salvation, but he would quickly add that nobody else does. The rest of us only *believe* in Him. We do not *know* Him. Tennyson fell into this Kantian trap when he wrote

> We have but faith: we cannot know;
> For knowledge is of things we see.
>
> *In Memoriam, Introduction*

This statement is not even Kantian; it is the extreme empiricism of Locke, Hume and Berkeley. Dr. Strong well says of Tennyson's remark, "This would make sensuous phenomena the only subjects of knowledge. Faith in supersensible realities, on the contrary, is the highest exercise of reason." (Augustus Hopkins Strong, *Systematic Theology,* I, 3).

The Reformed Theology rejects both the empiricism of Locke, Hume and Berkeley and the idealism of Kant and his followers, and declares our faith in the propositional revelation of the Greek New Testament. The New Testament is God's Word and we trust what it says as much as we would trust our eyes and ears if we had in fact seen and heard Jesus. Perhaps even more. The empiricist needs faith in a proposition that he cannot prove - that he is seeing straight and therefore that his senses can be trusted. Neither experience nor reason can bring us to Christ and the certitude which He provides. That is why knowledgeable evangelists do not waste time trying to convince unsaved people of the truth of Christianity, as if they could believe in Christ only because they were convinced that Christianity is the truth (1 Cor.12:3). Peter, Paul and the other evangelists of the Book of Acts witnessed for Him, by showing that He was the historic fulfillment of Moses and the Prophets, and then they dared their listeners to believe it.

But, although Christians do not become such either by sight, sound, touch, smell or taste, or by reason, when we do become such because God has given us the gift of His grace (Eph.2:8,9) we find that He is both experiential and reasonable. Christians should think about their supernatural experience of birth from above *after* they have had it. Jesus ordered Nicodemus not to think about it before (John 3:7). Little children (Mt.18:3) do not think before they choose; they believe.

What has all of this epistemology to do with our exposition of Romans 1:20?

God is justly angry with them. Why? Because they knew some things about Him because He revealed them. What things? They knew of divine power and the attributes of deity. How did they learn of these? They looked and listened to the "things which He had made." "The heavens declare the glory of God . . . " (Psalm 19:1-6). They saw and heard God's message in a language which is universal. One does not need a visit from a Christian missionary with a Bible to get this message. They saw visible sights, heard audible sounds, smelled pungent odors, both fragrant and malodorous, tasted pleasant and unpleasant flavors and touched tangible objects. Thus they were empiricists with Locke, Hume and Berkeley. But they thought about these experiences in terms of time and space relationships, with Kant, Leibniz, Spinoza and DesCartes. Thus they turned stimulii to organized sensation, perception, conception and knowledge. This knowledge was real and valid. It was the product of experience and reason. They were sure of it. They possessed certitude. But only about those things which they had experienced and thought about. What were these things? Paul tells us that they were the "invisible things" ($τὰ$ $ἀόρατα$) of God and that they learned them by observing the "things which had been created" ($τοῖς$ $ποιήμασιν$). He also tells us that this learning process had been going on since the day of creation. What, specifically, did they learn?

They learned of God's power. Only omnipotence could create matter out of nothing. They also learned of God's intelligence. Only omniscience could make a rational creation out of nothing. One does not need a Bible to tell him that the one who created the material worlds is all powerful. And once he has studied the material world he needs no one to tell him that the creator was intelligent. As scientists have examined the material world they have become convinced of two great facts: (1) the universal law of causation, and (2) the uniformity of nature. Radical empiricists and existentialists will challenge these principles, but they are the cornerstones of science. Without them no scientific research is possible. If we cannot be sure that causes cause results and that the same cause, under the same conditons causes the same result every time, we cannot have a controlled experiement. And an experiment that is not under control is not an experiment at all. The controlled experiment is one in which the same components are put together under the same conditions as before, except for one change, either in the component or in the condition under which it is introduced. The result will not be the same as in the previous experiment, and the scientist can be certain that the change in outcome of the experiment is the result of the one change which was introduced. If two or more changes in the experiment were made, we could not be sure, which of the two or more, caused the change in outcome. We would thus learn nothing from the experiment and science as we know it would not be possible. In a world where there is no relationship between cause and result and in which there is no uniformity of nature, there is nothing but randomness. It is to this conclusion that the radical existentialists have come and a few of them, (Jean Paul Sartes, for example) had the courage to behave as if they really believed it. But most people believe that nature acts the same way under the same circumstances every time. If I did not believe that I would not have the courage to crank my car, because I could not predict the result. I would hope that it would start and transport me without my effort to my destination. But unless we live in an ordered universe it might respond with a nuclear explosion or turn into a chocolate eclair.

There is something else that primitive man, enlightened only by his observations and thoughts about the material universe, and unenlightened by the message of the Bible, knew. He also knew that the intelligent God of power and creation had created him in the divine image. This was a great compliment to him. How did he arrive at this? If it were not true, he could not have followed God's thoughts and made them his own. Economics professors cannot teach economics to pigs, but we can teach the discipline to other human beings, or at least to many of them! This is because the student is made in the same image as the professors - and that is the image of God (Gen.1:26,26; Heb.2:6-8). Can primitive man create the universe and ordain its natural laws? No, because he too is a creature of God. But can he observe nature, derive its principles, at least in part, and come to manipulate it so as to make confident prediction? Indeed he could and did. The history of science tells us that this is so. We have invented the wheel, discovered the chemical properties of fire, split the atom and gone to the moon. The pigs have not done that. Nor will they. The conclusion must be that we are smarter than the pigs, and that because it was the Lord's desire that we should be. That is why He created us with that super-pig potential. In what area? Not in sense perception, for a pig can see and hear also and perhaps smell, though one might doubt it, judging from what he eats, but he cannot think about what he sees, hears, smells, tastes and touches. Man can.

Primitive man, aware that he was favored by God above other creatures, and also aware of the fact that though he could think he did not know as much as God, did not respond with the humility that God had every right to expect. He should have said to his Creator, "Tell me more. Teach me thy ways." This he did not do. On the contrary he ignored God and suppressed what he knew about Him. In what area did this suppression occur? . Paul says in Romans 1:18 that it was in the moral area - ἐν ἀδικίᾳ. I have taken the phrase as a locative of sphere, though we can interpret it as causal. When the question of man's relationship to

God came up, the concept of law could not be ignored. God is powerful in a way that man can never be, for He is creator. But man could become more powerful than he was at first, by becoming better educated than he was at first. He learned how to release the power in a lump of coal. For him greater knowledge meant more power. So great, indeed has his knowledge become, that he has been able to lift a rocket off the earth and send it roaring into outer space. Primitive man was happy to learn more about science and thus become more like God in intelligence and power. But he also knew that God was holy. He did not learn this from observation of things, nor even by thinking about what he saw. He learned this from his conscience - God placed in his breast the still small voice that always encourages the good and rebukes the evil. That is another dividend forthcoming from the fact that he is made in God's image. So it was when the question of law versus transgression, righteousness versus unrighteousness, goodness versus evil, purity versus the impure, obedeince versus disobedience, sin versus holiness - because of this ($\dot{\epsilon}\nu$ $\dot{\alpha}\delta\iota\kappa\dot{\iota}\alpha$ can be cause) and in the sphere of this issue (locative of sphere in $\dot{\epsilon}\nu$ $\dot{\alpha}\delta\iota\kappa\dot{\iota}\alpha$) primitive man decided that he could get along on this planet without God, if further fellowship with the Creator meant that he would have to give up his sins and live a holy life.

In essence the argument is this: primitive man looked about him at the earth and gained phenomenal knowledge. By his God given power of reason he gained noumenal knowledge. He became Cartesian. He achieved knowledge of reality by logic. Witness the evolution in mathematics, with an assist from DesCartes, from two-dimensional Euclidean geometry to tri-dimensional trigonometry and calculus and finally to four-dimensional Einsteinian relativity with its empirical evidence in astro-mathematics that put man on the moon with a precision that boggles the mind. The existentialist will find scant comfort here. Equipped in creation with the mental power to be logical about those things which he had the physical power to see and hear, he looked at the "things which had been made" and came to understand implicitly that a creature could exist only because a Creator had eternal power, plus infinite wisdom and knowledge. But he knew something else in the noumenal area. He knew that God was holy and that he was a transgressor. The still small voice within would not allow him to forget it.

Why did God arrange it like this? The clause that follows - $\epsilon\dot{\iota}\varsigma$ $\tau\dot{o}$ $\epsilon\dot{\iota}\nu\alpha\iota$ $\alpha\dot{\upsilon}\tau o\dot{\upsilon}\varsigma$ $\dot{\alpha}\nu\alpha\pi o\lambda o\gamma\dot{\eta}\tau o\upsilon\varsigma$ - is sub-final. It expresses both purpose and result, since, as Burton says result is only intended purpose. God's purpose in making man a Cartesian thinker and presenting him in creation with objective evidence was that he might either humbly accept the partial light of natural revelation and pray for more light, or, failing that, in the sad event that he would react irreverently and suppress the truth because he opted for his sin and lawlessness, he would be without excuse in a moral universe. Whether we take the $\epsilon\dot{\iota}\varsigma$ clause as pure purpose or quasi-purpose/result the exegesis is not changed. God's purpose was to equip His creature with intellectual power and objective stimulation to use it, so that he could either be humble and reverent, awe-struck by the majesty of creation and anxious to obey an inbuilt moral consciousness, thus to be clear in the judgment because he followed the light that he had, or when he chose to insult God, sin against the light and ignore the obvious truth, have no one to blame but himself.

Paul returns to this problem in Romans 2:12-16 and, as the passage develops we shall see that God is going to take into account how man has reacted to partial light.

*Verse 21 - "Because that, when they knew God they glorified him not as God, neither were thankful; but became vain in their imaginations, and their foolish heart was darkened."*

διότι γνόντες τὸν θεὸν οὐχ ὡς θεὸν ἐδόξασαν ἢ ηὐχαρίστησαν, ἀλλ' ἐματαιώθησαν ἐν τοῖς διαλογισμοῖς αὐτῶν καὶ ἐσκοτίσθη ἡ ἀσύνετος αὐτῶν καρδία.

διότι (causal particle) 1795.

γνόντες (aor.act.part.nom.pl.masc.of γινώσκω, adverbial, concessive) 131.

τὸν (acc.sing.masc.of the article in agreement with θεὸν) 9.

θεὸν (acc.sing.masc.of θεός, direct object of γνόντες) 124.

οὐχ (negative conjunction with the indicative) 130.

ὡς (conjunction in a comparative clause) 128.

θεὸν (acc.sing.masc.of θεός, predicate accusative) 124.

ἐδόξασαν (3d.per.pl.aor.act.ind.of δοξάζω, ingressive) 461.

ἢ (disjunctive) 465.

ηὐχαρίστησαν (3d.per.pl.aor.act.ind.of εὐχαριστέω, ingressive) 1185.

ἀλλ' (alternative conjunction) 342.

#3801 ἐματαιώθησαν (3d.per.pl.1st.aor.pass.ind.of ματαιόω, ingressive).

became vain - Romans 1:21.

*Meaning: Cf.* ματαιολογία (#4694), ματαιολόγος (#4882), μάταιος (#3321); ματαιότης (#3940) and μάτην (#1148). To make empty, vain, foolish, vacuous, vapid, insipid, devoid of serious content - Romans 1:21.

ἐν (preposition with the locative of sphere) 80.

τοῖς (loc.pl.masc.of the article in agreement with διαλογισμοῖς) 9.

διαλογισμοῖς (loc.pl.masc.of διαλογισμός, sphere) 1165.

αὐτῶν (gen.pl.masc.of αὐτός, possession) 16.

καὶ (continuative conjunction) 14.

ἐσκοτίσθη (3d.per.sing.aor.pass.ind.of σκοτίζω, culminative) 1504.

ἡ (nom.sing.fem.of the article in agreement with καρδία) 9.

ἀσύνετο (nom.sing.fem.of ἀσύνετος, in agreement with καρδία) 1159.

αὐτῶν (gen.pl.masc.of αὐτός, possession) 16.

καρδία (nom.sing.fem.of καρδία, subject of ἐσκοτίσθη) 432.

*Translation - ". . . the reason being that, although they knew God, they did not begin to glorify Him as such, nor did they become grateful. On the contrary they became vacuous in their discussions and their uncomprehending hearts became dark."*

**Comment:** διότι prepares us for the reason why the heathen are without excuse (verse 20). The participle γνόντες is concessive. They knew God, but, despite that fact, they did not react to Him in a way that He deserves. Verse 18 says that they were irreverent and unrighteous. The thought of verse 19 is repeated here. They did know God in an intellectual way. His partial revelation to them revealed His eternal power and the attributes of His divine nature. How did they come to know these things? They looked at the things which were created and deduced the concepts which could not be examined with sense perception. Examination of the visible brought a realization of concepts which were invisible. The phenomenal leads to the noumenal.

Early man was curious. He examined things upon the earth and gazed into the sky. Psalm 19:1-4 describes the curriculum which he studied. It is presented in God's universal language and is available to all - even to those who were never privileged to open a Bible or hear a missionary preach the gospel. This is natural theology. It is noumena through the medium of phenomena, a thing that is possible for man, but not for the beasts, since man was made in God's image and the animals were not. It is rational man who gazes at the Milky Way, the glory of the sunset, the dainty precision and breathtaking color of the rose petal, the quiet dignity of the harvest moon and the grace of the antelope. He is not an animal but a philosopher who listens to the roar of the waterfall, the sizzling zigzag of the lightning flash and the thunderous crash of the divine timpani. When he looks upon the microscopic stage and sees the mitotic process he is certain to ask why the human cell divides with such amazing regularity? What is life? How did it begin if indeed it is not eternal? What is its purpose? Man stands in awe as he examines, microscopically and telescopically, all that God created. He sees order and precision. He sees beauty and majesty. He sees unity in diversity. Every time he resumes his examination he sees these things again in God's handiwork. Day after day and night after night they utter speech and divulge information - not of God's love, mercy, grace, pardon, and forgiveness - not even of His holiness, though he learns about that from his conscience, but of His eternal power and infinite intelligence (verse 20).

This knowledge, though partial, is enough for man to take a preliminary step toward salvation. The first step is humility - the humility of a creature before his Creator and the sorrow for sins of which a built-in moral consciousness accuses him. This sense of moral, physical and intellectual inferiority, as he sees himself in contrast to God's holiness, intelligence and power, is enough to turn him into a philosophical babe (Mt.11:25). This is enough to make him "poor in spirit" (Mt.5:4). He should become a little child (Mt.18:3). If he did react like this, God would be morally obligated to give him more light for "a broken and a contrite heart God will not despise" (Psalm 51:17), especially when it comes from a poor savage who was born too soon or in too remote a spot of earth to hear the story of Jesus' love that drove Him to a cross.

But not many of them reacted like this. (Of course, most of them died in infancy.) For the rest, neither glory nor thanks, but irreverence and rebellion was their reaction. Why? Because they knew that this God of power, might and intelligence (attributes which they derived from their look at nature) was also a

God of moral perfection. The intensity and constancy of His love for man is matched by the fortitude and steadfastness of His hatred for sin and His sovereign determination not to be overthrown by it. This God will fight against the proud, but He will give grace to the humble (James 4:6; 1 Peter 5:5; Psalm 138:6).

Faced with the gravity of this dilemma and driven by an imperious compulsion for lawlessness, the heathen opted for the short-run pleasures of sin and against the long-run rewards of conformity to the nature of God. With "eternity's values in view" he chose the temporal vanities. But he had to live with himself. And this demanded a rationalization. He who does not wish to take God into account can tune Him out. This is what Paul tells us they did. If one does not wish to deal with God he can always rule that God does not exist. That this is totally irrational is obvious, but that is not the point. For the moment the decision to declare non-existent Him Who eternally and everlastingly exists, gives temporary relief from the panic which otherwise would drive us to insanity.

Some have questioned that κατέχω (#2071) means "to hold down" or "to suppress." Deissmann points to an ostracon text which reads Κρόνος ὁ κατέχων τὸν θυμὸν ὅλων τῶν ἀνθρώπων, which illuminates κατεχόντων of verse 18. "Cronos, thou who restrains the wrath of all men. . ." (Adolph Deissmann, *Light From the Ancient East*, 306). Thus the heathen held down (restrained, held in check, "smothered" - ((Montgomery)) ) the truth. That is, they refused to allow the truth to correct their morals and lead them to repentance. Their problem was not intellectual; it was moral. Rejected light results in darkness (Mt.6:23). Rejected wisdom is replaced by vacuous and vapid stupidity. Thus they became philosophical fools. When did they become thus foolish? When they sat down together to discuss it. It was during their philosophical dialogues (ἐν τοῖς διαλογισμοῖς). If one wishes with sufficient intensity to believe something which he knows is false, it is easier to accomplish this if he has the help of others who also wish the same thing. It is more difficult to brainwash one's self. One unregenerate philosopher alone can achieve stupidity but the ignorance grows in quantum leaps if he can share his thoughts with others who wish to arrive at the same godless conclusion. The result is that the uncomprehending heart is darkened (2 Cor.4:4).

It is ironic that man's mental capacity which enabled him first to know God then enabled him to rationalize his philosophy to reject God. The arbiter is his will. He wants to sin; he does not want to accept the moral commitment to a powerful, sovereign, intelligent and holy God. Man goes to hell, not because of intellectual incapacity, but because of a stubborn will to sin without regard to the consequences. "If any man will do his will he shall know of the doctrine. . . " (John 7:17). This also means that if any man wills not to do his will he shall not know. When the sinner wills to turn against God, the dynamo in his brain drives him to foolishness as quickly as it would have guided him to wisdom if he had willed in the other direction.

With reference to σκοτίζω see Romans 11:9,10; Eph.4:17,18. Since a sinner has a good mind he must use it to maintain his personal respectability. He must bring it into subjection to his depraved flesh. He must convince himself that God wants him to sin, or he must convince himself that God does not exist. Thus, in

*Verse 22 - "Professing themselves to be wise, they became fools."*

φάσκοντες εἶναι σοφοὶ ἐμωράνθησαν,

φάσκοντες (pres.act.part.nom.pl.masc.of φάσκω, adverbial, modal) 3622.
εἶναι (pres.inf.of εἰμί, object infinitive in indirect discourse) 86.
σοφοὶ (nom.pl.masc.of σοφός, predicate nominative) 949.
ἐμωράνθησαν (3d.per.pl.aor.pass.ind.of μωραίνω, ingressive) 444.

*Translation - "As they proclaimed themselves to be wise men, they were turned into fools."*

**Comment:** In the process of affirming that they were wise men, by that process they were turned into vapid fools. *Cf.*#'s 444 and 3622. φάσκω indicates great dogma. The psychologist, listening to the strident proclamations of notable erudtion by the atheist, who is trying to convince himself that there is no God, is reminded of the Queeen's observation to Hamlet as they sat watching the play. Hamlet had asked,

Madam, how like you this play?

to which she replied,

The lady doth protest too much, methinks.

Shakespeare, *Hamlet,* Acts III, Scene 2, line 242

The academic poverty of atheism, deism, agnosticism, existentialism and theological modernism is a phenomenon that elicits amazement. It was David who observed that only "the fool hath said in his heart, There is no God" (Psalm 14:1). The declaration that God does not exist is a dogma that requires evidential support. No true scientist would ever make such a statement. The best (or worst) that he could do, if he is honest and a true man of science, with the proper understanding of the scientific method, would be to say that he does not know whether there is a God or not. If he says that, we applaud his honesty and objectivity and pray that he may find by faith Him Whom he cannot find by empirical evidence. But if he should say, "There is no God" we should be required to ask for his evidence and insist that he confine it to sense perception. If he said that he made a careful search throughout the universe, both with microscope and telescope and found Him not, we could well suggest that while the scientist was looking in one place, God was in another. If the scientist replied that he had looked *everywhere at once,* he would be affirming that he was omnipresent. But omnipresence is an attribute of deity. Only God is omnipresent. So, if the scientist said that he was capable of being everywhere present at the same time he would be saying that he was God. A man, who says that he is a god, and then denies his own existence is a fool.

The only logical ground for the atheist is existentialism. For if God is not, but matter is, then mind is not and we live in a materialistic world of randomness. In such a world only fools will speak of the bifurcation between right and wrong, the just and the unjust, the true and the false. In such a world man is the helpless victim of an environment over which he has no control. He is responsible for nothing that he does and his notion that he thinks is only an illusion. There are no civil rights. The rule is that of the claw and fang. The strong will survive, but only until he encounters something stronger and then oblivion. This is the thinking of the radical empiricist.

And yet, if you should think that he is not a fool, hear him talk!

DesCartes, the father of modern rationalsim, bifurcated between subject and object. The subject is one entity; the object is the other. Existentialism denies this and attacks DesCartes with the dogmatic fervor, zeal and gusto unworthy of an existentialist who begins by saying that he is not sure of anything! If there is no difference between subject and object then communication is impossible, since words are only symbols that cannot convey true meaning. If this be true then the speaker is speaking only to himself and the listener is listening only to himself and no thought is conveyed from the one to the other. Phenomonology accounts for everything and there are no noumena. Since no two cultural backgrounds are identical each biped (we dare not call them men or suggest that they have minds) brings to each word he hears a different meaning. Words convey no meaning since there is no meaning in a random world. Therefore there is no difference between exegesis and eisegesis and the one who is trying to discover from his study of diction, grammar and syntax what was meant by what was said or written is wasting his time. For the existentialist the speaker or writer has no meaning for anyone other than himself and if he did have meaning for another he could not convey it.

Projective technique causes one phenomonologist to see one thing in Rorschach's ink blots and another something else, while neither is seeing anything that is really there. We bring to church or to the political rally our own construction upon all that we will hear and go away confirmed in our opinion that we were correct all along and that all others are fools and madmen. Hence life has no meaning, words can have no meaning and it is a waste of time to talk. It is also a waste of time to make signs, since a gesture is only a substitute for a word, be the gesture obscene or genteel.

All of this the speaker from Duke University told us in the conference on religion at Emory University. Yet when he told us with such persuasion that communication was impossible he was quite confident that he was communicating to us. The fact that I understood what he was trying to say, even though I did not believe a word of it, was proof that he was talking nonesense. For if he had been speaking truth his meaning would have escaped all of us who sat listening.

If the existentialists are correct and the atheist who says that he is sure that there is no God is correct, then they ought both to be stop talking. Since he does not - nay, verily he talks even more when he senses that he is not believed, his speech becomes that of a vapid, vacuous fool. One wishes to ask, "Whom are you trying to convince?"

*Verse 23 - "And changed the glory of the uncorruptible God into an image made like to corruptible man, and to birds, and fourfooted beasts, and creeping things."*

καὶ ἤλλαξαν τὴν δόξαν τοῦ ἀφθάρτου θεοῦ ἐν ὁμοιώματι εἰκόνος φθαρτοῦ ἀνθρώπου καὶ πετεινῶν καὶ πετραπόδων καὶ ἑρπετῶν.

καὶ (adjunctive conjunction joining verbs) 14.
ἤλλαξαν (3d.per.pl.aor.act.ind.of ἀλλάσσω, constative) 3097.
τὴν (acc.sing.fem.of the article in agreement with δόξαν) 9.
δόξαν (acc.sing.fem.of δόξα, direct object of ἤλλαξαν) 361.
τοῦ (gen.sing.masc.of the article in agreement with θεοῦ) 9.

#3802 ἀφθάρτου (gen.sing.masc.of ἄφθαρτος, in agreement with θεοῦ).

immortal - 1 Tim.1:17.
incorruptible - 1 Cor.9:25; 15:52; 1 Pet.1:4,23.
not corruptible - 1 Pet.3:4.
uncorruptible - Rom.1:23.

*Meaning:* α privative plus        φθαρτός (#3804), from φθείρω (#4119). Hence, incapable of being defiled, corrupted or destroyed. Viable. Non-degradable. Divine characteristic of God - Rom.1:23; 1 Tim.1:7; 1 Peter 1:23 (of the Holy Spirit); with reference to the Christian's reward - 1 Cor.9:25; 1 Pet.1:4; with reference to the resurrected body - 1 Cor.15:52; the human spirit of the Christian woman - 1 Pet.3:4.

θεοῦ (gen.sing.masc.of θεός, possession) 124.
ἐν (preposition with the locative, instrumental use) 80.

#3803 ὁμοιώματι (loc.sing.neut.of ὁμοίωμα, means).

shape - Rev.9:7.
likeness - Rom.6:5; 8:3; Phil.2:7.
made like - Rom.1:23.
similitude - Rom.5:14.

*Meaning: Cf.* ὁμοιόω (#575), ὅμοιοω   (#923); ὁμοίως (#1425); ὁμοίωσις (#5131); ὁμοιότης (#4950). Hence, that which has been made after the likeness of someone or something; a likeness. Followed by an ablative of comparison - corruptible man, birds, animals, serpents - Rom.1:23; Adam's sin - Rom.5:14; death - Rom.6:5; sinful flesh - Rom.8:3; of normal human nature - Phil.2:7; followed by ὅμοιοι and a dative of comparison - Rev.9:7.

εἰκόνος (abl.sing.fem.of εἰκών, comparison) 1421.

#3804 φθαρτοῦ (abl.sing.masc.of φθαρτός, in agreement with ἀνθρώπου).

corruptible - Rom.1:23; 1 Cor.9:25; 15:53,54; 1 Pet.1:23.
corruptible things - 1 Pet.1:18.

*Meaning: Cf.* ἄφθαρτος (#3802). Corruptible, destructible, non-viable, perishable. Always (except in 1 Pet.1:18) in the New Testament in opposition to ἄφθαρτος. With reference to man - Rom.1:23; a crown - 1 Cor.9:25; bodies of the dead - 1 Cor.15:53,54; human sperm - 1 Pet.1:23; silver and gold - 1 Pet.1:18.

ἀνθρώπου (abl.sing.masc.of ἄνθρωπος, comparison) 341.
καὶ (adjunctive conjunction joining nouns) 14.
πετεινῶν (abl.pl.neut.of πετεινόν, comparison) 615.
καὶ (adjunctive conjunction joining nouns) 14.
τετραπόδων (abl.pl.masc.of τετράπους, comparison) 3219.
καὶ (adjunctive conjunction joining nouns) 14.
ἑρπετῶν (abl.pl.neut.of ἑρπετόν, comparison) 3220.

*Translation - "And they exchanged the glory of the indestructible God for an image that looked like a biodegradable man and birds and fourfooted animals and serpents."*

**Comment:** ἐν ὁμοιώματι εἰκόνος - "by means of a likeness of an image of a destructible man . . ." God is immortal, imperishable, indestructible, changeless, viable, non-biodegradable. The opposite adjectives apply to the human species and to birds, animals and snakes and other forms of life that creep upon the earth.

The idolater has made God into his image. The irony is that in doing so he used the intellect that God gave to him when He created him in His image. Man has turned his highest gift from God - his power to reason - against God and used it to change God's glory of incorruptibility into the degradation of his own capacity for corruption. The idol is a god who maintains the same sordid moral standards of the man who made him.

If one does not wish to conform to the moral standards of his current deity, yet wishes to remain religious, he can accomplish this by changing deities. There are many deities - as many as the imagination of a fallen man can contrive. And each has its own level of morality. The advantage lies in the fact that man çan select the god whose morals are on the same level as his own. If his current god is too Victorian the man can always downgrade to one on his own selected level. To say, "I am religious and as good as god" is the same as "I am religious and god is no better than I am." The trick is to find the god whose moral standards are such as to allow me to live with them in comfort. Thus the inebriated Greek worshipped in the temple of Bacchus, a jolly, fat little fellow who never seemed to know when he had had enough. The belligerent bully with a penchant for knocking his brother-in-law's block off could always stop on the way to the field of battle at the temple of Mars, who was famous for pugilism. The nymphomaniac and her satyr escort poured out libations to Aphrodite. The Pantheon offered a wide choice. The roster of Greek and Roman deities contained the names of a depraved lot of reprobates who elevated to the level of godly dignity the sins which the Greeks and Romans were determined to commit. It is a convenient system! The worshipper can indulge his urge to be religious without the embarrassment of being rebuked for his sinful behavior. He is particularly proud of his accomplishment because he utilized his own resources in bringing it about. He arranged the system so by his own mental powers. What a brilliant idea! Of course, one must be religious - even Christian if one can find a way to change the definition of the term, although one need not bother, since the sociologists, given time, will change it for him, but one need not upgrade his ethics. It is so much easier to downgrade the ethics of the gods. In either case there is moral conformity.

In a strange and convoluted fashion some so-called holiness sects have done the same thing, although they have not intended to emulate the heathen. On the contrary they wish to be known not only as Christians, but as sinless Christians. Just as the Greeks and Romans said, "I am as holy as god" when they meant, "God is as sinful as I" so some holiness preachers say, "I do no sin" when what they mean is "Nothing that I do is sin." The difficulty with both the Greeks and the holiness preachers is that the sovereign God of the Bible has defined true holiness and man is not at liberty to change the definition. What some people call mistakes and weaknesses, the Bible calls sin.

Once the heathen had decided that since man could not be like god, it was proper for god to be like man. Once the deity is forced upon the toboggan slide the only direction possible is down. Thus it was not long until god ceased to look like a man. Now he looked like a bird - a peacock perhaps but later like a buzzard. But at least he was allowed to fly above the earth, until he was demoted again to the animal kingdom and ultimately to the snakes in the grass, going on his belly and eating dust.

In modern society the Pantheon roster is not composed of lifeless idols of stone, gold and silver. We put our gods upon a pedestal before they die - the stars of the silver screen, television personalities, football heros, electronic evangelists - even politicians!

Idolatry is material and phenomenal. Man must worship that which he can handle and see. His theology is phenomenal, not noumenal. Salesmen often speak of the difficulty in selling an intangible, like an insurance contract. It is so much easier to sell a new car or a bottle of wine or a banana split. Fallen man, dead to the supersensible realities and contemptuous of the long run analysis, bereft of faith and immune to true sophistication must worship, to be sure, but he must worship something tangible and sensuous. With no appreciation for the spiritual he is left only with the physical - a physical creature in a physical environment, characterized by too many people and too few resources to meet their needs - thus a society of scarcity where the law of the claw and fang must operate so that the fit can survive. Perhaps we can have a moment of silent meditation for those who did not.

Once the heathen decision to downgrade God was made, there was no remedy but judgment. If it has ever been supposed that man on the moral downgrade can select the spot where he will stop, never to descend to a lower level, let us read on.

*Verse 24 - "Wherefore God also gave them up to uncleanness through the lusts of their own hearts, to dishonour their own bodies between themselves."*

Διὸ παρέδωκεν αὐτοὺς ὁ θεὸς ἐν ταῖς ἐπιθυμίαις τῶν καρδιῶν αὐτῶν εἰς ἀκαθαρσίαν τοῦ ἀτιμάζεσθαι τὰ σώματα αὐτῶν ἐν αὐτοῖς,

Διό (consecutive conjunction) 1622.

παρέδωκεν (3d.per.sing.aor.act.ind.of παραδίδωμι, constative) 368.

αὐτοὺς (acc.pl.masc.of αὐτός, direct object of παρέδωκεν) 16.

ὁ (nom.sing.masc.of the article in agreement with θεός) 9.

θεὸς (nom.sing.masc.of θεός, subject of παρέδωκεν) 124.

ἐν (preposition with the locative, instrumental use) 80.

ταῖς (loc.pl.fem.of the article in agreement with ἐπιθυμίαις) 9.

ἐπιθυμίαις (loc.pl.fem.of ἐπιθυμία, cause) 2186.

τῶν (abl.pl.fem.of the article in agreement with καρδιῶν) 9.

καρδιῶν (abl.pl.fem.of καρδία, source) 432.

αὐτῶν (gen.pl.masc.of αὐτός, possession) 16.

εἰς (preposition with the accusative of extent) 140.

ἀκαθαρσίαν (acc.sing.fem.of ἀκαθαρσία, extent) 1467.

τοῦ (gen.sing.neut.of the article, articular infinitive, purpose) 9.

ἀτιμάζεσθαι (pres.pass.inf.of ἀτιμάζω, purpose) 2390.

τὰ (acc.pl.neut.of the article in agreement with σώματα) 9.

σώματα (acc.pl.neut.of σῶμα, general reference) 507.

αὐτῶν (gen.pl.masc.of αὐτός, possession) 16.

ἐν (preposition with the locative with plural pronouns) 80.

αὐτοῖς (loc.pl.masc.of αὐτός, place) 16.

*Translation - "Therefore God abandoned them unto uncleanness because of the lusts of their hearts with the result that their bodies are violated among themselves."*

**Comment:** Διό the consecutive conjunction introduces the result clause. God saw the decision of the heathen to reject His holiness. It was willfully arrived at, with full knowledge of the consequences (verse 32). It was an act of hypocrisy as they were intent upon maintaining their image as religious people. These people were neither agnostics nor atheists. They were polytheists, willing to create as many gods as necessary to meet their needs, even though they were aware that none of the gods they created were able to create the world with the scientific regularity and uniformity which they had observed. Nor had their substitute deities given them the power of reason.

Once a decision like this is made all moral standards are gone. There is nothing either good or evil. Situation ethics - the religion of the secular humanist becomes the rule. And as no two situations are alike, there can be no absolute standard of morality. This means that in their view every man was "free" (!) to do all that his heart suggested. τῶν καρδιῶν αὐτῶν - an ablative of source, tells us where the motivation for their thoughts and behavior came from. *Cf.* Mk.7:21-23; Jeremiah 17:9. Apparently there is no limit to the depths of degradation to which the unregenerate heart will not lead us. *Cf.* Gen.6:5,6. The depravity of sexual perversion knows no bounds. The physical drive to commit sin in intense. *Cf.*#2186 for the degree of intensity of temptation - it is more than desire; it is lust, in an evil sense. Once the mind has rejected God every ounce of bodily energy cries out for sin. The unregenerate libido is imperious in its demands.

Because of this (ἐν ταῖς ἐπιθυμίαις) God abandoned them to the slavery of their own fierce physical drives. Thus the people who wanted to be free ended up enslaved to themselves. *Cf.* Rom.6:16; John 8:33,34. τοῦ ἀτιμάζεσθαι is epexegetic, *i.e.* it serves to explain εἰς ἀκαθαρσίαν. There are many kinds of uncleanness. This type is homosexuality, an outrage against the human body. Other epexegetic uses of τοῦ and the infinitive are found in Rom.7:3; 8:12; 1 Cor.10:13. When a person rejects the God Who made him he has nothing left to respect expect himself. Yet, having rejected the Creator of his body, there is no reason why he should not disgrace and insult his own body also. The ultimate disgrace is suicide - a totally irrational act, but it is only the logical result of the irrationality involved in rejecting God. *Cf.* Romans 1:22.

Many modern sexologists, who pose as psychology and psychiatric authorities openly advocate the practice among consenting adults of anything and everything that gives pleasure, without regard to how bizarre, extragavent and eccentric the act might be. Once we redefine natural law and set its patterns of normality in paths beside those set by the Creator, there is no limit to their deviation. Paul discusses this further in verse 26.

*Verse 25 - "Who changed the truth of God into a lie, and worshipped and served the creature more than the Creator, who is blessed forever. Amen."*

οἵτινες μετήλλαξαν τὴν ἀλήθειαν τοῦ θεοῦ ἐν τῷ φεύδει, καὶ ἐσεβάσθησαν καὶ ἐλάτρευσαν τῇ κτίσει παρὰ τὸν κτίσαντα, ὅς ἐστιν εὐλογητὸς εἰς τοὺς αἰῶνας. ἀμήν.

οἵτινες (nom.pl.masc.of ὅστις, indefinite relative pronoun, subject of μετήλλαξαν) 163.

#3805 μετήλλαξαν (3d.per.pl.aor.act.ind.of μεταλλάσσω, constative).

change - Romans 1:25,26.

*Meaning:* A combination of μετά (#50) and ἀλλάσσω (#3097). Hence, to exchange one thing for another. God's truth for a lie - Rom.1:25; a heterosexual for a homosexual sex partner - Rom.1:26.

τὴν (acc.sing.fem.of the article in agreement with ἀλήθειαν) 9.
ἀλήθειαν (acc.sing.fem.of ἀλήθεια, direct object of μετήλλαξαν) 1416.
τοῦ (gen.sing.masc.of the article in agreement with θεοῦ) 9.
θεοῦ (gen.sing.masc.of θεός, possession) 124.
ἐν (preposition in a pregnant use with the locative) 80.
φεύδει (loc.sing.masc.of φεῦδος, means) 2388.
καὶ (adjunctive conjunction joining verbs) 14.

#3806 ἐσεβάσθησαν (3d.per.pl.1st.aor.mid.ind.of σεβάζομαι, ingressive).

worship - Romans 1:25.

*Meaning:* Cf. σέβας - "reverence." σέβασμα (#3411); σεβαστός (#3644); σέβω (#

1149). Hence, to fear; be afraid of; in later Greek, to honor religiously; worship. With reference to idol worship - Romans 1:25.

καὶ (adjunctive conjunction joining verbs) 14.

ἐλάτρευσαν (3d.per.pl.aor.act.ind.of λατρεύω, ingressive) 366.

τῇ (dat.sing.fem.of the article in agreement with κτίσει) 9.

κτίσει (dat.sing.fem.of κτίσις, indirect object of ἐλάτρευσαν) 2633.

παρὰ (preposition with the accusative - "rather than") 154.

τὸν (acc.sing.masc.of the article in agreement with κτίσαντα) 9.

κτίσαντα (1st.aor.act.part.acc.sing.masc.of κτίζω, substantival, extent) 1284.

ὅς (nom.sing.masc.of ὅς, definite relative pronoun, subject of ἐστιν) 65.

ἐστιν (3d.per.sing.pres.ind.ofd εἰμί, static) 86.

εὐλογητὸς (nom.sing.masc.of εὐλογητός, predicate adjective) 1849

εἰς (preposition with the accusative, time extent) 140.

τοὺς (acc.pl.masc.of the article in agreement with αἰῶνας) 9.

αἰῶνας (acc.pl.masc.of αἰών, time extent) 1002.

ἀμήν (explicative) 466.

*Translation - "Who traded the truth of God for a lie, and began to worship and serve the creature rather than the Creator, Who is blessed for ever! Amen!"*

**Comment:** οἵτινες is indefinite since Paul is talking about a class of people and not specifying individuals. Cf.#3805 - They exchanged (not changed) - *i.e.* they traded what they had (God's truth), because they did not like it, for its opposite (a lie) because the lie was in harmony with their inclinations. Thus Paul unmasks their intellectual harlotry. Honest sinners - and there are some - openly state that they would rather base their philosophy upon a lie so that they can indulge their lusts. But they do not worship the lie which they have received in the exchange. It is a lie and they know it and are not afraid to admit that it is false, but they are willing to accept the consequences. Karl Marx was honest enough to say that he did not believe in any god, either the God of the Bible or one of his own making. But the unfortunate clowns whom Paul is describing here insist upon being religious, even though it is upon their own terms. So they abandoned the God Whose power and intelligence they had come to appreciate as they examined what He had created, and of Whose holiness they were aware, when they listened to the voice of conscience, and began to bow before and worship a god of their own design. Now as creators of gods the gods they created were made in the image of the creators. The first units of the deity production line looked like men, but the models were improved as gods looking like birds, animals and snakes came from the factories. Demetrius of Ephesus was still putting out an old line, long since phased out by the more advanced designers. His goddess still looked like a human being. Apparently they felt that the progression from men, beyond birds and animals to snakes represented improvement. One is inclined to agree when we note the enormity of their sins. Neither ornithologists, zoologists or

herpetologists have reported homosexuality as characteristic behavior of birds, animals or reptiles. There are some things that a snake will not do. A god that looks like a snake therefore is better than one that looks like a man, but no god of human design is acceptable to the Creator of the universe.

Thus Mars, Baachus, Aphrodite, Zeus, Vulcan, Juno, Janus *et al* ⅃ the contributions of the Greeks and Romans, while the barbarians gave us Baal, Moloch, Ra, Ashtoreth and Ishtar. *Cf.* Acts 7:42.

Note παρά here with the accusative, meaning "rather than," "more than," or "better than."

Satan operates his program on lies (#2388) because he cannot abide the Truth (John 8:44). *Cf.* 2 Thess.2:9,11 for a reference to the "big lies" *e.g.* organic evolution, Anti-Christ is God, existentialism in its extreme form, ethical relativism, secular humanism, *et al.*. There will be no lies or liars in heaven, though all of us who will be there were liars before we found the truth in Christ (Rev.21:27; 22:15). Lies and liars are diametrically opposed to the truth (1 John 2:21,27).

"They traded . . . κ.τ.λ." It was a deliberate, conscious decision - an act of will about something they had thought about. They chose and God allowed their decision to stand and yield its inevitable results. None of them could have anticipated the result that would follow their rejection of God and the substitution of their own philosophy. This is because they assumed that their motives were pure and progressive since it is obvious that they thought that their minds were superior to God's. Why else would they have presumed to improve upon the Forever Blessed God of Creation? They overestimated their intelligence and they underestimated their capacity for depraved behavior and the social, economic and political chaos which was certain to follow. Nor do the "nice" infidels in modern times. Witness the homosexual, effeminate, existential modernist preacher or philosophy professor, who would not swat a fly or stoop to anything gross. If they are being "good" it is not for the right reasons. When the economics of overpopulation on this planet has brought about the struggle for survival, everywhere, as it already has in much of the world, the true potential for evil that lurks in the unregenerate heart will manifest itself.

One wonders if Walter Lippmann were still alive, would he look about him and defend his position that constructive morals need not be associated with Christianity, as fruit to root. It was his view that the secular world produced moral values, equal in lofty character to those of the New Testament, and that the decline of theism in an evolutionary world society need not signal the social chaos which Paul describes in our passage. *Cf. Public Opinion* (1922), *A Preface to Morals* (1929), *The Good Society* (1937) and *Essays in the Public Philosophy* (1955). Lippmann died in 1974.

One marvels at the naivete behind the optimism of Alvin Toffler, who warned us about *Future Shock* a decade ago and has recently calmed our fears with *The Third Wave.*

The postmillenialists, who still retain a modicum of confidence in "thus saith the Lord" although they do not understand what He said, are talking about "confident despair" and the "theology of hope." The scholarly social scientists outside of Christ are pessimistic. Occasionally one finds a Polly Anna who suggests that "Maybe we will think of something."

No one at this writing knows when the Lord will return, but though we do not know what is in the future, we know Who is in the future. The Christian therefore has adequate ground for optimism.

The growing incidence of homosexuality and the permissive if not exculpatory attitude of society toward it supports Paul's view in our passage that when man abandons the theology of the Word of God, moral standards decline and society disintegrates. The problem is not educational. As we approach the last days of the last days (Heb.1:2) travel and communication and therefore "knowledge shall be increased" (Dan.12:4). Men are "ever learning, and never able to come to the knowledge of the truth" (2 Tim.3:7). Science has made quantum leaps in the direction of omniscience, especially since the contribution of Einstein, but there seems to be an inverse relation between what unregenerate man knows and the way he behaves. The scientific genius becomes the moral moron. This is not to say that all super-intellectuals with advanced educational attainments have abandoned the moral standards of the New Testament. But the trend in modern society is in that direction. Sodom and Gomorrah are no longer only tragic stories of the past. They are front page copy. The morals of the antediluvians are emulated in the days of "the coming of the Son of Man" (Mt.25:37).

Verses 26 and 27 are devoted to a description of homosexuality that leaves little to the imagination.

*Verse 26 - "For this cause God gave them up unto vile affections: for even their women did change the natural use into that which is against nature."*

διὰ τοῦτο παρέδωκεν αὐτοὺς ὁ θεὸς εἰς πάθη ἀτιμίας. αἴ τε γὰρ θήλειαι αὐτῶν μετήλλαξαν τὴν φυσικὴν χρῆσιν εἰς τὴν παρὰ φύσιν,

διὰ (preposition with the accusative, cause) 118.
τοῦτο (acc.sing.neut.of οὗτος, cause) 93.
παρέδωκεν (3d.per.sing.aor.act.ind.of παραδίδωμι, constative) 368.
αὐτοὺς (acc.pl.masc.of αὐτός, direct object of παρέδωκεν) 16.
ὁ (nom.sing.masc.of the article in agreement with θεὸς) 9.
θεὸς (nom.sing.masc.of θεός, subject of παρέδωκεν) 124.
εἰς (preposition with the accusative of extent) 140.

#3807 πάθη (acc.pl.neut.of πάθος, extent).

affection- Rom.1:26.
inordinate affection - Col.3:5.
lust - 1 Thess.4:5.

*Meaning:* Cf. πάθημα (#3919) and παθητός (#3666). An affection, emotion, passion, intense desire. In profane Greek in either a good or evil sense. In the New Testament only in contexts indicating evil. Differs from ἐπιθυμία (#2186) which presents vice in action, whereas πάθος is passive. ἐπιθυμία is evil desire. πάθος is ungovernable desire (Thayer). Followed by a genitive of description - Rom.1:26; by an ablative of source - 1 Thess.4:5; absolutely in Col.3:5.

*(Note: At this point in the preliminary research for* The Renaissance New Testament, *a project that required more than ten years, the Revised Standard*

*Version of the New Testament appeared. While there was no anticipation of the decline in popularity of the King James Version, which decline happily has not developed, there was an expectation that the Revised Standard Version would be widely accepted. This expectation happily has also been realized. Accordingly the decision was made that, beginning with ἀτιμίας (#3808) and including all the Greek words which occur after this point, the exhaustive analytical concordance feature of the work would include the listings both of the King James and the Revised Standard Versions. It has been necessary for those who wish to study in depth all of the Greek vocabulary from #1 through #3807 to consult the King James Version. From this point on to the end of the work (#s 3808 through 5443 in Revelation 22:11) the student can use either one or both of the translations).*

**#3808** ἀτιμίας (gen.sing.fem.of ἀτιμία, description).

King James Version

dishonour - Romans 9:21; 1 Cor.15:43; 2 Cor.6:8; 2 Tim.2:20.
reproach - 2 Cor.11:21.
shame - 1 Cor.11:14.
vile - Romans 1:26.

Revised Standard Version

menial use - Romans 9:21.
dishonour - 1 Cor.15:43; 2 Cor.6:8.
ignoble - 2 Tim.2:20.
shame - 2 Cor.11:21.
degrading - 1 Cor.11:14.
dishonorable - Romans 1:26.

*Meaning: Cf.* ἄτιμος (#1102). A combination of α privative and τιμάω (#1142). Hence, without honor; disgraceful; opposed to τιμήν - Rom.9:21; 2 Tim.2:20; opposed to δόξα - 1 Cor.15:43; 2 Cor.6:8; shame - 2 Cor.11:21; 1 Cor.11:14.

αἱ (nom.pl.fem.of the article in agreement with θήλειαι) 9.
τε (ascensive particle) 1408.
γὰρ (emphatic conjunction) 105.
θήλειαι (nom.pl.fem.of θῆλυς, subject of μετήλλαξαν) 1287.
αὐτῶν (gen.pl.masc.of αὐτός, relationship) 16.
μετήλλαξαν (3d.per.pl.aor.act.ind.of μεταλλάσσω, constative) 3805.
τὴν (acc.sing.fem.of the article in agreement with φυσικήν) 9.

**#3809** φυσικὴν (acc.sing.fem.of φυσικός, in agreement with χρῆσιν).

King James Version

natural - Romans 1:26,27; 2 Peter 2:12.

Revised Standard Version

instinct - 2 Peter 2:12.

natural - Romans 1:26,27.

*Meaning: Cf.* φύσις (#3811). That which is produced by and therefore characteristic of nature; inborn; consistent with natural law; natural; instinctive. As an adjective - τὴν φυσικὴν χρῆσιν - *i.e.* the use normally to be expected in the nature of the case - Rom.1:26,27. Figuratively - "beasts of nature" *i.e.* men who act instinctively in keeping with their nature - 2 Peter 2:12.

**#3810** χρῆσιν (acc.sing.fem.of χρῆσις, direct object of μετήλλαξαν).

King James Version

use - Romans 1:26,27.

Revised Standard Version

relation - Romans 1:26,27.

*Meaning: Cf.* χράομαι (#2447). Use. With reference to the sexual function of women - Rom.1:26; of men - Rom.1:27.

εἰς (preposition with the accusative, predicate accusative, extent) 140.
τὴν (acc.sing.fem.of the article in agreement with φύσιν) 9.
παρά (preposition with the accusative, "beside the mark") 154.

**#3811** φύσιν (acc.sing.fem.of φύσις, predicate accusative, opposition).

King James Version

kind - James 3:7.
nature - Rom.1:26; 2:14,27; 11:24,24; 1 Cor.11:14; Gal.2:15; 4:8; Eph.2:3; 2 Peter 1:4.
natural - Rom.11:21,24.
mankind - James 3:7.

Revised Standard Version

unnatural - Rom.1:26.
natural - Rom.11:21,24.
nature - Rom.2:14; 11:24,24; 1 Cor.11:14; Gal.4:8; Eph.2:3; 2 Pet.1:4.
physically - Rom.2:27.
birth - Gal.2:15.
kind - James 3:7.
humankind - James 3:7.

*Meaning: Cf.* φύω (#2197). The nature of things; the force, laws, order or characteristics of nature. The way something should be - with παρά and the accusative - *i.e.* against or "beside the mark," - unnatural - Rom.1:26; in a taxonomy sense - James 3:7,7; Rom.2:27; 11:24,24; Gal.4:8; 2 Pet.1:4; Rom.11:24,24; James 3:7,7. In accord with human nature - Rom.2:14; natural instinct - 1 Cor.11:14; the nature one has by birth - Gal.2:15; Eph.2:3.

*Translation - "Because of this God abandoned them to ungovernable appetites of a dishonorable sort. In fact even their women exchanged the natural function for one that misappropriates nature."*

**Comment:** Paul is often accused of misogony. But he seems here to be surprized by the homosexual practices of women, as though he did not expect it of them as much as he did of men. This interpretation depends, of course, upon our taking τε as ascensive and καί as emphatic, which may or may not be justified, since we have the same idiom in verse 27 with reference to men. Whatever the exegesis here there is no evidence in Scripture that Paul hated women or that he thought of them as being essentially inferior to men. *Cf.* our discussion of the controversial passages *en loc.* Note the predicate use of εἰς πάθη ἀτιμίας and εἰς τὴν παρὰ φύσιν. Once God abandoned them, their depravity knew no bounds. τε is joined in verse 27 with ὁμοίως τε καί - "The women . . . likewise also the men." πάθη ἀτιμίας - an urge, out of control, to commit a degrading act. For παρά and the accusative in an opposition sense, *cf.* Rom.1:26; 4:18; Acts 18:13; Rom.11:24; 16:17. The etymology of παρά will help us. The Sanskrit is *para -* "distant," although Delbruck denies that it is the same word (*Vergl Synt*, I, 755, 761, as cited in Robertson, *Grammar*, 612). Brugmann connects it with the old word *pura* like the Latin *por—*, the Gothic *fayra*, the Anglo-Saxon *fore* and the German *vor.* (*Kurze Vergl.Gr.*, II, 474 and *Griech. Gr.*, 446, as cited in *Ibid.*). Giles thinks the same root furnishes παρός (gen.), παρά (instru.), παραί (dat.), περί (loc.). He also sees kinship in these to πέραν, πέρα and πρός (*Compartive Philology*, 342, as cited in *Ibid.*, 612, 613). We see the sense of παρά in the English *parallel* - "running alongside of" and therefore "missing the mark." A paralegal is not a lawyer, nor is a paramedic a physician, but they are competent within a given sphere of function, but only to a lesser degree. When a runner runs parallel to a path assigned to him in the shorter races of a track-and-field event, he is disqualified, despite the fact that he is running in the same direction as the winner. To hit a target near (alongside, parallel to) the bulls-eye is to miss the mark. Homosexuality is involved in a sex function, but the sex partner in the act places it outside of the natural purpose for which God created sex.

Men also are guilty of this perversion, as we learn in

*Verse 27 - "And likewise also the men, leaving the natural use of the woman, burned in their lust one toward another; men with men working that which is unseemly, and receiving in themselves that recompense of their error, which was meet."*

ὁμοίως τε καὶ οἱ ἄρσενες ἀφέντες τὴν φυσικὴν χρῆσιν τῆς θηλείας ἐξεκαύθησαν ἐν τῇ ὀρέξει αὐτῶν εἰς ἀλλήλους, ἄρσενες ἐν ἄρσεσιν τὴν ἀσχημοσύνην κατεργαζόμενοι καὶ τὴν ἀντιμισθίαν ἣν ἔδει τῆς πλάνης αὐτῶν ἐν ἑαυτοῖς ἀπολαμβάνοντες.

ὁμοίως (adverbial) 1425.

τε (continuative particle) 1408.

καὶ (adjunctive conjunction joining nouns) 14.
οἱ (nom.pl.masc.of the article in agreement with ἄρσενες) 9.
ἄρσενες (nom.pl.masc.of ἄρσην, subject of ἐξεκαύθησαν) 1286.
ἀφέντες (aor.act.part.nom.pl.masc.of ἀφίημι, adverbial, temporal) 319.
τὴν (acc.sing.fem.of the article in agreement with χρῆσιν) 9.
φυσικὴν (acc.sing.fem.of φυσικός, in agreement with χρῆσιν) 3809.
χρῆσιν (acc.sing.fem.of χρῆσις, direct object of ἀφέντες) 3810.
τῆς (gen.sing.fem.of the article in agreement with θηλείας) 9.
θηλείας (gen.sing.fem.of θῆλυς, description) 1287.

**#3812** ἐξεκαύθησαν (3d.per.pl.1st.aor.pass.ind.of ἐκκαίομαι, ingressive).

King James Version

burn - Romans 1:27.

Revised Standard Version

consume - Romans 1:27.

*Meaning:* A combination of ἐκ (#19) and καίω (#453). Literally, to burn up. Metaphorically, to be consumed. Followed by means or cause construction - Romans 1:27.

ἐν (preposition with the locative in an instrumental use) 80.
τῇ (loc.sing.fem.of the article in agreement with ὀρέξει) 9.

**#3813** ὀρέξει (loc.sing.fem.of ὄρεξις, means/cause).

King James Version

lust - Romans 1:27.

Revised Standard Version

passion - Romans 1:27.

*Meaning:* Cf. ὀρέγω (#4726). Desire, longing, craving, appetite, in an evil sense, lust. With reference to male homosexuality - Romans 1:27. The word does not denote evil *per se*, although the context in its only use in the New Testament indicates evil desire.

αὐτῶν (gen.pl.masc.of αὐτός, possession) 16.
εἰς (preposition with the accusative of extent) 140.
ἀλλήλους (acc.pl.masc.of ἀλλήλων, extent) 1487.
ἄρσενες (nom.pl.masc.of ἄρσην, nominative absolute) 1286.
ἐν (preposition with the locative in an instrumental use, association) 80.
ἄρσεσιν (loc.pl.masc.of ἄρσην, association) 1286.
τὴν (acc.sing.fem.of the article in agreement with ἀσχημοσύνην) 9.

**#3814** ἀσχημοσύνην (acc.sing.fem.of ἀσχημοσύνη, direct object of κατεργαζό-μενοι).

King James Version

shame - Revelation 16:15.
that which is unseemly - Romans 1:27.

Revised Standard Version

shameless acts - Romans 1:27.
exposed - Revelation 16:15.

*Meaning:* Cf. ἀσχήμων (#4218); ἀσχημονέω (#4168). Hence, that which is unseemly; an unseemly deed. In Romans 1:27, an unnatural sex act between men; in Rev.16:15, genitals in a metaphorical passage.

**#3815** κατεργαζόμενοι (pres.mid.part.nom.pl.masc.of κατεργάζω, adverbial, complementary).

King James Version

work - 1 Pet.4:3; Rom.7:8; 2 Cor.7:11; 12:12; Rom.15:18; 1:27; Phil.2:12; Rom.4:15; 5:3; 7:8; 2 Cor.7:10; James 1:3; Rom.7:13; 2 Cor.4:17; 7:11; 5:5.
do - Rom.7:15,17,20; Eph.6:13; Rom.2:9; 1 Cor.5:3.
perform - Rom.7:18.
cause - 2 Cor.9:11.

Revised Standard Version

work - Rom.7:8,13; 15:18.
do - 1 Pet.4:3; Rom.7:15; 7:17,18,20; Eph.6:13; Rom.2:9; 1 Cor.5:3.
produce - 2 Cor.7:10,11; James 1:3; 2 Cor.9:11; Rom.5:3.
perform - 2 Cor.12:12.
commit - Rom.1:27.
work out - Phil.2:12.
bring - Rom.4:15.
prepare - 2 Cor.4:17; 5:5.

*Meaning:* A combination of κατά (#98) and ἐργάζομαι (#691). To perform, do, accomplish, achieve -Rom.7:15,17,18,20; 15:18; Eph.6:13; 2 Cor.12:12; Rom.1:27; 2:9; 1 Cor.5:3; 1 Pet.4:3; to work out - Phil.2:12; Rom.4:15; 5:3; 7:8; 2 Cor.7:10; Jam.1:3; Rom.7:13; 2 Cor.4:17; 7:11; 9:11; to make one fit for a thing - 2 Cor.5:5.

καὶ (adjunctive conjunction joining participles) 14.
τὴν (acc.sing.fem.of the article in agreement with ἀντιμισθίαν) 9.

**#3816** ἀντιμισθίαν (acc.sing.fem.of ἀντιμισθία, direct object of ἀπολαμβάνοντες).

King James Version

recompence - Rom.1:27; 2 Cor.6:13.

Revised Standard Version

due penalty - Rom.1:27.
return - 2 Cor.6:13.

*Meaning:* A combination of ἀντί (#237) and μισθός (#441). Hence a reward; payment or recompence in return. That which was justly deserved in an evil sense - Rom.1:27; in a good sense - 2 Cor.6:13.

ἥν (acc.sing.fem.of ὅς, relative pronoun, in agreement with ἀντιμισθίαν) 65.
ἔδει (3d.per.sing.imp.of δεῖ) 1207.
τῆς (gen.sing.fem.of the article in agreement with πλάνης) 9.
πλάνης (gen.sing.fem.of πλάνη, description) 1684.
αὐτῶν (gen.pl.masc.of αὐτός, possession) 16.
ἐν (preposition with the locative with plural pronouns) 80.
ἑαυτοῖς (loc.pl.masc.of ἑαυτός, place) 288.
ἀπολαμβάνοντες (pres.act.part.nom.pl.masc.of ἀπολαμβάνω, adverbial, complementary) 2131.

*Translation - "And in the same way also the men, after they had abandoned the normal function of women, began to be consumed with their lust for one another - men with men engaging in degrading acts and receiving in return among themselves the consequences of their folly which was inevitable."*

**Comment:** ὁμοίως ties τε of verse 26 to τε καὶ of verse 27. The temporal participle ἀφέντες is also causal. When a man becomes unnatural in his relationship to God he tends to become unnatural, to some degree, in his relationship with others as well. God's order in nature, as it applies to the case before us, provides for a natural attracion of men for women and women for men. The male homosexual described here lost his desire for women. He sought instead for fulfillment in a way that God had not planned. He tried to "improve" upon natural law. In doing so he violated natural law. It was inevitable therefore that he should pay the price.

It has been said that one cannot eat onions and keep it a secret, which is a fanciful way to restate Romans 6:23 - "the wages of sin is death." No one breaks natural law, for natural law is still working perfectly despite the fact that it has been "broken" (transgressed) repeatedly. If all men and women were homosexuals and practised their lifestyle to the exclusion of heterosexuality God's covenant with Adam, that if he would populate the earth, God would provide one from the population who would redeem man from sin, would never have been fulfilled. Homosexuality therefore is a crime, both against God and the human race. One wonders where the homosexual would be if it were true that his father had adopted his lifestyle!

In recent years the homosexuals have mounted a civil rights campaign to assert that their appetites are normal and natural and that they should be accepted in society and protected from all discrimination, despite their lifestyle. The passage before us denies that homosexuality is normal and declares that it is a sin for which God will judge the offender. It was only after and because of man's repudiation of heterosexual love that he turned to homosexual expression. Though some of them make no public profession of faith in Christ, others insist that their conduct is consistent with Christianity, despite the clear teaching of the passage under discussion.

There is a difference between what is Christian and what is legal and/or socially acceptable in a democracy, where the power rests, not in the Bible, but in the will of the people. In view of the fact that the Scripture clearly teaches that at the close of the church age "evil men and seducers will wax worse and worse, deceiving and being deceived" (2 Tim.3:13), it is debateable whether or not Christians are properly advised to spend time, money and effort to use organized political power at the polls to "make American Christian." The so-called Moral Majority is to be congratulated for its zeal, though perhaps given lower marks for its wisdom. The problem lies in the fact that no one knows where we are on God's prophetic clock. Christians have a right to support at the polls men who are pledged to pass laws that follow lines of Christian deportment, but it is not the function of the state to impose standards of Christian morals upon the unsaved, except in cases where sinful freedoms affect the rights of others to life, liberty and property. If we are as close to the Second Coming of Messiah as some think, it is probably a waste of time to attempt to reform America along lines of Christian ethics.

The phrase $\ddot{\alpha}\rho\sigma\epsilon\nu\epsilon\varsigma$ $\dot{\epsilon}\nu$ $\ddot{\alpha}\rho\sigma\epsilon\nu\iota\nu$ is epexegetical. It serves to explain in more detail the clause which follows it - "performing the shameful" *i.e.* engaging in an act that a normal man would be ashamed to do, not because of social disapprobation, but ashamed even if no one ever knew except himself and his partner. Such acts are disgusting, revolting and outrageous to normal people. More than one homosexual has been knocked down for his solicitation. Violence on the part of the normal man solicited should not be condoned, but it can be easily understood and forgiven by other normal people.

The result of homosexuality is inevitable. It follows as the night the day. This is the force of $\mathring{\eta}\nu$ $\mathring{\epsilon}\delta\epsilon\iota$. One cannot transgress God's laws in the physical realm and escape the consequences in the psychological and social realms. Homosexuals become obvious. To the trained observer they stand out vividly in a crowd. If the practise did not come under divine judgment the human race would disappear.

*Verse 28 - "And even as they did not like to retain God in their knowledge, God gave them over to a reprobate mind, to do those things which were not convenient."*

$\kappa\alpha\grave{\iota}$ $\kappa\alpha\vartheta\grave{\omega}\varsigma$ $o\mathring{\upsilon}\kappa$ $\mathring{\epsilon}\delta o\kappa\acute{\iota}\mu\alpha\sigma\alpha\nu$ $\tau\grave{o}\nu$ $\vartheta\epsilon\grave{o}\nu$ $\mathring{\epsilon}\chi\epsilon\iota\nu$ $\mathring{\epsilon}\nu$ $\mathring{\epsilon}\pi\iota\gamma\nu\acute{\omega}\sigma\epsilon\iota$, $\pi\alpha\rho\acute{\epsilon}\delta\omega\kappa\epsilon\nu$ $\alpha\mathring{\upsilon}\tau o\grave{\upsilon}\varsigma$ $\acute{o}$ $\vartheta\epsilon\grave{o}\varsigma$ $\epsilon\mathring{\iota}\varsigma$ $\mathring{\alpha}\delta\acute{o}\kappa\iota\mu o\nu$ $\nu o\mathring{\upsilon}\nu$, $\pi o\iota\epsilon\mathring{\iota}\nu$ $\tau\grave{\alpha}$ $\mu\grave{\eta}$ $\kappa\alpha\vartheta\acute{\eta}\kappa o\nu\tau\alpha$,

*"And since they did not see fit to acknowledge God, God gave them up to a base mind and to improper conduct." - Revised Standard Version.*

καὶ (continuative conjunction) 14.

καθὼς (causal conjunction) 1348.

οὐκ (negative conjunction with the indicative) 130.

ἐδοκίμασαν (3d.per.pl.aor.act.ind.ofd δοκιμάζω, constative) 2493.

τὸν (acc.sing.masc.of the article in agreement with θεὸν) 9.

θεὸν (acc.sing.masc.of θεός, direct object of ἔχειν) 124.

ἔχειν (pres.act.inf.of ἔχω, direct object of ἐδοκίμασαν) 82.

ἐν (preposition with the locative, sphere) 80.

**#3817** ἐπιγνώσει (loc.sing.fem.of ἐπίγνωσις, sphere).

King James Version

knowledge - Phil.1:9; Col.3:10; Rom.10:2; Col.1:9; 1 Tim.2:4; 2 Tim.3:7; Heb.10:26; Rom.3:20; Eph.1:17; Col.1:10; 2 Pet.1:2,3; Eph.4:13; 2 Pet.1:8; 2:20; Rom.1:28.
acknowledgement - Col.2:2.
acknowledging - Philemon 6; 2 Tim.2:25; Titus 1:1.

Revised Standard Version

knowledge - Phil.1:9; Col.3:10; Col.1:9; 2:2; Philemon 6; 1 Tim.2:4; 2 Tim.3:7; Titus 1:1; Heb.10:26; Rom.3:20; Eph.1:17; Col.1:10; 2 Pet.1:2,3; Eph.4:13; 2 Pet.1:8; 2:20.
enlightened - Romans 10:2.
know the truth - 2 Tim.2:25.
acknowledge - Romans 1:28.

*Meaning:* A combination of ἐπί (#47) and γινώσκω (#131). *Cf.* also γνῶσις (#1856); γνώστης (#3652); γνωστός (#1917). An intensified, heightened and perfected knowledge. Used always in the New Testament of metaphysical concepts. Absolutely in Col.3:10; Rom.10:2; 1:28; with αἰσθήσει in Phil.1:9; with τοῦ θελήματος - Col.1:9; Rom.10:2; τοῦ μυστηρίου τοῦ θεοῦ in Col.2:2; παντὸς ἀγαθοῦ - Philemon 6; ἀληθείας in 1 Tim.2:4; 2 Tim.2:25; 3:7; Titus 1:1; Heb.10:26; ἁμαρτίας in Romans 3:20; αὐτοῦ in Eph.1:17; τοῦ θεοῦ in Col.1:10; 2 Pet.1:2,3; τοῦ υἱοῦ τοῦ θεοῦ in Eph.4:13; χριστοῦ in 2 Pet.1:8; τοῦ κυρίου χριστοῦ in 2 Pet.2:20.

παρέδωκεν (3d.per.sing.aor.act.ind.of παραδίδωμι, constative) 368.

αὐτοὺς (acc.pl.masc.of αὐτός, direct object of παρέδωκεν) 16.

ὁ (nom.sing.mac.of the article in agreement with θεὸς) 9.

θεὸς (nom.sing.masc.of θεός, subject of παρέδωκεν) 124.

εἰς (preposition with the accusative of extent) 140.

**#3818** ἀδόκιμον (acc.sing.masc.of ἀδόκιμος, in agreement with νοῦν).

King James Version

castaway - 1 Cor.9:27.

rejected - Heb.6:8.
reprobate - Rom.1:28; 2 Cor.13:5,6,7; 2 Tim.3:8; Titus 1:16.

Revised Standard Version

disqualified - 1 Cor.9:27.
worthless - Heb.6:8.
base - Romans 1:28.
rejected - 2 Tim.3:8.
unfit - Titus 1:16.
fail to meet test - 2 Cor.13:5.
to have failed - 2 Cor.13:7.

*Meaning:* A combination of α privative and δόκιμος (#4042). Hence, disapproved; unable to measure up to an approved standard; unfit. In a philosophical sense - Rom.1:28; 2 Tim.3:8; Titus 1:16; with reference to an infertile field - Heb.6:8; in terms of efficiency in Christian service - 1 Cor.9:27; 2 Cor.13:5,6,7.

νοῦν (acc.sing.masc.of νοῦς, predicate accusative) 2928.
ποιεῖν (pres.act.inf.of ποιέω, epexegetical) 127.
τὰ (acc.pl.neut.of the article in agreement with καθήκοντα) 9.
μὴ (negative conjunction with the participle) 87.
καθήκοντα (pres.part.acc.pl.neut.of καθήκω, substantival, direct object of ποιεῖν) 3582.

*Translation - "And because they decided against including God in their rationale, God abandoned them to a confused mind, to do the things which are indecent."*

**Comment:** The microscope of exegesis brings to light philosophical material that is best and most accurately understood in philosophic terms. καθώς is causal. *Cf.*#2493. They thought it over carefully. The decision was not the result of impulsive judgment. Their conclusion which they reached as a result of close reasoning was that they could not have God as a part of their philosophical system. God did not fit. Some of His characteristics they had come to know (verses 19-21). He was powerful; He was intelligent and He was holy. It was this about God that bothered them. They were not holy, and God's holiness stood in opposition to their desires. If they followed the light that they had about God, His righteous standards would destroy the philosophical model which they had chosen to build. By leaving God out of their system, they reasoned that their rationale possessed the inner consistency to make it viable. The builders rejected the foundation stone. To say that God, therefore abandoned them, is simply to mean that God allowed natural law to run its full course. A man with rational powers which are his because he was created in God's image, still possesses rational power after he rejects God. But alas, it is now a depraved mind, directed by a depraved will and driven by a depraved set of twisted emotions. Hence their mind became ἀδόκιμος (#3818). The infinitive clause is epexegetical. It explains what their depraved mind decided to do - indecent things. Thinking disjunctively because they left out the all-important component, they acted disjunctively. *Cf.* #3582 for the meaning. What they did was not "fit." That is, it introduced the eccentric activity and provided the seeds of their own personality disintegration. And, because their sinful flesh and twisted mind, directed by a perverted will, was a dynamo, they plumbed the depths of depravity described in verses 29-32.

μή with the participle, rather than οὐκ is an evidence of Paul's literary classical Greek scholarship. Most κοινή writers used οὐκ with the participle.

*Verse 29 - "Being filled with all unrighteousness, fornication, wickedness, covetousness, maliciousness: full of envy, murder, debate, deceit, malignity; whisperers, . . . "*

πεπληρωμένους πάσῃ ἀδικίᾳ πονηρίᾳ πλεονεξίᾳ κακίᾳ, μεστοὺς φθόνου φόνου ἔριδος δόλου κακοηθείας, ψιθυριστάς, . . .

*"They were filled with all manner of wickedness, evil, covetousness, malice. Full of envy, murder, strife, deceit, malignity, they are gossips, . . . "*     RSV

πεπληρωμένους (perf.pass.part.acc.pl.masc.of πληρόω, adverbial, causal) 115.

πάσῃ (instru.sing.fem.of πᾶς, in agreement with ἀδικίᾳ, πονηρίᾳ, πλεονεξίᾳ and κακίᾳ) 67.

ἀδικίᾳ (instru.sing.fem.of ἀδικία, means) 2367.

πονηρίᾳ (instru.sing.fem.of πονηρία, means) 1419.

πλεονεξίᾳ (instru.sing.fem.of πλεονεξία, means) 2302.

κακίᾳ (instru.sing.fem.of κακία, means) 641.

μεστοὺς (acc.pl.masc.of μεστός, predicate adjective in agreement with αὐτοὺς) 1468.

φθόνου (abl.sing.masc.of φθόνος, source) 1627.

φόνου (abl.sing.masc.of φόνος, source) 1166.

#3819 ἔριδος (abl.sing.fem.of ἔρις, source).

King James Version

strife - Phil.1:15; 2 Cor.12:20; Gal.5:20; Rom.13:13; 1 Cor.3:3; 1 Tim.6:4.
contention - 1 Cor.1:11; Titus 3:9.
debate - Romans 1:29.

Revised Standard Version

rivalry - Phil.1:15.
quarreling - 1 Cor.1:11; 2 Cor.12:20; Rom.13:13.
strife - Gal.5:20; Rom.1:29; 1 Cor.3:3.
dissension - Titus 3:9; 1 Tim.6:4.

*Meaning: Cf.* ἐριθεία (#3837); ἐρίζω (#983). Hence, brawling, raucous argument; strife of a vocal rather than physical nature. One of the works of the flesh - Gal.5:20; the logical result of apostasy - Romans 1:29; the mark of a backslidden Christian - 1 Cor.1:11; Rom.13:13; 1 Cor.3:3; 2 Cor.12:20; Phil.1:15; 1 Tim.6:4; Titus 3:9.

δόλου (abl.sing.masc.of δόλος, source) 1557.

**#3820** κακοηθείας (abl.sing.fem.of κακοήθεια, source).

King James Version

malignity - Romans 1:29.

Revised Standard Version

malignity - Romans 1:29.

*Meaning: Cf.* κακός (#1388) and ἔθος (#1788). Hence, bad character; depravity; malignant subtlety, malicious craftiness - Romans 1:29. Aristotle defined it - τὸ ἐπὶ τὸ χεῖρον ὑπολαμβάνειν πάντα - "taking everything in an evil way." Seeing evil in everything.

**#3821** ψιθυριστάς (acc.pl.masc.of ψιθυριατής, predicate accusative).

King James Version

whisperers - Romans 1:29.

Revised Standard Version

gossips - Romans 1:29.

*Meaning: Cf.* ψιθυρισμός (#4406). Hence, a whisperer; gossip; secret slanderer - Romans 1:29.

*Translation - "For they have been filled with all wickedness, active evil, greed, evil intent. They are full of envy, murder, strife, deceit, malignity. They are gossips. . . "*

**Comment:** This list of depraved characteristics in verses 29-31 is an example of asyndeton. Paul gains dramatic effect by switching from the instrumental of means to the ablative of source and then, without a copula to a list of substantives. "Filled with . . . κ.τ.λ.. . . Full of . . . κ.τ.λ.. . . Whisperers. . .κ.τ.λ." Note also parechesis (different words of similar sound) in φθόνου φόνου - "envy, murder." κακία is the evil disposition; πονηρία is the active manifestation of it. There is great variety of order of items in the manuscripts, but none of the items are omitted.

This is the inevitable development for apostates who rationalize God and His standards of ethics out of their lives.

*Verse 30 - ". . . backbiters, haters of God, despiteful, proud, boasters, inventors of evil things, disobedient to parents, . . . "*

καταλάλους, θεοστυγεῖς, ὑβριστάς, ὑπερηφάνους, ἀλαζόνας, ἐφευρετὰς κακῶν, γονεῦσιν ἀπειθεῖς,

". . . *slanderers, haters of God, insolent, haughty, boastful, inventors of evil, disobedient to parents,* . . . " *RSV.*

#3822 καταλάλους (acc.pl.masc.of κατάλαλος, predicate accusative, in agreement with αὐτούς).

King James Version

backbiter - Romans 1:30.

Revised Standard Version

slanderers - Romans 1:30.

*Meaning:* A combination of κατά (#98) and λάλος - "speaker". An evil speaker; character assassin; defamer; asperse critic; slur artist - Romans 1:30. This word has not been found outside the New Testament.

#3823 θεοστυγεῖς (acc.pl.masc.of θεοστυγής, predicate accusative, in agreement with αὐτούς).

King James Version

hater of God - Romans 1:30.

Revised Standard Version

haters of God - Romans 1:30.

*Meaning:* A combination of θεός (#124) and στυγέω - "to hate." *Cf.* στυγητός (#4901). Hence, one who hates God - Romans 1:30.

#3824 ὑβριστάς (acc.pl.masc.of ὑβριστής, predicate accusative, in agreement αὐτούς).

King James Version

despiteful - Romans 1:30.
injurious - 1 Tim.1:13.

Revised Standard Version

insolent - Romans 1:30.
insulted - 1 Tim.1:13.

*Meaning: Cf.* ὑβρίζω - "to insult." To offer an affront. "One who, uplifted with pride, either heaps insulting language upon others or does them some shameful act of wrong." (Fritzsche in Thayer, *Lexicon,* 633, 634) - Romans 1:30; 1 Tim.1:13.

ὑπερηφάνους (acc.pl.masc.of ὑπερήφανος, predicate accusative, in agreement with αὐτοὺς) 1830.

**#3825** ἀλαζόνας (acc.pl.masc.of ἀλάζων, predicate accusative, in agreement with αὐτοὺς).

King James Version

boaster - Romans 1:30; 2 Tim.3:2.

Revised Standard Version

boastful - Romans 1:30.
proud - 2 Tim.3:2.

*Meaning: Cf.* ἄλη - "wandering" or "roaming." An empty pretender; boaster, braggart, blowhard, Fourth-of-July orator - Romans 1:30; 2 Tim.3:2.

**#3826** ἐφευρετὰς (acc.pl.masc.of ἐφευρετής predicate accusative, in agreement with αὐτοὺς).

King James Version

inventor - Romans 1:30.

Revised Standard Version

inventor - Romans 1:30.

*Meaning:* A combination of ἐπί (#47) and εὑρετής - "inventor." *Cf.* ἐφευρίσκω - "to find out." An inventor; a contriver - Romans 1:30.

κακῶν (gen.pl.neut.of κακός, description) 1388.
γονεῦσιν (loc.pl.masc.of γονεύς, sphere) 878.
ἀπειθεῖς (acc.pl.masc.of ἀπειθής, predicate accusative, in agreement with αὐτοὺς) 1800.

*Translation - "... slanderers, haters of God, insolent, conceited, braggarts, promoters of evil, disobedient to parents, ..."*

**Comment:** Paul finishes his indictment with a list of substantives. These do not suffer so much from a lack of understanding of God (verses 18-23) as they do from a hatred of Him. Theophobia begins with fear of God and quickly turns to hatred. The braggart with his vain attempt to conceal his insecurity is trying to convince himself. He *sees* nothing that generates fear of God (Romans 3:18) but Paul did not say that he *feels* no fear of God.

Some men who feel inferior, as all should, in contemplation of God, develop fear and hatred. In others inferiority elicits humility, intellectual honesty, faith and love (2 Cor.2:15-17; Acts 13:48).

*Verse 31 - "... without understanding, covenantbreakers, without natural affection, implacable, unmerciful."*

ἀσυνέτους, ἀσυνθέτους, ἀστόργους, ἀνελεήμονας.

*"foolish, faithless, heartless, ruthless." RSV.*

ἀσυνέτους (acc.pl.masc.of ἀσύνετος, predicate accusative, in agreement with αὐτοὺς) 1159.

#3827 ἀσυνθέτους (acc.pl.masc.of ἀσύνθετος, predicate accusative, in agreement with αὐτοὺς).

King James Version

covenant breaker - Romans 1:31

Revised Standard Version

faithless - Romans 1:31.

*Meaning:* α privative plus σύν (#1542) plus θέτος - "placed," "set" from τίθημι (#455). Hence, not standing with. Inconstant. One who breaks his promise. One whose word cannot be trusted - Romans 1:31.

#3828 ἀστόργους (acc.pl.masc.of ἄστοργος, predicate adjective, in agreement with αὐτοὺς).

King James Version

without natural affection - Romans 1:31; 2 Tim.3:3.

Revised Standard Version

heartless - Romans 1:31.
inhuman - 2 Tim.3:3.

*Meaning:* α privative plus στοργή - "love of kindred." Hence, without the natural feelings of affection normally felt for one's family. Heartless, inhuman, cruelly indifferent - Romans 1:31; 2 Tim.3:3.

#3829 ἀνελεήμονας (acc.pl.masc.of ἀνελεήμων, predicate accusative, in agreement with αὐτοὺς).

King James Version

unmerciful - Romans 1:31.

Revised Standard Version

ruthless - Romans 1:31.

*Meaning:* α privative plus ἐλεήμων (#429). Hence, without mercy, merciless, ruthless - Romans 1:31.

*Translation - "Willfully stupid, unwilling to keep promises, heartless, showing no mercy."*

**Comment:** *Cf.* verse 21 for help in interpreting ἀσύνετο. It is active, not within itself etymologically, but because of context affiliation. It was not that they were unable to understand, but that they were unwilling to understand. Hence our translation. Verse 21 makes it clear that they did understand. Robertson supports this view. "Συνετός sometimes passive in sense in the old Greek, is always active in the N.T., as in Mt.11:25." (*Grammar*, 1097). But "ἀσύνθετος . . . is made from the middle συντίθημι . . ." which means "to make a covenant." (*Ibid.*) Thus ἀσυνθέτους is middle or passive. Once one has actively thrown God out of his rationale and thus has chosen to be stupid, he cannot avoid becoming the dishonest person that he is - one whose word cannot be trusted. That is why we have a strong and clear body of contract law. The banker has no way of knowing whether the borrower is one of the apostates being described by Paul or not. Thus the honest customer must suffer with the dishonest. Nobody borrows money at the bank without signing a contract which is considered sacrosanct in civil law. The apostate is a covenant breaker by nature. It is to his shortrun advantage to ignore the obligations of his promise. Thus he will do so if he can get away with it.

These accusations do not apply to all the unsaved, but only to those described in our context - *viz.* those who have made the conscious choice of rejecting God and His truth from consideration. Those whom the Holy Spirit will call to salvation are also dishonest on occasion  before they are saved, and many are not wholly honest even after they are saved. David admitted that he may have been hasty when he said that "all men are liars" (Psalm 116:11), but there is no evidence that he revised his estimate upon more mature reflection. In Paul's summation of his indictment against the human race in Romans 3:10-18 he said, ". . . with their tongues they have used deceit" (verse 13). This indictment applies to all of Adam's fallen race. But God's elect can be cured. The apostates described in Romans 1 cannot except by the miraculous application of the resurrection power of Christ. The psychopathic liar is not dangerous to society since his penchant for mendacity is well known. One would be naive indeed to trust his word. God's grace helps us. A Christian friend, prominent in the Production Credit Association, who loans billions of dollars of federal funds to qualified borrowers tells us that ministers of the gospel are among the better credit risks. Many bankers will be surprized to learn this. He also tells of a Kansas farmer who was such a big liar that he had to ask his neighbour to call his hogs!

2 Tim.3:1-3 indicates that these characteristics of early man (Romans 1:18-32) are also those of end-time apostates. Thus 6000 years of human acculturation have failed, the sociologists to the contrary notwithstanding.

The opposite set of characteristics listed in Galatians 5:22-23, are the fruits of the Holy Spirit, available to the elect, through regeneration.

ἀσυνέτους and ἀσυνθέτος are examples of parechesis or paronomasia. Grammarians differ. Winer defines paronamasia as words of similar sound, while Blass uses it of recurring words or word stems. Thus Blass would call this parechesis. *"Annominatio* deals with the *sense* as well as the sound." (Robertson, *Grammar*, 1201).

That the character so dismally portrayed (verses 29-31) is not due to ignorance but to man's free choice for himself, is clear in

*Verse 32 - "Who, knowing the judgment of God, that they which commit such things are worthy of death, not only do the same, but have pleasure in them that do them."*

οἵτινες τὸ δικαίωμα τοῦ θεοῦ ἐπιγνόντες, ὅτι οἱ τὰ τοιαῦτα πράσσοντες ἄξιοι θανάτου εἰσίν, οὐ μόνον αὐτὰ ποιοῦσιν ἀλλὰ καὶ συνευδοκοῦσιν τοῖς πράσσουσιν.

*"Though they know God's decree that those who do such things deserve to die, they not only do them but approve those who practice them." RSV.*

οἵτινες (nom.pl.masc.of ὅστις, indefinite relative pronoun, subject of ποιοῦσιν and συνευδοκοῦσιν) 163.

τὸ (acc.sing.neut.of the article in agreement with δικαίωμα) 9.

δικαίωμα (acc.sing.neut.of δικαίωμα, direct object of ἐπιγνόντες) 1781.

τοῦ (gen.sing.masc.of the article in agreement with θεοῦ) 9.

θεοῦ (gen.sing.masc.of θεός, description) 124.

ἐπιγνόντες (aor.act.part.nom.pl.masc.of ἐπιγινώσκω, adverbial, concessive) 675.

ὅτι (conjunction introducing an apposition clause in indirect discourse) 211.

οἱ (nom.pl.masc.of the article in agreement with πράσσοντες) 9.

τὰ (acc.pl.neut.of the article in agreement with τοιαῦτα) 9.

τοιαῦτα (acc.pl.neut.of τοιοῦτος, direct object of πράσοντες) 785.

πράσσοντες (pres.act.part.nom.pl.masc.of πράσσω, substantival, subject of εἰσίν) 1943.

ἄξιοι (nom.pl.masc.of ἄξιος, predicate adjective, in agreement with πράσσοντες) 285.

θανάτου (abl.sing.masc.of θάνατος, comparison) 381.

εἰσίν (3d.per.pl.pres.ind.of εἰμί, static) 86.

οὐ (negative conjunction with the indicative) 130.

μόνον (acc.sing.neut.of μόνος, adverbial) 339.

αὐτα (acc.pl.neut.of αὐτός, direct object of ποιοῦσιν) 16.

ποιοῦσιν (3d.per.pl.pres.act.ind.of ποιέω, progressive present) 127.

ἀλλὰ (alternative conjunction) 342.

καὶ (ascensive conjunction) 14.

συνευδοκοῦσιν (3d.per.pl.pres.act.ind.of συνευδοκέω, progressive duration, retroactive) 2468.

τοῖς (dat.pl.masc.of the article in agreement with πράσσουσιν) 9.

πράσσουσιν (pres.act.part.dat.pl.masc.of πράσσω, substantival, personal advantage) 1943.

*Translation - "Who, despite the fact that they are fully aware of the rule of divine law - that those who continue to practice such things are justly condemned to die, not only continue to do them, but even have always applauded those who are doing them."*

**Comment:** Again, as in verse 25, Paul uses the indefinite relative οἵτινες, because he is not specifying any particular individual, but rather a class of persons. ἐπιγνόντες is concessive. Note that it is the perfective form of the verb (#675 not #131). Although (concession) they had a clear understanding that should have given pause to the behavior, it did not. *Au contraire* they not only continued to practice deeds which they knew meant death, but had always applauded others who were always doing the same things. Note the linear action of the progressive present and the retroactive force of the progressive duration in συνευδοκοῦσιν. They had thorough knowledge of what they were doing and what the consequences would be. There was no mistake about it. What did they know? His power and divinity (verse 20). Yes, but far more. *That* they had learned by noumena deduced from phenomena (Ps.19:1-3) as Kant was later to discuss. They also were aware of God's moral standards. How? By the voice of conscience, a voice which spoke clearly to them about the difference between right and wrong, which, by the grace of the Creator, they possessed. It is this difference that elevates man above the animals. His ability to deduce some truth, though not the faith that saves from sin, and his ability to discern right from wrong constitutes evidence that he was made in God's image, a little lower than the angels.

If their consciences had not condemned them why did they find it necessary to exclude God from their model of rationality? We need not speculate. The text tells us why in verse 18. They suppressed the truth which they clearly understood because of lawlessness (ἐν ἀδικίᾳ). If they had not known that what they wanted to do was wicked, there would have been no need to suppress the truth, reject God and substitute a god of their own design who, by their design had moral standards more in keeping with their own. Their smitten conscience revealed clearly in the highest sense (#675) God's rule (#1781). Note in support of this, Rev.15:4 with the aorist passive tense in ἐφανερώθησαν - "Thy judgments have been made (punctiliar action in the past) manifest." This revelation was made, even to the heathen. Paul says that they knew them perfectly (Rom.1:32).

Lest some think that δικαίωμα does not include moral judgments, note the ὅτι clause in indirect discourse, which is epexegetical. It explains in detail the preceding clause. What judgments? "That the people who make a practice of doing such things (as were listed in verses 29-31) are worthy of death. Thus the ancients were asking for it, as indeed also are the end-time apostates. Note also Romans 5:18 with comment *en loc*. (Hint! Not upon babies since guilt is based upon ἐπιγινώσκω, Rom.5:16).

Note the disjunctive negative construction in οὐ μόνον . . . ἀλλὰ καί. Not only did they continue to sin despite their clear understanding of the eternal consequences, but they also applauded others who were doing the same thing.

Here we have an opportunity to study the difference between the apostate who sins and the Christian who also commits the same sins. Who can deny that the child of God is also guilty of many of the same sins listed in our passage (1 John 1:8). The apostate continues to commit sin, as the present progressive tenses in Romans 1:32 indicate. Transgression is his lifestyle in which he persists without intermittent periods of obedience. This agrees with 1 John 3:6b which says, ". . . whosoever continues to sin has never understood Him, neither known Him."

But 1 John 3:6a says, "Whosoever abideth in Him does not continue to sin, ... " and 1 John 3:9 adds, "Whosoever is born of God does not continue to sin (go on sinning; make a practice of sinning)." The point is that both in Romans 1:32 where the subject is the apostate and in 1 John 3:6a, 9, where the subject is the child of God, the verbs are in the present tense and denote continuous action. Christians sin, but they do not make a habit of it. Though they fall, they shall not be utterly cast down (Psalm 37:24). The Christian, with wrong views about holiness who says that he has not committed sin since he was "sanctified" deceives only himself (1 John 1:8). We may be sure that he is not deceiving his mother-in-law or his neighbours. But the man who says that he is a Christian and continues to practice lawlessness himself while he continues to applaud others who also go on sinning, is also deceiving himself.

The Calvinist, who understands this difference, need not sin occasionally in order to demonstrate that what the Scripture says about it, is indeed divinely inspired. There is no room for antinomianism in the debate. Indeed the antinomian is the cynic whom Paul is indicting before the bar of divine justice in Romans 1:18-32.

The relevance of the last clause of verse 32 is evident in the current late 20th century permissiveness, which flaunts itself in the name of democracy and looks to the United States Constitution for protection. Thus those who call themselves "Gay" (though not *Gay* as in *happy*, as one look at their miserably unhappy faces will attest) march in the streets of Washington and demonstrate in Lafayette Park. Freedom to sin is implicit in democracy if one is speaking of a democracy unfettered by a written constitution and fear from the police power that resides in organized government. If more people in a given area favor homosexuality, adultery, abortion, drug addiction, murder, rape, incest and robbery than oppose these things, democracy tells us that these things are in keeping with the will of God. But *vox populi vox Dei* is the slogan for mobocracy, not that of a constitutional democratic system of government such as we have in the United States. "The voice of the people" may or may not be "the voice of God." The voice of a people, such as those described in Romans 1:18-32 is not the voice of God. How often the sophomores in Political Science class have been told that democracy is a safe and humane system of government which can be depended upon to "establish justice, insure domestic tranquility, provide for the common defense, promote the general welfare, and secure the blessings of liberty. . . " if there is sufficient education for the people who vote. The unregenerate may say, "Education yes, but not morals." Thus we must settle the question as to whether education can be divorced from morals - whether ethics is or is not a branch of philosophy. If education provides morals then all democracy needs is education, but if not, successful democracy also needs morals. The heathen were well educated. Witness the Greeks and Romans. And some were as moral as many preachers are today. Witness Plato, Socrates and Aristotle all of whom believed in some restraint. On the day that all Ph.D.'s agree that the list of sins in Romans 1:24-32 are indeed sinful and no one defends them in the name of "personal liberty" and "civil rights" we may conclude that education indeed is all that is needed for successful democracy. But the apostates whose picture Paul has painted for us in Romans 1:18-32 were educated people, despite the fact that they did not go to Harvard. They understood the issues clearly, and then, with full knowledge of the consequences, they opted against God and morals and for sin and the inevitable social, economic and political consequences.

We need not rebut the view of the prophets of the "new morality" that moral standards are religious standards, as though all religions taught good morals. We need not even rebut the view that moral standards are Christian standards, although the New Testament is indeed a moral document. In fact, if Christian statesmen are smart, they will insist that the connection, if any, between morals and Christianity, is irrelevant to the discussion before the bar of public opinion. If one says that homosexuality, murder, rape and robbery are morally wrong and should be forbidden by the law of the secular state, because they are also unchristian, we run afoul of the first amendment which mandates that the ". . . Congress shall make no law respecting an establishment of religion or prohibiting the free exercise thereof . . . " The Christian statesman, for whom the standard of morals in the New Testament is the moral standard of God, must oppose those things which the Bible calls sin, but that the "new morality" calls freedom of expression, not because they are antireligious, but because they are inimical to the realization of those goals to which the nation aspires in the Preamble of the Constitution. Justice cannot be established, domestic tranquility cannot be insured, defense cannot be provided, the general welfare cannot be promoted and the blessings of liberty cannot be secured if men and women are free to be the kind of sinners described in Romans 1.

Both the state and the people are under social contract. Each side has its obligations. The people must obey the "general will" of the state as it has been determined by the democratic process of freedom of discussion in speech and press. The state in turn, pursuant to the goals of the Declaration of Independence, must recognize the self-evident truth that God created all men with an equality of opportunity which Heaven recognizes even though society does not. They were created by God. They were not evolved by means of the principle of survival of the fittest, as the law of claw and fang determined who should survive and who should not. The state is committed to the notion that some rights cannot be alienated as long as the citizen fulfills his side of the contract. Rights like life, liberty and property (which Thomas Jefferson called "pursuit of happiness") are sacred. It was to secure these rights that the founding fathers scrapped the Articles of Confederation which had proved inadequate to the task and replaced it with the Constitution that provides a federal government with powers competent to the realization of the goal. Can we have in the United States a society that provides the individual with protection from itself? Or must we, in the name of what misguided souls call freedom, allow some to do whatever they wish?. Must law-abiding citizens be deprived of their rights in order that criminals can be free? When a burglar enters my home and carries away my property, need I protest on the grounds that what he did was not Christian or can I say that what he did was not conducive to my "pursuit of happiness" ?

A failure to see this vital distinction has induced some who call themselves the "Moral Majority" to seek more control over the lives of the people than is warranted. We are well advised, in pursuit of our goals as set forth in our honored federal documents, to work for and request from the government, those laws which will militate against the erosion of our liberties. We are ill-advised to use the governments, either at the municipal, state or federal levels, to saddle upon citizens of the United States a way of life which conforms in all of its parts with our views of theology and morals. The laws of a secular state must oppose only those practices which have deleterious effects upon the social and economic conditions in which all must live and by which all are either made more or less free. For example, the Christian believes that the excessive intake of alcohol is sinful, because it results in drunkenness, which is expressly forbidden in the New Testament. But he does not ask for a law against drunkenness because it is a sin. He wants drunkenness curbed by the police power of the state because drunk drivers kill people on the highways. If a drunk can drink at home, stay at home and never cause trouble for someone else, then it is none of the Christian citizen's business, though as a Christian it may be some of his business, since he could wish that the inebriate could be saved from sin and saved for society. The state should forbid all "sins" which can be shown to have destructive effects upon society. Thus it is illegal to murder. Murder indeed is sin, but it is also destructive to human life. The uncontrolled use of drugs is sin, for our bodies are the temples of the Holy Spirit (1 Cor.6:19) but such is also a crime, since drug addicts do irrational things, when they are "high" such as raping little girls and old women. If a man wishes to destroy himself it is none of the state's business, but when in the process he destroys the property and even the lives of others, the state must move in to fulfill its promise to the innocent bystander.

If these distinctions are not made, the public pendulum will swing too far to the right and a law may be passed forbidding Coca Cola and coffee, since the Mormons teach that it is a sin to imbibe caffein. Or the Presbyterians may mandate that I sprinkle my baby, or the Baptists dictate that Presbyterians immerse theirs. From the Baptist point of view a sprinkled baby is an example of poor biblical exegesis and from the Presbyterian point of view, an immersed Christian is an unnecessary conformity to an unimportant hermeneutical detail, but neither sprinkled babies nor immersed Baptists are a threat to life, liberty and the pursuit of property or happiness.

Space forbids that we go over the list of sins in verses 26-31 and assess the social, economic and psychic impact of each upon the society in which we earthbound citizens of the world must live. The reader hopefully is social scientist enough to see which sins are harmful to society and therefore to the rights of others and which are not. Hint. What does disobedience to parents do to family life and how important is the home to American society? Can a homosexual practice his/her lifestyle without imposing upon the liberties of others? If so, then I cannot as a good citizen interfere, however much, as a Christian I may wish to help him. But if his lifestyle is a cancer that eats away at my civil liberties, then, as a good citizen I must ask the state to outlaw the way he lives. Another hint. What would happen in the world of business if all men were "covenant breakers"? A covenant breaker borrows money and refuses to pay it back. Sanctity of contract is a cornerstone of the business world. The

Constitution forbids the states to impair its obligation (Article I, Section 10, paragraph 1) Thus a covenant breaker transgresses the law and the police power of the state brings him into civil court where he is made to keep his promises. If this were not true the business man could not regard a contract, drawn in his favor, as an asset upon which he could depend in making investment decisions. Every accountant knows that Accounts Payable is an Asset, but it is not if covenant breaking is legal.

Thus it is clear that sin, as the New Testament defines it, is not only against the economy of God and His administration of the universe, but it is also against the economy of man as he struggles through his earth-bound existence in an economy of scarcity to achieve the good life. Kant's Categorical Imperative, which Jesus had already promulated, and which we call "The Golden Rule" (Mt.7:12) provides all of the guidance we need when we try to mark out the limits of the authority of the welfare state.

Democracy, which Winston Churchill described as the worst possible form of government except one - its alternative, and to which Plato gave a D, better only than anarchy, to which he gave an F, suffers from the fact that the small d democrats live in far greater conformity to the standards of Romans 1:18-32 than they do to the standards of the Sermon on the Mount. Almighty God, to Whom all power has been given (Mt.28:18) and before Whom every knee will bow (Phil.2:9-11) is no democrat. Or rather He is the only safe *DEMOCRAT*. He is Plato's Philosopher-King. When He comes democracy, the dream of the political scientists, will be realized at last, for He will write His laws upon our hearts (2 Cor.3:3) and "the earth shall be full of the knowledge of the Lord as the waters cover the sea." That is why, for the first time since Adam deliberately disobeyed God, ". . . they shall not hurt nor destroy" in all of His holy kingdom (Isa.11:9).

Paul's purpose in Romans is to show how a guilty transgressor of God's law can become just. It is only logical that he should first show that the entire human race is guilty of transgression. In Romans 1:18-32 the prosecuting attorney has successfully indicted the heathen world before the bar of divine justice. He turns his guns of prosecution now upon the civilized Gentiles, after which he will arraign the Jews in heaven's court and prove that even they, for all of the blessings of God's special treatment for them, are also sinners. His summation of man's guilt in Romans 3:9-20 completes the first section of the epistle. In the second section he expounds the good news of the gospel of Christ. Transgressors can be made righteous.

## The Righteous Judgment of God

*(Romans 2:1-16)*

*Romans 2:1 - "Therefore thou art inexcuseable, O man, whosoever thou art that judgest: for wherein thou judgest another, thou condemnest thyself; for thou that judgest doeth the same things."*

Διὸ ἀναπολόγητος εἶ, ὦ ἄνθρωπε πᾶς ὁ κρίνων, ἐν ᾧ γὰρ κρίνεις τὸν ἕτερον, σεαυτὸν κατακρίνεις, τὰ γὰρ αὐτὰ πράσσεις ὁ κρίνων.

*"Therefore you have no excuse, O man, whoever you are, when you judge another; for in passing judgment upon him you condemn yourself, because you, the judge, are doing the very same things."      RSV*

Διὸ (consecutive conjunction) 1622.

ἀναπολόγητος (nom.sing.masc.of ἀναπολόγητος, predicate adjective) 3800.

εἶ (2d.per.sing.pres.ind.of εἰμί, static) 86.

ὦ (exclamation) 1177.

ἄνθρωπε (voc.sing.masc.of ἄνθρωπος, address) 341.

πᾶς (voc.sing.masc.of πᾶς, in agreement with κρίνων) 67.

ὁ ( voc.sing.masc.of the article in agreement with κρίνων) 9.

κρίνων (pres.act.part.voc.sing.masc.of κρίνω, substantival, address) 531.

ἐν (preposition with the locative, sphere) 80.

ᾧ (loc.sing.neut.of ὅς, definite relative pronoun, sphere) 65.

γὰρ (causal conjunction) 105.

κρίνεις (2d.per.sing.pres.act.ind.of κρίνω, progressive duration, retroactive) 531.

τὸν (acc.sing.masc.of the article in agreement with ἕτερον) 9.

ἕτερον (acc.sing.masc.of ἕτερος, direct object of κρίνεις) 605.

σεαυτὸν (acc.sing.masc.of σεαυτοῦ, reflexive pronoun, direct object of κατακρίνεις) 347.

κατακρίνεις (2d.per.sing.pres.act.ind.of κατακρίνω, progressive duration, retroactive) 1012.

τὰ (acc.pl.neut.of the article in agreement with αὐτὰ) 9.

γὰρ (causal conjunction) 105.

αὐτὰ (acc.pl.neut.of αὐτός, in agreement with the substantive understood, intensive) 16.

πράσσεις (2d.per.sing.pres.act.ind.of πράσσω, progressive duration, retroactive) 1943.

ὁ (nom.sing.masc.of the article in agreement with κρίνων) 9.

κρίνων (pres.act.part.nom.sing.masc.of κρίνω, substantival, subject of πράσσεις) 531.

*Translation - "So there is no defense for you, O man - all you who have been criticizing. Because in the area of your criticism, you are condemning yourself, because the judge has been doing the very same things."*

**Comment:** Διὸ introduces the result clause. It depends upon the argument which has just been concluded in Romans 1:18-31. The same judgment that fell upon the heathen for their sins will fall upon the civilized world, since civilized people are guilty of the same sins. Paul will use his indictment of the uncivilized world based upon his psychological analysis of the reason for their moral decline to the gutter, as a basis for indicting other sinners who are equally guilty, but who tend to consider themselves more civilized. The "ethical" atheists, idolmakers, worshippers and servers look with disdain upon the heathen. But for no good reason. πᾶς ὁ κρίνων directs the charge against all who had been taking this superior attitude, while at the same time they were judging others, they were doing the "very same things" (intensive use of αὐτά). The phrase ἐν ᾧ can be taken, as I have, as a loctative of sphere, or, with equal grammatical justification, either as a locative of time point or as an instrumental of cause. It was when they were criticizing (time point) and because they were criticising (cause) and also when they were criticizing in the particular sphere of their criticism, that they were condemned. The sphere construction limits the criticism of the civilized world to a specific moral and philosophical areas described in Romans 1:18-32.

Why were they condemned? Because, although they appeared righteous by virtue of their objection to another's sins, as though they personally favored the moral standards of God, which the heathen had rejected, at the same time they were doing the same things.

They were worse sinners than those upon whom they sat in judgment. The heathen at least were not hypocrities. They openly repudiated God and His standards and substituted their own religious system and the life-style which resulted. But the civilized world professed to worship the God of creation and to approve of His ethics, while their lives reflected the same sordid moral pattern of those whom they criticized.

The only difference between the people of Romans 1:18-32 and those of Romans 2:1-16 is one of the degree of sophistication. The heathen had studied the natural law principles which they found in God's creation and had deduced from the phenomenal sensations, the noumena of supersensible reality, while they had noted the voice of conscience to understand that, in addition to being powerful and intelligent, the God of creation was also holy. They had advanced as far as Kant later thought anyone could, except those fortunate people who knew Jesus personally while He was here on earth. The people now under discussion in Romans 2:1-16 had gone further in the scientific development of their intellectual powers and enjoyed a higher standard of living and a higher degree of civilization than the heathen. They had television to amuse them and the possibility of going to the moon. But they had not advanced one whit in their appreciation of divine standards of behavior and their lives revealed that they were no better than those they criticized. The technologically advanced who have no saving faith in Christ, are no better in the morality sphere than the primitive cultures of earth. One cannot turn on ethics at an electric switch. Christian ethics results from a supernatural birth from above (John 3:1-8).

*Verse 2 - "But we are sure that the judgment of God is according to truth against them which commit such things."*

οἴδαμεν δὲ ὅτι τὸ κρίμα τοῦ θεοῦ ἐστιν κατὰ ἀλήθειαν ἐπὶ τοὺς τὰ τοιαῦτα πράσσοντας.

*"We know that the judgment of God rightly falls upon those who do such things." RSV.*

οἴδαμεν (1st.per.pl.perf.ind.of ὁράω, intensive) 144b.

δὲ (causal conjunction) 11.

ὅτι (conjunction introducing an object clause in indirect discourse) 211.

τὸ (nom.sing.neut.of the article in agreement with κρίμα) 9.

κρίμα (nom.sing.neut.of κρίμα, subject of ἐστιν) 642.

τοῦ (gen.sing.masc.of the article in agreement with θεοῦ) 9.

θεοῦ (gen.sing.masc.of θεός, description) 124.

ἐστιν (3d.per.sing.pres.ind.of εἰμί, static) 86.

κατὰ (preposition with the accusative, standard rule) 98.

ἀλήθειαν (acc.sing.fem.of ἀλήθεια, standard rule) 1416.

ἐπὶ (preposition with the accusative, reference) 47.

τοὺς (acc.pl.masc.of the article in agreement with πράσσοντας) 9.

τὰ (acc.pl.neut.of the article in agreement with τοιαῦτα) 9.

τοιαῦτα (acc.pl.neut.of τοιοῦτος, direct object of πράσσοντας) 785.

πράσσοντας (pres.act.part.acc.pl.masc.of πράσσω, substantival, reference) 1943.

*Translation - "Because we know that the judgment of God is in keeping with truth with reference to those who are doing such things."*

**Comment:** δὲ seems to be causal, as Paul moves to justify his strong statement of verse 1. God's judgments are always "right" (δίκαιος; Gen.18:25). Jesus Christ, Who is the Judge (John 5:22) is "the same, yesterday, today and forever" (Heb.13:8). Man's judgment is based upon the superficial observation (1 Samuel 16:7; 2 Cor.5:12; 10:7). The Judge Himself had served notice upon all those who stand accused in His court, from Whose decision there is no appeal to a higher jurisdiction, that that is how it will be (John 7:24).

οἴδαμεν is in intensive perfect tense. It places emphasis upon the state of Paul's knowledge at the time of writing, rather than upon the point in the past, when he had learned, once for all what, as a result, he now understands. Burton calls this "the Perfect of Existing State" (*New Testament Moods and Tenses,* 38). It is also proleptic (extends the state of knowledge into the future), but this is so, not because of the perfect tense, which is never proleptical, but because of the context. The judgments of our Lord, Who is the Judge (John 5:22) must always be consistent with His truth, since He is the same always.

ὅτι introduces the indirect discourse. The difference between κατὰ ἀλήθειαν and "accorinding to appearance" points up the fact that human observation is naive because superficial. P.T. Barnum understood this quite well and made a fortune off it. Only the sophisticated child of God with the Holy Spirit's discernment has the skepticism of the mature mind. Paul saw through the charade which he attacks. The civilized bum seeks to appear in the role of a gentleman, while he castigates as bums those who are committing no more sins than he, although he has hired a better public relations expert. But it is difficult to fool God! He knows the truth in all of its complexity about all of us and will hand down from the bench His decision in accord with what He knows.

*Verse 3 - "And thinkest thou this, O man, that judgest them which do such things, and doest the same, that thou shalt escape the judgment of God?"*

λογίζῃ δὲ τοῦτο, ωἰ ἄνθρωπε ὁ κρίνων τούς τὰ τοιαῦτα πράσσοντας καὶ ποιῶν αὐτά, ὅτι σὺ ἐκφεύξῃ τὸ κρίμα τοῦ θεοῦ; RSV

*"Do you suppose, O man, that when you judge those who do such things and yet do them yourself, you will escape the judgment of God?"*

λογίζῃ (2d.per.sing.pres.mid.ind.of λογίζομαι, direct question) 2611.
δὲ (continuative conjunction) 11.
τοῦτο (acc.sing.neut.of οὗτος, direct object of λογίζῃ) 93.
ωἰ (exclamation) 1177.
ἄνθρωπε (voc.sing.masc.of ἄνθρωπος, address) 341.
ὁ (nom.sing.masc.of the article in agreement with κρίνων) 9.
κρίνων (pres.act.part.nom.sing.masc.of κρίνω, substantival, in apposition with ἄνθρωπε) 531.
τοὺς (acc.pl.masc.of the article in agreement with πράσσοντας) 9.
τὰ (acc.pl.neut.of the article in agreement with τοιαῦτα) 9.
τοιαῦτα (acc.pl.neut.of τοιοῦτος, direct object of πράσσοντας) 785.
πράσσοντας (pres.act.part.acc.pl.masc.of πράσσω, substantival, direct object of κρίνων) 1943.
καὶ (concessive conjunction) 14.
ποιῶν (pres.act.part.nom.sing.masc.of ποιέω, substantival, in apposition with ἄνθρωπε) 127.
αὐτά (acc.pl.neut.of αὐτός, direct object of ποιῶν) 16.
ὅτι (conjunction introducing an object clause in indirect discourse) 211.
σὺ (nom.sing.masc.of σύ, subject of ἐκφεύξῃ, emphatic) 104.
ἐκφύξῃ (2d.per.sing.fut.mid.ind.of ἐκφεύγω, deliberative) 2740.
τὸ (acc.sing.neut.of the article in agreement with κρίμα) 9.
κρίμα (acc.sing.neut.of κρίμα, direct object of ἐκφεύξῃ) 642.
τοῦ (gen.sing.masc.of the article in agreement with θεοῦ) 9.
θεοῦ (gen.sing.masc.of θεός, description) 124.

*Translation - "And do you suppose this, O man, you who condemns those who are doing such things, despite the fact that you are doing the same things, that you will escape the judgment of God?"*

**Comment:** τοῦτο, the object of λογίζῃ is explained by the epexegetical objective ὅτι clause in indirect discourse. Did they suppose what? That they would escape the judgment of God. The generic man (ἄνθρωπε) is joined by two substantival participles in apposition. He is the man "who is judging" and also "who is doing." Thus concessive καὶ. There is scant consistency in criticizing others for doing the same things that the critic also is doing. The question is rhetorical. Paul seems amazed that anyone could imagine that God would allow anyone to get away with the attitude described.

Paul seems to be remembering Psalm 19:7-9 which significantly follows immediately after a description of the elements in natural revelation by which man knows God. *Cf.* Romans 1:18-20 with Psalm 19:1-6. Psalm 19:8 is parallel to Romans 2:2, just as Psalm 19:1-6 parallels Romans 1:18-20. There is enough truth in natural revelation to save the soul, if man reacts to it properly. The scientists and philosophers of Romans 1:18-20 were Kantian in their epsitemology. Observing phenomena, by discursive logic they deduced noumena. But they rejected what they had thus learned about God because of the moral question. If they had been content to abandon what they thought was the solid groun of Kantian certitude and ask by faith for the solider ground of New Testament certitude they would have been saved. Proof? Psalm 19:7-9. Indeed some, who never heard the historic account of the person and work of Jesus Christ may have moved on to this higher ground and gained the certitude which accompanies the birth from above. *Cf.* our discussion of Romans 2:10-16 *infra.*

*Verse 4 "Or despisest thou the riches of his goodness and forbearance and longsuffering; not knowing that the goodness of God leadeth thee to repentance?"*

ἤ τοῦ πλούτου τῆς χρηστότητος αὐτοῦ καὶ τῆς ἀνοχῆς καὶ τῆς μακροθυμίας καταφρονεῖς, ἀγνοῶν ὅτι τὸ χρηστὸν τοῦ θεοῦ εἰς μετάνοιάν σε ἄγει;

*"Or do you presume upon the riches of his kindness and forbearnace and patience? Do you not know that God's kindness is meant to lead you to repentance?"  RSV.*

ἤ (disjunctive) 465.
τοῦ (gen.sing.masc.of the article in agreement with πλούτου) 9.
πλούτου (gen.sing.masc.of πλοῦτος, objective genitive) 1050.
τῆς (gen.sing.fem.of the article in agreement with χρηστότητος) 9.

#3830 χρηστότητος (gen.sing.fem.of χρηστότης, description).

King James Version

gentleness - Gal.5:22.
good - Romans 3:12.
goodness - Romans 2:4; 11:22,22,22.
kindness - 2 Cor.6:6; Eph.2:7; Col.3:12; Titus 3:4.

Revised Standard Version

good - Romans 3:12.
goodness - Titus 3:4.
kindness - Gal.5:22; Rom.2:4; 11:22,22,22; 2 Cor.6:6; Eph.2:7; Col.3:12; Titus 3:4.

*Meaning: Cf.* χρηστός (#959). Hence, moral goodness, integrity - Romans 3:12; kindness, benignity - Gal.5:22; Rom.2:4; 11:22,22,22; 2 Cor.6:6; Eph.2:7; Col.3:12; Titus 3:4.

αὐτοῦ (gen.sing.masc.of αὐτός, possession) 16.
καὶ (adjunctive conjunction joining nouns) 14.
τῆς (gen.sing.fem.of the article in agreement with ἀνοχῆς) 9.

#3831 ἀνοχῆς (gen.sing.fem.of ἀνοχή, objective genitive).

King James Version

forbearance - Romans 2:4; 3:25.

Revised Standard Version

forbearance - Romans 2:4; 3:25.

*Meaning: Cf.* ἀνέχω (#1234).Hence, a "holding back," forbearance - Romans 2:4; 3:25. The decision of God to hold in abeyance the act of judgment in the hope that man would repent - Romans 2:4; until propitiation was provided in Christ - Romans 3:25.

καὶ (adjunctive conjunction joining nouns) 14.
τῆς (gen.sing.fem.of the article in agreement with μακροθυμίας) 9.

#3832 μακροθυμίας (gen.sing.fem.of μακροθυμία, objective genitive).

King James Version

long suffering - Romans 2:4; 9:22; 2 Cor.6:6; Gal.5:22; Eph.4:2; Col.1:11; 3:12; 1 Tim.1:16; 2 Tim.3:10; 4:2; 1 Pet.3:20; 2 Pet.3:15.
patience - Heb.6:12; James 5:10.

Revised Standard Version

patience - Romans 2:4; 9:22; Gal.5:22; Eph.4:2; Col.1:11; 3:12; 1 Tim,1:16; 2 Tim.3:10; 4:2; 1 Pet.3:20; Heb.6:12; James 5:10.
forbearance -   2 Cor.6:6; 2 Pet.3:15.

*Meaning: Cf.* μακροθυμέω (#1274), μακροθύμως (#3653). Patience, endurance, perseverance, constancy, steadfastness - Col.1:11; 2 Tim.3:10; Heb.6:12; James 5:10; 2 Cor.6:6; Gal.5:22. Forbearance, longsuffering - the quality that renders one slow to avenge a wrong - Romans 2:4; 9:22; Eph.4:2; Col.3:12; 1 Tim.1:16; 2 Tim.4:2; 1 Pet.3:20; 2 Pet.3:15. The word occurs in the same context with ὑπομενή in Col.1:11; 2 Cor.6:4,6; 2 Tim.3:10; James 5:10,11. "The differenceof meaning is best seen in their opposites. While ὑπομενή is the temper which does not easily succumb under suffering, μακ is the self-restraint which does not hastily retaliate a wrong. The one is opposed to cowardice or despondancy, the other to wrath or revenge (Prov.15:18; 16:32). . . . This distinction, though it applies generally, is not true without exception." (Trench, *New Testament Synonyms*, Para. liii).

καταφρονεῖς (2d.per.sing.pres.act.ind.of καταφρονέω, direct question) 607.
ἀγνοῶν (pres.act.part.nom.sing.masc.of ἀγνοέ, adverbial, concessive) 2345.
ὅτι (conjunction introducing the object clause in indirect discourse) 211.
τὸ (nom.sing.neut.of the article in agreement with χρηστὸν) 9.
χρηστὸν (nom.sing.masc.of χρηστός, subject of ἄγει) 959.

τοῦ (gen.sing.masc.of the article in agreement with θεοῦ) 9.
θεοῦ (gen.sing.masc.of θεός, possession) 124.
εἰς (preposition with the accusative of extent) 140.
μετάνοιάν (acc.sing.fem.of μετάνοια, metaphorical extent) 286.
σε (acc.sing.masc.of σύ, direct object of ἄγει) 104.
ἄγει (3d.per.sing.pres.act.ind.of ἄγω, inchoative) 876.

*Translation - "Or are you disdaining the abundance of His kindness and His forbearance and longsuffering, as if you were unaware of the fact that the kindness of God is His attempt to lead you to repentance?"*

**Comment:** Another rhetorical question. *Cf.* #607 for the meaning. They were looking down upon God's wealth of kindness, restraint and patience. They were taking it lightly and for granted and presuming upon it. They were indulging the selfish "give me an inch and I will take a mile" attitude. They were doing this as though they did not know what God's kindness was designed to do. See the inchoative present tense in ἄγει with emphasis upon the beginning of the attempt. God's restraint in holding back the judgment, which He has every just right to let fall without delay is the beginning (inchoative) of His attempt (conative) to induce the sinner to repent. *Cf.* Luke 6:35.

The neuter article τὸ with the adjective is common. As men indulge their lusts and rationalize God out of their philosophy He (1) showers them with kindness. This is the common grace that the Presbyterians talk about, which He gives to all men alike, without regard to their ultimate status in His kingdom - *viz.* sunshine, rain, familial love, happiness, health, finanical support for their needs. He (2) also resists the urge to smite, and meanwhile (3) He suffers as only Holiness must in the presence of sin. All of this - χρηστότης (#3830), ἀνοχή (#3831) and μακροθυμία (#3832) they were taking for granted. Because they misunderstood God's purpose in showering them with these evidences of His love and grace, they assumed that they would go on forever. But if God's common grace does not lead them to saving grace, judgment must result. This is the thought in

*Verse 5 - "But after thy hardness and impenitent heart treasurest up unto thyself wrath against the day of wrath and revelation of the righteous judgment of God."*

κατὰ δὲ τὴν σκληρότητά σου καὶ ἀμετανόητον καρδίαν θησαυρίζεις σεαυτῷ ὀργὴν ἐν ἡμέρᾳ ὀργῆς καὶ ἀποκαλύψεως δικαιοκρισίας τοῦ θεοῦ,

*"But by your hard and impenitent heart you are storing up wrath for yourself on*

*the day of wrath when God's righteous judgment will be revealed."*     RSV

κατὰ (preposition with the accusative, standard rule) 98.
δὲ (adversative conjunction) 11.
τὴν (acc.sing.fem.of the article in agreement with σκληρότητά) 9.

**#3833** σκληρότητά (acc.sing.neut.of σκληρότης, in agreement with καρδίαν).

King James Version

hardness - Romans 2:5.

Revised Standard Version

hard - Romans 2:5.

*Meaning: Cf.* σκληροκαρδία (#1293), σκληρός (#1537); σκληροτράχηλος (#3147),σκληρύνω (#3461) and σκληρός - "hard." Hence, hardness, obstinacny, stubbornness - Romans 2:5.

σου (gen.sing.masc.of σύ, possession) 104.
καὶ (adjunctive conjunction joining nouns) 14.

**#3834** ἀμετανόντον (acc.sing.neut.of ἀμετανόητος, in agreement with καρδίαν).

King James Version

impenitent - Romans 2:5.

Revised Standard Version

impenitent - Romans 2:5.

*Meaning:* α privative plus μετανοέω (#251). Hence, unrepentant, impenitent, obdurate, unwilling to admit a change of mind - Romans 2:5.

καρδίαν (acc.sing.fem.of καρδία, standard rule) 432.
θησαυρίζεις (2d.per.sing.pres.act.ind.of θησαυρίζω, progressive duration, retroactive) 591.
σεαυτῷ (dat.sing.masc.of σεαυτοῦ, reflexive pronoun, personal disadvantage) 347.
ὀργὴν (acc.sing.fem.of ὀργή, direct object of θησαυρίζεις) 283.
ἐν (preposition with the locative, time point) 80.
ἡμέρᾳ (loc.sing.fem.of ἡμέρα, time point) 135.
ὀργῆς (gen.sing.fem.of ὀργή, description) 282.
καὶ (adjunctive conjunction joining nouns) 14.
ἀποκαλύφεως (gen.sing.fem.of ἀποκαλύφις, description) 1902.

**#3835** δικαιοκρισίας (gen.sing.fem.of δικαιοκρισία, description).

King James Version

righteous judgment - Romans 2:5.

Revised Standard Version

righteous judgment - Romans 2:5.

*Meaning:* A combination of δίκαιος (#85) and κρίσις (#478). Hence righteous judgment. A court decision based properly upon all the facts and proper interpretation of the law. With reference to the judgment of God in the last day - Romans 2:5.

τοῦ (gen.sing.masc.of the article in agreement with θεοῦ) 9.
θεοῦ (gen.sing.masc.of θεός, description) 124.

*Translation - "But in keeping with the dictates of your hard and impenitent heart you have been storing up for yourself wrath on the day of wrath and revelation of the righteous judgment of God."*

**Comment:** δὲ is adversative. Instead of recognizing the reason for and significance of God's common grace they are adverse to it and remain impenitent. Thus they were, at the time that Paul wrote about it, and had been, since the moment of their first capacity to make a moral judgment, piling up wrath for themselves (progressive duration present in θησαυρίζεις, with its retroactive force). Why should they have been so unwise? It was in keeping with the dictates of their heart, which is described as hard and unrepentant. *Cf.#*'s 3833 and 3834. Note that because the mind is obdurate the heart is hard (Prov.23:7). The human soul will not long resist the dictates of the human mind. What we think, come to believe and settle upon soon reflects itsself in the desires of the emotional nature. Then, the intellect and the emotional nature unite to control the will. How important then it is that we should bring e . ery thought into captivity to the obedience of Christ (2 Cor.10:5). Paul observed that "evil communications corrupt good manners" (1 Cor.15:33). Those who do not remember that are deceived by the philosophers. If the reader enjoys the skepticism that is the hallmark of a mature mind he should read philosophy. But if he is a naive intellectual child who tends to believe everything he reads and play with every intellectual toy he finds, let him give the philosophers and their cranial vaporings a wide berth. We are to avoid conformation with this evil world and enjoy the transformation which the Holy Spirit gives us through the Word *"by the renewing of the mind"* (Romans 12:1-2). Only thus can we prove what God's good, acceptable and perfect will is.

Why is the mind obdurate? Because the flesh lusts after sin (Romans 1:18 - ἐν ἀδικία). Thus the sequence in the cause/result relationship is (1) depraved flesh, which causes (2) suppressed truth and an obdurate mind-set, which will not repent, which causes (3) a hard heart, which results in (4) a pile-up of wrath, which results in (5) damnation. The only force that can break this sequence is the grace of God.

Paul does not say that the wrath of God will fall immediately - or even soon. But he describes the day. It is the day of the revelation of the wrath of God at the close of the kingdom age, for the lost who have died before the second coming of our Lord. Those unsaved who are alive at the second coming will know His wrath that day (2 Thess.1:8-10; Rev.16:17) but the final disposition of their cases before the Great White Throne will occur at the end of the millenium (Rev.20:11-15). The student should consult all of the contexts in which ὀργή (#283) occurs and note those which speak of God's wrath at the second coming of Christ as opposed to those that speak of the Great White Throne judgment, one thousand years later. These days are characterized by the exhibit of divine wrath - ἡμέρα ὀργῆς καὶ ἀποκαλύψεως δικαιοκρισίας - "a day of wrath and revelation of righteous judgment." Note that when God is involved wrath is not inconsistent with righteous judgment. The drivel that in some incomprehensible manner passes in certain circles for wisdom to the effect that it is beneath the dignity of a loving God to be angry, forgets that the word δικαιοκρισίας - "righteous judgment" - means justice that is right in the sense that it is in keeping with the law. The same argument when applied to a court over which a human judge presides would merit a contempt citation. Righteous judgment must be wrathful if the defendant continues as a lawbreaker in a state of conscious impenitence. This is precisely what Paul says in

*Verse 6 - "Who will render to every man according to his deeds."*

ὃς ἀποδώσει ἑκάστῳ κατὰ τὰ ἔργα αὐτοῦ,

*"For he will render to every man according to his works:" RSV*

ὃς (nom.sing.masc.of ὅς, the relative pronoun, subject of ἀποδώσει) 65.
ἀποδώσει (3d.per.sing.fut.act.ind.of ἀποδίδωμι, predictive) 495.
ἑκάστῳ (dat.sing.masc.of ἕκαστος, indirect object of ἀποδώσει) 1217.
κατὰ (preposition with the accusative of standard rule) 98.
τὰ (acc.pl.neut.of the article in agreement with ἔργα) 9.
ἔργα (acc.pl.neut.of ἔργον, standard rule) 460.
αὐτοῦ (gen.sing.masc.of αὐτός, possession) 16.

*Translation - "Who will settle with every man in keeping with his record."*

**Comment:** Paul here quotes Psalm 62:12. The student should read the entire Psalm in the light of Romans 1:18 - 2:16. God's accounting is with each man/woman - on an individual basis (ἑκάστῳ - #1217).

Lest we read into this verse salvation by human merit, we must take verse 6 in the light of the epexegetical material that follows in verses 7-16. Do Christians perform only good works? By no means. Then does it follow that in saving the Christian God rewards only the good works while He ignores the evil works which appear on the Christian's record? Or do unregenerate sinners do only those things which are evil? Does God in condemning the sinner do so in punishment for his evil while ignoring the good, if any? These questions are both legitimate and without answers, if we have only the material in verse 6 for light. But the verses which follow explain how God can in justice save some and condemn others, even though Christians have a record of both the good deeds and evil (Gal.5:16-26), while the unregenerate, although they do things which society calls good, can really do nothing that God calls good (John 6:63a; Gal.5: 19-21; Mk.7:21-23; Rom.1:21-32; Psalm 7:11; Proverbs 21:4). Romans 2:6 well represents the reason why one cannot build a theology upon a proof text, until he has considered all of the light that shines upon it from other texts. This is true since no Scripture is of its own interpretation (2 Pet.1:20). *Cf.* our comment *en loc.*.

The entire salvation issue is contingent upon every man's reaction of will to (1) what he knows about God, and (2) what he knows and is willing to admit about himself. If Socrates had said Γνῶθι θεὸν καὶ γνῶθι σεαυτόν he would have been closer to the truth. In fact one cannot know himself until he knows God. He cannot react in the manner described in Romans 2:7 and Romans 2:10 until he knows both God and himself. Those who know neither God nor themselves react in the manner described in Romans 2:8,9. God, Who is the only one competent to Judge, and Who would appreciate it if mortals would keep out of His business, can be trusted to do the righteous thing (Romans 2:11).

*Verse 7 - "To them who by patient continuance in well doing seek for glory and honour and immortality, eternal life."*

τοῖς μὲν καθ' ὑπομονὴν ἔργου ἀγαθοῦ δόξαν καὶ τιμὴν καὶ ἀφθαρσίαν ζητοῦσιν, ζωὴν αἰώνιον,

*". . . to those who by patience in well-doing seek for glory and honor and immortality, he will give eternal life." RSV.*

τοῖς (dat.pl.masc.of the article in agreement with ζητοῦσιν) 9.
μὲν (particle of affirmation) 300.
καθ' (preposition with the accusative, standard rule) 98.
ὑπομονὴν (acc.sing.fem.of ὑπομονή, standard rule) 2204.
ἔργου (gen.sing.neut.of ἔργον, objective genitive) 460.
ἀγαθοῦ (gen.sing.masc.of ἀγαθός, in agreement with ἐργοῦ) 547.
δόξαν (acc.sing.fem.of δόξα, direct object of ζητοῦσιν) 361.
καὶ (adjunctive conjunction joining nouns) 14.
τιμὴν (acc.sing.fem.of τιμή, direct object of ζητοῦσιν) 1619.
καὶ (adjunctive conjunction joining nouns) 14.

#3836 ἀφθαρσίαν (acc.sing.fem.of ἀφθαρσία, direct object of ζητοῦσιν).

King James Version

immortality - Romans 2:7; 2 Tim.1:10.
incorruption - 1 Cor.15:42,50,53,54.
sincerity - Eph.6:24.

Revised Standard Version

immortality - Romans 2:7; 2 Tim.1:10.
live undying - Eph.6:24.

imperishable - 1 Cor.15:42,50,53,54.

*Meaning:* Cf. ἄφθαρτος (#3802). Perpetuity, sincerity, purity, incorruptibility. The quality which renders something viable. Absolutely in Romans 2:7; 2 Tim.1:10; 1 Cor.15:50; with reference to bodies - 1 Cor.15:42,53,54; adverbial in Eph.6:24.

ζητοῦσιν (pres.act.part.dat.pl.masc.of ζητέω, indirect object of ἀποδώσει) 207.

ζωὴν (acc.sing.fem.of ζωή, direct object of ἀποδώσει) 668.

αἰώνιον (acc.sing.fem.of αἰώνιος, in agreement with ζωὴν) 1255.

*Translation - "To those on the one hand who with patience seek good works, glory, true value and immortality, (He will give) eternal life."*

**Comment:** Note the μὲν . . . δὲ sequence in verses 7 and 8. It is antithetic parallelism - "On the one hand those who do one thing . . . on the other hand those who do the opposite." First, in verse 7 we have the sincere and humble people. What are their characteristics? In keeping with the standards of behavior and attitude which we expect from patience (καθ' ὑπομονὴν) they sought activities of a high ethical character. They saw the difference between their own standard of morals and that of God. They listened to their conscience and condemned their innate proclivities for evil. As a result they entered in upon a quest for glory, achievements of high value and the kind of life that is viable - glory, because the heavens which they could see at night declare the glory of God (Psalm 19:1) and their knowledge of the phenomenal led them in the quest for the noumenal glory of the mind. The man whom Paul here describes looks at the stars and sighs, "I wish that I could be as glorious as the God of glory." It is a divine discontent - a desire to be like God. Others, saw the difference and said, "I want God to be like me," and then proceeded to make a god that looked like him! Honor (τιμή, #1619) which means intrinsic value - the price that I am willing to pay because it is worth it. The word "honor" hides the basic idea from the English student. Honor comes to people who are considered "worth it" by those who honor them. These people whom Paul describes have their axiology straight. They seek only true value. They expend scarce personal resources only upon those things of greatest eternal value. Their priorities are ordered from a divine, heavenly and eternal point of view. Honors in the political, Hollywood or sports page sense are not necessarily the honors of Romans 2:7. Isaiah had the point in Isaiah 55:2. One who seeks τιμή has the heavenly point of view and is willing, in order to gain it in the long run, to forego it in the short run. His opposite looks only at the short run. The cocktail or the drug will make him forget his troubles now but there is a hangover in the morning. This is contrary to Isaiah's advice - this is spending money for that which is not "worth it."

Finally they seek viability (#3836). Anything with a disjunctive component cannot be viable. A machine or a philosophic system that carries within it the seeds of its own destruction is not immortal. The people in verse 7 are seeking long run consistency - philosophical perpetual motion. Perpetual motion in

physics would result if there were no friction. Such a system would be immortal.
In this sense eternal life is intellectual, physical and ethical perpetual motion.
The atheist cannot achieve it. His system is non-viable. Hell can be described as
everlasting disintegration in absence from the Lord (2 Thess.1:9). *Cf.* ὄλεϑρος
(#4135). Basicly its means disintegration. Hell is the place where everything will
"come unglued." No one in hell "puts it all together" because radical empiricism
says that the attempt to achieve consistency and concrescence ("putting it
together") is a tender minded and naive attempt to achieve the impossible. The
kind of thinking that achieves concresence and viability is noumenal. And that is
what the existentialist disdains. Phenomenology, which is all that the unbeliever
has, can never provide concrescent consistency and its reward - immortality.
Unbelievers pay throughout eternity the penalty for being philosophically and
theological wrong in time.

If the heathen reacts with humility to the noumena suggested to him by the
phenomena and consents to the "law of the Lord" that it is "perfect" (complete,
holistic) it "converts his soul" (Psalm 19:7). Similarly if he agrees that testimony
of the Lord is sure, the statutes of the Lord are right, the commandment of the
Lord is pure, the fear of the Lord is clean and that the judgments of the Lord are
true and righteous altogehter, they will not only convert his soul, but they will
make him wise, rejoice his heart and enlighten his eyes. Thus by yielding to the
light from God which began when he first looked at the stars and thought about
it, he not only became a Christian, but a philosopher and a man of science, with a
song in his heart. This is spiritual, intellectual and psychological good health,
because he has been made the total man - the dream that God had for him when
He created him in the garden in the first place.

That which is perfect, sure, right and pure converts the soul, makes wise the
simple, rejoices the heart and enlightens the eyes. For whom? For the man who
hears the entire Scriptural good news of salvation in the historic Jesus or, failing
that, in the savage who sees what Psalm 19;1-6 describes and reacts in keeping
with Romans 2:7. Obviously the latter as well as the former. This becomes
clearer in Romans 2:12-16.

The question arises - how many of the heathen reacted like that, instead of in
the manner described in Romans 2:8,9? And from whence came this proper
disposition of mind? Did he provide it from innate resources or not? It resulted,
if indeed he manifested it, from the election of God's grace and the question as to
who was given this gift and who was not is not a question for mortals to ask. Let
is also be kept in mind that the vast majority of the human race died in infancy. If
this were not true demographers tell us that the human race would long since
have starved to death on this planet as a result of extreme overpopulation.

Verses 8 and 9 describe a less fortunate group.

*Verse 8 - "But unto them that are contentious, and obey not the truth, but obey
unrighteousness, indignation and wrath."*

τοῖς δὲ ἐξ ἐριϑείας καὶ ἀπειϑοῦσαι τῇ ἀληϑείᾳ πειϑομένοις δὲ τῇ ἀδικίᾳ,
ὀργὴ καὶ ϑυμός —

"... *but for those who are factious and do not obey the truth, but obey wickedness, there will be wrath and fury.*" *RSV*

τοῖς (dat.pl.masc.of the article in agreement with πειθομένοις) 9.
δὲ (adversative conjunction) 11.
ἐξ (preposition with the partative genitive) 19.

#3837 ἐριθείας (gen.sing.fem.of ἐριθεία, partitive).

King James Version

contention - Phil.1:17.
strife - 1 Cor.12:20; Gal.5:20; Phil.2:3; James 3:14,16.
that are contentious - Romans 2:8.

Revised Standard Version

partisanship - Phil.1:17.
factious - Romans 2:8.
selfish ambition - James 3:14,16.
selfishness - 2 Cor.12:20; Gal.5:20; Phil.2:3.

*Meaning:* "ἐριθεύω - to spin wool, work in wool. Heliodoros 1,5; Mid.in the same sense, Tob. 2, 11; used of those who electioneer for office, courting popular applause by trickery and low arts, Aristotle, Polit.5,3. The verb is derived from ἔριθος, working for hire, a hireling; fr. the Maded.age down, a spinner or weaver, a worker in wool, Isa.38:12. LXX, a mean, sordid fellow, electioneering or intriguing for office. Aristot. Pol.5,2 and 3, (pp.1302b,4 and 1303a, 14). Hence, apparently in the N.T. a courting distinction, a desire to put one's self forward, a partisan and factious spirit which does not disdain low arts; partisanship, factiousness - James 3:14,16." (Thayer). In preaching the gospel in a way so as to promote one's self - Phil.1:17; generally in 2 Cor.12:20. Gal.5:20 and Phil.2:3 as a fruit of the flesh - with reference to the apostates - Romans 2:8.

καὶ (adjunctive conjunction) 14.
ἀπειθοῦσι (pres.act.part.dat.pl.masc.of ἀπείθω, substantival, indirect object of ἀποδώσει) 1996.
τῇ (dat.sing.fem.of the article in agreement with ἀληθείᾳ) 9.
ἀληθείᾳ (dat.sing.fem.of ἀλήθεια, dative of object) 1416.
πειθομένοις (pres.mid.part.dat.pl.masc.of πείθω, substantival, indirect object of ἀποδώσει) 1629.
δὲ (adversative conjunction) 11.
τῇ (dat.sing.fem.of the article in agreement with ἀδικίᾳ) 9.
ἀδικίᾳ (dat.sing.fem.of ἀδικία, dative of object) 2367.
ὀργή (nom.sing.fem.of ὀργή, *nominativus pendens*) 283.
καὶ (adjunctive conjunction joining nouns) 14.
θυμός (nom.sing.masc.of θυμός, *nominativus pendens*) 2034.

*Translation* - "... *but on the other hand to those factious persons who are disobeying the truth and acquiescing in lawlessness - indignation and wrath.*"

**Comment:**δὲ is adversative. The partitive genitive in ἐξ ἐριθείας (#3837) identifies the subjects and indicates the motivation for their attitude and behavior. Theirs was a desire for self promotion. These were the compulsive personalities who sought the spotlight for wicked reasons. A demonstration of bravado, particularly if one is waging a war against God and His word will gain attention in certain circles. God is not dead but a book written to that effect will enjoy a large sale and yield rich royalties. They took opposite attitudes toward the truth and lawlessness. The former they disobeyed, and to the latter they assented and gave their approval. Note Paul's suspended nominatives in ὀργή καὶ θυμός. ὀργή means slow burning, deep seated indignation that finally flames into θυμός which is divine anger. The former is covert; the latter is overt. God's anger burns against unrighteousness and finally explodes.

*Verse 9 - "Tribulation and anguish upon every soul of man that doeth evil, of the Jew first and also of the Gentiles."*

θλῖψις καὶ στενοχωρία ἐπὶ πᾶσαν ψυχὴν ἀνθρώπου τοῦ κατεργαζομένου τὸ κακόν, Ἰουδαίου τε πρῶτον καὶ Ἕλληνος.

*"There will be tribulation and distress for every human being who does evil, the Jew first and also the Greek, . . . " RSV*

θλῖψις (nom.sing.fem.of θλῖψις, suspended subject) 1046.

καὶ (adjunctive conjunction joining nouns) 14.

**#3838** στενοχωρία (nom.sing.fem.of στενοχωρία, suspended subject).

King James Version

anguish - Romans 2:9.
distress - Romans 8:35; 2 Cor.6:4; 12:10.

Revised Standard Version

distress - Romans 2:9; 8:35.
calamities - 2 Cor.6:4; 12:10.

*Meaning:* Cf. στενοχωρέω (#4300); στενός (#661). Cf. στενόχωρος - "narrowness of place." Metaphorically, dire calamity, extreme affliction, distress, anguish, pressure. With reference to the judgment of God upon unbelievers - Romans 2:9; with reference to the experiences of Christians in the world - Romans 8:38; 2 Cor.6:4; 12:10.

ἐπὶ (preposition with the accusative, extent) 47.
πᾶσαν (acc.sing.fem.of πᾶς, in agreement with ψυχὴν) 67.
ψυχὴν (acc.sing.fem.of ψυχή, extent) 233.
ἀνθρώπου (gen.sing.masc.of ἄνθρωπος, description) 341.
τοῦ (gen.sing.masc.of the article in agreement with κατεργαζομένου) 9.
κατεργαζομένου (pres.mid.part.gen.sing.masc.of κατεργάζομαι, adjectival,

restrictive, in agreement with φυχήν) 3815.

τό (acc.sing.neut.of the article in agreement with κακόν) 9.

κακόν (acc.sing.neut.of κακός, direct object of κατεργαζομένου) 1388.

'Ιουδαίου (gen.sing.masc.of 'Ιουδαῖος, in apposition) 143.

τε (correlative particle) 1408.

πρῶτον (acc.sing.neut.of πρῶτος, adverbial) 487.

καὶ (adjunctive conjunction joining nouns) 14.

Ἕλληνος (gen.sing.masc.of Ἕλλήν, in apposition) 2373.

*Translation - ". . . tribulation and distress upon every human soul who is doing evil, both the Jew first and also the Greek."*

**Comment:** Paul's thought is clear. His grammar needs improvement. There is no verb. Wrath and indignation from God brings tribulation and the pressures of social, economic and physical conditions upon the earth for those who transgress His laws, both moral and natural. The agonies of the dope addict who cannot find the money to support his habit are not inflicted by the hand of God directly. They are only the physical reaction to taking drugs. Note that natural law does not make a distinction between Jews and Greeks.

*Verse 10 - "But glory, honour, and peace to every man that worketh good, to the Jew first, and also to the Gentile."*

δόξα δὲ καὶ τιμὴ καὶ εἰρήνη παντὶ τῷ ἐργαζομένῳ τὸ ἀγατόν, 'Ιουδαίῳ τε πρῶτον καὶ Ἕλληνι.

*". . . but glory and honor and peace for every one who does good, the Jew first and also the Greek." RSV*

δόξα (nom.sing.fem.of δόξα, suspended subject) 361.

δὲ (adversative conjunction) 11.

καὶ (adjunctive conjunction joining nouns) 14.

τιμὴ (nom.sing.fem.of τιμή, suspended subject) 1619.

καὶ (adjunctive conjunction joining nouns) 14.

εἰρήνη (nom.sing.fem.of εἰρήνη, suspended subject) 865.

παντὶ (dat.sing.masc.of πᾶς, in agreement with ἐργαζομένῳ) 67.

τῷ (dat.sing.masc.of the article in agreement with ἐργαζομένῳ) 9.

ἐργαζομένῳ (pres.mid.part.dat.sing.masc.ofd ἐργάζομαι, substantival, indirect object) 691.

τὸ (acc.sing.neut.of the article in agreement with ἀγαθόν) 9.

ἀγαθόν (acc.sing.neut.of ἀγαθός, direct object of ἐργαζομένῳ) 574.

'Ιουδαίῳ (dat.sing.masc.of 'Ιουδαῖος, in apposition) 143.

τε (correlative particle) 1408.

πρῶτον (acc.sing.neut.of πρῶτος, adverbial) 487.

καὶ (adjunctive conjunction joining nouns) 14.

Ἕλληνι (dat.sing.masc.of Ἕλλήν, in apposition) 2373.

*Translation - ". . . but glory and honor and peace to everyone who works the good, both the Jew first and also the Greek."*

**Comment:** This repeats the statement of verse 7. Thus verses 7 and 10 contrast the attitudes, philosophies, lifestyles and destinies of two classes of people who each receive the same revelation of natural philosophy (Psalm 19:1-6) and are each possessed of the voice of conscience.

Paul does not say that all of the heathen turned against God's truth. Nor does he say that they all followed God's light to greater light. He does suggest that there is sufficient light in God's revelation to primitive man to lead to his salvation. This is explained in greater detail in verses 12-16. At this point Paul is only satisfied to make the case generally that God is compelled by the compulsions of His own holy nature to react in wrath toward sin and in reward toward compliance with His moral law, wherever He may find the one or the other. If any primitive man did the right thing in response to the light which he came to understand, we may be sure that he was impelled by a force outside himself. The exegete will balance παντὶ τῷ ἐργαζομένῳ τὸ ἀγαθόν of verse 10 with οὐκ ἔστιν ποιῶν χρηστότητα, οὐκ ἔστιν ἕως ἑνός of Romans 3:12b.

*Verse 11 - "For there is no respect of persons with God."*

οὐ γάρ ἐστιν προσωπολημφία παρὰ τῷ θεῷ.

*"For God shows no partiality."* RSV

οὐ (negative conjunction with the indicative) 130.
γάρ (causal conjunction) 105.
ἐστιν (3d.per.sing.pres.ind.of εἰμί, static) 86.

**#3839** προσωπολημφία (nom.sing.fem.of προσωπολημφία, subject of ἐστιν).

King James Version

respect of persons - Romans 2:11; Eph.6:9; Col.3:25; James 2:1.

Revised Standard Version

partiality - Romans 2:11; Eph.6:9; Col.3:25; James 2:1.

*Meaning:* respect of persons. The error of showing deference to outward circumstances of prestige rather than to intrinsic merit. Plural in James 2:1 to indicate numerous specific cases of partiality. In the sphere of God's judgment - Romans 2:8; Eph.6:9; Col.3:25.

παρὰ (preposition with the locative of sphere, with persons) 154.
τῷ (loc.sing.masc.of the article in agreement with θεῷ) 9.
θεῷ (loc.sing.masc.of θεός, sphere) 124.

*Translation - "For there is no partiality where God is concerned."*

**Comment:** Every case is decided strictly on its merits.

*Verse 12 - "For as many as have sinned without law shall also perish without law:*

*and as many as have sinned in the law shall be judged by the law."*

ὅσοι γὰρ ἀνόμως ἥμαρτον, ἀνόμως καὶ ἀπολοῦνται, καὶ ὅσοι ἐν νόμῳ ἥμαρτον, διὰ νόμου κριθήσονται.

*"All who have sinned without the law will also perish without the law, and all who have sinned under the law will be judged by the law." RSV*

ὅσοι (nom.pl.masc.of ὅσος, subject of ἥμαρτον and ἀπολοῦνται) 660.

γὰρ (inferential conjunction) 105.

#**3840** ἀνόμως (adverbial).

King James Version

without the law - Romans 2:12,12.

Revised Standard Version

without the law - Romans 2:12,12.

*Meaning:* α privative plus νόμος (#464) *Cf.* ἄνομος (#2772) and ἀνομία (#692). An adverb - "without law." In the absence of law. Without knowledge of the law - Romans 2:12,12.

ἥμαρτον (3d.per.pl.2d.aor.act.ind.of ἁμαρτάνω, culminative) 1260.
ἀνόμως (adverbial) 3840.
καὶ (adjunctive conjunction joining verbs) 14.
ἀπολοῦνται (3d.per.pl.fut.mid.ind.of ἀπόλλυμι, predictive) 208.
καὶ (continuative conjunction) 14.
ὅσοι (nom.pl.masc.of ὅσος, subject of ἥμαρτον and κριθήσονται) 660.
ἐν (preposition with the locative of sphere) 80.
νόμῳ (loc.sing.masc.of νόμος, sphere) 464.
ἥμαρτον (3d.per.pl.2d.aor.act.ind.of ἁμαρτάνω, culminative) 1260.
διὰ (preposition with the ablative of agent) 118.
νόμου (abl.sing.masc.of νόμος, agent) 464.
κριθήσονται (3d.per.pl.fut.pass.ind.of κρίνω, predictive) 531.

*Translation - "Therefore as many as have sinned without the law shall also perish without reference to the law, and as many as have sinned within the scope of the law will be judged by the law."*

**Comment:** The law (νόμος #464) here refers to the Mosaic Code. γὰρ is inferential. Paul's last thought in verse 11 is that with God there is no discrimination between Jew and Gentile. His comment in verse 12 covers the case of evil workers (verse 9, last clause) and good workers (verse 10, last clause) and the statement of verse 11. Since all men, Jew and Gentile have the voice of conscience, the distinguishing characteristic between Jew and Gentile is the fact the Jew has the Sinai Code, specifically given to him, while the Gentile does not. The thought is that when a man who never had the Mosaic Code dies, this fact will be taken into consideration by the righteous Judge, although the Judge will not overlook the fact that though the defendant did not have the Sinai Code he did have the voice of moral conscience, which all men have.

Conversely the Jew will be held up to the Sinai standard. If it were otherwise the Judge would be guilty of having respect of persons - something that verse 11 denies. God has another way to make His righteous judgment as we shall see. The use of ἀπολοῦνται (#208) does not always mean damnation, although that is its meaning in some contexts.

When the heathen, uninstructed by the Mosaic Code, dies the fact that he had never read or heard of the Ten Commandments is well known to the Judge. This does not mean that he is judged on a less exacting standard than the Jew. Neither Jew nor Gentile will be given a legal advantage over the other in God's righteous court. The next thought in verse 13 is causal.

*Verse 13 - "For not the hearers of the law are just before God, but the doers of the law shall be justified."*

οὐ γὰρ οἱ ἀκροαταὶ νόμου δίκαιοι παρὰ τῷ θεῷ, ἀλλ᾽ οἱ ποιηταὶ νόμου δικαιωθήσονται.

*"For it is not the hearers of the law who are righteous before God, but the doers of the law will be justified." RSV*

οὐ (negative conjunction with the indicative) 130.
γὰρ (causal conjunction) 105.
οἱ (nom.pl.masc.of the article in agreement with ἀκροαταὶ) 9.

#3841 ἀκροαταὶ (nom.pl.masc.of ἀκροατής, subject of the verb understood).

King James Version

hearer - Romans 2:13; James 1:22,23,25.

Revised Standard Version

hearer - Romans 2:13; James 1:22,23,25.

*Meaning:* Cf. ἀκροάομαι - "to hearken," "to listen to." Cf. also ἀκροατήριον (#3646). Hence, one who listens, hears and understands. Joined to an attributive genitive - νόμου in Romans 2:13; to λόγου - James 1:22,23; with νόμον τέλειον - James 1:25.

νόμου (gen.sing.masc.of νόμος, description) 464.
δίκαιοι (nom.pl.masc.of δίκαιος, predicate adjective) 85.
παρὰ (preposition with the locative of place, with persons) 154.
τῷ (loc.sing.masc.of the article in agreement with θεῷ) 9.
θεῷ (loc.sing.masc.of θεός, place, with persons) 124.
ἀλλ᾽ (alternative conjunction) 342.
οἱ (nom.pl.masc.of the article in agreement with ποιηταὶ) 9.

ποιηταὶ (nom.pl.masc.of ποιητής, subject of δικαιωϑήσονται) 3419.
νόμου (gen.sing.masc.of νόμος, description) 464.
δικαιωϑήσονται (3d.per.pl.fut.pass.ind.of δικαιόω, predictive) 933.

*Translation - "Because it is not those who hear the law who are righteous before God, but those who do what the law demands will be declared righteous."*

**Comment:** In verse 12 νόμος means the Mosaic Code. *Cf.* comment *en loc.* But notice that the article in missing before νόμου in verse 13. It is also absent in verse 12, but our argument there is based upon context. Robertson (*Grammar*, 796) says that it is "at least problematical" that Paul is speaking of Moses law specifically in verse 13 as in verse 12. The point is that he seems to be laying down a general principle that guides the Divine Judge. γὰρ is causal, as Paul prepares to explain why what he says in verse 12 is true. A Jew who has heard Moses read (or has read it for himself) is to be judged by it, since the rule of law is that doers are justified, not hearers, unless, of course, hearers are also doers. Note ποιηταί (#3419) - one whose life is characterized by the positive ethical implementation of the moral principles set forth in the law. A doer of the law is one whose life demonstrates in flesh and blood which is written on the tablets of stone (2 Cor.3:1-3). Otherwise if there is an advantage in hearing, even for one who does not obey, then the Jew has an advantage over the Gentile. But this violates verse 11. Thus we conclude that verse 13 argues the general principle to be applied to all law, which is therefore applied by God to the Mosaic law of verse 12 and also in verse 14. Note the strong contrast in the οὐ . . . ἀλλ' sequence.

*Verse 14 - "For when the Gentiles, which have not the law, do by nature the things contained in the law, these, having not the law, are a law unto themselves."*

ὅταν γὰρ ἔϑνη τὰ μὴ νόμον ἔχοντα φύσει τὰ τοῦ νόμου ποιῶσιν, οὗτοι νόμον μὴ ἔχοντες ἑαυτοῖς εἰσιν νόμος.

*"When Gentiles who hae not the law do by nature what the law requires, they are a law to themselves, even though they do not have the law."* RSV

ὅταν (temporal conjunction introducing the subjunctive in an indefinite temporal clause) 436.
γὰρ (inferential conjunction) 105.
ἔϑνη (nom.pl.neut.of ἔϑνος, subject of ποιῶσιν) 376.
τὰ (acc.pl.neut.of the article in agreement with ἔχοντα) 9.
μὴ (negative conjunction with the participle) 87.
νόμον (acc.sing.masc.of νόμος, direct object of ἔχοντα) 464.
ἔχοντα (pres.act.part.nom.pl.neut.of ἔχω, adjectival, restrictive, in agreement with ἔϑνη) 82.
φύσει (instru.sing.fem.of φύσις, means) 3811.
τὰ (acc.pl.neut.of the article, direct object of ποιῶσιν) 9.
τοῦ (gen.sing.masc.of the article in agreement with νόμου) 9.

*νόμου* (gen.sing.masc.of *νόμος*, description) 464.

*ποιῶσιν* (3d.per.pl.pres.act.subj.of *ποιέω*, indefinite temporal clause) 127.

*οὗτοι* (nom.pl.masc.of *οὗτος*, subject of *εἰσιν*) 93.

*νόμον* (acc.sing.masc.of *νόμος*, direct object of *ἔχοντες*) 464.

*μὴ* (negative conjunction with the participle) 87.

*ἔχοντες* (pres.act.part.nom.pl.masc.of *ἔχω*, adverbial, concessive) 82.

*ἑαυτοῖς* (dat.pl.masc.of *ἑαυτοῦ*, personal interest) 288.

*εἰσιν* (3d.per.pl.pres.ind.of *εἰμί*, static) 86.

*νόμος* (nom.sing.masc.of *νόμος*, predicate nominative) 464.

*Translation - "For when Gentiles who do not have the law, do naturally what the law requires, although they do not have the law, these are a law unto themselves."*

Comment: *γὰρ* is inferential as Paul supports what he said in the last clause of verse 13. Those who obey the law will be justified, but this does not mean that only Jews will be justified, since Jews are the only ones who received the Mosaic Code. How could a Gentile obey a law that he did not possess? Oh, but he does possess it, not on tablets of stone as did Moses and Israel, from the hand of God on Sinai, but in his conscience which is his by virtue of the fact that he is created in God's image.

*τὰ μὴ νόμον ἔχοντα* is the participial adjectival clause which defines *ἔθνη*. These Gentiles are "not having the law Gentiles." Note that *ὅταν* and the subjunctive is indefinite. Paul is not saying definitely that the Gentiles will obey their consciences. There is the usual element of contingency in the subjunctive mode. We do not know when or if they will but *if and when they do* they will have demonstrated that one does not need the Ten Commandments in order to know the difference between right and wrong. The fact that Gentiles never formally received the Mosaic Code will not prevent their being rewarded. Such persons (deictic *οὗτοι*), although they do not have the law (concessive *ἔχοντες*) are a law unto themselves.

How do Gentiles know and obey the law of God? It is by nature - *φύσει* - or "naturally." It is not the nature of fallen man to be good, but it is the nature of man, both before he fell and after, to know what the good is as distinct from the evil. *φύσει* here clearly teaches that man, created in God's image, not only can arrive at noumenal truth on the basis of phenomenal investigation but also has a built-in sense of God's concepts of right and wrong. When a heathen follows his conscience humbly, he refrains from the same sins that the Mosaic law condemns and wishes to do the good deeds which it applauds. His is a built-in code. Again we stress that Paul does not say here that anyone ever did this. He only says that if he did he would be showing the results of verse 15.

A missionary to the Sara Kaba tribe of disc-lipped women tells of an old woman who heard her first gospel sermon from his lips. He was the first white man that she had ever seen. She said, "I have believed ever since I was a little girl that there was a God like that."

*Verse 15 - "Which shew the work of the law written in their hearts, their conscience also bearing witness, and their thoughts the meanwhile accusing or else excusing one another. "*

οἵτινες ἐνδείκνυνται τὸ ἔργον τοῦ νόμου γραπτὸν ἐν ταῖς καρδίαις αὐτῶν, συμμαρτυρούσης αὐτῶν τῆς συνειδήσεως καὶ μεταξὺ ἀλλήλων τῶν λογισμῶν κατηγορούντων ἢ καὶ ἀπολογουμένων,

*"They show that what the law requires is written on their hearts, while their conscience also bears witness and their conflicting thoughts accuse or perhaps excuse them . . . " RSV*

οἵτινες (nom.pl.masc.of ὅστις, indefinite relative pronoun, subject of ἐνδείκνυνται) 163.

**#3842** ἐνδείκνυνται (3d.per.pl.pres.mid.ind.of ἐνδείκνυμαι, iterative).

King James Version

do - 2 Tim.4:14.
show - Romans 2:15; 9:17,22; 2 Cor.8:24; Eph.2:7; Titus 2:10; 3:2; Heb.6:10,11.
show forth - 1 Tim.1:16.

Revised Standard Version

show - Romans 2:15; 9:17,22; Eph.2:7; Titus 2:10; 3:2; Heb.6:10,11.
do - 2 Tim.4:14.
boast - 2 Cor.8:24.
display - 1 Tim.1:16.

*Meaning:* To point out; in the New Testament only in the middle voice. To demonstrate in one's self; show demonstrative proof - Rom.9:22; Eph.2:7; Titus 2:10; 3:2; Heb.6:11; Rom.2:15; 9:17; 1 Tim.1:16; Heb.6:10; 2 Cor.8:24; manifest, display - put forth - 2 Tim.4:14.

τὸ (acc.sing.neut.of the article in agreement with ἔργον) 9.
ἔργον (acc.sing.neut.of ἔργον, direct object of ἐνδείκνυνται) 460.
τοῦ (gen.sing.masc.of the article in agreement with νόμου) 9.
νόμου (gen.sing.masc.of νόμος, descriptive) 464.

**#3843** γραπτὸν (acc.sing.masc.of γραπτός, predicate adjective).

King James Version

written - Romans 2:15.

Revised Standard Version

written - Romans 2:15.

*Meaning: Cf.* γράφω (#156). Written - Romans 2:15.

ἐν (preposition with the locative of place) 80.
ταῖς (loc.pl.fem.of the article in agreement with καρδίαις) 9.
καρδίαις (loc.pl.fem.of καρδία, place where) 432.
αὐτῶν (gen.pl.masc.of αὐτός, possession) 16.

#3844 συμμαρτυρούσης (pres.act.part.gen.sing.fem.of συμμαρτυρέω, genitive absolute).

King James Version

bear witness - Romans 2:15.
bear witness also - Romans 9:1.
bear witness with - Romans 8:16.

Revised Standard Version

bear witness - Romans 2:15; 8:16; 9:1.

*Meaning:* A combination of σύν (#1542) and μαρτυρέω (#1471). Hence, to bear a corroborating witness; to give a joint witness with another; to support the testimony of another. The conscience supports what the will decides - Romans 2:15; 9:1. The Holy Spirit supports the witness of the believer - Romans 8:16.

αὐτῶν (gen.pl.masc.of  αὐτός, possession) 16.
τῆς (gen.sing.fem.of the article in agreement with συνείδησις) 9.
συνειδήσεως (gen.sing.fem.of συνείδησις, genitive absolute) 3590.
καὶ (continuative conjunction) 14.
μεταξὺ (improper preposition with the  genitive) 1262.
ἀλλήλων (gen.pl.masc.of ἀλλήλων, description) 1487.
τῶν (gen.pl.masc.of the article in agreement with λογισμῶν) 9.

#3845 λογισμῶν (gen.pl.masc.of λογισμός, genitive absolute).

King James Version

imagination - 2 Cor.10:5.
thought - Romans 2:15.

Revised Standard Version

conflicting thought - Romans 2:15.
arguments - 2 Cor.10:5.

*Meaning:* Cf. λογίζομαι (#2611). Hence, a reckoning; a computation; an argument; a line of reasoning; logical development - 2 Cor.10:4 (5). A judicial decision based upon a decision of the conscience - Romans 2:15.

κατηγορούντων (pres.act.part.gen.pl.masc.of κατηγορέω, genitive absolute) 974.
ἤ (disjunctive) 465.
καὶ (ascensive conjunction) 14.
ἀπολογουμένων (pres.act.part.gen.pl.masc.of ἀπολογέομαι, genitive

absolute) 2476.

*Translation - ".. . who reveal that the activity of the law has been written in their hearts, their conscience also bearing witness with them and their thoughts either accusing or justifying them."*

**Comment:**   Men do what they wish to do. Thus their covert behavior, the ethical lifestyle which they present to their peers for examination is a reflection of their thinking. The function of the law of God, whether it was discerned from the tablets of stone which God gave to Moses and to the nation Israel at Sinai or from the thoughts of the heart is to approbate the good and condemn the evil. Thus the conscience (#3590) of every man whispers to him the praise or blame of his Creator. The Jew has a double witness, for what he feels in his heart is also written in the law of Moses. If the tablets of stone had not been given to Israel, God would still have had a proper basis for judgment, since He had already witnessed to His chosen people His moral standards in the same way that He has witnessed to all the Gentiles.

It is significant that God's moral standards are revealed by nature (φῦσει - verse 14). Nature (φύσις) tells man what is right and wrong. This supports what Paul said in Romans 1:18-23, where we learned that those who had only the experimental knowledge derived from observation of the physical worlds knew, not only the noumena - divine power and attributes of deity - which cannot be discerned by sense perception, but also the distinction between that which was moral and that which was immoral. Thus when they indulged in homosexual activities which were said to be παρὰ φύσιν (Romans 1:26) they were beside the moral mark of divine law. Nor can they be excused on the grounds of ignorance, because it was φύσις which told them what was right and their conduct was παρὰ φύσιν - "beside or astray from the dicates of nature." When the homosexual tells us that he is a Christian and that his conduct is acceptable to God, he is in opposition to Romans 1:26 and Romans 2:14.

If a man falls into the category described in Romans 2:7,10, his conscience applauds and his peers sees his lifestyle in terms of verse 7. But if his behavior is described by verses 8 and 9, he knows while he follows that manner of life that he is sinning against the light of heart and mind.

Paul has not said that anyone has displayed the qualities that lead to eternal life, but the implication is there. Of course all who have died in infancy are safe from God's judgment. Their case is covered by Romans 4:15b. In view of the fact that in uncivilized cultures infant mortality sweeps away most of the children before they reach the age ot discretion means that even if every adult is lost (which this passage implies is not true) the vast majority of the human race will be saved.

*Verse 16 - "In the day when God shall judge the secrets of men by Jesus Christ according to my gospel."*

ἐν ᾗ ἡμέρᾳ κρίνει ὁ θεὸς τὰ κρυπτὰ τῶν ἀνθρώπων κατὰ τὸ εὐαγγέλιόν μου διὰ Ἰησοῦ Χριστοῦ.

"... *on that day when, according to my gospel, God judges the secrets of men by Christ Jesus."*    RSV

ἐν (preposition with the locative of time point) 80.

ᾗ (loc.sing.fem.of ὅς, relative pronoun, in agreement with ἡμέρᾳ) 65.

ἡμέρᾳ (loc.sing.fem.of ἡμέρα, time point) 135.

κρίνει (3d.per.sing.pres.act.ind.of κρίνω, futuristic) 531.

ὁ (nom.sing.masc.of the article in agreement with θεὸς) 9.

θεὸς (nom.sing.masc.of θεός, subject of κρίνει) 124.

τὰ (acc.pl.neut.of the article in agreement with κρυπτὰ) 9.

κρυπτὰ (acc.pl.neut.of κρυπτός, direct object of κρίνει) 565.

τῶν (gen.pl.masc.of the article in agreement with ἀνθρώπων) 9.

ἀνθρώπων (gen.pl.masc.of ἄνθρωπος, description) 341.

κατὰ (preposition with the accusative, standard rule) 98.

τὸ (acc.sing.neut.of the article in agreement with εὐαγγέλιον) 9.

εὐαγγέλιόν (acc.sing.neut.of εὐαγγέλιον, standard rule) 405.

μου (gen.sing.masc.of ἐγώ, possession) 123.

διὰ (preposition with the ablative of agent) 118.

Ἰησοῦ (abl.sing.masc.of Ἰησοῦς, agent) 3.

Χριστοῦ (abl.sing.masc.of Χριστός, apposition) 4.

*Translation - "On the day when God is going to judge the secrets of men in keeping with the terms of my gospel by Jesus Christ."*

**Comment:** Paul is pointing forward to a definite day of judgment. *Cf. Acts 17:31. Note the futuristic present in* κρίνει. The phrase κατὰ τὸ εὐαγγέλιόν μου means "on the terms of the gospel which I preach." Paul had never omitted the ultimate judgment phase of the gospel of Christ. *Cf.* Acts 24:25. A judgment day is to come when that which is secret to men, but which has never been secret to God, will be the factual basis upon which the decision of the court of heaven will be made. Paul leaves no doubt about Who the Judge will be. *Cf.* John 5:22.

*keeping with the terms of my gospel by Jesus Christ."*

**Comment:** Paul is pointing forward to a definite day of judgment. *Cf.* Acts 17:31. Note the futuristic present tense in κρίνει. The phrase κατὰ τὸ εὐαγγέλιόν μου means "on the terms of the gospel which I preach." Paul had never omitted the ultimate judgment phase of the gospel. *Cf.* Acts 24:25. A judgment day is scheduled when that which is secret to men, but which has never been secret to God, will be the factual basis upon which the Judge of heaven's court will hand down His decision. That Judge is Jesus Christ (John 5:22).

Generally we think of the secrets of men in terms of evil. Thus we speak darkly of "skeletons in the closet." But there is nothing in this context to suggest that all of the thoughts of men, known but to God, are thoughts of evil. How many whose outward demeanor would suggest only rebellion against God have at some time and in some secluded place approached the throne of grace on terms that fall within the parameters of the demands of the gospel of Christ? Whatever we may think about the chances for salvation of the heathen who lived and died without the gospel (*i.e.* of those who survived infancy), as though God will be influenced by what we think, and as though we thought that it was really some of our business, our Lord will make the proper judgment in that day. The implication is strong that some will fall into the category described in Romans 2:7,10, and that others will be judged on the basis of Romans 2:8,9. This implication in no way relieves the Church of the obligation to carry out the Great Commission of Matthew 28:18-20 and Acts 1:8. The rationalization that since a man can be saved if he reacts humbly to the truth which he has, and therefore we need not preach the gospel to him is a wicked and perverted attempt to justify our lack of zeal for missions. On the question as to how much theological truth is understood by the sinner at the moment he repents and accepts Christ, it is doubtful that his intellectual grasp is greater, or very little greater, than if he had never heard the gospel. Sinners exercise the gifts of repentance and faith with a spontaneity that precludes most philosophical examination of the terms upon which the gospel is offered.

No amount of rationalization on a disputed theological point is justification for outright disobedience. Our Lord said, "Go, disciple, baptize and teach." That should be all of the motivation a Christian needs.

Paul, who is cast in this scenario as a prosecuting attorney, has arraigned and indicted before the bar of divine justice two classes of Gentile society. He now calls the Jew to account for his sins in Romans 2:1-29.

# The Jews and the Law

*(Romans 2:17 - 3:8)*

*Verse 17 - "Behold, thou art called a Jew, and restest in the law, and makest thy boast of God."*

Εἰ δὲ σὺ Ἰουδαῖος ἐπονομάζῃ καὶ ἐπαναπαύῃ νόμῳ καὶ καυχᾶσαι ἐν θεῷ

*"But if you call yourself a Jew and rely upon the law and boast of your relation to God . . . " RSV*

Εἰ (conditional particle in a first-class condition) 337.
δὲ (explanatory conjunction) 11.
σὺ (nom.sing.masc.of σύ, subject of every verb through verse 20) 104.
Ἰουδαῖος (nom.sing.masc.of Ἰουδαῖος, predicate nominative) 143.

#3846 ἐπονομάζῃ (2d.per.sing.pres.pass.ind.of ἐπονομάζω, progressive duration, retroactive).

King James Version

call - Romans 2:17.

Revised Standard Version

call yourself - Romans 2:17.

*Meaning:* A combination of ἐπί (#47) and ὀνομάζω (#2115). Hence to name something or someone. In the middle, to call one's self. In the passive to be called by some name - Romans 2:17.

καὶ (adjunctive conjunction joining verbs) 14.
ἐπαναπαύῃ (2d.per.sing.pres.mid.ind.of ἐπαναπαύομαι, progressive duration, retroactive) 2413.

νόμῳ (loc.sing.masc.of νόμος, sphere) 464.
καὶ (adjunctive conjunction joining verbs) 14.

#3847 καυχᾶσαι (2d.per.sing.pres.ind.for καυχᾷ, of καύχάομαι, progressive present, retroactive).

King James Version

boast - 2 Cor.7:14; 9:2; 10:8,13,15,16; Eph.2:9.
boast one's self - 2 Cor.11:16.
burn - 1 Cor.13:3.
glory - Romans 5:3; 1 Cor.1:29,31,31; 3:21; 4:7; 2 Cor.5:12; 10:17,17; 11:12,18,18,30,30; 12:1,5,6,9; Gal.6:13,14.
joy - Romans 5:11.
make one's boast - Romans 2:17,23.
rejoice - Romans 5:2; Phil.3:3; James 1:9; 4:16.

Revised Standard Version

express pride - 2 Cor.7:14.
burn - 1 Cor.13:3.
boast - 2 Cor.9:2; 10:8,13,15,16; Eph.2:9; 2 Cor.11:16; 1 Cor.1:29,31,31; 3:21; 4:7; 2 Cor.10:17,17; 11:12,18,18,30,30; 12:1,5,5,6,9; Romans 2:17,23; James 1:9; 4:16.
rejoice - Romans 5:2,3,11.
pride themselves - 2 Cor.5:12.
glory - Gal.6:13,14; Phil.3:3.

*Meaning:* To glory in; derive satisfaction from; be proud of; boast of - whether with or without good reason. Followed by ὑπὲρ and the genitive - 2 Cor.7:14; 9:2; 5:12; 12:5a,b. Followed by περί -2 Cor.10:8; with the accusative - 2 Cor.10:13,15,16; 11:16,30b. Absolutely in Eph.2:9; 1 Cor.1:31a; 4:7; 2 Cor.10:17a; 11:18b,30a; 12:1a,b; James 1:9. With ἐν in Romans 5:3; 1 Cor.1:31b; 3:21; 2 Cor.10:17b; 11:12; 12:9; Gal.6:13,14; Rom.5:11; 2:17,23; Phil.3:3; James 4:16; with κατά in 2 Cor.11:18a; with ἐπί in Romans 5:2. With ἐνώπιον τοῦ θεοῦ in 1 Cor.1:29.

ἐν (preposition with the locative of sphere) 80.
θεῷ (loc.sing.masc.of θεός, sphere) 124.

*Translation - "Now since you are known as a Jew and you are depending upon the law and you are congratulating yourself about your relationship with God. . .*
"

Comment: Εἰ and the verbs in the indicative that follow through verse 20 comprise a long first-class condition. The assertions in this long protasis are assumed to be true, for the sake of the argument. Paul is being sarcastic. Everyone knew that the Jews were known as special people. They had been given the divine code of ethics, written with the finger of God upon tablets of stone. This presentation had been made under auspicious circumstances, the awesome display of which had made a lasting impression. On that occasion they had been introduced to the Eternal covenant making God, the Great I Am -'Εγὼ 'Ειμι, ὁ ὤν - Who later came to earth in incarnate preparation for redemption and the ultimate fulfillment of His promise to make them the greatest nation of earth. In the next three verses the other advantages which God gave to His chosen people are listed. This material consists of components of the protasis in the first-class condition introduced by Εἰ. Paul's point is not to deny that the Jews did in fact enjoy these advantages. Indeed they did. His point is that they had not reacted with humility before God and holy living as a result of them.

*Verse 18 - ". . . and knowest his will, and approvest the things that are more excellent, being instructed out of the law, . . . "*

καὶ γινώσκεις τὸ θέλημα καὶ δοκιμάζεις τὰ διαφέροντα κατηχούμενος ἐκ τοῦ νόμου,

*". . . and know his will and approve what is excellent, because you are instructed in the law, . . . "*   RSV

καὶ (adjunctive conjunction joining verbs) 14.
γινώσκεις (2d.per.sing.pres.act.ind.ofd γινώσκω, first-class condition, present progressive, retroactive) 131.
τὸ (acc.sing.neut.of the article in agreement with θέλημα) 9.
θέλημα (acc.sing.neut.of θέλημα, direct object of γινώσκεις) 577.
καὶ (adjunctive conjunction joining verbs) 14.
δοκιμάζεις (2d.per.sing.pres.act.ind.of δοκιμάζω, first-class condition, present progressive retroactive) 2493.
τὰ (acc.pl.neut.of the article in agreement with διαφέροντα) 9.
διαφέροντα (pres.act.part.acc.pl.neut.of διαφέρω, substantival, direct object of δοκιμάζεις) 620.
κατηχούμενος (pres.pass.part.nom.sing.masc.of κατηχέω, adverbial, causal) 1714.
ἐκ (preposition with the ablative of source) 19.
τοῦ (abl.sing.masc.of the article in agreement with νόμου) 9.
νόμου (abl.sing.masc.of νόμος, source) 464.

*Translation - " . . . and, since you have always known (God's) will, and have approbated the more important things, because you have been told by higher authority what is right . . . "*

**Comment:** Paul's sarcastic ennumeration of the professed advantages to which the Jew lays claims continues. These verbs are present progressives with retroactive force that extends backward in time to Sinai. Since that day fifteen centuries before when Moses was called up into the mountain that was rent with earthquake and surrounded by fire and smoke, the Jews had always known what the will of God was. They had their axiology straight. They had been able to distinguish between important matters (τὰ διαφέροντα #620) and trivialities, the former of which they professed to stress, while the latter were regarded as worthly of less attention. Their hypocrisy was apparent to Jesus who said that the Scribes and Pharisees had reversed this emphasis (Mt.23:23). Why were the Jews such superior teachers of ethics? The causal participle κατηχούμενος (#1714) tells us. They had been dictated to ("talked down to") by the God of Israel Himself. The source of their wisdom was lofty - beyond compare. That they knew this was to their credit. That they were proud of it and failed to allow the fact to humble them was not.

The greater the build-up, as Paul continues through verse 20, the greater the condemnation after verse 21.

*Verse 19 - "And art confident that thou thyself art a guide of the blind, a light of them which are in darkness, . . . "*

πέποιθάς τε σεαυτὸν ὁδηγὸν εἶναι τυφλῶν, φῶς τῶν ἐν σκότει, . . .

*". . . and if you are sure that you are a guide to the blind, a light to those who are in darkness . . . " RSV*

πέποιθάς (2d.per.sing.2d.perf.ind.of πείθω, intensive) 1629.
τε (adjunctive particle, joining verbs) 1408.
σεαυτὸν (acc.sing.masc.of σεαυτοῦ, general reference) 347.
ὁδηγὸν (acc.sing.masc.of ὁδηγός, predicate accusative) 1155.
εἶναι (pres.inf.of εἰμί, direct object of πέποιθάς, indirect discourse) 86.
τυφλῶν (gen.pl.masc.of τυφλός, description) 830.
φῶς (acc.sing.neut.of φῶς, predicate accusative) 379.
τῶν (gen.pl.masc.of the article, description) 9.
ἐν (preposition with the locative of place, metaphorical) 80.
σκότει (loc.sing.masc.of σκότος, metaphorical place) 602.

*Translation - ". . . and you have been persuaded (and are thus now positive) that you yourself are a guide to the blind, a light to those in darkness. . . "*

**Comment:** We are still involved in the first-class condition that began with Εἰ in verse 17. For the sake of his argument Paul is granting as true all that these verbs convey. The 2d.perfect tense in πέποιθάς has the same effect as the retroactive present progressive, since the perfect points to completed action in the past that results in a "finished product" (Mantey, *Manual*, 202). This was a present durative condition as a result of a preterite completed action. Once God had convinced a Jew that now he had the rule book and was qualified to be a guide to the blind, he was not likely to forget it. Of course, he assumed that his interpretation of the rule book was correct. "A guide to the blind"?!!!. *Cf.*Mt.23:16,24; 15:14; Luke 6:39. "A light to those in darkness"?!!! They crucified the Light of the World (John 8:12).

Paul's sarcasm gains momentum in

*Verse 20 - ". . . an instructor of the foolish, a teacher of babes, which hast the form of knowledge and of the truth in the law — "*

παιδευτὴν ἀφρόνων, διδάσκαλον νηπίων, ἔχοντα τὴν μόρφωσιν τῆς γνώσεως καὶ τῆς ἀηθείας ἐν τῷ νόμῳ — ... "

"... a corrector of the foolish, a teacher of children, having in the law the embodiment of knowledge and truth — ... " RSV

#3848 παιδευτὴν (acc.sing.masc.of παιδευτής, predicate accusative).

King James Version
instructor - Romans 2:20.
which correcteth - Hebrews 12:9.

Revised Standard Version

corrector - Romans 2:20.
to discipline - Hebrews 12:9.

*Meaning:* Cf. παιδαγωγός (#4131), παιδάριον (#2275) and παιδεύω (#2838). Hence, a teacher; an instructor - Romans 2:20; one who accompanies teaching with discipline - Hebrews 12:9.

ἀφρόνων (gen.pl.masc.of ἄφρων, description) 2462.
διδάσκαλον (acc.sing.masc.of διδάσκαλος, predicate accusative) 742.
νηπίων (gen.pl.masc.of νήπιος, description) 951.
ἔχοντα (pres.act.part.acc.sing.masc.of ἔχω, adverbial, causal, in agreement with σεαυτὸν) 82.
τὴν (acc.sing.fem.of the article in agreement with μόρφωσιν) 9.
μόρφωσιν (acc.sing.fem.of μορφή, direct object of ἔχοντα) 4843.
τῆς (gen.sing.fem.of the article in agreement with γνώσεως) 9.
γνώσεως (gen.sing.fem.of γνῶσις, description) 1856.
καὶ (adjunctive conjunction joining nouns) 14.
τῆς (gen.sing.fem.of the article in agreement with ἀληθείας) 9.
ἀληθείας (gen.sing.fem.of ἀλήθεια, description) 1416.
ἐν (preposition with the locative of place) 80.
τῷ (loc.sing.masc.of the article in agreement with νόμῳ) 9.
νόμῳ (loc.sing.masc.of νόμος, place) 464.

*Translation - "... an instructor of fools, a teacher of babies, because you have the formulation of knowledge and truth in the law ... "*

**Comment:** Thus the simple conditional sentence beginning with Εἰ in verse 17 ends. Paul is granting that each of the things that he says about the Jews is true, though he says them with withering sarcasm. He may have been thinking of his own arrogant hubris before he became a Christian (Phil.3:5,6; Acts 26:5).

There are advantages involved in being a Jew (Romans 3:1-2). The greater then is the condemnation when Jews, with all of the advantages which Paul lists, sin against their own professed superior knowledge. Note that he says that they had knowledge and truth, not in substance, but in formal formulation in the law code. The Jews could recite the Ten Commandments without a slip. Some of them could even discuss the wisdom and practical social value of the rules which the Great I Am laid down for Israel on Mount Sinai. But they made and worshipped a golden calf, they took the name of God lightly, they gathered sticks and manna on the Sabbath and ignored the economic regulations of the Jubilee, they disgraced and forsook their parents, they harbored hatred and lust in their hearts, they stole property and coveted that which they did not steal. They had the form of knowledge and of the truth, but they did not have the substance. He who possesses the substance of the Truth (John 14:6) and the knowledge which He gives, also has His lifestyle and His freedom (John 8:32,36).

The Jews were incurably religious and boundlessly convinced of their moral superiority. Their private lives emitted the fetid stench of the gutter and polluted society with the contaminations of the cess pool.

Every Christian who reads these lines should give some thought to the difference in his own life between the form and the substance of the knowledge and truth of the law of God, before he enjoys Paul's attack on other hypocrites too much.

Paul became so interested in his attack upon the Jews that he forgot his syntax and left the protasis of the first-class condition dangling without an apodosis, and started over in

*Verse 21 - "Thou therefore which teachest another, teachest thou not thyself: Thou that preachest a man should not steal, does thou steal?"*

ὁ οὖν διδάσκων ἕτερον σεαυτὸν οὐ διδάσκεις; ὁ κηρύσσων μὴ κλέπτειν κλέπτεις;

*". . . you then who teach others, will you not teach yourself? While you preach against stealing, do you steal?" RSV*

ὁ (voc.sing.masc.of the article in agreement with διδάσκων) 9.

οὖν (inferential conjunction) 68.

διδάσκων (pres.act.part.voc.sing.masc.of διδάσκω, substantival, address) 403.

ἕτερον (acc.sing.masc.of ἕτερος, direct object of διδάσκων) 605.

σεαυτὸν (acc.sing.masc.of σεαυτοῦ, reflexive pronoun, direct object of διδάσκεις) 347.

οὐ (negative conjunction with the indicative in rhetorical question for which a positive reply is expected) 130.

διδάσκεις (2d.per.sing.pres.act.ind.of διδάσκω, rhetorical question, positive reply expected) 403.

ὁ (voc.sing.masc.of the article in agreement with κηρύσσων) 9.

κηρύσσων (pres.act.part.voc.sing.masc.of κηρύσσω, substantival, address) 249.

μὴ (negative conjunction with the infinitive) 87.

κλέπτειν (pres.act.inf.of κλέπτω, direct object of κηρύσσων, indirect discourse) 597.

κλέπτεις (2d.per.sing.pres.act.ind.of κλέπτω, direct question) 597.

*Translation - "So, Teacher of others, you are teaching yourself are you not? Preacher who preaches against theft, are you a thief?"*

**Comment:** The literal translation says, "Do you steal?" We can find the subject, to whom these questions are directed implicit in the verbs διδάσκεις and κλέπτεις and take the participles as concessive, in which case we translate, "Although you teach and preach, you teach yourself do you not and . . . do you steal?" Thus Paul exposes the hypocrisy of the Jewish teachers and preachers. Their message which imposed ethical obligations upon others and pointed the way of God to the good life had no effect upon their own morals. It is also possible in this convoluted syntax to consider verses 21 and 22 as the apodosis of the conditional sentence which began in verse 17.

Paul continues to disrobe the hypocrites in

*Verse 22 - "Thou that sayest a man should not commit adultery, dost thou commit adultery? thou that abhorrest idols, dost thou commit sacrilege?"*

ὁ λέγων μὴ μοιχεύειν μοιχεύεις; ὁ βδελὑσσόμενος τὰ εἴδωλα ἱεροσυλεῖς;

*"You who say that one must not commit adultery, do you commit adultery? You who abhor idols, do you rob temples?" RSV*

ὁ (nom.sing.masc.of the article in agreement with λέγων) 9.
λέγων (pres.act.part.nom.sing.masc.of λέγω, adverbial, concessive) 66.
μὴ (negative conjunction with the infinitive) 87.
μοιχεύειν (pres.act.inf.of μοιχεύω, object of λέγων, indirect discourse) 498.
μοιχεύεις (2d.per.sing.pres.act.ind.of μοιχεύω, direct question) 498.
ὁ (nom.sing.masc.of the article in agreement with βδελυσσόμενος) 9.

#3849 βδελυσσόμενος (pres.mid.part.nom.sing.masc .of βδελύσσομαι, adverbial, concessive).

King James Version

abhor - Romans 2:22.
abominable - Revelation 21:8.

Revised Standard Version

abhor - Romans 2:22.
polluted - Revelation 21:8.

*Meaning: Cf.* βδέω - "to pass gas through the rectum." Hence, to react with abhorrence; to be offended. *Cf.* βδέλυγμα (#1492) and βδελυκτός (#4886). To be offended by the abomination of idol worship - Romans 2:22; generally in Revelation 21:8.

τὰ (acc.pl.neut.of the article in agreement with εἴδωλα) 9.
εἴδωλα (acc.pl.neut.of εἴδωλον, direct object of βδελυσσόμενος) 3138.

**#3850** ἱεροσυλεῖς (2d.per.sing.pres.act.ind.of ἱεροσυλέω, direct question).

King James Version

commit sacrilege - Romans 2:22.

Revised Standard Version

rob temples - Romans 2:22.

*Meaning: Cf.* ἱερόσυλος (#3494), ἱερόν (#346) and συλάω (#4373). Hence, to rob a temple of idols which were then offered for sale to idol worshippers. To traffic in idols - Romans 2:22.

*Translation - "Although you forbid adultery are you committing adultery? Do you who loathe idols rob their temples?"*

**Comment:**   Paul continues to address his audience with these participial substantives, as though they were in the vocative. Or *cf.* our comment on verse 21. The participles can be considered as concessive adverbs, in which case the sense is that despite what they said and what they detested, they transgressed the seventh commandment and, for a living, robbed the pagan temples of their idols, which they professed to abhor and sold them back for a profit. "You teachers! You preachers! You nay sayers! You offended people! You teach others; why do you not teach yourselves? You forbid stealing but you are thieves. You forbid adultery for others but indulge it for yourselves. Professing to be revolted by idol worship you find the sale of stolen idols a profitable business. What hypocrisy!"

And yet, for all of their transgressions of it, the Jews made loud protestations of their pride in and respect for the Mosaic Code. They even wore it upon their foreheads (Mt.23:5).

*Verse 23 - "Thou that makest thy boast of the law, through breaking the law, dishonourest thou God?"*

ὃς ἐν νόμῳ καυχᾶσαι, διὰ τῆς παραβάσεως τοῦ νόμου τὸν θεὸν ἀτιμάζεις;

*"You who boast in the law, do you dishonor God by breaking the law?"* RSV

ὃς (nom.sing.masc.of ὅς, relative pronoun, subject of καυχᾶσαι) 65.

ἐν (preposition with the locative of sphere) 80.

νόμῳ (loc.sing.masc.of νόμος, sphere) 464.

καυχᾶσαι (2d.per.sing.pres.ind.of καυχάομαι, present progressive retroactive) 3847.

διὰ (preposition with the ablative of manner) 118.

τῆς (abl.sing.fem.of the article in agreement with παραβάσεως) 9.

**#3851** παραβάσεως (abl.sing.fem.of παράβασις, manner).

King James Version

breaking - Romans 2:23.
transgression - Romans 4:15; 5:14; Gal.3:19; 1 Tim.2:14; Heb.2:2; 9:15.

Revised Standard Version

breaking - Romans 2:23.
transgression - Romans 4:15; 5:14; Gal.3:19; 1 Tim.2:14; Heb.2:2; 9:15.

*Meaning:* Cf. παραβαίνω (#1139). *Cf.*παρά in παρὰ φύσιν in Romans 1:26. To by-pass; disregard; to ignore some standard. Followed by the genitive of description - Romans 2:23; as a descriptive genitive in Romans 5:14; Heb.9:15. With χάριν and the genitive in a causal construction - Gal.3:19; absolutely in Romans 4:15; Heb.2:2; 1 Tim.2:14.

τοῦ (gen.sing.masc.of the article in agreement with νόμου) 9.
νόμου (gen.sing.masc.of νόμος, description) 464.
τὸν (acc.sing.masc.of the article in agreement with θεὸν) 9.
θεὸν (acc.sing.masc.of θεός, direct object of ἀτιμάζεις) 124.
ἀτιμάζεις (2d.per.sing.pres.act.ind.of ἀτιμάζω, direct question) 2390.

*Translation - "Do you who have always boasted about the law cheapen God by transgressing it?"*

**Comment:** Their boast had always been about their respect for the law of God, as though God had given it to Israel because He could trust them to observe it, while the law in unholy Gentile hands would be dishonored. Thus the Jews had always considered themselves superior to the Gentiles. Yet, by living daily as though the law did not exist or had no claim upon their allegiance, and that they could transgress it with impunity, they were insulting and cheapening God. Paul's cross examination of the Jews is now complete. Now he moves to the attack, not with questions, rhetorical and direct, but with direct assertion.

An example of παραβάσεως τοῦ νόμου - "moving forward parallel to the law" is found in the Jewish traditions which Jesus castigated in Mt.15:1-9; Mark 7:1-23, *q.v. en loc. The Renaissance New Testament,* II, 463-476; V, 519-547. The Jews were gnat strainers and camel swallowers. A good way to avoid meeting the financial needs of parents, something mandated by Moses in the fifth commandment, was to swear that the money had already been promised as a gift to the temple. The Pharisees were so eager to demonstrate their personal cleanliness that they criticized the disciples for eating without first washing their hands. One could not walk too far on the sabbath day lest he collected so much dirt on his shoes that it amounted to the labor of carrying it. Thus they honored the fourth commandment. Examples can be multiplied. This is the sanctity on parade which is the hallmark of the hypocrite whose private life belies what his public appearances attest.

Jewish hypocrisy is a stumbling block to the Gentiles. This is the thought of

*Verse 24 - "For the name of God is blasphemed among the Gentiles through you, as it is written."*

τὸ γὰρ ὄνομα τοῦ θεοῦ δι' ὑμᾶς βλασφημεῖται ἐν τοῖς ἔθνεσιν, καθὼς γέγραπται.

"For, as it is written, "The name of God is blasphemed among the Gentiles because of you.' " RSV

τὸ (nom.sing.neut.ofthe article in agreement with ὄνομα) 9.

γὰρ (inferential conjunction) 105.

ὄνομα (nom.sing.neut.of ὄνομα, subject of βλασφημεῖται) 108.

τοῦ (gen.sing.masc.of the article in agreement with θεοῦ) 9.

θεοῦ (gen.sing.masc.of θεός, possession) 124.

δι' (preposition with the accusative, cause) 118.

ὑμᾶς (acc.pl.masc.of σύ, cause) 104.

βλασφημεῖται (3d.per.sing.pres.pass.ind.of βλασφημέω, progressive retroaction) 781.

ἐν (preposition with the locative with plural nouns) 80.

τοῖς (loc.pl.neut.of the article in agreement with ἔθνεσιν) 9.

ἔθνεσιν (loc.pl.neut.of ἔθνος, place where) 376.

καθὼς (adverbial) 1348.

γέγραπται (3d.per.sing.perf.pass.ind.of γράφω, intensive) 156.

*Translation* - "And so the name of God because of you has been execrated among the Gentiles, as it is written."

**Comment:** The reference in Scripture is to Isaiah 52:5 and Ezekiel 36:20. The Jews insulted God with their disregard for His law and, as a result, the Gentiles profaned His name.

Paul has succeeded in reducing the Jews to the same sordid level of the heathen (Romans 1:18-28) and the civilized Gentiles (Romans 2:1-16). All have deliberately sinned against the light (Romans 1:21; 2:3; 2:17-24). The heathen had only the deductive noumena derived from phenomena, plus the light of a God created conscience. The civilized Gentiles had these, plus the advantages, if any, of the development of some human culture. The difference between a civilized and a heathen cannibal is that the former uses a knife and fork. The Jews had all that others had plus the direct revelation of the will of God on tablets of stone. Yet they all descended into the depths of the pit of moral degradation. Is there then any real advantage for the Gentile over the heathen, or for the Jew over the Gentile? This is the question which Paul now discusses for the next seven verses.

*Verse 25 - "For circumcision verily profiteth, if thou keep the law: but if thou be a breaker of the law, thy circumcision is made uncircumcision."*

περιτομὴ μὲν γὰρ ὠφελεῖ ἐὰν νόμον πράσσῃς, ἐὰν δὲ παραβάτης νόμου ᾖς, ἡ περιτομή σου ἀκροβυστία γέγονεν.

"Circumcision indeed is of value if you obey the law; but if you break the law, your circumcision becomes uncircumcision." RSV

περιτομή (nom.sing.fem.of περιτομή, subject of ὠφελεῖ) 2368.
μὲν (particle of affirmation) 300.
γὰρ (explanatory conjunction) 105.
ὠφελεῖ (3d.per.sing.pres.act.ind.of ὠφελέω, static) 1144.
ἐὰν (conditional particle in a third-class condition) 363.
νόμον (acc.sing.masc.of νόμος, direct object of πράσσῃς) 464.
πράσσῃς (2d.per.sing.pres.act.subj.of πράσσω, third-class condition) 1943.
ἐὰν (conditional particle in a third-class condition) 363.
δὲ (adversative conjunction) 11.

#3852 παραβάτης (nom.sing.masc.of παραβάτης, predicate nominative).

King James Version

breaker - Romans 2:25.
transgressor - Gal.2:18; James 2:9,11.
who doth transgress - Romans 2:27.

Revised Standard Version

break - Romans 2:25,27.
transgressor - Gal.2:18; James 2:9,11.

*Meaning:* Cf. παραβαίνω (#1139); παράβασις (#3851). Hence, one who by-passes. One who ignores or disregards by passing it by - Followed by νόμου - Romans 2:25,27; James 2:11; joined with νόμου in James 2:9; absolutely in Galatians 2:18.

νόμου (gen.sing.masc.of νόμος, description) 464.
ᾖς (2d.per.sing.pres.subj.of εἰμί, third-class condition) 86.
ἡ (nom.sing.fem.of the article in agreement with περιτομή) 9.
περιτομή (nom.sing.fem.of περιτομή, subject of γέγονεν) 2368.
σου (gen.sing.masc.of σύ, possession) 104.
ἀκροβυστία (nom.sing.fem.of ἀκροβυστία, predicate nominative) 3236.
γέγονεν (3d.per.sing.perf.ind.of γίνομαι, intensive) 113.

*Translation -* "*Now circumcision is indeed an asset if you obey the law; but if you are a violator of the law, your circumcision becomes uncircumcision.*"

**Comment:** We have a clear explanatory use of γὰρ. There are two third-class conditions. The conditions in the protases are undetermined, though each has the prospect of fulfillment. Either the Jew will keep the law or he will not. Paul does not venture to suggest which he will do, but the conclusions in the apodoses are dogmatic. A Jew who keeps the law of God has an advantage over a Gentile who also keeps the law of God. Paul does not here discuss what that advantage is, although he hints at it in Romans 3:2. His purpose here is to show the relative positions of the Jew *vis-a-vis* the Gentile, under conditions of compliance with the law on both sides, non-compliance on both sides and compliance on one side but not upon the other. Note the μὲν . . . δὲ sequence. Indeed the Jew is in a favored position if he keeps the law. But if he does not, his violation of the Mosaic code destroys any advantage which otherwise was his by his genetic connection with Abraham. Goodspeed says it well with his translation - "Circumcision will help you only if you observe the Law; but if you are a law-breaker, you might as well be uncircumcised." There is nothing said in the context about the situation if both Jew and Gentile break the law. Obviously they are both under condemnation before God. The Jew with his disobedience has forfeited whatever asset might have been his by virtue of his racial origin and the Gentile is in no worse condition for having been deprived of the rite of circumcision.

There is no doubt that God gave a great advantage to Israel by favoring them with the Mosaic Code, but this advantage has nothing to do with their individual salvation, since the Mosaic covenant was conditioned upon man's perfect obedience - an accomplishment of which no Jew has ever been capable, with the sole exception of Jesus of Nazareth. Thus the law became the legal ground upon which God will judge every transgressor, Jew and Gentile. The blessings which can result from obedience to the Mosaic Code are evident in human society. As long as Israel, as a nation, with an ordered social, economic and political pattern of life, obeyed the Ten Commandments the social, economic and political advantages manifested themselves. "Righteousness exalteth a nation: but sin is a reproach to any people" (Proverbs 14:34). It has never been tried so there is no real proof in history, but Social Scientists find it not difficult to show that a social and economic scenario based upon the morals of the Ten Commandments can provide a viable society, with the blessings of personal freedom and social progress and economic growth.

There is nothing in the Mosaic Code that promises the Jew that because he is descended from someone who stood at the foot of Mount Sinai one day he will be saved. *Au contraire* the law was given to awaken him to the fact that his moral record was such as not to be rewarded with salvation. Thus, when he understands the purpose which God had in giving the law, he will come to Christ and be saved by grace through faith (Gal.3

Nor is there anything in the covenant of circumcision which God gave to Abraham to guarantee eternal salvation     for anyone whose only connection with Abraham is that of genetics. To be sure the nation is promised perpetuity, but this promise does not descend automatically to individuals. Judas Iscariot was a Jew as were those whom Jesus addressed in John 8:44. Their circumcision became uncircumcision, not only because they had by-passed the morals of the Mosaic Code but also, and even more, because they murdered the Son of God, Who was the living embodiment of its morals (Matthew 5:17).

In Romans 2:13 we learned that those who keep the law, not because they read it from tablets of stone, but because they obeyed its dicates in their conscience will be justified in the final judgment. Paul expands on this thought in

*Verse 26 - "Therefore, if the uncircumcision keep the righteousness of the law, shall not his uncircumcision be counted for circumcision?"*

ἐὰν οὖν ἡ ἀκροβυστία τὰ δικαιώματα τοῦ νόμου φυλάσσῃ, οὐχὶ ἡ ἀκροβυστια αὐτοῦ εἰς περιτομὴν λογισθήσεται;

"So, if a man who is uncircumcised keeps the precepts of the law, will not his uncircumcision be regarded as circumcision?"                    RSV

ἐὰν (conditional particle in a third-class condition) 363.

οὖν (inferential conjunction) 68.

ἡ (nom.sing.fem.of the article in agreement with ἀκροβυστία) 9.

ἀκροβυστία (nom.sing.fem.of ἀκροβυστία, subject of φυλάσσῃ) 3236.

τὰ (acc.pl.neut.of the article in agreement with δικαιώματα) 9.

δικαιώματα (acc.pl.neut.of δικαίωμα, direct object of φυλάσσῃ) 1781.

τοῦ (gen.sing.masc.of the article in agreement with νόμου) 9.

νόμου (gen.sing.masc.of νόμος, description) 464.

φυλάσσῃ (3d.per.sing.pres.act.subj.of φυλάσσω, third-class condition) 1301.

οὐχὶ (negative conjunction with the indicative in rhetorical question with expectation of a postive reply) 130.

ἡ (nom.sing.fem.of the article in agreement with ἀκροβυστία) 9.

ἀκροβυστία (nom.sing.fem.of ἀκροβυστία, subject of λογισθήσεται) 3236.

αὐτοῦ (gen.sing.masc.of αὐτός, possession) 16.

εἰς (preposition with the accusative, purpose) 140.

περιτομὴν (acc.sing.fem.of περιτομή, predicate accusative) 2368.

λογισθήσεται (3d.per.sing.fut.pass.ind.of λογίζομαι, rhetorical question) 2611.

*Translation* - "So if the uncircumcision lives by the righteous principles of the law, his uncircumcision will be regarded as circumcision will it not?"

**Comment:** *Cf.* Romans 2:7,10. Let us suppose that a Gentile observes the righteous principles and follows the behavior pattern set forth in the law, even though he has never seen a copy nor heard its commandments read. In such a case he would be humbly following the dictates of his conscience which God gave to him by virtue of his having been created in the divine image. For the same God Who created a conscience in the heart of every man also inscribed upon tablets of stone the same principles of morality. God's law is written in his heart (verse 29). The important matter is not how he knew right from wrong, but how he reacted to the difference when he had it sorted out. When sociologists tell us that standards of right and wrong are the result of acculturation that occurs as man reacts to his environment, and that as environments differ, so then do standards of probity, they are basing this opinion upon the dogma of organic evolution and denying the Biblical view that man is here as a direct result of divine creation. Man, as the Bible knows him has dignity for the two capabilities, that, for the lack of which the animals do not. He is able to reason from the stimulus of sensation, through perception to conception and from conception to scientific knowledge, wisdom and the good life. He can also feel the approbation of his conscience when he does the right thing and the opprobrium which is his when he sins against his conscience. One does not require written law to tell the difference between what God calls right and what He calls evil. To argue otherwise is to argue that God did not create man with the capabilities which are essential if God is going to deal with him justly in a moral universe of law. God cannot in justice send the animals to hell, for they have no way of knowing what the will of the Creator is. But man does. Thus God will judge him in the same way that God will judge the Jew who not only had it in his heart, but also on tablets of stone or in a book. The Gentile's reaction to right and wrong, if it is in favor of the right, elevates him to a higher position in God's economy than that occupied by the Jew who disobeys the law, both that which is written and that which he has in his heart.

*Verse 27 - "And shall not uncircumcision which is by nature, if it fulfill the law, judge thee, who by the letter and circumcision dost transgress the law?"*

καὶ κρινεῖ ἡ ἐκ φύσεως ἀκροβυστία τὸν νόμον τελοῦσα σὲ τὸν διὰ γράμματος καὶ περιτομῆς παραβάτην νόμου.

*"Then those who are physically uncircumcised but keep the law will condemn you who have the written code and circumcision but break the law."*

καὶ (emphatic conjunction) 14.
κρινεῖ (3d.per.sing.fut.act.ind.of κρίνω, predictive) 531.
ἡ (nom.sing.fem.of the article in agreement with ἀκροβυστία) 9.
ἐκ (preposition with the ablative of source) 19.
φύσεως (abl.sing.fem.of φύσις, source) 3811.
ἀκροβυστία (nom.sing.fem.of ἀκροβυστία, subject of κρινεῖ) 3236.
τὸν (acc.sing.masc.of the article in agreement with νόμον) 9.
νόμον (acc.sing.masc.of νόμος, direct object of τελοῦσα) 464.
τελοῦσα (pres.act.part.nom.sing.fem.of τελέω, adjectival, restrictive, in agreement with ἀκροβυστία) 704.
σὲ (acc.sing.masc.of σύ, direct object of κρινεῖ) 104.
τὸν (acc.sing.masc.of the article in agreement with παραβάτην) 9.
διὰ (preposition with the ablative of manner) 118.
γράμματος (abl.sing.neut.of γράμμα, manner) 2100.
καὶ (adjunctive conjunction joining nouns) 14.
περιτομῆς (abl.sing.fem.of περιτομή, manner) 2368.
παραβάτην (acc.sing.masc.of παραβάτης, apposition) 3852.
νόμου (gen.sing.masc.of νόμος, description) 464.

*Translation - "In fact the uncircumcision (by virtue of having been born a Gentile) who fulfills the law will condemn you who, both by letter and by circumcision are a transgressor of the law."*

**Comment:** καὶ is emphatic as Paul intensifies the argument of verse 26. We can take τελοῦσα either as adverbial or adjectival. If the former it is conditional and the translation is "the circumcision by nature, if he fulfills the law... κ.τ.λ." If we think of it as an adjective it is restrictive, describing ἡ ἀκροβυστία and the translation is "The fulfilling of the law circumcision" or "The circumcision that fulfills the law." If we think of the construction as conditional then τελοῦσα serves like a verb in the protasis of either a first or third class condition, depending upon the degree of certainty or contingency that one has that a Gentile will fulfill the law. A first-class condition would have been written εἰ τελεῖ ("since he fulfils the law") with the apodosis having κρινεῖ. This would indicate that Paul had no doubt that some Gentiles would meet the conditions of the law. If third-class the protasis would read ἐὰν τελῇ ("if he fulfills the law and there is some doubt about it") with the same apodosis. This would indicate that Paul was not at all sure that such a case could be found, although if found, the result in the apodosis would be certain. In the light of Romans 2:7,10 it would appear that Paul entertained the idea that some Gentile would follow the voice of conscience and thus fulfill the law, despite his lack of advantages which the Jew has. The concessive idea is not in the text, but the context would seem to support it. Thus such a Gentile would be superior in standing to the transgressing Jew, who, despite his advantages, both circumcision and the written code (again no concession in the text) ignores God's claims upon his life. The phrase ἐκ φύσεως means "by virtue of his having been born in a Gentile culture that did not have a circumcision covenant with God." In an anatomical sense, all men are born by nature in uncircumcision.

Paul is now ready to give a moral and spiritual definition of a true Jew in

*Verse 28 - "For he is not a Jew, which is one outwardly; neither is that circumcision, which is outward in the flesh."*

οὐ γὰρ ὁ ἐν τῷ φανερῷ Ἰουδαῖός ἐστιν, οὐδὲ ἡ ἐν τῷ φανερῷ ἐν σαρκὶ περιτομή, . . .

*"For he is not a real Jew who is one outwardly, nor is true circumcision something external and physical." RSV*

οὐ (negative conjunction with the indicative) 130.
γὰρ (inferential conjunction) 105.
ὁ (nom.sing.masc.of the article, subject of ἐστιν) 9.
ἐν (preposition with the locative of sphere) 80.
τῷ (loc.sing.neut.of the article in agreement with φανερῷ) 9.
φανερῷ (loc.sing.neut.of φανερός, sphere) 981.
Ἰουδαῖος (nom.sing.masc.of Ἰουδαῖος, predicate nominative) 143.
ἐστιν (3d.per.sing.pres.ind.of εἰμί, static) 86.
οὐδὲ (disjunctive) 452.
ἡ (nom.sing.fem.of the article in agreement with περιτομή) 9.
ἐν (preposition with the locative of sphere) 80.
τῷ (loc.sing.neut.of the article in agreement with φανερῷ) 9.
φανερῷ (loc.sing.neut.of φανερός, sphere) 981.
ἐν (preposition with the locative, place where) 80.
σαρκὶ (loc.sing.fem.of σάρξ, place where) 1202.
περιτομή (nom.sing.fem.of περιτομή, subject of ἐστιν understood) 2368.

*Translation - "So he who appears to be a Jew is really not; neither is that which is apparent in the flesh real circumcision."*

**Comment:** Paul is placing spiritual, moral and ethical meanings upon the words Ἰουδαῖος and περιτομή. He does not deny that those Jews who acted and talked like Jews and who had been circumcised were physical descendants of Abraham, Isaac and Jacob. But he does deny that all of those physical children of Abraham are Jews in the spiritual sense. The other half of the thought, where Paul gives us his positive definitions of the words Ἰουδαῖος and περιτομή is in

*Verse 29 - "But he is a Jew, which is one inwardly; and circumcision is that of the heart, in the spirit and not in the letter, whose praise is not of men, but of God."*

ἀλλ' ὁ ἐν τῷ κρυπτῷ Ἰουδαῖος, καὶ περιτομὴ καρδίας ἐν πνεύματι οὐ γράμματι, οὗ ὁ ἔπαινος οὐκ ἐξ ἀνθρώπων ἀλλ' ἐκ τοῦ θεοῦ.

*"He is a Jew who is one inwardly, and real circumcision is a matter of the heart, spiritual and not literal. His praise is not from men but from God." RSV*

ἀλλ' (alternative conjunction) 342.
ὁ (nom.sing.masc.of the article, subject of ἐστιν understood) 9.
ἐν (preposition with the locative of sphere) 80.
τῷ (loc.sing.neut.of the article in agreement with κρυπτῷ) 9.
κρυπτῷ (loc.sing.neut.of κρυπτός, sphere) 565.
Ἰουδαῖος (nom.sing.masc.of Ἰουδαῖος, predicate nominative) 143.
καὶ (continuative conjunction) 14.
περιτομὴ (nom.sing.fem.of περιτομή, subject of ἐστιν understood) 2368.
καρδίας (gen.sing.fem.of καρδία, definition) 432.
ἐν (preposition with the locative in an instrumental use, means) 80.
πνεύματι (loc.sing.neut.of πνεῦμα, means) 83.
οὐ (negative conjunction with the indicative) 130.
γράμματι (loc.sing.neut.of γράμμα, means) 2100.
οὗ (gen.sing.masc.of ὅς, the relative pronoun, possession) 65.
ὁ (nom.sing.masc.of the article in agreement with ἔπαινος) 9.

#3853 ἔπαινος (nom.sing.masc.of ἔπαινος, subject of ἐστιν understood).

King James Version

praise - Romans 2:29; 13:3; 1 Cor.4:5; 2 Cor.8:18; Eph.1:6,12,14; Phil.1:11; 4:8; 1 Peter 1:7; 2:14.

Revised Standard Version

praise - Romans 2:29; Eph.1:6,12,14; Phil.1:11; 1 Peter 1:7; 2:14.
worthy of praise - Phil.4:8.
approval - Romans 13:3.
commendation - 1 Cor.4:5.
famous - 2 Cor.8:18.

*Meaning:* Cf. ἐπαινέω (#2568). A combination of ἐπί (#47) and αἶνος (#1362). Hence, a statement of approbation. Praise. From God - Romans 2:29; 1 Cor.4:5; 1 Pet.1:7; Praise to God - Eph.1:6,12,14; Phil.1:11; 1 Pet.2:14. Praise from God and man - Phil.4:8; Praise from man - 2 Cor.8:18. Praise specifically from a government official - Romans 13:3; 1 Pet.2:14.

οὐκ (negative conjunction with the indicative) 130.
ἐξ (preposition with the ablative of source) 19.
ἀνθρώπων (abl.pl.masc.of ἄνθρωπος, source) 341.
ἀλλ' (alternative conjunction) 342.
ἐκ (preposition with the ablative of source) 19.
τοῦ (abl.sing.masc.of the article in agreement with θεοῦ) 9.
θεοῦ (abl.sing.masc.of θεός, source) 124.

*Translation - "But the true Jewish character is inward, and heart circumcision is by means of the Spirit, not the letter, the praise for which is not from man but from God."*

**Comment:** Note the absence of the verbs. The true nature of Judaism, as intended by God when He chose an elect nation, entered into covenant relationships with Abraham and gave His law to Moses, was that they might be spiritually and therefore morally transformed from within. Circumcision was to be physical - in the flesh - to be sure, but only as physical evidence that the child was in genetic line from Abraham and that his father believed that God would keep His promises in the covenant. If he shared this faith with his father, who had circumcised him, he passed on the tradition to the next generation. But the true circumcision was a spiritual matter of the heart, and without the inward circumcision, that of the flesh meant nothing.

The true Jew therefore is not seeking approbation from men, by boasting of their exalted position, their adherence to laws or their national acquaintance with God. They wish only to receive commendation from God Who looks upon the heart. The horn blowers in the streets and the prayer orators in the synagogues have their rewards (Mt.6:2; Luke 18:1-14). The Pharisee in the story went down to his house *dignified*, but the publican went down to his house *justified*.

Paul's entire thought beginning in Romans 1:18 can be summed up like this: He divided the race into three main categories, depending upon the degree of enlightenment which each category had. The heathen (Romans 1:18-32) had the empirical testimony of nature, which, as they employed the light of reason they parlayed into a body of noumenal truth. They also had the voice of conscience which told them that God's moral standards were higher than their own. Thus he knew of God's eternal power, infinitive wisdom and knowledge and holiness. The Gentile civilized man had all of this and added the accumulation of social and economic elements in his culture (Romans 2:1-16). The Jew had all that the civilized Gentiles had and was given in addition the law of God on tablets of stone, the covenants, the rite of circumcision and the messages of the prophets (Romans 2:17-29). There is an ascending scale of the incidence and intensity of light. The Jew had more light than the Gentile sophisticate, who, in turn had more light than the heathen. Each group sinned deliberately against the light they had and the individual member of the group who rejected the light, because of its moral commitments was justly condemned. However, some individuals within each group may have reacted with humility and if so they were saved. This seems safely to be inferred from Romans 2:7,10 and Psalm 19:1-9.

In all cases, God, Who knows the individual heart, will judge with truth and justice (Psalm 19:9).

In all cases Paul is discussing those who reach the age of moral discretion. Most of the babies born to these three groups died in infancy. They are not in view in this passage.

The intensity of Paul's castigation of the Jews (Romans 2:17-29) might be interpreted by some to mean that God had no real purpose is singling out the Jew for special treatment. This false notion Paul now goes on to correct.

*Romans 3:1 - "What advantage then hath the Jew? Or what profit is there of circumcision?"*

Τί οὖν τὸ περισσὸν τοῦ Ἰουδαίου, ἢ τίς ἡ ὠφέλεια τῆς περιτομῆς;

*"Then what advantage has the Jew? Or what is the value of circumcision?"*
RSV

Τί (nom.sing.neut.of τίς, interrogative pronoun, predicate nominative, direct question) 281.

οὖν (inferential conjunction) 68.

τὸ (nom.sing.neut.of the article in agreement with περισσὸν) 9.

περισσὸν (nom.sing.neut.of περισσός, subject of ἐστιν understood) 525.

τοῦ (gen.sing.masc.of the article in agreement with Ἰουδαίου) 9.

Ἰουδαίου (gen.sing.masc.of Ἰουδαῖος, possession) 143.

ἢ (disjunctive) 465.

τίς (nom.sing.fem.of τίς, interrogative pronoun, predicate nominative, direct question) 281.

ἡ (nom.sing.fem.of the article in agreement with ὠφέλεια) 9.

#3854 ὠφέλεια (nom.sing.fem.of ὠφέλεια, subject of ἐστιν understood).

King James Version

advantage - Jude 16.
profit - Romans 3:1.

Revised Standard Version

advantage - Romans 3:1; Jude 16.

*Meaning:* Cf. ὠφελέω (#1144), ὠφέλιμος (#4754), ὠφελής - "gain." Hence, profit, advantage, utility, ophelimity. (*Cf.* the improvement and indifference curves of Vilfredo Pareto, *Cours d'economie politique,* 2 Vols., 1896, 1897. *Cf.* also Henry W. Spiegel, *The Growth of Economic Thought,* 556-561). The advantage inherent in being a Jew - Romans 3:1. Financial and social advantage to be gained by end-time apostates - Jude 16.

τῆς (abl.sing.fem.of the article in agreement with περιτομῆς) 9.
περιτομῆς (abl.sing.fem.of περιτομή, source) 2368.

*Translation - "What advantage then has the Jew? Or what utility is derived from circumcision?"*

**Comment:** These are direct questions as Paul poses them for pedagogical purposes. Note again the absence of the copula which really is not necessary. Note also the representative singular in ᾽Ιουδαίου. It would seem from Romans 2:17-29 that the Jew, who was given special treatment from God, had thrown away his advantage. On the contrary the divine purpose has been served.

*Verse 2 - "Much every way: chiefly because that unto them were committed the oracles of God."*

πολὺ κατὰ πάντα τρόπον. πρῶτον μὲν (γὰρ) ὅτι ἐπιστεύθησαν τὰ λόγια τοῦ θεοῦ.

*"Much in every way. To begin with, the Jews were entrusted with the oracles of God."* RSV

πολὺ (acc.sing.neut.of πολύς, adverbial) 228.
κατὰ (preposition with the accusative, adverbial) 98.
πάντα (acc.sing.masc.of πᾶς, in agreement with τρόπον) 67.
τρόπον (acc.sing.masc.of τρόπος, adverbial) 1477.
πρῶτον (acc.sing.neut.of πρῶτος, adverbial) 487.
μὲν (affirmative particle) 300.
(γὰρ) (causal conjunction) 105.
ὅτι (conjunction introducing an object clause in indirect discourse) 211.
ἐπιστεύθησαν (3d.per.pl.1st.aor.pass.ind.of πιστεύω, culminative) 734.
τὰ (nom.pl.neut.of the article in agreement with λόγια) 9.
λόγια (nom.pl.neut.of λόγιον, subject of ἐπιστεύθησαν) 3135.
τοῦ (gen.sing.masc.of the article in agreement with θεοῦ) 9.
θεοῦ (gen.sing.masc.of θεός, possession) 124.

*Translation - "Much every way. First of all, indeed, because (of the fact that) the sayings of God were entrusted to them."*

**Comment:** πολὺ, the adjective is used adverbially. *Cf.*#228. Note #98 for κατά with τρόπον and #1477 for the idiom with πᾶς - "A great deal from every point of view" or "Much, any way you look at it." πρῶτος, another adjective used adverbially. *Cf.* Acts 7:38 where Stephen pointed to the same advantage. Both the nominative and accusative cases make sense with this aorist passive verb. *Cf.*#734 for other cases.

While it was a great responsibility for the Jew to receive God's revelation at Sinai, with the charge to obey, protect and propogate it, it was also a very great advantage. The experience of having been visited and addressed by God Himself was unique, although this advantage accrued only to those who were at Sinai, all of whom, except Caleb and Joshua, died in the wilderness. The next generation, born in the wilderness, who entered the promised land as young men and women heard the story from Moses who passed the divine message on to them in his Deuteronomic message before he died. Thus they and all later generations were compelled to accept the saying of God by faith in the same way that New Testament Christians must take by faith the story of Jesus from those who knew Him personally in the first century of the Christian era. It is evident that for many in Israel the spiritual value of the tradition faded as time passed. History is seldom as compelling as current events, except for historians and philosophers.

The time point in the history of Israel when the Law was given is important to our assessment of its advantage. Two months before they had been slaves to a foreign power with not a foot of earth to call their own, except in contemplation of the promise of God to Abraham. Now they were a redeemed and liberated nation of three and one-half million people, on their way to Canaan. They had within their ranks a kingly line. The House of Judah was appointed by God to rule them (Genesis 49:8-12) and although Judah, the progenitor of the royal line, had forfeited his own right to rule, and had cast the curse of his indiscretion upon the next nine generations, the tenth generation produced David, with whom God reaffirmed the Royal covenant which promised perpetuity to the Son of David upon His throne forever (Genesis 38; Deuternomy 23:2; 2 Samuel 7:10-17). In the period that ensued, between Sinai and the coronation of the "Rod out of the stem of Jesse" (Isa.11:1), the nation was ruled, first by Moses, during the years of wilderness wandering, then by Joshua, who led them in victory across the Jordan and in partial conquest of the land, and then by a series of judges, raised up by Jehovah, each of whom, in his turn delivered them from their enemies, restored their political freedom and their respect for and obedience to their Law. Israel is the only nation with a Constitution, as the supreme law of the land, that was written by the God of heaven. The code was comprehensive. It included the moral precepts upon which all law must be based if it expects to survive, but these moral principles, stated in succinct terms in the Ten Commandments were applied in the areas of social, economic, political and even dietary regulations. Nutrition specialists have noted the wisdom of the restrictions upon the Jewish diet contained in Leviticus 11. Cancer was almost unknown among the Jews before Reformed Judaism overthrew the ban on pork. There were health and sanitation regulations to be observed at childbirth, in connection with leprosy and other diseases. Marriage relations and the ban upon adultery and homosexuality protected the home, strengthen the familial ties so important in the proper psychological development of children, and the law of the sabbath, had it been obeyed would have protected the economy from the evils of overproduction under the control of monopololists - a curse to the capitalism of the free market. Because Israel neglected the law of the sabbath, she spent seventy years in captivity in Babylon (Jer.25:10-12; 29:10). The sabbath law was so important that violation was a capital crime. A man gathered sticks on the sabbath and the Lord ordered him "stoned with stones without the camp" (Numbers 15:32-56). When some ignored Moses' order with reference to the gathering of the manna it spoiled, except that which was kept overnight on Friday night to provide food for the following day which was the Sabbath (Exodus 16:16-25). The law of the Sabbath included the provision that all land titles were to revert to the original owner every fifty years. This Jubilee land law thus prevented the consolidation of ownership of the public domain in the hands of a few. Thus the growth of the giant corporation, with its economic control over the nation was prevented and the small business man and farmer could survive. As long as the Mosaic Code was followed by Israel there was no need for economic assistance for the elderly, since the fifth commandment placed the responsibility for the care of aged parents upon the children.

A detailed study of the statutes which God dictated to Moses and which he recorded in the Pentateuch reveals that all of the moral principles which a God created conscience dictates to the man without the law, are spelled out in expanded form to provide the most comprehensive body of law ever promulgated for the guidance of a peaceful and prosperous society. Had Israel obeyed her laws she could not have failed to prosper. It was when she disobeyed them that she fell victim to the same social, political and economic disorders that have brought less fortunate nations down in defeat.

Israel also had the supernatural guidance of the Lord through the ministry of the Prophets. The Old Testament literature was part and parcel of Jewish culture and tradition. That many, charged with such holy and awesome responsibility, failed to live up to the challenge is not the point. The fact that some failed does not mean that all did. Culturally Israel possessed a great advantage. Witness Benjamin Disraeli's retort to a colleague in the House of Commons, when the Member of Parliament had spoken disparagingly of his Jewish ancestry. He said that his ancestors had produced the Old Testament when his critic's ancestors were naked savages chasing the wild boar through the frozen forests of northern Europe.

The oracle of God given to Israel, not only provided them with a comprehensive body of law designed, if obeyed, to guide the nation to great heights of peace and prosperity. God's revelation also provided the prophetic roots which grew to full plant and fruit development in the person and work of Jesus, the Messiah. The prophets expounded the law of Moses, rebuked sin, applauded righteousness, spoke to the social and economic issues of the day, directed foreign policy and pointed Israel forward to her Messiah. Thus the God Who spoke in former days unto the fathers by the prophets spoke in the last days through His Son (Heb.1:1,2) Who pointed out that His mission on earth was not something new (Luke 24:25-27). The Apostles never failed in their preaching to present Jesus of Nazareth as the Messiah Whose person and work fulfilled the Old Testament prophecies (Acts 2:14-36; 3:12-26; 7:2-53; 8:30-35, *et al*).

*Verse 3 - "For what if some did not believe? Shall their unbelief make the faith of God without effect?"*

τί γὰρ εἰ ἠπίστησάν τινες; μὴ ἡ ἀπιστία αὐτῶν τὴν πίστιν τοῦ θεοῦ καταργήσει;

*"What if some were unfaithful? Does their faithlessness nullify the faithfulness of God?" RSV*

τί (nom.sing.neut.of τίς, interrogartive pronoun, subject of γίνεται, understood) 281.

γὰρ (emphatic conjunction) 105.

εἰ (conditional particle in an elliptical condition) 337.

ἠπίστησαν (3d.per.pl.aor.act.ind.of ἀπιστέω, first-class condition) 2893.

τινες (nom.pl.masc.of τις, indefinite pronoun, subject of ἠπίστησαν) 486.

μὴ (negative conjunction with the indicative in rhetorical question which expects a negative response) 87.

ἡ (nom.sing.fem.of the article in agreement with ἀπιστία) 9.

ἀπιστία (nom.sing.fem.of ἀπιστία, subject of καταργήσει) 1103.

αὐτῶν (gen.pl.masc.of αὐτός, possession) 16.

τὴν (acc.sing.fem.of the article in agreement with πίστιν) 9.

πίστιν (acc.sing.fem.of πίστις, direct object of  καταργήσει) 728.

τοῦ (gen.sing.masc.of the article, in agreement with θεοῦ) 9.

θεοῦ (gen.sing.masc.of θεός, possession) 124.

καταργήσει (3d.per.sing.fut.act.ind.of καταργέω, deliberative, in rhetorical question) 2500.

*Translation* - *"Now really! What if some people did not believe? Their unbelief will not nullify the faith of God will it?"*

**Comment:** Note τί γὰρ in Mt.27:23; Rom.4:3. Paul is being rhetorical as Pilate was. What possible connection is there between the infidelity of some Jew and the objective reality of God's faithfulness as set forth in what He has said? Was God sincere when He said that if any man kept His law he would by that achievement earn eternal life? Or does the fact that the Jew transgressed the law make God dishonest in holding out the promise? The last question is rhetorical and expects a negative reply.

The intensity of Paul's feeling is apparent in

*Verse 4* - *"God forbid: yea, let God be true but every man a liar; as it is written, That thou mightest be justified in thy sayings, and mightest overcome when thou art judged."*

μὴ γένοιτο. γινέσθω δὲ ὁ θεὸς ἀληθής, πᾶς δὲ ἄνθρωπος ψεύστης, καθὼς γέγραπται, Ὅπως ἂν δικαιωθῇς ἐν τοῖς λόγοις σου καὶ νικήσεις ἐν τῷ κρίνεσθαί σε.

*"By no means! Let God be true though every man be false, as it is written, 'That thou mayest be justified in thy words, and prevail when thou art judged.'" RSV*

μὴ (negative conjunction with the optative) 87.

γένοιτο (3d.per.sing.aor.opt.of γίνομαι, voluntative) 113.

γινέσθω (3d.per.sing.pres.impv.of γίνομαι, entreaty) 113.

δὲ (adversative conjunction) 11.

ὁ (nom.sing.masc.of the article in agreement with θεὸς) 9.

θεὸς (nom.sing.masc.of θεός, subject of γινέσθω) 124.

ἀληθής (nom.sing.masc.of ἀληθής, predicate adjective) 1415.

πᾶς (nom.sing.masc.of πᾶς, in agreement with ἄνθρωπος) 67.

δὲ (adversative conjunction) 11.

ἄνθρωπος (nom.sing.masc.of ἄνθρωπος, subject of γινέσθω) 341.

φεύστης (nom.sing.masc.of φεύστης, predicate nominative) 2389.

καθὼς (adverbial) 1348.

γέγραπται (3d.per.sing.perf.pass.ind.of γράφω, intensive) 156.

ὅπως (conjunction introducing the subjunctive in a purpose clause) 177.

ἄν (contingency particle with ὅπως and the subjunctive in a purpose clause) 205.

δικαιωθῇς (2d.per.sing.aor.pass.subj.of δικαιόω, purpose clause) 933.

ἐν (preposition with the locative of sphere) 80.

τοῖς (loc.pl.masc.of the article in agreement with λόγοις) 9.

λόγοις (loc.pl.masc.of λόγος, sphere) 510.

σου (gen.sing.masc.of σύ, possession) 104.

καὶ (adjunctive conjunction joining verbs) 14.

νικήσεις (2d.per.sing.fut.act.ind.of νικάω, purpose) 2454.

ἐν (preposition with the locative of sphere) 80.

τῷ (loc.sing.neut.of the article, sphere) 9.

κρίνεσθαί (pres.pass.inf.of κρίνω, articular infinitive, loc.sing.neut., sphere) 531.

σε (acc.sing.masc.of σύ, general reference) 104.

*Translation - "Never! On the contrary let God be true but every man a liar, as it is written, 'In order that you may be justified in what you say and acquitted when you are called in judgment.' "*

**Comment:** μὴ γένοιτο (μὴ with the voluntative optative). *Cf.*#87 for other examples of μὴ γένοιτο. It is the strongest negative expression in the New Testament. Any English translation that expresses the strongest possible objection to what has been suggested in the context will do. Thus our "Never!" Goodspeed has "By no means!" Literally it translates to a prayer - "May it never be so!" The latest English idiom in America is "No way!" The reference is to Psalm 116:11. Can God's honor in any way be impugned because of man's infidelity? This is the rhetorical question of verse 3. "On the contrary" (adversative δὲ) "let God always be true, even though (ascensive or concessive δὲ) every man is shown to be a liar." The man who says that he has yielded perfect obedience to the law of God is a liar. No doubt about that. But that fact does not make God a liar also. God has never said that man could keep His law. But God did say that complete obedience to His law would result in justification, if and when it ever happened.

ὅπως ἄν with the aorist subjunctive and the future indicative is a double final clause. "The fut.ind.with ὅπως in pure final clauses has practically vanished from the N.T. The one example in Ro.3:4, ὅπως ἄν δικαιωθῆς καὶ νικήσεις, is a quotation from the LXX (Ps.51:6), but changed from subj.there." (Robertson, *Grammar*, 986). Paul is certain that when God's statements (locative of sphere in ἐν τοῖς λόγοις σου) are scrutinized He will be justified in what He said, and that if He is ever called into court and accused of false statements He will win the case and be acquitted. This is what David said in his prayer of confession and for forgiveness after his adultery with Bathsheba and the murder of her husband. David was the liar, the adulterer and the murderer and God, as always, was true and faithful. God has no fear that if man should ever be rash enough to indict Him for injustice, He will ever be proved guilty. That some men, all of whom are liars (Psalm 116:11; Romans 3:13), were indeed rash enough to suggest that God was mistaken, is clear as Paul moves in verse 5 to counter the sophistry of the antinomians.

*Verse 5 - "But if our unrighteousness commend the righteousness of God, what shall we say? Is God unrighteous who taketh vengeance? (I speak as a man)."*

εἰ δὲ ἡ ἀδικία ἡμῶν θεοῦ δικαιοσύνην συνίστησιν, τί ἐροῦμεν; μὴ ἄδικος ὁ θεὸς ὁ ἐπιφέρων τὴν ὀργήν; κατὰ ἄνθρωπον λέγω.

*"But if our wickedness serves to show the justice of God, what shall we say? That God is unjust to inflict wrath on us? (I speak in a human way)." RSV*

εἰ (conditional particle in a first-class condition) 337.

δὲ (adversative conjunction) 11.

ἡ (nom.sing.fem.of the article in agreement with ἀδικία) 9.

ἀδικία (nom.sing.fem.of ἀδικία, subject of συνίστησιν) 2367.

ἡμῶν (gen.pl.masc.of ἐγώ, possession) 123.

θεοῦ (gen.sing.masc.of θεός, possession) 124.

δικαιοσύνην (acc.sing.fem.of δικαιοσύνη, direct object of συνίστησιν) 322.

συνίστησιν (3d.per.sing.pres.act.ind.of συνίστημι, first-class condition) 2328.

τί (acc.sing.neut.of τίς, interrogative pronoun, direct object of ἐροῦμεν, direct question) 281.

ἐροῦμεν (1st.per.pl.fut.ind.of εἴρω, deliberative) 155.

μὴ (negative conjunction with the indicative in a rhetorical question which expects a negative response) 87.

ἄδικος (nom.sing.masc.of ἄδικος, predicate adjective) 549.

ὁ (nom.sing.masc.of the article in agreement with θεὸς) 9.

θεὸς (nom.sing.masc.of θεός, subject of ἐστιν understood) 124.

ὁ (nom.sing.masc.of the article in agreement with ἐπιφέρων) 9.

#3855 ἐπιφέρων (pres.act.part.nom.sing.masc.of ἐπιφέρω, substantival, in apposition).

King James Version

bring against - Jude 9.

take - Romans 3:5.

Revised Standard Version

inflict - Romans 3:5.
pronounce - Jude 9.

*Meaning:* A combination of ἐπί (#47) and φέρω (#683). Hence, to bear or carry to or upon. To inflict; impose. Followed by an accusative of the thing - τὴν ὀργήν in Romans 3:5; βλασφημίας in Jude 9. To visit with wrath upon the lost - Romans 3:5; to insult or at attack verbally - Jude 9.

τὴν (acc.sing.fem.of the article in agreement with ὀργήν) 9.
ὀργήν (acc.sing.fem.of ὀργή, direct object of ἐπιφέρων) 283.
κατά (preposition with the accusative, standard) 98.
ἄνθρωπον (acc.sing.masc.of ἄνθρωπος, standard) 341.
λέγω (1st.per.sing.pres.act.ind.ofd λέγω, aoristic) 66.

*Translation - "But since our unrighteousness makes God's justice apparent, what shall we say? God, Who visits His wrath (upon us) is not unjust, is He? I am speaking from a human point of view."*

**Comment:** There is no doubt about the truth of the statement in the protasis of this first-class condition. The contrast between man's unrighteousness and God's righteousness is obvious. All one needs to do is to look at the record and check it against the Ten Commandmends. The antinomians were granting this point, because they wanted to use it in their convoluted logic. They were saying that man was doing God a favor by sinning, since God was thus given an opportunity to reveal His justice by punishing sin. The same argument in a different form is found in Romans 6:1, as applied to the believer. The antinomians imply that God's justice can be manifested only in punishing sin rather than in rewarding righteousness. They also imply that God is happy that man has sinned because now He has the opportunity to show how He hates sin and is determined to punish it. It is true that God "is angry with the wicked every day" (Psalm 7:11), but there is no evidence that He is happy about it. On the contrary there is plenty of evidence that God is sorry about sin and its results (Gen.6:6; Mt.23:37,38).

But the antinomians pressed their point, as sophists also do. Man sins and puts God in a position to prove His justice by pouring out punishment. Now when God pours out His wrath upon the sinner is He not being unjust because He punishes the sinner, since He is indebted to the wretch for this golden opportunity? The argument is of a piece with the unregenerate human twists of logic, similar to that of Zeno, who replied to his slave's question, "Since I was predestined to steal your purse, why do you beat me for it?" by saying, "I was predestined to beat you for it." I have suggested the adequate answer to the question of the antinomians. God can as easily demonstrate His justice by rewarding good as by punishing evil. Thus if man wishes to give God an opportunity to display His justice, he can do so by doing good, since it is also God's righteous nature to reward good. Paul however passes up this reply and chooses rather to point out the logical result of his opponents' argument in verse six.

The antinomian argument is also a veiled attack upon the dignity of God. Is God so insecure that He needs to prove to Himself that He is righteous? Does He **therefore welcome** the chance to prove it, not only to Himself but also the man? How often insecure people rejoice when their opponents blunder in an argument by asking a question that can be used against them? The usual response is, "I am glad that you asked that question!" which means, "I am glad that you are stupid enough to walk into that trap, for it gives me the chance to show how wrong you are." No mature person is happy when another demonstrates his immaturity. Were we born into the world in order to humiliate others?

*Verse 6 - "God forbid: for then how shall God judge the world."*

μὴ γένοιτο. ἐπεὶ πῶς κρινεῖ ὁ θεὸς τὸν κόσμον;

*"By no means! For then how could God judge the world?" RSV*

μὴ (negative conjunction with the optative) 87.
γένοιτο (3d.per.sing.aor.optative, voluntative) 113.
ἐπεὶ (subordinating conjunction introducing a causal clause) 1281.
πῶς (interrogative conjunction) 627.
κρινεῖ (3d.per.sing.fut.act.ind.of κρίνω, deliberative) 531.
ὁ (nom.sing.masc.of the article in agreement with θεὸς) 9.
θεὸς (nom.sing.masc.of θεός, subject of κρινεῖ) 124.
τὸν (acc.sing.masc.of the article in agreement with κόσμον) 9.
κόσμον (acc.sing.masc.of κόσμος, direct object of κρινεῖ) 360.

*Translation - "Heaven forbid! Because if that were true, how could God judge the world?"*

**Comment:** Any translation that expresses intense abhorrence serves for μὴ γένοιτο. Instead of repeating the argument of verse 5, and using it as the protasis of a third-class condition, Paul uses ἐπεὶ and follows it with the deliberative future indicative. The Attic idiom would have used a potential optative.

The entire argument goes - "If it were true (which it is not) that our unrighteousness affords God an opportunity to demonstrate His wrath upon sinners and by so doing, His justice, then God is being unjust. He is punishing sinners in return for the favor which they have provided for Him. Thus God cannot in justice punish sin. He ought to be rewarding it."

Paul's basic position is that if the world is to survive there must be a discrimination between good and evil. If God cannot bifurcate between good and evil, rewarding the former and punishing the latter, then the world is sunk in a morass of existential relative morality which makes impossible its viability. Note in Revelation 21 and 22 that heaven is eternal only because evil is excluded.

*Cf.* Rev.21:8,27; 22:15. Man-made philosophy     (κατὰ ἄνθρωπον λέγω)
contrives all manner of circuitous logic in order to escape divine judgment upon
sin. Created in God's image he is capable of loftier intellectual heights than the
apes. No monkey ever understood the Pythagorean theorem. No monkey ever
even thought about it. Furthermore no monkey cares whether it is true or not.
Thus man is intellectually superior to monkeys, for God created him that way.
Capable of rising to intellectual heights to which monkeys do not aspire, he is
**also capable of descending** to deeper depths of stupidity. The antinomians under
discussion here are a case in point. One can appreciate the monkey's point of
view -

> Yes, man descended, the ornery cuss,
> But brother, he didn't descend from us!

Paul returns to his attack on the antinomians in verse 7 and 8.

*Verse 7 - "For if the truth of God hath more abounded through my lie unto his*
*glory; why yet am I also judged a sinner."*

εἰ γὰρ ἡ ἀλήθεια τοῦ θεοῦ ἐν τῷ ἐμῷ φεύσματι ἐπερίσσευσεν εἰς τὴν δόξαν
αὐτοῦ, τί ἔτι κἀγὼ ὡς ἁμαρτωλὸς κρίνομαι;

*"But if through my falsehood God's truthfulness abounds to his glory, why am*
*I still being condemned as a sinner."* RSV

εἰ (conditional particle in a first-class condition) 337.
γὰρ (adversative conjunction) 105.
ἡ (nom.sing.fem.of the article in agreement with ἀλήθεια) 9.
ἀλήθεια (nom.sing.fem.of ἀλήθεια, subject of ἐπερίσσευσεν) 1416.
τοῦ (gen.sing.masc.of the article in agreement with θεοῦ) 9.
θεοῦ (gen.sing.masc.of θεός, possession) 124.
ἐν (preposition with the locative in an instrumental use, means) 80.
τῷ (loc.sing.neut.of the article in agreement with φεύσματι) 9.
ἐμῷ (loc.sing.neut.of ἐμός, in agreement with φεύσματι) 1267.

#3856 φεύσματι (loc.sing.neut.of φεῦσμα, means).

King James Version

lie - Romans 3:7.

Revised Standard Version

falsehood - Romans 3:7.

*Meaning: Cf.* φεύδομαι (#439) and many other words in φευδ or φευστ (#2389).
A lie, falsehood. The broken promise of a false professor who has promised God
to do His will - Romans 3:7.

ἐπερίσσευσεν (3d.per.sing.aor.act.ind.of περισσεύω, culminative) 473.

εἰς (preposition with the accusative, purpose) 140.
τὴν (acc.sing.fem.of the article in agreement with δόξαν) 9.
δόξαν (acc.sing.fem.of δόξα, purpose) 361.
αὐτοῦ (gen.sing.masc.of αὐτός, possession) 16.
τί (acc.sing.neut.of τίς, interrogative pronoun, cause) 281.
ἔτι (adverbial) 448.
κἀγὼ (adjunctive conjunction and first personal pronoun, crasis) 178.
ὡς (connective particle in a comparative clause) 128.
ἁμαρτωλὸς (nom.sing.masc.of ἁμαρτωλός, predicate nominative) 791.
κρίνομαι (1st.per.sing.pres.pass.ind.of κρίνω, progressive retroaction) 531.

*Translation -* "*But if the truth of God by means of my lie has been magnified for His glory, why have I also been placed under indictment as a sinner?*"

**Comment:** Another first-class condition in which, for the sake of the argument, the statement of the protasis is assumed to be true, even though Paul knows that it is false. But the antinomian affirms that it is true. For him man's lie makes God's truth show up in brilliant contrast and that he (man) has lied in order to bring glory to God. If this is true (it is not, but the antinomian thinks it is) then the liar has performed a valuable service for God by glorifying His name in providing opportunity to show contrast. The conclusion to which he came **therefore was that the liar** should not be indicted in God's court. *Cf.* Romans 9:19 for Paul's use of τί ἔτι. Paul loved to string his particles together. τί ἔτι κἀγὼ ὡς with διά understood before τί - "on account of what" or "for what reason" or "why also have I been indicted as a sinner?" κρίνομαι is retroactive in its temporal force, for the sinner had indeed already been charged with violation of God's law - "Thou shalt not bear false witness" (Exodus 20:16). The liar is guilty before God because he has borne false witness and thus has transgressed God's holy law. The reason why he has lied, despite the excuse which he offers, is not an extenuating circumstance. Nobody glorifies God by breaking His commandments.

*Verse 8 - "And not rather (as we be slanderously reported, and as some affirm that we say) Let us do evil, that good may come? Whose damnation is just."*

καὶ μὴ καθὼς βλασφημούμεθα καὶ καυώς φασίν τινες ἡμᾶς λέγειν ὅτι Ποιήσωμεν τὰ κακὰ ἵνα ἔλθῃ τὰ ἀγαθά; ὧν τὸ κρίμα ἔνδικόν ἐστιν.

*"And why not do evil that good may come? — as some people slanderously charge us with saying. Their condemnation is just." RSV*

καὶ (continuative conjunction) 14.
μὴ (negative conjunction with the hortatory subjunctive) 87.
καθώς (adverbial) 1348.
βλασφημούμεθα (1st.per.pl.pres.pass.ind.of βλασφημέω, progessive retroaction) 781.
καὶ (ascensive conjunction) 14.
καθώς (adverbial) 1348.

φασίν (3d.per.pl.pres.ind.of φημί, iterative) 354.
τινες (nom.pl.masc.of τις, indefinite pronoun, subject of φασίν) 486.
ἡμᾶς (acc.pl.masc.of ἐγώ, general reference) 123.
λέγειν (pres.act.inf.of λέγω,object infinitive in indirect discourse) 66.
ὅτι (recitative) 211.

Ποιήσωμεν (1st.per.pl.aor.act.subj.of ποιέω, hortatory) 127.
τὰ (acc.pl.neut.of the article in agreement with κακά) 9.
κακά (acc.pl.neut.of κακός, direct object of ποιήσωμεν) 1388.
ἵνα (conjunction introducing the subjunctive, purpose) 114.
ἔλθῃ (3d.per.sing.aor.subj.of ἔρχομαι, purpose) 146.
τὰ (nom.pl.neut.of the article in agreement with ἀγαθά) 9.
ἀγαθά (nom.pl.neut.of ἀγαθός, subject of ἔλθῃ) 547.
ὧν (gen.pl.masc.of ὅς, relative pronoun, possession) 65.
τὸ (nom.sing.neut.of the article in agreement with κρίμα) 9.
κρίμα (nom.sing.neut.of κρίμα, subject of ἐστιν) 642.

#3857 ἔνδικόν (nom.sing.neut.of ἔνδικος, predicate adjective).

King James Version

just - Romans 3:8; Hebrews 2:2.

Revised Standard Version

just - Romans 3:8.
valid - Hebrews 2:2.

*Meaning:* A combination of ἐν (#80) and δίκη (#3761). Hence, according to right and justice; fair; legally proper; objective - Romans 3:8; Hebrews 2:2.

ἐστιν (3d.per.sing.pres.ind.of εἰμί, static) 86.

*Translation - "And why not do evil in order that good may come? - as some slanderously continue to charge that we say. Their condemnation is just."*

**Comment:** Note how the subordinate clauses dovetail into each other - καὶ καθὼς φασίν τινες ἡμᾶς λέγειν ὅτι . . . κ.τ.λ." ". . . even as some are saying that we are saying that . . . " There are other examples of what Robertson calls the richness of the Greek language. *Cf.* Mk.11:23; John 17:24; Acts 25:14-16; 3:19; 11:13; Lk.7:39; Mk.6:55; 1 Cor.11:23f., *etc.* (Robertson, *Grammar*, 1048, 1049).

Paul faced the existential confusion between good and evil, so prevalent in the 20th century, in his day. The attack upon DesCartes' bifurcation between subject and object leads to a loss of identity for each in the social mass and obscures the clear-cut dichotomy between right and wrong. All moral standards were relative, according to Paul's enemies. Good results from evil causes. The evil stimulation elicits the good response. This is so, according to the existentialists because both evil and good are part and parcel of the same monistic reality. Paul's observation is that the court of heaven, upon the judgment bench of which sits Jesus Christ, will in perfect justice condemn this philosophy and those who are deceived by it. ὧν, the relative pronoun, refers to the people who had been quoting him falsely, not to the false doctrines which they were teaching.

Paul's indictment of the human race as guilty before God is finished and he is now ready to begin his summation.

## There is None Righteous
### (Romans 3:9-19)

*Verse 9 - "What then? Are we better than they? No, in no wise: for we have before proved both Jews and Gentiles, that they are all under sin."*

Τί οὖν; προεχόμεθα; οὐ πάντως, προῃτιασάμεθα γὰρ Ἰουδαίους τε καὶ Ἕλληνας πάντας ὑφ' ἁμαρτίαν εἶναι,

*"What then? Are we Jews any better off? No, not at all; for I have already charged that all men, both Jews and Greeks, are under the power of sin,..."* RSV

Τί (nom.sing.neut.of τίς, interrogative pronoun, subject of ἐστιν understood) 281.

οὖν (inferential conjunction) 68.

#3858 προεχόμεθα (1st.per.pl.pres.mid.ind.of προέχω, aoristic).

King James Version

be better - Romans 3:9.

Revised Standard Version

any better off - Romans 3:9.

*Meaning:* A combination of πρό (#442) and ἔχω (#82). To have before or ahead; to have an advantage; to be in a better position; to be better, in whatever sense the context indicates. In Romans 3:9, were the Jews any better in their relation to God than Gentiles?

οὐ (negative conjunction with the indicative understood) 130.

πάντως (adverbial) 2029.

#3859 προῃτιασάμεθα (1st.per.pl.aor.mid.ind.of προαιτίαομαι, culminative).

King James Version

prove before - Romans 3:9.

Revised Standard Version
already charge - Romans 3:9.

*Meaning:* A combination of πρό (#442) and αἰτιάομαι - "to prove a charge."

Hence, with reference to something previously demonstrated to be true. Followed by the infinitive - Romans 3:9, with reference to Romans 1:18-32; 2:1-16; 17-29.

γὰρ (causal conjunction) 105.
Ἰουδαίους (acc.pl.masc.of Ἰουδαῖος, general reference) 143.
τε (correlative particle) 1408.
καὶ (adjunctive conjunction joining nouns) 14.
Ἕλληνας (acc.pl.masc.of Ἕλλήν, general reference) 2373.
πάντας (acc.pl.masc.of πᾶς, in agreement with Ἰουδαίους and Ἕλληνας) 67.
ὑφ' (preposition with the accusative, with the infinitive) 117.
ἁμαρτίαν (acc.sing.fem.of ἁμαρτία, metaphorical place) 111.
εἶναι (pres.inf.of εἰμί, object infinitive, of προῃτιασάμεθα) 86.

*Translation - "What then is the conclusion? Are we in a better position? Not at all. Because we have already established that all men, both Jews and Greeks are under (condemnation for ) sin."*

**Comment:** Note Paul's truncated question - τίοὖν - The predicate is missing. We can supply something like ". . . is the case?" or "is the conclusion?" προεχόμεθα is a one word sentence. "Do we come before?" Before in approbation or in opprobrium? Goodspeed thinks the latter and translates, "Are we Jews at a disadvantage?" The point cannot be settled and it does not make any difference, since neither Jew nor Gentile is either better of worse. When οὐ precedes the adverb, the force of the latter is lessened. *Cf.* 1 Cor.5:10. In this case it means "Not altogether" or "Not entirely." Paul had already said that from every point of view the Jew had an advantage, but only if he kept the law. Now he adds that though the Jew had an advantage to begin with, because he had received the Old Testament message with its law and prophect, he hads thrown the advantage away by sinning against even more light than had the Gentiles. The conclusion is that *ceteris paribus* the Jews is in a better position (Romans 3:1). If both Jews and Greeks had been sinless, then the Jew would have have an advantage in every way. But sin had become the great leveller. The Jew by his sin had reduced his status before God to that of the sinful Gentile. The uncivilized heathen had sinner (Romans 1:18-32). The civilized Gentile had sinned (Romans 2:1-16) and the Jews had sinned (Romans 2:17-29).

Now in a purple passage of fiery denunciation, the prosecuting attorney, representing the Kingdom of God brings forward the Old Testament to support his contention that the entire human race, with or without advantage, without regard to social origin or previous relation with God, is guilty. Of course, in this excoriation Paul did not exclude himself. Indeed later he was to say that he was the "chief of sinners" (1 Timothy 1:15) - a statement which those of us in the Body of Christ, who know ourselves best, are prepared to challenge.

*Verse 10 - "As it is written, There is none righteous, no, not one."*

καθὼς γέγραπται ὅτι Οὐχ ἔστιν δίκαιος οὐδὲ εἷς,

*". . . as it is written: 'None is righteous, no, not one;' " RSV*

καθώς (adverbial) 1348.

γέγραπται (3d.per.sing.perf.pass.ind.of γράφω, intensive) 156.

ὅτι (recitative) 211.

οὐκ (negative conjunction with the indicative) 103.

ἐστιν (3d.per.sing.pres.ind.of εἰμί, aoristic) 86.

δίκαιος (nom.sing.masc.of δίκαιος predicate adjective) 85.

οὐδὲ (disjunctive particle) 452.

εἷς (nom.sing.masc.of εἷς) 469.

*Translation - "As it is written, 'There is not one righteous man. Not even one.'"*

**Comment:** οὐδὲ εἷς is more emphatic than οὐδείς. The quotation is from Psalm 14:1-3. David gave us the statement of fact. Paul has given us the proof in detail.

*Verse 11 - "There is none that understandeth, there is none that seeketh after God."*

οὐκ ἐστιν ὁ συνίων, οὐκ ἐστιν ὁ ἐκζητῶν τὸν θεόν.

*"No one understands, no one seeks for God."* RSV

οὐκ (negative conjunction with the indicative) 130.

ἐστιν (3d.per.sing.pres.ind.of εἰμί, aoristic) 86.

ὁ (nom.sing.masc.of the article in agreement with συνίων) 9.

συνίων (pres.act.part.nom.sing.masc.of συνίημι, substantival, subject of ἐστιν) 1039.

οὐκ (negative conjunction with the indicative) 130.

ἐστιν (3d.per.sing.pres.ind.of εἰμί, aoristic) 86.

ὁ (nom.sing.masc.of the article in agreement with ἐκζητῶν) 9.

ἐκζητῶν (pres.act.part.nom.sing.masc.of ἐκζητέω, substantival, subject of ἐστιν) 2469.

τὸν (acc.sing.masc.of the article in agreement with θεόν) 9.

θεόν (acc.sing.masc.of θεός, direct object of ἐκζητῶν) 124.

*Translation - "There is not one who understands; there is not one who is seeking out God."*

**Comment:** The man who understands God or tries to find out about Him does not exist. *Cf.* Heb.11:6. The search for God is contingent upon man's faith that God exists and that He rewards them that seek Him. We have already seen that rather than search for God and receive His reward, man has already understood enough about God to see that a knowledge of God's eternal power and divine nature is incompatible with man's desire to sin (Romans 1:18-24). Hence he has deliberately avoided the search for God. Man's natural reasoning power - his by reason of the fact that he is created in God's image - is adequate for valid noumena, but his corrupt will and his depraved flesh do not permit him to reason his way to the light. The quotation is from Psalm 53:1-3.

Note the precise meaning of the participle συνίων #1039. To understand in this sense is to "put it all together." Such a thinker seeks and finds maximum concrescence. Truth is consistent, coherent and correspondant to reality. There are no parts of truth that oppose each other. Each part coheres with all other parts and all parts correspond to the real world. Truth in the abstract is theory without empirical investigation. It may indeed be true, but if it is experimentation will not refute it. Plato's idealism, Aristotle's mix of thought and observation and the sense perceptions of Locke, Hume and Berkeley, are not in conflict. If it is true in the real world it is possible to formulate an abstraction that comports with the facts. If the abstraction is to some degree false, the real world of experience will withhold its confirmation. The empiricists have begun their search from the wrong end. Only if one believes that there is order in the world can he put all of his sense perceptions in order. His only conclusion, after examining ten million sensory stimulations is that he lives in a random universe and that nothing means anything beyond the moment. He is not one who understands in the sense of Romans 3:11. Archimedes found that he could not move the universe unless he could find a place to stand, where he could put his fulcrum, outside of the universe. The concrescent philosopher who aspires to becoming ὁ συνίων must find his *pou sto* - his "place to stand" and that spot where he places his philosophical fulcrum to support his intellectual lever, with which he hopes to understand the universe, must be outside that universe. If he does not begin with God and creation and a universe of intelligent design and order, he has no way to "put it all together." He therefore proves the point in Romans 3:11. He does not understand because he does not seek after God. Thus he is a fool (2 Cor.10:12). Those who try to understand themselves by comparing themselves with themselves are οὐ συνιᾶσιν, which is a Greek euphemism for a fool. The student will find much interesting Biblical material on this point by running the references under # 1039. Even the Christian does not yet have it all together, but we have the right *pou sto*. Our point of reference is outside the objects of our investigation and we know at least where the treasure trove of all "wisdom and knowledge" is to be found. It is in Christ (Col.3:2). Without our *pou sto* the scientists will ever learn, but never come to a knowledge of the truth (2 Tim.3:7). Professing themselves to be wise, they become fools (Romans 1:22).

*Verse 12 - "They are all gone out of the way, they are together beome unprofitable; there is none that doeth good, no, not one."*

πάντες ἐξέκλιναν, ἅμα ἠχρειώθησαν, οὐ ἐστιν ποιῶν χρηστότητα, οὐκ ἐστιν ἕως ἑνός.

*"All have turned aside, together they have gone wrong; no one does good, not even one." RSV*

πάντες (nom.pl.masc.of πᾶς, subject of ἐξέκλιναν) 67.

#3860 ἐξέκλιναν (3d.per.pl.1st.aor.act.ind.of ἐκκλίνω, culminative).

King James Version

avoid - Romans 16:17.
eschew - 1 Peter 3:11.
go out of the way - Romans 3:12.

Revised Standard Version

turn aside - Romans 3:12.
avoid - Romans 16:17.
turn away - 1 Peter 3:11.

*Meaning:* A combination of ἐκ (#19) and κλίνω (#746). To incline out of or away from. To turn aside; to turn away from, thus to avoid. To avoid walking in God's moral paths - Romans 3:12; to avoid contentious brethren - Romans 16:17; in the imperative mode - to avoid evil - 1 Peter 3:11.

ἅμα (temporal adverb) 1063.

**#3861** ἠχρειώθησαν (3d.per.pl.aor.pass.ind.of ἀχρειάομαι, culminative).

King James Version

become unprofitable - Romans 3:12.

Revised Standard Version

go wrong - Romans 3:12.

*Meaning: Cf.* ἀχρεῖος (#1544). Hence, to render useless; to be made worthless - Romans 3:12.

οὐκ (negative conjunction with the indicative) 130.
ἔστιν (3d.per.sing.pres.ind.of εἰμί, aoristic) 86.
ποιῶν (pres.act.part.nom.sing.masc.of ποιέω, substantival, subject of ἔστιν) 127.
χρηστότητα (acc.sing.fem.of χρηστότης, direct object of ποιῶν) 3830.
οὐκ (negative conjunction with the indicative) 130.
ἔστιν (3d.per.sing.pres.ind.of εἰμί, aoristic) 86.
ἕως (preposition with the genitive of measure) 71.
ἑνός (gen.sing.masc.of εἷς, measure) 469.

*Translation - "All have turned aside; all have been made worthless; not one is doing good, not even one."*

**Comment:** ἐξέκλιναν denotes a deliberate act. *Cf.*#3860. They saw that they were on a collision course with God (Romans 1:18-32), and they turned aside in order to avoid Him. *Cf.*especially Romans 1:23. In association with each other, and at the same time (ἅμα) they became worthless. Godless men who have chosen not to go along with God cannot get along with each other. A society that turns aside from God cannot be productive in any viable way. Such a society divides labor, but turns out production which has no long-run utility. This is the meaning of ἅμα ἠχρειώθησαν (#3861). In their cooperative effort (division of labor - ἅμα) there is no long term net gain. Not one is able to do good. Just as οὐδὲ εἷς (verse 10) is stronger than οὐδείς, so also is οὐκ ἔστιν ἕως ἑνός - "not even one." For ἕως and the genitive, see Mark 14:34; Acts 1:8; 7:45. *Cf.* Eccles. 7:20.

*Verse 13 - "Their throat is an open sepulchre; with their tongues they have used deceit; the poison of asps is under their lips."*

τάφος ἀνεῳγμένος ὁ λάρυγξ αὐτῶν, ταῖς γλώσσαις αὐτῶν ἐδολιοῦσαν, ἰὸς ἀσπίδων ὑπὸ τὰ χείλη αὐτῶν,

" 'Their throat is an open grave, they use their tongues to deceive.' 'The venom of asps is under their lips.' " *RSV*

τάφος (nom.sing.masc.of τάφος, predicate nominative) 1463.

ἀνεῳγμένος (perf.pass.part.nom.sing.masc.of ἀνοίγω, adjectival, restrictive, in agreement with τάφος) 188.

ὁ (nom.sing.masc.of the article in agreement with λάρυγξ) 9.

**#3862** λάρυγξ (nom.sing.masc.of λάρυγξ, subject of ἐστιν understood).

King James Version

throat - Romans 3:13.

Revised Standard Version

throat - Romans 3:13.

*Meaning:* The organ of speech. In Romans 3:13 where the meaning is that their speech pours out the corruption and pollution of death upon others.

ταῖς (instru.pl.fem.of the article in agreement with γλώσσαις) 9.
γλώσσαις (instru.pl.fem.of γλῶσσα, means) 1846.
αὐτῶν (gen.pl.masc.of αὐτός, possession) 16.

**#3863** ἐδολιοῦσαν (3d.per.pl.imp.act.ind.of δολιόω, iterative).

King James Version

use deceit - Romans 3:13.

Revised Standard Version

use to deceive - Romans 3:13.

*Meaning: Cf.* δόλιος (#4377), δολόω (#4296), δόλος (#1557) δελεάζω (#5103). To deceive. In Romans 3:13 with reference to the lying tongues of men.

**#3864** ἰὸς (nom.sing.masc.of ἰός, subject of ἐστιν, understood).

King James Version

poison - Romans 3:13; James 3:8.
rust - James 5:3.

Revised Standard Version

venom - Romans 3:13.
poison - James 3:8.
rust - James 5:3.

*Meaning:* the poison of a deadly serpent. Metaphorically, of the deadly calumniations of unregenerate speech - Romans 3:13; James 3:8; of the deterioration of wealth - rust - James 5:3.

**#3865** ἀσπίδων (gen.pl.fem.of ἀσπίς, description).

King James Version

asps - Romans 3:13.

Revised Standard Version

asps - Romans 3:13.

*Meaning:* asp - a small and deadly venomous serpent. Its bite is fatal unless the part bitten is amputated immediately. In another metaphorical description of the deadly speech of the unregenerate - Romans 3:13.

ὑπὸ (preposition with the accusative of extent - "under") 117.
τὰ (acc.pl.neut.of the article in agreement with χείλη) 9.
χείλη (acc.pl.neut.of χεῖλος, place) 1146.
αὐτῶν (gen.pl.masc.of αὐτός, possession) 16.

*Translation - "Their throat is an open tomb; with their tongues they deceive again and again; the poison of asps is beneath their lips."*

**Comment:** *Cf.* Psalm 5:9; 140:3; Mark 7:21-23. A conference of New Testament scholars (!) in a graduate school of religion featured an existential exposition of the so-called "new hermeneutics" from a professor of another graduate school of religion. We were told that the bifurcation between subject and object of the Cartesians was all wrong and therefore, that there is no real difference between eisegesis and exegesis. His view was that no one can discern the true meaning of any text and therefore that the essence of all exposition is that which the interpreter has read into the text, as guided by his own subjectivity. His conclusion was that no truly sophisticated theologian should bother to seek for the true meaning of the Greek New Testament. Of course, from his existentialist point of view, he was correct. I did not argue with his logic - only with his premise. As I sat listening I thought of his throat as an open grave pouring out upon us for forty minutes the foul stench of the pollution of infidelity. Certainly he was using his tongue to deceive and under his lips, instead of the salivary glands that aid the digestion of the strong theological meat of the Greek New

Testament (Heb.5:12-14), lay the poison of secular humanism which came pouring out upon us. Few philosophical and theological deaths followed since, be it said to the everlasting credit of most of us who heard the speech, we did not swallow the poison. The normal function of the salivary glands - submaxillary, sublingual, buccal and parotid - is to secrete the alkaline fluid that moistens the mouth, softens food and aids digestion. Whatever may be said for the purity of the physical pepsin in the speaker's mouth, the philosophical and theological pepsin had turned to the poison of the snake that lied to Eve in the garden of Eden. As we sat listening, those in the audience with normal perception, recognized both the stench and the hiss of the serpent. Most of us were doubly insulated against his poison since we could not help wondering why he should have spent forty minutes trying to communicate to us the fact that no one can communicate anything to any other? If there is no distinction between subject and object the conference should never have been held, and we could have spent the time better upon the golf course.

No one denies that the task facing the 20th century Greek scholar as he faces a document that was written 1900 years ago is a challenge, but only those who are too intellectually lazy to try or those who are content to be the intellectual slave of another, will fail to accept it.

There is a social, economic and political point to be made here about the difference between poison and pepsin that flows from the mouths of those who speak to the great issues of the day. The poison of unregenerate philosophy has created the social, economic and political indigestion which has reduced modern society to the invalid status which we see all around the globe. How therapeutic the pepsin of the Word of God could be if it were given a chance! Let the reader reflect upon the remedial effects upon society that would result from the diligent application of the Golden Rule (Mt.7:12) and the Ten Commandments (Luke 10:29; Mt.22:35-40). Would there be any broken homes? Or psychotic young people? Or drug addicts? Or inflation? Or unemployment? Could downswings of the business cycle occur if everyone in the market lived by the precepts of New Testament ethics? But, just as both individual Gentiles and Jews have deliberately turned against the light of reason in order to indulge the insanity of sin, so has society. As the age continues and society swallows more and bigger doses of the "poison of asps" behind the lips of apostates, the social, economic and political systems of earth will sink into chaos, only to be rescued by the personal return of Plato's Philosopher-King, Who was given the name of Jesus because He would save His people from their sins.

Why should modern man follow the precepts of the Golden Rule? The only book that suggests it is the Bible, which society rejects as unscientific and therefore unreliable. Immanuel Kant's categorical imperative is a plagarism. He only demonstrated with good logic that Jesus' enunciation of the principle is good social ethics. But Kant provides no help. For the existentialists have not only rejected Jesus. They do not even believe Immanuel Kant!

*Verse 14 - "Whose mouth is full of cursing and bitterness."*

ὧν τὸ στόμα ἀρᾶς καὶ πικρίας γέμει,

*"Their mouth is full of curses and bitterness." RSV*

ὧν (gen.pl.masc.of ὅς, relative pronoun, possession) 65.
τὸ (nom.sing.neut.of the article in agreement with στόμα) 9.
στόμα (nom.sing.neut.of στόμα, subject of γέμει) 344.

#3866 ἀρᾶς (abl.sing.fem.of ἀρά, source).

King James Version

cursing - Romans 3:14.

Revised Standard Version

curses - Romans 3:14.

*Meaning:* In classical Greek the word meant a prayer or supplication more often than a curse. A malediction in Romans 3:14. *Cf.* Psalm 9:28 (10:7) and often in the LXX.

καὶ (adjunctive conjunction) 14.
πικρίας (abl.sing.fem.of πικρία, source) 3166.
γέμει (3d.per.sing.pres.act.ind.of γέμω, customary) 1457.

*Translation - "The mouth of whom is full of curses and bitterness."*

**Comment:** *Cf.* Psalm 10:7; Acts 8:23; Eph.4:31; Heb.12:15; 1 Cor.12:3.

*Verse 15 - "Their feet are swift to shed blood."*

ὀξεῖς οἱ πόδες αὐτῶν ἐκχέαι αἷμα,

*"Their feet are swift to shed blood, . . " RSV*

#3867 ὀξεῖς (nom.pl.masc.of ὀξύς, predicate adjective).

King James Version

sharp - Revelation 1:16; 2:12; 14:14,17,18,18; 19:15.
swift - Romans 3:15.

Revised Standard Version

swift - Romans 3:15.
sharp - Revelation 1:16; 2:12; 14:14,17,18a; 19:15.
not translated - Revelation 14:18b.

*Meaning:* sharp - Rev.1:16; 2:12; 14:14,17,18,18; 19:15; swift - Romans 3:15.

οἱ (nom.pl.masc.of the article in agreement with πόδες) 9.
πόδες (nom.pl.masc.of πούς, subject of εἰσί understood) 353.
αὐτῶν (gen.pl.masc.of αὐτός, possession) 16.

ἐκχέαι (1st.aor.act.inf.of ἐκχέω, purpose) 811.
αἷμα (acc.sing.neut.of αἷμα, direct object of ἐκχέαι) 1203.

*Translation - "Swift their feet for shedding blood!"*

**Comment:** Here we have the infinitive ἐκχέαι, but accompanied neither by τοῦ nor a preposition. However purpose can be represented by the simple infinitive as in Mt.5:17; 11:8; 22:3. Robertson suggests that the infinitive here is in the dative case "swift for shedding blood." *Cf.* Mt.5:17; Lk.12:58; Mt.7:11; 16:3; 2:2; John 21:3. (*Grammar*, 1062).

Ellipsis has been Paul's style in this series of Old Testament quotations. Romans 3:10-18; *Cf.* Isa.59:7.

A man in western Indiana told the author that he did not become a Christian because he did not believe the Bible to be trustworthy in this verse. He added that he abhorred bloodshed and always had. Then he was drafted into the army in 1917 and sent to France. His first experience in combat was hand-to-hand in a German trench. At first reluctant and frightened, he drew first blood with his bayonet and, after killing his first German, he felt a strange exhilaration. Until the fight was over he had great delight in the slaughter. To quote him, "I looked around for them!" When he calmed down his first thought was of Romans 3:15. When he came back home he became a Christian. His timidity about combat and his sudden enthusiasm for it were both the result of societal factors.

Most men hunt for the challenge and joy of killing, rather than for necessary food. Boxing matches are appreciated more if blood is shed. Auto races are more exciting if a car spins out and hits the wall.

A dear, little old Methodist lady with a sweet face, ringed with charming curls and a soft voice that was often heard in prayer and testimony at the Methodist mid-week prayer meeting, came to the wrestling matches every Saturday night, in Plainview, Texas where she occupied a ring-side seat. The memory lingers, distinct and clear. She often stood with her little fist clenched, screaming, "Tear his head off!"

Those who insist that they are never violent have never been placed in the proper environment to arouse hostility. The slap-stick comedians in Hollywood occasionally stage the pie fight between the aristocratic old ladies. It is hilarious because it is so close to the truth.

The result of bloody belligerence is destruction and misery, in

*Verse 16 - "Destruction and misery are in their ways."*

συντριμμα καὶ ταλαιπωρία ἐν ταῖς ὁδοῖς αὐτῶν,

" . . . in their paths are ruin and misery . . . "    **RSV**

**#3868** σύντριμμα (nom.sing.neut.of σύντριμμα, subject of εἰσί understood).

King James Version

destruction - Romans 3:16.

Revised Standard Version

ruin - Romans 3:16.

*Meaning:* Cf. συντρίβω (#985). Physical destruction, calamity, ruin, devastation, a laying waste, scorched earth policy. In the LXX for "wasting" (Hebrew *shode*) in Isa.59:7 - Romans 3:16.

καί (adjunctive conjunction joining nouns) 14.

#3869 ταλαιπωρία (nom.sing.fem.of ταλαιπωρία, subject of εἰσί, understood).

King James Version

misery - Romans 3:16; James 5:1.

Revised Standard Version

misery - Romans 3:16; James 5:1.

*Meaning:* Cf. ταλαιπωρέω (#5143); ταλαίωρπς (#3930), from ταλάω or τλᾶς

and πῶρος - callous. Cf. also περάω - "to endure toil." Hence, hardship, trouble, misery, calamity - Romans 3:16; James 5:1.

ἐν (preposition with the locative of place) 80.
ταῖς (loc.pl.fem.of the article in agreement with ὁδοῖς) 9.
ὁδοῖς (loc.pl.fem.of ὁδός, place) 199.
αὐτῶν (gen.pl.masc.of αὐτός, possession) 16.

*Translation* - *"Devastation and misery follow in their paths."*

**Comment:** Cf.#199 for what follows in the path of the unregenerate. Note especially Mt.7:13 - "the path that leads to destruction." James 1:8; 5:20; 2 Peter 2:15; Jude 11. Because man is unstable philosophically (James 1:8) he is destructive. If nothing consists (holds together) philosophically, as the existentialists say, why should anything consist physically? Thus the path of such leads to destruction (Mt.7:13) because it began with disintegration. The connection between disintegrative philosophy and disintegrative action is interesting. "Scoff, baby, scoff," which the modern university student hears in class every day, becomes, "Burn, baby, burn," as the students carry to a logical conclusion what the professor teaches.

Note the sequential results of the depravity of the unsaved in verse 10. It is philosophical (verse 11), pragmatic in terms of economic productivity and utility (verse 12a), ethical (verse 12b), verbally destructive (verses 13,14), physically destructive (verses 15,16), obdurate (verse 17) and unrepentant (verse 18).

What we believe is the root of which what we do is the fruit.

The socially disintegrative results flow from the philosophically disintegrative causes. Thus man in the late 20th century, in a universe that he has determined is random, deliberately hastens to total destruction (Revelation 18:19) and hell (2

Thess.1:9), where ὄλεθρος (#4135) occurs and where the random disintegration is permanent. The unsaved are so enthused about what they call freedom that they have opted for no rules whatever, whether in the social or the physical sciences. They will spend eternity where there are no rules. Existence will be eternally exciting and frustrating.

God will not destroy the world. He only waits until man has destroyed it.

If we are to avoid the devastation and misery of verse 16 we must have peace, but the path to peace is unknown according to

*Verse 17 - ". . . and the way of peace have they not known."*

καὶ ὁδὸν εἰρήνης οὐ ἔγνωσαν.

*". . . and the way of peace they do not know."* RSV

καὶ (continuative conjunction) 14.
ὁδὸν (acc.sing.fem.of ὁδός, direct object of ἔγνωσαν) 99.
εἰρήνης (gen.sing.fem.of εἰρήνη, description) 865.
οὐκ (negative conjunction with the indicative) 130.
ἔγνωσαν (3d.per.pl.2d.aor.act.ind.of γινώσκω, ingressive) 131.

*Translation - "And a path to peace they have never discovered."*

**Comment:** Note the ingressive aorist in ἔγνωσαν. Hence, our translation. Note the contrast between the two ways (ὁδοῖς, verse 16) and (ὁδὸν, verse 17). Man's path is strewn with the results of his agression. Devastation and the misery which must follow it abounds on every hand. Witness the human degradation and misery that follows in the war ravaged areas of the world. The ways of man (a) destruction and (b) misery, as opposed to the way of God (c)peace, they have mastered, by virtue of constant practice. They have sought but failed to find the way of peace. The implication here is that unregenerate society knows that something is wrong. The bleeding hearts write editorials about it in every issue of the paper. Where is the path to peace? It is no wonder that Paul was so angry with Bar-Jesus (Acts 13:10)!

There is enough preaching here to keep the pastor busy for a month. Why did the unsaved never discover the path to peace? The answer is in Romans 1:18-23. At one time they did know it, but they exchanged it for an opposite way, which was more compatible with their love of sin. And the heathen decision to trade God's way for the way of his own "God in his image" is the decision of every unsaved person. The difficulty is in the will (John 7:17).

The cry for world peace has become strident. Diplomats confer in frantic search for the economic formula that will prevent the nuclear war in which no one wins. One wonders whether they are more motivated by their desire for the positive blessings of peace in terms of economic development and social progress or by their fear of the horrible results of the holocaust which promises to make no distinction between combatants and non-combatants. The universal cry is "Peace, peace" but "there is no peace" (Ezek.13:10,16).

It is ironic in the extreme. They fear the results of war and cry for peace, but they do not fear God, Who is the only One Who can give them peace. (Lev.26:6; Numbers 6:26; Psalm 4:8; 29:11; 85:8; Isa.9:6: 26:3: Luke 2:14; John 14:27; 16:33; Rom.5:1; 14:17; Gal.5:22; Eph.2:14; Phil.4:7).

The human animal is at war with others in the jungle because he is at war with himself (James 4:1). Internal conflict leads to social conflict in a world of scarcity. Isaiah could speak of a day when "they shall not hurt nor destroy in all my holy mountain" - and for good reason, because "the earth shall be full of the knowledge of the Lord as the waters cover the sea" (Isaiah 11:9) because the mind of man will be stayed upon the Lord and God will keep him in perfect peace (Isa.26:3).

*Verse 18 - "There is no fear of God before their eyes."*

οὐκ ἔστιν φόβος θεοῦ ἀπέναντι τῶν ὀφθαλμῶν αὐτῶν.

*"There is no fear of God before their eyes." RSV*

οὐκ (negative conjunction with the indicative) 130.
ἔστιν (3d.per.sing.pres.ind.of εἰμί, aoristic) 86.
φόβος (nom.sing.masc.of φόβος, subject of ἔστιν) 1131.
θεοῦ (gen.sing.masc.of θεός, objective genitive) 124.
ἀπέναντι (improper preposition with the genitive of place description) 1679.
τῶν (gen.pl.masc.of the article in agreement with ὀφθαλμῶν) 9.
ὀφθαλμῶν (gen.pl.masc.of ὀφθαλμός, place description) 501.
αὐτῶν (gen.pl.masc.of αὐτός, possession) 16.

*Translation - "There is no reverence for God before their eyes."*

**Comment:** ἀπέναντι τῶν ὀφθαλμῶν αὐτῶν in a metaphorical sense. One cannot literally (in the βλέπω sense) "see" fear. The meaning is that the philosophical model of those whom Paul has been describing (verses 10-18) does not admit the concept of fear of or reverence for God. Him they have long since traded off (Romans 1:23) for one who does not frighten them. Nor does he command their reverence, or even their respect, since they created him!

A Mexican Baptist told the author that when he was a child, the village priest took a tree trunk from his back yard, upon which he had played for years and made it into an idol for the parish church. The man remembered well his boyish reaction. He said that he knew that old tree trunk too well to have any reverence for it! For one thing it had his initials carved upon it. Thus unregenerate man has carved God down to his size. Why should he fear the god of his creation? As for the true God, Whom he ought to fear, He is ruled out of consideration. For the results of holy fear, which is reverence *cf.* # 1131, (2).

*Verse 19 - "Now we know that what things soever the law saith, it saith to them who are under the law: that every mouth may be stopped, and all the world may become guilty before God."*

Οἴδαμεν δὲ ὅτι ὅσα ὁ νόμος λέγει τοῖς ἐν τῷ νόμῳ λαλεῖ, ἵνα πᾶν στόμα φραγῇ καὶ ὑπόδικος γένηται πᾶς ὁ κόσμος τῷ θεῷ.

*"Now we know that whatever the law says it speaks to those who are under the law, so that every mouth may be stopped, and the whole world may be held accountable to God." RSV*

Οἴδαμεν (1st.per.pl.perf.act.ind.of ὁράω, intensive) 144b.
δὲ (explanatory conjunction) 11.
ὅτι (conjunction introducing an object clause in indirect discourse) 211.
ὅσα (acc.pl.neut.of ὅσος, indefinite relative pronoun, direct object of λέγει) 660.
ὁ (nom.sing.masc.of the article in agreement with νόμος) 9.
νόμος (nom.sing.masc.of νόμος, subject of λέγει) 464.
λέγει (3d.per.sing.pres.act.ind.of λέγω, aoristic) 66.
τοῖς (dat.pl.masc.of the article, indirect object of λαλεῖ) 9.
ἐν (preposition with the locative of sphere) 80.
τῷ (loc.sing.masc.of the article in agreement with νόμῳ) 9.
νόμῳ (loc.sing.masc.of νόμος, sphere) 464.
λαλεῖ (3d.per.sing.pres.act.ind.of λαλέω, aoristic) 815.
ἵνα (conjunction with the subjunctive, sub-final) 114.
πᾶν (acc.sing.neut.of πᾶς, in agreement with στόμα) 67.
στόμα (acc.sing.neut.of στόμα, subject ofd φραγῇ) 344.

#3870 φραγῇ (3d.per.sing.2d.aor.pass.subj.of φράσσω, sub-final).

King James Version

stop - Romans 3:19; 2 Cor.11:10; Heb.17:33.

Revised Standard Version

stop - Romans 3:19; Heb.11:33.
silence - 2 Cor.11:10.

*Meaning:* To fence in; block; stop; close up. To stop the mouth, *i.e.* remove all justification for speaking a certain thing; put to silence - Romans 3:19; 2 Cor.11:10; in a literal sense with reference to the miracle of the lions' mouths - (Daniel 6:22) - Heb.11:33.

καὶ (adjunctive conjunction joining verbs) 14.

#3871 ὑπόδικος (nom.sing.masc.of ὑπόδικος, predicate adjective).

King James Version

guilty - Romans 3:19.

Revised Standard Version

held accountable - Romans 3:19.

*Meaning:* A combination of ὑπό (#117) and δίκη (#3761)   ὑπὸ δίκην ὤν - under condemnation; the legal position of the defendant who has lost his case; legally guilty - Romans 3:19.

γένηται (3d.per.sing.aor.subj.of γίνομαι, sub-final) 113.

πᾶς (nom.sing.masc.of πᾶς, in agreement with κόσμος) 67.

ὁ (nom.sing.masc.of the article in agreement with κόσμος) 9.

κόσμος (nom.sing.masc.of κόσμος, subject of γένηται) 360.

τῷ (dat.sing.masc.of the article in agreement with θεῷ) 9.

θεῷ (dat.sing.masc.of θεός, personal interest) 124.

*Translation - "Now we know that whatever the law is saying it is speaking it to those under its jurisdiction in order (and with the result) that every mouth may be stopped and the entire world may become guilty before God."*

**Comment:** δὲ is explanatory, as Paul prepares to make his final summation of the evidence before he presents the remedy for man's plight in the gospel of Christ, of which he was so proud (Romans 1:16). οἴδαμεν, the intensive perfect, emphasizes the present durative result, though also calling attention to the past fact of learning that has resulted in what he knows now. "We know now because we have learned in the past . . . κ.τ.λ." If Paul had not wished us to contemplate the preterite force of the perfect, he would have used the present tense. He points us back to a previous learning experience. When in the Book of Romans did "we" (editorial) learn this? The answer is found in Romans 1:18 - 3:18. In other words Paul is basing his present conclusion, expressed in οἴδαμεν and the indirect discourse object clause which follows, upon the immediately preceding argument.

The law says whatever it has to say to those within its jurisdiction. This is the force of the locative of sphere in ἐν τῷ νόμῳ. What does the law say? "Thou shalt not . . . κ.τ.λ." It holds up an ethical standard beyond the reach of fallen man. Why then, if this be so, does it say what it says to the group to whom it says it? For a definite purpose that also will be certain to yield a definite result. The purpose clauses in which God is involved are always sub-final, for the purposes of God always yield the results which He willed. Thus ἵνα and the two subjunctives, φραγῇ and γένηται comprise a double sub-final clause - both divine purpose and inevitable result. Every mouth is stopped and the entire race is declared guilty before God.

Not a single argument for the defense will prevail in God's court of perfect justice. But some will say that the law was given formally only to the Jew - τοῖς ἐν τῷ νόμῳ. Why should God declare the Gentile guilty because of a Jew's inability to keep the law?

The answer to this logical question lies in the fact that, while God selected from the human family one man, Abraham, made a covenant with him and from his loins singled out a single genetic line, for His own special purposes, Abraham was descended from Adam and Eve also. Thus, though the Jew is special in the economy of God, he has Adam's blood in his veins just as do the Gentiles, who, in terms of the Abrahamic covenant are beyond the pale. The Jew, to whom the tablets of stone were given at Sinai is special, but he is also common. He is unique, but only in the sense that he is a member of a selected family of the human race, for whom God has a special mission. He is in no sense unique in terms of his physical descent from Adam, the genetic head of the race. The Prince of Wales is a member of a select family of kings and queens and as such destined to reign over the British Empire, but he is also a member of the human family, and must suffer the disabilities inherent in that fact along with the rest of us. Thus the Jew is involved in a human homogeneity, for which one can say nothing in terms of moral perfection. He is one member of God's chosen nation, but he is also one of Adam's fallen race.

An analogy will help. A farmer owns one hundred acres of infertile and unproductive land. He doubts that it will respond to scientific treatment, such as fertilization, irrigation and cultivation. To treat it all would be financially prohibitive, unless he could be certain in advance that it would respond to treatment. He selects ten representative acres and irrigates, fertilizes and cultivates diligently. The ten acres do not repond. The farmer grows nothing. He therefore concludes that the untreated ninety acres are like the ten which got the treatment. God gave the law to Israel. She failed the test. Even as Moses was in conference with the Lord on Mount Sinai receiving the divine code, the children of Israel at the foot of the mountain were transgressing it. The Jews who broke the law were no different genetically than the Gentiles who never saw the tablets of stone. Israel is God's ten acres. The entire race is guilty. If Israel could not keep the law, neither could the Gentile.

But there is another reason why the entire race is guilty before God. Paul has already shown that the same moral precepts which are spelled out in the Mosaic code, which only the Jews had available, are written into the conscience of every human being, on the fleshly tablets of the human heart. Since man is God's crowning achievement in creation, the ethical mark of the Creator is upon the heart of the creature, just as the intellectual mark of the Creator is upon him. God does not have two moral standards - one for the Jew, who will be given special help in order that he can attain it, and the other at some lower ethical level for the Gentile. His moral laws are the same for all. The voice of conscience has always spoken to the Gentile world, and, depending upon how each man responds to it, that voice will either accuse or excuse him before the bar of judgment. This is the clear teaching of Romans 2:6-16. Not all men are under the law in the formal Mosaic sense, but all men are under the jurisdiction of the law due to the light of conscience. (Psalm 19:1-3).

Thus the prosecutor has arraigned the entire race before the bar of God and indicted every discrete son and daughter of Adam. And he has secured a guilty verdict. How can any man, then, be declared legally righteous? The answer to this question will occupy Paul in the next five chapters. But he tells us in one verse how it is *not* done. It is not by the law.

*Verse 20 - "Therefore by the deeds of the law there shall no flesh be justified in his sight, for by the law is the knowledge of sin."*

διότι ἐξ ἔργων νόμου οὐ δικαιωθήσεται πᾶσα σάρξ ἐνώπιον αὐτοῦ, διὰ γὰρ νόμου ἐπίγνωσις ἁμαρτίας.

*"For no human being will be justified in his sight by works of the law, since through the law comes knowledge of sin." RSV*

διότι (subordinating conjunction introducing a causal clause) 1795.

ἐξ (preposition with the ablative of source) 19.

ἔργων (abl.pl.neut.of ἔργον, source) 460.

νόμου (gen.sing.masc.of νόμος, description) 464.

οὐ (negative conjunction with the indicative) 130.

δικαιωθήσεται (3d.per.sing.fut.pass.ind.of δικαιόω, predictive) 933.

πᾶσα (nom.sing.fem.of πᾶς, in agreement with σάρξ) 67.

σὰρξ (nom.sing.fem.of σάρξ, subject of δικαιωθήσεται) 1202.

ἐνώπιον (improper preposition with the genitive, with persons, place description) 1798.

αὐτοῦ (gen.sing.masc.of αὐτός, place description) 16.

διὰ (preposition with the ablative of means) 118.

γὰρ (causal conjunction) 105.

νόμου (abl.sing.masc.of νόμος, means) 464.

ἐπίγνωσις (nom.sing.fem.of ἐπίγνωσις, subject of the verb understood) 3817.

ἁμαρτίας (gen.sing.fem.of ἁμαρτία, description) 111.

*Translation - "Because by means of legal activity no flesh is going to be declared righteous before Him, for it is by the law that we have an awareness of sin."*

**Comment:** οὐ πᾶς means "not all" or "some" but when we have οὐ . . . πᾶς, the negative οὐ is joined with the verb, not with the substantive. Thus the subject of the verb is πᾶσα σάρξ and the verb is οὐ δικαιωθήσεται - "all flesh is not justified" which means that no flesh will be justified, as though οὐδείς were used with a positive verb. The subordinating conjunction διότι introduces the causal clause. Paul is about to give the reason for his statement of verse 19, which was to the effect that it is the law of God that stops the mouths of all men and proves that all are guilty before God. Obviously then if it is the law that is used against me in court to prove that I am guilty of having transgressed it, I cannot use that same law to gain the legal status described as righteousness. The law holds out hope to no man that by means of the activities which it demands he can be justified. If a defendant cannot be declared righteous by the law, then its only function is to condemn him.

God's court, as all courts should, but more than any other operates on the legal principles of truth and justice. The law therefore acts upon the defendant in one of two ways: it either acquits him and declares him just, or it convicts him and pronounces him condemned. Its decision is a function of the truth in the case being tried. If a man is innocent of all transgression in a negative way, and if he also can be credited with total obedience to all of the law's positive demands  - if he has done nothing that the law forbids and everything that the law demands - then the law declares that he is righteous. If he is guilty of a single transgression and/or if it can be shown that he has failed to perform a single good work which it mandates, then the same law that would have declared him righteous pronounces upon him the sentence of death.

A superficial view of righteousness might lead some to conclude that righteousness consists of having done nothing wrong, even though he who has done nothing wrong has also done nothing right. The Ten Commandments specifies areas of human conduct and attitudes which are forbidden. They could not specify, except in general terms, the areas where human conduct is mandated. Jesus did so many good things that John has said that if he recorded them all the world would not hold the books that could be written (John 21:25). Divine love not only prevents transgression of the law, which transgression would harm our neighbour, but it also mandates and motivates countless positive acts and attitudes. "Therefore love is the fulfilling of the law" (Romans 13:10). Thus it is clear that righteousness by the law which enjoins against sin and mandates love is impossible for a sinner, who can neither love steadfastly and selflessly nor avoid sinning.

The law tells every man that he is both a sinner and a transgressor - a sinner because he lacks conformity to the nature of God and a transgressor because he is an outlaw by his own choice. If he conformed to God's nature he would lack nothing. This is what we mean by holiness (wholeness). God is holy because He is holistic (perfect, complete, lacking nothing)

Thus it should be clear that the same law that tells me that I am a transgressor cannot tell me at the same time that I am legally righteous in the judgment of the court. *Cf.* #933 for all of the uses of δικαιόω, which means to be declared, not only as righteous as though I had never transgressed, but also that in a positive way I have fulfilled all of the ethical precepts which it demands. To be thus justified is nothing less than to have imputed to me the positive righteousness of Jesus Christ.

The gloom of sin's night and the fury of the storm of divine judgment has descended upon Paul's page at the close of verse 20. The entire race is deliberately guilty of having transgressed God's law even though we sinned with full knowledge of the eternal consequences. The law thus condemns and can never justify. Is there no way then for a guilty man to be justified? Thank God there is, and Paul now presents the gospel of Christ on the terms of which God, the righteous Judge, with legal correctitude can nevertheless declare the guilty transgressor righteous.

Homer, the Epic Greek poet, was skilled in involving his heros in the most hopeless predicaments, if only to give himself the opportunity to show how cleverly he could devise the means for their rescue. Thus Odysseus and his friends were captured by Polyphemus, the one-eyed giant in his cave, who planned to eat them. No doubt Odysseus trembled as did Jack of beanstalk fame when he heard the giant say

Fee, fie, fo fum!

But we read on breathlessly to learn that Odysseus blinded the giant with a sharpened stick that had been heated in the fire and rode out of the cave to safety clinging to the shaggy under-belly of a ram.

So Paul has reduced the human race to utter hopelessness with his scathing indictment, but only in order that he may now present the plan of salvation by which men, lost in sin, with no hope of gaining salvation by his own efforts, can possess the righteousness of Jesus Christ.

The difference is that Homer was only telling a story. What Paul has to tell us is true.

## Righteousness Through Faith

*(Romans 3:21-31)*

*Verse 21 - "But now the righteousness of God without the law is manifested, being witnessed by the law and the prophets."*

Νυνὶ δε χωρὶς νόμου δικαιοσύνη θεοῦ πεφανέρωται, μαρτυρουμένη ὑπὸ τοῦ νόμου καὶ τῶν προφητῶν,

*"But now the righteousness of God has been manifested apart from law, although the law and the prophets bear witness to it, . . . " RSV*

Νυνὶ (temporal adverb) 1497.

δὲ (adversative conjunction) 11.

χωρὶς (improper preposition with the ablative of separation, in an abstract relation) 1077.

νόμου (abl.sing.masc.of νόμος, separation) 464.

δικαιοσύνη (nom.sing.fem.of δικαιοσύνη, subject of πεφανέρωται) 322.

θεοῦ (abl.sing.masc.of θεός, source) 124.

πεφανέρωται (3d.per.sing.perf.pass.ind.of φανερόω, intensive) 1960.

μαρτυρουμένη (pres.pass.part.nom.sing.fem.of μαρτυρέω, adverbial, concessive) 1471.

ὑπὸ (preposition with the ablative of agent) 117.

τοῦ (abl.sing.masc.of the article in agreement with νόμου) 9.

νόμου (abl.sing.masc.of νόμος, agent) 464.

καὶ (adjunctive conjunction joining nouns) 14.

τῶν (abl.pl.masc.of the article in agreement with προφητῶν) 9.

προφητῶν (abl.pl.masc.of προφήτης, agent) 119.

*Translation - "But now apart from law a righteousness from God is apparent, although the law and the prophets bear witness to it, . . . "*

**Comment:** δὲ is one of the most fortunate adversatives in the New Testament, equal in importance to the one in Ephesians 2:4, and for the same reason. They stand between the damnation of mankind and the salvation which only God can provide. Paul, having only a moment before proved that the entire race was hopelessly lost, now reveals a way to be saved. A few years ago some Bible teacher wrote a book called, "Hopeless. Yet There is Hope." The title effectively illustrates the adversative conjunction in Romans 3:21 and Ephesians 2:4. The book might more accurately have been entitled "Hopeless Yet There is Assurance."

In Romans 3:21 it is the righteousness of God that intervenes to rescue us from the condemnation imposed upon us by the broken law. In Ephesians 2:4 it is the mercy of God. These concepts are not incompatible. If God could not justly extend His mercy and love to us - if His mercy, love and justice were arranged upon a scale whereon justice perforce takes precedence over love and mercy - if He could not be merciful, loving and just at the same time, then justice would prevail and He would have to forget mercy and love. But such is not the case. The justice of God and His love and mercy make equal claims upon His attention and He has devised a way to honor both. That is why the gospel is "good news." It is not only good news to the sinner, who learns that the imperious correctitude of the court of heaven does not prevent the Judge from granting forgiveness to the condemned defendant, but it is also fortunate for the Judge Himself, although it is not news to Him for He has always known about it. At the cross of Jesus Christ "mercy and truth met together; righteousness and peace kissed each other" (Psalm 85:10). The good news is that God has a way to be "just and the justifier of him who beieves in Jesus" (Rom.3:26).

Note that χωρὶς νόμου is emphasized ahead of δικαιοσύνη. This δικαιοσύνη is totally separate from the law (ablative of separation in νόμου). This must be since the law has already been shown to be the source of condemnation for man. The same law cannot condemn and justify us at the same time. This does not mean that God's righteousness is χωρὶς νόμου, for He could never be said to be righteous if He acted against His law. When God justifies us He acts justly for that is the only way *a fortiori* He can act. But the justice which is involved in the salvation equation which justifies the transgressor is not that justice which grows out of our obedience to the law. It grows out of the obedience to the law which was the sole achievement of the Judge, Who died for us. Because Jesus Christ was righteous in His incarnation (Mt.5:17) and beause that Righteous Man died as though He had violated every precept of His own law, he can, with perfect justice justify us. Whatever God has done to save us was done in perfect consistency with His law, but not because of our consistency with His law. *Au contraire* it was done in His grace *despite* our inconsistency with His law.

The phrase χωρὶς νόμου is enough Greek grammar to lay to rest all theological systems that base man's claim to salvation upon human merit. This righteousness has God as its source. It is His righteousness which meets the holy standard and for which He alone is responsible. We can draw this conclusion whether we consider δικαιοσύνη θεοῦ an ablative of source, a genitive of description or a genitive of possession. If it is His possession, then it describes Him. If a rose possesses beauty then beauty describes the rose. And if God possesses righteousness then He is a righteous God. Thus θεοῦ in the genitive also becomes θεοῦ in the ablative. For if God possesses the righteousness which describes Him, and man does not, as indeed he does not (Rom.3:10), then if righteousness exists at all in the universe it resides only in God and he is the sole source of it. The argument among the grammarians, if indeed one exists, over whether ϑεοῦ in this context is ablative or genitive, and, if genitive, whether it is possession or description, is a needless and annoying quibble. Here is an excellent example of the fact that the logic of the context takes precedence over the grammar. Normally we say that if the substantive in the genitive follows the substantive in the nominative without the intervening article, it is descriptive and thus we can translate "but apart from the law a divine righteousness has been revealed." This fills the bill grammatically and meets all of the requirements of the context.

Paul adds that this divine righteousness is here for all to see. It has been revealed (made manifest) having been forecast, both by the law, of which Moses is the representative, and also by the Prophets, of whom we can think of Elijah as the spokesman (Luke 9:30; 16:16; Mt.11:7-15). The perfect passive indicative, πεφανέρωται "looks at both ends of the action." (Gildersleeve, *Syntax*, 99, as cited in Robertson, *Grammar*, 893). It is preterite. It points to a punctiliar action in the past. There was once a definite time point when God first revealed this righteousness of His. He has always had it, for the character of God is as eternal as God Himself, but there was the time point when he first revealed it. The perfect tense is also durative and therefore continuously present. As a result of the preterite completed revelation it is still apparent and it will always be apparent. Because we have had it revealed to us in the past we know about it now. The action of the perfect tense can be shown as a definite beginning from which flows a continuous result (*———). Of course our perception of it will continue into the future, but this is because of the nature of our mind's ability to remember, not because of anything which the perfect tense tells us, for the perfect tense is never proleptical *per se*. The emphasis of Νυνὶ and the durative result of πεφανέρωται seems to say that previous to the time that Paul wrote (or at least before the gospel revelation came in Jesus Christ) men could not have understood about this δικαιοσύνη. This is why Paul adds the concessive participle in μαρτυρουμένη - "despite the fact that this righteousness has always been witnessed by the law and the prophets."

The law cannot save (verse 19,20), but the law can point us forward to a righteousness which can save. So also with the Prophets. Throughout Old Testament history the law of Moses was condemning all men, by revealing through the contrast between its own holy standard and man's sinful performance, his sin. But at the same time the law was pointing man forward to Jesus Christ Who is the incarnate embodiment of the righteousness of God (Mt.3:17; 5:17; John 8:29) - "Not through the law, as man strives without success to obey the law, but through the righteousness of Jesus Christ, Who fulfilled the law of Moses, including even the vowel points in the Hebrew language" (Mt.5:18). At the same time that the law diagnoses the case and pronounces the patient incurable, since the medicine required is not available to him, it points the patient to a better physician.

So also did the Prophets. *Cf.* our comment on Mt.17;3; Mk.9:4 and Lk.9:31 where the law (Moses) and the Prophets (Elijah), each having failed to redeem Israel, appeared to Jesus and admonished Him not to fail. Thus we see that the

Old Testament, with its legal regulations and its prophetic pronouncements is not a means of salvation but a living evangel pointing forward to Him, the Great Prophet (Deut.18:15; John 1:21) Who fulfilled the law (Mt.5:17) and died as though He had transgressed every part, in order that we who believe might stand ". . . dressed in His righteousness alone, faultless to stand before the throne."

*Verse 22 - "Even the righteousness of God which is by faith of Jesus Christ unto all and upon all them that believe; for there is no difference:"*

δικαιοσύνη δὲ θεοῦ διὰ πίστεως Ἰησοῦ Χριστοῦ, εἰς πάντας τοὺς πιστεύοντας, οὐ γάρ ἐστιν διαστολή,

*". . . the righteousness of God through faith in Jesus Christ for all who believe. For there is no distinction:" RSV*

δικαιοσύνη (nom.sing.fem.of δικαιοσύνη, apposition) 322.
δὲ (adversative conjunction) 11.
θεοῦ (abl.sing.masc.of θεός, source) 124.
διὰ (preposition with the ablative of means) 118.
πίστεως (abl.sing.fem.of πίστις, means) 728.
Ἰησοῦ (abl.sing.masc.of Ἰησοῦς, source) 3.
Χριστοῦ (abl.sing.masc.of Χριστός, apposition) 4.
εἰς (preposition with the accusative of extent) 140.
πάντας (acc.pl.masc.of πᾶς, in agreement with πιστεύοντας) 67.
τοὺς (acc.pl.masc.of the article in agreement with πιστεύοντας) 9.
πιστεύοντας (pres.act.part.acc.pl.masc.of πιστεύω, substantival, extent) 734.
οὐ (negative conjunction with the indicative) 130.
γάρ (causal conjunction) 105.
ἐστιν (3d.per.sing.pres.ind.of εἰμί, aoristic) 86.

#3872 διαστολή (nom.sing.fem.of διαστολή, subject of ἐστιν).

King James Version

difference - Romans 3:22; 10:12.
distinction - 1 Cor.14:7.

Revised Standard Version

distinction - Romans 3:22; 10:12.
distinct - 1 Cor.14:7.

*Meaning: Cf.* διαστέλλομαι (#2244). Hence a thorough (διά) change; a difference; a distinction. Between men in reference to sin - Romans 3:22; between Jew and Gentile in reference to salvation - Romans 10:12. In the tones of a musical instrument playing a melody - 1 Cor.14:7.

*Translation - "But it is a divine righteousness (appropriated) by faith that comes from Jesus Christ unto all the believers. Because there is no distinction."*

**Comment:** δικαιοσύνη, the subject of verse 21 is repeated with δὲ for emphasis. Paul adds more information about this righteousness. In verse 21 we learn that
it has God as its source (ablative case), that it belongs to God (genitive of possession) and that it describes Him (genitive of description). We also learn that it is not to be obtained by obedience to the law. Further that although it was the subject of the witness of both the law and the prophets in the Old Testament age, it has now, that Jesus has come and the New Testament is being written, been revealed in its totality. There will be no further need for revelation of the nature of this righteousness when the New Testament canon of scripture has been completed.

Having learned how we do not get this righteousness - we do not get it by keeping the law - we now learn how we do get it. We get it by the faith of Jesus Christ. We also learn that it is available to Gentiles as well as to Jews, subject only to their acceptance of and commitment to it. This must be true, if it is to be available at all, since there is no difference between the heathen of Romans 1:18-31, the civilized Gentile of Romans 2:1-16 and the Jew of Romans 2:17- 3:8. The entire human race is condemned (Romans 3:9-20). The prosecuting attorney has done his work well. If we are to believe that salvation from sin is by grace through faith alone, we must first understand that otherwise it would not be available to any man on any other basis. The sophisticated Gentile, for all of his cultural advantages, is no less a transgressor of God's law than his heathen cousin, and the Jew, despite his status as one individual within a chosen nation to which God gave His law and to whose people God sent His prophets, is also lost in sin. If anything his condemnation would be greater since he sinned against greater light, although all men have transgressed against enough light to condemn them. The voice of conscience forbids the same acts that are forbidden in the Ten Commandmends. Thus Paul destroys all distinctions of sociological origin between men. Heaven's Judge of all the earth (Gen.18:25; John 5:22; Acts 17:31) will not be asking the defendant which fork he used to eat his salad, or whether or not he graduated from Harvard. He will be asking (as if He did not already know) whether or not the defendant had transgressed the moral law of the universe.

This δικαιοσύνη has God as it source and it can be obtained only by faith (Rom.10:9-17; Acts 13:38,39; 16:31). Faith has Jesus Christ as its source. *Cf.*#3013 and note Heb.12:2. Note also that Jesus is the divine origin of life (Acts 3:15) and salvation (Heb.2:14). *Cf.* our comments on the use of ἀρχηγός in these passages.

*Verse 23 - "For all have sinned, and come short of the glory of God."*

πάντες γὰρ ἥμαρτον καὶ ὑστεροῦνται τῆς δόξης τοῦ θεοῦ,

*". . . since all have sinned and fall short of the glory of God, . . . " RSV*

πάντες (nom.pl.masc.of πᾶς, subject of ἥμαρτον and ὑστεροῦνται) 67.
γὰρ (causal conjunction) 105.
ἥμαρτον (3d.per.pl.2d.aor.act.ind.of ἁμαρτάνω, culminative) 1260.

καὶ (adjunctive conjunction joining verbs) 14.
ὑστεροῦνται (3d.per.pl.pres.mid.ind.of ὑστερέω, iterative) 1302.
τῆς (abl.sing.fem.of the article in agreement with δόξης) 9.
δόξῆς (abl.sing.fem.of δόξη, separation) 361.
τοῦ (gen.sing.masc.of the article in agreement with θεοῦ) 9.
θεοῦ (gen.sing.masc.of θεός, description) 124.

Translation - *"Because all have sinned and fall short of the glory of God again and again."*

Comment: γὰρ is causal as Paul explains why the plan of salvation, as described in verse 22, involves only faith - not by the law (verse 20), but by faith alone (verses 21,22) because (γὰρ) all men, Jew and Gentile alike, are in the same condition. They have sinned and, as a result, they repeatedly fall short of God's glory (ablative of separation).

If we take the verb ὑστεροῦνται as meaning specific overt transgressions of the law, then it is iterative. Thus our translation. Transgressors do not transgress continuously. They do not sin when they are asleep. But it is human nature, to which even Christians often yield compliance, for us to sin again and again. But if we take ὑστεροῦνται in the sense of man's lack of conformity to the holy nature of God, then it should be considered as a present progressive with retroactive force, since there has never been a moment since Adam deliberately disobeyed God's command in Eden that man has not fallen short of the divine standard.

Similarly, ἥμαρτον may be gnomic - *i.e.* a timeless aorist. If so, we can make nothing out of the time distinction between ἥμαρτον which is aorist and ὑστεροῦνται which is present. If ἥμαρτον is gnomic, the only distinction is that ἥμαρτον is punctiliar and ὑστεροῦνται is durative. All have sinned, in a completed act of will, mind and body and now all are continuing to stop short of the divine glory.

The Greeks employed what Robertson calls a "spontaneous variety" of tenses, unlike modern English which strives for uniformity of tense in narration. On the point, P. Thomson (*The Greek Tenses in the New Testament*, 17, as cited in Robertson, *Grammar*, 847) says, "When they wished to narrate a fact, or to convey a meaning, there is good ground for holding that they employed the tense appropriate for the purpose, and that they employed it just because of such appropriateness." Whether ἥμαρτον is gnomic or not, the distinction in the type of action is sufficient to warrant the interpretation that the verb ἥμαρτον refers to the fall in Adam, while ὑστεροῦνται refers to the succession of transgressions, as a result. Only in Adam could the entire human race (πάντες) have sinned in one completed act. Thus Paul is teaching what he mentions in 1 Cor.15:22 and discusses at length in Romans 5:12-21. The entire race was in Adam, genetically when he sinned with the conscious deliberation described in 1 Tim.2:14. Note this same concept in Heb.7:7-10. This does not mean that God condemns anyone but Adam for Adam's sin, but genetics dictates that all the race inherited from Adam an innate disposition to sin deliberately as Adam did (Romans 1:18-25).

Thus all discrete people (those who have reached the age after which they make morally responsible choices) sin as Adam did (Rom.5:14), and God condemns each one severally for his own deliberate transgression. The race did not inherit Adam's *guilt* but it did inherit Adam's *nature* - a nature which is continuously and sinfully short of the glory of God and which transgresses His law repeatedly (Gal.5:19-21; Mark 7:21-23).

It is hardly necessary to point out that the source of the rejection of the Scripturally established dogma of the depravity of man is the dogma of the type of organic evolution which rejects categorically the Genesis account of creation with its corrolary of the physical headship of the race in Adam. Evolutionists do not believe in "federal headship" theology (death in Adam and life in Christ, the Second Adam) because they do not believe that the human race originated in Adam's sperm. If this is not true, then the various strains of human beings evolved under varying environmental conditions, and man is "good", "bad" or "indifferent" only because he is the child of environmental factors, over none of which he had control. If this is true then it follows that he is not morally responsible for what he does or does not do.

Thus we have the materialistic behaviorism of Watsonian Stimulus-Response, situation ethics, B.F.Skinner's "box" and a solid foundation for the Marxian interpretation of history. The canon of error is as logically consistent as the canon of truth. Infidels, in reference to Bible theology, have great "faith" in their system and are sure that the human race must evolve to perfection beause the alternative is future chaos. Witness Alfin Toffler, *Future Shock* and *The Third Wave*. The difference between the materialistic and Biblical scenarios is that the former does not include a sovereign gracious God of love who wrote a Bible. To the hard-headed, mature and therefore skeptical Christian intellectual, the infidel's "faith" is fantastic - something that could be indulged only by a fanatic.

It is also vital to say that since the entire race originated in Adam, there is no Biblical basis for the intolerant and Fascistic discrimination on the grounds of race or skin color. It is ironic in the extreme, though not surprizing, when one considers the educational level of those involved, that race prejudice has its strongest support in the so-called "Bible belt" where opposition to evolution is the most strident! Consistency may not be a jewel but it is something worth developing. Those who reject the totally unproved theory of organic evolution as suggested by Charles Darwin and espoused by his disciples, affirm the Biblical principle that in the genetic sense, all of Adam's family are brothers and sisters and that each has the dignity and whatever civil rights should follow that results from the fact that God created man in His image.

*Verse 24 - "Being justified freely by his grace through the redemption that is in Christ Jesus."*

δικαιούμενοι δωρεὰν τῇ αὐτοῦ χάριτι διὰ τῆς ἀπολυτρώσεως τῆς ἐν Χριστῷ Ἰησοῦ.

*"they are justified by his grace as a gift, through the redemption which is in Christ Jesus, . . . " . . . RSV*

δικαιούμενοι (pres.pass.part.nom.pl.masc.of δικαιόω, adverbial, concessive) 933.

δωρεὰν (adverbial) 858.

τῇ (instru.sing.fem.of the article in agreement with χάριτι) 9.

αὐτοῦ (gen.sing.masc.of αὐτός, possession) 16.

χάριτι (instru.sing.fem.of χάρις, cause) 1700.

διὰ (preposition with the ablative of means) 118.

τῆς (abl.sing.fem.of the article in agreement with ἀπολυτρώσεως) 9.

ἀπολυτρώσεως (abl.sing.fem.of ἀπολύτρωσις, means) 2732.

τῆς (abl.sing.fem.of the article in agreement with ἀπολυτρώσεως) 9.

ἐν (preposition with the locative of place) 80.

Χριστῷ (loc.sing.masc.of Χριστός, place) 4.

Ἰησοῦ (loc.sing.masc.of Ἰησοῦς, apposition) 3.

*Translation - "Although declared righteous, not on the basis of personal merit, but because of His grace, through the redemption which is in Christ Jesus."*

**Comment:** δωρεὰν is in reference to the merits of the sinner. The decision of the court of heaven is made without regard to the merits of the defendant. If it were, he would most certainly be condemned. δωρεὰν in verse 24 has the same force as χωρὶς νόμου in verse 21. What then is the reason for the justification? His grace (instrumental of cause in τῇ χάριτι). What is the ground? The redemption in Christ Jesus (ablative of means in διὰ τῆς ἀπολυτρώσεως). *Cf.* #1700. Grace is not unmerited favor. It is more than that. It is favor *vis a vis* demerit. The defendant has only demerit. God gives a gift. God does things through grace because His love impels Him to be kind to unfortunate people whose sins merit only judgment. But what God does in grace cannot conflict with what He does in righteousness. For both δικαιοσύνη (#322) and χάρις (#1700) are fundamental characteristics of God. He must do right and He will be gracious only if He can find a way to do so without involving Himself in unrighteousness. This is so because unrighteousness involves compromise with evil and God cannot compromise with evil. This is the dilemma which the death of Jesus Christ resolved (Psalm 85:10). The means is the legal transaction of redemption. *Cf.* #2732 for its basic meaning. The payment required for a legal ransom, demanded by the court for the deliverance of the defendant. This ransom Jesus paid.

*Verse 25 - "Whom God hath set forth to be a propitiation through faith in his blood, to declare his righteousness for the remission of sins that are past, through the forbearance of God. . . . "*

ὃν προέθετο ὁ θεὸς ἱλαστήριον διὰ πίστεως ἐν τῷ αὐτοῦ αἵματι εἰς ἔνδειξιν τῆς δικαιοσύνης αὐτοῦ διὰ τὴν πάρεσιν τῶν προγεγονότων ἁμαρτημάτων. . "

*". . . whom God put forward as an expiation by his blood, to be received by faith. This was to show God's righteousness, because in his divine forbearance he has passed over former sins, . . . " RSV*

ὃν (acc.sing.masc.of ὅς, relative pronoun, direct object of προέθετο) 65.

προέθετο (3d.per.sing.2d.aor.mid.ind.of προτίθημι, culminative) 3793.
ὁ (nom.sing.masc.of the article in agreement with θεὸς) 9.
θεὸς (nom.sing.masc.of θεός, subject of προέθετο) 124.

#3873 ἱλαστήριον (acc.sing.masc.of ἱλαστήριος, predicate accusative).

King James Version

mercy seat - Heb.9:5.
propitiation - Rom.3:25.

Revised Standard Version

expiation - Rom.3:25.
mercy seat - Heb.9:5.

*Meaning: Cf.* ἱλάσκομαι (#2632), ἱλασμός (#5289) and ἵλεως (#1211). The mercy seat, which was the cover of the Ark of the Covenant (Exodus 25:19-22) between the cherubim, upon which the blood of the animal sacrifice was sprinkled. Here, and on the basis of the death of the sacrifice, as made evident by the shed blood, God has agreed to meet and fellowship with sinners who trusted in the blood of the coming true Lamb of God (Heb.9:5; John 1:29). Thus Christ is the propitiation - Romans 3:25. An expiatory sacrifice; the victim who took the punishment exacted by the sentence of a righteous Court, thus to free the Judge to declare the defendant for whom the sacrifice was made, legally just.

διὰ (preposition with the ablative of means) 118.
πίστεως (abl.sing.fem.of πίστις, means) 728.
ἐν (preposition with the locative of sphere) 80.
τῷ (loc.sing.neut.of the article in agreement with αἵματι) 9.
αὐτοῦ (gen.sing.masc.of αὐτός, possession) 16.
αἵματι (loc.sing.neut.of αἷμα, sphere) 1203.
εἰς (preposition with the accusative, purpose) 140.

#3874 ἔνδειξιν (acc.sing.fem.of ἔνδειξις, purpose).

King James Version

evident token - Phil.1:28.
proof - 2 Cor.8:24.
declare - Rom.3:25,26.

Revisded Standard Version

show - Rom.3:25.
prove - Rom.3:26.
proof - 2 Cor.8:24.
clear omen - Phil.1:28.

*Meaning:* A combination of ἐν (#80) and δείκνυμι (#359). *Cf.* ἐνδείκνυμι (#3842).

Demonstrated evidence, proof. Followed by a genitive of description - Rom.3:25,26 - with reference to the righteousness of God; 2 Cor.8:24, of the love of the Corinthian christians for the Lord and of Paul's confidence in them; Phil.1:28 - proof of perdition.

τῆς (gen.sing.fem.of the article in agreement with δικαιωσύνης) 9.
δικαιωσύνης (gen.sing.fem.of δικαιωσύνη, description) 322.
αὐτοῦ (gen.sing.masc.of αὐτός, possession) 16.
διὰ (preposition with the accusative, cause) 118.
τὴν (acc.sing.fem.of the article in agreement with πάρεσιν) 9.

#3875 πάρεσιν (acc.sing.fem.of πάρεσις, cause).

King James Version

remission - Rom.3:25.

Revised Standard Version

pass over - Rom.3:25..

*Meaning:* Cf. παρίημι (#5070). A passing over; the act of disregarding. *Cf.* comment on Rom.3:25 *infra.*

τῶν (gen.pl.neut.of the article in agreement with ἁμαρτημάτων) 9.

#3876 προγεγονότων (perf.part.gen.pl.neut.of προγίνομαι, adjectival, ascriptive).

King James Version

be past - Rom.3:25.

Revised Standard Version

former - Rom.3:25.

*Meaning:* A combination of πρό (#442) and γίνομαι (#113). Previously occurring; former. With reference to the sins committed before the death of Christ - Rom.3:25.

ἁμαρτημάτων (gen.pl.neut.of ἁμάρτημα, description) 2182.

*Translation -* "*Whom God previously designated as an expiation, by means of His blood, to be appropriated by faith, in order to vindicate His righteousness, in question because of the forgiveness of sins previously committed.*"

**Comment:**ὅν, the relative pronoun, refers to Χριστῷ Ἰησοῦ of verse 24. He is set forth as the Propitiator. *Cf.*carefully #3873 and see our comments on Luke 18:13. This propitiation is accomplished by the shedding of Jesus' blood, for since "the wages of sin is death" (Rom.3:23), the Propitiator must die in order to perform this function. The finished work of propitiation is appropriated by faith. Why the advance designation of a coming Propitiator? It was necessary in order for God to justify His acts of forgiveness in the Old Testament period of transgressions committed before the debt was paid.

Some elect Jews faced the problem of their sins honestly and humbly and brought the Levitical offerings prescribed by the law, with faith, not in the blood of bulls and goats *per se*, but faith that looked forward in time to Him Who was typfied by the animal sacrifices (John 1:29). Their sins were "passed by" (#3875). When they died they went to Paradise along with Abraham and the beggar of Luke 16. There may also have been Gentiles whose attitudes are described in Rom.2:7-10. There may also have been heathen who did *not* suppress what they knew about God (Rom.1:18). Certainly there were millions of children in the Old Testament period who died in infancy. The transgressions of all of these adults and the sinful natures of all of these infants were by-passed as God exercised His patience, but only because He had already provided that their sin debt would in fact be paid by the Propitiator. God saved them, as it were, on credit. But there was no doubt that in the execution of the eternal decrees of God, the debt would be paid. Thus God defended Himself against the charge that a holy God forgave sins without regard to the legal demands of a transgressed law.

In connection with all of this *cf.* our comment on Eph.4:8-10. By faith Old Testament transgressors looked forward in anticipation to the same cross toward which New Testament transgressors look back in contemplation. They believed that Christ would die for their sins and they were saved by that faith. We believe that Christ did die for our sins and we are saved by the same faith. It takes no more faith to believe God's prophecy than to believe God's history. This may be why Jesus did not establish the fact of His resurrection among unsaved historical sources in such fashion as to render it as certain as other well established historical facts of the same period. Had He done so, sinners who believed after the fact would have had a scientific ground for their commitment which sinners before the fact could not have had. Faith based upon evidence is not the kind of faith that saves. Saving faith accepts God's statement without question because it is God's statement. Christian evidences belong in the curriculum of those who are already saved. They have no place in an evangelistic meeting. The evangelist who seeks to implant the truth of the gospel of Christ in the sinner's heart by an approach through his head, cheapens it. Biblical evangelists do not try to prove to the sinner that the gospel story is true. They tell the story of the gospel of Christ and dare the audience to believe it. Only the Holy Spirit can enable one who is "dead in trespasses and sins" (Eph.2:1) to believe that which, at first blush, is "foolishness unto him" (1 Cor.1:18).

All references to time and space as they seem to relate to God must be viewed as accommodations to human thinking. God is eternal and omnipresent and thus He knows nothing of the categories of Immanuel Kant, which relate to relative matters. For God the creation of the universe, His decree to permit the fall of man, His provision for redemption and the historical implementation of all of these matters which men call history, was viewed in His eternal present. The Lamb of God was slain "from the foundation of the world" (Rev.13:8). Furthermore a sovereign God is not required to justify what He does for human skeptics.

*Verse 26 - "To declare, I say, at this time his righteousness: that he might be just and the justifier of him that believeth on Jesus."*

ἐν τῇ ἀνοχῇ τοῦ θεοῦ, πρὸς τὴν ἔνδειξιν τῆς δικαιοσύνης αὐτοῦ ἐν τῷ νῦν καιρῷ, εἰς τὸ εἶναι αὐτὸν δίκαιον καὶ δικαιοῦνται τὸν ἐκ πίστεως Ἰησοῦ.

*"... it was to prove at the present time that he himself is righteous and that he justifies him who has faith in Jesus." RSV*

ἐν (preposition with the locative, time period) 80.
τῇ (loc.sing.fem.of the article in agreement with ἀνοχῇ) 9.
ἀνοχῇ (loc.sing.fem.of ἀνοχή, time period) 3831.
τοῦ (gen.sing.masc.of the article in agreement with θεοῦ) 9.
θεοῦ (gen.sing.masc.of θεός, possession) 124.
πρὸς (preposition with the accusative, purpose) 197.
τὴν (acc.sing.fem.of the article in agreement with ἔνδειξιν) 9.
ἔνδειξιν (acc.sing.fem.of ἔνδειξις, purpose) 3874.
τῆς (gen.sing.fem.of the article in agreement with δικαιωσύνης) 9.
δικαιωσύνης (gen.sing.fem.of δικαιωσύνη, description) 322.
αὐτοῦ (gen.sing.masc.of αὐτός, possession) 16.
ἐν (preposition with the locative of time point) 80.
τῷ (loc.sing.masc.of the article in agreement with καιρῷ) 9.
νῦν (loc.adverbial modifier) 1497.
καιρῷ (loc.sing.masc.of καιρός, time point) 767.
εἰς (preposition with the accusative, purpose) 140.
τὸ (acc.sing.neut.of the article, with the articular infinitive, purpose) 9.
εἶναι (pres.inf.of εἰμί, accusative, purpose) 86.
αὐτὸν (acc.sing.masc.of αὐτός, general reference) 16.
δίκαιον (acc.sing.masc.of δίκαιος, predicate adjective) 85.
καὶ (ascensive conjunction) 14.                    ιιε a
δικαιοῦντα (pres.act.part.acc.sing.masc.of δικαιόω, adverbial, concessive) 933.
τὸν (acc.sing.masc.of the article direct object of δικαιοῦντα) 9.
ἐκ (preposition with the partitive ablative) 19.
πίστεως (abl.sing.fem.of πίστις, partitive) 728.
Ἰησοῦ (abl.sing.fem.of Ἰησοῦς, source) 3.

*Translation - "... during the period of God's forbearance in order to demonstrate His righteousness at the present time so that He may be adjudged just even though He declares him who has faith in Jesus just."*

**Comment:** The ἐν ... θεοῦ phrase is joined to verse 25 in the KJV. God passed over former sins, in the Old Testament age, at a time in human history before redemption was made. This was the time of His forbearance. He demonstrated His justice by establishing Christ as the propitiation in Old Testament times. He now demonstrates it again ἐν τῷ νῦν καιρῷ. The foreordained Saviour became the historic Saviour. God's eternal plan, conceived and planned in eternity past, and announced in the Old Testament period, was implemented when Jesus died on the cross. Both the designation (προέθετο) in eternity (verse 25) and the incarnation and death (verse 26) in time demonstrate God's righteousness. The cross was not an afterthought with God, for God cannot have afterthoughts. That He recognized that redemption was necessary if transgressors were to be justified indicates that God has proper regard to the canons of holiness and the justice without which holiness could not be protected. Having recognized this fact, God announced it before the historic fact, both by the law of Moses and by the prophets (Rom.3:21), and having announced that the legal basis for man's forgiveness would be provided, He did in fact provide it. Type was lost in Antitype. Prophecy was fulfilled in history. The law and the prophets said that God would at some future time settle the sin account in perfect justice for those whose sins He passed over. History says that He did.

εἰς introduces the purpose clause. καὶ is ascenive in introduction of the concessive participle. God is just, even (ascensive καὶ) though (concessive δικαιοῦντα) He justifes men of faith.

For other examples like ἐκ πίστεως, see John 18:37 - ὁ ὢν ἐκ τῆς ἀληθείας; Rom.4:14 - οἱ ἐκ νόμοι; Acts 11:2 - οἱ ἐκ περιτομῆς and Rom.2:8 - οἱ ἐκ ἐριθίας. These are partitive ablative uses of ἐκ. Those persons selected from the entire human race who are of faith, God has declared righteous. And this He has been able to do without prejudice to His own standards of righteousness.

Thus, after proving that the entire human race stands condemned before the bar of divine justice (Romans 1:18 - 3:19), Paul has now shown how it was possible for God in perfect justice and thus with no compromise of His holiness, to save some. It is obvious for those who understand the grounds for justification that there is nothing in the system to suggest to the transgressor who now, despite his transgressions, is declared righteous, that he should congratulate himself or announce to others that they should congratulate him. For such the material of verses 27 and 28 is unnecessary. But for the obtuse Paul goes over the ground again!

*Verse 27 - "Where is boasting then? It is excluded. By what law? Of works? Nay: but by the law of faith."*

Ποῦ οὖν ἡ καύχησις; ἐξεκλείσθη. διὰ ποίου νόμου; τῶν ἔργων; οὐχί, ἀλλὰ διὰ νόμου πίστεως.

*"Then what becomes of our boasting? It is excluded. On that principle? On the principle of works? No, but on the principle of faith."*    RSV

Ποῦ (interrogative adverb of place) 142.

οὖν (inferential conjunction) 68.

ἡ (nom.sing.fem.of the article in agreement with καύχησις) 9.

#3877 καύχησις (nom.sing.fem.of καύχησις, subject of verb understood).

King James Version

boasting - Rom.3:27; 2 Cor.7:14; 8:24; 11:10,17.

glorying - 2 Cor.7:4.
rejoicing - 1 Cor.15:31; 2 Cor.1:12; 1 Thess.2:19; James 4:16.
whereof I may glory - Rom.15:17.

Revised Standard Version

boasting - Rom.3:27; 2 Cor.7:14; 8:24; 1 Thess.2:19; James 4:16.
boast - 2 Cor.1:12; 11:10.
boastful confidence - 2 Cor.11:17.
pride - 2 Cor.7:4; 1 Cor.15:31.
be proud - Rom.15:17.

*Meaning: Cf.* καυχάομαι (#3847) and καύχημα (#3881). Boasting; pride in; rejoicing because of accomplishment - one's own or that of others. The boasting of the legalist and his works - Rom.3:27; the glory which is Christ's - 1 Cor.15:31; Paul's boast of his own Christian experience - 2 Cor.1:12; Rom.15:17; Paul's boast of the Corinthians - 2 Cor.7:4,14; 8:24; of the Thessalonians - 1 Thess.2:19; Paul's boast of his qualifications as an apostle - 2 Cor.11:10,17; with reference to the self-willed Christian outside of God's will - James 4:16.

**#3878** ἐξεκλείσθη (3d.per.sing.1st.aor.pass.ind.of ἐκκλείω, culminative).

King James Version

exclude - Rom.3:27; Gal.4:17.

Revised Standard Version

exclude - Rom.3:27.
shut out - Gal.4:17.

*Meaning:* A combination of ἐκ (#19) and κλείω (#570). Hence, to shut out; to exclude; to rule out. In logical argument, to rule out as inadmissible - Rom.3:27; to prevent access - Gal.4:17.

διὰ (preposition with the ablative  of agent) 118.
ποίου (abl.sing.masc.of ποῖος, in agreement with νόμου) 1298.
νόμου (abl.sing.masc.of νόμος, agent) 464.
τῶν (gen.pl.neut.of the article in agreement with ἔργων) 9.
ἔργων (gen.pl.neut.ofd ἔργον, description) 460.
οὐχί (negative conjunction with the indicative) 130.
ἀλλὰ (alternative conjunction) 342.
διὰ (preposition with the ablative of agent) 118.
νόμου (abl.sing.masc.of νόμος, agent) 464.
πίστεως (gen.sing.fem.of πίστις, description) 728.

*Translation - "Where then is boasting? It has been ruled out. By what principle? Of works? No! But by the faith principle."*

**Comment:** The intensity of Paul's feeling is evident. He has asked three questions and made three statements. And yet there is only one verb in the lot. οὖν is inferential and depends for its force upon the foregoing argument of Rom.3:19-26. The exclusion here is logical. No man can boast about his having been given a gift. Paul develops this in greater detail in Romans 4:1-7. No one who understands the basis upon which God saves a sinner could ever boast about it. We have involved here the agency of two opposite principles. One operates on law; the other on faith. One depends upon what a man does; the other upon what he believes and, what is equally important, how humbly he believes it. The law principle says that salvation is something to be gained through human merit. The faith principle says that salvation is through humble acknowledgment of one's own worthlessness, followed by a child-like acceptance of the grace of God by faith.

There are only two kinds of religion in the world - the one built upon the word DO; the other upon the word DONE. All systems except Christianity demand that man must earn his salvation. They differ only in what they demand that he do. There is no real difference between the Arminian determination to "hold out faithful and gain a home in heaven" and the Moslem determination to make it to Mecca. This is not to say that an Arminian with the grace of God in his heart is not a Christian. It is to say that though he has the grace of God in his heart he lacks the theology of God in his head. God be thanked that He saves us, not upon the basis of what we understand, but upon the basis of whom we trust. One can speak about comparative religions, but he should not consider Christianity as one of them. Unsaved people throughout the world are weighted down with religion. Christians are free. We have accepted a gift.

Paul is now ready to present a logical conclusion. When a lawyer and logician of Paul's stature reaches a conclusion and announces it, the world had better listen.

*Verse 28 - "Therefore we conclude that a man is justified by faith without the deeds of the law."*

λογιζόμεθα γὰρ δικαιοῦσθαι πίστει ἄνθρωπον χωρὶς ἔργων νόμου.

*"For we hold that a man is justified by faith apart from the works of law."* RSV

λογιζόμεθα (1st.per.pl.pres.mid.ind.of λογίζομαι, culminative) 2611.

γὰρ (inferential conjunction) 105.

δικαιοῦσθαι (pres.pass.inf.of δικαιόω, noun use, object of λογιζόμεθα in indirect discourse) 933.

πίστει (instru.sing.fem.of πίστις, means) 728.

ἄνθρωπον (acc.sing.masc.of ἄνθρωπος, general reference) 341.

χωρὶς (preposition with the ablative of separation) 1077.

ἔργων (abl.pl.neut.ofd ἔργον, separation) 460.

νόμου (gen.sing.masc.ofd νόμος, description) 464.

*Translation - "So we have arrived by logic at this conclusion: a man is declared righteous by means of faith, apart from works of law."*

**Comment:** γάρ is inferential. BCD$_c$KP 33 88 104 181 330 451 614 629 1241 1877 1984 1985 2495 *Byz* syr$_{p,y}$ Ephraem Chrysostom Euthalius Theodoret Ps-Oecumenius and Theophylact have οὖν, while *Lect* omits the conjunction. The context permits either a causal or inferential interpretation. *Cf.* #2611 - "to reach a logical conclusion." Note the infinitive in indirect discourse. The instrumental πίστει and the ablative phrase χωρὶς ἔργων νόμου are the poles apart. Paul is really being tautological, but he does it for emphasis. Goodspeed correctly translates, "The observance of the law has nothing to do with it."

Thus Paul opposes the legalistic Judaizers and the Gnostic ascetics as he will continue to do in Romans, Galatians, Ephesians, Philippians and Colossians especially. Thus Augustine, in the best of Pauline traditions, opposed Pelagius. Thus Luther and Calvin withstood Arminius and Erasmus. And thus modern Calvinists oppose those who today deny human depravity and teach that man really needs no salvation beyond what he can achieve for himself. It is not strange that modernists should refer to the death of Jesus on the cross as a miscarriage of justice, for "if righteousness is come by the law then Christ is dead in vain" (Gal.2:21).

Two more questions come to mind as we consider what Paul has said thus far in this epistle. He deals with the first of these in verses 29 and 30 and with the second in verse 31.

*Verse 29 - "If he the God of the Jews only? Is he not also of the Gentiles? Yes, of the Gentiles also."*

ἢ ᾽Ιουδαίων ὁ θεὸς μόνον; οὐχὶ καὶ ἐθνῶν; ωαὶ καὶ ἐθνῶν,

*"Or is God the God of Jews only? Is he not the God of Gentiles also? Yes, of Gentiles also, . . . " RSV*

ἢ (disjunctive) 465.
᾽Ιουδαίων (gen.pl.masc.of ᾽Ιουδαῖος, relationship) 143.
ὁ (nom.sing.masc.of the article in agreement with θεὸς) 9.
θεὸς (nom.sing.masc.of θεός, subject of ἔστιν understood) 124.
μόνον (acc.sing.neut.of μόνος, adverbial) 339.
οὐχὶ (negative conjunction with the indicative in rhetorical question, which expects an affirmative reply) 130.
καὶ (adjunctive conjunction) 14.
ἐθνῶν (gen.pl.neut.of ἔθνος, relationship) 376.
ναὶ (affirmative particle) 524.
καὶ (adjunctive conjunction) 14.
ἐθνῶν (gen.pl.neut.of ἔθνος, relationship) 376.

*Translation - "Or does God relate only to Jews? Does He not relate also to Gentiles?. Yes, also to Gentiles."*

**Comment:** Note ἢ here in introduction of a question. The second question is rhetorical. We expect the answer to be in the affirmative. ναὶ καὶ ἐθνῶν is confirmatory. The reasons for this is clear from verse 30.

*Verse 30 - "Seeing it is God which shall justify the circumcision by faith, and uncircumcision through faith."*

εἴπερ εἷς ὁ θεός, ὃς δικαιώσει περιτομὴν ἐκ πἰστεως καὶ ἀκροβυστίαν διὰ τῆς πίστεως.

*". . . since God is one; and he will justify the circumcised on the ground of their faith and the uncircumcised through their faith."*

**#3879** εἴπερ (intensive conditional particle).

King James Version

if so be that - Rom.8:9,17; 1 Cor.15:15; 1 Pet.2:3.
seeing - 2 Thess.1:6; Rom.3:30.
though - 1 Cor.8:5.

Revised Standard Version

since - Rom.3:30; 2 Thess.1:6.
if - Rom.8:9.
provided - Rom.8:17.
if it is true - 1 Cor.15:15.
for - 1 Pet.2:3.
as indeed - 1 Cor.8:5.

*Meaning:* A combination of εἰ (#337) and intensive περ. Since εἰ can introduce a first-class condition with the fact in the protasis not in doubt, assumed to be true, stated as though true but in fact rejected, or with great doubt, (when used with the optative), the context of εἴπερ determines its meaning within the range of εἰ as listed. περ simply intensifies (and sometimes extensifies) εἰ. "Since, in fact" - Rom.3:30; 2 Thess.1:6; "if, in fact" - Rom.8:9,17; 1 Pet.2:3; "if indeed" (in an argumentative hypothesis) in 1 Cor.15:15. In a concessive sense - "though" or "despite the fact that" - 1 Cor.8:5.

εἷς (nom.sing.masc.of εἷς, predicate adjective) 469.
ὁ (nom.sing.masc.of the article in agreement with θεός) 9.
θεός (nom.sing.masc.of θεός, subject of ἐστιν understood) 124.
ὃς (nom.sing.masc.of ὅς, relative pronoun, subject of δικαιώσει) 65.
δικαιώσει (3d.per.sing.fut.act.ind.of δικαιόω, predictive) 933.
περιτομὴν (acc.sing.fem.of περιτομή, direct object of δικαιώσει) 2368.
ἐκ (preposition with the ablative, cause) 19.
πίστεως (abl.sing.fem.of πίστις, cause) 728.
καὶ (adjunctive conjunction joining nouns) 14.
ἀκροβυστίαν (acc.sing.fem.of ἀκροβυστία, direct object of δικαιώσει) 3236.
διὰ (preposition with the ablative of means) 118.
τῆς (abl.sing.fem.of the article in agreement with πίστεως) 9.
πίστεως (abl.sing.fem.of πίστις, means) 728.

*Translation - "Since, in fact God is one He will declare the circumcised righteous because of their faith and the uncircumcised righteous by means of their faith."*

**Comment:** *Cf.#3879.* In this passage εἰ (in εἴπερ) introduces an elliptical condition (with the apodosis missing) of the simple first-class, which accepts as true the condition stated, *viz.* that God is one. He does not have two or more policies to guide Him in His dealings with Jews and Gentiles. Paul is answering the question of verse 29. God justifies Jews on the ground of their faith and Gentiles by means of their faith. It could be no other way, since we have only two choices. Man is saved either by the works of the law or by faith. Paul has before proved that both Jews and Gentiles are hopelessly depraved. Neither Jew nor Gentile could hope to please God by human merit. Thus it must be by faith and this principle must apply both to Jews and to Gentiles.

There is a hint here that brings to mind the supposed advantage that the Jew has over the Gentile (Rom.3:1-2). The Jew received a revelation from God that was not given to the Gentile. But the advantage was not such as to enable him to gain his own salvation. He had the moral law of God codified and inscribed on tablets of stone. The Mosaic Code also laid down guidelines for the ordering of Jewish society under the theocracy, with its twin administrators of kings and priests. Thus Jewish society should have been superior in social, economic and political matters, and indeed it would have been better in these areas than that of the pagans, if the Jews had obeyed the code. But Jews are no better than Gentiles. Thus they transgressed the law of God as much as the Gentiles, even though they had the elements of this law written down.

It is also true that the Gentile had the law of God written into his conscience as much as did the Jew and that he was blessed with the power of reason to the same degree as did the Jew, since both were created in Adam in the image of God. Both had the advantage of Psalm 19:1-9. We have already seen that the greater light which gives salvation was given to those, whether Jew or Gentile, who showed the disposition to follow the light which they already posssessed. Thus the Gentile could be saved as easily as could the Jew, particularly in view of the fact that the latter not only sinned against the light of his conscience, but also against the letter of the law of Moses and the admonitions of the prophets. Both Moses and the Prophets pointed the Jew forward to another righteousness (Rom.3:21), but that was of advantage to him only if he responded to the message. If by reading Moses and the Prophets (Rom.10:17) he found faith in Christ generated in his heart, his faith became the cause of God's justification. Faith in the Gentile heart, generated only by his reaction to natural theological revelation (Psalm 19:1-9; Rom.2:7-10) is the means of God's act of justification for him.

In summation the fact that the Jew is as depraved as a result of the fall of the race in Adam, as is the Gentile, any advantage which he might have gained in the Mosaic Law and the message of the Prophets, was rendered nugatory. He sinned willingly as did the Gentile. In fact he sinned against more light than did the heathen nations of the race.

One more question arises which Paul answers in

*Verse 31 - "Do we then make void the law through faith? God forbid: Yea, we establish the law."*

νόμον οὖν καταργοῦμεν διὰ τῆς πίστεως; μὴ γένοιτο, ἀλλὰ νόμον
ἱστάνομεν.

*"Do we then overthrow the law by this faith? By no means! On the contrary,
we uphold the law."*    RSV

νόμεν (acc.sing.masc.of νόμος, direct object of καταργοῦμεν) 464.
οὖν (inferential conjunction) 68.
καταργοῦμεν (1st.per.pl.pres.act.ind.of καταργέω, aoristic) 2500.
διὰ (preposition with the ablative of means) 118.
τῆς (abl.sing.fem.of the article in agreement with πίστεως) 9.
πίστεως (abl.sing.fem.of πίστις, means) 728.
μὴ (negative conjunction with the optative) 87.
γένοιτο (3d.per.sing.aor.optative of γίνομαι, voluntative) 113.
ἀλλὰ (alternative conjunction) 342.
νόμον (acc.sing.masc.of νόμος, direct object of ἱστάνομεν) 464.
ἱστάνομεν (1st.per.pl.pres.act.ind.of ἱστάνω, for ἵστημι) 180.

*Translation - "Are we then abrogating law by means of faith? Not at all! On the
contrary, we are establishing law."*

**Comment:** *Cf.*#2500. Since law cannot save but faith can, the superficial
conclusion is that faith renders law nugatory. But this would be so only if God's
purpose for the law had been to use it to save men. This is not God's purpose
(Rom.3:20; Gal.3:19-25). The fact that justification is by faith χωρὶς νόμου
establishes and honors the law because it has performed its two-fold task well. It
has convinced the transgressor, be he Jew or Gentile, that he is a transgressor
(Rom.3:20) and it has also witnessed about another righteousness which was
displayed in the person and work of the Lord Jesus Christ, God incarnate.

The Mosaic Code is an ethical expression of the holiness of God on a stone
tablet. Jesus Christ is an ethical expression of the holiness of God in a man. And
it is His righteousness which is imputed unto the believer who is now, and will
forever be, a member of His living body (2 Cor.5:21; Rom.4:6). Thus, so far from
concluding that salvation by faith means that the law failed in its mission and is
therefore no longer important, on the contrary (ἀλλὰ) salvation by faith results
in seeing the law's righteous standard honored to its last jot and tittle in Jesus
Christ historically (Mt.5:17), in the believer positionally when he is saved
(Rom.4:6) and ultimately both in the glorified believer and in the social order of
the kingdom age.

This concludes Paul's legal argument on the plan of salvation. What follows is
epexegetical. First, he illustrates salvation by grace through faith χωρὶς νόμου in
the lives of Abraham and David in Romans 4:1-25.

# The Example of Abraham

*(Romans 4:1-12)*

*Romans 4:1* - *"What shall we say then that Abraham our father, as pertaining to the flesh, hath found?"*

Τί οὖν ἐροῦμεν εὑρηκέναι Ἀβραὰμ τὸν προπάτοορα ἡμῶν κατὰ σάρκα;

*"What then shall we say about Abraham, our forefather according to the flesh?"*　　　*RSV*

Τί (acc.sing.neut.of τίς, interrogative pronoun, direct object of ἐροῦμεν) 281.
οὖν (inferential conjunction) 68.
ἐροῦμεν (1st.per.pl.fut.act.ind.of εἴρω, deliberative) 155.
εὑρηκέναι (perf.act.inf.of εὑρίσκω, object of ἐροῦμεν, indirect discourse) 79.
Ἀβραὰμ (acc.sing.masc.of Ἀβραάμ, general reference) 7.
τὸν (acc.sing.masc.of the article in agreement with προπάτορα) 9.

#**3880** προπάτορα (acc.sing.masc.of προπάτωρ, apposition).

King James Version

father - Rom.4:1.

Revised Standard Version

forefather - Rom.4:1.

*Meaning:* A combination of πρό (#442) and πατήρ (#238). Hence, forefather, progenitor. With reference to Abraham, the federal head of the Jewish people - Romans 4:1.

ἡμῶν (gen.pl.masc.of ἐγώ, relationship) 123.
κατὰ (preposition with the accusative, standard) 98.
σάρκα (acc.sing.fem.of σάρξ, standard) 1202.

*Translation* - *"What then shall we say about what Abraham, our forefather, has experienced?"*

**Comment:** οὖν is inferential and depends for its force upon the preceding argument. Paul has just established a principle to the effect that salvation is attainable only by grace through faith and not by law. Therefore (οὖν), he suggests, we ought to apply this principle to Abraham's experience and see what can be said about it, either to confirm or deny. Note the indirect discourse after ἐροῦμεν, a deliberative future in a direct question, with the perfect infinitive εὑρηκέναι. At the time of Paul's writing, Abraham had been long since dead. But the perfect infinitive has in view both Abraham's original experience and the knowledge that resulted from it which he understood to the day of his death. In other words, the perfect infinitive idea of time and action is in relation to Abraham, not to Paul. What did Abraham continue to understand throughout his regenerate life as a result of his preterite punctiliar experience? That Paul knew what Abraham knew is due to his knowledge of Abraham's history, not to any proleptical force of the perfect infinitive εὑρηκέναι. κατὰ σάρκα is joined to τὸν προπάτορα ἡμῶν and refers to the human genetic connection of every Jew to Abraham. What was Abraham's experience, and what theological conclusions can be drawn from it? The entire fourth chapter is devoted to answering this question. Some readings have πατέρα rather than προπάτορα and with a different word order.

*Verse 2 - "For if Abraham were justified by works, he hath whereof to glory; but not before God."*

εἰ γὰρ Ἀβραὰμ ἐξ ἔργων ἐδικαιώθη, ἔχει καύχημα, ἀλλ' οὐ πρὸς θεόν.

*"For if Abraham was justified by works, he has something to boast about, but not before God." RSV*

εἰ (conditional particle in a first-class condition) 337.
γὰρ (causal conjunction) 105.
Ἀβραὰμ (nom.sing.masc.of Ἀβραάμ, subject of ἐδικαιώθη) 7.
ἐξ (preposition with the ablative of means) 19.
ἔργων (abl.pl.neut.of ἔργον, means) 460.
ἐδικαιώθη (3d.per.sing.aor.pass.ind.of δικαιόω, first-class condition) 933.
ἔχει (3d.per.sing.pres.act.ind.of ἔχω, static, in a first-class condition) 82.

#**3881** καύχημα (acc.sing.neut.of καύχημα, direct object of ἔχει).

King James Version

boasting - 2 Cor.9:3.
glorying - 1 Cor.5:6; 9:15.
rejoicing - 2 Cor.1:14; Gal.6:4; Phil.1:26; Heb.3:6.
rejoice - Phil.2:16.
whereof to glory - Rom.4:2; 2 Cor.5:12.
nothing to glory of - 1 Cor.9:16.

Revised Standard Version

something to boast about - Rom.4:2.
boasting - 1 Cor.5:6; 2 Cor.9:3.
ground for boasting - 1 Cor.9:15,16.
cause to be proud of - 2 Cor.1:14; Phil.2:16.
reason to boast - Gal.6:4.
cause to glory - Phil.1:26.
pride in our hope - Heb.3:6.

*Meaning:* Cf. καυχάομαι (#3847) and καύχησις (#3877). Grounds for boasting; reason to be proud. Each context is clear. Differs from #3877 by virtue of the result suffix μα.

ἀλλ' (adversative conjunction) 342.
οὐ (negative conjunction) 130.

πρός (preposition with the accusative of extent) 197.
θεόν (acc.sing.masc.of θεός, extent) 124.

*Translation - "For if Abraham was made righteous by works, he has grounds for boasting. But not in God's presence."*

**Comment:** γάρ is causal as Paul establishes a hypothetical case in point. The first-class condition with εἰ, though untrue, is assumed to be true for the sake of the argument. If the premise is true, the conclusion is also true. Otherwise not. Paul goes on to declare in verse 2 and prove in later verses, that the conclusion is not true. Therefore the premise is also false. Abraham was not justified by his good works. If he had been so justified it could not have been the good works of the law because Abraham lived 430 years before the law was given (Gal.3:17). Thus the motivation for Abraham's good works, if he had offered them to God in exchange for salvation, would have been the promptings of his moral conscience. But Abraham was not made righteous because of good works, either those of his own devising or those in obedience to express divine commands.

But Paul asks us to suppose that Abraham worked his way into the good graces of God. What then? The conclusion in such a case would be that Abraham now had grounds for personal pride in his accomplishment and probably was, at the very moment of Paul's writing (present tense in ἔχει) strutting up and down the streets of glory! This would be the logical conclusion to be drawn in the apodosis to fit the assumption in the protasis. Anyone who can work his way into God's favor by his own good works has a right to be proud. Actually such an achievement, if Abraham had accomplished it, would have proved that Abraham was as good as God. The Pharisee of Luke 18:9-12 illustrates the point. Paul quickly adds that Abraham was not boasting about his accomplishment - ἀλλ᾽ οὐ πρὸς θεόν - "but not in God's presence." Abraham is now as humble in heaven as he *finally* came to be on earth. Paul gives the details of Abraham's experience, which shed great light upon the Old Testament story, later in the chapter, with an additional shaft of heavenly light from Heb.11:17-19.

*Verse 3 - "For what saith the scripture? Abraham believed God and it was counted unto him for righteousness."*

τί γὰρ ἡ γραφὴ λέγει; Ἐπίστευσεν δὲ Ἀβραὰμ τῷ θεῷ, καὶ ἐλογίσθη αὐτῷ εἰς δικαιοσύνην.

*"For what does the scripture say? 'Abraham believed God, and it was reckoned to him as righteousness.'" RSV*

τί (acc.sing.neut.of τίς, interrogative pronoun, direct object of λέγει) 281.
γάρ (causal conjunction) 105.
ἡ (nom.sing.fem.of the article in agreement with γραφή) 9.
γραφή (nom.sing.fem.of γραφή, subject of λέγει) 1389.
λέγει (3d.per.sing.pres.act.ind.of λέγω, aoristic) 66.
Ἐπίστευσεν (3d.per.sing.aor.act.ind.of πιστεύω, constative) 734.
δὲ (continuative conjunction) 11.

'Αβραάμ (nom.sing.masc.of 'Αβραάμ, subject of ἐπίστευσεν) 9.
τῷ (dat.sing.masc.of the article in agreement with θεῷ) 9.
θεῷ (dat.sing.masc.of θεός, personal interest) 124.
καὶ (continuative conjunction) 14.
ἐλογίσθη (3d.per.sing.aor.pass.ind.of λογίζομαι, constative) 2611.
αὐτῷ (dat.sing.masc.of αὐτός, indirect object of ἐλογίσθη) 16.
εἰς (preposition with the accusative, predicate accusative) 140.
δικαιοσύνην (acc.sing.fem.of δικαιοσύνη, purpose) 322.

*Translation - "For what does the scripture say?'And Abraham believed God and it was credited to his account as righteousness.' "*

**Comment:** γὰρ is causal as Paul appeals to Genesis 15:6 in support of his previous statement that Abraham was not boasting before God. *Cf.* Gal.3:6 and James 2:23 and comment *en loc.*

Abraham had just received an unconditional promise from God.. Though Genesis 15:6 says that he believed God, it does not say that he believed God *at that time,* although he probably thought he did. Paul deals with the entire story in greater detail in Romans 4:10-25 and we shall defer further comments until later. All that Paul says now is that Abraham was declared righteous, not because he obeyed God, but because he believed God. He was saved by faith, not by works.

We get further exploration of the thought with an analogy in verses 4 and 5. *Cf.*#2611, III, for λογίζομαι in an accounting sense, as it is used here.

*Verse 4 - "Now to him that worketh is the reward not reckoned of grace, but of debt."*

τῷ δὲ ἐργαζομένῳ ὁ μισθός οὐ λογίζεται κατὰ χάριν ἀλλὰ κατὰ ὀφείλημα.

*"Now to one who works, his wages are not reckoned as a gift but as his due."* RSV

τῷ (dat.sing.masc.of the article in agreement with ἐργαζομένῳ) 9.
δὲ (explanatory conjunction) 11.
ἐργαζομένῳ (pres.mid.part.dat.sing.masc.of ἐργάζομαι, substantival, personal advantage) 691.
ὁ (nom.sing.masc.of the article in agreement with μισθὸς) 9.
μισθὸς (nom.sing.masc.of μισθός, subject of λογίζεται) 441.
οὐ (negative conjunction with the indicative) 130.
λογίζεται (3d.per.sing.pres.pass.ind.of λογίζομαι, customary) 2611.
κατὰ (preposition with the accusative standard) 98.
χάριν (acc.sing.fem.of χάρις, standard) 1700.
ἀλλὰ (alternative conjunction) 342.
κατὰ (preposition with the accusative, standard) 98.
ὀφείλημα (acc.sing.neut.of ὀφείλημα, standard) 580.

*Translation - "Now the reward paid to the worker is not regarded as a gift, but is paid according to the extent of obligation."*

**Comment:** δὲ is explanatory. The relationship between an employer and his employee is a business relationship. The employer hires; the employee works; there is an agreement as to the wage. When the work is done a cash settlement is made in which the employer is debtor and the employee is creditor. The money paid by the employer to the employee is not a gift. It is the payment of a debt. This relationship is not grace and a gift. It is works and a payment. As Paul states the opposite proposition the analogy fades into its application of the theology of justification in

*Verse 5 - "But to him that worketh not, but believeth on him that justifieth the ungodly, his faith is counted for righteousness."*

τῷ δὲ μὴ ἐργαζομένῳ, πιστεύοντι δὲ ἐπὶ τὸν δικαιοῦντα τὸν ἀσεβῆ, λογίζεται ἡ πίστις αὐτοῦ εἰς δικαιοσύνην,

*"And to one who does not work but trusts him who justifies the ungodly, his faith is reckoned as righteousness."*   RSV

τῷ (dat.sing.masc.of the article in agreement with ἐργαζομένῳ) 9.
δὲ (adversative conjunction) 11.
μὴ (negative conjunction with the participle) 87.
ἐργαζομένῳ (pres.mid.part.dat.sing.masc.of ἐργάζομαι, substantival, personal reference) 691.
πιστεύοντι (pres.act.part.dat.sing.masc.of πιστεύω, substnatival, personal reference) 734.
δὲ (adversative conjunction) 11.
ἐπὶ (preposition with the accusative, metaphorical extent) 47.
τὸν (acc.sing.masc.of the article in agreement with δικαιοῦντα) 9.
δικαιοῦντα (pres.act.part.acc.sing.masc.of δικαιόω, substantival, extent) 933.
τὸν (acc.sing.masc.of the article in agreement with ἀσεβῆ) 9.

#3882 ἀσεβῆ (acc.sing.masc.of ἀσεβής, direct object of δικαιοῦντα).

King James Version

ungodly - Rom.4:5; 5:6; 1 Tim.1:9; 1 Pet.2:5,6; 3:7; Jude 4,15′,15.

Revised Standard Version

ungodly - Rom.4:5; 5:6; 1 Tim.1:9; 2 Pet.2:5,6; 3:7; Jude 4,15,15.
impious - 1 Pet.4:18.

*Meaning:* A combination of α privative and σέβω (#1149). Destitute of reverence. As a noun - one with no awe or respect for God.

λογίζεται (3d.per.sing.pres.pass.ind.of λογίζομαι, static) 2611.
ἡ (nom.sing.fem.of the article in agreement with πίστις) 9.
πίστις (nom.sing.fem.of πίστις, subject of λογίζεται) 728.

αὐτοῦ (gen.sing.masc.of αὐτός, possession) 16.
εἰς (preposition with the accusative, predicate use) 140.
δικαιοσύνην (acc.sing.fem.of δικαιοσύνη, predicate accusative, purpose) 322.

*Translation - "But with reference to the one who does not work, but rather believes upon Him Who declares the ungodly righteous - his faith is credited to his account as righteousness."*

Comment: δὲ is adversative as Paul suggests the opposite hypothesis to that of verse 4. The non-worker, who, however (adversative δὲ) believes upon the God Who has a way to declare an ungodly man righteous is representative of the opposite side of the illustration. What is the situation with reference to him? Note the anacoluthon. Paul leaves the first clause dangling. But the meaning is clear - "with reference to the non-worker - his faith is credited to his account and he is declared righteous." Again we have λογίζεται in an accounting sense. *Cf.*#2611, III.

This is ironical and paradoxical. It is contrary to human ideas. The capitalist world believes that a worker should be rewarded. A drone who does no work but trusts instead for a handout should starve. Thus man reasons, but Isaiah 55:8 suggests that God is not governed by human thought patterns. Under law the worker is paid and the believer gets nothing. Under grace the believer gets the gift of eternal life, while the worker who chooses the legal relation with the court goes to hell as a lawbreaker.

And yet when we consider the quality of the work performed by the unbelieving worker in the analogy the philosophy is not contrary to human thinking, for, although the workers imagines that his work is profitable to God, it is not. He can offer nothing but the exercises of the flesh and it yields no profit (John 6:63). All that he can do is to break the law. There is no altruism in the heart of the unregenerate. All his thoughts and deeds are in opposition to God. His is an adversary relation *vis a vis* the God of heaven, just as the buyer and the seller occupy opposite sides of the counter in the business world.

Salvation is not for sale in God's bargain basement. If it were, even at reduced prices, man could not buy it. He does not have the coin of the realm. The primary characteristic of money is acceptability. Nothing that man can offer is acceptable to God. He may view what he brings to the market as good, but God sees it as counterfeit, but when God looked at what His Son had to offer in payment in the covenant of redemption He was "well pleased" (Mt.3:17).

Paul now supports his thought with a quotation from David in

*Verse 6 - "Even as David also describeth the blessedness of the man, unto whom God imputeth righteousness without works."*

καθάπερ καὶ Δαυὶδ λέγει τὸν μακαρισμὸν τοῦ ἀνθρώπου ᾧ ὁ θεὸς λογίζεται δικαιοσύνην χωρὶς ἔργων,

*"So also David pronounces a blessing upon the man to whom God reckons righteousness apart from works: . . . " RSV*

**#3883** καθάπερ (intensive comparative particle).

King James Version

as - Rom.12:4; 1 Cor.10:10; 12:12; 2 Cor.3:13; 8:11; 1 Thess.2:11; 3:6; Heb.5:4.
as well as - Heb.4:2.
even as - Rom.4:6; 2 Cor.1:14; 3:18; 1 Thess.3:12; 4:5.

Revised Standard Version

so also - Rom.4:6.
just as - 1 Cor.12:12; Heb.4:2; 5:4.
as - 2 Cor.1:14; 1 Thess.3:6,12; 1 Cor.10:10; 1 Thess.4:5.
for this comes - 2 Cor.3:18.
like - 2 Cor.3:13; 1 Thess.2:11.
may be matched - 2 Cor.8:11.

*Meaning:* A combination of καθώς (#1348) and περ, from περί (#173). περ intensifies the force of καθώς - precisely as; exactly as. In comparative clauses.

καὶ (adjunctive conjunction) 14.
Δαυὶδ (nom.sing.masc.of Δαυίδ, subject of λέγει) 6.
λέγει (3d.per.sing.pres.act.ind.of λέγω, aoristic) 66.
τὸν (acc.sing.masc.of the article in agreement with μακαρισμὸν) 9.

**#3884** μακαρισμὸν (acc.sing.masc.of μακαρισμός, reference).

King James Version

blessedness - Rom.4:6,9; Gal.4:15.

Revised Standard Version

blessing - Rom.4:6,9.
satisfaction - Gal.4:15.

*Meaning:* Cf. μακάριος (#422) and μακαρίζω (#1827). Blessing - Romans 4:6, where μακαρισμὸν is an accusative of general reference following λέγει - "he speaks with reference to the blessing. . . κ.τ.λ." With reference to the blessedness (happy state) itself - Rom.4:9; Gal.4:15.

τοῦ (gen.sing.masc.of the article in agreement with ἀνθρώπου) 9.
ἀνθρώπου (gen.sing.masc.of ἄνθρωπος, possession) 341.
ᾧ (dat.sing.masc.of ὅς, indirect object of λογίζεται) 65.
ὁ (nom.sing.masc.of the article in agreement with θεὸς) 9.
θεὸς (nom.sing.masc.of θεός, subject of λογίζεται) 124.
λογίζεται (3d.per.sing.pres.mid.ind.of λογίζομαι, customary) 2611.
δικαιοσύνην (acc.sing.fem.of δικαιοσύνη, direct object of λογίζεται) 322.
χωρὶς (preposition with the ablative of separation) 1077.
ἔργων (abl.pl.neut.of ἔργον, separation) 460.

*Translation - "Precisely as David also speaks about the blessing of the man to whom God credits righteousness apart from works."*

**Comment:** Abraham is one illustration of Paul's argument (Rom.4:1-5, 9-25). David's comment in Psalm 32:1-2 is another.

*Verse 7 - "Saying, Blessed are they whose iniquities are forgiven, and whose sins are covered."*

Μακάριοι ὧν ἀφέθησαν αἱ ἀνομίαι καὶ ὧν ἐπεκαλύφθησαν αἱ ἁμαρτίαι.

*"Blessed are those whose iniquities are forgiven, and whose sins are covered."* RSV

μακάριοι (nom.pl.masc.of μακάριος, predicate adjective) 422.
ὧν (gen.pl.masc.of ὅς, the relative pronoun, possession) 65.
ἀφέθησαν (3d.per.pl.aor.pass.ind.of ἀφίημι, culminative) 319.
αἱ (nom.pl.fem.of the article in agreement with ἀνομίαι) 9.
ἀνομίαι (nom.pl.fem.of ἀνομία, subject of ἀφέθησαν) 692.
καὶ (adjunctive conjunction joining nouns) 14.
ὧν (gen.pl.masc.of ὅς, the relative pronoun, possession) 65.

#3885 ἐπεκαλύφθησαν (3d.per.pl.aor.pass.ind.of ἐπικαλύπτω, culminative).

    King James Version

cover - Rom.4:7.

    Revised Standard Version

cover - Rom.4:7.

*Meaning:* A combination of ἐπί (#47) and καλύπτω (#753). Hence, covered over; hidden; totally obscured from view. A stronger verb than #753 - Rom.4:7.

αἱ (nom.pl.fem.of the article in agreement with ἁμαρτίαι) 9.
ἁμαρτίαι (nom.pl.fem.of ἁμαρτία, subject of ἐπεκαλύφθησαν) 111.

*Translation - "Happy are they whose lawless acts have been forgiven and whose sins have been covered."*

**Comment:** The antecedent of ὧν is the unexpressed οὗτοι, the subject of the unexpressed εἰσίν. μακάριοι is the predicate adjective of the main clause, all of which is unexpressed except μακάριοι. The meaning is - "These whose violations of the law are forgiven are happy . . . " The quotation is from Psalm 32:1,2. The Hebrew poetic parallelism is apparent. Acts against the law have been forgiven. Sins have been covered. Note the culminative aorists, with emphasis upon the result of the completed action.

    A purely legal relationship between Judge and defendant would demand death for transgression, unless propitiation intervenes, as it does in Christ. The transgressor is an outlaw, with all civil rights forfeited in the universe over which the Judge has jurisdiction, until his debt is paid and reconcilation is made. But David says that the Judge will forgive ("stand away from" - #319) sin and cover it - *i.e.* He will refuse to charge it against the account of the sinner. This thought follows in

*Verse 8 - "Blessed is the man to whom the Lord will not impute sin."*

μακάριος ἀνὴρ οὗ οὐ μὴ λογίσηται κύριος ἁμαρτίαν.

μακάριος (nom.sing.masc.of μακάριος, predicate adjective) 422.
ἀνὴρ (nom.sing.masc.of ἀνήρ, subject of ἐστιν understood) 63.
οὗ (gen.sing.masc.of ὅς, relative pronoun, possession) 65.
οὐ (negative conjunction with μὴ and the subjunctive) 130.
μὴ (negative conjunction with οὐ and the subjunctive, emphatic negation) 87.
λογίσηται (3d.per.sing.1st.aor.mid.subj.of λογίζομαι, emphatic negation) 2611.
κύριος (nom.sing.masc.of κύριος, subject of λογίσηται) 97.
ἁμαρτίαν (acc.sing.fem.of ἁμαρτία, direct object of λογίσηται) 111.

*Translation - "The man whose sin the Lord will never charge to his account is happy."*

**Comment:** μακάριος is emphasized. Note the emphatic negation of the double negative οὐ μὴ with the aorist subjunctive. Transgressions of the moral law of the universe must be imputed to some account and fully paid. Otherwise the holiness of God is compromised, which is another way of saying that God does not exist. If sins are not imputed to the sinner to whom are they imputed? To the Propitiator (Isa.53:5,6; 1 Peter 2:24). Once imputed to the account of the Substitute and the full penalty of the law exacted, the matter is closed. There is no double jeopardy in Heaven's court.

> Oh to grace how great a debtor
> Daily I'm constrained to be!
> Let thy goodness like a fetter
> Bind my wandering heart to thee."

*Verse 9 - "Cometh this blessedness then upon the circumcision only, or upon the uncircumcision also? For we say that faith was reckoned to Abraham for righteousness."*

ὁ μακαρισμὸς οὖν οὗτος ἐπὶ τὴν περιτομὴν ἢ καὶ ἐπὶ τὴν ἀκροβυστίαν; λέγομεν γάρ, Ἐλογίσθη τῷ Ἀβραὰμ ἡ πίστις εἰς δικαιοσύνην.

*"Is this blessing pronounced only upon the circumcised, or also upon the uncircumcised? We say that faith was reckoned to Abraham as righteousness."*

ὁ (nom.sing.masc.of the article in agreement with μακαρισμὸς) 9.　　*RSV* μακαρισμὸς (nom.sing.masc.of μακαρισμός, subject of verb understood) 3884.

οὖν (inferential conjunction) 68.

οὗτος (nom.sing.masc.of οὗτος, in agreement with μακαρισμὸς) 93.

ἐπὶ (preposition with the accusative of extent, place) 47.

τὴν (acc.sing.fem.of the article in agreement with περιτομὴν) 9.

περιτομὴν (acc.sing.fem.of περιτομή, place) 2368.

ἤ (disjunctive) 465.

καὶ (adjunctive conjunction joining prepositional phrases) 14.

ἐπὶ (preposition with the accusative of extent, place) 47.

τὴν (acc.sing.fem.of the article in agreement with ἀκροβυστίαν) 9.

ἀκροβυστίαν (acc.sing.fem.of ἀκροβυστία, place) 3236.

λέγομεν (1st.per.pl.pres.act.ind.of λέγω, progressive duration, retroactive) 66.

γάρ (causal conjunction) 105.

Ἐλογίσθη (3d.per.sing.aor.pass.ind.of λογίζομαι, constative) 2611.

τῷ (dat.sing.masc.of the article in agreement with Ἀβραὰμ) 9.

Ἀβραὰμ (dat.sing.masc.of Ἀβραάμ, indirect object of ἐλογίσθη) 7.

ἡ (nom.sing.fem.of the article in agreement with πίστις) 9.

πίστις (nom.sing.fem.of πίστις, subject of ἐλογίσθη) 728.

εἰς (preposition with the accusative, predicate use, purpose) 140.

δικαιοσύνην (acc.sing.fem.of δικαιοσύνη, predicate use, purpose) 322.

*Translation - "Is this blessing granted then to the circumcision only, or also to the uncircumcision? Because we have been saying, 'The faith was credited to Abraham as righteousness.' "*

**Comment:** Paul's two examples from Old Testament Scripture which exemplify justification by faith involved Abraham and David, both of whom are associated with the Jew. Lest this lead some to ask if this policy applies only to Jews, whose distinguishing mark is circumcision, he now anticipates the question and answers it. Abraham's experience was deliberately chosen by Paul to make his point, because Abraham, better than any other Old Testament character, could make the point. As a matter of fact no one but Abraham could be cited to make the point that Jews and Gentiles alike are justified by faith χωρὶς νόμου and χωρὶς ἔργων. Note how the context allows us to translate λέγομεν as a present progressive retroactive. Paul calls the attention of the reader to something that he had said before. He now asks how and when this imputation of divine righteousness was given to Abraham, and then replies to his own question. Finally, in verses 11 and 12, Paul uses the facts of Abraham's case to show that God has included in His redemption plan those individuals of every branch of the human family.

*Verse 10 - "How was it then reckoned? When he was in circumcision or in uncircumcision? Not in circumcision but in uncircumcision."*

πῶς οὖν ἐλογίσθη; ἐν περιτομῇ ὄντι ἤ ἐν ἀκροβυστίᾳ; οὐκ ἐν περιτομῇ ἀλλ᾽

ἐν ἀκροβυστίᾳ.

"*How then was it reckoned to him? Was it before or after he had been circumcised? If was not after, but before he was circumcised.*" RSV

πῶς (interrogative conjunction) 627.
οὖν (inferential conjunction) 68.
ἐλογίσθη (3d.per.sing.aor.pass.ind.of λογίζομαι, constative) 2611.
ἐν (preposition with the locative of time point) 80.
περιτομῇ (loc.sing.fem.of περιτομή, time point) 2368.
ὄντι (pres.part.loc.sing.masc.of εἰμί, adverbial, temporal) 86.
ἤ (disjunctive) 465.
ἐν (preposition with the locative of time point) 80.
ἀκροβυστίᾳ (loc.sing.fem.of ἀκροβυστία, time point) 3236.
οὐκ (negative conjunction with the indicative) 130.
ἐν (preposition with the locative of time point) 80.
περιτομῇ (loc.sing.fem.of περιτομή, time point) 2368.
ἀλλ' (alternative conjunction) 342.
ἐν (preposition with the locative of time point) 80.
ἀκροβυστίᾳ (loc.sing.fem.of ἀκροβυστία, time point) 3236.

*Translation* - "*Under what circumstances then was it credited? After he was circumcised or before? Not after, but before.*"

**Comment:** Blass observes that Paul's skillful use of rhetorical question recalls the oratorical style of the late Attic period. (Blass, *Grammar of New Testament Greek*, 304 as cited in Robertston, *Grammar*, 1198). The locatives are all time point. Was Abraham circumcised before or after he was saved? He was circumcised after he was saved. He had not received the covenant of circumcision when he was saved. Therefore circumcision, whatever benefit it may bestow upon the Jew, has nothing to do with salvation. That which comes after the fact cannot cause the fact. Both circumcision and the giving of the law came later - in the case of the law 430 years later (Gal.3:17).

All of this raises a logical question. If Abraham was saved by faith when he was yet uncircumcised, why did he receive circumcision? The same question will be raised with reference to the law in Gal.3:19 and we must wait until then for Paul's answer, but he answers the first question in verses 11 and 12.

*Verse 11 - "And he received the sign of circumcision, a seal of the righteousness of the faith which he had being uncircumcised; that he might be the father of all them that believe, though they be not circumcised; that righteousness might be imputed unto them also.*"

καὶ σημεῖον ἔλαβεν περιτομῆς, σφραγῖδα τῆς δικαιοσύνης τῆς πίστεσο τῆς ἐν τῇ ἀκροβυστίᾳ, εἰς τὸ εἶναι αὐτὸν πατέρα πάντων τῶν πιστευόντων δι' ἀκροβυστίας, εἰς τὸ λογισθῆναι αὐτοῖς (τὴν) δικαιοσύνην,

"*He received circumcision as a sign or seal of the righteousness which he had by faith while he was till uncircumcised. The purpose was to make him the father*

*of all who believe without being circumcised and who thus have righteousness
reckoned to them, . . . "     RSV*

καὶ (continuative conjunction) 14.

σημεῖον (acc.sing.neut.of σημεῖον, direct object of ἔλαβεν) 1005.

ἔλαβεν (3d.per.sing.aor.act.ind.of λαμβάνω, constative) 533.

περιτομῆς (gen.sing.fem.of περιτομή, definition) 2368.

#3886 σφραγῖδα (acc.sing.fem.of σφραγίς, apposition).

King James Version

seal - Rom.4:11; 1 Cor.9:2; 2 Tim.2:19; Rev.5:1,2,5,9; 6:1,3,5,7,9,12; 7:2; 8:1;
9:4.

Revised Standard Version

seal - Rom.4:11; 1 Cor.9:2; 2 Tim.2:19; Rev.5:1,2,5,9; 6:1,3,5,7,9,12; 7:2; 8:1;
9:4.

*Meaning:* possibly from φράσσω (#3870). φραγνῦμι equals φράσσω, in the
sense that a seal is a mark of ownership which warns intruders not to intrude. A
mark of permanent ownership. Physical circumcision was a sign of
righteousness by faith - Rom.4:11; metaphorically in 2 Tim.2:19; Rev.7:2; 9:4.
The Corinthian christians were living evidence that Paul was an Apostle - 1
Cor.9:2. With reference to the seals upon the book, sealed in Daniel (Daniel
12:9) but opened in Revelation - Rev.5:1,2,5,9; 6:1,3,5,7,9,12; 8:1.

τῆς (gen.sing.fem.of the article in agreement with δικαιοσύνης) 9.

δικαιοσύνης (gen.sing.fem.of δικαιοσύνη, description) 322.

τῆς (abl.sing.fem.of the article in agreement with πίστεως) 9.

πίστεως (abl.sing.fem.of πίστις, source) 728.

τῆς (abl.sing.fem.of the article in agreement with πίστεως) 9.

ἐν (preposition with the locative of time point) 80.

τῇ (loc.sing.fem.of the article in agreement with ἀκροβυστίᾳ) 9.

ἀκροβυστίᾳ (loc.sing.fem.of ἀκροβυστία, time point) 3236.

εἰς (preposition with the accusative of purpose) 140.

τὸ (acc.sing.neut.of the article, purpose) 9.

εἶναι (pres.inf.of εἰμί, noun use, purpose) 86.

αὐτὸν (acc.sing.masc.of αὐτός, general reference) 16.

πατέρα (acc.sing.masc.of πατήρ, predicate accusative) 238.

πάντων (gen.pl.masc.of πᾶς, in agreement with πιστευόντων) 67.

τῶν (gen.pl.masc.of the article in agreement with πιστευόντων) 9.

πιστευόντων (pres.act.part.gen.pl.masc.of πιστεύω, substantival, relationship) 734.

δι' (preposition with the ablative in a time expression) 118.

ἀκροβυστίας (abl.sing.fem.of ἀκροβυστία, time expression) 3236.

εἰς (preposition with the accusative, purpose) 140.

τὸ (acc.sing.neut.of the article, purpose) 9.

λογισθῆναι (aor.pass.inf.of λογίζομαι, purpose) 2611.
αὐτοῖς (dat.pl.masc.of αὐτός, indirect object of λογισθῆναι) 16.
τὴν (acc.sing.fem.of the article in agreement with δικαιοσύνην) 9.
δικαιοσύνην (acc.sing.fem.of δικαιοσύνη, general reference) 322.

*Translation - "And he received a circumcision symbol, a mark that signifies the righteousness that comes from the faith which he had when he was still uncircumcised, so that he might be the father of all who believe when they are uncircumcised, in order that righteousness might be credited to their account."*

**Comment:** The sentence goes on through verse 12. This half says that after Abraham was justified by faith he was circumcised. Why should he be circumcised if he was already saved? Obviously the rite is not prerequisite to or a cause or condition of justification. Salvation for Abraham was not made contingent upon circumcision, but upon faith. We must look elsewhere for the purpose of circumcision. It was a seal (#3886) - an evidence of God's ownership - a certification that something is true, like a notarized sworn statement. Of what? That Abraham already had righteousness (#322). Where did he get it? It's source was faith (ablative of source in τῆς πίστεως). When did Abraham receive this imputation of righteousness? When he was still uncircumcised as the temporal prepositional phrase ἐν τῇ ἀκροβυστίᾳ indicates.

The fact that he was circumcised *after* he was saved forever testifies and attests to the fact that he was already justified by faith. Why go to all the trouble? A purpose clause follows with εἰς τὸ εἶναι. . . δι' ἀκροβυστίας - "in order that he might be the father of all believers, who, like Abraham, their spiritual father (Gal.3:6,7), were saved when they too were uncircumcised. For διά and the ablative in a time expression *cf.* Mark 2:1; Mt.26:61; Acts 27:17; Gal.2:1; Acts 10:2. Why? Another purpose clause in εἰς τὸ λογισθῆναι . . . τὴν δικαιοσύνην - "In order that they might have righteousness imputed to their accounts" despite the fact that when they believed they lacked circumcision. This is of no consequence, since Abraham, their spiritual father, also lacked circumcision when he believed, but that fact did not prevent him from receiving the imputation of righteousness to his account.

Thus physical circumcision is an after-the-fact permanent evidence of a previous salvation experience, which is therefore in no way based upon circumcision but solely upon faith. The purpose of circumcision for Abraham is similar to the purpose of immersion in water for the believer. Both are public evidences in a ceremonial way of a spiritual experience. Paul makes this point in Romans 2:28,29. Regeneration may be thought of as spiritual circumcision of the heart and only those so regenerated should receive the physical evidence, which in Christian circles is immersion in water.

That Jewish infants are circumcised cannot be adduced as proof that Gentile infants should be baptized. Circumcision was also the seal of God that the child belonged to a chosen race of people who are destined to reign with their Messiah in the Kingdom Age. The racial solidarity of the Jewish people, which began to disintegrate only with the rise of reformed Judaism, even though the Jews were dispersed throughout the Gentile world, and subjected to great discrimination and persecution, is attributed to the rite of circumcision and to the religious dogmas with which it is associated. God's promise to Abraham was not that he would save all of his descendants who were circumcised, but that He would preserve the nation Israel and select from their numbers those who would comprise His special administrative nation in the Kingdom Age. The promise which Peter cited to the Jews in Jerusalem at Pentecost which was given "unto you, and to your children, and to all that are afar off. . . " is qualified by the phrase, ". . . even as many as the Lord our God shall call." (Acts 2:39). God has not promised to save every infant who has participated in a pedo-baptism ceremony, whether he was sprinkled, poured or immersed, any more than He has promised to save every Jewish boy who was circumcised in infancy. The covenant theology that equates circumcision in the Old Testament with baptism in the New Testament is not taught in these passages. Regeneration must come first. Those who reverse the order cannot influence the eternal counsels of God.

Christian baptism, which is conducted by immersing the candidate in water, is a public attestation of the same experience to which Abraham gave testimony when he was circumcised. We have seen why Abraham was circumcised even though he was already saved and needed no further action to assure his salvation. Why should we immerse a Christian in water if he is already saved? The order of events as set forth in the Great Commission of Mt.28:18-20 demands that we go to the ends of the earth with the gospel witness and (a) disciple, (b) immerse and (c) teach those who receive the message. The disciple is one who has become a humble learner. Thus he is regenerated. He has received the divine light of the gospel and has begun a long experience of learning more and more of the Way. The immersion ordinance is a public witness that the candidate has already been saved, though not yet immersed, and that now he wishes to be taught all of the wonderful truths to be found in the curriculum of Christian Education. Thus the unsaved who witness this ordinance are made to understand that they too can believe and be saved, though as yet not immersed. But the ordinance also teaches that others who, like them, were saved without immersion in water, should nevertheless submit to the ordinance, and add their testimony that, although they were not baptized in water they were in fact baptized by the Holy Spirit into the Body of Christ (1 Cor.12:13). The baptism of the Holy Spirit is what Paul in Romans 2:29 calls the circumcision of the sinner's heart and what Jesus calls being born "from above" (John 3:3,7,8). Similarly water baptism for the Christian and circumcision for Abraham were physical evidences which attest to an inner spiritual experience.

The dogma of baptismal regeneration, which says that immersion in water is a necessary means, rather than a subsequent demonstration, of salvation already possessed is a doctrine that says that Abraham was circumcised as a means of salvation rather than to demonstrate that he had already entered into saving relationships with God by faith. This, verse 11 expressly denies. Water baptism is important to the Christian, as a means of showing willingness to obey the divine command of our Lord, just as circumcision was important to Abraham, but only in relation to the divine purpose for which it was instituted. To confuse this purpose is to destroy the entire Abrahamic covenant, as it relates to soteriology.

*Verse 12* - *"And the father of circumcision to them who are not of the circumcision only, but who also walk in the steps of that faith of our father Abraham, which he had being yet uncircumcised."*

καὶ πατέρα περιτομῆς τοῖς οὐκ ἐκ περιτομῆς μόνον ἀλλὰ καὶ τοῖς στοιχοῦσιν τοῖς ἴχνεσιν τῆς ἐν ἀκροβυστίᾳ πίστεως τοῦ πατρὸς ἡμῶν Ἀβραάμ.

*". . . and likewise the father of the circumcised who are not merely circumcised but also follow the example of the faith which our father Abraham had before he was circumcised."* RSV

καὶ (adjunctive conjunction joining nouns) 14.
πατέρα (acc.sing.masc.of πατήρ, general reference) 238.
περιτομῆς (gen.sing.fem.of περιτομή, relationship) 2368.
τοῖς (dat.pl.masc.of the article, personal advantage) 9.
οὐκ (negative conjunction with the indicative) 130.
ἐκ (preposition with the ablative, partitive) 19.
περιτομῆς (gen.sing.fem.of περιτομή, description) 2368.
μόνον (acc.sing.neut.of μόνος, adverbial) 339.
ἀλλὰ (alternative conjunction) 342.
καὶ (adjunctive conjunction joining substantives) 14.
τοῖς (dat.pl.masc.of the article in agreement with στοιχοῦσιν) 9.
στοιχοῦσιν (pres.act.part.dat.pl.masc.of στοιχέω, substantival) 3557.
τοῖς (instru.pl.neut.of the article in agreement with ἴχνεσιν) 9.

#3887 ἴχνεσιν (instru.pl.neut.of ἴχνος, means).

King James Version

step - Rom.4:12; 2 Cor.12:18; 1 Pet.2:21.

Revised Standard Version

example - Rom.4:12.
step - 2 Cor.12:18; 1 Pet.2:21.

*Meaning: Cf.* ἵκω - "to go" and ἱκνέομαι, a lengthened form of ἵκω. Hence, a footstep or a track. Metaphorically, an example. With reference to those who emulate the faith experience of Abraham - Rom.4:12; the suffering Christian is emulating Christ's suffering - 1 Pet.2:21. Paul personally followed Titus' policy - not to take money from the Corinthians - 2 Cor.12:18.

τῆς (gen.sing.fem.of the article in agreement with πίστεως) 9.
ἐν (preposition with the locative of time point) 80.
ἀκροβυστίᾳ (loc.sing.fem.of ἀκροβυστία, time point) 3236.
πίστεως (gen.sing.fem.of πίστις, description) 728.
τοῦ (gen.sing.masc.of the article, in agreement with πατρὸς) 9.
πατρὸς (gen.sing.masc.of πατήρ, description) 238.

ἡμῶν (gen.pl.masc.of ἐγώ, relationship) 123.

'Αβραάμ (gen.sing.masc.of 'Αβραάμ, apposition) 7.

*Translation - "And the father of the circumcised, who are not merely circumcised but also those who are walking in the steps of the faith of our father Abraham which he had before he was circumcised."*

**Comment:** The verse is the remainder of the purpose clause, begun in verse 11 with εἰ τὸ εἶναι. God ordered Abraham's experience with its prescribed sequence of events (faith first and justification by means of it and then circumcision) for a purpose. Abraham is God's example of a circumcised Jew who was a Christian first and who later became a Jew. Thus he is the spiritual father of Gentiles who believe as Abraham did, for he was a Gentile when he first believed (Gal.3:6,7). He is also the genetic father of all Jews, who kept the national solidarity intact by circumcising their infant sons, and who are members of the nation whose King Messiah will return to earth to rule in His Kingdom of the Heavens forever upon this earth. Further Abraham is the spiritual father of those Jews, who were circumcised physically and who later believed as he did and became circumcised in heart (Rom.2:29). Abraham, born a Gentile, became a Christian (although they were not called Christians until the first century A.D.) before he became a Jew. Many Gentiles by birth, who can never become Jews, are nevertheless spiritual children of Abraham, with the circumcision of the heart and who are thus justified by faith as he was. Thus Paul makes his point that to become a "son" of Abraham one must believe as he did. Once that is done and the righteousness of Christ is credited to his account, physical circumcision is not necessary to complete an already completed salvation. Similarly physical circumcision is insufficient to bring justification. It is neither a help nor a hindrance. A circumcised Jew can still be saved, but only if he believes on Christ and His sacrifice alone, which rules out any confidence that he might otherwise have in the fact that he is a Jew. A Hebrew Christian can point to Abraham and say, "I, in circumcision, acquired his faith and he in faith acquired my circumcision." A Christian Gentile can point to Abraham as father and say, "I, though uncircumcised, have the same faith that he had when he too was uncircumcised." Abraham's circumcision, subsequently acquired, did nothing to add to his already perfect salvation. Nor will it add to the salvation of any other Christian. Nor will water baptism, nor church attendance, nor participation at the Lord's communion table, nor tithing, nor moral reformation. Those are things that we ought to do not *in order to* be saved, but *because* we are saved.

Paul now states the same proposition in slightly different terms.

# The Promise Realized through Faith

*(Romans 4:13-25)*

*Verse 13 - "For the promise that he should be the heir of the world, was not to Abraham, or to his seed, through the law, but through the righteousness of faith."*

Οὐ γὰρ διὰ νόμου ἡ ἐπαγγελία τῷ ᾽Αβραὰμ ἢ τῷ σπέρματι αὐτοῦ, τὸ κληρονόμον αὐτὸν εἶναι κόσμου, ἀλλὰ διὰ δικαιοσύνης πίστεως.

"The promise to Abraham and his descendants, that they should inherit the world, did not come through the law but through the righteousness of faith." RSV

Οὐ (negative conjunction with the indicative) 130.
γὰρ (causal conjunction) 105.
διὰ (preposition with the ablative of source) 118.
νόμου (abl.sing.masc.of νόμος, source) 464.
ἡ (nom.sing.fem.of the article in agreement with ἐπαγγελία) 9.
ἐπαγγελία (nom.sing.fem.of ἐπαγγελία, subject of ἦν understood) 2929.
τῷ (dat.sing.masc.of the article in agreement with ᾽Αβραὰμ) 9.
᾽Αβραὰμ (dat.sing.masc.of ᾽Αβραάμ, indirect object) 7.
ἢ (disjunctive) 465.
τῷ (dat.sing.neut.of the article in agreement with σπέρματι) 9.
σπέρματι (dat.sing.neut.of σπέρμα, indirect object) 1056.
αὐτοῦ (gen.sing.masc.of αὐτός, relationship) 16.
τὸ (acc.sing.neut.of the article in the articular infinitive) 9.
κληρονόμον (acc.sing.masc.of κληρονόμος, predicate accusative) 1386.
αὐτὸν (acc.sing.masc.of αὐτός, general reference) 16.
εἶναι (pres.inf.of εἰμί, apposition) 86.
κόσμου (gen.sing.masc.of κόσμος, definition) 360.
ἀλλὰ (alternative conjunction) 342.
διὰ (preposition with the ablative of source) 118.
δικαιοσύνης (abl.sing.fem.of δικαιοσύνη, source) 322.
πίστεως (abl.sing.fem.of πίστις, source) 728.

*Translation - "Because it was not from law that the promise came to Abraham or to his descendants that he would be the heir of the world, but it was from righteousness which has its source in faith."*

**Comment:** If the promise had its origin in the law (ablative of source in νόμου) then Abraham could not have had it until he was circumcised, a fact which Genesis 15:6 controverts. If by νόμου we mean the Mosaic Code, Abraham could not have had it at all, since the law post-dated the Abrahamic promise by 430 years (Gal.3:17). If by νόμου we mean the voice of conscience - the innate sense of the distinction between moral right and moral evil, which every man created in the image of God possesses, then Abraham could never inherit the world because, like the rest of the race, depraved in Adam, he could not live in keeping with the law's ethical demands. Only the incarnate Lord did that (Mt.5:17). Thus there is no hope for anyone in the world, be he Jew or Gentile, before or after circumcision, however sincerely motivated and thorougly sophisticated, if the world is to be owned and enjoyed only by those who keep the law of God.

What is this promise? The infinitive clause τὸ κληρονόμον αὐτὸν εἶναι is epexegetic, in apposition to ἡ ἐπαγγελία. It explains more fully what the promise is. *Cf.* Gen.12:1-3; 15:18-21; 18:18; 22:17-18; Gal.3:29. Abraham and his spiritual children are heirs of the universe; heirs to all that is viable because of orderly arrangement (*cf.*#360). Abraham, saved by grace through faith, and all of his posterity, Jew and Gentile, who have Abraham's faith χωρὶς ἔργων shall own the entire universe with all of its orderly arrangement and hence its eternal viability. Such is the promise. (1 Cor.3:21-23).

Under what circumstances did Abraham receive this legacy? What, if anything, did he have to do in order to gain the promise? Was the promise of God conditional or unconditional? Is there an if-clause in it? Is the implementation of its terms contingent upon anything that Abraham must do first? Paul's statement with reference to these matters is strong and clear. The promise and its fulfillment has nothing to do with law. It's source is righteousness (ablative in δικαιοσύνης) which, in turn has its source in faith (ablative of source in πίστεως). God gave the faith (Eph.2:8,9; Heb.12:2); faith produced the righteousness; righteousness produced the promise. Is that not the sequence? ἡ ἐπαγγελία . . . δικαιοσύνης . . . πίστεως.

Note 1 Thess.4:3 and 1 Pet.2:15 where we have infinitives in apposition to the substantive as τὸ εἶναι is to ἡ ἐπαγγελία here. *Cf.* also Acts 15:28 and James 1:27. When a noun follows another noun for greater clarity we call it apposition; the same relation between two verbs we call epexegesis. But since an infinitive is both noun and verb, its relation to either noun or verb which precedes it, is both appositional, if the substantive aspect is in view or epexegetical if we think of the infinitive more as a verb than as a noun. It is a matter of emphasis, which derives from the way in which the context impacts upon the infinitive. The two ideas are really the same. What the writer is after is a fuller explanation. The promise in this case was that Abraham and his descendants should fall heir to everything God has created. Of course it seems hardly necessary to point out that we are speaking of Abraham's spiritual descendants, not of his genetic posterity as such, though, thanks to the election of grace, many of his physical children are also his spiritual children. If this seems too good to be true, let us remember that if we are children of God, then we are heirs also; heirs of God and joint-heirs with Christ (Romans 8:17). All that He has is ours also. And what of Him? Read carefully Philippians 2:9-11 and Ephesians 1:17-23 and rejoice.

That the two orders - law and faith - are antithetical in their impact upon man's standing before God, is clear from

*Verse 14 - "For if they which are of the law be heirs, faith is made void, and the promise made of none effect."*

εἰ γὰρ οἱ ἐκ νόμου κληρονόμοι, κεκένωται ἡ πίστις καὶ κατήργηται ἡ ἐπαγγελία.

*"If it is the adherents of the law who are to be the heirs, faith is null and the promise is void." RSV*

εἰ (conditional particle in a first-class condition) 337.

γάρ (causal conjunction) 105.

οἱ (nom.pl.masc.of the article, subject of the verb understood) 9.

ἐκ (preposition with the ablative of source) 19.

νόμου (abl.sing.masc.of νόμος, source) 464.

κληρονόμοι (nom.pl.masc.of κληρονόμος, predicate nominative) 1386.

#3888 κεκένωται (3d.per.sing.perf.pass.ind.of κενόω, intensive).

King James Version

make of none effect - 1 Cor.1:17.
make of no reputation - Phil.2:7.
make void - Rom.4:14; 1 Cor.9:15.
be in vain - 2 Cor.9:3.

Revised Standard Version

null - Rom.4:14.
emptied of his power - 1 Cor.1:17.
deprive me of my ground - 1 Cor.9:15.
in vain - 2 Cor.9:3.
empty - Phil.2:7.

*Meaning:* To empty to pour out completely; to divest totally. Christ laid aside His heavenly glory in incarnation - Phil.2:7; to render nugatory, useless, ineffective; to deprive of force. Thus faith is useless if salvation is by law - Rom.4:14; the cross of Christ was needless if salvation is by water - 1 Cor.1:17; to make void; to cause a thing to be empty, hollow, vain - with reference to Paul's boast of the Corinthians - 2 Cor.9:3; of himself - 1 Cor.9:15.

ἡ (nom.sing.fem.of the article in agreement with πίστις) 9.

πίστις (nom.sing.fem.of πίστις, subject of κεκένωται) 728.

καὶ (continuative conjunction) 14.

κατήργηται (3d.per.sing.perf.pass.ind.of καταργέω, intensive) 2500.

ἡ (nom.sing.fem.of the article in agreement with ἐπαγγελία) 9.

ἐπαγγελία (nom.sing.fem.of ἐπαγγελία, subject of κατήργηται) 2929.

*Translation - "Because if those followers of the law be heirs, faith is nothing and the promise if worthless."*

**Comment:** The conclusion of verse 14 follows inferentially from the statement of verse 13. Paul is drawing an inference in theology from a fact of history. οἱ ἐκ νόμου - "those who are depending upon law." *Cf.* John 18:37; Rom.3:26; Acts 11:2; Rom.2:8 for other instances. εἰ with the indicative (though the copula is ellided) introduces a first-class condition in which the statement in the apodosis is true only if the statement in the protasis is also true. Otherwise it is false. It is an argumentative device. The statement in the premise is false, but it is assumed to be true, for the sake of the argument. Paul has just said in verse 13 that those of the law cannot be heirs. Now he hypothesizes. "If they were (and they are not) then the conclusion would follow, that faith has been nullified and the promise has been made worthless." The two passive perfect verbs in the apodosis are intensive - *i.e.* they speak of a present condition as a result of a past completed action. God's promises are null and our faith in them is void. The student should research both of these verbs thoroughly - #'s 2500 and 3888. The results will reveal the wickedness of the cults. Legalists will observe that the preaching that salvation is obtainable through human merit - circumcision, water baptism, sabbath observance, the practice of high ethical standards, *et al* make the death of Jesus Christ upon the cross unnecessary. If it was unnecessary then the modernists are right - God is a vicious bully when He allowed His Son to undergo the agony of the cross to accomplish that which can be accomplished by the sociologists.

Law which means works and faith which means trust and rest are totally antithetical. Paul reaches this same conclusion in Galatians 2:20,21. *Cf.*#2164 for the use of ἀθετέω in the New Testament.

Antitheses produce antithetical effects. Faith saves. Law condemns because it generates the wrath of God. This is the thought in

*Verse 15 - "Because the law worketh wrath: for where no law is, there is no transgression."*

ὁ γὰρ νόμος ὀργὴν κατεργάζεται, οὗ δὲ οὐκ ἔστιν νόμος, οὐδὲ παράβασις.

*"For the law brings wrath, but where there is no law there is no transgression."* RSV

ὁ (nom.sing.masc.of the article in agreement with νόμος) 9.

γὰρ (causal conjunction) 105.

νόμος (nom.sing.masc.of νόμος, subject of κατεργάζεται) 464.

ὀργὴν (acc.sing.fem.of ὀργή, direct object of κατεργάζεται) 283.

κατεργάζεται (3d.per.sing.pres.mid.ind.of κατεργάζομαι, present progressive retroactive) 3815.

οὗ (gen.sing.neut.of ὅς - *cf.*#132) 65.

δὲ (concessive conjunction) 11.

οὐκ (negative conjunction with the indicative) 130.

ἔστιν (3d.per.sing.pres.ind.of εἰμί, aoristic) 86.

νόμος (nom.sing.masc.of νόμος, subject of ἔστιν) 464.

οὐδὲ (disjunctive particle) 452.

παράβασις (nom.sing.fem.of παράβασις, subject of ἔστιν understood) 3851.

*Translation - "Because the law generates wrath, although where there is no law neither is there transgression."*

**Comment:** Paul is proving his contention of verse 14 that if law keepers are heirs, God's promise becomes vacant. Why? Because the law, instead of making a man an heir, makes him a criminal who deserves God's wrath. Goodspeed translates, "For the law only brings down God's wrath; where there is no law there is no violation of it." The law of God forbids those things which it is man's fallen nature to do. The law is the legal expression of the holiness of God. It tells us what God considers right and wrong. It mandates the former and forbids the latter. We can neither obey the mandate nor avoid doing what it forbids. The law of God is holy, just and good and by contrast man's nature is unholy, unjust and evil. Thus the law produces the basis by which God can charge man with transgression and visit His wrath upon him. Law enforcement, in a society where only good laws are enacted and where men are evil, is essential if the society is to remain viable. Thus God must enforce His moral laws in the universe because lax enforcement reduces the universe to chaos.

The stern pronouncement of legalism, with its message of salvation by character, is not a gospel. It is not "good news." It's message is that God's holy standard is beyond the reach of every man. Under its rule all men are lost and none can ever be saved. Else God is not holy. The God who can accept and incorporate into His society the best than man can do is not the God Who can assure that the Heavenly City and the society that surrounds it will go on forever. One infinitesimal percent of man's capacity for evil would turn heaven into hell in a short time. That is why God must judge sin and banish transgressors from heaven.

Though faith brings justification with its imputation of Christ's righteousness to the balance sheet of the believer, it does not immediately bring sinlessness, but it assures sinlessness after glorification. Only when we see Him at His return shall we be like Him because then we shall see Him as He is (1 John 3:2). The believer was foreknown and therefore predestined, called and justified. All of that is history. He is also scheduled for glorification. That is in the future. In the meantime he is warned not to say that he has no sin, for to say that is to deceive ourselves and to demonstrate that the truth is not in us (1 John 1:8). As we await glorification we have the potential for sinless living. We need only to walk in the Spirit in order to avoid the sins of the flesh (Gal.5:16). Since the Holy Spirit baptized us into the Body of Christ (1 Cor.12:13; Gal.3:27) we have had all of Him, but unfortunately too often He has not had all of us. It is in those times of defeat that we transgress God's law. But these lapses from the divine standard affect only our state - never our standing, which is always inviolate in Christ (Rom.5:1-2). We sing with our black brethren in Christ

> Sometimes I's up, sometimes I's down
> Oh yes, Lord!
> Sometimes I's almost to the ground,
> Oh yes, Lord!

But even in our "down times" we are never out. For our position in the Body of Christ depends upon His righteousness, not upon our own, for we have none of ourselves.

Paul's added observation that where there is no law there is no transgression is the ground for the view that all who die in infancy are safe. More on this in our comment on Romans 5:14.

*Verse 16 - "Therefore it is of faith, that it might be by grace; to the end the*

*promise might be sure to all the seed; not to that only which is of the law, but to*
*that also which is of the faith of Abraham, who is the father of us all."*

διὰ τοῦτο ἐκ πίστεως, ἵνα κατὰ χάριν, εἰς τὸ εἶναι βεβαίαν τὴν ἐπαγγελίαν
παντὶ τῷ σπέρματι, οὐ τῷ ἐκ τοῦ νόμου μόνον ἀλλὰ καὶ τῷ ἐκ πίστεως Ἀβραάμ
(ὅς ἐστιν πατὴρ πάντων ἡμῶν, . . .

*"That is why it depends on faith, in order that the promise may rest on grace*
*and be guaranteed to all his descendants — not only to the adherents of the law*
*but also to those who share the faith of Abraham, for he is the father of us all. . . .*
*" RSV.*

διὰ (preposition with the accusative, cause) 118.
τοῦτο (acc.sing.neut.of οὗτος, cause) 93.
ἐκ (preposition with the ablative of source) 19.
πίστεως (abl.sing.fem.of πίστις, source) 728.
ἵνα (conjunction with the subjunctive understood, in a sub-final clause) 114.
κατὰ (preposition with the accusative, standard) 98.
χάριν (acc.sing.fem.of χάρις, standard) 1700.
εἰς (preposition with the accusative, purpose) 140.
τὸ (acc.sing.neut.of the article in the articular infinitive, purpose) 9.
εἶναι (pres.inf.of εἰμί, acc.sing.neut., purpose) 86.

#3889 βεβαίαν (acc.sing.fem.of βέβαιος,  in agreement with ἐπαγγελίαν,
predicate adjective).

King James Version

of force - Heb.9:17.
stedfast - 2 Cor.1:7; Heb.2:2; 3:14; 6:19.
sure - Rom.4:16; 2 Pet.1:10,19.

Revised Standard Version

valid - Heb.2:2.
steadfast - Heb.6:19.
take effect - Heb.9:17.
unshaken - 2 Cor.1:7.
be guaranteed - Rom.4:16.
confirm - 2 Pet.1:10.
make more sure - 2 Pet.1:19.

*Meaning:* Cf. βαω equals βαίνω. Cf. βεβαιόω (#2932 and βεβαίωσις (#4540).
Firm, steady, unmoveable, dependable. God's covenant promise is certain to be
fulfilled - Rom.4:16; Heb.6:19; 2 Pet.1:19. Angelic words are trustworthy - 2
Pet.1:10; Heb.2:2. Christians are not to waver in their faith - Heb.3:14. Wills are
executable after the death of the testator upon probation - Heb.9:17. With
reference to Paul's faith in the Corinthians - 2 Cor.1:7.

τὴν (acc.sing.fem.of the article in agreement with ἐπαγγελίαν) 9.

ἐπαγγελίαν (acc.sing.fem.of ἐπαγγελία, general reference) 2929.
πάντι (dat.sing.neut.of πᾶς, in agreement with σπέρματι) 67.
τῷ (dat.sing.neut.of the article in agreement with σπέρματι) 9.
σπέρματι (dat.sing.neut.of σπέρμα, personal advantage) 1056.
οὐ (negative conjunction with the indicative) 130.
τῷ (dat.sing.masc.of the article, personal advantage) 9.
ἐκ (preposition with the ablative of source) 19.
τοῦ (abl.sing.masc.of the article in agreement with νόμου) 9.
νόμου (abl.sing.masc.of νόμος, source) 464.
μόνον (acc.sing.neut.of μόνος, adverbial) 339.
ἀλλὰ (alternative conjunction) 342.
καὶ (adjunctive conjunction, joining substantives) 14.
τῷ (dat.sing.masc.of the article, personal advantage) 9.
ἐκ (preposition with the ablative of source) 19.
πίστεως (abl.sing.fem.of πίστις, source) 728.
'Αβραάμ (gen.sing.masc.of 'Αβραάμ, description) 7.
(ὅς (nom.sing.masc.of ὅς, relative pronoun, subject of ἔστιν) 65.
ἔστιν (3d.per.sing.pres.ind.of εἰμί, aoristic) 86.
πατὴρ (nom.sing.masc.of πατήρ, predicate nominative) 238.
πάντων (gen.pl.masc.of πᾶς, in agreement with ἡμῶν) 67.
ἡμῶν (gen.pl.masc.of ἐγώ, relationship) 123.

*Translation - "This is why it is based on faith - in order that it may be according to grace, with the result that the promise is certain to be realized for all the descendants, not for those of the law only, but also for those who share Abraham's faith, (who is the father of all of us."*

**Comment:** διὰ τοῦτο - "because of this" - depends for its thrust upon verse 15. Since the law generates only the wrath of God which must fall upon the hapless heads of transgressors, a promise of God to man could never be made contingent upon man's obedience, if the fulfillment of the promise is to be expected. God's promise on that basis could never be sure to anyone, either Jew or Gentile. But, because salvation depends only upon God's gift (κατὰ χάριν), a sure result flows from this fact. We need not say "free gift" unless we wish to indulge in tautology. If it is not free it is not a gift. The clause εἰς τὸ εἶναι ... τῷ σπέρματι is sub-final - both purpose and result, since result is only intended purpose, and, when God's purpose is in view, there is no doubt that result will conform to purpose. God wanted to make His promise sure. So He put salvation on a grace basis. There is therefore no reason why what He purposes to do for Abraham and his spiritual descendants, both Jew and Gentile, cannot result. *Cf.*#3889. (Gal.3:6,7; Rom.4:11,12). Job had scant faith in man when he asked, "What is man that he should be clean? And he that is born of a woman, that he should be righteous?" (Job.15:14). He went on to add that God doesn't even trust His saints (Job.15:15). Indeed He does not - not at least until He has finished His work of glorification for us. That is why He cannot leave the issue of our salvation in our hands.

Paul makes a special point out of saying that since the salvation covenant between God and man is upon a grace basis, the assurance of salvation is the same for the Hebrew Christian as for the Gentile Christian. Since Jew and Gentile alike have been proved totally depraved, whatever advantage the Jew may have had by virtue of the fact that it was to him that the oracles of God were given — both those incorporated in the Mosaic Code and those from the sermons of the prophets, they did nothing to enhance his ability to earn salvation by his own good works (Rom.3:1-2). The Jew should have known better than to behave as he did, since God gave to him His law written on tablets of stone and also sent to him numerous prophets with their divine inspiration, but he did not. He sinned against the light, but so also did the Gentile , who heard the precepts of the Ten Commandments in the still small voice of his conscience. The fall of man was total and his plight was such as not to yield to social and environmental influences. Since all have sinned and continue to transgress God's law (Rom.3:23) all are alike and must be treated alike. So salvation is by grace through faith alone, and totally divorced from human merit. And this plan is for the Jew with his advantages as well as for the disadvantaged Gentile.

*Verse 17 - ("As it is written, I have made thee a father of many nations") before him whom he believed, even God, who quickeneth the dead, and calleth those things which be not as though they were."*

καθὼς γέγραπται ὅτι Πατέρα πολλῶν ἐθνῶν τέθεικά σε) κατέναντι οὗ ἐπίστευσεν θεοῦ τοῦ ζωοποιοῦντος τοὺς νεκροὺς καὶ καλοῦντος τὰ μὴ ὄντα ὡς ὄντα.

*". . . as it is written, 'I have made you the father of many nations' — in the presence of God in whom he believed, who gives life to the dead and calls into existence the things that do not exist."    RSV*

καθὼς (adverb introducing a comparative clause) 1348.
γέγραπται (3d.per.sing.perf.pass.ind.of γράφω, intensive) 156.
ὅτι (recitative) 211.
Πατέρα (acc.sing.masc.of πατήρ, predicate accusative) 238.
πολλῶν (gen.pl.neut.of πολύς, in agreement with ἐθνῶν) 228.
ἐθνῶν (gen.pl.neut.of ἐθνός, relationship) 376.
τέθεικά (1st.per.sing.perf.act.ind.of τίθημι, intensive) 455.
σε (acc.sing.masc.of σύ, direct object of τέθεικά) 104.
κατέναντι (improper preposition with the genitive of place description) 1342.
οὗ (gen.sing.masc.of ὅς, objective genitive) 65.
ἐπίστευσεν (3d.per.sing.aor.act.ind.of πιστεύω, ingressive) 734.
θεοῦ (gen.sing.masc.of θεός, place description, after κατέναντι) 124.
τοῦ (gen.sing.masc.of the article in agreement with πωοποιοῦντος) 9.
ζωοποιοῦντος (pres.act.part.gen.sing.masc.of ζωοποιέω, substantival, apposition) 2098.
τοὺς (acc.pl.masc.of the article in agreement with νεκροὺς) 9.
νεκροὺς (acc.pl.masc.of νεκρός, direct object of ζωοποιοῦντος) 749.

καὶ (adjunctive conjunction joining participles) 14.

καλοῦντος (pres.act.part.gen.sing.masc.of καλέω, apposition) 107.

τά (acc.pl.neut.of the article in agreement with ὄντα) 9.

μὴ (negative conjunction with the participle) 87.

ὄντα (pres.part.acc.pl.neut.of εἰμί, substantival, direct object of καλοῦντος) 86.

ὡς (comparative particle) 128.

ὄντα (pres.part.nom.pl.neut.of εἰμί, predicate nominative) 86.

*Translation - "As it is written, 'I have established you a father of many nations') - He believed God Who visited him - the God who brings the dead to life and calls into being that which does not exist."*

**Comment:** Paul calls Abraham the father of all true believers, whether they be Jew or Gentile (Gal.3:7) and supports the contention with Genesis 17:5, the statement God made to Abraham when God rejected his presumptuous act of begetting Ishmael of Hagar, a younger woman (Gen.16:1-16) when he was still sufficiently virile to beget him. The promise was that Sarah, who was now 89 should bear a son (Gen.17:16), who would be fathered by Abraham who was now 99 (Gen.17:1). Paul develops this thought in verses 18-22.

The promise was made firm (εἰς τὸ εἶναι βεβαίαν τὴν ἐπαγγελίαν) in the very presence of God (κατέναντι . . . θεοῦ). Why was the promise firm? Because it was God's promise and thus, in the nature of the case, was already accomplished as far as God was concerned. Any promise made κατέναντι θεοῦ is βεβαίαν. This is the promise that Abraham believed.

Robertson points to οὗ as a case of incorporation with the genitive of θεοῦ, from the ᾧ which normally would be its case with ἐπίστευσεν. Perhaps, or we can take οὗ as an objective genitive with ἐπίστευσεν and explain θεοῦ as a genitive of place description after κατέναντι. In any case the relative pronoun οὗ refers to θεοῦ and is the object of Abraham's faith.

Although the record shows that Abraham did not believe God when the promise was first made (Gen.12:2,3; 15:1-6).Note Gen.15:2,3 where Abraham suggests to God that, according to ancient custom, any child born in his house could be called his heir. But God assured him that the promised heir should be his, by virtue also of being his "seed." (Gen.15:4). Though Gen.15:6 says that Abraham believed God and was declared righteous, it does not say that he believed God *at that time.* Moses has telescoped the story. Eventually Abraham believed God, but not in Genesis 15. If he had the sad and sordid story of Genesis 16:1-16 would not have taken place. Convinced by God's promise that he would father a child (Gen.15:4) he nevertheless doubted Sarah's ability at her advanced age to bear him, particularly in view of her long history; for she had never given him a son. This is why he married Hagar. The faith that saved Abraham, referred to in Romans 4:17, was exercised in Genesis 17. Why should Abraham have believed God when he was 99 and Sarah ten years younger, when he could not believe it when he was 85 and Sarah 75? Because he now understood Who this God is. Note the perfect tense in τέθεικά σε - "In the eternal counsels of my will I have made you a father of many nations (the preterite idea in the perfect), and, as a result, you are now the father of many nations" (the present durative result of the punctiliar action in the past). At the time that God said this (Gen.17:5) Abraham had a son who was sixteen years old, who would try to kill Isaac, the miracle baby, and the descendants of whom are still trying to kill all of the descendants of the miracle baby. But he had no son whom God would recognize as the legitimate heir to the spiritual blessings which flow from the Abrahamic covenant, although God recognizes Ishmael and the Arab world as Abraham's physical descendants, albeit illegitimate. The Arabs are the harvest of the seeds of unbelief which Abraham sowed in his affair with Hagar - an affair that would never have taken place if Abraham had believed God in the first place. The patriarch interpreted God's promise in the light of what he thought he knew about gynecology. This know-it-all scientist (!) was certain that he could father a child, but he knew that Sarah could not conceive one. Gnostics have been interpreting God's Word in conformity with what they think they know ever since. The Bible demands that we accept the supernatural. Intellectual honesty would dictate that we recognize this fact and openly declare that since we do not believe in the supernatural, we therefore reject the Bible. But the social and economic cost of such blatant infidelity is too great for the modernist to bear. There is a better way. One can have his cake and eat it too. The theological cake is interpreted in terms of modern science, as the audience is assured that of course the passage does not mean what it says, since that is not possible, but the passage is a beautiful figure of speech. We must look beneath the text, which is obviously unscientific, for the true figurative meaning, which is in line with the latest scholarship. That this sort of infidelity is nothing new is obvious when we remember that Origen was teaching hermeneutics like this 1700 years ago.

We do not associate Abraham with infidels, except for the first 99 years of his life. He was given the gift of faith and, as a result, he conceived an idea of God more in keeping with the facts. Indeed, he had some faith when, at 85, he left Ur and travelled to Bethel on the promise that God would give him the country, but God's promise at that time did not call for him to believe that his aged wife would be the mother of the sons and daughters to whom he would bequeath the world when he died. All of the truly supernatural evidences of the faith of Abraham came after he was 99.

To a man, 99 years old, God promised that he would father a son by a women, 89 years old. And this time Abraham believed it - something that he had rejected 14 years before. What made the difference? The answer is two-fold. Abraham finally understood and accepted the concept of an omnipotent God, and he also was brought to the place where he was forced to recognize and accept his own helplessness in the situation. Thus he trusted God because he was forced to do so. He could no longer trust himself. Paul says this in verse 19.

This God is described in the substantival participles which are found in apposition to θεοῦ. He is the God τοῦ ζωοποιοῦντος τοὺς νεκροὺς καὶ καλοῦντος τὰ μὴ ὄντα ὡς ὄντα - "Who makes the dead alive and declares those things which do not exist as existing." He is thus the God of resurrection, the mighty victor over death and also the God of creation. The Creator to whom matter, if it could think, should be eternally indebted for its very existence, and

Who, in sovereign wisdom permitted sin and death to exercise temporary influence in His universe, is competent to solve whatever problems they may create.

The God Who makes the dead alive announced to Abraham that he would restore Sarah's youth and correct whatever had been the cause of her previous inability to conceive, and that he would also revitalize Abraham's virility, which had fallen into disorder in the previous fourteen years. Abraham believed this because he had to believe it. Fourteen years before he felt competent to help God out of a dilemma into which the Deity had blundered! Sarah could not have a baby, but he could father one. *Voila!* An affair with the cook in the kitchen. That was the essence of Abraham's faith when he was 85. He believed in God but he rejected the supernatural. A year later Hagar bore his son Ishmael (Gen.16:16). For thirteen years God hid His face from Abraham (Gen.17:1). What a harvest of the flesh! But God could not ignore him forever, for He was committed unto him. Now Abraham is 99, Ishmael is 13 and Sarah is 89. If Abraham could not believe God fourteen years before when his own reproduction facility was unimpaired, how could he believe Him now when his own body, as well as Sarah's was "dead" (verse 19)? The unregenerate never believe the promises of God as long as there is the slightest hope that they can do for themselves what must be done. That is why moralistic preaching is not evangelism. The evangelist who spends his time scolding the inebriate about his intemperate addiction to liquor, arouses in his prospect the desire to reform and the conviction that he can effect the reformation. The only sin for which there is no redemption is the sin of rebuffing the Holy Spirit when He comes to convince that God can forgive all other transgressions, but He cannot forgive a rejection of His Son (John 16:7-11).

The second participle in apposition is καλοῦντος. God, the Creator is able to call non-existent things (τὰ μὴ ὄντα) into existence (ὄντα). That which has no existence will exist if God says so! Once God spoke and the universe came into being. Now he speaks again to Abraham and a new nation in the family of nations is born. The God Who said "Light, exist!" (Gen.1:3) saw that light existed and He said that it was good. The same God "who commanded the light to shine out of darkness, hath shined in our hearts, to give the light of the knowledge of the glory of God in the face of Jesus Christ" (2 Cor.4:6), and on that day He shined His light into the heart of Abraham.

That the above is the proper exegesis will become clear in verses 18-25.

Abraham's original concept of God was that God could perform His promises only in scientific ways as understood by man. This was the error of the people described in Rom.1:18-25. They rejected the supernatural God and exchanged Him for one of their design, whose ways they could understand. Abraham's understanding of the problem evolved along the following lines: (1) I am too old to have a baby and so is Sarah. Therefore God will keep His promise to me by counting as my heir one born in my house to a younger man and wife (Gen.12:1-3; 15:1-3). (2) God will restore my youth but not Sarah's. So I will marry Hagar, the cook (Gen.16:1-16). (3) God will restore to me and Sarah our youth to give us Isaac, the miracle baby. Only in Genesis 17, when he finally accepted God as τοῦ ζωοποιοῦντος τὸς νεκροὺς καὶ καλοῦντος τὰ μὴ ὄντα ὡς ὄντα did he have real saving faith. There was a fourth step in Abraham's spiritual development. The God Who makes the dead alive could restore his "dead" body and heal "the deadness of Sarah's womb" (verse 19). That he understood, at last. But a few years later, when Isaac was old enough to carry firewood up the slopes of Mount Moriah, Abraham came to believe that God, Who had given to him and Sarah this miracle baby, in whom the hopes of the world for a Redeemer-Messiah rested, would raise him from the dead after his father had stabbed him to the heart, cut his throat, shed his blood and burned his body upon an altar (Heb.11:17-19). That Abraham fully intended to kill Isaac is clear from what he said to his servants in Genesis 22:5. He and the lad would go; he and the lad would worship; he and the lad would return. Thus saving faith, as exemplified in Abraham, our spiritual father, includes faith in the resurrection of the body.

Those in whose minds the issues are raised, who wish to be saved, must believe in three miracles that relate to birth. They must believe that Sarah had a baby when she was ninety years old. That was a miracle that only God could perform. They must also believe that Mary had a baby without a husband. That also is a miracle which only God can perform. They must also believe in the reality of their own "birth from above" (John 3:3,7). That also is a miracle that only God can perform. I have not said that everyone who comes seeking salvation must be catechized and faced with the challenge which these three issues present. But the one faced with the question dare not reject this supernatural element in his conception of God. If he does he makes the same mistake as those described in Romans 1:18-25 and the mistake that Abraham made until he was 99 years old.

Faith leads us to a naive, childlike view of God that no sophisticated scientist, *qua* scientist, can accept. Scientists, who pin all of their hopes for certitude upon measureable observation, thus profess themselves to be wise only to become fools (Rom.1:22) and miss salvation in the bargain, while Christians, admitting themselves to be babes and fools become wise unto salvation (Mt.11:25,26; 1 Cor11:18-25; 2:1-12; Mt.5:3; Psalm 19:7; Mt.18:3; 1 Cor.3:18; 4:10). Christians understand the scientific method of investigation, applaud its use and accept the conclusions to which it leads, when it is properly applied, with due regard to its limitations. But Christians abhor the dogma that no true scientist would dare defend that there are no supersensible realities.

Saving faith for Abraham, which enabled him to believe in miracle babies and a miraculous resurrection from the dead of his murdered son, came to Abraham in the same way that it comes for all of God's elect. The salvation experience of which faith is a vital part, and without which it could not occur, is the gift of God (Eph.2:8,9) not of works, but the gift is held out to us only when we become, like Abraham, willing to abandon our own highly regarded understanding of epistemology and accept as little children that which seems to us like nonesense. "Faith is knowledge, and a higher sort of knowledge ... faith is yet a cognitive act of the reason, and may be defined as certitude with respect to matters in which verification is unattainable. ... Faith in supersensible realities, on the contrary, is the highest exercise of reason." (Augustus Hopkins Strong, *Systematic Theology*, I, 3, *et passim*). The difference between γνῶσις (#1856) and ἐπίγνωσις (#3817) and between γινώσκω (#131) and ἐπιγινώσκω (#675) is to be noted. The intensified forms, both of noun and verb, speak of certitude which is unattainable by empirical authentication. A knowledge of God is not unscientific; it is superscientific. Many humble scientists have come to Christ by faith that leads to a commitment that cannot be explained by his concept of *scientific* truth or reality. The tragedy is that many scientists worship themselves and grant commitment only to that certitude available to them at the moment from their own scientific investigation. Since no scientist has ever seen God - nor has any philosopher or theologian for that matter - or analyzed Him in a test-tube, science has nothing to say about God, one way or the other. He can only say that he does not know whether God exists or not. This is honest agnosticism. If he becomes a Christian he then believes in a God who does "unscientific things." This may cost him a measure of respect among his colleagues, but it will assure him of eternal salvation, which, after all is not a bad tradeoff. Nor was it for Abraham, even though he never lived on earth to see the fulfillment of God's promise. He wandered until he died as a sojourner in a strange country, even though he was the heir to every foot of it. When Sarah died he had to buy a burial plot from the sons of Heth, for which he paid four hundred shekels of silver, which was the acceptable coin of the local market, but he looked for a city "which hath foundations, whose builder and maker is God" (Heb.11:10).

In verses 18-22 Paul discusses in more detail the elements of Abraham's faith. The passage illustrates the fact that man's extremity is God's opportunity. It was from a condition of helplessness and frustration that Abraham came to exercise saving faith.

*Verse 18 - "Who against hope believed in hope, that he might become the father of many nations, according to that which was spoken, So shall thy seed be."*

ὃς παρ' ἐλπίδα ἐπ' ἐλπίδι ἐπίστευσεν εἰς τὸ γενέσθαι αὐτὸν πατέρα πολλῶν ἐθνῶν κατὰ τὸ εἰρημένον, Οὕτως ἔσται τὸ σπέρμα σου.

*"In hope he believed against hope, that he should become the father of many nations; as he had been told, 'So shall your descendants be.' "* RSV

ὃς (nom.sing.masc.of ὅς, the relative pronoun, subject of ἐπίστευσεν) 65.
παρ' (preposition with the accusative, "near to") 154.
ἐλπίδα (acc.sing.fem.of ἐλπίς, "near to", in contrast with ἐπ' ἐλπίδι) 2994.
ἐπ' (preposition with the instrumental of means) 47.
ἐλπίδι (instru.sing.fem.of ἐλπίς, means) 2994.
ἐπίστευσεν (3d.per.sing.aor.act.ind.of πιστεύω, ingressive) 734.
εἰς (preposition with the accusative, purpose) 140.
τὸ (acc.sing.neut.of the article in the articular infinitive, purpose) 9.
γενέσθαι (aor.mid.inf.of γίνομαι, purpose) 113.
αὐτὸν (acc.sing.masc.of αὐτός, general reference) 16.
πατέρα (acc.sing.masc.of πατήρ, predicate accusative) 238.
πολλῶν (gen.pl.masc.of πολύς, in agreement with ἐθνῶν) 228.
ἐθνῶν (gen.pl.neut.of ἔθνος, relationship) 376.
κατὰ (preposition with the accusative, standard) 98.

τό (acc.sing.neut.of the article, in agreement with εἰρημένον) 9.

εἰρημένον (perf.pass.part.acc.sing.neut.of ῥέω, standard) 116.

Οὕτως (comparative particle) 74.

ἔσται (3d.per.sing.fut.ind.of εἰμί, predictive) 86.

τό (nom.sing.neut.of the article in agreement with σπέρμα) 9.

σπέρμα (nom.sing.neut.of σπέρμα, subject of ἔσται) 1056.

σου (gen.sing.masc.of σύ, relationship) 104.

*Translation - "Who, despite his doubts kept on hoping in order that he might become the father of many nations, in keeping with that which had been spoken, 'Thus shall your descendants be.' "*

**Comment:** ὅς, the subject of ἐπίστευσεν, has Ἀβραάμ of verse 16 as its antecedent. παρ' ἐλπίδα ἐπ' ἐλπίδι - "With less than hope" (*i.e.* with doubts) "by means of hope." παρ' ἐλπίδα means "contrary to hope" just as παρὰ φύσιν in Romans 1:26 means "contrary to nature." It seemed so futile to Abraham to hope that God's promise could and would be fulfilled. Yet he used his hope as a means of faith. The difference between "I hope that it will happen" and "I know that it will happen" is a difference in degree, not in kind. That which was against his better scienfitic judgment became the instrument of his faith. The first step which the empiricist must take if he becomes a Christian is to exercise some healthy doubt about empiricism, as the sole source of certitude.

Why did Abraham believe? The purpose clause with εἰς and the articular infinitive tells us. εἰς τὸ γενέσθαι αὐτὸν πατέρα πολλῶν ἐθνῶν - "in order that he might become the father of many nations." This was in keeping with God's spoken promise. οὕτως depends for its force upon the number of stars in the sky (Gen.15:5). That is a lot of saints saved by grace! "Hope against hope and by means of hope" is a dramatic way to describe the struggle in Abraham's mind as he balanced the reasonableness of God's promise from a human point of view against the faith that, if God said it, He was able to willing to do it. In the same way the Christian intellectual believes in the virgin birth, the miracles, the vicarious death of Jesus, His bodily resurrection and second coming and the supernatural new birth. None of these make any more scientific sense than the proposition that a 99 year old man and his 89 year old wife would become the parents of a miracle baby named Isaac. How did Abraham do it? He rejected the scientific method.

*Verse 19 - "And being not weak in faith he considered not his own body now dead, when he was about an hundred years old, neither yet the deadness of Sarah's womb."*

καὶ μὴ ἀσθενήσας τῇ πίστει κατενόησεν τὸ ἑαυτοῦ σῶμα ἤδη νενεκρωμένον, ἑκατονταετής που ὑπάρχων, καὶ τὴν νέκρωσιν τῆς μήτρας Σάρρας,

*"He did not weaken in faith when he considered his own body, which was as good as dead because he was about a hundred years old, or when he considered the barrenness of Sarah's womb." RSV*

καί (continuative conjunction) 14.

μή (negative conjunction with the participle) 87.

ἀσθενήσας (aor.act.part.nom.sing.masc.of ἀσθενέω, adverbial, causal) 857.

τῇ (loc.sing.fem.of the article in agreement with πίστει) 9.

πίστει (loc.sing.fem.of πίστις, sphere) 728.

κατενόησεν (3d.per.sing.aor.act.ind.of κατανοέω, constative) 648.

τό (acc.sing.neut.of the article in agreement with σῶμα) 9.

ἑαυτοῦ (gen.sing.masc.of ἑαυτοῦ, possession) 288.

σῶμα (acc.sing.neut.of σῶμα, direct object of κατενόησεν) 507.

ἤδη (temporal adverb) 291.

**#3890** νενεκρωμένον     (perf.pass.part.acc.sing.neut.of νεκρόω, adverbial, circumstantial).

King James Version

mortify - Col.3:5.
dead - Rom.4:19; Heb.11:12.

Revised Standard Version

as good as dead - Rom.4:19; Heb.11:12.
put to death - Col.3:5.

*Meaning:* Cf. νεκρός (#749) and νέκρωσις (#3893). To be dead; to be ineffective, as though dead. With reference to the sexual impotence of Abraham at 100 years of age - "as good as dead" - Rom.4:19; Heb.11:12. To deprive the Adamic nature of its power to commit sin - Col.3:5.

**#3891** ἑκατονταετής (nom.sing.masc.of ἑκατονταετής, predicate nominative).

King James Version

an hundred years old - Rom.4:19.

Revised Standard Version

an hundred years old - Rom.4:19.

*Meaning:* A combination of ἑκατόν (#1035) and ἔτος (#821). One hundred years old - Rom.4:19.

**#3892** που (enclitic particle).

King James Version

about - Rom.4:19.
in a certain place - Heb.2:6; 4:4.

Revised Standard Version

about - Rom.4:19.
somewhere - Heb.2:6; 4:4.

*Meaning:* an enclitic particle. Somewhere, with reference to a passage of Scripture - Heb.2:6; 4:4    with a numeral - somewhere near; about; approximately - Rom.4:19.

ὑπάρχων (pres.part.nom.sing.masc.of ὑπάρχω, adverbial, causal) 1303.
καὶ (adjunctive conjunction joining nouns) 14.
τὴν (acc.sing.fem.of the article in agreement with νέκρωσιν) 9.

#3893 νέκρωσιν (acc.sing.fem.of νέκρωσις, direct object of κατενόησεν) 9.

King James Version

deadness - Rom.4:19.
dying - 2 Cor.4:10.

Revised Standard Version

barrenness - Rom.4:19.
death - 2 Cor.4:10.

*Meaning: Cf.* νεκρός (#749) and νεκρόω (#3890). A putting to death; slaughter; murder. With reference to Jesus - 2 Cor.4:10; a condition of death; ineffectiveness; barrenness - of Sarah's womb - Rom.4:19.

τῆς (gen.sing.fem.of the article in agreement with μήτρας) 9.
μήτρας (gen.sing.fem.of μήτρα, description) 1889.

#3894 Σάρρας (gen.sing.fem.of Σάρρα, possession).

King James Version

Sarah - Rom.4:19; 9:9; Heb.11:11; 1 Pet.3:6.

Revised Standard Version

Sarah - Rom.4:19; 9:9; Heb.11:11; 1 Pet.3:6.

*Meaning:* Sarah. The English transliterates the Hebrew, *Sarah,* which means "Princess." The wife of Abraham and mother of Isaac - Rom.4:19; 9:9; Heb.11:11; 1 Pet.3:6.

*Translation -* "*And because he was not weak in faith he paid no attention to his own body already as good as dead, since he was about one hundred years old, and he disregarded the fact that Sarah was barren.*"

**Comment:** To read into this passage any element of concession, it seems to me, is to miss the point.

It was because his body was already as good as dead, for purposes of paternity, and it was because Sarah could not be depended upon for motherhood that Abraham ruled out the possibility that God's promise could be fulfilled by natural law. And that is why he was not weak in faith. He had to believe in the supernatural since the natural means was no longer available. The participle ὑπάρχων is also causal, as it explains why his own body was already as good as dead. Since God had spoken the biological consideration need not be taken seriously. To say that Abraham considered his own body and concluded that since he was impotent he needed to strengthen his faith, is to say that the action of the aorist participle is subsequent to that of κατενόησεν, the main verb. This is not good Greek and it is idle to accuse Paul of all writers of a Hebraism, as Burton does (*Moods and Tenses,* 66).It was the other way around. Abraham's faith, since it was not weak, ruled out, as totally irrelevant, anything that science or human reason might wish to say about it. I am taking κατανοέω here to mean "rule out" or "rule against," though the word (#648) means simply to "study closely." Abraham took a careful look at the scientific facts of the case. He was almost one hundred years old. Sarah, who had never had children, was almost ninety. The text says that he considered both facts carefully. It does not say that what he concluded affected his decision. Note ἤδη νενεκρωμένον, where ἤδη is pleonastic, since the perfect passive participle carries the idea of a preterite action resulting in Abraham's current condition of impotence. Some MSS omit ἤδη. Just when Abraham's body "died" the text does not say. It was alive when he was 85, fourteen years before (Gen.16:1-16). But now, when he is approaching one hundred, it is as good as dead. κατενόησεν has two objects - τὸ ἑαυτοῦ σῶμα and τὴν νέκρωσιν. He had considered the latter fourteen years before. It is false exegesis to say that Abraham's faith was the result of his helplessness. Abraham's faith was the gift of God. His helplessness was the factor that put him into a position of humility required of those who are willing to accept a gift from God. When God said, "So shall thy seed be," and "Sarah shall have a son" (Gen.17:16; 15:5) science cried out, "It is impossible." Abraham rejected the voice of reason although he listened carefully to what it said. So the Christian hears God's statement that the virgin had a son, who lived sinlessly, died vicariously, arose victoriously and is coming triumphantly. Science says, "It is impossible." The Christian listens to the protest of science and then rejects it, just as Abraham considered the biological impossibility of any further paternity for himself, but because of his faith, he rejected it. Paul says this twice more in verses 20 and 21. *Cf.* Heb.11:12.

*Verse 20 - "He staggered not at the promise of God through unbelief; but was strong in faith, giving glory to God,"*

εἰς δὲ τὴν ἐπαγγελίαν τοῦ θεοῦ οὐ διεκρίθη τῇ ἀπιστίᾳ ἀλλ' ἐνεδυναμώθη τῇ πίστει, δοὺς δόξαν τῷ θεῷ . . .

*"No distrust made him waver concerning the promise of God, but he grew strong in his faith as he gave glory to God, . . . " RSV*

εἰς (preposition with the accusative, cause) 140.

δὲ (continuative conjunction) 11.

τὴν (acc.sing.fem.of the article in agreement with ἐπαγγελίαν) 9.

ἐπαγγελίαν (acc.sing.fem.of ἐπαγγελία, cause) 2929.

τοῦ (gen.sing.masc.of the article in agreement with θεοῦ) 9.

θεοῦ (gen.sing.masc.of θεός, possession) 124.

οὐ (negative conjunction with the indicative) 130.

διεκρίθη (3d.per.sing.aor.pass.ind.of διακρίνομαι, constative) 1195.

τῇ (instrumental sing.fem.of the article in agreement with ἀπιστίᾳ) 9.

ἀπιστίᾳ (instru.sing.fem.of ἀπιστία, cause) 1103.

ἀλλ' (alternative conjunction) 342.

ἐνεδυναμώθη (3d.per.sing.1st.aor.pass.ind.of ἐνδυναμόω, culminative) 3193.

τῇ (loc.sing.fem.of the article in agreement with πίστει) 9.

πίστει (loc.sing.fem.of πίστις, sphere) 728.

δοὺς (aor.act.part.nom.sing.masc.of δίδωμι, adverbial, causal) 362.

δόξαν (acc.sing.fem.of δόξα, direct object of δοὺς) 361.

τῷ (dat.sing.masc.of the article in agreement with θεῷ) 9.

θεῷ (dat.sing.masc.of θεός, indirect object of δοὺς) 124.

*Translation - "And because of the promise of God he was never in doubt through unbelief, but was made strong in his faith, because he had given glory to God."*

**Comment:** The εἰς clause is causal. It was the promise of God that started Abraham thinking. God's promise that Abraham would inherit the world and that the promise would be carried out through his heir who would be Sarah's son, not Ishmael, the son of Hagar, forced Abraham to look at the possibilities. *Cf.*#1195 - a thorough examination of any matter may lead to uncertainty in judgment. But Abraham was not made uncertain. Natural law argued against God's promise (verse 19) but the character of God, Who made the promise was not uncertain (verse 17). The KJV "stagger" in a metaphorical sense is good. "Waver" is a good word to use. Why not simply say that he was not in doubt. If he had entertained any doubts it would have been because of his unbelief (τῇ ἀπιστίᾳ). Doubts about God and His promises are the evil results of unbelief. On the contrary Abraham was made strong in the sphere of faith. Who gave him this strength of faith and why? It was God (Eph.2:8,9) and the reason is that Abraham had given glory to God (the aorist participle in δοὺς, which indicates time prior to that of the main verb ἐνεδυναμώθη). God will strengthen the faith of any honest doubter who glorifies Him by trading off the uncertainties of science for the certitude of "thus saith the Lord."

Note that faith in a grace covenant is what glorifies God, while human performance under a works covenant glorifies man (Rom.4:1-3). The text does not say who made Abraham strong in faith, but Paul supplies the answer in Eph.2:8,9. It does say that Abraham did not strengthen his own faith. The verb ἐνεδυναμώθη is passive.

*Verse 21 - "And being fully persuaded that, what he had promised, he was able also to perform."*

καὶ πληροφορηθεὶς ὅτι ὃ ἐπήγγελται δυνατός ἐστιν καὶ ποιῆσαι.

"... *fully convinced that God was able to do what he had promised.*"   RSV

καὶ (adjunctive conjunction joining participles) 14.
πληροφορηθεὶς (aor.pass.part.nom.sing.masc.of πληροφορέω, adverbial, causal) 1708.
ὅτι (conjunction introducing an object clause in indirect discourse) 211.
ὃ (acc.sing.neut.of ὅς, relative pronoun, direct object of ποιῆσαι) 65.
ἐπήγγελται (3d.per.sing.perf.pass.ind.of ἐπαγγέλλω, consummative) 2752.
δυνατός (nom.sing.masc.of δυνατός, predicate adjective) 1311.
ἐστιν (3d.per.sing.pres.ind.of εἰμί, static) 86.
καὶ (ascensive conjunction) 14.
ποιῆσαι (aor.act.inf.of ποιέω, epexegetical) 127.

*Translation* - "*and because he was thoroughly convinced that He was able to do even that which had been promised.*"

Comment: καὶ, the adjunctive conjunction joins the two causal participles, δοὺς and πληροφορηθεὶς. Here we have the second reason why Abraham was made strong in faith (verse 20). He gave glory to God and he was convinced that science had nothing to do with it. Abraham did not make himself strong in faith. Nor did he convince himself. Both ἐνεδυναμώθη and πληροφορηθεὶς are passive. ὅτι introduces the object clause in indirect discourse. The tense is present as it would be in direct discourse. To what conclusion did Abraham come as he thought about the problem? God had said that he would have a son and that Sarah would be the child's mother. It was on the fulfillment of this promise that Abraham had been told to base his hopes that he would be the heir of the world. But human wisdom dictated that it was impossible. If it happened it would be a miracle. Did God perform miracles? Was He able to do what He had promised? Abraham was made thoroughly dogmatic about it. He came to believe that the God Who created science, and Who normally allows its principles to operate in ways that scientists can understand, and upon the basis of which they can predict,   is not shut up to such means. The Creator   of science can transcend its limits if He chooses to do so. In other words, Abraham came to believe in the reality of the supernatural. That this was a leap of faith for him is clear from the ascensive use of καὶ, joined to the infinitive. God is able *even* to do what He had promised, however skeptical scientists might be. ἐπήγγελται is perfect, calling attention as always to the past completed act of promising (Gen.12:1-3; 15:1-5), and also to the fact that the past promise has an enduring current result. God had promised it and His promise was still in force. *Cf.* Acts 7:5; Tit.1:2; 1 John 2:25; James 1:12; 2:5; Gal.3:19; Heb.12:26; 6:13; 10:23; 11:11. This cross reference material on ἐπαγγέλλω is highly productive of good sermon material.

In summation, Abraham's saving faith went back for its basis to the omnipotence and integrity of God, - something that is revealed in the heavens (Rom.1:18-20; Ps.19:1-11), which some once understood, only to reject, thus to become fools in the profession of their sophistication (Rom.2:22). Abraham accepted it and the simple was made wise unto salvation.

The question as to why Abraham reacted one way and his condemned contemporaries in the opposite way is inscrutable, except as we accept the decrees of God (Acts 13:48).

*Verse 22 - "And therefore it was imputed to him for righteousness."*

διὸ καὶ ἐλογίσθη αὐτῷ εἰς διακιοσύνην.

*"That is why his faith was 'reckoned to him as righteousness.' "*    RSV

διὸ (conjunction introducing a result clause) 1622.

καὶ (continuative conjunction) 14.

ἐλογίσθη (3d.per.sing.aor.pass.ind.of λογίζομαι, constative) 2611.

αὐτῷ (dat.sing.masc.of αὐτός, indirect object of ἐλογίσθη) 16.

εἰς (preposition with the accusative, predicate accusative) 140.

δικαιοσύνην (acc.sing.fem.of δικαιοσύνη, predicate accusative) 322.

*Translation - "And the result is that it was credited to his account as righteousness."*

**Comment:** διὸ depends for its force upon Paul's analysis of Abraham's psychology as he acted and reacted in a particular situation. Faced with a promise from God that he was to become the progenitor of a vast company of descendants, through whom the world would be blessed, but having received this promise long after he could reasonably be expected to sire a child of Sarah, his aged wife, Abraham acted and reacted in the way described in verses 18-21. Therefore righteousness was entered upon the books of heaven as an asset held by him and credited to his account.

Abraham's way of being saved is the way, indeed the only way that all discrete sinners can be saved. The elements are as follows: (1) a promise from God which, viewed from a scientific point of view, cannot be fulfilled; (2) a view of God as One powerful enough as not to be frustrated by what man's wisdom calls impossibility (verse 17); (3) a thorough, critical, objective look at the human side of the equation (verse 19); (4) the reception of the gift of faith which made him strong (verse 20) and convinced him totally (verse 21) that God could and would keep His promise; (5) a rejection of the conclusion arrived at in step 3 (verse 20) and thus (6) a reception of God's promise and complete anticipation of its practical fulfillment.

Abraham's faith was based upon the power and integrity of God. His skepticism was directed against his own ability to evaluate a scientific situation. He trusted God and he distrusted himself. One cannot do the former without first doing the latter.

DesCartes (*Meditations*, I) doubted that sense perception always led to certitude. Perhaps he was in fact asleep in his bed and only dreaming that he sat before the fire in his dressing gown. Mad men think that they are kings or pumpkins. Thus DesCartes concluded that physics, astronomy, medicine and other scientific disciplines that deal in observation, measurement and classification of sensory data, may lead to conclusions "very dubious and uncertain." After suggesting that perhaps arithmetic, geometry and sciences involved in basic research are more productive of certitude, so that whether he was awake or asleep, the sum of two and three is five and a square can have only four sides, he suggests the possibility that even the deductive approach to certitude may fail of reality. Perhaps even here DesCartes was a victim of deception. He asks, ". . . how do I know that I am not deceived every time that I add two and three, or count the sides of a square. . . ?" He concludes by bifurcating between the self (cogito), which is the subject and everything else, which thus becomes object. The cogito says that two plus three equals five; the objects, sodium and chloride, when mixed together, seem to sense perception to be the components of table salt. Neither induction (observation of objects) nor deduction (thought processes of the subject) are thus safe guides to reality. Guided by thought or observation, or both, one may arrive at certitude, but certitude may not be the same as reality. Perhaps DesCartes had been the victim of a two-faced hoax!

Abraham's reason (cogito, self, subject) said that he and Sarah would never have a child. Abraham's scientific investigation (object, his senile body and Sarah's infertile womb) agreed. He rejected both opinions. He believed that which was neither scientific nor reasonable. Thus in the opinion of the world he became a fool. But God credited his account with righteousness.

DesCartes' cogito and the things that it can "know" is similar to Kant's noumena, while DesCartes' object (everything outside the cogito, *i.e.* the world of sense perceptions) is analogous to Kant's phenomena. Kant attempted to show that the isolated and individualistic bits and pieces of phenomenal data, gathered from sense perception, could by noumenal synthesis, be validly connected to produce a valid and truthful concept or reality — an achievement which Hume regarded as an impossibility. Hume's statement, "In short there are two principles which I cannot render consistent, nor is it in my power to renounce either of them, *viz.* that all our distinct perceptions are distinct existences, and that the mind never perceives any real connections among distinct existences. Did our perceptions either inhere in something simple or individual, or did the mind perceive some real connection among them, there would be no difficulty in the case." (David Hume, App. to *Treatise of Human Nature,* as cited in *E.B.* 13, 268). Kant however later doubted that even noumena was as good a guide to reality as "faith" by which he meant something beyond knowledge, something indeed possibly irrational. Thus the existentialist view, so prevalent in modern theology, that since salvation is by faith alone, and, since, as Kant has shown, faith need not be faith in anything that the mind can grasp, everyone has faith in something, and that there is no rational content in the gospel of Jesus Christ at all.

But, though Abraham examined the phenomenal objects involved in his problem and concluded, noumenally that Isaac's birth was impossible, his faith, nonetheless, was based upon a rational proposition, *viz.* that God who made the promise to him is One who gives life to the dead and declares existent those things which are non-existent (verse 17). Thus Abraham's faith was a reasonable faith which he could describe. He could tell you what he believed in. He believed in the omnipotence and integrity of God. He could not spell it out as thoroughly as we do when we exegete the Greek New Testament, but though he knew *in part* he did *know* in part, just as do we all, who believe. Saving faith need not come to grips with all that there is to know about revealed theology, but the part which it does understand is reasonable. What Christian can say that he was a mature theologian with a mature philosophical and theological system worked out when he was regenerated? But no one ever believed to the saving of the soul who believed in everything and therefore believed in nothing. Kant's antiChristian influence has come down to us in the thinking of Barth, Brunner, Kierkegaard, Tillich and their satellites. Greek New Testament exegetes can refute this influence by showing that the Greek text makes saving faith reasonable to the human mind, once it has been revealed and that faith (πίστις, #728) is not inconsistent with knowledge (γνῶσις #1856 and ἐπίγνωσις #3817). *Cf.* 1John 5:13.

This long exposition of the spiritual experiences of David and Abraham in salvation (Rom.4:1-22) would be deprived of its point, if Paul had not related it to all other sinners saved by grace through faith. This he does in the remainder of the chapter.

*Verse 23 - "Now it was not written for his sake alone, that it was imputed to him."*

Οὐκ ἐγράφη δὲ δι' αὐτὸν μόνον ὅτι ἐλογίσθη αὐτῷ.

*"But the words, 'it was reckoned to him,' were written not for his sake alone, . . . . ."    RSV*

Οὐκ (negative conjunction with the indicative) 130.
ἐγράφη (3d.per.sing.2d.aor.pass.ind.of γράφω, intensive) 156.
δὲ (adversative conjunction) 11.
δι' (preposition with the accusative, cause) 118.
αὐτὸν (acc.sing.masc.of αὐτός, cause) 16.
μόνον (acc.sing.neut.of μόνος, adverbial) 339.
ὅτι (conjunction introducing an object clause in indirect discourse) 211.
ἐλογίσθη (3d.per.sing.aor.pass.ind.of λογίζομαι, culminative, indirect discourse) 2611.
αὐτῷ (dat.sing.masc.of αὐτός, indirect object of ἐλογίσθη) 16.

*Translation - "But it was not written because of him alone, that it was credited to his account."*

**Comment:** δὲ is adversative. Οὐκ . . . μόνον is matched by ἀλλὰ καὶ in verse 24 - "But not only . . . but also . . . κ.τ.λ." The subject of ἐγράφη is the quotation ἐλογίσθη αὐτῷ εἰς δικαιοσύνην of verse 22.   Paul has told the story of Abraham's conversion in great psychological detail and in a way that carries us to the bottom of the great epistemological questions raised by Locke, Hume, Leibnitz, DesCartes, Berkeley, Kant, Hegel, Kierkegaard, Barth, Brunner and

Tillich, to mention a few. But this is not the only reason that Moses told the story and that Paul commented about it. Why else?

*Verse 24 - "But for us also, to whom it shall be imputed, if we believe on him that raised up Jesus our Lord from the dead."*

ἀλλὰ καὶ δι' ἡμᾶς οἷς μέλλει λογίζεσθαι, τοῖς πιστεύουσιν ἐπὶ τὸν ἐγείραντα Ἰησοῦν τὸν κύριον ἡμῶν ἐκ νεκρῶν,

*". . . but for ours also. It will be reckoned to us who believe in him that raised from the dead Jesus our Lord, . . . " RSV*

ἀλλὰ (alternative conjunction) 342.

καὶ (adjunctive conjunction joining pronouns) 14.

δι' (preposition with the accusative, cause) 118.

ἡμᾶς (acc.pl.masc.of ἐγώ, cause) 123.

οἷς (dat.pl.masc.of ὅς, relative pronoun, indirect object of λογίζεσθαι) 65.

μέλλει (3d.per.sing.pres.act.ind.of μέλλω, futuristic) 206.

λογίζεσθαι (pres.pass.inf.of λογίζομαι, epexegetical) 2611.

τοῖς (dat.pl.masc.of the article in agreement with πιστεύουσιν) 9.

πιστεύουσιν (pres.act.part.dat.pl.masc.of πιστεύω, in apposition with οἷς) 734.

ἐπὶ (preposition with the accusative, extent) 47.

τὸν (acc.sing.masc.of the article in agreement with ἐγείραντα) 9.

ἐγείραντα (1st.aor.act.part.acc.sing.masc.of ἐγείρω, substantival, extent) 125.

Ἰησοῦν (acc.sing.masc.of Ἰησοῦς, direct object of ἐγείραντα) 3.

τὸν (acc.sing.masc.of the article in agreement with κύριον) 9.

κύριον (acc.sing.masc.of κύριος, apposition) 97.

ἡμῶν (gen.pl.masc.of ἐγώ, relationship) 123.

ἐκ (preposition with the ablative of separation) 19.

νεκρῶν (abl.pl.masc.of νεκρός, separation) 749.

*Translation - "But also because of us to whom it is going to be imputed - those who will believe upon the One Who raised Jesus our Lord from the dead."*

**Comment:** οὐκ . . . μόνον . . . ἀλλὰ καὶ - "not only because of Abraham, but also because of us." We are to be saved for precisely the same reasons that Abraham was saved. Abraham's story, in addition to its historic value, is a lesson to us. As he was credited with righteousness so also will we be credited. How then was he thus credited? Because Abraham believed in the God of resurrection (Rom.4:17; Gen.22:5). The dogma of religious evolution is thus here demolished. Faced with these passages those who teach that man's concept of God grew gradually and that Abraham lived in a day when the concept of resurrection of the body was not yet known, reply that the New Testament passages (Rom.4:17; Heb.11:17-19) are true but that they cannot be applied to Abraham's experience. But Paul says in Romans 4:17 that Abraham believed in the God of resurrection. The question thus becomes this: did Abraham realize that his faith in God embraced also the notion that God could raise the dead? It is possible to interpret Romans 4:17 in a way that permits a negative reply to the question. The verse says that Abraham believed God, in whose presence he had stood and heard the divine promise. It also says that the God whom he believed is a God who raises the dead. It does not say that Abraham knew that the God in whom He trusted was a God who raised dead bodies from the grave. But Heb.11:17-19 says that he did. Note the meaning of #2611, the word used in Heb.11:19. Abraham thought about it and came to the conclusion that God was able to raise Isaac from the dead after he had killed him. Thus if we allow the light of Heb.11:17-19 to shine upon Romans 4:17 we conclude that the religious evolutionists are wrong when they say that Abraham could not have known about resurrection in his day since his contemporaries did not. It may or may not be true that religious people generally in Abraham's day knew about the resurrection of the body, but that is beside the point. The question is not what they knew or did not know, but what Abraham knew. If he knew more about resurrection than his contemporaries that is because he was the object of God's special grace in revelation and salvation, and, as such became a model for all believers, Jew and Gentile, who as children of faith are the "children of Abraham." (Gal.3:6,7).

If we grant the dogma of those who say that Abraham and his contemporaries had no concept of resurrection, except in the sense that immortality of the body was realized through one's descendants, we have no way of explaining what Abraham said to his servants in Gen.22:5. When Abraham was saved he believed in an omnipotent God (Rom.4:17). After he was saved he actually tried to put his faith to work. Ordered by the Lord to kill Isaac, the son designated by God as the heir through whom the promise would be fulfilled, he did not hesitate. Enroute to the place of sacrifice on Mount Moriah, he told his servants that he and Isaac would go on to Moriah while they waited there for their return. He said that he and the lad would go, and that, after they had worshipped, he and the lad would return. The LXX for Gen.22:5 has ἐγὼ δὲ καὶ τὸ παιδίον διελευσόμεθα (plural) ἕως ὧδε καὶ προσκυνήσαντες (a plural participle) ἀναστρέφωμεν (plural). The participle for worship is plural as are the verbs for going and returning. Two would go, and after two had worshipped, two would return. Yet at that time Abraham did not know that God would interrupt his act of obedience. Thus he was resolved to follow God's order to the letter, as his behavior on the mountain revealed. If God had not stopped him Abraham would have killed his son and burned his body upon the altar of sacrifice. Yet he told his servants that Isaac would be back. Heb.11:19 gives us the explanation - λογισάμενος ὅτι καὶ ἐκ νεκρῶν ἐγείρειν δυνατὸς ὁ θεός - "Having reasoned it out (a logical bit of noumena, no thanks to Immanuel Kant) that God also was able to raise him up from the dead." Thus those who contend that Abraham knew nothing of resurrection of the dead since none of his contemporaries did are guilty of interpreting the Book by something they read out of a book. I do not know whether any of Abraham's friends and neighbours knew about resurrection or not. I do know that Abraham understood it.

It is strange as well as tragic that the interpretation of the Bible is made to conform to the writings of the theologians. Should it not be the other way around?

This lays to rest Tillich's nonesense that saving faith need not be faith in anything specific. Is the group to whom righteousness shall be imputed a specific group? Indeed it is. It is a group who, as Abraham did, believe in something specific. They believe in the One Who raised Jesus our Lord from the grave. The sinner who cannot accept the fact of the historical resurrection of Jesus of Nazareth, is one who has exchanged the God of revelation for one of his own construction. Thus in Kantian "wisdom" which he professes he becomes a fool (Rom.2:22). Obviously Tillich's theology is not the theology of the Apostle Paul. The doctrine of substitutionary atonement, linked to Jesus' bodily resurrection, is also a part of the picture, in

*Verse 25 - "Who was delivered for our offences, and was raised again for our justification."*

ὃς παρεδόθη διὰ τὰ παραπτώματα ἡμῶν καὶ ἠγέρθη διὰ τὴν δικαίωσιν ἡμῶν.

*". . . who was put to death for our trespasses and raised for our justification"*. . *RSV*

ὃς (nom.sing.masc.of ὅς, relative pronoun, subject of παρεδόθη and ἠγέρθη) 65.

παρεδόθη (3d.per.sing.aor.pass.ind.of παραδίδωμι, constative) 368.

διὰ (preposition with the accusative, cause) 118.

τὰ (acc.pl.neut.of the article in agreement with παραπτώματα) 9.

παραπτώματα (acc.pl.neut.of παράπτωμα, cause) 585.

ἡμῶν (gen.pl.masc.of ἐγώ, possession) 123.

καὶ (adjunctive conjunction joining verbs) 14.

ἠγέρθη (3d.per.sing.aor.pass.ind.of ἐγείρω, constative) 125.

διὰ (preposition with the accusative, cause) 118.

τὴν (acc.sing.fem.of the article in agreement with δικαίωσιν) 9.

**#3895** δικαίωσιν (acc.sing.fem.of δικαίωσις, cause).

King James Version

justification - Rom.4:25; 5:18.

Revised Standard Version

justification - Rom.4:25.
acquittal - Rom.5:18.

*Meaning: Cf.* δικαιοσύνη (#322), δικαίως (#2855), δίκαιος (#85), δικαιόω (#933) and others with δίκ. The act of God which imputes δικαιοσύνην. Acquittal - Rom.4:25; 5:18. The decision of heaven's court that Christ's righteousness is imputed to us as a result of His assumption of our guilt.

ἡμῶν (gen.pl.masc.of ἐγώ, possession) 123.

*Translation - "Who was delivered to death because of our moral lapses and was raised up because of our justification."*

**Comment:** *Cf.* #118. διά with the accusative in most contexts is clearly causal. Thus we have translated it here. "For the sake of" is a similar idea. If He died for the sake of our sins, He died because we had sinned. To die for sinners necessarily is to die because of sinners, because if the sinners did not exist as sinners, there would be no need for Christ to die (Rom.3:24,25). Because we fell by the wayside (παρεδόθη #368) He was delivered to death.

But that is not the end of the story. "And (adjunctive καὶ) He was raised up . . . " Why? Because in His death He secured our justification. Christ was not raised from the dead in order to justify those for whom He died, but because in His death He had actually justified them. Is the resurrection of Jesus the cause of our justification or is our justification the cause of His resurrection? It is the latter, not the former. Thus Paul's theology includes vicarious atonement, with its reconciliation as well as the bodily resurrection. But note that Paul does not say that we must understand the Anselmic view of the atonement in order to be saved. That view, we believe to be the true view, but it is understood in all of its theological implications of soteriology only after the sinner comes to Christ. An intellectual appreciation of the theology of the Christian faith comes only after long years of study. No sinner at an altar of repentance for the first time can be expected to understand *how* God can save. But he must believe in the God Who raised Jesus up from the dead (verse 24). This is what Abraham believed and thus he becomes the pattern for all who came after him.

In the next eleven verses Paul discusses the results of justification.

## Results of Justification

*(Romans 5:1-11)*

*Romans 5:1 - "Therefore being justified by faith, we have peace with God through our Lord Jesus Christ."*

Δικαιωθέντες οὖν ἐκ πίστεως εἰρήνην ἔχομεν πρὸς τὸν θεὸν διὰ τοῦ κυρίου ἡμῶν Ἰησοῦ Χριστοῦ,

*"Therefore, since we are justified by faith, we have peace with God through our Lord Jesus Christ." . . . RSV*

Δικαιωθέντες (aor.pass.part.nom.pl.masc.of δικαιόω, adverbial, causal) 933.
οὖν (inferential conjunction) 68.
ἐκ (preposition with the ablative of source) 19.
πίστεως (abl.sing.fem.of πίστις, source) 728.
εἰρήνην (acc.sing.fem.of εἰρήνη, direct object of ἔχομεν) 865.
ἔχομεν (1st.per.pl.pres.act.ind.of ἔχω, aoristic) 82.

πρός (preposition with the accusative of extent) 197.

τὸν (acc.sing.masc.of the article in agreement with θεὸν) 9.

θεὸν (acc.sing.masc.of θεός, extent, metaphorical) 124.

διὰ (preposition with the ablative of agent) 118.

τοῦ (abl.sing.masc.of the article in agreement with κυρίου) 9.

κυρίου (abl.sing.masc.of κύριος, agent) 97.

ἡμῶν (gen.pl.masc.of ἐγώ, relationship) 123.

'Ιησοῦ (abl.sing.masc.of 'Ιησοῦς, apposition) 3.

Χριστοῦ (abl.sing.masc.of Χριστός, apposition) 4.

*Translation* - "*Therefore because we have been declared righteous by faith, we have peace with God through the agency of our Lord, Jesus Christ.*"

**Comment:** οὖν is inferential. Paul has established the fact that the believer has been declared righteous; thus he is now righteous, as a result of the past decision and declaration of the court. The participle δικαιωθέντες is an effective aorist - *i.e.* it calls attention to the result of the action in the past, not the beginning of the action. Having been declared righteous we are now standing in God's presence with the righteousness of Christ credited to our account. Our sins are "covered" (Rom.4:7b). ἐκ πίστεως is source which is closely allied to cause. Faith is both the source and the cause of justification. Either translation will do.

Aland, *et al* have opted for Sinaiticus a B3 Ggr P Φ 0220vid 88 104 326 330 451 629 1241 1739 1877 1984 2127 2492 2495 *Byz Lect* it ar vid? z* syrh copsa Ephrraem Didymus Epiphanius Cyril3/4 and Sedulius-Scotus for ἔχομεν the present active indicative of ἔχω rather than for the hortatory subjunctive ἔχωμεν, which is shown in Sinaiticus• A B* C D K and a smaller number of miniscules and Fathers, though only with a C degree of certitude. Robertson is sure (*Grammar*, 200) that ἔχωμεν has the best support. Thus Goodspeed has "let us live in peace," Montgomery has "let us continue to enjoy the peace" and Weymouth agrees. The Oxford RSV translates the indicative mode.

Both ideas are true. *Cf.*#865. Peace can be defined both as absence of war and absence of worry. Whichever one of these two ideas is taught in Romans 5:1, the other is also taught elsewhere in Scripture. Since "the Word of God" consists of all writings which are "God breathed" (2 Tim.3:16) and since no such Scripture is of its own interpretation (2 Pet.1:20), the result of these two facts is that the divine Scriptures combine into a inerrant mosaic of divine revelation. The New Testament is a divine gestalt - a heavenly jigsaw puzzle, in which every portion is allowed to shed its light upon every other portion to reveal the entire message of God. This is why no theologian builds his system upon a proof text. Rather we depend upon the total message which emerges when we "study to show ourselves approved unto God - workmen that need never to be ashamed, because we rightly divided (and fitted together) the Word of Truth" (2 Tim.2:15). *Cf.* our comment on 2 Tim.2:15.

Thus the believer enjoys both peace in the sense of absence of war and also in the sense of absence of worry, whether we read ἔχομεν, the indicative mode statement of fact or ἔχωμεν the subjunctive mode exhortation to enjoy the peace of mind which comes from knowing that we are saved.

That a holy God is at war with sinners is clearly taught in Scripture. *Cf.* 2 Thess.1:7-9; Rev.6:12-18; Rom.2:8,9; Psalm 7:11 *et al.* But there is no war between God and the justified Christian. The war ended at Calvary. A story, possibly apocryphal, tells of a Confederate soldier in the closing days of the Civil War who realized that the Southern cause was lost. He was hungry. He deserted to the Union forces near by in the hope that, although he would be a prisoner of war, at least he would be fed, only to be rejected by the Union sentry who told him to go back to his outfit because the Yankees did not intend to feed any more prisoners. He dared not return to his place within the Confederate lines and face a firing squad as a deserter, so he hid in the woods and somehow survived. Finally, however, he determined to return, confess his desertion and ask, at least, that if he was to be shot for deserting he might first of all be fed. He was told, "The war is over. Lee surrendered to Grant at Appomattox Court House two weeks ago." Many unsaved sinners are wandering in the world, sick, hungry, homeless and ready to die, who do not know that the war between them and God is over. It ended at the cross.

Note where we enjoy this peace. It is πρὸς τὸν θεὸν (Rom.5:1), which is the same place where the λόγος, Who "became flesh and dwelt among us" (John 1:14) has his position of intimacy with the Father (John 1:1). The transgressor, once alienated from God, but now declared righteous, cannot get any closer to God than that (John 17:21).

Psychological peace is one of the fruits of the Spirit (Gal.5:22). How could one be distressed when he enjoys a position with Christ in a place described as πρὸς τὸν θεὸν? *Cf.* also πρὸς τὸν πατέρα in 1 John 1:2; Eph.2:18 . This nearness to God with its intimacy (John 17:21) is through the agency of our Lord Jesus Christ - διὰ τοῦ κυρίου'Ιησοῦ Χριστοῦ. διά with the ablative is often used of our relation with Christ. *Cf.* Rom.1:8; John 14:6. There are many more instances. Find them by running all of the references where διά is followed by the ablative - *Cf*.#118.

Thus the first result of justification is the peace that exists between the believer and God and also the peace of mind which floods the soul of the child of God. The second result is the intimacy of association between the justified believer and the Godhead.

*Verse 2 - "By whom also we have access by faith into this grace wherein we stand, and rejoice in hope of the glory of God."*

δι' οὗ καὶ τὴν προσαγωγὴν ἐσχήκαμεν (τῇ πίστει) εἰς τὴν χάριν ταύτην ἐν ᾗ ἐστήκαμεν, καὶ καυχώμεθα ἐπ' ἐλπίδι τῆς δόξης τοῦ θεοῦ.

*"Through him we have obtained access to this grace in which we stand, and we rejoice in our hope of sharing the glory of God."     RSV*

δι' (preposition with the ablative of agency) 118.
οὗ (abl.sing.masc.of ὅς, relative pronoun, agency) 65.
καὶ (adjunctive conjunction joining verbs) 14.

τὴν (acc.sing.fem.of the article in agreement with προσαγωγὴν) 9.

**#3896** προσαγωγὴν (acc.sing.fem.of προσαγωγή, direct object of ἐσχήκαμεν).

King James Version

access - Rom.5:2; Eph.2:18; 3:12.

Revised Standard Version

access - Rom.5:2; Eph.2:18; 3:12.

*Meaning:* A combination of πρός (#197) and ἄγω (#876). *Cf.* προσάγω (#2343) and ἀγωγή (#4852). Hence, the act of bringing or leading to; in the New Testament, access, approach. Followed by εἰς and the accusative in Rom.5:2; followed by πρὸς τὸν πατέρα in Eph.2:18; absolutely in Eph.3:12.

ἐσχήκαμεν (1st.per.pl.perf.act.ind.ofd ἔχω, intensive) 82.
(τῇ (instru.sing.fem.of the article in agreement with πίστει) 9.
πίστει) (instru.sing.fem.of πίστις, means) 728.
εἰς (preposition with the accusative of extent) 140.
τὴν (acc.sing.fem.of the article in agreement with χάριν) 9.
χάριν (acc.sing.fem.of χάρις, extent) 1700.
ταύτην (acc.sing.fem.of οὗτος, in agreement with χάριν) 93.
ἐν (preposition with the locative of place) 80.
ᾗ (loc.sing.fem.of ὅς, relative pronoun, place) 65.
ἑστήκαμεν (1st.per.pl.perf.act.ind.of ἵστημι, intensive) 180.
καὶ (adjunctive conjunction joining verbs) 14.
καυχώμεθα (1st.per.pl.pres.ind.of καυχάομαι, present progressive, retroactive) 3847.
ἐπ' (preposition with the instrumental, cause) 47.
ἐλπίδι (instru.sing.fem.of ἐλπίς, cause) 2994.
τῆς (gen.sing.fem.of the article in agreement with δόξης) 9.
δόξης (gen.sing.fem.of δόξα, description) 361.
τοῦ (gen.sing.masc.of the article in agreement with θεοῦ) 9.
θεοῦ (gen.sing.masc.of θεός, description) 124.

*Translation - "Through whom also we have been given access by means of faith into this grace in which we have been standing, and we have been exulting because we anticipate the glory of God."*

**Comment:** δι' οὗ in a similar sense as διὰ τοῦ κυρίου in verse 1. ἐσχήκαμεν and ἑστήκαμεν are perfect tenses. The first indicates present possession of access as a result of a previous act of God in granting it; and ἑστήκαμεν indicates a present standing as a result of a previous positioning. God has stood the believer in His grace and has given Him access to the throne. Now, as a result, the believer has a standing before God that provides him with a permanent access to God's unmerited favor. Christ is the Divine Agent, through Whom all of this has been done, and we have appropriated it "by means of faith" - τῇ πίστει. Such wonderful standing results in the delight that began with Paul when he was saved, and with each Christian when he is saved, and once begun the child of God is never without it. This is the force of the present progressive in καυχώμεθα, which is also retroactive. The reason for this abounding joy (ἐπ' ἐλπίδι) is our anticipation that at His return we shall also participate in the glory of God. We are going to share His glory (Col.3:4; 2 Thess.1:10). *Cf.*#3847. The Christian who understands his position in God's grace before heaven's court, as being totally justified with sins forgiven and covered, is indeed happy (Rom.4:7,8). His joy (Gal.5:22) is due to a sense of relief that his sin debt is cancelled and he will never face it; and also, as he looks into the future and anticipates his participation with Christ in glory (1 Pet.5:4).

With such a positive faith and a positive psychology which it supports even tribulation is a blessing. As long as there is the slightest doubt about the Christian's standing, as he listens to the Arminian warning that salvation once enjoyed can be forever lost, he cannot identify with the chain reaction of experiences which we find in verses 3-5.

*Verse 3 - "And not only so, but we glory in tribulations also: knowing that tribulation worketh patience;"*

οὐ μόνον δέ, ἀλλὰ καὶ καυχώμεθα ἐν ταῖς θλίψεσιν, εἰδότες ὅτι ἡ θλῖψις ὑπομονὴν κατεργάζεται,

*"More than that, we rejoice in our sufferings, knowing that suffering produces endurance, . . . "*     RSV

οὐ (negative conjunction with the indicative) 130.
μόνον (acc.sing.neut.of μόνος, adverbial) 339.
δέ (continuative conjunction) 11.
ἀλλὰ (alternative conjunction) 342.
καὶ (ascensive conjunction) 14
καυχώμεθα (1st.per.pl.pres.mid.ind.of καυχάομαι, present progressive, retroactive) 3847.
ἐν (preposition with the locative of sphere) 80.
ταῖς (loc.pl.fem.of the article in agreement with θλίψεσιν) 9.
θλίψεσιν (loc.pl.fem.of θλῖψις, sphere) 1046.
εἰδότες (aor.act.part.nom.pl.masc.ofd ὁράω, adverbial, causal) 144b.
ὅτι (conjunction introducing an object clause in indirect discourse) 211.
ἡ (nom.sing.fem.of the article in agreement with θλῖψις) 9.
θλῖψις (nom.sing.fem.of θλῖψις, subject of κατεργάζεται) 1046.
ὑπομονὴν (acc.sing.fem.of ὑπομονή, direct object of κατεργάζεται) 2204.
κατεργάζεται (3d.per.sing.pres.mid.ind.of κατεργάζομαι, customary) 3815.

*Translation - "And not only do we rejoice, but we even rejoice because of hardships, because we realize that trouble generates patience, . . . "*

**Comment:** We must supply καυχώμεθα with οὐ μόνον δέ. Νοτε οὐ μόνον . . . ἀλλὰ καὶ - "not only . . . but even" (ascensive καὶ). ἐν ταῖς θλίψεσιν can be causal, accompanying circumstance or sphere - we even rejoice because of, or as accompanying circumstance dictates, or in the sphere of our experience that is characterized by suffering - it is all the same idea.

Why should a Christian react toward tribulation in the same way he reacts toward the thrilling prospect of eternal heavenly glory? This is an example of superrationalization that the unsaved world can never understand. The assurance of eternal glory thrills us, and we rejoice. We are even happy when trials beset our path. The causal participle εἰδότες tells us. It is "because we have learned that tribulation generates patience which, in turn, generates experience which, in its turn generates more hope (verse 4). It is not the tribulation (θλίφις) that we enjoy *per se* but the knowledge that it generates more joy for the future. This is what Peter meant by "growth in grace" (2 Pet.3:18).

*Verse 4 - "And patience, experience; and experience, hope."*

ἡ δὲ ὑπομονὴ δοκιμήν, ἡ δὲ δοκιμὴ ἐλπίδα.

*". . . and endurance produces character, and character produces hope, . . .* RSV

ἡ (nom.sing.fem.of the article in agreement with ὑπομονή) 9.

δὲ (continuative conjunction) 11.

ὑπομονή (nom.sing.fem.of ὑπομονή, subject of κατεργάζεται, understood) 2204.

#3897 δοκιμήν (acc.sing.fem.of δοκιμή, direct object of κατεργάζεται, understood).

King James Version

experience - Rom.5:4,4.
experiment - 2 Cor.9:13.
proof - 2 Cor.2:9; 13:3; Phil.2:22.
trial - 2 Cor.8:2.

Revised Standard Version

character - Rom.5:4,4.
test - 2 Cor.2:9; 8:2; 9:13.
proof - 2 Cor.13:3.
worth - Phil.2:22.

*Meaning:* Cf. δοκέω (#287), δοκιμάζω (#2493), δοκίμιον (#5091); δόκιμος (#4042). A trial or test - 2 Cor.8:2; character that has emerged out of trial - that was designed to prove the quality or character of one tested and has stood the test and stands approved - Rom.5:4a,b; 2 Cor.2:9; Phil.2:22; 2 Cor.9:13. A proof - an example of worth that has been tested - 2 Cor.13:3.

ἡ (nom.sing.fem.of the article in agreement with δοκιμή) 9.

δὲ (continuative conjunction) 11.

δοκιμή (nom.sing.fem.of δοκιμή, subject of κατεργάζεται, understood) 3897.

ἐλπίδα (acc.sing.fem.of ἐλπίς, direct object of κατεργάζεται) 2994.

*Translation - ". . . and patience develops character, and character generates hope."*

**Comment:** A severe test of character is its ability to continue to trust in an unseen God and His promise of a better future, solely by faith, when tribulation abounds. Patience (#2204, the quality of remaining under the load) demands that we continue to bear the burden, whatever it may be, and for whatever length of time required, and faith in an unseen future furnishes the rationale why we should. "Though he slay me yet will I trust in him" is the statement of a tormented man who was patiently enduring the trial because he was trusting God to bring it all out in the end for His glory. This practice builds character (Job 13:15). One should reflect frequently upon Romans 8:18 - ". . . the sufferings of this present time are not worthy to be compared with the glory which shall be revealed in us" and 2 Cor.4:17 - "For our light affliction, which is but for a moment, worketh for us a far more exceeding and eternal weight of glory." *Cf.* our comment on these passages, *en loc.*

Tribulation with its demand for patience builds christian character because patience demands great faith and faith is the source of righteousness (Rom.5:1). Anything that causes us to exercise faith in God develops character, for faith transcends the world of sense perception and anchors our souls in eternity where "God shall wipe away all tears from our eyes." (Rev.21:4).

Now we are in a position to note the circular causation. Abraham believed by means of hope (Rom.4:18); hence hope produces faith; faith provides righteousness (Rom.5:1), access and standing (Rom.5:2). Because of the hope that gave us faith we rejoice (Rom.5:2). But tribulation came to the christian (John 16:33). Thank God for it (Eph.5:20; 1 Thess.5:18), because it demands patience, which demands faith and thus builds character, and character, because its faith is now strengthened by practice, produces hope. That is how Abraham started (Rom.4:18). This explains how Paul could write Romans 8:28; 2 Cor.2:14; 1 Thess.5:16,18 and Phil.4:4.

In James 1:2-4 the writer, with his usual pragmatic approach leaves out the details and goes straight to the point. A philosophy that enables a Christian to be as happy about his trials on earth as he is about his anticipation of joys in heaven did not originate on the earth which, according to Voltaire, is inhabited by "tormented atoms in a bed of mud" !

There is one more step in Paul's sequence.

*Verse 5 - "And hope maketh not ashamed, because the love of God is shed abroad in our hearts by the Holy Ghost which is given to us."*

ἡ δὲ ἐλπὶς οὐ καταισχύνει, ὅτι ἡ ἀγάπη τοῦ θεοῦ ἐκκέχυται ἐν ταῖς καρδίαις ἡμῶν διὰ πνεύματος ἁγίου τοῦ δοθέντος ἡμῖν,

*". . . and hope does not disappoint us, because God's love has been poured into our hearts through the Holy Spirit which has been given to us." RSV*

ἡ (nom.sing.fem.of the article in agreement with ἐλπὶς) 9.

δὲ (continuative conjunction) 11.

ἐλπὶς (nom.sing.fem.of ἐλπίς, subject of καταισχύνει) 2994.

οὐ (negative conjunction with the indicative) 130.

καταισχύνει (3d.per.sing.pres.act.ind.of καταισχύνω, static) 2505.

ὅτι (conjunction introducing a causal clause) 211.

ἡ (nom.sing.fem.of the article in agreement with ἀγάπη) 9.

ἀγάπη (nom.sing.fem.of ἀγάπη, subject of ἐκκέχυται) 1490.

τοῦ (gen.sing.masc.of the article in agreement with θεοῦ) 9.

θεοῦ (gen.sing.masc.of θεός, description) 124.

ἐκκέχυται (3d.per.sing.perf.pass.ind.of ἐκχέω, intensive) 811.

ἐν (preposition with the locative of place) 80.

ταῖς (loc.pl.fem.of the article in agreement with καρδίαις) 9.

καρδίαις (loc.pl.fem.of καρδία, place where) 432.

ἡμῶν (gen.pl.masc.of ἐγώ, possession) 123.

διὰ (preposition with the ablative of agent) 118.

πνεύματος (abl.sing.neut.of πνεῦμα, agent) 83.

ἀγίου (abl.sing.neut.of ἅγιος, in agreement with πνεῦμα) 84.

τοῦ (abl.sing.neut.of the article in agreement with δοθέντος) 9.

δοθέντος (1st.aor.pass.part.abl.sing.neut.of δίδωμι, adjectival, ascriptive) 362.

ἡμῖν (dat.pl.masc.of ἐγώ, indirect object of δοθέντος) 123.

*Translation - "And the hope never embarrasses us because the love of God has been flooded into our hearts by the Holy Spirit Who has been given to us."*

**Comment:** *Cf.*#2505 for other uses. When the christian, burdened down with tribulation, nevertheless remains patient and continues to express his faith in the promises of God and to indulge his hope for God's future reward, he becomes the object of scorn from the unsaved, who feel that a more sophisticated view is that life is hopeless. Witness the advice of Job's wife to her husband (Job 2:9). Why was not Job, and why indeed are not all Christians in similar circumstances ashamed to appear so utterly naive? The ὅτι clause is causal. It tells us why. The love of God has been flooded into our hearts and has innundated us with rivers of living water (John 7:38,39 with Gal.5:22) - hence, "rivers of love." Note Arthur Way's translation - "brimming river of the love of God." ἐκκέχυται is an intensive perfect indicating the continuing present result of a completed process, like this . . . . . *———————————*. We are the recipients of a constant flow of God's love. The administering agent is the Holy Spirit Who is described as the One Who have been given to us who are saved (Eph.1:13). τοῦ θεοῦ is both a genitive of description and an ablative of source. God is the source of the love that floods our hearts and this love is divine. Both ideas are grammatically possible and both ideas are true. Hope-faith-justification-the gift of the Holy Spirit-God's love-tribulation-patience-character-hope-love — What a sequence! Let the Watsonian behaviorists or Pavlov's slobbering dog explain this one!! Note the force of ἐκχέω by checking its various uses under #811.

*Verse 6 - "For when we were yet without strength, in due time Christ died for the ungodly."*

ἔτι γὰρ Χριστὸς ὄντων ἡμῶν ἀσθενῶν ἔτι κατὰ καιρὸν ὑπὲρ ἀσεβῶν ἀπέθανεν.

*"While we were yet helpless, at the right time Christ died for the ungodly."* RSV

ἔτι (temporal adverb) 448.

γὰρ (causal conjunction) 105.

Χριστὸς (nom.sing.masc.of Χριστός, subject of ἀπέθανεν) 4.

ὄντων (pres.part.gen.pl.masc.of εἰμί, genitive absolute, adverbial, temporal) 86.

ἡμῶν (gen.pl.masc.of ἐγώ, genitive absolute) 123.

ἀσθενῶν (gen.pl.masc.of ἀσθενῶν, predicate adjective, genitive absolute) 1551.

ἔτι (temporal adverb) 448.

κατὰ (preposition with the accusative, standard) 98.

καιρὸν (acc.sing.masc.of καιρός, standard) 767.

ὑπὲρ (preposition with the ablative - "instead of") 545.

ἀσεβῶν (abl.pl.masc.of ἀσεβής, "in instead of") 3882.

ἀπέθανεν (3d.per.sing.aor.act.ind.of ἀποθνήσκω, constative) 774.

*Translation - "Because at a time when we were helpless, on the appointed day and at the appointed hour, Christ died instead of the ungodly."*

**Comment:** Untaught Christians are sometimes seduced into attributing undue and sometimes fanatical importance to events which others might explain as examples of coincidental serendipity. This zeal for playing up the importance of what to us seems *unusual* can lead to a mysticism for which there is no Scriptural warrant. In extreme cases it has led to the voodooism of devil worship. It is at least interesting, however, and worthy of mention that today is Good Friday (9 April 1982) and the hour is 9:38 A.M. And I am exegeting one of the verses in the New Testament that speaks of our Lord's vicarious death. Nineteen hundred, fifty-three years ago today, at this hour it was 4:38 P.M. (Jerusalem is seven hours ahead of Washington, D.C.) Our Lord cried with a loud voice and dismissed his human spirit into the hands of the Father. It was a supernatural death. No man took His life from Him but He laid it down of Himself (John 10:18). A short time before He had suffered the anguish of hell in total helplessness as His Father broke all ties of fellowship between them for three dreadful hours. That is when and how He paid my debt and made it possible for Him to declare me righteous. Having fulfilled the covenant of redemption (Τετέλεσται - "It has been finished") He then demonstrated His contempt for physical death by invoking it. He had the power to lay down His life and that is why He had the power to take it up again. Of course God is not interested in the coincidences of time events since He is eternal and in His divine purpose the Lamb of God was slain "from the foundation of the world" (Rev.13:8).

This verse has served many preaching purposes as well it can. The helplessness of sinners is set forth; thus the verse supports the T in the Tulip (Total depravity). The fact of vicarious atonement is here. That Jesus appeared and died "on time" is supported here (Gal.4:4; John 2:4; 12:27, *et al*). This is the thrust of κατὰ καιρὸν, the accusative of standard or rule. But in context, the verse is a part of Paul's preceding argument which began in verse 3. His line of thought need not be repeated here. Go back and read the comment on verse 3-5. Now note causal γὰρ in verse 6. Why should a Christian, beset with tribulation, react as Paul describes? Because there was a time in his life when he was even in a worse condition than he is currently. Then, before he was saved, he was totally without strength. Now he is justified. Then he was an alien. Now he has standing. Once he was barred from God's presence. Now he has access. Then he was hopeless, helpless and hapless. Now he has a hope of participation in the glory of God. Out of touch with the lifegiving regenerating power of God, he had no patience and no character. Now he is "born from above" (John 3:3,7) and he knows that tribulation is a blessing because it requires patience which builds character. He has troubles now, but he also had them then. The difference is that, now there is amelioration. Then there was none.

Paul's argument will procede like this: If, when he was totally miserable and undone, not only physically, socially, economically and politically, but also morally, theologically, philosophically and psychologically, God loved him enough to send Christ to die for him, how much more does God love him now? What was then only the results of his own folly, as he suffered under the penalties and pains of broken universal law, now becomes a tool in the hands of God, his Father, Jesus Christ, his Saviour and the Holy Spirit, his Teacher, to make him like Christ. This is the line of thought developed in verses 7-11.

Note ὑπέρ with the ablative for substitution like ἀντὶ πολλῶν (Mt.20:28) and περὶ πολλῶν (Mt.26:28). Different prepositions with the same case, or the same preposition with different cases is all in harmony with good Greek idiom. Thus we see the versatility of the Greek to enrich the text, while the context always guards the exegete against eisegesis. If we pay due regard to diction, grammar, syntax and *zeitgeist*, and put the concept, thus derived into the context, we will never be guilty of reading into the divine text something which the Holy Spirit did not intend.

ὑπέρ with the ablative means "instead of" because "In most cases one who acts 'in behalf of' takes his place" (Winer, *A Treatise on the Grammar of New Testament Greek*, Moulton edition, 479). For ὑπὲρ σοῦ in the sense of "instead of" *cf*. Plato, *Giorgias*, 5152; Thucydides, I, 141. For ὑπέρ meaning "substitution" *cf*. Xenophon, 7, 4,9.

In verses 7 and 8 Paul reinforces his point that the Christian, beset with troubles now can be victorious over them and turn them to his advantage, since we know what God did for us when we were worthy of nothing but death and hell.

*Verse 7 - "For scarcely for a righteous man will one die: yet peradventure for a good man some would even dare to die."*

μόλις γὰρ ὑπὲρ δικαίου τις ἀποθανεῖται, ὑπὲρ γὰρ τοῦ ἀγαθοῦ τάχα τις καὶ τολμᾷ ἀποθανεῖν,

*"Why, one will hardly die for a righteous man — though perhaps for a good man one will dare even to die."*    RSV

μόλις (adverbial) 2342.
γὰρ (explanatory conjunction) 105.
ὑπὲρ (preposition with the ablative - "instead of") 545.
δικαίου (abl.sing.masc.of δίκαιος, "instead of") 85.
τις (nom.sing.masc.of τις, indefinite pronoun, subject of ἀποθανεῖται) 486.
ἀποθανεῖται (3d.per.sing.fut.mid.ind.of ἀποθνήσκω, predictive) 774.
ὑπὲρ (preposition with the ablative "instead of") 545.
γὰρ (concessive conjunction) 105.
τοῦ (abl.sing.masc.of the article in agreement with ἀγαθοῦ) 9.
ἀγαθοῦ (abl.sing.masc.of ἀγαθός, "instead of") 547.

**#3898** τάχα (adverbial).

King James Version

peradventure - Rom.5:7.
perhaps - Philemon 15.

Revised Standard Version

perhaps - Rom.5:7; Philemon 15.

*Meaning:* An adverb. In early Greek, hastily, quickly, readily, soon. Since Herodotus and in the New Testament - perhaps - Rom.5:7; Philemon 15. *Cf.#*'s 2531, 5232, 2767, 3397, 2626 and 491.

τις (nom.sing.masc.of τις, indefinite pronoun, subject of τολμᾷ) 486.
καὶ (ascensive conjunction) 14.
τολμᾷ (3d.per.sing.pres.act.subj.of τολμάω, deliberative) 1430.
ἀποθανεῖν (2d.aor.act.inf.of ἀποθνήσκω, epexegetical) 774.

*Translation - "Now it is not likely that anyone would sacrifice his life for a righteous man, although for a good man some might even have the courage to die . . . "*

**Comment:** The first γὰρ is explanatory and the second, at the beginning of the second clause is concessive, a rare use. The difference between anarthrous δικαίου and τοῦ ἀγαθοῦ is the emphasis in the second case and the lack of it in the first. If a man were really good (τοῦ ἀγαθοῦ) some might (deliberative subjunctive in τολμᾷ) even (ascensive καὶ) have courage to die for him, though (concessive γὰρ) it is possible that such could be found. The point is that only the very best of human goodness could be rewarded by being allowed to live while another died for him. If he were good enough to merit a willing substitute he probably would not be condemned to die. All of this is for the purpose of contrast with what follows in

*Verse 8 - "But God commendeth his love toward us, in that, while we were yet sinners, Christ died for us."*

συνίστησιν δὲ τὴν ἑαυτοῦ ἀγάπην εἰς ἡμᾶς ὁ θεὸς ὅτι ἔτι ἁμαρτωλῶν ὄντων ἡμῶν Χριστὸς ὑπὲρ ἡμῶν ἀπέθανεν.

*"But God shows his love for us in that while we were yet sinners Christ died for us." RSV*

συνίστησιν (3d.per.sing.pres.act.ind.of συνίστημι, present progressive, retroactive) 2328.

δὲ (adversative conjunction) 11.

τὴν (acc.sing.fem.of the article in agreement with ἀγάπην) 9.

ἑαυτοῦ (gen.sing.masc.of ἑαυτοῦ, reflexive pronoun, possession) 288.

ἀγάπην (acc.sing.fem.of ἀγάπη, direct object of συνίστησιν) 1490.

εἰς (preposition with the accusative, like a dative) 140.

ἡμᾶς (acc.pl.masc.of ἐγώ, like a dative of personal advantage) 123.

ὁ (nom.sing.masc.of the article in agreement with θεὸς) 9.

θεὸς (nom.sing.masc.of θεός, subject of συνίστησιν) 124.

ὅτι (conjunction introducing a causal clause) 211.

ἔτι (temporal adverb) 448.

ἁμαρτωλῶν (gen.pl.masc.of ἁμαρτωλός, genitive absolute) 791.

ὄντων (pres.part.gen.pl.masc.of εἰμί, genitive absolute, adverbial, temporal) 86.

ἡμῶν (gen.pl.masc.of ἐγώ, genitive absolute) 123.

Χριστὸς (nom.sing.masc.of Χριστός, subject of ἀπέθανεν) 4.

ὑπὲρ (preposition with the ablative - " instead of") 545.

ἡμῶν (abl.pl.masc.of ἐγώ, "instead of") 123.

ἀπέθανεν (3d.per.sing.aor.act.ind.of ἀποθνήσκω, constative) 774.

*Translation - "But God has been proving His own love for us, because while we were still sinners Christ died in our place."*

**Comment:** δὲ is adversative. The hypothetical case of verse 7 was highly unlikely, although in rare cases one might find one who would be willing to die for a truly good man, but the true story of the gospel of Christ is not like that at all. Christ died, not for good men, but for men who at the time of His death were sinners, some of whom stood at the cross upon which He died and hurled their obscene insults into His face. Thus God demonstrated (see the full meaning of #2328) with an argument in history that is conclusive that He loves uss. εἰς ἡμᾶς is joined, not to ἀγαπήν, but to the verb συνίστησιν. Thus εἰς ἡμᾶς, though accusative, is used like a dative of personal advantage. In this idiom "disposition or attitude of mind is set forth" (Robertson, *Grammar,* 594). *Cf.* 1 Cor.16:1; Acts 14:23; Rom.10:12; Phil.4:17; Acts 24:17; Rom.15:16; Heb.11:26; Acts 2:25;

Mt.5:34; Rom.12:16; Mt.18:6; Eph.4:32. "If the attitude is hostile the translation is 'against' but εἰς does not mean 'against.' " (*Ibid.*) The hostile idea comes from the context; *e.g.* Lk.12:10; Mt.12:32; Acts 9:1. ἔτι... ἡμῶν, the genitive absolute in the present tense indicates the time point and under what circumstances Christ died for us. It was not when we were justified saints, oppressed with afflictions (verses 3-5) but when we were still guilty transgressors with no legal rights in heaven's court.

The statement of verse 8 forms the foundation for Paul's πολλῷ οὖν μᾶλλον - "much more therefore" argument of

*Verse 9 - "Much more then, being now justified by his blood, we shall be saved from wrath through him."*

πολλῷ οὖν μᾶλλον δικαιωθέντες νῦν ἐν τῷ αἵματι αὐτοῦ σωθησόμεθα δι' αὐτοῦ ἀπὸ τῆς ὀργῆς.

*"Since, therefore, we are now justified by his blood, much more shall we be saved by him from the wrath of God."*

πολλῷ (associative-instrumental sing.neut.of πολύς, adverbial) 228.

οὖν (inferential conjunction) 68.

μᾶλλον (adverbial) 619.

δικαιωθέντες (aor.pass.part.nom.pl.masc.of δικαιόω, adverbial, temporal, causal) 933.

νῦν (temporal adverb) 1497.

ἐν (preposition with the locative, instrumental use, means) 80.

τῷ (loc.sing.neut.of the article in agreement with αἵματι) 9.

αἵματι (loc.sing.neut.of αἷμα, means) 1203.

αὐτοῦ (gen.sing.masc.of αὐτός, possession) 16.

σωθησόμεθα (1st.per.pl.fut.pass.ind.of σώζω, predictive) 109.

δι' (preposition with the ablative, agent) 118.

αὐτοῦ (abl.sing.masc.of αὐτός, agent) 16.

ἀπὸ (preposition with the ablative of separation) 70.

τῆς (abl.sing.fem.of the article in agreement with ὀργῆς) 9.

ὀργῆς (abl.sing.fem.of ὀργή, separation) 283.

*Translation - "Much more, then, now that we have been declared righteous by His blood, we shall be delivered through His agency from the wrath."*

**Comment:** If Jesus loved us enough to die for us when we were guilty sinners (verse 8) shall He love us less, now that we have been justified? The Greek is not in the form of rhetorical question, nor is my translation of it. But the first sentence in the Comment is and, of course, the answer is "No." Paul states it positively in verse 9. The participle δικαιωθέντες is temporally and causally adverbial and its thrust is culminative, with emphasis upon the result. The temporal idea is reinforced by νῦν in contrast to ἔτι ἁμαρτωλῶν ὄντων in verse 8, which speaks of the time when we were sinners, as contrasted with the present time (νῦν) *after* we are justified. The contrast is between the former state of our wicked warfare against God and the current state of our reconciliation, now that we are ". . . justified from all things, from which (we) could not be justified by the law of Moses" (Acts 13:39), at peace with the Judge of all the earth (Gen.18:25; John 5:22) and with the perfect standing before the court which is enjoyed by the Judge Himself (Rom.5:1). The text does not say that the wrath to which reference is made is the divine wrath, but the context supplies the idea. It may also refer to some of the tribulation of verse 3. God permits His children to suffer the wrath of the unregenerate world. Indeed Jesus predicted that this would be so (John 16:33), but such experiences work the results set forth in verses 3-5.

Verse 10 is essentially a restatement of the argument.

*Verse 10 - "For if, when we were enemies, we were reconciled to God by the death of His Son, much more, being reconciled, we shall be saved by His life."*

εἰ γὰρ ἐχθροὶ ὄντες κατηλλάγημεν τῷ θεῷ διὰ τοῦ θανάτου τοῦ υἱοῦ αὐτοῦ, πολλῷ μᾶλλον καταλλαγέντες σωθησόμεθα ἐν τῇ ζωῇ αὐτοῦ.

*"For if while we were enemies we were reconciled to God by the death of his Son, much more, now that we are reconciled, shall we be saved by his life."*

εἰ (conditional particle in a first-class condition) 337.　　　　RSV
γὰρ (causal conjunction) 105.
ἐχθροὶ (nom.pl.masc.of ἐχθρός, predicate nominative) 543.
ὄντες (pres.part.nom.pl.masc.of εἰμί, adverbial, temporal) 86.

**#3899** κατηλλάγημεν (1st.per.pl.2d.aor.pass.ind.of καταλλάσσω, first-class condition).

King James Version

reconcile - 2 Cor.5:18,19,20; Rom.5:10,10; 1 Cor.7:11.

Revised Standard Version

reconcile - Rom.5:10,10; 1 Cor.7:11; 2 Cor.5:18,19,20.

*Meaning:* A combination of κατά (#98) and ἀλλάσσω (#3097). Hence, to exchange - as coins for others of equal value. Hence, to reconcile. God is reconciled to sinners - 2 Cor.5:18,19; sinners are reconciled to God - 2 Cor.5:20; Rom.5:10,10. A wife is reconciled to her husband - 1 Cor.7:11.

τῷ (associative-instrumental sing.masc.of the article in agreement with θεῷ) 9.
θεῷ (associative-instrumental sing.masc.of θεός, association) 124.
διὰ (preposition with the ablative of means) 118.
τοῦ (abl.sing.masc.of the article in agreement with θανάτου) 9.
θανάτου (abl.sing.masc.of θάνατος, means) 381.
τοῦ (gen.sing.masc.of the article in agreement with υἱοῦ) 9.
υἱοῦ (gen.sing.masc.of υἱός, description) 5.
αὐτοῦ (gen.sing.masc.of αὐτός, relationship) 16.

πολλῷ (associative-instrumental neut.of πολύς, adverbial) 228.

μᾶλλον (adverbial) 619.

καταλλαγέντες (2d.aor.pass.part.nom.pl.masc.of καταλλάσσω, adverbial, temporal, causal) 3899.

σωθησόμεθα (1st.per.pl.fut.pass.ind.of σώζω, predictive) 109.

ἐν (preposition with the locative, instrumental use) 80.

τῇ (loc.sing.fem.of the article in agreement with ζωῇ) 9.

ζωῇ (loc.sing.fem.of ζωή, instrumental use, means) 668.

αὐτοῦ (gen.sing.masc.of αὐτός, possession) 16.

*Translation - "For since when we were enemies we were reconciled to God through the death of His Son, much more, now that we are reconciled, we shall be saved by His life."*

**Comment:** γὰρ is causal. εἰ introduces the first-class condition - in which the condition in the protasis is assumed, for the sake of the argument, to be true. In this case it is indeed true. We were enemies of God when God's love provided our salvation through the death of His Son. Because of His death we have been reconciled. Because this is true, the statement in the result clause is also true. *Cf.*#3899 for the basic meaning of καταλλάσσω. God found in the righteous record of His Son - a record which He established upon earth after His incarnation (Mt.3:17), something which He could accept. This Son died and paid the redemptive price in the coin of the realm. By means of the death of Jesus, under the penalty of man's sin, God found a way to exchange Christ's righteousness for our sins. Hence there was a reconciliation which met the full demand for payment required by the moral standards of heaven's court.

By imputing Christ's righteousness to us, God reconciled the two, so that there is no difference. Printers speak of "reconciliation" by which they mean the process of bringing into line with each other two or more press runs of a multi-colored printing job, with the result that the viewer cannot tell one press line from another, thus to give the impression that it was all printed in one press run. Thus God looks at His former enemies and sees only Christ's righteousness. Now that this is so the conclusion in the apodosis is that we former enemies, now reconciled, shall live as we participate in the resurrection life of Jesus Christ. Note the culminative aorists in δικαιωθέντες ἐν τῷ αἵματι αὐτοῦ (verse 9) and κατηλλάγημεν διὰ τοῦ θανάτου αὐτοῦ (verse 10). They speak about the result of the finished transaction. We were justified, once and for all time, and the end result is that we are declared forever righteous. We were reconciled by His death and the result is that we enjoy a standing before Him of total peace - both the absence of war and the absence of worry.

The result of this new relationship with our Lord is one of joy as we see in

*Verse 11 - "And not only so but we also joy in God through our Lord Jesus Christ by whom we have now received the atonement."*

οὐ μόνον δέ, ἀλλὰ καὶ καὶ καυχώμενοι ἐν τῷ θεῷ διὰ τοῦ κυρίου ἡμῶν Ἰησοῦ Χριστοῦ, δι' οὗ νῦν τὴν καταλλαγὴν ἐλάβομεν.

*"Not only so, but we also rejoice in God through our Lord Jesus Christ, through whom we have now received our reconciliation." RSV*

οὐ (negative conjunction with the indicative) 130.
μόνον (acc.sing.neut.of μόνος, adverbial) 339.
δέ (continuative conjunction) 11.
ἀλλά (alternative conjunction) 342.
καὶ (adjunctive conjunction joining verbs) 14.
καυχώμενοι (pres.act.part.nom.pl.masc.of καυχάομαι, adverbial, complementary) 3847.
ἐν (preposition with the locative, in an associative use) 80.
τῷ (loc.sing.masc.of the article in agreement with θεῷ) 9.
θεῷ (loc.sing.masc.of θεός, association) 124.
διά (preposition with the ablative of agent) 118.
τοῦ (abl.sing.masc.of the article in agreement with κυρίου) 9.
κυρίου (abl.sing.masc.of κύριος, agent) 97.
ἡμῶν (gen.pl.masc.of ἐγώ, relationship) 123.
Ἰησοῦ (abl.sing.masc.of Ἰησοῦς, apposition) 3.
Χριστοῦ (abl.sing.masc.of Χριστός, apposition) 4.
δι' (preposition with the ablative of agent) 118.
οὗ (abl.sing.masc.of ὅς, relative pronoun, agent) 65.
νῦν (temporal adverb) 1497.
τὴν (acc.sing.fem.of the article in agreement with καταλλαγήν) 9.

#3900 καταλλαγὴν (acc.sing.fem.of καταλλαγή, direct object of ἐλάβομεν).

King James Version

atonement - Rom.5:11.
reconciliation - 2 Cor.5:18,19.
reconciling - Rom.11:15.

Revised Standard Version

reconciliation - Rom.5:11; 11;15; 2 Cor.5:18,19.

*Meaning:* Cf. καταλλάσσω (#3899). Exchange; the business of the money changer who is involved in changing assets of equal value. Hence, reconciliation. The process of negotiation that results in the adjustment of differences; reconciliation between opposing parties. With reference to the relationship between sinners and God - Rom.5:11; 11:15; 2 Cor.5:18,19.

ἐλάβομεν (1st.per.pl.aor.act.ind.of λαμβάνω, culminative) 533.

*Translation - "And that is not all. We shall be saved as we rejoice with God through our Lord Jesus Christ, through Whom we have now received the reconciliation."*

**Comment:** σωθη σόμεθα must be supplied with οὐ μόνον δέ. Note the οὐ μόνον.

... ἀλλὰ καὶ sequence - "not only . . . but also." We can regard καυχώμενοι as a complementary participle. The fact of our salvation is accompanied by great joy. Not only will we be rescued from this life of temptation and trial by the first resurrection, but also, in anticipation of that great event we are rejoicing. God shares our joy, which is ours through the agency of the Lord Jesus Christ, through Whose agency we also received the reconciliation.

Thus at the end of this section the argument has brought us back to the joy with which we began it in verse 3.

Paul's great statement of federal headship theology follows in verses 12-21.

# Adam and Christ

### (Romans 5:12-21)

*Verse 12 - "Wherefore as by one man sin entered into the world, and death by sin; and so death passed upon all men, for that all have sinned."*

Διὰ τοῦτο ὥσπερ δι᾽ ἑνὸς ἀνθρώπου ἡ ἁμαρτία εἰς τὸν κόσμον εἰσῆλθεν καὶ διὰ τῆς ἁμαρτίας ὁ θάνατος, καὶ οὕτως εἰς πάντας ἀνθρώπους ὁ θάνατος διῆλθεν, ἐφ᾽ ᾧ πάντες ἥμαρτον —

*"Therefore as sin came into the world through one man and death through sin, and so death spread to all men because all men sinned —"    RSV*

Διὰ (preposition with the accusative, cause) 118.

τοῦτο (acc.sing.neut.of οὗτος, cause) 93.

ὥσπερ (intensive particle introducing a comparative clause) 560.

δι᾽ (preposition with the ablative of agent) 118.

ἑνὸς (abl.sing.masc.of εἷς, in agreement with ἀνθρώπου) 469.

ἀνθρώπου (abl.sing.masc.of ἄνθρωπος, agent) 341.

ἡ (nom.sing.fem.of the article in agreement with ἁμαρτία) 9.

ἁμαρτία (nom.sing.fem.of ἁμαρτία, subject of εἰσῆλθεν) 111.

εἰς (preposition with the accusative of extent) 140.

τὸν (acc.sing.masc.of the article in agreement with κόσμον) 9.

κόσμον (acc.sing.masc.of κόσμος, extent) 360.

εἰσῆλθεν (3d.per.sing.aor.ind.of εἰσέρχομαι, constative) 234.

καὶ (adjunctive conjunction joining nouns) 14.

διὰ (preposition with the ablative of agent) 118.

τῆς (abl.sing.fem.of the article in agreement with ἁμαρτίας) 9.

ἁμαρτίας (abl.sing.fem.of ἁμαρτία, agent) 111.

ὁ (nom.sing.masc.of the article in agreement with θάνατος) 9.

θάνατος (nom.sing.masc.of θάνατος, subject of εἰσῆλθεν) 381.

καὶ (continuative conjunction) 14.

οὕτως (demonstrative adverb) 74.

εἰς (preposition with the accusative of extent) 140.

πάντας (acc.pl.masc.of πᾶς, in agreement with ἀνθρώπους) 67.

ἀνθρώπους (acc.pl.masc.of ἄνθρωπος, extent) 341.

ὁ (nom.sing.masc.of the article in agreement with θάνατος) 9.
θάνατος (nom.sing.masc.of θάνατος, subject of διῆλθεν) 381.
διῆλθεν (3d.per.sing.aor.ind.of διέρχομαι, culminative) 1017.
ἐφ' (preposition with the instrumental, cause) 47.
ᾧ (instru.sing.neut.of ὅς, relative pronoun, cause) 65.
πάντες (nom.pl.masc.of πᾶς, subject of ἥμαρτον) 67.
ἥμαρτον (3d.per.pl.aor.act.ind.of ἁμαρτάνω, constative) 1260.

*Translation - "Due to the fact that just as by one man sin entered into the world and, by sin, death, and thus unto all men came death, in view of the fact that all have sinned —"*

**Comment:** Διὰ τοῦτο is causal, as always - "on account of this" and seems out of place until we recognize a striking anacoluthon. Paul lost his trend of thought temporarily, having introduced the ὥσπερ clause for which he provided no apodosis. We rejoice with God, having been reconciled, because of federal headship truth. In verse 19 he returns to the ὥσπερ clause and completes the thought. The entire basis of reconciliation, with its psychological fruitage — joy, peace, hope, patience, love, character building, etc. (verses 3-11), is the fact that, though in Adam we died, in Christ we are reconciled to live forever. In verse 19 he starts the sentence again and finishes it, with a summation of everything in between in verses 13-18.

ὥσπερ is intensified ὡς. Precisely as Adam was the agent through whom sin entered the world, so Christ is the Agent through Whose obedience the elect are declared righteous (verse 19).

We dare not overlook 1 Tim.2:14 and the light which it sheds upon Romans 5:12. Adam is charged with the responsibility for the fall of man, not Eve, because he, unlike Eve, was not deceived, whereas Eve thought that she was doing the right thing when she transgressed the rule of the Edenic covenant. Adam sinned deliberately. *Cf.* our comment on 1 Tim.2:14 *en loc.*

Paul returns to this point in verse 14. Adam's deliberate and rational decision to transgress was copied by those described in Rom.1:18-22. Theirs also was a deliberate choice. It was a case of the will acting contrary to clear intellectual light. As Adam did, they sinned because they wanted to and with the full knowledge of the consequences.

διὰ τῆς ἁμαρτίας - an ablative of means. (Gen.2:17; 3:3; Rom.6:23; James 1:15; Ezek.18:4). Death as a consequence of sin refers both to physical and spiritual death - total separation from God but not unconscious oblivion. Paul adds that Adam's sin and Adam's death thus (οὕτως) brought death upon all. That one man's sin should be used in court to condemn the race is not the point. Adam died spiritually when he ate the forbidden fruit. We shall leave for our discussion of 1 Tim.2:14 the rationale of his decision. However noble his motives may have seemed to Adam the fact remains that when he ate of the forbidden fruit he knew that he was doing that which God had forbidden, and he also knew that when he ate he would suffer the penalty of spiritual death. But he lived physically for 930 years and "begat sons and daughters" (Gen.5:4) each of whom inherited Adam's fallen and depraved nature and thus, when they achieved the intellectual maturation necessary to make discrete choice, they also sinned deliberately as Adam did. However there is one difference. When Adam sinned he was not prompted to do so by a fallen nature. Adam was not depraved; he was motivated to transgress God's order by other considerations. His descendants, condemned by genetics to contend with a fallen nature which can produce nothing but sin (Gal.5:19-21; Mk.7:21-23) and brainwashed by Satan (2 Cor.4:4) follow in his sinful and illegal steps. This is why death, the wages of sin (Rom.6:23) passed upon all the race. The curse that rests upon the human race is not the fact that God holds us responsible for something that Adam did before we were born, but that Adam is the progenitor of all of us. Just as genetics dictates hair and eye color, skin pigmentation, intelligence and everything else about us that is physical, it also dictates our propensity to disobey God, despite the fact that when we sin we do so with the full knowledge of the consequences, just as Adam did.

The only progeny of Adam who, having inherited his sinful nature, nevertheless escapes his penalty, are the infants who die before they reach the age of discretion. Paul deals with the question of the salvation of those who die physically in infancy in verses 13 and 14. He explains the fact that death comes to all men with the ἐφ' ᾧ clause - "because all have sinned," not because Adam sinned. All sin and each dies because each sinned; no man dies because Adam sinned, except Adam. *Cf.* comment on Rom.3:23 where we have the same thought.

The question of the salvation of infants occupies us in verses 13 and 14.

*Verse 13 - "(For until the law sin was in the world; but sin is not imputed when there is no law."*

ἄχρι γὰρ νόμου ἁμαρτία ἦν ἐν κόσμῳ, ἁμαρτία δὲ οὐκ ἐλλογεῖται μὴ ὄντος νόμου.

"... sin indeed was in the world before the law was given, but sin is not counted where there is no law."     RSV

ἄχρι (preposition with the genitive in a time expression) 1517.
γὰρ (concessive conjunction) 105.
νόμου (gen.sing.masc.of νόμος, time description) 464.
ἁμαρτία (nom.sing.fem.of ἁμαρτία, subject of ἦν) 111.
ἦν (3d.per.sing.imp.ind.of εἰμί, progressive description) 86.
ἐν (preposition with the locative of place) 80.
κόσμῳ (loc.sing.masc.of κόσμος, place where) 360.
ἁμαρτία (nom.sing.fem.of ἁμαρτία, subject of ἐλλογεῖται) 111.
δὲ (adversative conjunction) 11.
οὐκ (negative conjunction with the indicative) 130.

#3901 ἐλλογεῖται (3d.per.sing.pres.pass.ind.of ἐλλογέω, customary).

King James Version

impute - Rom.5:13.

put on one's account - Philemon 18.

Revised Standard Version

counted - Rom.5:13.

charge to my account - Philemon 18.

*Meaning:* A combination of ἐν (ἐλ before λ) (#80) and λόγος (#510). To charge to one's account. With reference to a financial obligation - Philemon 18; with reference to the judicial reckoning of deliberate transgression - Rom.5:13.

μὴ (negative conjunction with the participle) 87.

ὄντος (pres.part.gen.sing.masc.of εἰμί, adverbial, temporal, genitive absolute) 86.

νόμου (gen.sing.masc.of νόμος, genitive absolute) 464.

*Translation - ". . . although before the law, sin was in the world, but sin is not charged against the sinner in the absence of law."*

**Comment:** Paul breaks off the thought begun in verse 12 to explore other aspects of the problem. γάρ here is either explanatory or concessive. Let the student try it both ways and determine which better fits the context. ἄχρι with the genitive in a time expression. *Cf.* #1517.

That Paul means the Mosaic Code, not the moral code written upon the conscience of every man, seems clear from verse 14, where he defines the historic time period which he has in view. It is the period beginning with the creation and closing with Moses' Sinai encounter at the burning bush - a long period of 2600 years. During this time sin continued in the world, since it entered by Adam's deliberate transgression in Eden. Although sin was present (concessive γάρ), there is no imputation of guilt, since there was no transgression. It is a matter of definition. Sin is any want of conformity to the holy nature of God. Transgression is deliberate violation of a legal code. There was no such code until Sinai, although the moral standards of the court of heaven, spelled out in the Ten Commandments, are written into the conscience. Thus all who are old enough to make rational decisions know the difference between what God calls right and what He calls wrong, even though they may never have seen a copy of the Mosaic Code. They know this difference because "they show the work of the law written in their hearts, their conscience also bearing them witness, and their thoughts the mean while accusing or else excusing one another" (Rom.2:15). That is why we cannot conclude that no one was lost before Moses received the law and explain it by saying that heaven's court cannot charge a man with sin if no law exists. Paul had already shown that God's moral law has existed in the heart of man since He created man in His image. But we can conclude that those who die in infancy are not *transgressors* and thus are *safe* even though by definition they are *sinners.* Infants are sinners but they are not guilty sinners. If they were they would also be transgressors, like adults.

*Verse 14 - "Nevertheless death reigned from Adam to Moses, even over them that had not sinned after the similitude of Adam's transgression, who is the figure of him that was to come."*

ἀλλὰ ἐβασίλευσεν ὁ θάνατος ἀπὸ 'Αδὰμ μέχρι Μωϋσέως καὶ ἐπὶ τοὺς μὴ ἁμαρτήσαντας ἐπὶ τῷ ὁμοιώματι τῆς παραβάσεως 'Αδάμ, ὅς ἐστιν τύπος τοῦ μέλλοντος.

*"Yet death reigned from Adam to Moses, even over those whose sins were not like the transgression of Adam, who was a type of the one who was to come."*

RSV

ἀλλὰ (concessive conjunction) 342.

ἐβασίλευσεν (3d.per.sing.aor.act.ind.of βασιλεύω, constative) 236.

ὁ (nom.sing.masc.of the article in agreement with θάνατος) 9.

θάνατος (nom.sing.masc.of θάνατος, subject of ἐβασίλευσεν) 381.

ἀπὸ (preposition with the genitive, time expression) 70.

'Αδὰμ (gen.sing.masc.of 'Αδάμ (indeclin.) time expression) 1774.

μέχρι (preposition with the genitive, time expression) 948.

Μωϋσέως (gen.sing.masc.of Μωϋσῆς, time expression) 715.

καὶ (ascensive conjunction) 14.

ἐπὶ (preposition with the accusative of extent) 47.

τοὺς (acc.pl.masc.of the article in agreement with ἁμαρτήσαντας) 9.

μὴ (negative conjunction with the participle) 87.

ἁμαρτήσαντας (aor.act.part.acc.pl.masc. of ἁμαρτάνω, substantival, extent) 1260.

ἐπὶ (preposition with the locative of sphere) 47.

τῷ (loc.sing.neut.of the article in agreement with ὁμοιώματι) 9.

ὁμοιώματι (loc.sing.neut.of ὁμοίωμα, sphere) 3803.

τῆς (gen.sing.fem.of the article in agreement with παραβάσεως) 9.

παραβάσεως (gen.sing.fem.of παράβασις, description) 3851.

'Αδάμ (gen.sing.masc.of 'Αδάμ, (indeclin.) description) 1774.

ὅς (nom.sing.masc.of ὅς, relative pronoun, subject of ἐστιν) 65.

ἐστιν (3d.per.sing.pres.ind.of εἰμί, aoristic) 86.

τύπος (nom.sing.masc.ofd τύπος, predicate nominative) 2917.

τοῦ (gen.sing.masc.of the article in agreement with μέλλοντος) 9.

μέλλοντος (pres.act.part.gen.sing.masc.of μέλλω, substantival, description) 206.

*Translation - ". . . although death reigned from Adam until Moses, even over those who had not sinned in a manner similar to the transgression of Adam, who is a type of the Coming One."*

**Comment:** Although infants died physically they were not condemned to eternal spiritual death. There was no formal law code before Moses. God's law was written into human hearts, but its message could not be discerned by infants and thus could not with deliberation be transgressed by them. Yet babies died physically in infancy, just as adults also died physically, during this period. *Cf.* Gen.5:5,8,11,14,17,20,27i,31. καὶ is ascensive.. Even *sinners* before Moses died, who were not *transgressors* since they could not have sinned according to the manner in which Adam did. *Cf.* Lk.1:59 for ἐπί and the locative in this same sense. How did Adam sin? Deliberately - 1 Tim.2:14. In the face of an express command which was accompanied by a clear warning that to do so meant death (Gen.2:17). Some commentators argue that adults in the "Adam to Moses" period are meant, since they did not have the express knowledge of the consequences. In rebuttal we cite Romans 1:32. Those men did sin in full knowledge of the consequences. Hence Paul can be speaking only of infants who died in infancy, and of others who grew up physically but were mental infants due to mental retardation. They were the victims of physical death because of Adam's sin, but safe from God's condemnation, since where there is no understanding of the law, sin is not imputed (Romans 5:13). Such infants (and that includes infants who die in infancy in whatever period) are not *saved*, since they were never lost, but they are *safe*.

Adam is a type of the Last Adam, Christ the Coming One. The race fell in its physical federal head. The elect are saved through its spiritual head, Jesus Christ.

In contemplation of the fact that Adam is said to be a type of Christ, the question may be raised as to why Adam sinned. We know why Eve did. She was deceived. But her husband was not deceived (1 Tim.2:14). Each acted contrary to the divine ban laid down by their Creator, but with different motives. Eve knew no better. She believed the devil's lie that if she ate she would be "as Elohim" (Gen.3:5) with full knowledge of good and evil. Adam not only knew the consequences which would follow if he ate of the fruit, but he also knew the consequences which had followed as a result of the fact that Eve had already transgressed the law. She was "dead" and destined to be driven from the garden. Thus they would be forever separated, unless he too, with total knowledge of the consequences, also ate. Adam faced a choice. Should he reject the offered fruit, continue to obey God and continue to enjoy God's fellowship in the garden? If he did he would be forever denied further fellowship with the woman whom he loved. If he ate the fruit, his fellowship with God would cease, but he would be free to leave the garden and live out his life, however depraved and miserable it might be, with Eve. Faced with this choice Adam said, "Goodbye, God" and to Eve he said, "Give me that fruit." Thus for the love of his bride Adam deliberately stepped out of Paradise and down to her sordid and tragedy ridden level. Thus Adam became a type of Christ who also left heaven's paradise and came to earth to become "sin for us" (2 Cor.5:21), because He loved us (Gal.2:20; Rev.1:5). The difference is that the Last Adam knew before He came to earth to live for God and to die for us, that after His death He would rise again, never to suffer another death and that in His resurrection He would forever rescue His bride. Did the first Adam entertain the thought that if he stepped down to Eve's level he could rescue both himself and her in some sort of self-redemption? The Scriptures are silent on the point, but if he did he was mistaken.

*Verse 15 - "But not as the offence, so also is the free gift. For if through the offence of one many be dead, much more the grace of God and the gift by grace, which is by one man, Jesus Christ, hath abounded unto many."*

'Αλλ' οὐχ ὡς τὸ παράπτωμα, οὕτως καὶ τὸ χάρισμα, εἰ γὰρ τῷ τοῦ ἑνὸς παραπτώματι ὁ πολλοὶ ἀπέθανον, πολλῷ μᾶλλον ἡ χάρις τοῦ θεοῦ καὶ ἡ δωρεὰ ἐν χάριτι τῇ τοῦ ἑνὸς ἀνθρώπου Ἰησοῦ Χριστοῦ εἰς τοὺς πολλοὺς ἐπερίσσευσεν.

*"But the free gift is not like the trespass. For if many died through one man's trespass, much more have the grace of God and the free gift in the grace of that one man Jesus Christ abounded for many."*　　RSV

'Αλλ' (adversative conjunction) 342.

οὐχ (negative conjunction with the indicative) 130.

ὡς (particle introducing a comparative clause) 128.

τὸ (nom.sing.neut.of the article in agreement with παράπτωμα) 9.

παράπτωμα (nom.sing.neut.of παράπτωμα, subject of verb understood) 585.

οὕτως (demonstrative adverb) 74.

καὶ (adjunctive conjunction joining nouns) 14.

τὸ (nom.sing.neut.of the article in agreement with χάρισμα) 9.

χάρισμα (nom.sing.neut.of χάρισμα, subject of verb understood) 3790.

εἰ (conditional particle in a first-class condition) 337.

γὰρ (causal conjunction) 105.

τῷ (instru.sing.neut.of the article in agreement with παραπτώματι) 9.

τοῦ (gen.sing.masc.of the article in agreement with ἑνὸς) 9.

ἑνὸς (gen.sing.masc.of εἷς, description) 469.

παραπτώματι (instru.sing.neut.of παράπτωμα, cause) 585.

οἱ (nom.pl.masc.of the article in agreement with πολλοὶ) 9.

πολλοὶ (nom.pl.masc.of πολύς, subject of ἀπέθανον) 228.

ἀπέθανον (3d.per.pl.aor.act.ind.of ἀποθνήσκω, culminative) 774.

πολλῷ (instru.sing.neut.of πολύς, measure) 228.

μᾶλλον (adverbial) 619.

ἡ (nom.sing.fem.of the article in agreement with χάρις) 9.

χάρις (nom.sing.fem.of χάρις, subject of ἐπερίσσευσεν) 1700.

τοῦ (gen.sing.masc.of the article in agreement with θεοῦ) 9.

θεοῦ (gen.sing.masc.of θεός, possession) 124.

καὶ (adjunctive conjunction joining nouns) 14.

ἡ (nom.sing.fem.of the article in agreement with δωρεὰ) 9.

δωρεὰ (nom.sing.fem.of δωρεά, subject of ἐπερίσσευσεν) 2004.

ἐν (preposition with the locative, instrumental use, means) 80.

χάριτι (instru.sing.fem.of χάρις, means) 1700.

τῇ (instru.sing.fem.of the article in agreement with χάριτι) 9.

τοῦ (gen.sing.masc.of the article in agreement with ἀνθρώπου) 9.

ἑνὸς (gen.sing.masc.of εἷς, in agreement with ἀνθρώπου) 469.

ἀνθρώπου (gen.sing.masc.of ἄνθρωπος, possession) 341.

Ἰησοῦ (gen.sing.masc.of Ἰησοῦς, apposition) 3.

Χριστοῦ (gen.sing.masc.of Χριστός, apposition) 4.

εἰς (preposition with the accusative, extent, predicate accusative) 140.

τοὺς (acc.pl.masc.of the article in agreement with πολλούς) 9.
πολλούς (acc.pl.masc.of πολύς, extent) 228.
ἐπερίσσευσεν (3d.per.sing.aor.act.ind.of περισσεύω, culminative) 473.

Translation - "But the trespass and the gift do not produce the same results. For, since, because of the fall of one man the many have died, in a greater and more positive way, the grace of God and the gift by means of the grace of one man, Jesus Christ, abounds unto the many."

Comment: Paul has just said that Adam is a type of Christ. But types can be carried too far. Paul thus hastens to tell us that the type and his trespass reacted one way upon mankind, while the Antitype and His righteousness reacted in the opposite way and also to a greater extent (ἐπερίσσευσεν). This is the thrust of ἀλλ' οὐχ ὡς . . . οὕτως καὶ. The transgression and the gift worked in opposite ways. How? γὰρ introduces the causal clause in explanation. We have εἰ and a simple first-class condition with no doubt about the truth of the condition in the protasis. Since, as a result of Adam's fall (cf.#585 - "to fall by the wayside") the mass of mankind died - - (now for the inverse effect and a more positive slope of the curve) God's grace and the gift of eternal life through the grace of Jesus Christ, is poured out in greater abundance (πολλῷ μᾶλλον and ἐπερίσσευσεν) upon many.

God's grace goes beyond a simple restoration of man to the Edenic state of innocence from which he might fall again. This is not a case of giving the redeemed a second chance. Our position is much superior to that. We possess in Jesus Christ the imputation of the righteousness and the standing before the throne which He Himself possesses (Rom.5:1,2; John 17:21; 2 Cor.5:21).

Verse 16 - "And not as it was by one that sinned, so is the gift: for the judgment was by one to condemnation, but the free gift is of many offences unto justification."

καὶ οὐκ ὡς δι' ἑνὸς ἁμαρτήσαντος τὸ δώρημα. τὸ μὲν γὰρ κρίμα ἐξ ἑνὸς εἰς κατάκριμα, τὸ δὲ χάρισμα ἐκ πολλῶν παραπτωμάτων εἰς δικαίωμα.

"And the free gift is not like the effect of that one man's sin. For the judgment following one trespass brought condemnation, but the free gift following many trespasses brings justification."     RSV

καὶ (continuative conjunction) 14.
οὐκ (negative conjunction with the indicative) 130.
ὡς (comparative particle) 128.
δι' (preposition with the ablative of agent) 118.
ἑνὸς (abl.sing.masc.of εἷς, in agreement with ἁμαρτήσαντος) 469.
ἁμαρτήσαντος (aor.act.part.abl.sing.masc.of ἁμαρτάνω, substantival, agent) 1260.
τὸ (nom.sing.neut.of the article in agreement with δώρημα) 9.

#3902 δώρημα (nom.sing.neut.of δώρημα, subject of ἐστιν understood).

King James Version

gift - Rom.5:16; James 1:17.

Revised Standard Version

free gift - Rom.5:16.
perfect gift - James 1:17.

*Meaning: Cf.* δωρέω (#2874) plus μα, the result suffix. The result of giving; hence, a gift. Eternal life - Rom.5:16; every gift is from heaven - James 1:17.

τό (nom.sing.neut.of the article in agreement with κρίμα) 9.
μὲν (particle of affirmation) 300.
γὰρ (causal conjunction) 105.
κρίμα (nom.sing.neut.of κρίμα, subject of ἐστιν understood) 642.
ἐξ (preposition with the ablative of source) 19.
ἑνὸς (abl.sing.neut.of εἷς, in agreement with παράπτωμα understood) 469.
εἰς (preposition with the accusative, result) 140.

**#3903** κατάκριμα (acc.sing.neut.of κατάκριμα, result).

King James Version

condemnation - Rom.5:16,18; 8:1.

Revised Standard Version

judgment - Rom.5:16.
condemnation - Rom.5:18; 8:1.

*Meaning:* A combination of κατά (#98) and κρίμα (#642). Hence, condemnation; a legal judgment of guilt and accompanying order for punishment. *Cf.* κατακρίνω (#1012). Romans 5:16, 18; 8:1.

τό (nom.sing.neut.of the article in agreement with χάρισμα) 9.
δὲ (adversative conjunction) 11.
χάρισμα (nom.sing.neut.of χάρισμα, subject of the verb understood) 3790.
ἐκ (preposition with the ablative of source) 19.
πολλῶν (abl.pl.neut.of πολύς, in agreement with παραπτωμάτων) 228.
παραπτωμάτων (abl.pl.neut.of παράπτωμα, source) 585.
εἰς (preposition with the accusative, result) 140.
δικαίωμα (acc.sing.neut.of δικαίωμα, result) 1781.

*Translation - "Furthermore, the gift is not as though it were the result of the act of one sinner, because in fact the legal decision to condemn resulted from one man, but the gift of justification came after many transgressions."*

**Comment:** The dissimilarity between type and Antitype of verse 15 was that Adam brought death to the race while Christ brought life. Another dissimilarity is now added. Hence we have translated καὶ as "Furthermore" or "In addition."

What God has done for the race He did, not because Adam sinned, but because of the fact that, as a result of Adam's sin and his genetic bequest of a sinful nature to posterity, all of Adam's seed have sinned many times. Adam sinned deliberately (1 Tim.2:14) on a neutral choice at a time when he was not influenced by a depraved nature. He sinned from a stance of neutral innocence. All of the race since, to be sure, have sinned with deliberation, but from a stance of anti-God depravity. Adam was indeed the "free moral agent" that the Arminians like to talk about. He was totally free from the motivation that rises from the depraved nature of all of his posterity. No man since Adam has been a free moral agent. We were born with an innate predisposition to sin. And this drive to sin is so compelling that it overrules the conscious conviction that "they which commit such things are worthy of death" (Rom.1:32). In fact, the drive to sin is so imperious that for the moment it drives from the thinking of the deviant the fear of punishment and replaces it with an enthusiasm for the act and for those partners who share in the sin (Rom.1:32b). Those who sinned with discretion (after reaching the age of accountability) but who then repented and sought divine help will be judged in truth and justice according to Rom.2:-16. Those who sinned with discretion and then persisted in their evil ways and traded the true concept of a holy God for one of their own sordid creation (Rom.1:23) will also be judged truthfully and with justice. Man's moral predicament, *viz.* that he is genetically predisposed to sin, is a result of Adam's fall in Eden, an event which occurred before he was born. Adam's decision to transgress was upon the basis of his own decision, and not upon the decision of any of his depraved posterity. Divine justice cannot hold the reader responsible for what Adam chose to do. Thus God in grace provides the gift of justification by faith apart from the works of the law. The "many transgressions" from which we have been justified by faith were charged to the account of our Substitute on the cross. There the debt was paid in full.

Thus Paul refutes the charge that the entire race collectively, is condemned because of what Adam did representatively. Adam sinned once and acquired a fallen nature. After that, for the next 930 years, he sinned again and again. And then he died, but not before he trusted the promise of God that salvation would be his through the heel bruising death upon the cross of the "seed of the woman" (Gen.3:15). There is good reason to believe that Adam was saved by the faith which he exercised when, after listening to the promise of Gen.3:15 he named his wife Eve, which means "The mother of all living."

Adam's children have also sinned many times, but there is grace more abundant (verse 20).

*Verse 17 - "For if by one man's offence, death reigned by one; much more they which receive abundance of grace and of the gift of righteousness shall reign in life by one, Jesus Christ."*

εἰ γὰρ τῷ τοῦ ἑνὸς παραπτώματι ὁ θάνατος ἐβασίλευσεν διὰ τοῦ ἑνός, πολλῷ μᾶλλον οἱ τὴν περισσείαν τῆς χάριτος καὶ τῆς δωρεᾶς τῆς δικαιοσύνης λαμβάνοντες ἐν ζωῇ βασιλεύσουσιν διὰ τοῦ ἑνὸς Ἰησοῦ Χριστοῦ.

*"If, because of one man's trespass, death reigned through that one man, much*

*more will those who receive the abundance of grace and the free gift of righteousness reign in life through the one man Jesus Christ."*   RSV

εἰ (conditional particle in a first-class condition) 337.

γὰρ (causal conjunction) 105.

τῷ (instru.sing.neut.of the article in agreement with παραπτώματι) 9.

τοῦ (gen.sing.masc.of the article in agreement with ἑνὸς) 9.

ἑνὸς (gen.sing.masc.of εἷς, possession) 469.

παραπτώματι (instru.sing.neut.of παράπτωμα, cause) 585.

ὁ (nom.sing.masc.of the article in agreement with θάνατος) 9.

θάνατος (nom.sing.masc.of θάνατος, subject of ἐβασίλευσεν) 381.

ἐβασίλευσεν (3d.per.sing.aor.act.ind.of βασιλεύω, culminative) 236.

διὰ (preposition with the ablative of agent) 118.

τοῦ (abl.sing.masc.of the article in agreement with ἑνός) 9.

ἑνός (abl.sing.masc.of εἷς, agent) 469.

πολλῷ (instru.sing.neut.of πολύς, measure, adverbial) 228.

μᾶλλον (adverbial) 619.

οἱ (nom.pl.masc.of the article in agreement with λαμβάνοντες) 9.

τὴν (acc.sing.fem.of the article in agreement with περισσείαν) 9.

#3904 περισσείαν (acc.sing.fem.of περισσεία, direct object of λαμβάνοντες).

King James Version

abundance - Rom.5:17; 2 Cor.8:2.
superfluity - James 1:21.
abundantly - 2 Cor.10:15.

Revised Standard Version

abundance - Rom.5:17; 2 Cor.8:2.
be greatly enlarged - 2 Cor.10:15.
rank growth - James 1:21.

*Meaning:* Cf. περίσσευμα (#1003), περισσεύω (#473), περισσός (#525) and περισσῶς (#1630). Hence, abundance, superfluity, over-supply. Followed by a genitive of description - τῆς χάριτος - Rom.5:17; τῆς χαρᾶς - 2 Cor.8:2; κακίας - James 1:21; adverbially - εἰς περισσείαν - 2 Cor.10:15.

τῆς (gen.sing.fem.of the article in agreement with χάριτος) 9.

χάριτος (gen.sing.fem.of χάρις, description) 1700.

καὶ (adjunctive conjunction joining nouns) 14.

τῆς (gen.sing.fem.of the article in agreement with δωρεᾶς) 9.

δωρεᾶς (gen.sing.fem.of δωρεά, description) 2004.

τῆς (gen.sing.fem.of the article in agreement with δικαιοσύνης) 9.

δικαιοσύνης (gen.sing.fem.of δικαιοσύνη, description) 322.

λαμβάνοντες (pres.act.part.nom.pl.masc.of λαμβάνω, substantival, subject of βασιλεύσουσιν) 533.

ἐν (preposition with the locative, instrumental use) 80.

ζωῇ (loc.sing.fem.of ζωή, means) 668.

βασιλεύσουσιν (3d.per.pl.fut.act.ind.of βασιλεύω, predictive) 236.

διὰ (preposition with the ablative of agent) 118.

τοῦ (abl.sing.masc.of the article in agreement with ἑνὸς) 9.

ἑνὸς (abl.sing.masc.of εἷς, agent) 469.

Ἰησοῦ (abl.sing.masc.of Ἰησοῦς, apposition) 3.

Χριστοῦ (abl.sing.masc.of Χριστός, apposition) 4.

*Translation* - *"For since because of the fall of one man death ruled through the one man, much more those receiving the abundance of grace and of the gift of righteousness shall rule by means of life through the one man, Jesus Christ."*

**Comment:** The contrast here between Adam, the type and Christ, the Antitype, is in terms of the dictatorship of death versus the hegemony of life. Death indeed rules all through the agency of Adam who fathered the race and passed down to posterity the immoral propensities of the flesh (διὰ τοῦ ἑνὸς) and because of his fall (τῷ τοῦ ἑνὸς παραπτώματι). Adam and his fall resulted in the universal rule of death. Death dominates the race, both physically and spiritually. The first-class condition with εἰ and the indicative ἐβασίλευσεν in the protasis, leaves no doubt about the premise. Since that is so the conclusion in the apodosis follows. In a much greater way (πολλῷ μᾶλλον) those who receive overwhelming floods of grace and the gift of imputed righteousness will reign through the agency of the Last Adam, Jesus Christ. The reign of life is greater than the dictatorship of death. This is obviously true, since the gift of Jesus Christ, the Creator, is greater than the legacy of Adam, the creature. (1 John 4:4).

A variant reading has τὴν δωρεάν, making it the object of λαμβάνοντες instead of the genitive of description of περισσείαν. The thought is the same in either case.

*Verse 18* - *"Therefore, as by the offence of one judgment came upon all men to condemnation, even so by the righteousness of one the free gift came upon all men unto justification of life."*

Ἄρα οὖν ὡς δι' ἑνὸς παραπτώματος εἰς πάντας ἀνθρώπους εἰς κατάκριμα, οὕτως καὶ δι' ἑνὸς δικαιώματος εἰς πάντας ἀνθρώπους εἰς δικαίωσιν ζωῆς.

*"Then as one man's trespass led to condemnation for all men, so one man's act of righteousness leads to acquittal and life for all men."* RSV

Ἄρα (illative particle, with οὖν in an inferential clause) 995.

οὖν (inferential conjunction) 68.

ὡς (comparative particle) 128.

δι' (preposition with the ablative, means) 118.

ἑνὸς (gen.sing.masc.of εἷς, description) 469.

παραπτώματος (abl.sing.neut.of παράπτωμα, means) 585.

εἰς (preposition with the accusative of extent, predicate use) 140.

πάντας (acc.pl.masc.of πᾶς, in agreement with ἀνθρώπους) 67.

ἀνϑρώπους (acc.pl.masc.of ἄνϑρωπος, extent) 341.
εἰς (preposition with the accusative, result) 140.
κατάκριμα (acc.sing.neut.of κατάκριμα, result) 3903.
οὕτως (demonstrative adverb) 74.
καὶ (continuative conjunction) 14.
δι' (preposition with the ablative of means) 118.
ἑνὸς (gen.sing.masc.of εἷς, description) 469.
δικαιώματος (abl.sing.neut.of δικαίωμα, means) 1781.
εἰς (preposition with the accusative of extent, predicate use) 140.
πάντας (acc.pl.masc.of πᾶς in agreement with ἀνϑρώπους) 67.
ἀνϑρώπους (acc.pl.masc.of ἄνϑρωπος, extent, predicate use) 341.
εἰς (preposition with the accusative, result) 140.
δικαίωσιν (acc.sing.fem.of δικαίωσις, result) 3895.
ζωῆς (gen.sing.fem.of ζωή, description) 668.

*Translation - "Accordingly therefore, as by means of the fall of one man, condemnation came to all men, so also by the righteous act of one came justification of life to all men."*

**Comment:** Paul has been involved in anacoluthon since verse 12, though his thought is perfectly clear. He omitted the apodosis of the ὥσπερ clause in verse 12. Now, in verse 18, he starts again and this time he brings the thought to conclusion. Ἄρα οὖν - "accordingly therefore." *Cf.* #68 for other ἄρα οὖν examples. "In the light of what I have said since verse 12, therefore . . . κ.τ.λ."

Verse 18 is a summation of his federal headship teaching. Paul omits the verbs. Winer suggests ἀπέβη for the first clause and ἀποβήσεται for the second. (*Cf.*#2042). Judgment came upon all men by Adam's fall and justification came to all men and will come, if they believe, because of the obedient act of righteousness in Christ (John 8:29).

*Verse 19 - "For as by one man's disobedience many were made sinners, so by the obedience of one shall many be made righteous."*

ὥσπερ γὰρ διὰ τῆς παρακοῆς τοῦ ἑνὸς ἀνϑρώπου ἁμαρτωλοὶ κατεστάϑησαν οἱ πολλοί, οὕτως καὶ διὰ τῆς ὑπακοῆς τοῦ ἑνὸς δίκαιοι κατασταϑήσονται οἱ πολλοί.

*"For as by one man's disobedience many were made sinners, so by one man's obedience many will be made righteous."*    RSV

ὥσπερ (intensive comparative particle) 560.
γὰρ (causal conjunction) 105.
διὰ (preposition with the ablative of means) 118.
τῆς (abl.sing.fem.of the article in agreement with παρακοῆς) 9.

**#3905** παρακοῆς (abl.sing.fem.of παρακοή, means).

King James Version

disobedience - Rom.5:19; 2 Cor.10:6; Heb.2:2.

Revised Standard Version

disobedience - Rom.5:19; 2 Cor.10:6; Heb.2:2.

*Meaning:* A combination of παρά (#154) and ἀκοή (#409). Hence a hearing amiss; action that is beside (not conformable to) the hearing of an order. Hence disobedience. With reference to Adam's sin - Rom.5:19; *cf.* also 2 Cor.10:6; Heb.2:2, - unwillingness to hear.

τοῦ (gen.sing.masc.of the article in agreement with ἀνθρώπου) 9.
ἑνὸς (gen.sing.masc.of εἷς, in agreement with ἀνθρώπου) 469.
ἀνθρώπου (gen.sing.masc.of ἄνθρωπος, description) 341.
ἁμαρτωλοὶ (nom.pl.masc.of ἁμαρτωλός, predicate nominative) 791.
κατεστάθησαν (3d.per.pl.aor.pass.ind.of καθίστημι, culminative) 1523.
οἱ (nom.pl.masc.of the article in agreement with πολλοί) 9.
πολλοί (nom.pl.masc.of πολύς, subject of κατεστάθησαν) 228.
οὕτως (demonstrative adverb) 74.
καὶ (adjunctive conjunction joining substantives) 14.
διὰ (preposition with the ablative of means) 118.
τῆς (abl.sing.fem.of the article in agreement with ὑπακοῆς) 9.
ὑπακοῆς (abl.sing.fem.of ὑπακοή, means) 3785.
τοῦ (gen.sing.masc.of the article in agreement with ἑνὸς) 9.
ἑνὸς (gen.sing.masc.of εἷς, description) 469.
δίκαιοι (nom.pl.masc.of δίκαιος, predicate adjective) 85.
κατασταθήσονται (3d.per.pl.fut.pass.ind.of καθίστημι, predictive) 1523.
οἱ (nom.pl.masc.of the article in agreement with πολλοί) 9.
πολλοί (nom.pl.masc.of πολύς, subject of κατασταθήσονται) 228.

*Translation - "Because just as it was by the disobedience of the one man that the many were made sinners, so also by the obedience of the One, the many will be made righteous."*

**Comment:** Note ὥσπερ, the comparative particle with the correlative οὕτως - "precisely as . . . even so." Here is a perfectly balanced equation. Adam's willful disobedience made the rest of the race, of which he was the federal head, sinners. In the same way the willing obedience of Jesus makes the elect, of whom He is the federal head as righteous as He. Natural birth passes the genetic characteristics of parent to child. Thus we fell in Adam. Supernatural birth (John 3:3,7; 1 Pet.1:23) makes the believer like Christ. Thus we are justified in Christ.

*Verse 20 - "Moreover the law entered that the offence might abound. But where sin abounded, grace did much more abound."*

νόμος δὲ παρεισῆλθεν ἵνα πλεονάσῃ τὸ παράπτωμα, οὗ δὲ ἐπλεόνασεν ἡ ἁμαρτία, ὑπερεπερίσσευσεν ἡ χάρις,

*"Law came in to increase the trespass; but where sin increased, grace*

*abounded all the more, . . . "     RSV*

νόμος (nom.sing.masc.of νόμος, subject of παρεισῆλθεν) 464.
δὲ (explanatory conjunction) 11.

**#3906** παρεισῆλθεν (3d.per.sing.aor.ind.of παρεισέρχομαι, constative).

King James Version

came in privily - Gal.2:4.
enter - Rom.5:20.

Revised Standard Version

came in - Rom.5:20.
secretly brought in - Gal.2:4.

*Meaning:* A combination of παρά (#154) and εἰσέρχομαι (#234); to come in (or be brought in) beside. The law was introduced into the life of Israel after, and in addition to, the grace covenant - Rom.5:20; with reference to false teachers imported into Galatia after Paul left the region - Gal.2:4.

ἵνα (conjunction introducing the subjunctive in a sub-final clause) 114.

**#3907** πλεονάσῃ (3d.per.sing.aor.act.subj.of πλεονάζω, sub-final).

King James Version

abound - Rom.5:20,20; 6:1; Phil.4:17; 2 Thess.1:3; 2 Pet.1:8.
make to increase - 1 Thess.3:12.
abundant - 2 Cor.4:15.
have nothing over - 2 Cor.8:15.

Revised Standard Version

increase - Rom.5:20,20; Phil.4:17; 2 Thess.1:3; 1 Thess.3:12; 2 Cor.4:15.
abound - Rom.6:1; 2 Pet.1:8.
have nothing over - 2 Cor.8:15.

*Meaning: Cf.* πλέον equals πλήν - "in addition to." Superabundance. Hence, to have more of something than is needed. To have an abundance. To cause a supply to increase. With reference to the consciousness of sin - Rom.5:20,20; grace - Rom.6:1; 2 Cor.4:15; the fruitage of Christian service - Phil.4:17; charity - 2 Thess.1:3; Christian virtues generally - 2 Pet.1:8; 1 Thess.3:12, followed by a locative of sphere; of an abundance of manna - 2 Cor.8:15.

τὸ (nom.sing.neut.of the article in agreement with παράπτωμα) 9.
παράπτωμα (nom.sing.neut.of παράπτωμα, subject of πλεονάσῃ) 585.
οὗ (gen.sing.masc.of ὅς, relative pronoun, genitive of place description) 65.
δὲ (adversative conjunction) 11.
ἐπλεόνασεν (3d.per.sing.aor.act.ind.of πλεονάζω, constative) 3907.

ἡ (nom.sing.fem.of the article in agreement with ἁμαρτία) 9.
ἁμαρτία (nom.sing.fem.of ἁμαρτία, subject of ἐπλεόνασεν) 111.

#3908 ὑπερεπερίσσευσεν (3d.per.sing.aor.act.ind.of ὑπερπερισσεύω, constative).

King James Version

abound much more - Rom.5:20.
be exceeding joyful - 2 Cor.7:4.

Revised Standard Version

abound all the more - Rom.5:20.
be overjoyed - 2 Cor.7:4.

*Meaning:* A combination of ὑπέρ (#545) and περισσεύω (#473). Hence, to abound or to be more abundant - in a comparative degree. Followed by a locative of sphere - 2 Cor.7:4; with reference to grace - Rom.5:20.

ἡ (nom.sing.fem.of the article in agreement with χάρις) 9.
χάρις (nom.sing.fem.of χάρις, subject of ὑπερεπερίσσευσεν) 1700.

*Translation -* "*Now law was introduced in order (and with the result) that the transgression might be accented, but though sin grew more sinful, grace was supplied even more.*"

**Comment:** δὲ is explanatory. In verse 14 Paul had alluded to the period between Adam and Moses - from the creation to Sinai, where the Mosaic law was given to Israel. But he had already made it clear that the moral law of God, of which the Mosaic Code was but a codified and formal statement, was written in the hearts of men (Rom.2:15). The question arises, therefore, as to why the law was given at Sinai? *Cf.*Gal.3:19-26, where Paul raises this question again and gives a complete answer. He says here that it was for the purpose of accenting the fact that men are transgressors and that transgression of the law of God is a serious matter.

The grammarians are divided as to whether the ἵνα clause here is final (purpose), consecutive (result) or sub-final (a blend of purpose and result). Robertson says, "As a matter of fact the various points of view shade off into one another very easily and sometimes quite imperceptibly." (Robertson, *Grammar*, 980). I have translated the sub-final idea, because what God purposes always follows as result. ἵνα clauses with the subjunctive that do not involve the purposes of God are not necessarily sub-final. Man purposes many things which, fortunately, do not follow as result. But God's purposes are never frustrated (Eph.1:11).

Both the purpose of God and the result which He intended are found at Sinai. The children of Israel came to realize how sinful they were. A study of Exodus 19-32 will bear this out. At the very time that God and Moses were upon the mountain, the people were in the foothills transgressing every one of the ten commandments. The giving of the Mosaic Code did not necessarily contribute to their depravity, nor to the enormity of their transgressions of it, but, though they already knew that they were sinners - the voice of conscience, which was the "work of the law written in their hearts" (Rom.2:15) had told them that - they were now confronted with the written and spoken moral code by which their lives would be judged. It is easier to resist the voice of conscience than to disobey a plainly written statement in a legal code. Behavior which is not necessarily immoral before a law is passed to forbid it becomes illegal when it is prohibited by the statute. For example, it is not necessarily immoral to drive an automobile in excess of fifty-five miles per hour, but it is illegal.

A careful reading of Exodus 19 suggests that Israel should have begged God to continue His gracious treatment described by Him as "eagles' wings" (Exodus 19:4). Instead, with rash overconfidence they promised complete obedience to the divine will (Exodus 19:8). Thus it can be argued that God gave the law so that (purpose) they would come to understand their true condition of depravity. That they did so come to understand it argues of course that the ἵνα clause is also consecutive. Thus we have called it sub-final. Actually as Burton says, "purpose is intended result" (Burton, *Moods and Tenses*, 148). God wanted to humble Israel that she might throw herself upon His grace and mercy. The passage in Galatians 3:19-26 seems to suggest that this was His purpose in giving the law. God's eternal purpose in history always leads to His intended result. Thus when God is involved ἵνα with the subjunctive is both purpose and ecbatic (result).

But an overwhelming sense of guilt for sin was met with an even greater overwhelming flood of grace. God's Mosaic Code became the basis for the allegation of guilt and the indictment in heaven's court. Adam sinned against an express command and died. Men after Adam and before Moses sinned against the voice of conscience and died. Since Moses, men have sinned both against the voice of conscience and the Mosaic Code and they have died. But grace has superabounded. The "Judge of all the earth" (Gen.18:25; Acts 17:31; John 5:22) fulfilled the law (Mt.5:17) and died as though He had broken it all, thus to make His righteous achievement available to the believer as a gift of His grace. But no sinner ever asks God for grace until he is convinced that he is a transgressor with a sin debt to God too great for him to pay. This is what he comes to understand when he compares his own moral record with the spotless standard demanded by the law of God.

*Verse 21 - "That as sin hath reigned unto death, even so might grace reign through righteousness unto eternal life by Jesus Christ our Lord.*

ἵνα ὥσπερ ἐβασίλευσεν ἡ ἁμαρτία ἐν τῷ θανάτῳ, οὕτως καὶ ἡ χάρις βασιλεύσῃ διὰ δικαιοσύνης εἰς ζωὴν αἰώνιον διὰ Ἰησοῦ Χριστοῦ τοῦ κυρίου ἡμῶν.

*". . . so that, as sin reigned in death, grace also might reign through righteousness to eternal life through Jesus Christ our Lord." . . . RSV*

ἵνα (conjunction with the subjunctive in a sub-final clause) 114.
ὥσπερ (intensive comparative particle) 560.

ἐβασίλευσεν (3d.per.sing.aor.act.ind.of βασιλεύω, constative) 236.
ἡ (nom.sing.fem.of the article in agreement with ἁμαρτία) 9.
ἁμαρτία (nom.sing.fem.of ἁμαρτία, subject of ἐβασίλευσεν) 111.
ἐν (preposition with the locative, instrumental use, means) 80.
τῷ (loc.sing.masc.of the article in agreement with θανάτῳ) 9.
θανάτῳ (loc.sing.masc.of θάνατος, means) 381.
οὕτως (demonstrative adverb) 74.
καὶ (adjunctive conjunction joining nouns) 14.
ἡ (nom.sing.fem.of the article in agreement with χάρις) 9.
χάρις (nom.sing.fem.of χάρις, subject of βασιλεύσῃ) 1700.
βασιλεύσῃ (3d.per.sing.aor.act.subj.of βασιλεύω, sub-final) 236.
διὰ (preposition with the ablative of agent) 118.
δικαιοσύνης (abl.sing.fem.of δικαιοσύνη, agent) 322.
εἰς (preposition with the accusative, result) 140.
ζωὴν (acc.sing.fem.of ζωή, result) 668.
αἰώνιον (acc.sing.fem.of αἰώνιος, in agreement with ζωὴν) 1255.
διὰ (preposition with the ablative of agent) 118.
Ἰησοῦ (abl.sing.masc.of Ἰησοῦς, agent) 3.
Χριστοῦ (abl.sing.masc.of Χριστός, apposition) 4.
τοῦ (abl.sing.masc.of the article in agreement with κυρίου) 9.
κυρίου (abl.sing.masc.of κύριος, apposition) 97.
ἡμῶν (gen.pl.masc.of ἐγώ, relationship) 123.

*Translation - "In order that in precisely the way that sin enforced its reign through death, so also grace might establish its reign by means of righteousness with a result of eternal life through Jesus Christ our Lord."*

**Comment:** We have another sub-final clause with ἵνα and the subjunctive in βασιλεύσῃ. Here we have the contrasts between sin and righteousness, life and death set forth again. Sin is the tyrant that dominates the lives of its victims and enforces its grisly hegemony by means of death - both physical and spiritual. The grace of God, in contrast brings justification and enforces its rule through righteousness, both imputed and practical (as we shall see in Chapter 6) and the result is that those who are foreknown, predestined, called, justified and glorified (Rom.8:29,30) will live eternally. Life that is eternal is so because its viability results from its total compliance with universal law. Everlasting existence is the fate of those whose lives are in violation of universal law. Death in hell is total separation from God and total transgression of every principle of science and ethics decreed by our Lord in creation.

The benevolent reign of grace can be maintained only by means of righteousness (διὰ δικαιοσύνης) and is given only through the agency of Jesus Christ our Lord. Christ, through grace reigns in righteousness and the result is eternal life, described both in quantitative and qualitative terms. In precisely the same way sin exercises its rule over men by means of death. ὥσπερ is ὡς with intensity - "in exactly the same way as . . . κ.τ.λ."

The issue is finally decided on the basis that though sin, already heinous enough to condemn sinners, was made more malevolent when the law came, since now every mouth is stopped and the entire race is guilty before God (except babies), grace abounded even more. Sin uses death to subdue men. The grim reaper heads the hit squad of the prince of darkness. Grace through Christ's righteousness uses eternal life to rescue them. It is important for the student to understand these two rules of verse 21 - the rule of sin by death versus the rule of grace to eternal life since Paul uses this distinction, as the foundation for his teaching of the victorious life in chapter six.

## Dead to Sin but Alive in Christ

### (Romans 6:1-14)

*Romans 6:1 - "What shall we say then? Shall we continue in sin, that grace may abound?"*

Τί οὖν ἐροῦμεν; ἐπιμένωμεν τῇ ἁμαρτίᾳ, ἵνα ἡ χάρις πλεονάσῃ;

*"What shall we say then? Are we to continue in sin that grace may abound?"*
                                                                          RSV

Τί (acc.sing.neut.of τίς, direct object of ἐροῦμεν) 281.
οὖν (inferential conjunction) 68.
ἐροῦμεν (1st.per.pl.fut.act.ind.of ἔρω, deliberative) 155.
ἐπιμένωμεν (1st.per.pl.pres.act.subj.of ἐπιμένω, deliberative) 2379.
τῇ (loc.sing.fem.of the article in agreement with ἁμαρτίᾳ) 9.
ἁμαρτίᾳ (loc.sing.fem.of ἁμαρτία, sphere) 111.
ἵνα (conjunction with the subjunctive, purpose) 114.
ἡ (nom.sing.fem.of the article in agreement with χάρις) 9.
χάρις (nom.sing.fem.of χάρις, subject of πλεονάσῃ) 1700.
πλεονάσῃ (3d.per.sing.aor.act.subj.of πλεονάζω, purpose) 3907.

*Translation - "What then shall we say? Are we to continue in sin in order that grace may abound?"*

**Comment:** The two questions are deliberative - the first with the future; the second with the subjunctive. Both express great doubt.

Paul apparently was raising a question that had been posed. It represents the argument of the antinomians ("against the law" proponents). The argument runs like this: If, as Paul has just argued in chapter five, God is determined to demonstrate the superabundance of grace over sin, then the greater the sin, the greater must be the grace. Now, since God is glorified by His grace, we should perform for Him the service of sinning more, thus to give Him an even greater opportunity to demonstrate His even greater grace. Thus, it was concluded, that sin in the life of the Christian glorifies God. Stated conversely, the believer who lives the victorious life does God a disservice since he gives God little opportunity to demonstrate His grace. All of this seemed to be a logical extrapolation of verse 20 of chapter 5. That it is tortured logic is clear, as Paul points out so clearly in the remainder of this chapter. Antinomians, due to their misguided because unregenerate hearts consider their position an extrapolation of Romans 5:20b. That it is tortured logic is clear as Paul refutes it by applying the higher ethical principle of Romans 5:21. *Cf.* Rom.11:22,23; Col.1:23; 1 Tim.4:16; Acts 13:43.

Arminians often allude to antinomianism as a lethal weapon against the P in the Calvinistic TULIP - the Preservation of the saints. How often have we heard it - "If I believed in eternal security I would . . . ." Decency forbids me to finish the quotation! The proper rejoinder to which is "You would?!" Such a confession is an honest statement of the real reason why some church members try to live a decent life. Severely induced to evil as all Christians, short of glorification are, they struggle to exemplify the Christian ethic, not because they think that the victorious life in Christ is superior to a life of sin, but because they fear the eternal consequences of repeated transgressions of the law of God. Thus they are working for themselves out of a sense of fear, not working for the Lord out of a sense of love and gratitude. The true regenerate dreads sin and recoils in shame and repentance after he commits it. The antinomian strives mightily to avoid sin, all the while ardently wishing for the freedom to commit it and deterred only by the fear of punishment.

*Verse 2 - "God forbid. How shall we that are dead to sin, live any longer therein?"*

μὴ γένοιτο. οἵτινες ἀπεθάνομεν τῇ ἁμαρτίᾳ, πῶς ἔτι ζήσομεν ἐν αὐτῇ;

*"By no means! How can we who died to sin still live in it?"*     RSV

μὴ (negative conjunction with the optative) 87.

γένοιτο (3d.per.sing.2d.aor.opt.of γίνομαι, voluntative) 113.

οἵτινες (nom.pl.masc.of ὅστις, relative pronoun in a causal clause, subject of ἀπεθάνομεν) 163.

ἀπεθάνομεν (1st.per.pl.aor.act.ind.of ἀποθνῄσκω, culminative) 774.

τῇ (loc.sing.fem.of the article in agreement with ἁμαρτίᾳ) 9.

ἁμαρτίᾳ (loc.sing.fem.of ἁμαρτία, sphere) 111.

πῶς (interrogative conjunction) 627.

ἔτι (temporal adverb) 448.

ζήσομεν (1st.per.pl.fut.act.ind.of ζάω, deliberative) 340.

ἐν (preposition with the locative of sphere) 80.

αὐτῇ (loc.sing.fem.of αὐτός, sphere) 16.

*Translation - "Perish the thought! How can we go on living in sin in view of the fact that we are dead to it?"*

**Comment:** The literal translation of μὴ γένοιτο - "may it not be so!" will do, but there are other ways to express dismay. Goodspeed has, "Certainly not!" The RSV has "By no means!" Montgomery - "No indeed;" Williams has "Not at all!" The current idiom which developed five years ago and which expresses the abhorrence which one feels for the antinomian position is "No way!"

"The phrase μὴ γένοιτο is an Optative of Wishing which strongly deprecates something suggested by a previous question or assertion. Fourteen of the fifteen New

Testament instances are in Paul's writings, and in twelve of these it expresses the apostle's abhorrence of an inference which he fears may be (falsely) drawn from his argument." (Burton, *Moods and Tenses*, 79).

The relative clause οἵτινες ἀπεθάνομεν is causal. The fact is that the Christian is living under the hegemony of grace and the administrative implementation of the kingdom principle is righteousness. The Executive Head of the Body (Eph.1:22,23) and the King of the Kingdom is the Lord Jesus Christ, unto Whom all power in heaven and in earth has been given (Mt.28:18; Phil.2:9-11; Eph.1:19-23). He is not only the Administrator of righteousness.   He is the Source of it (Mt.5:17; John 8:29). The result of all of this is eternal life which is defined in terms both of quantity and quality. The Christian has been rescued from the rule of sin which held him in thralldom through death (Rom.5:21a), both physical and spiritual. The child of God is now liberated. In Christ he died with respect to sin. The future question is deliberative. How did we die to sin? Paul tells us in

*Verse 3 - "Know ye not that so many of us as were baptized into Jesus Christ were baptized into his death?"*

ἢ ἀγνοεῖτε ὅτι ὅσοι ἐβαπτίσθημεν εἰς Χριστὸν Ἰησοῦν εἰς τὸν θάνατον αὐτοῦ ἐβαπτίσθημεν;

*"Do you not know that all of us who have been baptized into Christ Jesus were baptized into his death?"*

ἢ (disjunctive conjunction) 465.
ἀγνοεῖτε (2d.per.pl.pres.act.ind.of ἀγνοέω, direct question) 2345.
ὅτι (conjunction introducing an object clause in indirect discourse) 211.
ὅσοι (nom.pl.masc.of ὅσος, relative pronoun, subject of ἐβαπτίσθημεν) 660.
ἐβαπτίσθημεν (1st.per.pl.aor.pass.ind.of βαπτίζω, constative) 273.
εἰς (preposition with the accusative of extent) 140.
Χριστὸν (acc.sing.masc.of Χριστός, extent) 4.
Ἰησοῦν (acc.sing.masc.of Ἰησοῦς, apposition) 3.
εἰς (preposition with the accusative of extent) 140.
τὸν (acc.sing.masc.of the article in agreement with θάνατον) 9.
θάνατον (acc.sing.masc.of θάνατος, extent) 381.
αὐτοῦ (gen.sing.masc.of αὐτός, designation) 16.
ἐβαπτίσθημεν (1st.per.pl.aor.pass.ind.of βαπτίζω, constative) 273.

*Translation - "Or are you unaware that those of us who were immersed into Christ Jesus were identified with His death?"*

**Comment:** Paul is attempting to discover the reason for the misunderstanding of the antinomians (*cf.* comment on verses 1,2 *supra).* Perhaps they did not know what he tells us with ὅτι and the object clause in indirect discourse. Whoever is totally involved (immersed, innundated, overwhelmed, totally surrounded by, overcome - the basic meaning of βαπτίζω - *cf*.#273) with Christ is thus totally involved in *all* of His experience, which includes His death on Calvary and His resurrection. Sin, which dominates Adam's race (Romans 5:21a) exercises its rule by means of death. Men have sinned and men die physically and those outside of Christ who died spiritually when they first deliberately transgressed God's law, spend eternity in hell. Sin did its worst against Jesus on the cross, but there it met its match. He took all of the punishment which it had to offer, assumed its total guilt and suffered the agonies of eternal separation from His Father in the three dreadful hours upon the cross. Thus He ransomed the elect, and as a result Satan has no further ultimate control over those for whom Christ died. But Jesus, having paid the spiritual wages for sin was still alive. Did physical death conquer Him? Not at all. He conquered physical death (John 10:17,18 comment upon which *cf. en loc.*). "Through death (spiritual) He destroyed him that has the power of death (both physical and spiritual) that is the devil and delivered . . . . " those for whom He died (Heb.2:14). Sin had no further weapon to employ after its ultimate weapon had been thrown into the battle.

Paul seems to express some surprize that they did not know that when Christ died the believer also died in Him. But how can the believer be identified with Jesus in a historical event which, in the case of the Old Testament saints, occured after they were dead and, in the case of the rest of us, centuries before we were born? By the elective choice of God the believer is a member of the body of Christ. Hence, when Christ died His spiritual body died with Him. Paul says this clearly in Gal.2:20. We must keep in mind the fact that as creatures of time and space we are subject to these categories, and we must remember that God is eternal and omnipresent and that He knows nothing of time and space. All is for Him present, both spatially and temporally.

But how does the believer in his own time become subjectively and thus historically identified with Christ's body? Paul tells us that it is by baptism. Water? And we can be sure that the baptismal regenerationists and other sacerdotalists will answer in the affirmative. But *cf.* Galatians 3:27; 1 Cor.12:13. Gal.3:27 is explained by Gal.3:26 and that Paul means the Holy Spirit in 1 Cor.12:13 is evident from the context. He had been speaking in 1 Cor.12 of no one else. But if some object that there is no such thing as the baptism of the Holy Spirit, since there can be no doubt that water baptism is enjoined and thus there is only water baptism, since Eph.4:5 says that there is only *one* baptism, we reply that there is indeed only one true baptism and that baptism  is of the Holy Spirit, while immersion in water is only a picture of it. There has only been one George Washington also, but his picture is on every dollar bill.

Whoever in historic time is baptized by the Holy Spirit into the Body of Christ (1 Cor.12:13) thus makes true for himself subjectively what God made true for him objectively in the death of Jesus Christ upon the cross. Let the reader reflect upon the time and place when and where he was brought by the Holy Spirit into the Body of Christ. For him it was an overwhelming and totally dominating experience (Luke 12:50). For him it was a baptism (immersion, innundation) And it killed him (Gal.2:20). It paid his sin debt. But he also rose from the dead when Christ arose. Hence neither spiritual nor physical death can exercise further control over us (Romans 6:9).

God's glory is not served when Christians, who apart from the death of Christ would be slaves to sin, the enforcement agent of which is death, but who are now set forever free, both from sin and its eternal results, return to serve the old slave driver. So complete is the believer's identification with the Body of Christ, as a result of Holy Spirit baptism (1 Cor.12:13) that his identification includes, in addition to death, Jesus' burial and resurrection. This is Paul's thought in

*Verse 4 - "Therefore we are buried with him by baptism into death: that like as Christ was raised up from the dead by the glory of the Father, even so we also should walk in newness of life."*

συνετάφημεν οὖν αὐτῷ διὰ τοῦ βαπτίσματος εἰς τὸν θάνατον, ἵνα ὥσπερ ἠγέρθη Χριστὸς ἐκ νεκρῶν διὰ τῆς δόξης τοῦ πατρός, οὕτως καὶ ἡμεῖς ἐν καινότητι ζωῆς περιπατήσωμεν.

*"We were buried therefore with him by baptism into death, so that as Christ was raised from the dead by the glory of the Father, we too might walk in newness of life."     RSV*

#3909 συνετάφημεν (1st.per.pl.2d.aor.pass.ind.of συνθάπτω, culminative).

King James Version

bury with - Rom.6:4; Col.2:12.

Revised Standard Version

bury with - Rom.6:4; Col.2:12.

*Meaning:* A combination of σύν (#1542) and θάπτω (#748). Hence, to bury with another. In the passive, to share another's grave. In a spiritual sense, with reference to the believer's identify with Christ in His burial - Rom.6:4; Col.2:12.

οὖν (inferential conjunction) 68.
αὐτῷ (instru.sing.masc.of αὐτός, association, after σύν in composition) 16.
διὰ (preposition with the ablative of manner) 118.
τοῦ (abl.sing.neut.of the article in agreement with βαπτίσματος) 9.
βαπτίσματος (abl.sing.neut.of βάπτισμα, manner) 278.
εἰς (preposition with the accusative, cause) 140.
τὸν (acc.sing.masc.of the article in agreement with θάνατον) 9.
θάνατον (acc.sing.masc.of θάνατος, cause) 381.
ἵνα (conjunction with the subjunctive, purpose) 114.
ὥσπερ (intensive comparative particle) 560.
ἠγέρθη (3d.per.sing.aor.pass.ind.of ἐγείρω, constative) 125.
Χριστὸς (nom.sing.masc.of Χριστός, subject of ἠγέρθη) 4.
ἐκ (preposition with the ablative of separation) 19.
νεκρῶν (abl.pl.masc.of νεκρός, separation) 749.
διὰ (preposition with the ablative, manner) 118.
τῆς (abl.sing.fem.of the article in agreement with δόξης) 9.

δόξης (abl.sing.fem.of δόξα, manner) 361.
τοῦ (gen.sing.masc.of the article in agreement with πατρός) 9.
πατρός (gen.sing.masc.of πατήρ, possession) 238.
οὕτως (demonstrative adverb) 74.
καὶ (adjunctive conjunction joining substantives) 14.
ἡμεῖς (nom.pl.masc.of ἐγώ, subject of περιπατήσωμεν) 123.
ἐν (preposition with the locative, instrumental use, manner) 80.

#3910 καινότητι (loc.sing.masc.of καινότης, manner).

King James Version

newness - Rom.6:4; 7:6.

Revised Standard Version

newness - Rom.6:4.
new life - Rom.7:6.

*Meaning:* Cf. καινός (#812). Newness. Followed by a genitive of description - ζωῆς - Rom.6:4; by an ablative of source - πνεύματος - Rom.7:6.

ζωῆς (gen.sing.fem.of ζωή, description) 668.
περιπατήσωμεν (1st.per.pl.1st.aor.act.subj.of περιπατέω, purpose) 384.

*Translation - "Therefore we have been buried with Him by the immersion unto death, in order that, just as Christ was raised from the dead amid the glory of the Father, so also we may begin to walk around in a new lifestyle."*

**Comment:** The phrase εἰς τὸν θάνατον is joined, not to συνετάφημεν (verse 4), but to ἐβαπτίσθημεν. The Spirit baptism was unto death, not unto the burial. But since He was buried after He died, and we, by Spirit baptism were identified with Him in death, we also are buried with him. We shared His cross; we also shared His tomb. Why? So that (ἵνα... περιπατήσωμεν, the purpose clause) we may walk about in the world, powered by the resurrection power that provides us with a new lifestyle. Once buried, Christ rose from the dead, and we with Him (Gal.2:20).

It is plain that Paul is still speaking of Spirit baptism in vese 4, not water baptism. Else he is saying that immersion in water is prerequisite to the victorious life. It is indeed essential to complete obedience to our Lord's divine command (Mt.28:19,20), but to read water baptism into verse 4 is to say that only immersed believers walk in the world in the newness of life that characterizes the born from above believer.

There is an abundance of Scripture to support the truth that all believers should, as a matter of obedience submit to the ordinance of immersion in water as a means of publicly identifying with the cause of Christ and as a prerequisite to local church membership. To read water baptism into Romans 6:1-4, however, is to destroy Paul's argument against the antinomians. The believer is a living member of the body of Christ (1 Cor.12:12,13) and, as such, enjoys total identification with Him in His death, burial and resurrection. We died with Christ on the cross (verse 3); we were also buried with Him, and raised again from the dead. This was so because God reckoned us as a part of His body. We identified with Christ in our own experience by the baptism of the Holy Spirit (1 Cor.12:13; Gal.3:27). It is not our emergence from the waters of immersion that gives us newness of life. It is the fact that we came up, just as Christ did, out of death.

*Verse 5 - "For if we have been planted together in the likeness of his death, we shall be also in the likeness of his resurrection."*

εἰ γὰρ σύμφυτοι γεγόναμεν τῷ ὁμοιώματι τοῦ θανάτου αὐτοῦ, ἀλλὰ καὶ τῆς ἀναστάσεως ἐσόμεθα.

*"For if we have been united with him in a death like his, we shall certainly be united with him in a resurrection like his." RSV*

εἰ (conditional particle in a first-class condition) 337.
γὰρ (inferential conjunction) 105.

#3911 σύμφυτοι (nom.pl.masc.of σύμφυτος, predicate adjective).

King James Version

planted together - Rom.6:5.

Revised Standard Version

united with - Rom.6:5.

*Meaning: Cf.* συμφύω (#2199). Hence, grown with; congenitally connected with. Identified with. Followed by a locative of sphere - τῷ ὁμοιώματι τοῦ θανάτου αὐτοῦ - Rom.6:5. The word indicates total identification of the believer with Christ in His death, burial and resurrection.

γεγόναμεν (1st.per.pl.2d.perf.ind.of γίνομαι, intensive) 113.
τῷ (loc.sing.neut.of the article in agreement with ὁμοιώματι) 9.
ὁμοιώματι (loc.sing.neut.of ὁμοίωμα, sphere) 3803.
τοῦ (gen.sing.masc.of the article in agreement with θανάτου) 9.
θανάτου (gen.sing.masc.of θάνατος, description) 381.
αὐτοῦ (gen.sing.masc.of αὐτός, possession) 16.
ἀλλὰ (confirmatory conjunction) 342.
καὶ (adjunctive conjunction joining nouns) 14.
τῆς (gen.sing.fem.of the article in agreement with ἀναστάσεως) 9.
ἀναστάσεως (gen.sing.fem.of ἀνάστασις, description) 1423.
ἐσόμεθα (1st.per.pl.fut.ind.of εἰμί, predictive) 86.

*Translation - "Therefore since we have been organically connected with Him in the sphere of His death, we shall doubtless also be in the sphere of the resurrection."*

**Comment:** It is a first-class condition. The assumption in the protasis is, in fact, true. It follows then that the statement in the apodosis is also true. The unity of the believer in God and Christ is here expressed in σύμφυτοι. This is in keeping with our Lord's prayer of John 17:21. Note the second perfect passive form in γεγόναμεν. Our union with Christ is said to have been completed in the past. The present and continuing result is that the union still exists and will always exist, like grains of corn merging in the hill into one stock. So complete has been our identification with Him that we shared His death and therefore we died to sin, by taking its complete and final thrust. Thus sin can do no more to lord it over us. The Christian will yield to the demand to commit sin only if he chooses to do so.

Such complete union with Christ carried us beyond His cross to our association with Him in His tomb and even beyond that. The statement in the apodosis is that we shall also identify with Him in His resurrection.

Can the resurrected Christ commit sin? No more will we, when, at some future time (future tense in ἐσόμεθα) we will be glorified (1 Thess.4:13-18; 1 Cor.15:51-58; Phil.3:20,21; Col.3:3-4; 1 John 3:1-3; Rom.8:11).

Paul is not suggesting that the believer is glorified at the moment of regeneration, but he is saying that glorification for the believer is as certain at the Second Coming of our Lord, when the dead in Christ shall rise and the living saints shall be raptured, as it was for Jesus at His resurrection. In the meantime Christians are to reflect upon the certitude of future sinlessness as a spur to dedication now. This is why Paul has used the future tense (ἐσόμεθα) to refer to the time of the resurrection and glorification of the believer. In Romans 8:29,30, where he is speaking of the eternal purposes of God, he refers to the foreknowledge, predestination, calling, justification and glorification of the elect in the aorist tense. For as God views His decrees they are all complete in what men call "the past" and are therefore certain to be implemented. But in Romans 6 Paul is speaking of the Christian experience as it is to be implemented in our lives in historic time. The chronological order of the events which God has planned for us is not in view in Romans 8:29,30. In Romans 6 the chronology is important. Christians are twice born people. Our flesh, the product of our first birth, is no different, now that we are born "from above" (John 3:3,7) than it was before we were saved. It profits nothing (John 6:63). It can but produce its works (Gal.5:19-21). The motivation of the unregenerated heart is in terms of nothing but sin (Mark 7:21-23). Thus the Christian, for all of his glorious prospect of future sinlessness, which will be his at and after the rapture, can live the victorious life only as he yields to the indwelling Holy Spirit Who inhabits his physical body like a temple (1 Cor.6:19,20). It is only when we "walk in the Spirit that (we) will not fulfill the lust of the flesh" (Gal.5:16). There is no sinless perfection for the child of God until glorification. Those who say otherwise about themselves "deceive (themselves) and the truth is not in (them)" (1 John 1:8). It is all a matter of definition. Those Christians who speak of sinlessness before glorification have their own definition of sin, which does not conform to the Biblical definition. When they say, "I do no sin" they mean "Nothing that I do is sin." The difficulty is that what they call mistakes the Word of God calls sin.

*Verse 6 - "Knowing this, that our old man is crucified with him, that the body of sin might be destroyed, that henceforth we should not serve sin."*

τοῦτο γινώσκοντες, ὅτι ὁ παλαιὸς ἡμῶν ἄνθρωπος συνεσταυρώθη, ἵνα καταργηθῇ τὸ σῶμα τῆς ἁμαρτίας, τοῦ μηκέτι δουλεύειν ἡμᾶς τῇ ἁμαρτίᾳ.

*"We know that our old self was crucified with him so that the sinful body might be destroyed, and we might no longer be enslaved to sin."*    RSV

τοῦτο (acc.sing.neut.of οὗτος, direct object of γινώσκοντες) 93.

γινώσκοντες (pres.act.part.nom.pl.masc.of γινώσκω, adverbial, causal) 131.

ὅτι (conjunction introducing an object clause in indirect discourse) 211.

ὁ (nom.sing.masc.of the article in agreement with ἄνθρωπος) 9.

παλαιὸς (nom.sing.masc.of παλαιός, in agreement with ἄνθρωπος) 804.

ἄνθρωπος (nom.sing.masc.of ἄνθρωπος, subject of συνεταυρώθη) 341.

συνεταυρώθη (3d.per.sing.aor.pass.ind.of συσταυρόω, culminative) 1650.

ἵνα (conjunction with the subjunctive in a purpose clause) 114.

καταργηθῇ (3d.per.sing.aor.pass.subj.of καταργέω, purpose) 2500.

τὸ (nom.sing.neut.of the article in agreement with σῶμα) 9.

σῶμα (nom.sing.neut.of σῶμα, subject of καταργηθῇ) 507.

τῆς (gen.sing.fem.of the article in agreement with ἁμαρτίας) 9.

ἁμαρτίας (gen.sing.fem.of ἁμαρτία, description) 111.

τοῦ (gen.sing.neut.of the article, articular infinitive, purpose) 9.

μηκέτι (temporal adverb) 1368.

δουλεύειν (pres.act.inf.of δουλεύω, gen.sing.neut., articular infinitive, purpose) 604.

ἡμᾶς (acc.pl.masc.of ἐγώ, general reference) 123.

τῇ (loc.sing.fem.of the article in agreement with ἁμαρτίᾳ) 9.

ἁμαρτίᾳ (loc.sing.fem.of ἁμαρτία, sphere) 111.

*Translation - "Because we know this - that our old man was crucified with Him, in order that the body of sin might be repudiated, so that we need not longer be enslaved by sin."*

**Comment:** Here Paul calls the flesh τὸ σῶμα τῆς ἁμαρτίας. In Romans 7:24 he calls it σώματος τοῦ θανάτου τούτου - "the body of this death." *Cf.* Rom.8:10,13. It is the body in which we must live out our lives for Christ until the glorification of the rapture and resurrection. It is still depraved - as evil as it was before we were saved. It is still capable of producing its wicked works (Gal.5:17-21). It was the source of Paul's wretchedness (Rom.7:24) but it is destined to be changed at His coming (1 Cor.15:51; Phil.3:21; 1 John 3:1-3). *Cf.* Eph.4:22 and Col.3:9 for "the old man" in the same sense. *Cf.* Titus 3:3 for δουλεύω in this same sense.

These passages indicate that our representative resurrection in the body of Christ with Him, and/or even our historic experience of repentance, faith, regeneration and Holy Spirit baptism (1 Cor.12:13) by which, in a subjective way, we are co-victors with Christ over sin, does not actually render us incapable of sinning. Our victory will be complete at the transfiguration. In the meantime we derive guidance, strength and encouragement to yield to the Holy Spirit, thus to avoid yielding to the flesh (Gal.5:16). We understand now that we are already delivered from sin's penalty and can be delivered from its power because some day we will be delivered from its presence. The "body of sin" will be destroyed and transfigured into a body of glory (Phil.3:21), and this because in Christ we rose again on the third day. Total victory over sin is certain, even though as yet it is in the future. "Whom he justified them he also glorified" (Rom.8:30). With the eternal God all of His decrees are looked upon as having already been accomplished. Since we shall not serve sin after the rapture, why should we serve it now?

*Verse 7 - "For he that is dead is freed from sin."*

ὁ γὰρ ἀποθανὼν δεδικαίωται ἀπὸ τῆς ἁμαρτίας.

*"For he who has died is freed from sin."*    *RSV*

ὁ (nom.sing.masc.of the article in agreement with ἀποθανὼν) 9.

γὰρ (causal conjunction) 105.

ἀποθανὼν (2d.aor.part.nom.sing.masc.of ἀποθνῄσκω, substantival, subject of δεδικαίωται) 774.

δεδικαίωται (3d.per.sing.perf.pass.ind.of δικαιόω, intensive) 933.

ἀπὸ (preposition with the ablative of separation) 70.

τῆς (abl.sing.fem.of the article in agreement with ἁμαρτίας) 9.

ἁμαρτίας (abl.sing.fem.of ἁμαρτία, separation) 111.

*Translation - "Because the dead man is free from any further subjection to sin."*

**Comment:** The point here is the principle of double jeopardy. When the defendant, indicted for alleged transgression of the law, is convicted upon the preponderance of the evidence, condemned and executed, the law can do no more. One cannot tempt a dead man to further sin, nor convict him again on the same charge on which he was tried before. He has paid his debt and cannot again be brought into court. Sin can kill. Indeed sin uses death as its instrument of administration in the kingdom of darkness (Rom.5:21a), but after it has killed, it has no further weapon to use. If the dead man rises from the grave sin and death have no further resources against him. Christ died for our sins and we were in Him representatively when He died. Thus we also died (Gal.2:20). Sin did its worst and the defendant is dead. But we also arose in Christ. Sin has forever lost its power over us (Rom.5:21). Note the perfect tense in δεδικαίωται - "having been justified we are now declared righteous."

The child of God can look back upon his unregenerate days and reflect upon the wretched state of his slavery to sin and error. How we served Satan and his demonic henchmen! How we yielded to the impulses of our darkened hearts, deluded minds and arrogant wills! What craven slaves we were to yield to every lust of our depraved flesh! To reflect upon this slavery, the pit from which we were rescued by God's grace and the eternal hell where we would have spent eternity but for His sovereign intervention is to develop the strongest contempt for Satan and all his works and a great desire to redeem whatever time is left to us to glorify God and promote His gospel. Why then, does the Christian fall into sin? Perhaps he is caught off guard because of his lack of understanding of the potential for ungodliness of his fleshly nature. It is fatal to believe that regeneration has done anything to change the nature of the flesh. Glorification is coming for every child of God, to be sure, but we are not yet made sinless, nor beyond the sweep and scope of temptation. Perhaps those who know their Bibles well enough to recognize that the flesh is never to be trusted have grown careless. Peter has warned the Christian to be "sober and vigilant because your adversary the devil, as a roaring lion lion, walketh about, seeking whom he may devour" (1 Pet.5:8). If we forget to be on our guard we may neglect to employ the panoply of defense (Eph.6:10-18) which is provided. Armed with truth, righteousness, the gospel of peace, the shield of faith, the helmet of salvation and the sword of the Spirit, the weakest Christian is invincible, but there are days when we were too busy with inconsequential matters to pray, too confident of our ability to resist evil with the energy of our own human resources, too eager to take our lives into our own hands as if we were in a position to improve upon the scenario which our Lord has designed for us (Eph.2:10). The road ahead is unknown even to the most erudite child of God. It is folly therefore for him to drive. Let him retire to the back seat and withhold his advice while the nail pierced hands rest upon the steering wheel. Wreckage with great loss of opportunity to serve God, great pain, to ourselves and those we love the most, and even loss of life for some is sure to result when we take the wrong turn and get on the wrong road. "All things work together for good" to be sure, but this promise is reserved for those who love the Lord enough to allow Him to guide their lives and who are therefore "the called ones *according to His purpose*" (Romans 8:28).

Verse 7 has established that the Christian who died with Christ on the cross is immune to the eternal results of sin and death. Verse 8 adds that the Christian who lives with Christ is invincible. Thus the victorious life is the life that is lived every moment of every hour of every day of the rest of our lives in the resurrection power and glory of Him Who demonstrated His power over a tomb.

*Verse 8 - "Now if we be dead with Christ, we believe that we shall also live with him."*

εἰ δὲ ἀπεθάνομεν σὺν Χριστῷ, πιστεύομεν ὅτι καὶ συζήσομεν αὐτῷ.

*"But if we have died with Christ, we believe that we shall also live with him."*
RSV

εἰ (conditional particle in a first-class condition) 337.
δὲ (explanatory conjunction) 11.
ἀπεθάνομεν (1st.per.pl.2d.aor.ind.of ἀποθνήσκω, culminative) 774.
σὺν (preposition with the instrumental of association) 1542.
Χριστῷ (instru.sing.masc.of Χριστός, association) 4.
πιστεύομεν (1st.per.pl.pres.act.ind.of πιστεύω, aoristic) 734.

ὅτι (conjunction introducing an object clause in indirect discourse) 211.
καὶ (adjunctive conjunction joining verbs) 14.

**#3912** συζήσομεν (1st.per.pl.fut.act.ind.of συζάω, predictive).

King James Version

live with - Rom.6:8; 2 Cor.7:3; 2 Tim.2:11.

Revised Standard Version

live with - Rom.6:8; 2 Tim.2:11.
live together - 2 Cor.7:3.

*Meaning:* A combination of σύν (#1542) and ζάω (#340). Hence, to live together. In a physical sense - 2 Cor.7:3; to live a life in spiritual fellowship with the risen Lord - Rom.6:8; 2 Tim.2:11.

αὐτῷ (instru.sing.masc.of αὐτός, association) 16.

*Translation - "Now since we died with Christ we believe that we shall also live with Him."*

**Comment:** Paul has said repeatedly that the believer died with Christ (verses 2,3,4,5,6,7). εἰ therefore assumes as true the condition in the protasis and thus we translate "Since" not "If", as though the issue were still in doubt. The conclusion in the apodosis follows. The child of God who understands federal headship theology knows where, when and in Whom he died to pay his sin debt. Since we were "in Christ" when He died and also "in Him" when they buried Him in Joseph's tomb, we were still "In Him" when He arose from the tomb. We share then in all of His resurrection victory. The full benefit of this victory has not yet been realized by the members of His body. The tense in the indirect discourse in the ὅτι clause is future - the same tense as in the direct. What was said in direct discourse? "We shall live with Him!" This points us forward to the rapture and the resurrection "at the last trump" (1 Cor.15:52). In the meantime however we have available to us "the power of His resurrection" (Phil.3:10), as we walk in the light "as He is in the light" (1 John 1:7) and perform "the good works which He hath before ordained that we should walk in them" (Eph.2:10). This Christian walk yields "fellowship one with another" and the constant cleansing by the blood of Jesus Christ from all sin. But it also involves "the fellowship of His suffering" (Phil.3:10; John 16:33) and conformity to His death. To walk with Him always is to die with Him daily (1 Cor.15:31). That is precisely what the Christian wants because "he that is dead is freed from sin" (Rom.6:7). That is why Paul later tells us to "reckon (ourselves) to be dead indeed unto sin, but alive unto God through Jesus Christ our Lord" (Rom.6:11).

As we go on living in association with Him Who is alive, we enjoy His victory over sin and death. The point becomes stronger in verse 9. We shall indeed live with Christ, since we died with Him. But for how long?

*Verse 9 - "Knowing that Christ being raised from the dead dieth no more; death hath no more dominion over him."*

εἰδότες ὅτι Χριστὸς ἐγερθεὶς ἐκ νεκρῶν οὐκέτι ἀποθνῄσκει, θάνατος αὐτοῦ οὐκέτι κυριεύει.

*"For we know that Christ being raised from the dead will never die again; death no longer has dominion over him."   RSV*

εἰδότες (2d.perf.part.nom.pl.masc.of οἶδα, adverbial, causal) 144b.
ὅτι (conjunction introducing an object clause in indirect discourse) 211.
Χριστὸς (nom.sing.masc.of Χριστός, subject of ἀποθνῄσκει) 4.
ἐγερθεὶς (aor.pass.part.nom.sing.masc.of ἐγείρω, adverbial, causal) 125.
ἐκ (preposition with the ablative of separation) 19.
νεκρῶν (abl.pl.masc.of νεκρός, separation) 749.
οὐκέτι (temporal adverb) 1289.
ἀποθνῄσκει (3d.per.sing.pres.act.ind.of ἀποθνῄσκω, futuristic) 774.
θάνατος (nom.sing.masc.of θάνατος, subject of κυριεύει) 381.
αὐτοῦ (gen.sing.masc.of αὐτός, objective genitive) 16.
οὐκέτι (temporal adverb) 1289.
κυειεύει (3d.per.sing.pres.act.ind.of κυριεύω, progressive present, retroactive) 2776.

*Translation - "Because we know that Christ, having been raised from the dead, will never again be subject to its dominion."*

**Comment:** The 2d.perfect participle εἰδότες is causal. It speaks of current knowledge possessed on the basis of past completed realization. In the past we learned that Jesus Christ arose from the dead and thus we know it now. That is why we know what Paul told us in verse 8. What do we know? The indirect discourse tells us. Christ, once resurrected from the dead will never die again. Death which held Him in its grisly grasp for thirty-six hours has forever lost its hold over Him. Even during this period, while Jesus was in the heart of the earth, in Paradise (Eph.4:9; Luke 23:43), assembling the multitude of Old Testament saints whose debt He had just paid on the cross, preparatory to taking them with Him to the Paradise at the right hand of God (2 Cor.12:1-4), death held His body only by His sovereign permission. Let no man say that physical death dominated a helpless Jesus (John 10:17,18). Paul's use of κυριεύει here is an accommodated usage. Death dominated Him because He chose to permit it to do so. In His death "He destroyed him that has the power of death, that is the devil" (Heb.2:14). When Jesus said Τετέλεσται (John 19:30) He had bruised the head of the serpent (Gen.3:15). The redemption covenant was fulfilled and in place and Satan was henceforth powerless to prevent its implementation. One little matter needed yet to be attended to. What was Jesus going to do about this pesky trifle known as physical death? It is such a gruesome, aggravating, malodorous and noxious nuisance. It had been Satan's weapon by which he maintained control over his hellish kingdom of wrath and tears. Now that he had lost control over the destinies of those for whom the Son of God died, our Lord might as well dispose of it. Thus "the last enemy that shall be destroyed is death" (1 Cor.15:26). The "grim reaper" is nothing but an unfortunate and ineffectual clown for those who know what Jesus did to him.

Our Lord's victory over death is gloriously conclusive. There will be no successful counterattack. Screwtape and the other little demons, along with their deluded Gnostic dupes, may as well forget it.

*Verse 10 - "For in that he died, he died unto sin once: but in that he liveth, he liveth unto God."*

ὃ γὰρ ἀπέθανεν, τῇ ἁμαρτίᾳ ἀπέθανεν ἐφάπαξ, ὃ δὲ ζῇ, ζῇ τῷ θεῷ.

*"The death he died he died to sin, once for all, but the life he lives he lives to God."*     RSV

ὃ (acc.sing.neut.of ὅς, relative pronoun, cognate accusative) 65.
γὰρ (causal conjunction) 105.
ἀπέθανεν (3d.per.sing.aor.act.ind.of ἀποθνῄσκω, constative) 774.
τῇ (dat.sing.fem.of the article in agreement with ἁμαρτίᾳ) 9.
ἁμαρτίᾳ (dat.sing.fem.of ἁμαρτία, reference) 111.
ἀπέθανεν (3d.per.sing.aor.act.ind.of ἀποθνῄσκω, culminative) 774.

#3913 ἐφάπαξ (temporal adverb).

King James Version

at once - 1 Cor.15:6.
once - Rom.6:10; Heb.7:27; 9:12.
once for all - Heb.10:10.

Revised Standard Version

once for all - Rom.6:10; Heb.7:27; 9:12; 10:10.
at one time - 1 Cor.15:6.

*Meaning:* A combination of ἐπί (#47), an intensive prefix and ἅπαξ (#4383). Hence, once, once for all, only one time ever. With reference to Christ's death - Rom.6:10; Heb.7:27; 9:12; 10:10. All at one time, with reference to the witnesses of Christ's resurrection - 1 Cor.15:6.

ὃ (acc.sing.neut.of ὅς, relative pronoun, cognate accusative) 65.
δὲ (adversative conjunction) 11.
ζῇ (3d.per.sing.pres.act.ind.of ζάω, present progressive retroactive) 340.
ζῇ (3d.per.sing.pres.act.ind.of ζάω, present progressive retroactive) 340.
τῷ (instru.sing.masc.of the article in agreement with θεῷ) 9.
θεῷ (instru.sing.masc.of θεός, association) 124.

*Translation - "Because when He died, He died with reference to sin, once for all, but now that He has been alive, He will live forever in association with God."*

**Comment:** Although the relative pronouns can be looked upon as adverbial, they are cognate accusatives, since "in reality (they reproduce) the idea of the verb." (Robertson, *Grammar*, 715) - "the death which He died . . .but the life which He lives . . . κ.τ.λ."

The same is true of δ ζῶ in Gal.2:20.

Note the distinction between the constative and the culminative aorists in ἀπέθανεν. In the first clause we are contemplating the action in its entirety, while in the second, although we still view the action in its entirety we "regard it from the viewpoint of its existing results." (Mantey, *Manual*, 196). The culminative idea is supported by ἐφάπαξ. His death was in reference to the problem which sin caused in the counsels of the court of heaven. In His death He paid the wages of sin (Rom.4:25; 6:23) and cleared the way for His own judicial ruling that sin could be forgiven and righteousness imputed to the believer without compromise to the standards of holiness. His death robbed sin of its slaves and removed the sting from death, by which Satan had previously enforced his edicts in his kingdom of darkness. This is why Christ needed to die only once. *Cf.* Heb.7:27; 9:12; 10:10. Unlike Aaron, who brought an animal (as a type of Christ - John 1:29; 1 Cor.5:7) every day, Christ died only once (Heb.7:27). Satan's tool by which he ruled his kingdom was death. Once death has been suffered and conquered, sin has no further tool to use against the elect. Death is sin's ultimate weapon. Defuse it and sin has lost its dominance. Jesus' life before the cross was lived in reference to and in contemplation of His encounter with sin. Everything He did and said pointed forward to this encounter. Note His repeated reference to His "hour." (*Cf.*#735). Until that hour came He lived in reference to what He was going to do about sin. Once that was done and Jesus was alive again, He resumed the eternal life in association with His Father. This is the same eternal relationship which He enjoyed with the Father and the Holy Spirit before the foundation of the world (John 1:1).

The argument of the rest of the chapter is that the believer whose happy position in Christ has just been described, and whose standing as a child of God and a vital member of the body of Christ can never be in jeopardy, should use this knowledge to help him to resist the inroads of sin in his personal life. Once the Christian learns his soteriology and reflects upon it daily he has a psychological weapon against antinomianism. This is not to say that Calvinists are less sinful than Arminians, whose view of the atonement provides less assurance of salvation. Many Arminians live lives more in harmony with the will of God than do Calvinists. The victorious life is a function of momentary submission to the Holy Spirit Who lives within the body of the saint, not a function of what the child of God may have in his head about soteriology.

However the assurance of salvation (the P in the TULIP) provides the psychic support for the Christian who has fallen by the wayside temporarily and who then has the courage to make a comeback. If sin in the life of the Christian negates all that Christ had previously done for him and puts him back where he was before he repented the first time, it would seem that there would be little courage left to try again. What assurance would he have that he could succed the next time, in view of repeated failures in the past?

Paul now tells the Roman Christians, and us that the way to live the victorious life is to accept the doctrine of justification as he has laid it down in Romans 3:21-6:10, and to regard it as the truth.

*Verse 11 - "Likewise reckon ye also yourselves to be dead indeed unto sin, but alive unto God through Jesus Christ our Lord."*

οὕτως καὶ ὑμεῖς λογίζεσθε ἑαυτοὺς (εἶναι) νεκροὺς μὲν τῇ ἁμαρτίᾳ ζῶντας δὲ τῷ θεῷ ἐν Χριστῷ Ἰησοῦ.

*"So you also must consider yourselves dead to sin and alive to God in Christ Jesus." RSV*

οὕτως (demonstrative adverb) 74.
καὶ (adjunctive conjunction) 14.
ὑμεῖς (nom.pl.masc.of σύ, subject of λογίζεσθε) 104.
λογίζεσθε (2d.per.pl.pres.mid.impv.of λογίζομαι, command) 2611.
ἑαυτοὺς (acc.pl.masc.of ἑαυτοῦ, general reference) 288.
(εἶναι) (pres.inf.of εἰμί, indirect discourse) 86.
νεκροὺς (acc.pl.masc.of νεκρός, predicate adjective, in agreement with ἑαυτοὺς) 749.
μὲν (particle of affirmation) 300.
τῇ (dat.sing.fem.of the article in agreement with ἁμαρτίᾳ) 9.
ἁμαρτίᾳ (dat.sing.fem.of ἁμαρτία, reference) 111.
ζῶντας (pres.act.part.acc.pl.masc.of ζάω, adjectival in the predicate) 340.
δὲ (adversative conjunction) 11.
τῷ (instru.sing.masc.of the article in agreement with θεῷ) 9.
θεῷ (instru.sing.masc.of θεός, association) 124.
ἐν (preposition with the locative, mystical place where) 80.
Χριστῷ (loc.sing.masc.of Χριστός, mystical place where) 4.
Ἰησοῦ (loc.sing.masc.of Ἰησοῦς, apposition) 3.

*Translation - "So also you must consider yourselves to be really dead with reference to sin but alive in association with God in Christ Jesus."*

**Comment:** οὕτως καὶ - "In the same way also. . . ." That is, apply to yourself the same truth that you have just applied to Jesus Christ in verse 10, because you are "in Him" - ἐν Χριστῷ Ἰησοῦ. "The classic discussion of the matter is, of course, Deissmann's *Die Neutestamentliche Formel "in Christo Jesu"* (1892) in which by careful study of the LXX and the N.T. he shows the depth and originality of Paul's idea in the use of ἐν Χριστῷ" (Robertson, *Grammar*, 588). This mystic indwelling was our Lord's own idea as expressed in His highly priestly prayer (John 17:21) and was adopted by Paul.

Since we are identified with Christ by the baptism of the Holy Spirit (1 Cor.12:13; Gal.3:27; Rom.6:3,4) whatever is true of Him (verse 10) is true of us (verse 11), at least as matters relate to sin and salvation, life and death and our association with the Father. We need only to register this fact in our mental accounting procedure. *Cf.* #2611 for the instances where God imputes Christ's righteousness to the account of the believer. Now, let that believer think about it and do some accounting of his own. This means to make note of, accept, agree with and utilize by acting upon the fact that in God's estimate, you are forever finished with sin. Note the infinitive in indirect discourse - Dead with reference to sin, but alive in association with God, since you are in Christ Jesus and hence involved in the intimate relationship for which He prayed in John 17:21. It is when we forget this glorious fact that we fall victim to the Adamic human nature (Gal.5:17-21) that lurks inside to embarrass us. No Christian ever knowingly committed sin while he was reflecting upon the fact that God the Father, Jesus Christ, the Saviour and Lord and the Holy Spirit (1 Cor.6:19,20), the indwelling Guide and Comforter would also be involved in his sin. Victory over the temptations of the flesh is always available to the twice-born child of God while we await the Second Coming of our Lord and the glorification which will transfigure "our vile bodies and fashion them like unto His body of glory" (Phil.3:21). After that there will be no further victory over the flesh since there will be no battle with the flesh. When we speak of sinless perfection in its most complete sense, we are speaking of our life with Christ after the resurrection. Before that day the victorious life is available and possible, but no Christian achieves it to the fullest possible extent. Those who say that they have deceive themselves (1 John 1:8).

*Verse 12 - "Let not sin therefore reign in your mortal body, that ye should obey it in the lusts thereof."*

Μὴ οὖν βασιλευέτω ἡ ἁμαρτία ἐν τῷ θνητῷ ὑμῶν σώματι εἰς τὸ ὑπακούειν ταῖς ἐπιθυμίαις αὐτοῦ,

*"Let not sin therefore reign in your mortal bodies, to make you obey their passions." . . . RSV*

Μή (negative conjunction with the imperative) 87.

οὖν (inferential conjunction) 68.

βασιλευέτω (3d.per.sing.pres.impv.of βασιλεύω, prohibition) 236.

ἡ (nom.sing.fem.of the article in agreement with ἁμαρτία) 9.

ἁμαρτία (nom.sing.fem.of ἁμαρτία, subject of βασιλευέτω) 111.

ἐν (preposition with the locative of place where) 80.

τῷ (loc.sing.neut.of the article in agreement with σώματι) 9.

#3914 θνητῷ (loc.sing.neut.of θνητός, in agreement with σώματι).

King James Version

mortal - Rom.6:12; 8:11; 1 Cor.15:53,54; 2 Cor.4:11.
mortality - 2 Cor.5:4.

Revised Standard Version

mortal - Rom.6:12; 8:11; 1 Cor.15:54; 2 Cor.4:11.
mortal nature - 1 Cor.15:53.
what is mortal - 2 Cor.5:4.

*Meaning:* Cf. θνήσκω (#232). Hence, liable to death; mortal. With reference to the body of the believer prior to the first resurrection - Rom.6:12; 8:11; 1 Cor.15:53,54; 2 Cor.4:11; 5:4.

ὑμῶν (gen.pl.masc.of σύ, possession) 104.

σώματι (loc.sing.neut.of σῶμα, place where) 507.

εἰς (preposition with the accusative, articular infinitive,  sub-final) 140.

τὸ (acc.sing.neut.of the article, purpose) 9.

ὑπακούειν (pres.act.inf.of ὑπακούω, accusative of  purpose and result) 760.

ταῖς (loc.pl.fem.of the article in agreement with ἐπιθυμίαις) 9.

ἐπιθυμίαις (loc.pl.fem.of ἐπιθυμία, sphere) 2186.

αὐτοῦ (gen.sing.neut.of αὐτός, description) 16.

*Translation - "Therefore sin must not have its way in your mortal body in order (and with the result) that you obey its intense passions."*

**Comment:** Since we are ordered to consider ourselves to be as dead to sin and as alive in God's personal presence as the resurrected Christ Himself, it follows that sin should not continue to dominate our bodies, even though they are still mortal and liable to sin, disease and physical death. That the inclination to sin is still present in the Christian is apparent from the language of this prohibition. Note especially ἐπιθυμίαις (#2186) with its basic meaning. If some visitation of the Holy Spirit, subsequent to regeneration, by which the Christian is made impervious to temptation and incapable of committing sin is possible, then the language of this verse is without point. But this is not to say that there is nothing in Scripture about the victorious life in Christ.

The prohibition continues in verse 13 as Paul introduces the economic concept of opportunity cost.

*Verse 13 - "Neither yield ye your members as instruments of unrighteousness unto sin: but yield yourselves unto God, as those that are alive from the dead, and your members as instruments of righteousness unto God."*

μηδὲ παριστάνετε τὰ μέλη ὑμῶν ὅπλα ἀδικίας τῇ ἁμαρτίᾳ, ἀλλὰ παραστήσατε ἑαυτοὺς τῷ θεῷ ὡσεὶ ἐκ νεκρῶν ζῶντας καὶ τὰ μέλη ὑμῶν ὅπλα δικαιοσύνης τῷ θεῷ.

*"Do not yield your members to sin as instruments of wickedness, but yield yourselves to God as men who have been brought from death to life, and your members to God as instruments of righteousness."    RSV*

μηδὲ (negative continuative particle) 612.

#3915 παριστάνετε (2d.per.pl.pres.act.impv.of παριστάνω, prohibition).

King James Version

yield - Rom.6:13,13,16,19,19.

Revised Standard Version

yield - Rom.6:13,13,16,19,19.

*Meaning: Cf.* παρίστημι (#1596). To stand alongside; to make available. To employ the human body in sinful practices - Rom.6:13,13,16,19,19.

τὰ (acc.pl.neut.of the article in agreement with μέλη) 9.

μέλη (acc.pl.neut.of μέλος, direct object of παριστάνετε) 506.

ὑμῶν (gen.pl.masc.of σύ, possession) 104.

ὅπλα (nom.pl.neut.of ὅπλον, predicate nominative) 2804.

ἀδικίας (gen.sing.fem.of ἀδικία, description) 2367.

τῇ (loc.sing.fem.of the article in agreement with ἁμαρτίᾳ) 9.

ἁμαρτίᾳ (loc.sing.fem.of ἁμαρτία, sphere) 111.

ἀλλὰ (alternative conjunction) 342.

παραστήσατε (2d.per.pl.aor.act.impv.of παριστάνω, command) 3915.

ἑαυτοὺς (acc.pl.masc.of ἑαυτοῦ, direct object of παραστήσατε) 288.

τῷ (dat.sing.masc.of the article in agreement with θεῷ) 9.

θεῷ (dat.sing.masc.of θεός, indirect object of παραστήσατε) 124.

ὡσεὶ (comparative particle) 325.

ἐκ (preposition with the ablative of separation) 19.

νεκρῶν (abl.pl.masc.of νεκρός, separation) 749.

ζῶντας (pres.act.part.acc.pl.masc.of ζάω, substantival, predicate accusative) 340.

καὶ (adjunctive conjunction joining substantives) 14.

τὰ (acc.pl.neut.of the article in agreement with μέλη) 9.

μέλη (acc.pl.neut.of μέλος, direct object of παραστήσατε) 506.

ὑμῶν (gen.pl.masc.of σύ, possession) 104.

ὅπλα (acc.pl.neut.of ὅπλον, predicate accusative) 2804.

δικαιοσύνης (gen.sing.fem.of δικαιοσύνη, description) 322.

τῷ (dat.sing.masc.of the article in agreement with θεῷ) 9.

θεῷ (dat.sing.masc.of θεός, indirect object of παραστήσατε) 124.

*Translation - "And stop making your members available as tools of unrighteousness for sin; rather offer yourselves to God as alive from the dead and your members as instruments of righteousness to Him."*

**Comment:** The μὴ . . . μηδὲ disjunctive sequence connects a passive submission to sin (verse 12) with an active participation in it (verse 13). *Cf.#3915.* We are not to submit meekly to the demands of the flesh (verse 12), nor are we to actively cooperate with it. The verb indicates an act of making something available. This suggests that a Christian might actively promote a situation that would result in sinful behavior. Nothing that belongs to the believer, be it physical, mental, financial or technical should be made available as a tool for ungodliness. We are not to help implement Satan's program.

On the contrary (alternative ἀλλὰ) all of our resources are to be made available to God for the purpose (and with the result) of allowing God to use our talents as tools of righteouness. This is because we are alive from the dead.

There is a war in progress. Satan with his program of lawlessness is arrayed against God and righteousness. The Christian should never forget which side he is on.

The economic concept of opportunity cost will help us to grasp Paul's point.

Economics is the science of scarcity. Resources of production upon which the supply schedule depends are limited, while we face an indefinite expansibility of human wants for goods and services. There is never enough resources to supply the demand. Hence cost is involved in production and this production cost must be covered by price or there will be no production. Thus there are few "free goods" available. A "free good" is one which is so abundant relative to the demand for it that it can be provided without price because no cost is involved in its production. Sand in the Sahara Desert is a free good and water in the middle of the Pacific Ocean is also free, not to mention ice and snow at the South Pole. But in the struggle for survival "there is no such thing as a free lunch." Salvation from sin is free to the believer, but it cost the Son of God His life on a cross.

The Christian has limited resources. He has only two hands and two feet, one mind, one voice, one quantity of skills, a limited amount of money and physical strength, and the same amount of time as all others, *viz.* twenty-four hours in the day. He will probably live to reach the age of 70 years or, by the grace of God, a little more. He cannot be in two different places at the same time and he can only perform one function at a time. These obvious facts introduce us to the concept of opportunity cost. If I play golf for two hours the financial cost will be in terms of the green fee and the golf balls that I may lose. But what is the opportunity cost? It will cost me the benefit of what I could have done during those two hours if I had not chosen to play golf. The sixty seconds required to read this page could have been spent by the reader in sleeping or gardening or in reading some other page. Since we can only do one thing at a time, if we choose to perform task A we do so at the cost of foregoing task B.

The Christian has only one body with its various members and only one life to live. If he employs himself in the sphere of sin he has lost the opportunity to employ himself during the same time period in the sphere of righteousness. It was Abraham Lincoln who counselled that we should not waste time since "time is the stuff from which life is made." Thus everything we do for Satan robs God of the service which we could have performed for Him, and conversely when we are serving God we cannot serve Satan at the same time and with the same resources.

> "Only one life, 'twill soon be past.
> Only what's done for Christ will last."

The child of God must decide how this battle between God and the devil is going to end. Who will be vanquished and who will prevail? Which of the two systems that are locked in mortal combat is viable? He is told to decide these questions on the basis of the fact that in Christ he is alive from the dead. This being the case, he is on God's side and he will reap the rewards of God's victory when the battle is over. These rewards will be available to him throughout eternity, for he is a part of a society where there is no death.

It should not be difficult for a Christian, armed with these assurances, to see which side he is on. And he should be able to reduce his opportunity costs to a minimum. That is the way to maximize utility.

Any Christian who remembers the period of his slavery to sin and Satan, who pays off his slaves only with death, physical and spiritual, in a place called hell, where the devil, far from being the king is hell's chief victim, and who also appreciates his present position in Christ and the certainty of life everlasting in a society characterized by perfect righteousness, with all of the ripple effects in the social sciences working to make Heaven the Holy City, must see the folly of giving any further aid and comfort to the enemy. Why should any Christian serve the devil? What has he ever done for us? Nothing! But let us not forget what he tried to do to us!

The victorious life is a function of keeping "eternity's values in view" thus to minimize to the vanishing point, if it were possible, the opportunity cost.

*Verse 14 - "For sin shall not have dominion over you: for ye are not under the law, but under grace."*

ἁμαρτία γὰρ ὑμῶν οὐ κυριεύσει, οὐ γάρ ἐστε ὑπὸ νόμον ἀλλὰ ὑπὸ χάριν.

*"For sin will have no dominion over you, since you are not under law but under grace."* . . . RSV

ἁμαρτία (nom.sing.fem.of ἁμαρτία, subject of κυριεύσει) 111.
γὰρ (inferential conjunction) 105.
ὑμῶν (gen.pl.masc.of σύ, objective genitive) 104.
οὐ (negative conjunction with the indicative) 130.
κυριεύσει (3d.per.sing.fut.act.ind.of κυριεύω, predictive) 2776.
οὐ (negative conjunction with the indicative) 130.
γάρ (causal conjunction) 105.
ἐστε (2d.per.pl.pres.ind.of εἰμί, aoristic) 86.
ὑπὸ (preposition with the accusative, with ἐστε) 117.
νόμον (acc.sing.masc.of νόμος, with ἐστε) 464.
ἀλλὰ (alternative conjunction) 342.
ὑπὸ (preposition with the accusative, with ἐστε) 117.
χάριν (acc.sing.fem.of χάρις, with ἐστε) 1700.

*Translation - "Thus sin shall not dominate you, because you are not under law, but under grace."*

**Comment:** The result of the Christian compliance with the rule of verse 13 is that sin will dictate neither the scenario of his life nor determine his destiny. The grace relationship with God calls the resources of heaven to his aid. "Though he fall, he shall not be utterly cast down: for the Lord upholdeth him with his hand" (Psalm 37:24). Grace means sonship with God and heirship with Jesus Christ (John 1:12; Rom.8:16,17). Our Lord has an investment in us and we may be sure that He will move to protect it. Greater love for us could no man demonstrate than His love which drove Him to a cross (John 15:13), and "Whom the Lord loveth He chasteneth and scourgeth every son whom He receiveth" (Heb.12:6). He is determined to bring us to glory, though the path be strewn with many experiences of chastening. These only prove that He loves us, and that we are His by right of purchase (Acts 20:28) and also by right of conquest (Heb.2:14,15).

The mention of grace in verse 14 brings to Paul's mind again the philosophy of the antinomians, the subject to which he addresses himself again in

*

## Slaves of Righteousness

*(Romans 6:15-23)*

*Verse 15 - "What then? Shall we sin because we are not under law, but under grace? God forbid."*

Τί οὖν; ἁμαρτήσωμεν ὅτι οὐκ ἐσμὲν ὑπὸ νόμον ἀλλὰ ὑπὸ χάριν; μὴ γένοιτο.

*"What then? Are we to sin because we are not under law but under grace? By no means!" . . . RSV*

Τί (nom.sing.neut.of τίς, interrogative pronoun, subject of verb understood) 281.

οὖν (inferential) 68.

ἁμαρτήσωμεν (1st.per.pl.aor.act.subj.of ἁμαρτάνω, deliberative) 1260.

ὅτι (conjunction introducing a causal clause) 211.

οὐκ (negative conjunction with the indicative) 130.

ἐσμὲν (1st.per.pl.pres.ind.of εἰμί, aoristic) 86.

ὑπὸ (preposition with the accusative, with ἐσμὲν) 117.

νόμον (acc.sing.masc.of νόμος, with ἐσμὲν) 464.

ἀλλὰ (alternative conjunction) 342.

ὑπὸ (preposition with the accusative, with ἐσμὲν) 117.

χάριν (acc.sing.fem.of χάρις, with ἐσμὲν) 1700.

μὴ (negative conjunction with the optative) 87.

γένοιτο (3d.per.sing.aor.opt.of γίνομαι, voluntative) 113.

*Translation - "What then? Shall we commit sin because we are not under law, but under grace? Certainly not!"*

**Comment:** Unbelievers reject Jesus Christ for a variety of surface reasons, although the basic reason is that they are brainwashed by the devil (Eph.2:1-3; 2 Cor.4:4; 1 John 5:19b). Many reason that they do not need Jesus Christ since they are capable of earning heaven by their own good works. Heaven is obligated to reward righteousness wherever it can be found. If it were true that those who are "dead in trespasses and sins" (Eph.2:1) could perform deeds of righteousness, justice demands that they be rewarded. However the only resource of the unregenerate is the flesh, for he has had only one birth and the result is that "the flesh profiteth nothing" (John 6:63). But the same justice that must reward the good must condemn the evil. Thus if a man kept the entire law of God and yet offended in only one part, the decision of heaven must be that he is guilty of all (James 2:10). This is why sin can have no dominion over us who are under grace. If we were under law, with the perfect record of obedience, but for one isolated transgression, that one sin would have dictated our unhappy destiny.

But we are not under law. Our relationship with God is grace, and grace means the gift of Christ's own righteousness imputed to us and credited to our account. Grace means sonship with God and joint heirship with Jesus Christ. Grace means that even though, in fact we have transgressed all of God's law, yet we are not cast out, since those transgressions were pardoned on the righteous basis of His redemption. And grace means that God has made Himself responsbile for us. He provides whatever we need to bring us safely to our heavenly destiny. This often means chastening, the evidence of the Father's love and watchcare over us.

In his previous attack upon the antinomians Paul used the present subjunctive ἐπιμένωμεν - Rom.6:1 - "shall we continue sinning?" Now he asks, "Shall we sin even once?" (aorist subjunctive in ἁμαρτήσωμεν). Some might agree that a life characterized only by repeated sinning is out of harmony with the life of grace, but that, since our debt is paid and we, as objects of grace are not under the law, an occasional sin could do no harm! But Paul reacts to this as emphatically as he did before - μὴ γένοιτο (*Cf.* Rom.6:1). Why? What is the principle behind this?

*Verse 16 - "Know ye not that to whom ye yield yourselves servants to obey, his servants ye are to whom ye obey; whether of sin unto death, or of obedience unto righteousness."*

οὐκ οἴδατε ὅτι ᾧ παριστάνετε ἑαυτοὺς δούλους εἰς ὑπακοήν, δοῦλοί ἐστε ᾧ ὑπακούετε, ἤτοι ἁμαρτίας εἰς θάνατον ἢ ὑπακοῆς εἰς δικαιοσύνην;

*"Do you not know that if you yield yourselves to any one as obedient slaves, you are slaves of the one whom you obey, either of sin, which leads to death, or of obedience, which leads to righteousness?"    RSV*

οὐκ (negative conjunction with the indicative, in rhetorical question, expecting an affirmative reply) 130.

οἴδατε (2d.per.pl.perf.ind.of οἶδα, intensive) 144b.

ὅτι (conjunction introducing an object clause in indirect discourse) 211.

ᾧ (dat.sing.masc.of ὅς, relative pronoun, indirect object of παριστάνετε) 65.

παριστάνετε (2d.per.pl.pres.act.ind.of παριστάνω, aoristic) 3915.

ἑαυτοὺς (acc.pl.masc.of ἑαυτοῦ, direct object of παριστάνετε) 288.

δούλους (acc.pl.masc.of δοῦλος, predicate accusative) 725.

εἰς (preposition with the accusative, purpose) 140.

ὑπακοήν (acc.sing.fem.of ὑπακοή, purpose) 3785.

δοῦλοί (nom.pl.masc.of δοῦλος, predicate nominative) 725.

ἐστε (2d.per.pl.pres.ind.of εἰμί, aoristic) 86.

ᾧ (dat.sing.masc.of ὅς, relative pronoun, possession) 65.

ὑπακούετε (2d.per.pl.pres.act.ind.of ὑπακούω, aoristic) 760.

#3916 ἤτοι (correlative particle).

King James Version

whether - Rom.6:16.

Revised Standard Version

either - Rom.6:16.

*Meaning:* In the sequence ἤτοι . . . ἤ - "either indeed . . . or" - Rom.6:16.

ἁμαρτίας (gen.sing.fem.of ἁμαρτία, description) 111.
εἰς (preposition with the predicate accusative) 140.
θάνατον (acc.sing.masc.of θάνατος, predicate accusative) 381.
ἤ (disjunctive particle) 465.
ὑπακοῆς (gen.sing.fem.of ὑπακοή, description) 3785.
εἰς (preposition with the predicate accusative) 140.
δικαιοσύνην (acc.sing.fem.of δικαιοσύνη, predicate accusative) 322.

*Translation - "You do know, do you not, that to whom you make yourselves available as slaves to obey, you are slaves of those whom you obey, whether it be of sin unto death or obedience unto righteousness?"*

**Comment:** Keep in mind that Paul distinguishes clearly between the sin that the Christian commits because he was dominated by it (verse 12) and the sin that he commits by deliberately putting himself at sin's disposal (verse 13). In verse 16 it is the deliberate sin that is in view. The transgressor is the initiator of this action. παριστάνετε is in the active voice. If one places himself alongside sin as a servant, for the express purpose of obeying sin's dictate, he has made himself the slave of sin. Submission to another by an act of one's own will, whether such submission results in transgression unto death or obedience unto righteousness makes the one who submits the servant of the one to whom he submits. Paul is speaking here of willful decision and action. In such a case we cast our lot either with the forces of sin or the forces of righteousness. The two principles are set here in juxtaposition - sin and death; obedience and righteousness. The antinomian has deliberately constructed a rationale which satisfies him by which he can sin either once (verse 15) or many times (verse 1) because grace forgives all and he can therefore "get away with it." Thus he indicates that he would rather sin than obey God. Thus he congratulates himself that he has stolen a march on God, which strongly suggests that he thinks that he is more intelligent than God. This is the reasoning of the unregenerate man.

This decision to sin smugly and triumphantly with a presumption upon God's grace is wholly different from the sin of the tortured saint described in Romans 7:15-25, comment upon which *cf. en loc.* The psychology of the defeated Christian described by Paul in Romans 7:15-25 is not the psychology of the antinomian..

The heart and mind of the born again believer is favorably disposed toward the gospel of Christ, as we see in

*Verse 17 - "But God be thanked that ye were the servants of sin, but ye have obeyed from the heart that form of doctrine which was delivered you."*

χάρις δὲ τῷ θεῷ ὅτι ἦτε δοῦλοι τῆς ἁμαρτίας ὑπηκούσατε δὲ ἐκ καρδίας εἰς ὃν παρεδόθητε τύπον διδαχῆς,

*"But thanks be to God that you who were once slaves of sin have become*

*obedient from the heart to the standard of teaching to which you were committed." RSV*

χάρις (nom.sing.fem.of χάρις, suspended subject) 1700.
δὲ (adversative conjunction) 11.
τῷ (dat.sing.masc.of the article in agreement with θεῷ) 9.
θεῷ (dat.sing.masc.of θεός, indirect object of verb understood) 124.
ὅτι (conjunction introducing a causal clause) 211.
ἦτε (2d.per.pl.imp.ind.of εἰμί, progressive description) 86.
δοῦλοι (nom.pl.masc.of δοῦλος, predicate nominative) 725.
τῆς (gen.sing.fem.of the article in agreement with ἁμαρτίας) 9.
ἁμαρτίας (gen.sing.fem.of ἁμαρτία, description) 111.
ὑπηκούσατε (2d.per.pl.aor.act.ind.of ὑπακούω, constative) 760.
δὲ (adversative conjunction) 11.
ἐκ (preposition with the ablative, source) 19.
καρδίας (abl.sing.fem.of καρδία, source) 432.
εἰς (preposition with the accusative of extent) 140.
ὃν (acc.sing.masc.of ὅς, relative pronoun, extent) 65.
παρεδόθητε (2d.per.pl.aor.pass.ind.of παραδίδωμι, constative) 368.
τύπον (acc.sing.masc.of τύπος, direct object of ὑπηκούσατε) 2917.
διδαχῆς (gen.sing.fem.of διδαχή, description) 706.

*Translation - "But thanks be to God because, although you used to be slaves of sin, you have obeyed from the heart the system of doctrine to which you were introduced."*

**Comment:** Paul here tells the Roman christians that his attack upon the rationale of the antinomians did not apply to them. Theirs was a heart-based (ἐκ καρδίας) obedience to the gospel which they heard and to which they were committed. Paul is grateful to God because of this, although of course before they were saved they were slaves of sin. In other words they had had a supernatural change of heart. Before regeneration they had consistently served sin (imperfect tense in ἦτε). But (adversative δὲ) their regeneration experience changed all of that. They would still have a skirmish or two with the flesh (Rom.7:15-25) which, although scheduled for glorification at the Second Coming (Phil.3:20,21; 1 Thess.4:13-18; 1 Cor.15:51-58; 1 John 3:1-3), was still very much with them and seeking to seduce them into sin (Gal.5:17-21), but their heart would not be in it, because since the moment they were saved, their new nature was permanently on God's side.

But though they had been rescued from the slavery to sin, they had become servants of another despot. This is the thought of

*Verse 18 - "Being then made free from sin, ye became the servants of righteousness."*

ἐλευθερωθέντες δὲ ἀπὸ τῆς ἁμαρτίας ἐδουλώθητε τῇ δικαιοσύνῃ.

*". . . and, having been set free from sin, have become slaves of righteousness."*

*RSV*

ἐλευθερωθέντες (aor.pass.part.nom.pl.masc.of ἐλευθερόω, adverbial, temporal) 2385.
δὲ (continuative conjunction) 11.
ἀπὸ (preposition with the ablative of separation) 70.
τῆς (abl.sing.fem.of the article in agreement with ἁμαρτίας) 9.
ἁμαρτίας (abl.sing.fem.of ἁμαρτία, separation) 111.
ἐδουλώθητε (2d.per.pl.aor.pass.ind.of δουλόω, culminative) 3103.
τῇ (loc.sing.fem.of the article in agreement with δικαιοσύνῃ) 9.
δικαιοσύνῃ (loc.sing.fem.of δικαιοσύνη, sphere) 322.

*Translation - "And having been made free from sin, you are enslaved to righteousness."*

**Comment:** δὲ is continuative as Paul ties the two clauses (verses 17 and 18) together. The aorist passive participle ἐλευθερωθέντες indicates action which can be either antecedent to or simultaneous with the action of the main verb ἐδουλώθητε. The aorist participle is never proleptical. In this context the action is simultaneous. When a Christian is saved he trades his slavery to sin for slavery to righteousness. To be saved is to forever escape the bondage of sin and it wages, which is death, both physical and spiritual. And at the same moment of escape from sin we find ourselves faced with the compelling demands upon our wills to perform the righteous acts which God has before prepared "that we should walk in them." (Eph.2:10). *Cf.* verse 22 where these two verbs occur again. *Cf.* John 8:32,36; Gal.5:1; Rom.6:22; 8:2,21.

That δικαιοσύνη (#322) should be referred to as having placed one under bondage (ἐδουλώθητε) is only a human manner of speaking, as Paul points out in verses 19 and 20. Actually deliverance from sin results in the "glorious liberty of the children of God" (Rom.8:21). The child of God who has experienced His "glorious liberty" understands completely that it is not a liberty to do that which one does not wish to do. Liberty exists when one does what he wishes to do. The Spirit-filled Christian enjoys this glorious liberty. There is no comfort here for antinomianism.

Note who sets us free - the Truth (John 8:32); the Son (John 8:36). The Son is the Truth (John 14:6). Justification with its liberation from sin therefore is contingent upon a cognitive faith in the essential deity of the historic Jesus of Cross and Empty Tomb, Tillich, Boultmann *et al* with their salvation by "courageous ignorance" to the contrary notwithstanding. Saving faith is not faith in faith but faith in objective cognitive reality. If salvation is to be had by the process of submitting to brainwash, without reference to the subject matter in which one's brain has been laved, then everyone is saved for there is no one who does not have "faith" in something - the stars, Joseph Smith, Charles Russell, Quakers on the moon, boojums or the Reverend Mr.Moon.

*Verse 19 - "I speak after the manner of men because of the infirmity of your flesh: for as ye have yielded your members servants to uncleanness and to iniquity unto iniquity; even so now yield your members servants to righteousness unto holiness."*

ἀνθρώπινον λέγω διὰ τὴν ἀσθένειαν τῆς σαρκὸς ὑμῶν. ὥσπερ γὰρ παρεστήσατε τὰ μέλη ὑμῶν δοῦλα τῇ ἀκαθαρσίᾳ καὶ τῇ ἀνομίᾳ εἰς τὴν ἀνομίαν, οὕτως νῦν παρασθήσατε τὰ μέλη ὑμῶν δοῦλα τῇ δικαιοσύνῃ εἰς ἁγιασμόν.

*"I am speaking in human terms, because of your natural limitations. For just as you once yielded your members to impurity and to greater and greater iniquity, so now yield your members to righteousness for sanctification."* RSV

ἀνθρώπινον (acc.sing.neut.of ἀνθρώπινος, adverbial) 3415.

λέγω (1st.per.sing.pres.act.ind.of λέγω, aoristic) 66

διὰ (preposition with the accusative, cause) 118.

τὴν (acc.sing.fem.of the article in agreement with ἀσθένειαν) 9.

ἀσθένειαν (acc.sing.fem.of ἀσθένεια, cause) 740.

τῆς (gen.sing.fem.of the article in agreement with σαρκὸς) 9.

σαρκὸς (gen.sing.fem.of σάρξ, description) 1202.

ὑμῶν (gen.pl.masc.of σύ, possession) 104.

ὥσπερ (intensive comparative conjunction) 560.

γὰρ (causal conjunction) 105.

παρεστήσατε (2d.per.pl.aor.act.ind.of παριστάνω, constative) 3915.

τὰ (acc.pl.neut.of the article in agreeement with μέλη) 9.

μέλη (acc.pl.neut.of μέλος, direct object of παρεστήσατε) 506.

ὑμῶν (gen.pl.masc.of σύ, possession) 104.

δοῦλα (acc.pl.neut.of δοῦλος, predicate accusative) 725.

τῇ (loc.sing.fem.of the article in agreement with ἀκαθαρσίᾳ) 9.

ἀκαθαρσίᾳ (loc.sing.fem.of ἀκαθαρσία, sphere) 1467.

καὶ (adjunctive conjunction, joining nouns) 14.

τῇ (loc.sing.fem.of the article in agreement with ἀνομίᾳ) 9.

ἀνομίᾳ (loc.sing.fem.of ἀνομία, sphere) 692.

εἰς (preposition with the accusative of extent) 140.

ἀνομίαν (acc.sing.fem.of ἀνομία, extent) 692.

οὕτως (demonstrative adverb) 74.

νῦν (temporal adverb) 1497.

παραστήσατε (2d.per.pl.aor.act.impv.of παριστάνω, command) 3915.

τὰ (acc.pl.neut.of the article in agreement with μέλη) 9.

μέλη (acc.pl.neut.of μέλος, direct object of παραστήσατε) 506.

ὑμῶν (gen.pl.masc.of σύ, possession) 104.

δοῦλα (acc.pl.neut.of δοῦλος, predicate accusative) 725.

τῇ (loc.sing.fem.of the article in agreement with δικαιοσύνῃ) 9.

δικαιοσύνῃ (loc.sing.fem.of δικαιοσύνη, sphere) 322.

εἰς (preposition with the accusative, result) 140.

#3917 ἁγιασμόν (acc.sing.masc.of ἁγιασμός, result).

King James Version

holiness - Rom.6:19,22; 1 Thess.4:7; 1 Tim.2:15; Heb.12:14.

sanctification - 1 Cor.1:30; 1 Thess.4:3,4; 2 Thess.2;13; 1 Pet.1:2.

Revised Standard Version

sanctification - Rom.6:19,22; 1 Cor.1:30; 1 Thess.4:3; 2 Thess.2:13.
holiness - 1 Thess.4:7; 1 Tim.2:15; Heb.12:14; 1 Thess.4:4.
sanctified - 1 Pet.1:2.

*Meaning: Cf.* ἁγιάζω (#576), ἅγιος (#84), ἁγιωσύνη (#3784), ἁγιότης (#5068).
Hence, the result of allocating one's resources to a single function or purpose.
The behavior of one set apart for a single purpose. Absolutely in Rom.6:19,22; 1
Cor.1:30; in apposition - 1 Thess.4:3,4; followed by an ablative of agent - 2
Thess.2:13; 1 Pet.1:2. In opposition to ἀκαθαρσίᾳ in 1 Thess.4:7; joined with
ἀγάπη and σωφροσύνης in 1 Tim.2:15; prerequisite to a victorious life -
Heb.12:14.

*Translation - "I speak in human terms because of the weakness of your flesh.*
*Because just as you made your members available to uncleanness and*
*more and more lawlessness, even so now you must make your members available*
*as servants for the purpose of righteousness and the result - holiness."*

**Comment:** The analogy to slaves and slavish obedience to a master was familiar
to the Roman Christians. Once they had set themselves wholly at the disposal of
impurity and lawlessness for the purpose of serving its every dictate. Now that
they have been regenerated they are in a different realm and they are ordered to
devote themselves wholly to concentration (*cf.*#3917 for its complete meaning of
dedication to one task). Once they concentrated on sin; now they are to
concentrate on holiness.

Paul pursues the analogy even further in

*Verse 20 - "For when ye were the servants of sin, you were free from*
*righteousness."*

ὅτε γὰρ δοῦλοι ἦτε τῆς ἁμαρτίας, ἐλεύθεροι ἦτε τῇ δικαιοσύνῃ.

*"When you were slaves in sin, you were free in regard to righteousness."* RSV

ὅτε (particle introducing a contemporaneous temporal clause) 703.
γὰρ (causal conjunction) 105.
δοῦλοι (nom.pl.masc.of δοῦλος, predicate nominative) 725.
ἦτε (2d.per.pl.imp.ind.of εἰμί, progressive description) 86.
τῆς (gen.sing.fem.of the article in agreement with ἁμαρτίας) 9.
ἁμαρτίας (gen.sing.fem.of ἁμαρτία, description) 111.
ἐλεύθεροι (nom.pl.masc.of ἐλεύθερος, predicate adjective) 1245.
ἦτε (2d.per.pl.imp.ind.of εἰμί, progressive description) 86.
τῇ (loc.sing.fem.of the article in agreement with δικαιοσύνῃ) 9.
δικαιοσύνῃ (loc.sing.fem.of δικαιοσύνη, sphere) 322.

*Translation - "Because when you were slaves of sin you were free from*
*righteousness."*

Comment: The particle ὅτε, translated "when" or "at the time that" indicates simultaneous time to that of the main verb. In the former days of their unregeneracy they were slaves to sin. They gave slavish obedience to every evil impulse. That was also the time when they were totally unresponsive to the impulse to be righteous. They needed to do nothing righteous.. They were totally dedicated to sin and wholly free  from God's will. So now, though Paul does not say what he implies, being slaves to God's righteousness they should be totally impervious to the impulse to sin. The blatant unbeliever whose dedication to evil is cordial is never criticized for his moral life. He is not a hypocrite. He is committed to Satan and all of his works and he will devote all of his resources to the promotion of the ends which his master desires.

Why should he show the same devotion to the righteous implementation of the will of God, now that he has become God's child? It is a practical matter. Paul now asks for an assessment of the utility which they derived from their slavery to sin. When they were in thralldom to Satan he paid them for their services. In what coin and with what eternal result? This is the question of verse 21. In verse 22 Paul asks the same question with reference to their new life in Christ.

*Verse 21 - "What fruit had ye then in those things whereof ye are now ashamed? for the end of those things is death."*

τίνα οὖν καρπὸν εἴχετε τότε ἐφ' οἷς νῦν ἐπαισχύνεσθε; τὸ γὰρ τέλος ἐκείνων θάνατος.

*"But then what return did you get from the things of which you are now ashamed? The end of those things is death."    RSV*

τίνα (acc.sing.masc.of τίς, interrogative pronoun, in agreement with καρπὸν) 281.

οὖν (inferential conjunction) 68.

καρπὸν (acc.sing.masc.of καρπός, direct object of εἴχετε) 284.

εἴχετε (2d.per.pl.imp.act.ind.of ἔχω, progressive description) 82.

τότε (temporal conjunction) 166.

ἐφ' (preposition with the instrumental, cause) 47.

οἷς (instru.pl.masc.of ὅς, relative pronoun, causal) 65.

νῦν (temporal conjunction) 1497.

ἐπαισχύνεσθε (2d.per.pl.pres.mid.ind.of ἐπαισχύνομαι, static) 2318.

τὸ (nom.sing.neut.of the article in agreement with τέλος) 9.

γὰρ (causal conjunction) 105.

τέλος (nom.sing.neut.of τέλος, subject of ἐστιν understood) 881.

ἐκείνων (gen.pl.neut.of ἐκεῖνος, description) 246.

θάνατος (nom.sing.masc.of θάνατος, predicate nominative) 381.

*Translation - "What benefit then did you reap in those days because of those things of which you are now ashamed? Because the end of those things is death."*

Comment: οὖν is inferential, since τότε is also present to supply the temporal clause. Note the contrast between τότε and νῦν - "then" as opposed to "now."

This passage will make little sense to those who confuse social reform for spiritual regeneration. Those who succeed in qualifying for membership in the Boy Scouts, the Rotary Club or Alcoholics Anonymous are not necessarily ashamed of their former life style because there has been no fundamental change in their lives. There are also many who regard church membership only as a social obligation to society, since they regard the local church only as a social institution. Children whose lives before they joined the church were exemplary, but only because of parental control or because they were too young to have become notorious sinners will see little superficial and no basic difference in their outlook on life before and after the event.

But the Christian whose life style before his conversion was characterized by real slavery to the lusts of the flesh and who is now genuinely regenerated will understand the contrast. Before he was saved when he considered himself fortunate to be so gloriously (!) free from righteousness, what were his advantages? How well did sin reward him for his faithful service? What was in it for him? Then he looked upon sin as his Lord and he served it as a slave. Now he is ashamed of his former lord and master who paid him daily in terms of poverty, hangovers, disease, sleepless nights and social disgrace, and the final payment, had not the grace of God intervened would have been death. *Cf.* Phil.3:19; Heb.6:8; 1 Pet.1:9; 4:17; Mk.3:26; Rom.6:21,22; 2 Cor.3:13; 11:15 for τέλος in this same sense (#881). A check of these verses indicates that the claims of the gospel are very pragmatic in terms of end results. Faith and obedience to righteousness has a result. Unbelief and slavery to sin also has its result. What we have are the short and long-term analyses.

*Verse 22 - "But now being made free from sin, and become servants of God, ye have your fruit unto holiness, and the end everlasting life."*

νυνὶ δέ, ἐλευθερωθέντες ἀπὸ τῆς ἁμαρτίας δουλωθέντες δὲ τῷ θεῷ, ἔχετε τὸν καρπὸν ὑμῶν εἰς ἁγιασμόν, τὸ δὲ τέλος ζωὴν αἰώνιον.

*"But now that you have been set free from sin and have become slaves of God, the return you get is sanctification and its end, eternal life."*    RSV

νυνὶ (temporal adverb) 1497.

δὲ (adversative conjunction) 11.

ἐλευθερωθέντες (aor.pass.part.nom.pl.masc.of ἐλευθερόω, adverbial, temporal/causal) 2385.

ἀπὸ (preposition with the ablative of separation) 70.

τῆς (abl.sing.fem.of the article in agreement with ἁμαρτίας) 9.

ἁμαρτίας (abl.sing.fem.of ἁμαρτία, separation) 111.

δουλωθέντες (aor.pass.part.nom.pl.masc.of δουλόω, adverbial, temporal/causal) 3103.

δὲ (adjunctive conjunction joining participles) 11.

τῷ (loc.sing.masc.of the article in agreement with θεῷ) 9.

θεῷ (loc.sing.masc.of θεός, sphere) 124.

ἔχετε (2d.per.pl.pres.act.ind.of ἔχω, static) 82.

τὸν (acc.sing.masc.of the article in agreement with καρπὸν) 9.
καρπὸν (acc.sing.masc.of καρπός, direct object of ἔχετε) 284.
εἰς (preposition with the accusative, result) 140.
ἁγιασμόν (acc.sing.masc.of ἁγιασμός, result) 3917.
τὸ (acc.sing.neut.of the article in agreement with τέλος) 9.
δὲ (adjunctive conjunction joining nouns) 11.
τέλος (acc.sing.neut.of τέλος, direct object of ἔχετε) 881.
ζωὴν (acc.sing.fem.of ζωή, apposition) 668.
αἰώνιον (acc.sing.fem.of αἰώνιος, in agreement with ζωὴν) 1255.

*Translation - "But now, having been liberated from sin, and have been enslaved to God, you have your fruit which results in holiness and the end result - everlasting life."*

**Comment:** Paul's contrast is between the fruit of sin (verse 21) and the fruit of righteousness (verse 22). Enslaved to sin in former days, the slave could look forward only to death as the harvest. But now (νυνὶ δέ) - "But now" in contrast to then (τότε) the believer has found that grace has forged new chains which he is humbly proud to wear. His allegiance has been shifted from verse 20 to verse 22. Then he was free from righteousness and a slave to sin. Now he is enslaved to God and as a result serves righteousness. The harvest for the Christian is two fold: (1) concentration (consecration) upon a single positive ethic and (2) everlasting life. The unsaved sinner with his concentration upon sin impacts upon society with devastating effect. Thus we see the connection between the theological and the social gospel. The Christian with his concentration upon the good works which have been marked out for him (Eph.2:10) and thrilled in his personal life with the fruits of the Holy Spirit (Gal.5:22,23) is a positive blessing to society.

We need not think of Spinoza's block universe with its cause and effect relations in the pantheistic sense in which he conceived it, in order to recognize that cause and effect principles are foundational to the science of which our Lord is the Master Designer and Creator. Since in Christ "are hid all of the treasures of science and philosophy" (Col.2:3) it follows that sin can be defined as any transgression of any of His laws. The adulterer, the murderer and the thief has transgressed the moral law of the universe and perpetrated an affront to God, but he has also set loose in society the ripple effects of social, economic and political law. A sinless society in a perfect universe, governed by Christ's perfect scientific principles would thus be viable. That is why Paul says that obedience to the moral law of God through concentration on obedience to His will results in eternal life, conceived both in its qualitative and quantitative aspects. Everlasting existence in a society rent with the horrors that result from sin is hell. But everlasting existence in heaven's society with the blessings that result from obedience to God's moral laws is the eternal life which the Christian is destined to enjoy forever. Paul changes the figure. He has just spoken in terms of the fruits of sin or righteousness. Now he speaks of wages in contrast to a gift.

*Verse 23 - "For the wages of sin is death; but the gift of God is eternal life through Jesus Christ our Lord."*

τὰ γὰρ ὀφώνια τῆς ἁμαρτίας θάνατος, τὸ δὲ χάρισμα τοῦ θεοῦ ζωὴ αἰώνιος ἐν Χριστῷ Ἰησοῦ τῷ κυρίῳ ἡμῶν.

*"For the wages of sin is death, but the free gift of God is eternal life in Christ Jesus our Lord."* RSV

τὰ (nom.pl.neut.of the article in agreement with ὀφώνια) 9.
γὰρ (causal conjunction) 105.
ὀφώνια (nom.pl.neut.of ὀφώνιον, subject of ἐστιν understood) 1947.
τῆς (gen.sing.fem.of the article in agreement with ἁμαρτίας) 9.
ἁμαρτίας (gen.sing.fem.of ἁμαρτία, description) 111.
θάνατος (nom.sing.masc.of θάνατος, predicate nomintive) 381.
τὸ (nom.sing.neut.of the article in agreement with χάρισμα) 9.
δὲ (adversative conjunction) 11.
χάρισμα (nom.sing.neut.of χάρισμα, subject of ἐστιν understood) 3790.
τοῦ (gen.sing.masc.of the article in agreement with θεοῦ) 9.
θεοῦ (gen.sing.masc.of θεός, description) 124.
ζωὴ (nom.sing.fem.of ζωή, predicate nominative) 668.
αἰώνιος (nom.sing.fem.of αἰώνιος, in agreement with ζωή) 1255.
ἐν (preposition with the locative) 80.
Χριστῷ (loc.sing.masc.of Χριστός, mystic union) 4.
Ἰησοῦ (loc.sing.masc.of Ἰησοῦς, apposition) 3.
τῷ (loc.sing.masc.of the article in agreement with κυρίῳ) 9.
κυρίῳ (loc.sing.masc.of κύριος, apposition) 97.
ἡμῶν (gen.pl.masc.of ἐγώ, relationship) 123.

*Translation - "Because the reward that sin gives is death, but the gift from God is eternal life in Christ Jesus our Lord."*

**Comment:** Thus Paul sums up the argument. The antinomians should be thoroughly silenced. Their position reveals a clear lack of understanding of the dramatic difference between the spheres of sin and grace. Sin means slavery, servitude, impurity, iniquity, lawlessness, rebellion against God and all of His universal laws, and, in the end, it means death, both physical and spiritual. Grace means holiness, concentration in the positive affairs of God, righteousness and life. To accept the gift of God and continue to presume upon His grace to serve sin is preposterous. The presumption comes in committing sin as a result of a positive decision to do so. The antinomian decision is deliberate. He decides to commit sin and thus he makes himself available to the services of sin as a result of his reasoned argument that if he sins God's grace will cover the transgression. This is not to say that Christians with a full commitment to God and His grace do not at times yield to fleshly indulgence. But in these cases it is the flesh and not the mind and will. This will become clear in the seventh chapter.

# An Analogy from Marriage

*(Romans 7:1-6)*

*Romans 7:1* - *"Know ye not, brethren, (for I speak to them that know the law,) how that the law hath dominion over a man as long as he liveth?"*

Ἦ ἀγνοεῖτε ἀδελφοί, γινώσκουσιν γὰρ νόμον λαλῶ, ὅτι ὁ νόμος κυριεύει τοῦ ἀνθρώπου ἐφ᾽ ὅσον χρόνον ζῇ;

*"Do you not know, brethren — for I am speaking to those who know the law — that the law is binding on a person only during his life?"* RSV

Ἦ (disjunctive conjunction) 465.
ἀγνοεῖτε (2d.per.pl.pres.ind.of ἀγνοέω, direct question) 2345.
ἀδελφοί (voc.pl.masc.of ἀδελφός, address) 15.
γινώσκουσιν (pres.act.part.dat.pl.masc.of γινώσκω, substantival, indirect object of λαλῶ) 131.
γὰρ (causal conjunction) 105.
νόμον (acc.sing.masc.of νόμος, direct object of γινώσκουσιν) 464.
λαλῶ (1st.per.sing.pres.act.ind.of λαλέω, aoristic) 815.
ὅτι (conjunction introducing an object clause in indirect discourse) 211.
ὁ (nom.sing.masc.of the article in agreement with νόμος) 9.
νόμος (nom.sing.masc.of νόμος, subject of κυριεύει) 464.
κυριεύει (3d.per.sing.pres.act.ind.of κυριεύω, customary) 2776.
τοῦ (gen.sing.masc.of the article in agreement with ἀνθρώπου) 9.
ἀνθρώπου (gen.sing.masc.of ἄνθρωπος, objective genitive) 341.
ἐφ᾽ (preposition with the accusative of time extent) 47.
ὅσον (acc.sing.masc.of ὅσος, in agreement with χρόνον) 660.
χρόνον (acc.sing.masc.of χρόνος, time extent) 168.
ζῇ (2d.per.sing.pres.ind.of ζάω, in a relative indefinite temporal clause) 340.

*Translation* - *"Or do you not know, brethren (for I am speaking to those who know the law) that the law exercises authority over the man for such time as he lives under its jurisdiction?"*

**Comment:** The statement simply establishes the fact that law imposes the obligation of compliance, obedience and acceptance of regulation upon those who live within its jurisdiction. The emphasis is upon the verb ζῇ. The relative pronoun ὅσον with the preposition ἐφ᾽ before it expresses the temporal idea, but the time span is indefinite. It covers only the time when the man is alive. When he dies the law has no more jurisdiction over him. *Cf.*#660 for other instances of ἐπί with ὅσος and χρόνον in an indefinite temporal phrase.

It is rhetorical question. Of course, those to whom Paul directs his question, know the law enough to reply in the affirmative.

*Verse 2* - *"For the woman which hath an husband is bound by the law to her husband so long as he liveth; but if the husband be dead, she is loosed from the law of her husband."*

ἡ γὰρ ὕπανδρος γυνὴ τῷ ζῶντι ἀνδρὶ δέδεται νόμῳ. ἐὰν δὲ ἀποθάνῃ ὁ ἀνήρ, κατήργηται ἀπὸ τοῦ νόμου τοῦ ἀνδρός.

*"Thus a married woman is bound by law to her husband as long as he lives; but if her husband dies she is discharged from the law concerning her husband."* ...
RSV

ἡ (nom.sing.fem.of the article in agreement with γυνή) 9.
γὰρ (explanatory conjunction) 105.

**#3918** ὕπανδρος (nom.sing.fem.of ὕπανδρος, in agreement with γυνή).

King James Version

which hath an husband - Rom.7:2.

Revised Standard Version

married - Rom.7:2.

*Meaning:* A combination of ὑπό (#117) and ἀνήρ (#63). Hence, under a man's jurisdiction; married - Rom.7:2.

γυνὴ (nom.sing.fem.of γυνή, subject of δέδεται) 103.
τῷ (instru.sing.masc.of the article in agreement with ἀνδρὶ) 9.
ζῶντι (pres.act.part.instru.sing.masc.of ζάω, adjectival, ascriptive, in agreement with ἀνδρὶ) 340.
ἀνδρὶ (instru.sing.masc.of ἀνήρ, association) 63.
δέδεται (3d.per.sing.perf.pass.ind.of δέω, intensive) 998.
νόμῳ (instru.sing.masc.of νόμος, means) 464.
ἐὰν (conditional particle with the subjunctive in a third-class condition) 363.
δὲ (adversative conjunction) 11.
ἀποθάνῃ (3d.per.sing.aor.pass.subj.of ἀποθνήσκω, third-class condition) 774.
ὁ (nom.sing.masc.of the article in agreement with ἀνήρ) 9.
ἀνήρ (nom.sing.masc.of ἀνήρ, subject of ἀποθάνῃ) 63.
κατήργηται (3d.per.sing.perf.pass.ind.of καταργέω, intensive) 2500.
ἀπὸ (preposition with the ablative of separation) 70.
τοῦ (abl.sing.masc.of the article in agreement with νόμου) 9.
νόμου (abl.sing.masc.of νόμος, separation) 464.
τοῦ (gen.sing.masc.of the article in agreement with ἀνδρός) 9.
ἀνδρός (gen.sing.masc.of ἀνήρ, description) 63.

*Translation - "Thus the married woman has been bound by law to her living husband; but if the man should die she is released from the law of marriage."*

**Comment:** γὰρ is explanatory. A well known legal principle was laid down in verse 1. Verse 2 is a specific illustration of the principle. Note the attributive adjective ὕπανδρος and the adjectival participle ζῶντι in the ascriptive attributive position - "the married woman" and her "living husband." She was bound by the marriage law when she took the vows, and she is still bound, but only as long as she has a living husband. δὲ introduces the adverse third-class condition. The condition is unfulfilled in Paul's illustration but with some prospect of fulfillment. Her husband may or may not die before she does. Nothing dogmatic is asserted. In the event that he predeceases her the statement in the result clause becomes true. At his death she is released from the law with reference to marriage and is therefore free.

Paul employs the third verse to complete the details of the analogy which he will then apply in verse 4.

*Verse 3 - "So then if, while her husband liveth she be married to another man, she shall be called an adultress; but if her husband be dead she is free from that law; so that she is no adultress, though she be married to another man."*

ἄρα οὖν ζῶντος τοῦ ἀνδρὸς μοιχαλὶς χρηματίσει ἐὰν γένηται ἀνδρὶ ἑτέρῳ. ἐὰν δὲ ἀποθάνῃ ὁ ἀνήρ, ἐλευθέρα ἐστὶν ἀπὸ τοῦ νόμου, τοῦ μὴ εἶναι αὐτὴν μοιχαλίδα γενομένην ἀνδρὶ ἑτέρῳ.

*"Accordingly, she will be called an adulteress if she lives with another man while her husband is alive. But if her husband dies she is free from that law, and if she marries another man she is not an adulteress." . . . RSV*

ἄρα (illative particle) 995.

οὖν (inferential conjunction) 68.

ζῶντος (pres.act.part.gen.sing.masc.of ζάω, genitive absolute, adverbial, conditional) 340.

τοῦ (gen.sing.masc.of the article in agreement with ἀνδρὸς) 9.

ἀνδρὸς (gen.sing.masc.of ἀνήρ, genitive absolute) 63.

μοιχαλὶς (nom.sing.fem.of μοιχαλίς, predicate nominative) 1006.

χρηματίσει (3d.per.sing.fut.act.ind.of χρηματίζω, predictive) 195.

ἐὰν (conditional particle in a third-class condition) 363.

γένηται (3d.per.sing.aor.subj.of γίνομαι, third-class condition) 113.

ἀνδρὶ (instru.sing.masc.of ἀνήρ, association) 63.

ἑτέρῳ (instru.sing.masc.of ἕτερος, in agreement with ἀνδρὶ) 605.

ἐὰν (conditional particle in a third-class condition) 363.

δὲ (adversative conjunction) 11.

ἀποθάνῃ (3d.per.sing.aor.act.subj.of ἀποθνήσκω, third-class condition) 774.

ὁ (nom.sing.masc.of the article in agreement with ἀνήρ) 9.

ἀνήρ (nom.sing.masc.of ἀνήρ, subject of ἀποθάνῃ) 63.

ἐλευθέρα (nom.sing.fem.of ἐλεύτερος, predicate adjective) 1245.

ἐστὶν (3d.per.sing.pres.ind.of εἰμί, static) 86.

ἀπὸ (preposition with the ablative of separation) 70.

τοῦ (abl.sing.masc.of the article in agreement with νόμου) 9.

νόμου (abl.sing.masc.of νόμος, separation) 464.

τοῦ (gen.sing.neut.of the article in an articular infinitive of result) 9.

μὴ (negative conjunction with the infinitive) 87.
εἶναι (pres.inf.of εἰμί, consecutive) 86.
αὐτὴν (acc.sing.fem.of αὐτός, general reference) 16.
μοιχαλίδα (acc.sing.fem.of μοιχαλίς, predicate accusative) 1006.
γενομένην (aor.mid.part.acc.sing.fem.of γίνομαι, adverbial, concessive) 113.
ἀνδρὶ (instru.sing.masc.of ἀνήρ, association) 63.
ἑτέρῳ (instru.sing.masc.of ἕτερος, in agreement with ἀνδρὶ) 605.

*Translation - "It follows then that as long as her husband lives she will be called an adulteress if she is associated with another man; but if the man dies she is free from the law, with the result that she is not an adulteress though married to another man."*

**Comment:** Meyer, who could never agree that τοῦ and the infinitive can be consecutive comments on τοῦ μὴ εἶναι κ.τ.λ. "Not a more precise definition (Th. Schott); *nor yet a consequence* (my italics) (as *usually* rendered) (Meyer's italics), which is never correct, not even in Acts vii.19 . . . but rather: *in order that she be not an adulteress.* That is the *purpose*, involved in the divine legal ordinance, of her freedom from the law." (Meyer, *Commentary on the New Testament, Romans*, 261). To which Robertson responds, "Meyer on Ro.7:3, τοῦ μὴ εἶναι, argues that τοῦ and the inf.never expresses result, a position which I once held. But the evidence is too strong to resist." (Robertson, *Grammar*, 1002). The principles of grammar and syntax in such matters are to be observed, to be sure, and if Meyer had said that τοῦ and the infinitive in a result sense is rare he would certainly have been correct. But the context is the final arbiter. To force a well established rule upon a clear context is to derive a tortured interpretation. In our passage the woman's first husband did not die for the purpose of allowing her to associate with another man without the stigma of adultery. He died and the result of his death was that she was free from the law, which also resulted in her freedom to marry again. The infinitive is also epexegetic (explanatory) as well as consecutive (result). This clause explains the phrase ἐλευθέρα ἀπὸ τοῦ νόμου.

Paul's concern is not to teach the law of marriage so much as to set up the analogy to make clear the believer's relation to the law as opposed to his position in the body of Christ.

*Verse 4 - "Wherefore, my brethren, ye also are become dead to the law by the body of Christ; that ye should be married to another, even to him who is raised from the dead, that we should bring forth fruit unto God."*

ὥστε, ἀδελφοί μου, καὶ ὑμεῖς ἐθανατώθητε τῷ νόμῳ διὰ τοῦ σώματος τοῦ Χριστοῦ, εἰς τὸ γενέσθαι ὑμᾶς ἑτέρῳ, τῷ ἐκ νεκρῶν ἐγερθέντι, ἵνα καρποφορήσωμεν τῷ θεῷ.

*"Likewise, my brethren, you have died to the law through the body of Christ, so that you may belong to another, to him who has been raised from the dead in order that we may bear fruit for God."* . . . RSV

ὥστε (conjunction introducing a result clause) 752.

ἀδελφοί (voc.pl.masc.of ἀδελφός, address) 15.

μου (gen.sing.masc.of ἐγώ, relationship) 123.

καὶ (adjunctive conjunction joining substantives) 14.

ὑμεῖς (nom.pl.masc.of σύ, subject of ἐθανατώθητε) 104.

ἐθανατώθητε (2d.per.pl.aor.pass.ind.of θανατόω, culminative) 879.

τῷ (loc.sing.masc.of the article in agreement with νόμῳ) 9.

νόμῳ (loc.sing.masc.of νόμος, sphere) 464.

διὰ (preposition with the ablative of agent) 118.

τοῦ (abl.sing.neut.of the article in agreement with σώματος) 9.

σώματος (abl.sing.neut.of σῶμα, agent) 507.

τοῦ (gen.sing.masc.of the article in agreement with Χριστοῦ) 9.

Χριστοῦ (gen.sing.masc.of Χριστός, possession) 4.

εἰς (preposition with the articular infinitive, accusative, result) 140.

τὸ (acc.sing.neut.of the article with the consecutive infinitive) 9.

γενέσθαι (aor.inf.acc.sing.neut.of γίνομαι, result) 113.

ὑμᾶς (acc.pl.masc.of σύ, general reference) 104.

ἑτέρῳ (instru.sing.masc.of ἕτερος, association) 605.

τῷ (instru.sing.masc.of the article in agreement with ἐγερθέντι) 9.

ἐκ (preposition with the ablative of separation) 19.

νεκρῶν (abl.pl.masc.of νεκρός, separation) 749.

ἐγερθέντι (aor.pass.part.instru.sing.masc.of ἐγείρω, substantival, apposition) 125.

ἵνα (conjunction introducing the subjunctive in a final clause) 114.

καρποφορήσωμεν (1st.per.pl.1st.aor.act.subj.of καρποφορέω, final clause) 1054.

τῷ (dat.sing.masc.of the article in agreement with θεῷ) 9.

θεῷ (dat.sing.masc.of θεός, personal advantage) 124.

*Translation - "The result, my brothers, is that you were put to death with reference to the law by the body of Christ with the result that you have come to be associated with another - the One who was raised from the dead in order that we might bear fruit for God."*

**Comment:** ὥστε introduces another result clause. Paul is applying the analogy of the marriage code. The believer in his unregenerate days was married to the law and thus bound by it. But we died when Christ died (Gal.2:20) because we had been "baptized by the Holy Spirit into the body of Christ" (1 Cor.12:13) and thus we were associated with Him (1 Peter 2:24). We are thus free from any further obligation to the law, because, in Christ, we paid the penalty.

We also shared His resurrection and thus are now, like Him, in resurrection victory able to be "married" to the One Who is raised from the dead. This victory in Christ is (a) for His glory (Eph.2:7), (b) for the benefits of eternal salvation that accrue to us, and (c) in order that we might bear fruit for our new Bridegroom (Mt.25:6; Eph.2:10; Heb.6:7).

The law stands in relation to the Christian as a former husband does to a wife to whom he has died and who has died to him.

In verse 5 Paul discusses the fruit of the former marriage and in verse 6 the fruit of the new marriage.

*Verse 5 - "For when we were in the flesh, the motions of sins, which were by the law, did work in our members to bring forth fruit unto death."*

ὅτε γὰρ ἦμεν ἐν τῇ σαρκί, τὰ παθήματα τῶν ἁμαρτιῶν τὰ διὰ τοῦ νόμου ἐνηργεῖτο ἐν τοῖς μέλεσιν ἡμῶν εἰς τὸ καρποφορῆσαι τῷ θανάτῳ

*"While we were living in the flesh, our sinful passions, aroused by the law, were at work in our members to bear fruit for death."* . . . *RSV*

ὅτε (particle introducing a contemporaneous temporal clause) 703.
γὰρ (causal conjunction) 105.
ἦμεν (1st.per.pl.imp.ind.of εἰμί, progressive description) 86.
ἐν (preposition with the locative of sphere) 80.
τῇ (loc.sing.fem.of the article in agreement with σαρκί) 9.
σαρκί (loc.sing.fem.of σάρξ, sphere) 1202.
τὰ (nom.pl.neut.of the article in agreement with παθήματα) 9.

#3919 παθήματα (nom.pl.neut.of πάθημα, subject of ἐνηργεῖτο).

King James Version

affection - Gal.5:24.
affliction - 2 Tim.3:11; Heb.10:32; 1 Pet.5:9.
motion - Rom.7:5.
suffering - Rom.8:18; 2 Cor.1:5,6,7; Phil.3:10; Col.1:24; Heb.2:9,10; 1 Pet.1:11; 4:13; 5:1.

Revised Standard Version

passions - Rom.7:5; Gal.5:24.
sufferings - Rom.8:18; 2 Cor.1:5,6,7; Phil.3:10; Col.1:24; Heb.2:9,10; 1 Pet.1:11; 4:13; 5:1; 2 Tim.3:11; Heb.10:22; 1 Pet.5:9.

*Meaning: Cf.* πάσχω (#1208). That which one suffers in fellowship with the sufferings of Christ - Rom.8:18; 2 Cor.1:5,6,7; Phil.3:10; Col.1:24; 1 Pet.4:13; 5:1; 2 Tim.3:11; Heb.10:32; 1 Pet.5:9. With reference to Christ's sufferings upon the cross - Heb.2:9; in incarnation - Heb.2:10; 1 Pet.1:11. Of the internal drive of the unregenerate to commit sin - Rom.7:5; Gal.5:24.

τῶν (gen.pl.fem.of the article in agreement with ἁμαρτιῶν) 9.
ἁμαρτιῶν (gen.pl.fem.of ἁμαρτία, description) 111.
τὰ (nom.pl.neut.of the article in agreement with παθήματα) 9.
διὰ (preposition with the ablative of means) 118.
τοῦ (abl.sing.masc.of the article in agreement with νόμου) 9.
νόμου (abl.sing.masc.of νόμος, means) 464.
ἐνηργεῖτο (3d.per.sing.imp.mid.ind.of ἐνεργέω, iterative) 1105.

ἐν (preposition with the locative, instrumental use, means) 80.
τοῖς (loc.pl.neut.of the article in agreement with μέλεσιν) 9.
μέλεσιν (loc.pl.neut.of μέλος, means) 506.
ἡμῶν (gen.pl.masc.of ἐγώ, possession) 123.
εἰς (preposition with the accusative, purpose) 140.
τό (acc.sing.neut.of the article in agreement with καρποφορῆσαι) 9.
καρποφορῆσαι (aor.act.inf.of καρποφορέω, purpose) 1054.
τῷ (loc.sing.masc.of the article in agreement with θανάτῳ) 9.
θανάτῳ (loc.sing.masc.of θάνατος, sphere) 381.

*Translation - "Because when we were in the sphere of the flesh, the propensities
to sin, enflamed by the law, operated in the organs of our bodies to produce fruit
unto death."*

**Comment:** The former marriage, in the analogy of verses 2,3 was fruitful. We
lived in the fleshly sphere - the sphere into which we were born (John 3:5). The
flesh had complete control of our bodies and a scenario to enact which lacked
nothing in the category of depravity. It was well equipped to produce (1
Cor.15:56). It built up a cumulative intensity (cf.#1105). The tools were the
members of our physical body and the fruit of its activity led to death (Mk.7:21-
23; Gal.5:17-21). Note ἐνεργέω in an evil sense also in Eph.2:2 and 2 Thess.2:7.
But God also energizes the believer. Cf.#1105 for the list of references. Thus,
married once to the law we served sin faithfully and fruitfully and received sin's
reward which is death - both physical and spiritual.

*Verse 6 - "But now we are delivered from the law, that being dead wherein we
were held; that we should serve in newness of spirit, and not in the oldness of the
letter."*

νυνὶ δὲ κατηργήθημεν ἀπὸ τοῦ νόμου, ἀποθανόντες ἐν ᾧ κατειχόμεθα, ὥστε
δουλεύειν ἡμᾶς ἐν καινότητι πνεύματος καὶ οὐ παλαιότητι γράμματος.

*"But now we are discharged from the law, dead to that which held us captive,
so that we serve not under the old written code but in the new life of the Spirit."..
RSV*

νυνὶ (temporal adverb) 1497.
δὲ (adversative conjunction) 11.
κατηργήθημεν (1st.per.pl.aor.pass.ind.of καταργέω, culminative) 2500.
ἀπὸ (preposition with the ablative of separation) 70.
τοῦ (abl.sing.masc.of the article in agreement with νόμου) 9.
νόμου (abl.sing.masc.of νόμος, separation) 464.
ἀποθανόντες (aor.pass.part.nom.pl.masc. of ἀποθνήσκω, adverbial,
temporal/causal) 774.
ἐν (preposition with the locative of sphere) 80.
ᾧ (loc.sing.neut.of ὅς, sphere) 65.
κατειχόμεθα (1st.per.pl.imp.pass.ind.of κατέχω, progressive description)
2071.
ὥστε (conjunction introducing a consecutive clause) 752.

δουλεύειν (pres.act.inf.of δουλεύω, result) 604.

ἡμᾶς (acc.pl.masc.of ἐγώ, general reference) 123.

ἐν (preposition with the locative, instrumental use, manner) 80.

καινότητι (loc.sing.masc.of καινότης, manner) 3910.

πνεύματος (abl.sing.neut.of πνεῦμα, source) 83.

καὶ (adversative conjunction) 14.

οὐ (negative conjunction with the indicative) 130.

γράμματος (gen.sing.neut.of γράμμα, description) 2100.

#**3920** παλαιότητι (loc.sing.masc.of παλαιότης, manner).

King James Version

oldness - Rom.7:6.

Revised Standard Version

old code - Rom.7:6.

*Meaning: Cf.* πάλαι (#941); παλαιόω (#2483); παλαιός (#804). Hence, oldness; the characteristic of being old. Followed by a genitive of description - Rom.7:6.

*Translation - "But now we have been rescued from the law, because we have died to that by which we were being held captive. The result is that now we serve with a newness born of the Spirit and not by the old written code."*

**Comment:** As a woman is free from her former husband when he dies, to marry another, so the believer is free from his former condition of legal bondage to the law, when he dies and rises again to enjoy a new relationship with another way of life. The law did not die; it still lives on to enslave millions. We died with reference to it. Because of it we were in a constant state of bondage. Note κατειχόμεθα - a continuous state of bondage in past time. This slavery ended at the cross, when the law's ability to enslave us any further was brought to an end, since, in Christ, we paid the full legal penalty for our transgressions of it. Note καταργέω (#2500) used to say that the law was superceded by grace in 2 Cor.3:7,11,13,14. The law is not voided in the sense that it is stripped of its authority (Rom.3:31). On the contrary the fact that a sinner can be justified to measure up to its righteous standard only by faith, is the fact that dignifies the law. It is superceded in the sense that it is rendered incapable of condemning the believer because of the substitution of another federal headship in Christ (Eph.2:15). Note that all of these verses use καραργέω (#2500).

The believer is free from any further bondage imposed by the law, our former tyrant, since the law did its worst in exacting the extreme penalty at our expense, when we died representatively in the person of our substitute, Jesus Christ. Now that we are alive in Christ the old relation is forever gone. Our new resurrection life is spent in serving with a verve, eclat and aplomb that is forever new since it has the Holy Spirit as its eternal and heavenly Source.

The Christian never again serves in slavish obedience to a written legal code. Nothing that he does is done as a means of being saved. Everything good that he does is done as a result of the fact that he has been saved. Thus the victorious life is available to him and he can live it only if he exercises constant care to allow his ethics to be guided by his knowledge of his once-for-all deliverance from legal bondage and his present continuous and eternal connection by grace through faith with the risen mystical body of Christ. Though his flesh is scheduled for glorification at the Second Coming he is not yet actually rid of a fleshly body which, since it is genetically descended from Adam, can produce nothing but sin (Gal.5:19-21). His old nature is still with him. Another new nature, the result of his new birth (John 3:3,7;1 Pet.1:23) now is his. Thus a struggle ensues between the two natures. (Rom.7:14-25; Gal.5:16-23).

Paul now discusses the problem of indwelling sin in the liberated Christian in verses 7-25.

## The Problem of Indwelling Sin

*(Romans 7:7-25)*

*Verse 7 - "What shall we say then? Is the law sin? God forbid. Nay, I had not known sin, but by the law: for I had not known lust, except the law had said, Thou shalt not covet,"*

Τί οὖν ἐροῦμεν; ὁ νόμος ἁμαρτία; μὴ γένοιτο. ἀλλὰ τὴν ἁμαρτίαν οὐκ ἔγνων εἰ μὴ διὰ νόμου, τήν τε γὰρ ἐπιθυμίαν οὐκ ᾔδειν εἰ μὴ ὁ νόμος ἔλεγεν, Οὐκ ἐπιθυμήσεις.

*"What then shall we say? That the law is sin? By no means! Yet, if it had not been for the law, I should not have known sin. I should not have known what it is to covet if the law had not said, 'You shall not covet.' " . . . RSV*

Τί (acc.sing.neut.of τίς, interrogative pronoun, direct object of ἐροῦμεν, in direct question) 281.

οὖν (inferential conjunction) 68.

ἐροῦμεν (1st.per.pl.fut.act.ind.of εἶπον, deliberative) 155.

ὁ (nom.sing.masc.of the article in agreement with νόμος) 9.

νόμος (nom.sing.masc.of νόμος, subject of ἐστιν understood) 464.

ἁμαρτία (nom.sing.fem.of ἁμαρτία, predicate nominative) 111.

μὴ (negative conjunction with the optative) 87.

γένοιτο (3d.per.sing.aor.opt.of γίνομαι, voluntative) 113.

ἀλλὰ (confirmatory conjunction) 342.

τὴν (acc.sing.fem.of the article in agreement with ἁμαρτίαν) 9.

ἁμαρτίαν (acc.sing.fem.of ἁμαρτία, direct object of ἔγνων) 111.

οὐκ (negative conjunction with the indicative) 130.

ἔγνων (1st.per.sing.2d.aor.act.ind.of γινώσκω, ingressive) 131.

εἰ (conditional particle in a second-class condition) 337.

μὴ (negative conjunction with the indicative in a contrary to fact condition) 87.

διὰ (preposition with the ablative of means) 118.

νόμου (abl.sing.masc.of νόμος, means) 464.

τήν (acc.sing.fem.of the article in agreement with ἐπιθυμίαν) 9.

τε (correlative particle) 1408.

γὰρ (causal conjunction) 105.

ἐπιθυμίαν (acc.sing.fem.of ἐπιθυμία, direct object of ἤδειν) 2186.

οὐκ (negative conjunction with the indicative) 130.

ἤδειν (1st.per.sing.pluperf.ind.of οἶδα, consummative, in a second-class condition) 144b.

εἰ (conditional particle in a second-class condition) 337.

μὴ (negative conjunction in a second-class condition) 87.

ὁ (nom.sing.masc.of the article in agreement with νόμος) 9.

νόμος (nom.sing.masc.of νόμος, subject of ἔλεγεν) 464.

ἔλεγεν (3d.per.sing.imp.act.ind.of λέγω, progressive description) 66.

Οὐκ (negative conjunction with the indicative) 130.

ἐπιθυμήσεις (2d.per.sing.fut.act.ind.of ἐπιθυμέω, imperatival) 500.

*Translation - "What then shall we say? Is the law sin? Certainly not! On the contrary I did not recognize sin except by the law, for I had never understood the depths of intense desire but for the fact that the law has always said, 'You shall not covet.' "*

**Comment:** Paul is fond of τί οὖν - (Rom.6:1,15; 7:7; 8:31 etc). The εἰ μὴ clauses are second-class conditions with the assumption contrary to fact. "I did not know sin if not by the law, but it was by the law that I did know sin." And "If the law had not been saying . . . but it was saying . . . κ.τ.λ."

The law, so far from being sin, is the pure reflection of God's moral character, so that the contrast between the demands of the law and the moral character of my performance is the way that we know what sin is. Paul then gave an example. He had not understand that the intense passion to possess something was a sin until he read in the law, Οὐκ ἐπιθυμήσεις (*cf.* Ex.2017; Deut.5:21). It is when the law reveals to man that what he does is immoral and hence forbidden in God's moral order that it provides God with legal justification for condemnation. Hence the law enslaves. A driver may drive his car down the road at the rate of 60 miles per hour on two successive days. On the evening of the first day the legislature passes a statute and posts a sign which reads, "55 miles per hour." The second day, the driver, performing precisely as he did the day before is a law-breaker and subject to prosecution and punishment. Thus the law kills. But the moral principle behind the law is not to blame, if, in fact, safety on the highway requires a 55 miles per hour speed limit.

God's law are moral and therefore reasonable, else God would not have imposed them. God has not arbitrarily forbidden harmless actions of men in order to show His authority. Nor should men. God says, "No" only in order that He may say a bigger and eternal "Yes."

But in Rom.7:5 Paul said that the evil passions of our flesh were aroused and intensified by the law. The law forbids me to do a certain thing, but why does it intensify my desire to do it? We must remember that in Adam we are born enemies of God. Already annoyed because of the divine limitations upon what the unsaved sinner calls his "liberty" he strikes out at God to express his frustration and to prove to himself that he is a real, macho theophobe. How often child psychologists have warned parents against the possibility that when they forbid a certain practice, they only succeed in suggesting it to the child, who otherwise might not have thought of it. Thus we do not say to our obstreperous offspring, "Don't paint the dog with sorghum molasses." Red Skleton in his portrayal of "the bad little kid" when he was planning some bit of deviltry used to say, "If I do it, I get a whipping. I do it!" One good way for the misguided sinner to get even with God is to do something that God has forbidden, not because he wishes to do it especially but because God has forbidden it.

*Verse 8 - "But sin, taking occasion by the commandment, wrought in me all manner of concupiscence. For without the law sin was dead."*

ἀφορμὴν δὲ λαβοῦσα ἡ ἁμαρτία διὰ τῆς ἐντολῆς κατειργάσατο ἐν ἐμοὶ πᾶσαν ἐπιθυμίαν. χωρὶς γὰρ νόμου ἁμαρτία νεκρά.

*"But sin, finding opportunity in the commandment, wrought in me all kinds of covetousness. Apart from the law sin lies dead." . . . RSV*

#3921 ἀφορμὴν (acc.sing.fem.of ἀφορμή, direct object of λαβοῦσα).

King James Version

occasion - Rom.7:8,11; 2 Cor.5:12; 11:12,12; Gal.5:13; 1 Tim.5:14.

Revised Standard Version

cause - 2 Cor.5:12.
claim - 2 Cor.11:12,12.
occasion - 1 Tim.5:14.

*Meaning:* A combination of ἀπό (#70) and ὁρμή (#3309). Properly, a place from which a military movement or attack is made; a base of operations; beach-head. Metaphorically, whatever stimulates an endeavor and by which it is made; incentive; opportunity, stimulation, suggestion, supposed justification for some thought or action. The law provided the basis for proving Paul a sinner - Rom.7:8,11. Christian liberty should not be rationalized as a reason to sin - Gal.5:13; Paul hoped that his performance would supply the Corinthians with a sound basis for praising him - 2 Cor.5:12; also to deprive his enemies of grounds for attacking him - 2 Cor.11:12,12. Christian women should provide no ground for criticism - 1 Tim.5:14.

δὲ (adversative conjunction) 11.
λαβοῦσα (aor.act.part.nom.sing.fem.of λαμβάνω, adverbial, modal) 533.
ἡ (nom.sing.fem.of the article in agreement with ἁμαρτία) 9.
ἁμαρτία (nom.sing.fem.of ἁμαρτία, subject of κατειργάσατο) 111.
διὰ (preposition with the ablative of means) 118.
τῆς (abl.sing.fem.of the article in agreement with ἐντολῆς) 9.

ἐντολῆς (abl.sing.fem.of ἐντολή, means) 472.
κατειργάσατο (3d.per.sing.aor.mid.ind.of κατεργάζομαι, constative) 3815.
ἐν (preposition with the locative of place) 80.
ἐμοὶ (loc.sing.masc.of ἐμός, place) 1267.
πᾶσαν (acc.sing.fem.of πᾶς, in agreement with ἐπιθυμίαν) 67.
ἐπιθυμίαν (acc.sing.fem.of ἐπιθυμία, direct object of κατειργάσατο) 2186.
χωρὶς (preposition with the ablative of separation) 1077.
γὰρ (causal conjunction) 105.
νόμου (abl.sing.masc.of νόμος, separation) 464.
ἁμαρτία (nom.sing.fem.of ἁμαρτία, subject of ἐστιν understood) 111.
νεκρά (nom.sing.fem.of νεκρός, predicate adjective) 749.

*Translation - "But sin by seizing opportunity through the commandment produced in me every evil passion. For apart from law sin is dead."*

**Comment:** Study the new word ἀφορμήν (#3921) carefully. Sin was in the world before law in the period which Paul describes as "from Adam to Moses" (Romans 5:14) and during this period it reigned relentlessly, enforcing its grisly will by means of death. Infants escaped the eternal consequences of transgression, but even they paid the wages of physical death. But evil desire, a natural result of Adam's fall and our inherent propensity to indulge it, was not recognized as such until God's codified law forbade certain things. The law therefore provided sin with its ground for accusation. We suddenly knew that doing what came naturally to a depraved man displeased God. This extends to all evil passion. Paul illustrated this in verse 7 with the tenth commandment and he expands his explanation in verses 9-11.

Covetousness is condemned by the law and idolatry is covetousness (Col.3:5. cf.#2302). Covetousness is the desire, heated to incandescence, to possess everything. The law began by forbidding idolatry (Exod.20:3-6). Primitive man's first reaction to intuitive truth was idolatry (Rom.1:18-23). The law then proceded to specify what covetousness is - false worship, disrespect for self and for parents, murder, adultery, theft, and false witness and then closed by forbidding all covetousness. Thus the Decalogue swings full circle, beginning, proceeding and ending with ἐπιθυμία and Paul agrees, by saying κατειργάσατο ἐν ἐμοὶ πᾶσαν ἐπιθυμίαν.

Sin, unable to condemn without the law, is revived when the law comes as we see in

*Verse 9 - "For I was alive without the law once: but when the commandment came, sin revived, and I died."*

ἐγὼ δὲ ἔζων χωρὶς νόμου ποτέ, ἐλθούσης δὲ τῆς ἐντολῆς ἡ ἁμαρτία ἀνέζησεν, . . .

*"I was once alive apart from the law, but when the commandment came, sin revived and I died;" . . . RSV*

ἐγὼ (nom.sing.masc.of ἐγώ, subject of ἔζων) 123.
δὲ (explanatory conjunction) 11.

ἔζων (1st.per.sing.imp.act.ind.of ζάω, progressive description) 340.

χωρὶς (preposition with the ablative of separation) 1077.

νόμου (abl.sing.masc.of νόμος, separation) 464.

ποτέ (temporal adverb) 2399.

ἐλθούσης (aor.part.gen.sing.fem.of ἔρχομαι, adverbial, temporal/causal, genitive absolute) 146.

δὲ (adversative conjunction) 11.

τῆς (gen.sing.fem.of the article in agreement with ἐντολῆς) 9.

ἐντολῆς (gen.sing.fem.of ἐντολή, genitive absolute) 472.

ἡ (nom.sing.fem.of the article in agreement with ἁμαρτία) 9.

ἁμαρτία (nom.sing.fem.of ἁμαρτία, subject of ἀνέζησεν) 111.

ἀνέζησεν (3d.per.sing.aor.act.ind.of ἀναζάω, constative) 2556.

*Translation - "Now once I lived apart from the law, but when (and because) the commandment came, sin was invigorated . . . "*

Comment:The last clause of the KJV, "and I died" is in verse 10 in the Greek text. *Cf.* comment on Rom.2:7,10,11,12,13,14,15,16. For one who followed in honest humility whatever light he had, however scant, God's justice provided more light. Paul says that in his case his condemnation came when the law came and specifically defined sin so that he then recognized himself as a transgressor. *Cf.* our discussion of verses 7 and 8. Paul supports this in 1 Cor.15:56.

The commandment forbidding covetousness is the last of ten. But the Mosaic Code did not define covetousness as idolatry as Paul later did (Col.3:5). Thus transgression of the first three commandments is transgression of the tenth and all of the others as well. Saul of Tarsus, the Pharisee, who made a professional career out of "keeping the law" (Phil.3:4-6) did so only because of his superficial view of it. His moral "score card" was spotless in categories one through nine. He had no other gods ahead of Jehovah. He had made no graven images. He had not taken God's name in vain. He was a sabbath observer. He provided for his parents. He had neither killed, committed adultery, stolen nor borne false witness. At the end of the ninth inning there were no errors. Came the tenth - "You must not even want to do any of these things." Covetousness is not overt. It is covert. The desire for that which is not one's own originates in the heart (Jer.17:9; Mk.7:21-23; Gal.5:17-21). Saul had done none of the things which were forbidden in the first nine commandments. But he had wanted to do all of them. Jesus pointed out that adultery, murder, theft and all other sins originate in the evil heart of man which can be rescued only by regeneration (Mt.5:17-48). Thus the righteousness which is recognized as such in the Kingdom of the Heavens must exceed that of which Saul boasted before Saul became Paul (Mt.5:20).

Those who reject Jesus Christ on the grounds that they do not need Him since they are capable of keeping the law of God make the same mistake that Saul of Tarsus did. Theirs is a superficial and therefore false understanding of the standard of righteousness which the law demands. Once they realize this, they "die" as Paul says he did in

*Verse 10 - "And the commandment, which was ordained to life, I found to be unto death."*

ἐγὼ δὲ ἀπέθανον, καὶ εὑρέθη μοι ἡ ἐντολὴ ἡ εἰς ζωὴν αὕτν εἰς θάνατον.

*"The very commandment which promised life proved to be death to me."*
RSV

ἐγὼ (nom.sing.masc.of ἐγώ, subject of ἀπέθανον) 123.
δὲ (continuative conjunction) 11.
ἀπέθανον (1st.per.sing.aor.ind.of ἀποθνήσκω, constative) 774.
καὶ (continuative conjunction) 14.
εὑρέθη (3d.per.sing.aor.pass.ind.of εὑρίσκω, constative) 79.
μοι (dat.sing.masc.of ἐγώ, personal disadvantage) 123.
ἡ (nom.sing.fem.of the article in agreement with ἐντολή) 9.
ἐντολὴ (nom.sing.fem.of ἐντολή, subject of εὑρέθη) 472.
ἡ (nom.sing.fem.of the article in agreement with ἐντολή) 9.
εἰς (preposition with the accusative, purpose) 140.
ζωὴν (acc.sing.fem.of ζωή, purpose) 668.
αὕτη (nom.sing.fem.of οὗτος, anaphoric, subject of verb understood) 93.
εἰς (preposition with the accusative, result) 381.

θάνατον (acc.sing.masc.of θάνατος, result) 381.

*Translation - "... and I died; and the commandment which I supposed to be for life resulted in death."*

**Comment:** The clause ἐγὼ δὲ ἀπέθανον, a part of the ninth verse in the KJV is in verse 10 in the Greek.

The remainder of the verse and verse 11 explains why the coming of the law meant death to one who, without the law, thought himself alive. Purpose (εἰς ζωὴν) and result (εἰς θάνατον) are here set forth. Saul thought the law was for the former purpose, but found that it brought the opposite result. Recall Israel's confident promise to God at Sinai (Exodus 19:8). Apparently they also thought that the Mosaic Code administered on Sinai was designed to give them life as they obeyed it. They also found that it resulted in death as they disobeyed (Exodus 32:1-35; 1 Cor.10:5-12).

Note the anaphoric use of αὕτη. It is resumptive, recalling attention to ἡ ἐντολή.

*Verse 11 - "For sin, taking occasion by the commandment, deceived me, and by it slew me."*

ἡ γὰρ ἁμαρτία ἀφορμὴν λαβοῦσα διὰ τῆς ἐντολῆς ἐξηπάτησέν με καὶ δι' αὐτῆς ἀπέκτεινεν.

*"For sin, finding opportunity in the commandment, deceived me and by it killed me." ... RSV*

ἥ (nom.sing.fem.of the article in agreement with ἁμαρτία) 9.
γὰρ (causal conjunction) 105.
ἁμαρτία (nom.sing.fem.of ἁμαρτία, subject of ἐξηπάτησεν and ἀπέκτεινεν) 111.
ἀφορμὴν (acc.sing.fem.of ἀφορμή, direct object of λαβοῦσα) 3921.
λαβοῦσα (2d.aor.act.part.nom.sing.fem.of λαμβάνω, adverbial, modal) 533.
διὰ (preposition with the ablative, means) 118.
τῆς (abl.sing.fem.of the article in agreement with ἐντολῆς) 9.
ἐντολῆς (abl.sing.fem.of ἐντολή, means) 472.

#3922 ἐξηπάτησέν (3d.per.sing.aor.act.ind.of ἐξαπατάω, constative).

King James Version

beguile - 2 Cor.11:3.
deceive - Rom.7:11; 16:18; 1 Cor.3:18; 2 Thess.2:3; 1 Tim.2:14.

Revised Standard Version

deceive - Rom.7:11; 16:18; 1 Cor.3:18; 2 Cor.11:3; 2 Thess.2:3; 1 Tim.2:14.

*Meaning:* A combination of ἐκ (#19) and ἀπατάω (#4511). An intensified form of ἀπατάω. To deceive. Sin deceived Paul by suggesting to him that he was good enough to keep the commandment of God - Rom.7:11; false teachers deceive the saints - Rom.16:18; 1 Cor.3:18; 2 Thess.2:3. Satan deceived Eve - 2 Cor.11:3; 1 Tim.2:14.

με (acc.sing.masc.of ἐγώ, direct object of ἐξηπάτησεν) 123.
καὶ (adjunctive conjunction joining verbs) 14.
δι' (preposition with the ablative of means) 118.
αὐτῆς (abl.sing.fem.of αὐτός, means) 16.
ἀπέκτεινεν (3d.per.sing.aor.act.ind.of ἀποκτείνω, constative) 889.

*Translation - "Because sin, having seized the opportunity offered by the commandment, deceived me and with it killed me."*

**Comment:** The law is not the culprit. Sin is the deceiver and the killer, not the law. Sin used the law as its base of operations (*cf.*#3921) from which it launched its attack upon Paul, who was first deceived into thinking that, in his natural state, he was able to keep the law. He was totally deceived on the point and, as a result, he worked hard to justify himself by keeping the law (Acts 22:3-5; 26:4-5; Phil.3:4-6).

It is a sinful presumption to assume that one's natural standard of ethics is sufficiently holy to satisfy God's law. One who says, "I am able to be as good as God wants me to be" is really saying, "God does not want me to be any better than I can be." And this really says, "God is no better than I am." Thus they trade the real God for one of their own design. This man is deceived and he is going to get killed. To advance as acceptable to God one's own ethical standards is to commit sin. Actually to assume such an attitude is to play God. Thus Saul of

Tarsus, for all of his self-righteous Phariseeism died under the attack of sin, which used the law as its weapon. *Cf.* 2 Cor.3:6.

*Verse 12 - "Wherefore the law is holy, and the commandment holy, and just and good."*

ὥστε ὁ μὲν νόμος ἅγιος, καὶ ἡ ἐντολὴ ἁγία καὶ δικαία καὶ ἀγαθή.

*"So the law is holy, and the commandment is holy and just and good."*.. *RSV*

ὥστε (consecutive conjunction) 752.
ὁ (nom.sing.masc.of the article in agreement with νόμος) 9.
μὲν (correlative affirmative conjunction) 300.
νόμος (nom.sing.masc.of νόμος, subject of ἐστίν understood) 464.
ἅγιος (nom.sing.masc.of ἅγιος, predicate adjective) 84.
καὶ (continuative conjunction) 14.
ἡ (nom.sing.fem.of the article in agreement with ἐντολή) 9.
ἐντολὴ (nom.sing.fem.of ἐντολή, subject of ἐστίν,understood) 472.
ἁγία (nom.sing.fem.of ἅγιος, predicate adjective) 84.
καὶ (adjunctive conjunction joining adjectives) 14.
δικαία (nom.sing.fem.of δίκαιος, predicate adjective) 85.
καὶ (adjunctive conjunction joining adjectives) 14.
ἀγαθή (nom.sing.fem.of ἀγαθός, predicate adjective) 547.

*Translation - "The result is that the law is holy, and the commandment holy and just and good."*

**Comment:** μὲν here finally finds it correlative δὲ in verse 14 - "The law on the one hand is holy (verse 12) and spiritual (verse 14), but (δὲ) I am carnal. . ." (verse 14).

Paul moves to block the argument that since sin used the law to deceive and kill him (verse 11), then the law must be sinful. Only that which is holy (ἅγιος) can meet the standard of justice (δικαία) demanded before the bench of the Judge of heaven's court. And only a holistic code, which embraces all of that which is true, not only in the moral sphere, but also in the spheres of natural, physical and social science, could be good, thus to yield the positive and therefore viable ripple effects in heaven's society. Paul's statement here clearly reveals the necessary connection between the theological and the social gospels. Society will never be "good" until it is governed by the *total* canon of truth as that canon was established in creation. The eccentricities of error which are intermixed with truth in the natural, physical and social sciences are not to be differentiated from the eccentricity of sin in the moral realm. It is sin and therefore destructive to be wrong about anything. That is why we will never be sinless as long as we are in error about anything, and that is why we can never have a viable society until the King of Kings returns to establish and administer it.

Paul pursues this point in

*Verse 13 - "Was then that which is good made death unto me? God forbid. But sin, that it might appear sin, working death in me by that which is good; that sin by the commandment might become exceeding sinful."*

Τὸ οὖν ἀγαθὸν ἐμοὶ ἐγένετο θάνατος; μὴ γένοιτο. ἀλλὰ ἡ ἁμαρτία, ἵνα φανῇ ἁμαρτία, διὰ τοῦ ἀγαθοῦ μοι κατεργαζομένη θάνατον. ἵνα γένηται καθ᾽ ὑπερβολὴν ἁμαρτωλὸς ἡ ἁμαρτία διὰ τῆς ἐντολῆς.

*"Did that which is good, then, bring death to me? By no means! It was sin, working death in me through what is good, in order that sin might be shown to be sin, and through the commandment might become sinful beyond measure."*

RSV

Τὸ (nom.sing.neut.of the article in agreement with ἀγαθὸν) 9.
οὖν (inferential conjunction) 68.
ἀγαθὸν (nom.sing.neut.of ἀγαθός, subject of ἐγένετο) 547.
ἐμοὶ (dat.sing.masc.of ἐμός, reference) 1267.
ἐγένετο (3d.per.sing.aor.ind.of γίνομαι, constative) 113.
θάνατος (nom.sing.masc.of θάνατος, predicate nominative) 381.
μὴ (negative conjunction with the optative) 87.
γένοιτο (3d.per.sing.aor.opt.of γίνομαι, voluntative) 113.
ἀλλὰ (alternative conjunction) 342.
ἡ (nom.sing.fem.of the article in agreement with ἁμαρτία) 9.
ἁμαρτία (nom.sing.fem.of ἁμαρτία, subject of κατεργαζομένη) 111.
ἵνα (conjunction with the sujunctive, purpose) 114.
φανῇ (3d.per.sing.aor.act.ind.of φαίνω, purpose) 100.
ἁμαρτία (nom.sing.fem.of ἁμαρτία, predicate nomintive) 111.
διὰ (preposition with the ablative of comparison) 118.
τοῦ (abl.sing.masc.of the article in agreement with ἀγαθοῦ) 9.
ἀγαθοῦ (abl.sing.masc.of ἀγαθός, comparison) 547.
μοι (dat.sing.masc.of ἐμοί, personal disadvantage) 1267.
κατεργαζομένη (pres.mid.part.nom.sing.fem.of κατεργάζομαι, nom.sing.
fem. of κατεργάζομαι, adverbial, modal) 3815.
ἵνα (conjunction with the subjunctive, purpose) 114.
γένηται (3d.per.sing.aor.subj.of γίνομαι, purpose) 113.
καθ᾽ (preposition with the accusative, measure) 98.

#3923 ὑπερβολὴν (acc.sing.fem.of ὑπερβολή, measure).

King James Version

abundance - 2 Cor.12:7.
excellency - 2 Cor.4:7.
beyond meausre - Gal.1:13.
exceeding - Rom.7:13.
far more exceeding - 2 Cor.4:17,17.
more excellent - 1 Cor.12:31.
out of measure - 2 Cor.1:8.

Revised Standard Version

beyond measure - Rom.7:13.
still more excellent - 1 Cor.12:31.
utterly - 2 Cor.1:8.
transcendant - 2 Cor.4:7.
beyond all comparison - 2 Cor.4:17,17.
abundance - 2 Cor.12:7.
violently - Gal.1:13.

*Meaning: Cf.* ὑπερβάλλω (#4290) and ὑπερβαλλόντως (#4381). Hence, a throwing (projection) beyond or above. A superior achievement, in whatever way the context dictates as ὑπερβάλλω is joined to adjuncts. In the idiom καθ' ὑπερβολήν - Rom.7:13 (great sin); 1 Cor.12:31 (a better way); 2 Cor.1:8 (great trouble); 2 Cor.4:17,17 (great glory); Gal.1:13 (great zeal in persecution). Followed by a genitive of specification in 2 Cor.4:7 (great divine power) and 2 Cor.12:7 (great volume of revelation).

ἁμαρτωλὸς (nom.sing.masc.of ἁμαρτωλός, predicate adjective) 791.
ἡ (nom.sing.fem.of the article in agreement with ἁμαρτία) 9.
ἁμαρτία (nom.sing.fem.of ἁμαρτία, subject of γένηται) 111.
διὰ (preposition with the ablative, comparison) 118.
τῆς (abl.sing.fem.of the article in agreement with ἐντολῆς) 9.
ἐντολῆς (abl.sing.fem.of ἐντολή, comparison) 472.

*Translation - "Did then the good thing become death to me? Of course not! But sin, in order that it might be recognized as sin in contrast to the good, wrought death in me, in order that sin in contrast with the commandment might be sinful beyond all measure."*

**Comment:** In verse 11, Paul said that sin used the law as a means to kill him. In verse 12 he insisted that the law, a tool in the hands of sin, was nevertheless holy, just and good. To superficial observation this appears to be inconsistent. The danger is that we confuse agency with means - the actor with his tools. The law of God, which Paul in verse 13 calls Τὸ ἀγαθὸν - "the good thing," did not produce death for Paul. After his characteristic emotional disclaimer, μὴ γένοιτο (*cf.* Rom.3:4,6,31;1 6:2,17; 7:7,13; 9:14, *etc. cf.*#113), Paul adds the alternative ἀλλὰ - "but sin . . . producing death." Why? The first ἵνα final clause (purpose) tells why - "in order that it might stand out prominently as sin." (*cf.*#100 for the basic idea in φαίνω). And thus (now the second ἵνα clause) sin in its contrast with the commandment (διὰ τῆς ἐντολῆς) becomes inexpressibly sinful.

How can sin become more sinful than it already is? What is more sinful than idolatry, adultery, murder, theft, disregard for parents, false witness, *etc.*? There is one sin even more heinous than the overt transgression of God's law. That is the covert pride in one's native goodness that leads the sinner to assume that his personal moral standard and performance in compliance with it is as lofty as that of God, as expressed in the Ten Commandments! When Israel, encamped in the foothills of Sinai, said, "All that the Lord hath spoken we will do" (Exodus 19:8) she plumbed the depths of depravity. Paul made the same mistake during his preregenerate days as he zealously "obeyed" the law (Phil.3:4-6). So does every moralist who rejects Christ on the ground that he does not need Him. This is why unbelief, ultimately persisted in, is the unpardonable sin - the only sin for which there is no propitiation.

The enormity of the sin of human pride is brought out (ἵνα φανῇ ἁμαρτία) and sin is made "sinful beyond measure" (ἵνα γένηται καθ᾽ ὑπερβολὴν ἁμαρτωλὸς ἡ ἁμαρτία διὰ τῆς ἐντολῆς) when the law appears and man chooses to seek salvation by human meritorious observance of God's moral code. As though he were able to do so! The law of God is not in league with sin, for the result of its introduction is that the blackness, hideousness and blasphemous nature of sin in intensified beyond description by the contrast between man's performance and the standard that God demands. The greater the efficiency of the mirror to reflect light, the clearer is the nature and degree of dirt on the face of him who gazes into it. The ultimate Pharisee says, "Mirror, mirror on the wall, Who's the fairest of them all?" and expects the mirror to reply in his favor.

This is worse than sinful. It is inexpressibly stupid.

*Verse 14 - "For we know that the law is spiritual: but I am carnal, sold under sin."*

οἴδαμεν γὰρ ὅτι ὁ νόμος πνευματικός ἐστιν. ἐγὼ δὲ σάρκινός εἰμι, πεπραμένος ὑπὸ τὴν ἁμαρτίαν.

*"We know that the law is spiritual; but I am carnal, sold under sin."* . . . RSV

οἴδαμεν (1st.per.pl.perf.ind.of οἶδα, intensive) 144b.
γὰρ (causal conjunction) 105.
ὅτι (conjunction introducing an object clause in indirect discourse) 211.
ὁ (nom.sing.masc.of the article in agreement with νόμος) 9.
νόμος (nom.sing.masc.of νόμος, subject of ἐστιν) 464.
πνευματικός (nom.sing.masc.of πνευματικός, predicate adjective) 3791.
ἐστιν (3d.per.sing.pres.ind.of εἰμί, aoristic) 86.
ἐγὼ (nom.sing.masc.of ἐγώ, subject of εἰμί) 123.
δὲ (adversative conjunction) 11.

#3924 σάρκινός (nom.sing.masc.of σάρκινος, predicate adjective).

King James Version

fleshly - 2 Cor.3:3.
carnal - Rom.7:14; 1 Cor.3:1; Heb.7:16.

Revised Standard Version

carnal - Rom.7:14; 1 Cor.3:1; Heb.7:16.
human - 2 Cor.3:3.

*Meaning: Cf.* σάρξ (#1202) and σαρκικός (#4058). Pertaining to the flesh; to the human or other animal body. Psychologically in reference to human emotions - 2 Cor.3:3; with reference to human depravity in Rom.7:14; 1 Cor.3:1, where Paul might have used σαρκικός in contrast to πνευματικός. It seems that Paul used σαρκινός and σαρκικός interchangeably, unless, as Thayer suggests, the former is a heightened form of the latter. Note that in Romans 7:14 it is followed by epexegesis to explain the depraved nature of the flesh. The Aaronic Priesthood and the Mosaic Law in Heb.7:16.

εἰμι (1st.per.sing.pres.ind.of εἰμί, aoristic) 86.

πεπραμένος (perf.pass.part.nom.sing.masc.of πιπράσκω, adjectival, predicate position in agreement with ἐγώ) 1088.

ὑπό (preposition with the accusative, predicate usage) 117.

τὴν (acc.sing.fem.of the article in agreement with ἁμαρτίαν) 9.

ἁμαρτίαν (acc.sing.fem.of ἁμαρτία, predicate usage) 111.

*Translation - "Because we know that the law is spiritual, but I am carnal, sold into slavery to sin."*

**Comment:** Here the contrast between the ethical standards of the law of God and of man is made clear. The law is dominated by the Holy Spirit, Who is its heavenly source and Whose moral standards it expresses. On the contrary Paul is dominated by and follows the dictates of his earthly source, the fallen flesh of Adam. As Saul of Tarsus he did not always know this. But now, as Paul the Christian, he is well aware of it. This is the force of the intensive perfect tense in οἴδαμεν. Now he knows as a result of a past experience of learning. The perfect tense, as always, has both ends of the action in view. What does he know now? The ὅτι clause in indirect discourse tells us. He knows that the law is spiritual and thus it holds up a moral standard which is inaccessible to the flesh (John 6:63; Gal.5:16-23).

Lack of respect for God and His law lies at the bottom of man's pride and lack of repentance. (*cf.* Isa.6:1-5, with particular attention to Isaiah's reason for confession in the last clause of verse 5). All learning begins with the humility which comes from a proper respect for the superiority of the teacher over the student. (*cf.* 2 Peter 1:5 where the virtue referred to is the intellectual humiltiy. *cf. en loc.*). When Paul realized the heavenly, spiritual nature of the law, he came to understand his own wretched carnality.

δέ here is correlative to μέν in verse 12 - "The law is holy but I am carnal." The participle πεπραμένος in the perfect tense is adjectival as a further description of Paul's depravity. Or we can also take it as a causal adverb because it tells us why Paul was carnal. It indicates preterite action; it is punctiliar in nature and it yields a durative current result. Having been sold into slavery (Mt.18:25), Paul was now a slave under the domination of sin (Rom.6:17). However he does not mean that he is still a slave to sin in a judicial sense, for in the atonement he became dead to sin in the body of Christ. He means that he still has a fleshly nature which is no different, now that he is saved, than it was before he was saved. Then he had only one nature, because he had had only one birth. All the components of his personality - will, intellect and emotion, were subject to his carnal nature. Since he had no spiritual nature to make its demands upon him there was no conflict. Now, having been "born from above" (John 3:3,7; 1 Pet.1:23), Paul has a new nature which makes demands upon his will, intellect and emotions. These demands are in conflict with the demands of the old nature. This conflict he now describes in verses 15-25. Regenerate man is duophysite and duothelite - two natures and two wills, since he has had two births. The heavenly (πνευματικός) and the carnal (σαρκινός) war against each other (Gal.5:17). This battle will continue until the second coming of our Lord when the carnal nature will be glorified (Phil.3:21). Then all conflict between the flesh and the Spirit will be resolved in favor of the Holy Spirit (1 Cor.15:44).

It is the argument of the context that leads me to the conclusion that what follows in the remainder of the chapter is a description of the experience of the Christian, not a description of his moral ambivalence before he was saved. There is also internal evidence available to support this view.

*Verse 15 - "For that which I do, I allow not: for what I would, that do I not; but what I hate, that do I."*

ὁ γὰρ κατεργάζομαι οὐ γινώσκω, οὐ γὰρ ὁ θέλω τοῦτο πράσσω, ἀλλ' ὁ μισῶ τοῦτο ποιῶ.

*"I do not understand my own actions. For I do not do what I want, but I do the very thing I hate." . . . RSV*

ὁ (acc.sing.neut.of ὅς, relative pronoun, direct object of γινώσκω) 65.

γὰρ (causal conjunction) 105.

κατεργάζομαι (1st.per.sing.pres.mid.ind.of κατεργάζομαι, customary) 3815.

οὐ (negative conjunction with the indicative) 130.

γινώσκω (1st.per.sing.pres.act.ind.of γινώσκω, aoristic) 131.

οὐ (negative conjunction with the indicative) 130.

γὰρ (causal conjunction) 105.

ὁ (acc.sing.neut.of ὅς, relative pronoun, direct object of θέλω) 65.

θέλω (1st.per.sing.pres.act.ind.of θέλω, customary) 88.

τοῦτο (acc.sing.neut.of οὗτος, direct object of πράσσω, resumptive, in agreement with ὁ) 93.

πράσσω (1st.per.sing.pres.act.ind.of πράσσω, customary) 1943.

ἀλλ' (adversative conjunction) 342.

ὁ (acc.sing.neut.of ὅς, relative pronoun, direct object of μισῶ) 65.

μισῶ (1st.per.sing.pres.act.ind.of μισέω, customary) 542.

τοῦτο (acc.sing.neut.of οὗτος, direct object of ποιῶ, resumptive, in agreement with ὁ) 93.

ποιῶ (1st.per.sing.pres.act.ind.of ποιέω, customary) 127.

*Translation - "Because I never understand what I am always doing. For I do not do what I want to do, but what I hate is what I do."*

**Comment:** Here are two natures in conflict with the result that Paul confesses that he does not understand his actions. His actions (ὃ κατεργάζομαι) are in conflict with his regenerated will, which has the mind of Christ. Why should a Christian behave like an unbeliever? His regenerated will, taking orders from his new nature wants to do the will of God, but he admits that he does not obey it. On the contrary, his carnal will orders what his carnal mind approves and his carnal body obeys. But his regenerate will disapproves because his action is out of harmony with his regenerate mind. His unregenerate body responds to his unregenerate will and intellect in a way that his entire regenerate personality deplores. Saul and Paul are at loggerheads. This is not schizophrenia because neither the regenerate nor the unregenerate personalities are split. This is a split between two personalities, each of which *must* take orders from the nature which produced it. These two natures, the result of two births, occupy the same body.

*Verse 16 - "If then I do that which I would not, I consent unto the law that it is good."*

εἰ δὲ ὃ οὐ θέλω τοῦτο ποιῶ, σύμφημι τῷ νόμῳ ὅτι καλός.

*"Now if I do what I do not want, I agree that the law is good."* . . . *RSV*

εἰ (conditional particle in a first-class condition) 337.
δὲ (explanatory conjunction) 11.
ὃ (acc.sing.neut.of ὅς, relative pronoun, direct object of θέλω) 65.
οὐ (negative conjunction with the indicative) 130.
θέλω (1st.per.sing.pres.act.ind.of θέλω, present progressive) 88.
τοῦτο (acc.sing.neut.of οὗτος, resumptive, direct object of ποιῶ) 93.
ποιῶ (1st.per.sing.pres.act.ind.of ποιέω, customary) 127.

#3925 σύμφημι (1st.per.sing.pres.act.ind.of σύμφημι, static).

King James Version

consent unto - Rom.7:16.

Revised Standard Version

agree - Romans 7:16.

*Meaning:* A combination of σύν (#1542) and φημί (#354). Hence, to affirm or to agree with another. To consent - followed by ὅτι and indirect discourse in Rom.7:16.

τῷ (instru.sing.masc.of the article in agreement with νόμῳ) 9.
νόμῳ (instru.sing.masc.of νόμος, association after σύν in composition) 464.
ὅτι (conjunction introducing an object clause in indirect discourse) 211.
καλός (nom.sing.masc.of καλός, predicate adjective) 296.

*Translation - "But since I do not wish to do that which I am doing, I am in agreement with the law that it is good."*

**Comment:** For purposes of discussion we shall refer to the carnal nature as Saul and    to the spiritual nature as Paul. Since (εἰ in a first-class condition) Paul does not wish to do what Saul is doing, Paul is agreeing with God's law which forbids what Saul is doing and is thus affirming that the law of God is good. Before Paul existed, Saul agreed with all that Saul did, all the while affirming that what he did was in keeping with the law. Thus Saul was saying that the law was good but look what he was calling "good"! Murder by stoning! When a bad man says that what he does is in keeping with God's law, he is either saying that he is not bad or that God's law is not good. This is the exceeding sinfullness of sin. It requires the gift of God, called repentance, to change the thinking of the depraved man. Note what repentance did in his thinking as Saul became Paul for now Paul, the Christian, agrees that God's law is good and that he is bad.

*Verse 17 - "Now then it is no more I that do it, but sin that dwelleth in me."*

νυνὶ δὲ οὐκετι ἐγὼ κατεργάζομαι αὐτὸ ἀλλὰ ἡ οἰκοῦσα ἐν ἐμοὶ ἁμαρτία.

*"So then it is no longer I that do it, but sin which dwells within me."* . . . *RSV*

νυνὶ (temporal conjunction) 1497.
δὲ (explanatory conjunction) 11.
οὐκετι (negative temporal conjunction) 1289.
ἐγὼ (nom.sing.masc.of ἐγώ, subject of κατεργάζομαι) 123.
αὐτὸ (acc.sing.neut.of αὐτός, direct object of κατεργάζομαι) 16.
ἀλλὰ (alternative conjunction) 342.
ἡ (nom.sing.fem.of the article in agreement with ἁμαρτία) 9.

**#3926** οἰκοῦσα (pres.act.part.nom.sing.fem.of οἰκέω, adjectival, ascriptive, in agreement with ἁμαρτία).

King James Version

dwell - Rom.7:17,18,20; 8:9,11; 1 Cor.3:16; 7:12,13; 1 Tim.6:16.

Revised Standard Version

dwell - Rom.7:17,18,20; 8:9,11; 1 Cor.3:16; 1 Tim.6:16.
live - 1 Cor.7:12,13.

*Meaning:* Cf. οἰκία (#186) and others in οἰκ (*e.g.*οἰκεῖος (#4456), οἴκημα (#3246), οἰκητήριον (#4305), οἰκέτης (#2572), οἰκιακός (#885), οἶκος (#784), *etc.* To dwell in or with. In a physical sense of two people living in the same house - 1 Cor.7:12,13. With reference to the carnal sin principle present in the believer - Rom.7:17,18,20; the Holy Spirit indwells the believer - Rom.8:9,11; 1 Cor.3:16. Intransitively of God's dwelling - 1 Tim.6:16.

ἐν (preposition with the locative of place) 80.
ἐμοὶ (loc.sing.masc.of ἐμός, place) 1267.
ἁμαρτία (nom.sing.fem.of ἁμαρτία, subject of κατεργάζεται understood).

*Translation - "Now it follows that no longer is it I doing it, but the indwelling sin."*

**Comment:** *νυνὶ δὲ* is explanatory. Paul is drawing a conclusion from his assertion in verse 16 that when Paul disapproves of what Saul does, Paul is agreeing with God. Therefore in reality Paul did not commit the sin, but Saul who still occupies the same house in which he has always lived. When Paul came in (the new birth) Saul was not asked to leave, though he will be expelled at the rapture (1 Cor.15:44,51; Phil.3:21). It is a case of two incompatible personalities living in the same house. This verse sheds light on 1 John 3:8 ,9, although it is probable that the point there is in the present continuous action of the verb. *ἐγὼ* emphasizes the contrast between Paul (*ἐγώ*) and Saul (*ἁμαρτία*). *ἐγώ* in contrast can be seen in John 5:31,34; 10:30; Eph.5:32; Phil.4:11, *etc.*

Although Paul seeks to disassociate himself from his fleshly body, through the agency of which he had committed sin, he does not mean to say that he is not responsible before God for what he allowed his fleshly Saul nature to do to embarrass him, dishonor God and grieve the Holy Spirit. The Christian does not "get away with" his sins after he is saved, but the penalty is not death in hell. The child of God pays a heavy opportunity cost in terms of loss of reward for what he could have been doing for Christ with the time and strength resources which he expended in the service of sin. The old carnal nature of Saul is slated for physical death, but promised resurrection and glorification, but Paul's appreciation of heaven and its eternal blessings will be less than it could have been otherwise, if he had not allowed his flesh to corrupt his testimony, crucify the Son of God afresh and put Him to an open shame (Heb.6:6).

*Verse 18 - "For I know that in me (that is, in my flesh,) dwelleth no good thing: for to will is present with me, but how to perform that which is good I find not."*

οἶδα γὰρ ὅτι οὐκ οἰκεῖ ἐν ἐμοί, τοῦτ' ἔστιν ἐν τῇ σαρκί μου, ἀγαθόν. τὸ γὰρ θέλειν παράκειταί μοι, τὸ δὲ κατεργάζεσθαι τὸ καλὸν οὔ.

*"For I know that nothing good dwells within me, that is, in my flesh. I can will what is right, but I cannot do it."*

οἶδα (1st.per.sing.perf.act.ind.of οἶδα, intensive) 144b.

γὰρ (causal conjunction) 105.

ὅτι (conjunction introducing an object clause in indirect discourse) 211.

οὐκ (negative conjunction with the indicative) 130.

οἰκεῖ (3d.per.sing.pres.act.ind.of οἰκέω, present progressive, retroactive) 3926.

ἐν (preposition with the locative of place) 80.

ἐμοί (loc.sing.masc.of ἐμός, place) 1267.

τοῦτ' (nom.sing.neut.of οὗτος, subject of ἔστιν) 93.

ἔστιν (3d.per.sing.pres.ind.of εἰμί, aoristic) 86.

ἐν (preposition with the locative of place) 80.

τῇ (loc.sing.fem.of the article in agreement with σαρκί) 9.

σαρκί (loc.sing.fem.of σάρξ, place) 202.

μου (gen.sing.masc.ofd ἐγώ, possession) 123.

ἀγαθόν (nom.sing.neut.of ἀγαθός, subject of οἰκεῖ) 547.

τὸ (nom.sing.neut.of the article in agreement with θέλειν) 9.
γὰρ (causal conjunction) 105.
θέλειν (pres.act.inf.of θέλω, noun use, subject of παράκειται) 88.

#3927 παράκειται (3d.per.sing.pres.mid.ind.of παράκειμαι, aoristic).

King James Version

be present with - Rom.7:18,21.

Revised Standard Version

I can will - Rom.7:18.
lies close at hand - Rom.7:21.

*Meaning:* A combination of παρά (#154) and κεῖμαι (#295). Hence, to be present; to be at hand; to be placed alongside. With reference to the presence of the will of the regenerated nature to do that which is good - Rom.7:18,21.

μοι (instru.sing.masc.of ἐγώ, association) 123..
τὸ (nom.sing.neut.of the article in agreement with κατεργάζεσθαι) 9.
δὲ (adversative conjunction) 11.
κατεργάζεσθαι (pres.mid.inf.of κατεργάζομαι, noun use, subject of παράκειται) 3815.
τὸ (acc.sing.neut.of the article in agreement with καλὸν) 9.
καλὸν (acc.sing.neut.of καλός, direct object of κατεργάζεσθαι) 296.
οὔ (negative conjunction with the indicative) 130.

*Translation - "Because I have learned that there dwells in me, that is in my flesh, nothing good; for the will is present with me, but the performance of the good is not."*

**Comment:** Again Paul has used a perfect tense to indicate his past learning experience. Since he says that there is *nothing good* in him, he must qualify the statement. Otherwise he is saying that the indwelling Holy Spirit (1 Cor.6:19) and the new nature, the result of his birth from above (John 3:3,7; 1 Pet.1:23) is not good. Hence the qualification τουτ' ἐστιν ἐν τῇ σαρκί μου, explains ἐν ἐμοί. When he says that he now realizes what he did not know in his old days as Saul, namely that there was nothing good in him, he means the Saul nature. Here is some of the internal evidence that Paul is not describing his experiences in his unregenerate days. If he were, the qualifying clause τουτ' ἐστιν ἐν τῇ σαρκί μου would be without point, for there is nothing good in the unsaved man, be it flesh, will, intellect or emotion (John 6:63; Eph.2:1-3). But there is something good in Paul, the Christian. He has a new personality, the result of his birth from above, with a will that wants to do good, an intellect that recognizes the utility of doing good and the folly of doing bad and an emotional nature to match. Paul wants to obey God, but Saul cannot do it. Here we have a clear-cut distinction between the new nature (the will) and the old nature (the performance).

"The abrupt termination of the sentence with οὗ (Sinaiticus A B C 81 1739 cop<sub>sa,bo</sub> goth arm *al*) prompted copyists to add some kind of supplement: (a) εὑρίσκω (D G K P Φ 33 88* 614 *Byz Lect)*, or (b) γινώσκω (88<sub>mg</sub> 2127), or (c) *is not in me (*eth)." (Metzger, *A Textual Commentary on the Greek New Testament*, 514).

*Verse 19 - "For the good that I would I do not: but the evil which I would not, that I do."*

οὐ γὰρ ὃ θέλω ποιῶ αγαθόν, ἀλλὰ ὃ οὐ θέλω κακὸν τοῦτο πράσσω.

*"For I do not do the good I want, but the evil I do not want is what I do."*..
                                                              *RSV*

οὐ (negative conjunction with the indicative) 130.
γὰρ (causal conjunction) 105.
ὃ (acc.sing.neut.of ὅς, relative pronoun, direct object of ποιῶ) 65.
θέλω (1st.per.sing.pres.act.ind.of θέλω, static) 88.
ποιῶ (1st.per.sing.pres.act.ind.of ποιέω, progressive description) 127.
ἀγαθόν (acc.sing.masc.of ἀγαθός, direct object of ποιῶ) 547.
ἀλλὰ (adversative conjunction) 342.
ὃ (acc.sing.neut.of ὅς, relative pronoun, direct object of θέλω) 65.
οὐ (negative conjunction with the indicative) 130.
θέλω (1st.per.sing.pres.act.ind.of θέλω, static) 88.
κακὸν (acc.sing.neut.of κακός, direct object of πράσσω) 1388.
τοῦτο (acc.sing.neut.of οὗτος, anaphoric) 93.
πράσσω (1st.per.sing.pres.act.ind.of πράσσω, present description) 1943.

*Translation - "I do not do the good that I wish to do, but the evil that I do not wish is what I always do."*

**Comment:** This is in part a repetition of verse 16, and he follows it with a restatement of verse 17 in verse 20.

If the reader is concerned that Paul seems to be describing the scenario of the defeated Christian life, as though there were no alternative in terms of the victorious life in Christ, let him be patient. Paul cannot tell it all at once. In Romans 8 we have a full discussion of the victorious life.

*Verse 20 - "Now if I do that I would not, it is no more I that do it, but sin that dwelleth in me."*

εἰ δὲ ὃ οὐ θέλω (ἐγὼ) τοῦτο ποιῶ, οὐκέτι ἐγὼ κατεργάζομαι αὐτὸ ἀλλὰ ἡ οἰκοῦσα ἐν ἐμοὶ ἁμαρτία.

*"Now if I do what I do not want, it is no longer I that do it, but sin which dwells within me." . . . RSV*

εἰ (conditional particle in a first-class condition) 337.

δὲ (explanatory conjunction) 11.

ὃ (acc.sing.neut.of ὅς, relative pronoun, direct object of θέλω) 65.

οὐ (negative conjunction with the indicative) 130.

θέλω (1st.per.sing.pres.act.ind.of θέλω, aoristic) 88.

(ἐγὼ) (nom.sing.masc.of ἐγώ, subject of ποιῶ) 123.

τοῦτο (acc.sing.neut.of οὗτος, direct object of ποιῶ) 93.

ποιῶ (1st.per.sing.pres.act.ind.of ποιέω, aoristic, in a first-class condition) 127.

οὐκέτι (negative temporal conjunction) 1289.

ἐγὼ (nom.sing.masc.of ἐγώ, subject of κατεργάζομαι) 123.

κατεργάζομαι (1st.per.sing.pres.mid.ind.of κατεργάζομαι, aoristic) 3815.

αὐτὸ (acc.sing.neut.of αὐτός, direct object of κατεργάζομαι, anaphoric) 16.

ἀλλὰ (alternative conjunction) 342.

ἡ (nom.sing.fem.of the article in agreement with ἁμαρτία) 9.

οἰκοῦσα (pres.act.part.nom.sing.fem.of οἰκέω, adjectival, ascriptive, in agreement with ἁμαρτία) 3926.

ἐν (preposition with the locative of place) 80.

ἐμοὶ (loc.sing.masc.of ἐμός, place) 1267.

ἁμαρτία (nom.sing.fem.of ἁμαρτία, subject of ποιεῖ understood) 111.

*Translation* - "*Now since I do that which I do not wish to do, it is no longer I who does it, but the sin which dwells within me.*"

**Comment:** δὲ is explanatory. εἰ introduces a first-class condition with the indicative in the protasis. Paul is stating a fact. He has already said that he does not approve of what he does. That is, Saul, with his unregenerate will, orders his flesh, which, until glorification is eager to manifest its evil works (Gal.5:19-21) in compliance with the dictates of his will, the reasoning of his unregenerate intellect and the drive of his unregenerate emotions. But Paul disapproves. His regenerate will, intellect and emotional nature, the products of his new birth, the baptism of the Holy Spirit into union in the Body of Christ, abhors what his flesh is doing. Since the premise is true the conclusion in the apodosis follows. Paul is not the one who commits the sin. It is Saul. This conflict between the flesh and the Spirit (Gal.5:16,17) leads Paul to the enunciation of a principle which follows in

*Verse 21* - "*I find then a law, that, when I would do good, evil is present with me.*"

Εὑρίσκω ἄρα τὸν νόμον τῷ θέλοντι ἐμοὶ ποιεῖν τὸ καλὸν ὅτι ἐμοὶ τό κακὸν παράκειται.

"*So I find it to be a law that when I want to do right, evil lies close at hand.*"...
RSV

Εὑρίσκω (1st.per.sing.pres.act.ind.of εὑρίσκω, static) 79.

ἄρα (illative particle) 995.

τὸν (acc.sing.masc.of the article in agreement with νόμον) 9.

νόμον (acc.sing.masc.of νόμος, direct object of εὑρίσκω) 464.

τῷ (loc.sing.neut.of the article in a locative absolute construction) 9.

θέλοντι (pres.act.part.loc.sing.neut.of θέλω, adverbial, concessive) 88.

ἐμοὶ (loc.sing.masc.of ἐμός, locative absolute) 1267.

ποιεῖν (pres.act.inf.of ποιέω, epexegetical) 127.

τὸ (acc.sing.neut.of the article in agreement with καλὸν) 9.

καλὸν (acc.sing.neut.of καλός, direct object of ποιεῖν) 296.

ὅτι (conjunction introducing an object clause in indirect discourse) 211.

ἐμοὶ (instru.sing.masc.of ἐμός, association) 1267.

τὸ (nom.sing.neut.of the article in agreement with κακὸν) 9.

κακὸν (nom.sing.neut.of κακός, subject of παράκειται) 1388.

παράκειται (3d.per.sing.pres.mid.ind.of παράκειμαι, static) 3927.

*Translation - "So I find the principle that, despite the fact that I am willing to do right, evil lies nearby."*

**Comment:** ἄρα is illative. *Cf.* #995. νόμον in the sense of "principle" or "rule of life." This governing principle seems to prevail - that (ὅτι and indirect discourse), despite the fact that (concessive participle in θέλοντι) I am always wishing to do the right thing, evil is present. The will of Paul cannot banish from his presence the evil desires of the flesh of Saul.

In the terms of our discussion Paul and Saul live together in the same body and are operating at cross purposes, for Saul is dead in Adam and Paul is born from above in Christ. The Christian is not ambivalent since Paul and Saul are not opposite tendencies of the same will, intellect and emotion. The Christian does not love and hate the same thing at the same time. When he is dominated by Saul he loves sin and evil totally. The way to the victorious life is to seek permanent ascendancy of Paul over Saul. This is done as we "Walk in the Spirit" and thus do not "fulfil the lust of the flesh." (Gal.5:16). The Holy Spirit, Who indwells the body of the Christian (1 Cor.6:19) is sovereign and will always win the contest with the flesh, *if we permit Him to do so.* But He will not interfere with the works of the flesh unless He is invited  into the fight.

That this contest between flesh and Spirit, between Saul and Paul, between evil and good, will not go on forever is clear when we learn in Romans 8:11 and Phil.3:21 that our fleshly bodies will be glorified at the rapture/resurrection of the Second Coming of our Lord (1 Thess.4:13-18; 1 Cor.15:51-58). Until glorification there is no such thing as sinless perfection in the truest sense of the term, although the formula for the victorious life is clear in Romans 8.

Paul describes this conflict again in verses 22 and 23.

*Verse 22 - "For I delight in the law of God after the inward man."*

συνήδομαι γὰρ τῷ νόμῳ τοῦ θεοῦ κατὰ τὸν ἔσω ἄνθρωπον,

*"For I delight in the law of God, in my inmost self, . . . "* . . . RSV

#3928 συνήδομαι (1st.per.sing.pres.mid.ind.of συνήδομαι, aoristic).

King James Version

delight in - Rom.7:22.

Revised Standard Version

delight in - Rom.7:22.

*Meaning:* A combination of σύν (#1542) and ἥδομαι; hence, to take pleasure in; to delight in; to enjoy. Followed by a locative of sphere in Rom.7:22.

γὰρ (causal conjunction) 105.
τῷ (loc.sing.masc.of the article in agreement with νόμῳ) 9.
νόμῳ (loc.sing.masc.of νόμος, sphere) 464.
τοῦ (gen.sing.masc.of the article in agreement with θεοῦ) 9.
θεοῦ (gen.sing.masc.of θεός, description) 124.
κατὰ (preposition with the accusative, standard) 98.
τὸν (acc.sing.masc.of the article in agreement with ἄνθρωπον) 9.
ἔσω (adverbial, used like an adjective in the attributive position) 1601.
ἄνθρωπον (acc.sing.masc.of ἄνθρωπος, standard) 341.

*Translation - "Because I am delighted with the law of God insofar as the inner man is concerned."*

**Comment:** Verses 22 and 23 further explain verse 21. Paul found opposing tendencies within him. The "inner man" (τὸν ἔσω ἄνθρωπον), which is the result of the birth from above (John 3:3,7; 1 Pet.1:23) finds compatibility in and is delighted with the law of God. There is complete harmony between the two.

Exegetes have debated whether Paul in Romans 7 is describing his experience before or after his regeneration, and whether, therefore, this is a description of a regenerate person or a lost sinner. Who is speaking here? Saul or Paul? Verse 22 seems conclusive that Paul is talking about his experience after he was saved. No unregenerate person has an "inner man" (ἔσω ἄνθρωπον) that delights in the law of God. *Cf.* verse 18. If Paul meant the unsaved in verse 22 he was mistaken in verse 18 and the doctrine of total depravity must be abandoned, as we all return to the position of Thomas Aquinas and the Jesuits. The "inner man" is Paul. Verse 23 describes Saul. Since Paul delights in God's law, he needs to be strengthened in his struggle against Saul. *Cf.* Eph.3:16 where the phrase ἔσω ἄνθρωπον occurs in the same sense. The inner man is Paul, born from above (John 3:3,7) of incorruptible seed (1 Pet.1:23). He (the inner man) cannot sin because he is born of God (1 John 3:9). His fruits are listed in Gal.5:22,23. Paul loves God's law. Saul hates it.

*Verse 23 - "But I see another law in my members, warring against the law of my mind, and bringing me into captivity of the law of sin which is in my members."*

βλέπω δὲ ἕτερον νόμον ἐν τοῖς μέλεσίν μου ἀντιστρατευόμενον τῷ νόμῳ τοῦ νοός μου καὶ αἰχμαλωτίζοντά με ἐν τῷ νόμῳ τῆς ἁμαρτίας τῷ ὄντι ἐν τοῖς μέλεσίν μου.

"... but I see in my members another law at war with the law of my mind and making me captive to the law of sin which dwells in my members." ... RSV

βλέπω (1st.per.sing.pres.act.ind.of βλέπω, present progressive, retroactive) 499.

δὲ (adversative conjunction) 11.

ἕτερον (acc.sing.masc.of ἕτερος, in agreement with νόμον) 605.

νόμον (acc.sing.masc.of νόμος, direct object of βλέπω) 464.

ἐν (preposition with the locative of place) 80.

τοῖς (loc.pl.neut.of the article in agreement with μέλεσίν) 9.

μέλεσίν (loc.pl.neut.of μέλος, place) 506.

μου (gen.sing.masc.of ἐγώ, possession) 123.

#3929 ἀντιστρατευόμενον (pres.mid.part.acc.sing.masc.of ἀντιστρατεύομαι, adjectival, restrictive).

King James Version

war against - Rom.7:23.

Revised Standard Version

at war with - Rom.7:23.

*Meaning:* A combination of ἀντί (#237) and στρατεύω (#1944). Hence, to make war against; to fight; to resist; to seek to overcome; to take the field as in a military expedition. With reference to the opposition of the flesh to the new nature in the believer - Rom.7:23.

τῷ (dat.sing.masc.of the article in agreement with νόμῳ) 9.

νόμῳ (dat.sing.masc.of νόμος, personal disadvantage) 464.

τοῦ (gen.sing.masc.of the article in agreement with νοός) 9.

νοός (gen.sing.masc.of νοῦς, description) 2928.

μου (gen.sing.masc.of ἐγώ, possession) 123.

καὶ (adjunctive conjunction joining participles) 14.

αἰχμαλωτίζοντά (pres.act.part.acc.sing.masc.of αἰχμαλωτίζω, adjectival, restrictive) 2726.

με (acc.sing.masc.of ἐγώ, direct object of αἰχμαλωτίζοντά) 123.

ἐν (preposition with the locative of sphere) 80.

τῷ (loc.sing.masc.of the article in agreement with νόμῳ) 9.

νόμῳ (loc.sing.masc.of νόμος, sphere) 464.

τῆς (gen.sing.fem.of the article in agreement with ἁμαρτίας) 9.

ἁμαρτίας (gen.sing.fem.of ἁμαρτία, description) 111.

τῷ (loc.sing.masc.of the article in agreement with νόμῳ) 9.

ὄντι (pres.act.part.loc.sing.masc.of εἰμί, adjectival, restrictive, in agreement with νόμῳ) 86.

ἐν (preposition with the locative of place) 80.

τοῖς (loc.pl.masc.of the article in agreement with μέλεσίν) 9.

μέλεσίν (loc.pl.masc.ofd μέλος, place) 506.

μου (gen.sing.masc.of ἐγώ, possession) 123.

*Translation - "But I see another principle in my body at war with the principle of my mind and bringing me into captivity to the principle of sin which exists in my body."*

**Comment:** δὲ is adversative and places verse 23 in contrast to verse 22. Paul delights in the law of God (verse 22) but Paul is always aware of the presence of Saul, the other basic actor in the drama, working in his physical body and waging war against Paul (the principle of the regenerate mind). Saul not only wages war against Paul, but he also wins the battle. The two participles are adjectival. They define ἕτερον νόμον ἐν τοῖς μέλεσίν μου. Saul's body, the result of his first birth in Adam, an aggregation of fleshly organs in which there is no profit and which can only produce its works (ἔργα, Gal.5:19-21; John 6:63) is at war with Paul's regenerate mind. The body is, as yet, unchanged by regeneration, although it too will be delivered by glorification "from the bondage of corruption into the glorious liberty of the children of God" (Rom.8:21). Paul's mind had been changed since repentance (μετανοία - "a change of the mind") is identified with faith. The will of the Christian follows the will of the redeemed mind, while his unregenerate will (the will of Saul) is attracted to the temptations of sin in the body. If the will of the inner man (verse 22) always prevailed we could speak objectively about sinless perfection for the Christian prior to glorification. But verse 22 is modified by verse 23. Until our Lord returns the two natures will contend, and, in those moments when the Christian forgets that he has within him his most dangerous enemy, and thus forgets to pray and appeal to the indwelling Holy Spirit for victory, he is going to be defeated, with disastrous results, both to himself, his loved ones, the body of Christ as a whole and with embarrassment to His Lord, the glorified Head of the Body in heaven.

Paul understood this conflict all too well, not only by revelation but also by sad experience. Thus his cry of anguish in

*Verse 24 - "O wretched man that I am! Who shall deliver me from the body of death?"*

ταλαίπωρος ἐγὼ ἄνθρωπος. τίς με ῥύσεται ἐκ τοῦ σώματος τοῦ θανάτου τούτου;

*"Wretched man that I am! Who will deliver me from this body of death?"* . . .
*RSV*

#3930 ταλαίπωρος (nom.sing.masc.of ταλαίπωρος, predicate adjective).

King James Version

wretched - Rom.7:24. Rev.3:17.

Revised Standard Version

wretched - Rom.7:24. Rev.3:17.

*Meaning:* from ταλάω - "to bear" and πῶρος - "a callous." The result of having undergone long suffering. Wretched. Psychologically - Rom.7:24; generally - Rev.3:17.

ἐγώ (nom.sing.masc.of ἐγώ, subject of εἰμί understood) 123.

ἄνθρωπος (nom.sing.masc.of ἄνθρωπος, predicate nominative) 341.

τίς (nom.sing.masc.of τίς, interrogative pronoun, subject of ῥύσεται) 281.

ῥύσεται (3d.per.sing.fut.mid.ind.of ῥύομαι, deliberative in direct question) 584.

ἐκ (preposition with the ablative of separation) 19.

τοῦ (abl.sing.neut.of the article in agreement with σώματος) 9.

σώματος (abl.sing.neut.of σῶμα, separation) 507.

τοῦ (gen.sing.masc.of the article in agreement with θανάτου) 9.

θανάτου (gen.sing.masc.of θάνατος, description) 381.

τούτου (abl.sing.neut.of οὗτος, in agreement with σώματος) 93.

*Translation - "What a wretched man I am! Who is going to deliver me from this body of death?"*

**Comment:** ταλαίπωρος ἐγώ ἄνθρωπος - an interjectional nominative. The question is rhetorical, asked in human desperation. Paul regarded his body as one that could only produce death, because it has its source in Adam in whom the human race died (1 Cor.15:22; Rom.5:12).

The answer to Paul's question can never come from a human source. Heaven's power is required to deliver us from the body of death.

It is important that we do not construe this passage in Gnostic terms. The Gnostics thought of the human body as inherently evil because it was material. Thus glorification could not change its evil nature, because after glorification it would still be material and hence evil. The glorified body of the Christian will no longer be a "body of death."

Paul's designation of the body as a "body of death" is consistent with entropy, the second law of thermodynamics, which provides that the energy to maintain the human body after maturity will become increasingly unavailable. There is a point at which synthesis becomes analysis. At that point complexity tends toward simplicity and entropy is increased until the vital organs of the body cannot function. This is physical death. After physical death the process of simplification continues until the whole has succombed to biodegradability. Paul touches on this point again in Romans 8:20,21 and applies it, not only to the physical bodies of the saints, but to the entire material creation as well.

Paul has an answer for his rhetorical question which he develops fully in the eighth chapter. The Great Deliverer is Jesus Christ our Lord.

*Verse 25 - "I thank God through Jesus Christ our Lord. So then with the mind I myself serve the law of God: but with the flesh, the law of sin."*

χάρις δὲ τῷ θεῷ διὰ Ἰησοῦ Χριστοῦ τοῦ κυρίου ἡμῶν. ἄρα οὖν αὐτὸς ἐγὼ τῷ μὲν νοῒ δουλεύω νόμῳ θεοῦ, τῇ δὲ σαρκὶ νόμῳ ἁμαρτίας.

*"Thanks be to God through Jesus Christ our Lord! So then I myself serve the law of God with my mind, but with my flesh I serve the law of sin."* RSV

χάρις (nom.sing.fem.of χάρις, nominative interjection) 1700
δὲ (continuative conjunction) 11.
τῷ (dat.sing.masc.of the article in agreement with θεῷ) 9.
θεῷ (dat.sing.masc.of θεός, indirect object) 124.
διὰ (preposition with the ablative of agent) 118.
Ἰησοῦ (abl.sing.masc.of Ἰησοῦς, agent) 3.
Χριστοῦ (abl.sing.masc.of Χριστός, apposition) 4.
τοῦ (abl.sing.masc.of the article in agreement with κυρίου) 9.
κυρίου (abl.sing.masc.of κύριος, apposition) 97.
ἡμῶν (gen.pl.masc.of ἐγώ, relationship) 123.
ἄρα (illative particle with οὖν) 995.
οὖν (illative conjunction) 68.
αὐτὸς (nom.sing.masc.of αὐτός, intensive) 16.
ἐγὼ (nom.sing.masc.of ἐγώ, subject of δουλεύω, 123).
τῷ (instru.sing.masc.of the article in agreement with νοῒ) 9.
μὲν (correlative particle of affirmation) 300.
νοῒ (instru.sing.masc.of νοῦς, means) 2928.
δουλεύω (1st.per.sing.pres.act.ind.of δουλεύω, present progressive retroactive) 604.
νόμῳ (dat.sing.masc.of νόμος, indirect object) 464.
θεοῦ (gen.sing.masc.of θεός, description) 124.
τῇ (instru.sing.fem.of the article in agreement with σαρκὶ) 9.
δὲ (adversative conjunction) 11.
σαρκὶ (instru.sing.fem.of σάρξ, means) 1202.
νόμῳ (dat.sing.masc.of νόμος, indirect object) 464.
ἁμαρτίας (gen.sing.fem.of ἁμαρτία, description) 111.

*Translation - "Thanks be to God, through Jesus Christ, our Lord. So then I myself on the one hand, with the mind serve the divine law, but, on the other hand, with the flesh the sin principle."*

**Comment:** Final deliverance from the body of death will come at the first resurrection (1 Cor.15:51; Phil.3:21). The delivering agent will be Jesus Christ our Lord (1 John 3:1-4). In the meantime the battle continues between the regenerate mind of the child of God and his depraved flesh. The mind, the product of his birth from above can serve only the divine principles by which the universe is orchestrated. These principles will of course ultimately prevail. The flesh, due to its human origin, can only continue in its activities of sin (Gal.5:17-19). How the will follows the one to holiness or the other in sin is the basic problem of the victorious life of the believer.

This is the great subject of the eighth chapter.

## Live in the Spirit
### *(Romans 8:1-17)*

*Romans 8:1 - "There is therefore now no condemnation to them which are in Christ Jesus, who walk not after the flesh but after the Spirit."*

Οὐδὲν ἄρα νῦν κατάκριμα τοῖς ἐν Χριστῷ Ἰησοῦ.

*"There is therefore now no condemnation for those who are in Christ Jesus.".*
                                                                        RSV

Οὐδὲν (nom.sing.neut.of οὐδείς, in agreement with κατάκριμα) 446.
ἄρα (illative particle) 995.
νῦν (temporal conjunction) 1497.
κατάκριμα (nom.sing.neut.of κατάκριμα, subject of ἐστίν understood) 3903.
τοῖς (dat.pl.masc.of the article, personal interest) 9.
ἐν (preposition with the locative, like an instrumental of association) 80.
Χριστῷ (instrumental sing. masc.of Χριστός, association) 4.
Ἰησοῦ (instrumental sing.masc.of Ἰησοῦς, apposition) 3.

*Translation - "There is therefore now no other judgment against those in association with Christ Jesus."*

**Comment:** ἄρα is illative. νῦν *i.e.* since the cross. οὐδὲν κατάκριμα - "not a single instance of condemnation." Satan, who makes it his business to slander the saints before the court of heaven (Job 1:9-11; 2:7) will never win a case against those for whom Christ died, since our Advocate pleads the efficacy of His shed blood (1 John 2:1,2).

It is significant that Paul should open this section on the victorious life with this assurance of salvation for those who are in the body of Christ. He has just finished his discussion of sin in the life of the believer and has admitted that in his own case, he was not always victorious. What assurance then has the child of God that he is even rescued from the penalty of sin, much less rescued from its power and presence? The Arminian threat that hangs over the head of the Christian who is defeated would seem to militate against his having the courage to struggle onward to the victorious life. But if we are assured that we are eternally secure in Christ, even though we have sinned, we somehow have the courage after a fall to get up and go on for the Lord. John's admonition to the saints that they not "go on sinning" is followed by his assurance that if they do, their lapse does not affect their *standing* in Christ (Rom.5:1,2) however destructive it may be to their *state* (1 John 2:1,2).

The class of persons is well defined by the phrase τοῖς ἐν Χριστῷ Ἰησοῦ - those in association with (instrumental) or in union with (Goodspeed) Christ Jesus. This phrase is understood in the light of John 17:21; 1 Cor.12:13. Note all other uses of ἐν Χριστῷ. The United Bible Societies' Committee has rejected the variant reading which in the KJV supports the last relative clause. Their degree of certitude is graded A. The language omitted here occurs in verse 4, where it harmonizes with the context. Its inclusion here was a natural copyist error. "The shorter text, which makes the more general statement without the qualification that is appropriate enough at ver.4, is strongly supported by early representatives of both the Alexandrian and the Western types of text (Sinaiticus * B C₂ D* G 1739 itd*, g copsa,bo armmss al)." Metzger, *A Textual Commentary on the Greek New Testament*, 515).

The concept of union with Christ by simple repentance and faith and its result of total freedom from condemnation, is unpalatable to the natural mind, which is incapable of grasping the genius of gospel truth. The legalist will wish to make the promise of freedom from condemnation contingent upon personal merit. Calvinists have no difficulty with the passage. It destroys Pelagianism, Arminianism and the modern counterpart - the modernistic doctrine of relative salvation by relative ethics. Paul explains in verse 2 why the statement in verse one is true.

*Verse 2 - "For the law of the spirit of life in Christ Jesus hath made me free from the law of sin and death."*

ὁ γὰρ νόμος τοῦ πνεύματος τῆς ζωῆς ἐν Χριστῷ Ἰησοῦ ἠλευθέρωσέν με ἀπὸ τοῦ νόμου τῆς ἁμαρτίας καὶ τοῦ θανάτου.

*"For the law of the Spirit of life in Christ Jesus has set me free from the law of sin and death."* . . . RSV

ὁ (nom.sing.masc.of the article in agreement with νόμος) 9.

γὰρ (causal conjunction) 105.

νόμος (nom.sing.masc.of νόμος, subject of ἠλευθέρωσεν) 464.

τοῦ (gen.sing.neut.of the article in agreement with πνεύματος) 9.

πνεύματος (gen.sing.neut.of πνεῦμα, description) 83.

τῆς (gen.sing.fem.of the article in agreement with ζωῆς) 9.

ζωῆς (gen.sing.fem.of ζωή, description) 668.

ἐν (preposition with the locative, like an instrumental of association) 80.

Χριστῷ (instrumental sing.masc.of Χριστός, association) 4.

Ἰησοῦ (instru.sing.masc.of Ἰησοῦς, apposition) 3.

ἠλευθέρωσέν (3d.per.sing.aor.act.ind.of ἐλευθερόω, culminative) 2385.

με (acc.sing.masc.of ἐγώ, direct object of ἠλευθέρωσέν) 123.

ἀπὸ (preposition with the ablative of separation) 70.

τοῦ (abl.sing.masc.of the article in agreement with νόμου) 9.

νόμου (abl.sing.masc.of νόμος, separation) 464.

τῆς (gen.sing.fem.of the article in agreement with ἁμαρτίας) 9.

ἁμαρτίας (gen.sing.fem.of ἁμαρτία, description) 111.

καὶ (adjunctive conjunction joining nouns) 14.

τοῦ (gen.sing.masc.of the article in agreement with θανάτου) 9.

θανάτου (gen.sing.masc.of θάνατος, description) 381.

*Translation - "Because the law of the Spirit of life in association with Christ*

*Jesus has rescued me from the law of sin and death."*

**Comment:** No condemnation in Christ? Why? Because (causal γὰρ) one law has operated to free me from the toils of another opposite law. The law of the Spirit of life is opposed to the law of sin and death. No two principles could be more diametrically antithetical than these. How does the Spirit's law make me free? The prepositional phrase ἐν Χριστῷ Ἰησοῦ is joined, not to ζωῆς but to the verb ἠλευθέρωσέν. Whatever the Holy Spirit does for us He does because of our association with Christ Jesus - both with reference to His person and also to His work. Indeed it is by the baptism of the Holy Spirit (1 Cor.12:13; Gal.3:27) that the believer has become associated with Christ. *Cf.* Rom.5:15,16,17,18,19,20,21; 6:18-20,22; 7:5,8,24,25.

Note the connection of the Holy Spirit with Jesus' incarnation - Luke 1:34,35; His sinless life - Heb.9:14; His death - Heb.9;14; His resurrection - 1 Pet.3:18; Rom.8:11. Thus this same Spirit of Life did for us, when He liberated us from the chains of sin and death, what He did for Christ Jesus. As the Holy Spirit fathered the human nature of Jesus (Luke 1:34,35), so He has fathered our new nature (John 3:5b). As He kept Jesus sinless (Heb.9:14) so He is able to keep us from the works of the flesh (Gal.5:16). As He raised Jesus from the dead (Rom.8:11) so indeed will He raise us up. Thus the Holy Spirit of life identifies the believer with the body of Christ (1 Cor.12:13). Only thus, by His supernatural function in the division of labor in the Godhead, could we be thus rescued.

The law of Moses could not do it because the law's reflection of the holiness of God stood in stark contrast to the behavior of fallen man, with the result that the law could not save - only condemn.

*Verse 3 - "For what the law could not do, in that it was weak through the flesh, God, sending His own Son in the likeness of sinful flesh, and for sin, condemned sin in the flesh."*

τὸ γὰρ ἀδύνατον τοῦ νόμου, ἐν ᾧ ἠσθένει διὰ τῆς σαρκός, ὁ θεὸς τὸν ἑαυτοῦ υἱὸν πέμψας ἐν ὁμοιώματι σαρκὸς ἁμαρτίας καὶ περὶ ἁμαρτίας κατέκρινεν τὴν ἁμαρτίαν ἐν τῇ σαρκί,

"For God has done what the law, weakened by the flesh, could not do: sending his own Son in the likeness of sinful flesh and for sin, he condemned sin in the flesh, . . . " . . . RSV

τὸ (nom.sing.neut.of the article in agreement with ἀδύνατον) 9.
γὰρ (causal conjunction) 105.
ἀδύνατον (nom.sing.neut.of ἀδύνατος, suspended nominative) 1310.
του (gen.sing.masc.of the article in agreement with νόμου) 9.
νόμου (gen.sing.masc.of νόμος, description) 464.
ἐν (preposition with the locative, like an instrumental of cause) 80.
ᾧ (instru.sing.neut.of ὅς, cause) 65.
ἠσθένει (3d.per.sing.imp.ind.of ἀσθενέω, progressive description) 857.
διὰ (preposition with the ablative, agency) 118.

τῆς (abl.sing.fem.of the article in agreement with σαρκὸς) 9.

σαρκὸς (abl.sing.fem.of σάρξ, agency) 1202.

ὁ (nom.sing.masc.of the article in agreement with ϑεὸς) 9.

ϑεὸς (nom.sing.masc.of ϑεός, subject of κατέκρινεν) 124.

τὸν (acc.sing.masc.of the article in agreement with υἱὸν) 9.

ἑαυτοῦ (gen.sing.masc.of ἑαυτός, relationship) 288.

υἱὸν (acc.sing.masc.of υἱός, direct object of πέμψας) 5.

πέμψας (aor.act.part.nom.sing.masc.of πέμπω, adverbial, modal) 169.

ἐν (preposition with the locative of sphere) 80.

ὁμοιώματι (loc.sing.neut.of ὁμοίωμα, sphere) 3803.

σαρκὸς (gen.sing.fem.of σάρξ, description) 1202.

ἀμαρτίας (gen.sing.fem.of ἀμαρτία, description) 111.

καὶ (adversative conjunction) 14.

περὶ (preposition with the ablative of separation) 173.

ἀμαρτίας (abl.sing.fem.of ἀμαρτία, separation) 111.

κατέκρινεν (3d.per.sing.aor.act.ind.of κατακρίνω, culminative) 1012.

τὴν (acc.sing.fem.of the article in agreement with ἀμαρτίαν) 9.

ἀμαρτίαν (acc.sing.fem.of ἀμαρτία, direct object of κατέκρινεν) 11.

ἐν (preposition with the locative of place) 80.

τῇ (loc.sing.fem.of the article in agreement with σαρκί) 9.

σαρκί (loc.sing.fem.of σάρξ, place) 1202.

*Translation* - "*Because, in view of the impotence of the law, weak as it had always been through the agency of the flesh, God, after He had sent His own Son in the likeness of sinful flesh, but separate from sin, condemned sin in the flesh.*"

**Comment:** "As to τὸ ἀδύνατον τοῦ νόμου . . . we have either the *nominativus pendens*, the accusative in apposition with the object of the sentence, the accusative of general reference or an instance of anacoluthon." (S.G.Green, *Handbook to the Grammar of the Greek New Testament*, 234, as cited in Robertson, *Grammar*, 490). Any of these are grammatically possible. In any case the sense is clear. What was impossible of accomplishment through the law, God accomplished through His Son. ἐν ᾧ is causal. The law is unable to release sinners from the principle of sin and death. Why? The weakness is in the flesh, not in the law. The law is not weak. It upholds an ethical standard which the flesh, through its weakness cannot achieve. Mankind would never have been enslaved by the principle of sin and death if we had been able to live in keeping with the standard of holiness demanded by the law of God. If we had been able, salvation would have been by the law. More precisely, there would have been no need for salvation. It is man's transgression of the law of God that makes him a universal outlaw, in need of salvation (Gal.3:21). Paul made this clear in Acts 13:38,39.

God's plan, carried out because the the flesh of depraved man cannot attain to the holy standard of the law, involves the incarnation. Thus God had to send His own Son (John 3:16; Gal.4:4). How? Into the fleshly sphere, but only in the likeness of sinful flesh, not sinful flesh in reality. This is the force of ἐν ὁμοιώματι σαρκὸς ἁμαρτίας. Jesus' flesh in incarnation was human flesh in reality but it was not sinful flesh. This is the force of περὶ ἁμαρτίας - "near to but separate from" sin. Thus καὶ is adversative. Cf. Heb.7:26.

The incarnation was followed by the cross where God condemned sin in the flesh. The prepositional phrase ἐν τῇ σαρκί is predicate, not attributive, though we reach this conclusion, not as a grammarian, but as a theologian. Grammatically the phrase can be either attributive or predicate. This is an exegetical question. "Sometimes it is quite important for doctrinal reasons to be careful to note whether the adjunct is attributive or predicate. Thus in Ro.8:3, κατέκρινε τὴν ἁμαρτίαν ἐν τῇ σαρκί, if ἐν τῇ σαρκί is attributive with ἁμαρτίαν, there is a definite assertion of sin in the flesh of Jesus. But if the phrase is predicate and is to be construed with κατέκρινε, no such statement is made. Here the grammarian is helpless to decide the point. The interpreter must step in and appeal to the context or other passages for light. One conversant with Paul's theology will feel sure that ἐν σαρκί is here meant to be taken as predicate." (Robertson, *Grammar*, 784).

This is why the statement in verse 1 is true. There is no condemnation for the believer, because the condemnation has already taken place upon the cross. This is the soteriology of it (the science of salvation). There is also a practical and ethical purpose, in

*Verse 4 - "That the righteousness of the law might be fulfilled in us, who walk not after the flesh, but after the spirit."*

ἵνα τὸ δικαίωμα τοῦ νόμου πληρωθῇ ἐν ἡμῖν τοῖς μὴ κατὰ σάρκα περιπατοῦσιν ἀλλὰ κατὰ πνεῦμα.

". . . in order that the just requirement of the law might be fulfilled in us, who walk not according to the flesh but according to the Spirit." . . . RSV

ἵνα (conjunction with the subjunctive in a sub-final clause) 114,
τὸ (nom.sing.neut.of the article in agreement with δικαίωμα) 9.
δικαίωμα (nom.sing.neut.of δικαίωμα, subject of πληρωθῇ) 1781.
τοῦ (gen.sing.masc.of the article in agreement with νόμου) 9.
νόμου (gen.sing.masc.of νόμος, description) 464.
πληρωθῇ (3d.per.sing.aor.pass.subj.of πληρόω, sub-final) 115.
ἐν (preposition with the locative of sphere) 80.
ἡμῖν (loc.pl.masc.of ἐγώ, sphere) 123.
τοῖς (loc.pl.masc.of the article in agreement with περιπατοῦσιν) 9.
μὴ (negative conjunction with the participle) 87.
κατὰ (preposition with the accusative, standard) 98.
σάρκα (acc.sing.fem.of σάρξ, standard) 1202.
περιπατοῦσιν (pres.act.part.loc.pl.masc.of πατιπατέω, substantival, in apposition with ἡμῖν) 384.
ἀλλὰ (alternative conjunction) 342.

κατά (preposition with the accusative, standard) 98.
πνεῦμα (acc.sing.neut.of πνεῦμα, standard) 83.

*Translation - "In order (and with the result) that the righteous acts of the law may be fulfilled in us - the ones who are walking not according to the flesh, but according to the Spirit."*

**Comment:** Since God's sovereign purpose is in view in the incarnation and atoning death of Christ (verse 3) the sure result of that purpose is also in view. Thus ἵνα and the subjunctive in this case is sub-final. The ultimate divine purpose in redemption is not only that the elect shall be declared righteous in the judicial sense, but also that we shall live lives that fulfill in an ethical sense the fullest demands of His law, which is "holy and just and good." (Romans 7:12). ἐν ἡμῖν - "in us." Who is "us"? The substantival participle περιπατοῦσιν is in apposition to further explain ἡμῖν (epexegetical if a verb instead of a pronoun had been involved). Paul has reference to the elect saints who yield themselves to the Holy Spirit at all times (present tense durative action in περιπατοῦσιν) and thus live victorious lives (Gal.5:16, 22-23). This is God's desire for us and His purpose in the cross, though none of the elect succeed in this lofty moral achievement to the fullest extent, until we have been glorified. Ultimately (after the rapture and resurrection at the Second Coming of our Lord) we will have bodies like His (Phil.3:21; 1 John 3:1-4; 1 Cor.15:44,51 *et al*). Then His purpose will be realized fully. Although sinless perfection is God's ideal purpose for the saints, it is not attainable before glorification, except in periods when we are filled with the Holy Spirit.

Thus two results flow from the incarnation and death of Jesus Christ. His substitutionary act of redemption satisfied the full demand of the law and made it possible for Him, as the Judge of all the earth (Gen.18:25; John 5:22; Acts 17:31) to dismiss the indictment of transgression against the elect and declare that we are as righteous as the Judge Himself (2 Cor.5:21). He took our sin and paid the debt upon the cross. In the exchange we are given His righteousness.

> *"Dressed in His righteousness alone*
> *Faultless to stand before the throne."*

Now that the judicial question is settled the problem remains of translating this judicial righteousness into practical, day to day and moment by moment behavior that measures up to the divine standard. To effect this achievement, the Holy Spirit overwhelms the elect, in His act which 1 Cor.12:13 calls "baptism" and the result is the new birth from above (John 3:3,7; 1 Pet.1:23). Now we are in the body of Christ, the recipients of the benefits of His high priestly prayer of John 17:21. Our bodies are now the temple of the Holy Spirit (1 Cor.6:19) and the garden in which His fruits can grow (Gal.5:22,23) if we allow Him to manifest them. If we do not He is grieved (Eph.4:30) but He is not grieved away, since He has also sealed us as God's property and that seal cannot be broken. It will remain intact until the "day of redemption" when our Lord, Who made us His judicially at the cross, will make us His in sinless perfection forever. Thus the ἵνα clause is sub-final - both final and consecutive, purpose and result. It is unthinkable that anything which our Sovereign God purposes should not result. It is precisely because we know that we shall be sinless in our glorified bodies, and that this glorification is the work of the indwelling Holy Spirit, Who baptized us into the body of Christ, bestowed upon us His gifts, directed our minds to a better understanding of His Word, and grew His garden of fruit in us, and will "quicken our mortal bodies" (Rom.8:11) to a life of glorified sinlessness, that we are encouraged to walk at His direction now (Gal.5:16). And because we know what He has done and will do for us, we are devastated when we grieve Him. Christians often mind the things of the flesh, rather than the things of the Spirit (verse 5), but no Christian who dishonors the body of Christ does so without the soul sorrow that follows, which is another way of saying that the church member who professes to be saved, who can transgress the law of God with impunity indicates by his lack of concern for his wasted life that he is only a church member, not a Christian, and that he only professes that which he does not possess. No child of God escapes His chastening. Those false professors who do escape are thus demonstrated to be illegitimate (Heb.12:5-8). It is to be regretted that some Christians have little assurance of their salvation except in periods following transgression of the Father's principles of righteousness, when they feel the rod of divine chastisement.

*Verse 5 - "For they that are after the flesh do mind the things of the flesh; but they that are after the spirit the things of the spirit."*

οἱ γὰρ κατὰ σάρκα ὄντες τὰ τῆς σαρκὸς φρονοῦσιν, οἱ δὲ κατὰ πνεῦμα τὰ τοῦ πνεύματος.

*"For those who live according to the flesh set their minds on the things of the flesh, but those who live according to the Spirit set their minds on the things of the Spirit." . . . RSV*

οἱ (nom.pl.masc.of the article in agreement with ὄντες) 9.
γὰρ (explanatory conjunction) 105.
κατὰ (preposition with the accusative, standard) 98.
σάρκα (acc.sing.fem.of σάρξ, standard) 1202.
ὄντες (pres.act.part.nom.pl.masc.of εἰμί, substantival, subject of φρονοῦσιν) 86.
τὰ (acc.pl.neut.of the article, direct object of φρονοῦσιν) 9.
τῆς (abl.sing.fem.of the article in agreement with σαρκὸς) 9.
σαρκὸς (abl.sing.fem.of σάρξ, source) 1202.
φρονοῦσιν (3d.per.pl.pres.act.ind.of φρονέω, customary) 1212.
οἱ (nom.pl.masc.of the article in agreement with ὄντες understood) 9.
δὲ (adversative conjunction) 11.
κατὰ (preposition with the accusative, standard) 98.
πνεῦμα (acc.sing.neut.of πνεῦμα, standard) 83.
τὰ (acc.pl.neut.of the article, direct object of φρονοῦσιν) 9.
τοῦ (abl.sing.neut.of the article in agreement with πνεύματος) 9.

πνεύματος (abl.sing.neut.of πνεῦμα, source) 83.

*Translation - "Now those who live according to the flesh have regard for the things that originate in the flesh, but those of the Spirit, the things that the Spirit produces."*

**Comment:** Once again Paul emphasizes the dichotomy between the two realms: Adam vs. Christ (Rom.5:12); death vs. life (Rom.5:17); condemnation vs. justification (Rom.5:18); sin vs. righteousness (Rom.5:19); law vs. grace (Rom.5:20); slavery vs. freedom (Rom.6:17,18); flesh vs. Spirit (Rom.8:5). The trend of Paul's thought from verse 5 through verse 8 must be seen in the light of verse 9. The student should read verse 9 immediately after having read each of verses 5,6,7 and 8. Those whose philosophy and lives are based upon materialism can consider only the flesh, because for them, there is nothing else to consider. Thus it is natural that they are interested in, have an understanding of and are devoted to the works of the flesh- *i.e.* the activities which have the flesh as their source (Gal.5:17-19). Just why we should expect the unregenerate to be interested in anything else defies analysis. That is why it is abundantly clear that when we allow the unsaved, with their fleshly materialistic outlook, to dominate the planet, society is characterized by little else than "adultery, fornication, uncleanness, lasciviousness, idolatry, witchcraft, hatred, variance, emulations, wrath, strife, seditions, heresies, envyings, muders, drunkenness, revelings and all of the rest of the filth that Paul chose not to list (Gal.5:17-19). That is why British and Argentine soldiers are dying today in the icy waters of the South Atlantic over a few small islands that nobody really wants, and only because a small junta of warlords with racial views that recall Adolf Hitler are afflicted with delusions of grandeur about a future that Argentina will never have, while the British continue to dream of the grandeur that was once hers and which she will never have again. The world now is hastening on its ways to the psychopathic ward, reserved for the criminally insane, because the world, outside of Christ is "of the flesh" and therefore can think only in terms of those things which originate in the flesh.

It should be interjected at this point, lest some think that the divine purpose for the world in this age has come to nought, that it is not God's purpose now to "save" world society, but to save the elect. This He is doing as the Holy Spirit directs the worldwide missionary enterprise, to "visit the Gentiles, to take out of them a people for his name." In the meantime God is not particularly concerned with the forms of government which vie for supremacy among world leaders, be they dictatorship, oligarchy, democracy or anarchy. Whichever system of government men choose those in control are going to "mind the things of the flesh." Hitler gave us dictatorship while, at the opposite end of the continuum can be seen the conditions that prevail on some university campuses when the moon is full. In between are the oligarchs who are only slightly less vicious than Hitler and whose powers are only inferior to his, while democracy, which assumes intelligence in the "small d" democrats, as taught by the "cult of the common man" illustrates the fact that the politicians and the people deserve each other.

Although the regenerate child of God must wait with patience for the day of glorification and, in the meantime struggle with the old motivations that once dominated him before he was saved, he now has the new nature and is attracted to the things that have the Holy Spirit as their divine source. These fruits of the Spirit are listed in Gal.5:22,23. He finds in this list, if he will only allow them to grow uninhibited the perfect answers to his psychic disequilibria which otherwise take the glow off his witness for Christ and the sharp edge of his testimony. Verse 6 teaches us that the unregenerate are dead before they die and that the Christian is alive and at peace with the universe and its Creator before glorification sets him free from the loathsome thing which Paul called "the body of death."

*Verse 6 - "For to be carnally minded is death; but to be spiritually minded is life and peace."*

τὸ γὰρ φρόνημα τῆς σαρκὸς θάνατος, τὸ δὲ φρόνημα τοῦ πνεύματος ζωὴ καὶ εἰρήνη.

*"To set the mind on the flesh is death, but to set the mind on the Spirit is life and peace." . . . RSV*

τὸ (nom.sing.neut.of the article in agreement with φρόνημα) 9.
γὰρ (inferential conjunction) 105.

#3931 φρόνημα (nom.sing.neut.of φρόνημα, subject of ἐστίν understood).

King James Version

mind - Rom.8:7,27.
to be minded - Rom.8:6,6.

Revised Standard Version

set the mind on - Rom.8:6,6.
mind - Rom.8:7,27.

*Meaning: Cf.* φρονέω (#1212); φρόνησις (#1801); φρόνιμος (#693); φρονίμως (#2569); φροντίζω (#4902). The root φρόν, plus the result suffix μα - the result of thinking. Attitude; way of thinking; philosophy. Followed by the ablative of source - Rom.8:6,6,7,27.

τῆς (abl.sing.fem.of the article in agreement with σαρκὸς) 9.
σαρκὸς (abl.sing.fem.of σάρξ, source) 1202.
θάνατος (nom.sing.masc.of θάνατος, predicate nominative) 381.
τὸ (nom.sing.neut.of the article in agreement with φρόνημα) 9.
δὲ (adversative conjunction) 11.
φρόνημα (nom.sing.neut.of φρόνημα, subject of ἐστίν understood) 3931.
τοῦ (abl.sing.neut.of the article in agreement with πνεύματος) 9.
πνεύματος (abl.sing.neut.of πνεῦμα, source) 83.

ζωή (nom.sing.fem.of ζωή, predicate nominative) 668.

καί (adjunctive conjunction joining nouns) 14.

εἰρήνη (nom.sing.fem.of εἰρήνη, predicate nominative) 865.

*Translation - "Thus the philosophy based upon the flesh results in death, but the philosophy that originates with the Spirit yields life and peace."*

**Comment:** The ablatives indicate source. Both the flesh and the Holy Spirit produce an attitude and a mind-set. The flesh can only teach us that our destiny is death and that the animal life which we enjoy only temporarily is without meaning. The flesh is subject to the chemical analysis known as biodegradibility. Its complexity can only become simplicity as the second law of thermodynamics dictates that available energy (entropy) is lessened to the point where the vital organs of the body can no longer function. Once the body is clinically and legally dead the state demands that we bury it, in the interest of the maintenance of public health for those who survive. In the grave, some growth continues as hair, fingernails and toenails continue to grow for a short time, but entropy relentlessly continues the disintegration until what was once a philosopher of materialism is now only the dust from which the Lord God made the body in the first place.

The materialist believes that life in its varied forms was synthesized by chance. Amino acids united by sheer random selection to form peptides, dipeptides and quadripeptides, which in turn synthesize to form the proteins of life. For the NeoDarwinian there is no teleonomy involved. No genetic programs were devised by extramaterial intelligence to fit genetic codes, provide constraints against entropy and finally bring the mutations that we see in the plant, animal and human worlds. All is chance and they believe this with a tenacity that amazes those acquainted with probability theory and cybernetics.

With physics and chemistry like that as a base what sort of metaphysics can be had? Certainly not the kind that produces life, joy and peace. Certainly not a conviction that the intelligence Who created the universe is great enough and powerful enough to bring His kingdom through the crisis of man's rebellion to the perfect day when He will create a "new heaven and a new earth wherein dwelleth righteousness."

Materialists who pose as theologians speak much of "confident despair" and "the theology of hope" which can only mean that they are big boys and girls now and are not going to cry although they very much feel like crying. The Christian views all of this nonesense, marvels at the credulity, which they call faith, which enables them to believe in blind chance as the explanation of the origin of life, despite the exponential character of the odds (!), notes the chaos that results in individual lives and in society, and understands quite well that the philosophy that depends only upon the flesh results in death.

But the philosophy and life which originates with the Holy Spirit produces both life and peace. This is a life of peace. If it were not a life of peace, we could not call it life at all. Attitudes and philosophies come either from the flesh (Rom.8:6a,7) or from the Holy Spirit (Rom.8:6b,27).

*Verse 7 - "Because the carnal mind is enmity against God: for it is not subject to the law of God, neither indeed can be."*

διότι τὸ φρόνημα τῆς σαρκὸς ἔχθρα εἰς θεόν, τῷ γὰρ νόμῳ τοῦ θεοῦ οὐχ ὑποτάσσεται, οὐδὲ γὰ δύναται.

*"For the mind that is set on the flesh is hostile to God; it does not submit to God's law, indeed it cannot." . . . RSV*

διότι (compound particle introducing a causal clause) 1795.
τὸ (nom.sing.neut.of the article in agreement with φρόνημα) 9.
φρόνημα (nom.sing.neut.of φρόνημα, subject of ἐστίν understood) 3931.
τῆς (gen.sing.fem.of the article in agreement with σαρκὸς) 9.
σαρκὸς (abl.sing.fem.of σάρξ, source) 1202.
ἔχθρα (nom.sing.fem.of ἔχθρα, predicate nominative) 2834.
εἰς (preposition with the accusative of extent) 140.
θεόν (acc.sing.masc.of θεός, metaphorical extent) 124.
τῷ (dat.sing.masc.of the article in agreement with νόμῳ) 9.
γὰρ (causal conjunction) 105.
νόμῳ (dat.sing.masc.of νόμος, reference) 464.
τοῦ (gen.sing.masc.of the article in agreement with θεοῦ) 9.
θεοῦ (gen.sing.masc.of θεός, possession) 124.
οὐχ (negative conjunction with the indicative) 130.
ὑποτάσσεται (3d.per.sing.pres.pass.ind.of ὑποτάσσω, static) 1921.
οὐδὲ (disjunctive particle) 452.
γὰρ (emphatic conjunction) 105.
δύναται (3d.per.sing.pres.mid.ind.of δύναμαι, static) 289.

*Translation - ". . . the reason being that the mind of the flesh is hostile to God, because it is never subject to the law of God - in fact, it never can be."*

**Comment:** If we understand the verse properly we would not expect the unregenerate world to follow the pattern of Christian morality. The extent to which the country is unChristian is the extent to which attempts to legislate morality must fail. The thinking that has its roots in the unregenerate nature of man is, in the nature of the case, hostile to God. Thus it never bows in submission to the law of God because it cannot. It is contrary to human nature to be "good." Modern education theory, based of course upon the unproved and unprovable hypothesis of NeoDarwinism, that insists that "there are no bad children" is clearly unscriptural. In fact "bad children" is the only type we have outside of Christ. Human institutions which are not based upon the regenerating power of the Holy Spirit, however lofty their ethical aims are destined to fail. Fish swim; birds fly; the flesh hates God. Frenetic attempts to provide a sound basis for morals apart from New Testament theology indicate the author's attempt to disclaim logical association with his bedfellow. There are many examples - for one Walter Lippmann's *A Preface to Morals* (1929). He is generally credited with the suggestion to Woodrow Wilson that resulted in the famous Fourteen Points of the Versailles Treaty. The cynical response of Georges Clemenceau, the French "Tiger" to Wilson's Fourteen Points makes the point. He said, "Fourteen points? Almighty God only had ten!"

Lippmann, who was not a Christian but who believed that the thinking that originates in unregenerate human nature is capable to writing the scenario that leads to world peace, gave his ideas to Wilson who was. But the world at large, cruelly ravaged by four years of blood, rejected idealism and thought only of revenge. Thus we paraded to the tune of "Hang the Kaiser" and "Squeeze the orange until the pips squeak." With no regard for the record of history we wrote into the treaty Article 231 which said,

*The Allied and Associated Governments affirm and Germany accepts the responsibility of Germany and her allies for causing all the loss and damage to which the Allied and Associated Governments and their nationals have been subjected as a consequence of the war imposed upon them by the agreesion of Germany and her allies."*

Philip Mason Burnet, *The Paris Peace Conference; History and Documents,* I, 142, as cited in Paul Birdsall, *Versailles Twenty Years After,* 254.

The Versailles talks saw the clash between the Presbyterian idealism and self-sacrifice of the American President, who derived the basis for his dream of lasting world peace, both from his New Testament and from Lippmann's misguided notion that unsaved thinkers can show the way to plough shares rather than swords and pruning hooks rather than spears. Wilson was right in pointing the world to the New Testament. He and Lippmann were wrong in expecting an unsaved world to accept that kind of idealism.

"A hard-boiled and disillusioned age is quick to gibe about cant and hypocrisy." (Birdsall, *Versailles,* 5). John Maynard Keynes, who looked forward to World War II in his book *The Economic Consequences of the Peace* remarked that the Presbyterian theocrat was "bamboozled by Clemenceau and Lloyd George and could not be debamboozled." (Keynes, *The Economic Consequences of the Peace,* 27-55 *et passim,* as cited in *Ibid*) and Harold Nicolson wrote of the "arid revivalism" of the "American Prophet" in whose pronouncements Nicolson observed "a slight tinge of revivalism, a touch of Methodist arrogance, more than a touch of Presbyterian vanity." (Harold Nicolson, *Peacemaking 1919,* 37, as cited in *Ibid.*)

President Wilson's efforts to make good on his promise that World War I was the war to end all wars, efforts which cost him his life, is honored for his zeal, but he earns somewhat lower marks for his failure to note that the same Bible that teaches idealism, peace and prosperity in a theocratic state, which our Lord called "The Kingdom of the Heavens" also teaches that it is futile to force the mind of the flesh into submission to the law of God.

We have learned much by the sad experiences of world history since 1919. The lessons of experience are the same lessons which were clearly written into the New Testament. Only the mentally deprived now continue to insist that unregenerate man will still learn to subject himself to the law of God. If President Wilson had read Matthew 24:6,7 and taken it seriously he would have faced his diplomatic tasks at Versailles more realistically.

*Verse 8 - "So then they that are in the flesh cannot please God."*

οἱ δὲ ἐν σαρκὶ ὄντες θεῷ ἀρέσαι οὐ δύνανται.

"... *and those who are in the flesh cannot please God."* ... *RSV*

οἱ (nom.pl.masc.of the article in agreement with ὄντες) 9.
δὲ (inferential conjunction) 11.
ἐν (preposition with the locative of sphere) 80.
σαρκὶ (loc.sing.fem.of σάρξ, sphere) 1202.
ὄντες (pres.part.nom.pl.masc.of εἰμί, substantival, subject of δύνανται) 86.
θεῷ (dat.sing.masc.of θεός, personal advantage) 124.
ἀρέσαι (aor.act.inf.of ἀρέσκω, complementary) 1110.
οὐ (negative conjunction with the indicative) 130.
δύνανται (3d.per.sing.pres.mid.ind.of δύναμαι, static) 289.

*Translation* - "*So those who are in the flesh are not able to please God."*

**Comment:** This is Paul's conclusion. The realm of the flesh is unregenerate. It is hostile to God, disobedient to Him and totally unable to please Him. *Cf.* Heb.11:6. The mind of the flesh knows nothing of faith and hence nothing of justification. *Cf.* 1 Cor.2:14

Our comment on verse 5 (p.519) was that "The trend of Paul's thought from verse 5 through verse 8 must be seen in the light of verse 9." In verse 9 we learn that Paul was not speaking of Christians in verses 5-8.

*Verse 9* - "*But ye are not in the flesh but in the Spirit, if so be that the Spirit of God dwell in you. Now if any man have not the Spirit of Christ, he is none of his."*

ὑμεῖς δὲ οὐκ ἐστὲ ἐν σαρκὶ ἀλλὰ ἐν πνεύματι, εἴπερ πνεῦμα θεοῦ οἰκεῖ ἐν ὑμῖν. εἰ δέ τις πνεῦμα Χριστοῦ οὐκ ἔχει, οὗτος οὐκ ἔστιν αὐτοῦ.

"*But you are not in the flesh, you are in the Spirit, if the Spirit of God really dwells in you. Any one who does not have the Spirit of Christ does not belong to him."* ... *RSV*

ὑμεῖς (nom.pl.masc.of σύ, subject of ἐστὲ) 104.
δὲ (adversative conjunction) 11.
οὐκ (negative conjunction with the indicative) 130.
ἐστὲ (2d.per.pl.pres.ind.of εἰμί, aoristic) 86.
ἐν (preposition with the locative of sphere) 80.
σαρκὶ (loc.sing.fem.of σάρξ, sphere) 1202.
ἀλλὰ (alternative conjunction) 342.
ἐν (preposition with the locative of sphere) 80.
πνεύματι (loc.sing.neut.of πνεῦμα, sphere) 83.
εἴπερ (intensive conditional particle, in a first-class condition) 3879.
πνεῦμα (nom.sing.neut.of πνεῦμα, subject of οἰκεῖ) 83.
θεοῦ (gen.sing.masc.of θεός, description) 124.
οἰκεῖ (3d.per.sing.pres.act.ind.of οἰκέω, first-class condition) 3926.
ἐν (preposition with the locative of place) 80.
ὑμῖν (loc.pl.masc.of σύ, place) 104.

εἰ (conditional particle in a first-class condition) 337.

δέ (adversative conjunction) 11.

τις (nom.sing.masc.of τις, indefinite pronoun, subject of ἔχει) 486.

πνεῦμα (acc.sing.neut.of πνεῦμα, direct object of ἔχει) 83.

Χριστοῦ (gen.sing.masc.of Χριστός, possession) 4.

οὐκ (negative conjunction with the indicative) 130.

ἔχει (3d.per.sing.pres.act.ind.of ἔχω, aoristic) 86.

οὗτος (nom.sing.masc.of οὗτος, subject of ἔστιν, deictic) 93.

οὐκ (negative conjunction with the indicative) 130.

ἔστιν (3d.per.sing.pres.ind.of εἰμί, aoristic) 86.

αὐτοῦ (gen.sing.masc.of αὐτός, relationship) 16.

*Translation* - *"But you are not in the flesh but in the Spirit, if, in fact, the Spirit of God dwells in you. But if any one does not have the Spirit of Christ, that one is not His."*

**Comment:** Here Paul makes clear that the statements on both sides of the question in verses 5-8 are general statements - not to be applied to any particular person. In verse 9 he assures the Roman Christians (and all others who read his words) that the one great question is - "Does the Spirit of God dwell in you?" If so, you are not living in the sphere governed by the flesh and thus you are not attending to fleshly things (verse 5), or meriting death (verse 6), or at enmity with God (verse 7), or unable to please God (verse 8). On the contrary, the practical righteousness of God's will may be perfected in you (verse 4) as you attend to spiritual things (verse 5) with life and peace as the result (verse 6). How does the Christian receive the Spirit of God and Christ? *Cf.* John 20:22; Acts 1:8; John 14:16,17,26; John 7:38,39; 2 Tim.1:14; 1 Cor.3:16; 12:13; Eph.1:13; 1 Cor.6:19,20. Reception of the Holy Spirit is contingent upon repentance and faith and He brings the new birth (John 3:3,7; 1 Pet.1:23) and baptizes us into the body of Christ (1 Cor.12:13; Gal.3:27). Conversely those who have not the Holy Spirit are unregenerate. *Cf.* Acts 19:1-6. Verse 9 provides us with a definition of φυχικοί in Jude 19. *Cf.*our discussion of 1 Cor.2:14.

*Verse 10* - *"And if Christ be in you, the body is dead because of sin: but the spirit is life because of righteousness."*

εἰ δὲ Χριστὸς ἐν ὑμῖν, τὸ μὲν σῶμα νεκρὸν διὰ ἁμαρτίαν, τὸ δὲ πνεῦμα ζωὴ διὰ δικαιοσύνην.

*"But if Christ is in you, although your bodies are dead because of sin, your spirits are alive because of righteousness."* . . . RSV

εἰ (conditional particle in a first-class condition) 337.

δὲ (adversative conjunction) 11.

Χριστὸς (nom.sing.masc.of Χριστός, subject of ἔστιν understood) 4.

ἐν (preposition with the locative of place) 80.

ὑμῖν (loc.pl.masc.of σύ, place) 104.

τὸ (nom.sing.neut.of the article in agreement with σῶμα) 9.

μὲν (correlative affirmative particle) 300.
σῶμα (nom.sing.neut.of σῶμα, subject of ἔστιν understood) 507.
νεκρὸν (nom.sing.neut.of νεκρός, predicate adjective) 749.
διὰ (preposition with the accusative, cause) 118.
ἁμαρτίαν (acc.sing.fem.of ἁμαρτία, cause) 111.
τὸ (nom.sing.neut.of the article in agreement with πνεῦμα) 9.
δὲ (adversative conjunction) 11.
πνεῦμα (nom.sing.neut.of πνεῦμα, subject of ἔστιν understood) 83.
ζωὴ (nom.sing.fem.of ζωή, predicate nominative) 668.
διὰ (preposition with the accusative, cause) 118.
δικαιοσύνην (acc.sing.fem.of δικαιοσύνη, cause) 322.

*Translation - "But since Christ is in you, although the body indeed is dead because of sin the spirit is life because of righteousness."*

**Comment:** The first-class condition assumes nothing either way in the protasis. It depends upon how the reader qualifies as a child of God when tested by verse 9. If the first clause of verse 9 describes the reader then verse 10 should translate, "Since Christ is in you. . . " If He is then the two conclusions in the apodosis are true.. The body of flesh is dead but the Holy Spirit is life. The body of flesh, sin and death are associated. So also are the Holy Spirit, the spirit of the regenerated Christian, life and righteousness. Note Romans 4:25. Christ was dead beause of our sin, but alive again because of our justification. We shared His crucifixion and resurrection (Gal.2:20; 1 Cor.12:13). Hence, since Christ lives in us (Gal.2:20) our bodies of sin are already judged as dead. This is the basis of Paul's advice in Romans 6:11. Our bodies are not actually physically dead yet, but they have been adjudged so by God and are already in the process of disintegration. Why should we not agree with God and call our body "a body of death"? (Rom.7:24).

Now that Paul has said that our bodies are dead because of sin and God's judgment upon it, the question naturally arises as to the ultimate destiny of our bodies, which, after all are the temples of the Holy Spirit (1 Cor.6:19,20). They shall also be rescued from death as we learn in

*Verse 11 - "But if the spirit of Him that raised up Jesus from the dead dwell in you, He that raised up Christ from the dead shall also quicken your mortal bodies by His Spirit that dwelleth in you."*

εἰ δὲ τὸ πνεῦμα τοῦ ἐγείραντος τὸν Ἰησοῦν ἐκ νεκρῶν οἰκεῖ ἐν ὑμῖν, ὁ ἐγείρας (τὸν) Χριστόν ἐκ νεκρῶν ζωοποιήσει καὶ τὰ θνητὰ σώματα ὑμῶν διὰ τοῦ ἐνοικοῦντος αὐτοῦ πνεύματος ἐν ὑμῖν.

*"If the Spirit of him who raised Jesus from the dead dwells in you, he who raised Christ Jesus from the dead will give life to your mortal bodies also through his Spirit which dwells in you." . . . RSV*

εἰ (conditional particle in a first-class condition) 337.
δὲ (explanatory conjunction) 11.

τὸ (nom.sing.neut.of the article in agreement with πνεῦμα) 9.

πνεῦμα (nom.sing.neut.of πνεῦμα, subject of οἰκεῖ) 83.

τοῦ (gen.sing.masc.of the article in agreement with ἐγείραντος) 9.

ἐγείραντος (aor.act.part.gen.sing.masc.of ἐγείρω, substantival, possession) 125.

(τὸν) (acc.sing.masc.of the article in agreement with Ἰησοῦν) 9.

Ἰησοῦν (acc.sing.masc.of Ἰησοῦς, direct object of ἐγείραντος) 3.

ἐκ (preposition with the ablative of separation) 19.

νεκρῶν (abl.pl.masc.of νεκρός, separation) 749.

οἰκεῖ (3d.per.sing.pres.act.ind.of οἰκέω, first-class condition) 3926.

ἐν (preposition with the locative of place) 80.

ὑμῖν (loc.pl.masc.of σύ, place) 104.

ὁ (nom.sing.masc.of the article in agreement with ἐγείρας) 9.

ἐγείρας (aor.act.part.nom.sing.masc.of ἐγείρω, substantival, subject of ζωοποιήσει) 125.

τὸν (acc.sing.masc.of the article in agreement with Χριστὸν) 9.

Χριστὸν (acc.sing.masc.of Χριστός, direct object of ἐγείρας) 4.

ἐκ (preposition with the ablative of separation) 19.

νεκρῶν (abl.pl.masc.of νεκρός, separation) 749.

ζωοποιήσει (3d.per.sing.fut.act.ind.of ζωοποιέω, predictive) 2098.

καὶ (adjunctive conjunction joining nouns) 14.

τὰ (acc.pl.neut.of the article in agreement with σώματα) 9.

θνητὰ (acc.pl.neut.of θνητός, in agreement with σώματα) 3914.

σώματα (acc.pl.neut.of σῶμα, direct object of ζωοποιήσει) 507.

ὑμῶν (gen.pl.masc.of σύ, possession) 104.

διὰ (preposition with the ablative of agent) 118.

τοῦ (abl.sing.neut.of the article in agreement with πνεύματος) 9.

#3932 ἐνοικοῦντος (pres.act.part.abl.sing.neut.of ἐνοικέω, adjectival, restrictive, in agreement with πνεύματος).

King James Version

dwell in - Rom.8:11; 2 Cor.6:16; Col.3:16; 2 Tim.1:5,14.

Revised Standard Version

dwells in - Rom.8:11; Col.3:16; 2 Tim.1:5,14.
live in - 2 Cor.6:16.

*Meaning:* A combination of ἐν (#80) and οἰκέω (#3926). Hence, to dwell in. Metaphorically. The Holy Spirit dwells in the believer - Rom.8:11; 2 Tim.1:14; 2 Cor.6:16. The word of Christ in the believer - Col.3:16; faith in the believer - 2 Tim.1:5. In all passages it refers to the mystic union of Christ and the believer.

αὐτοῦ (gen.sing.masc.of αὐτός, relationship) 16.

πνεύματος (abl.sing.neut.of πνεῦμα, agent) 83.

ἐν (preposition with the locative of place) 80.

ὑμῖν (loc.pl.masc.of σύ, place) 104.

*Translation - "Now since the Spirit of the One who raised Jesus from the dead is living in you, He who raised Christ from the dead will also give life to your mortal bodies through the agency of His indwelling Spirit in you."*

**Comment:** A first-class condition if we assume that Paul is speaking to Christians who qualify under the terms of verse 9. The condition is that the Holy Spirit of the Heavenly Father must dwell in the believer. The Father is identified as the One who raised up Christ from the dead. (Psalm 2:7; 16:10; Acts 13:30-35). The conclusion in the apodosis is sure. He who raised Jesus from the dead will do the same for our bodies, now fleshly and totally unable to please Him in their present fallen state. Now they are in unrelenting rebellion against God. But He will give them life. *Cf.#2098* and run the references where the word applies to God's resurrection power in the bodies of believers. Note especially 2 Cor.3:6; John 6:63; 1 Pet.3:18; John 5:21,21; 1 Cor.15:45; 1 Tim.6:13.

God is unwilling that Satan should enjoy even a partial victory over the elect. Even our bodies will be redeemed by the resurrection power from the curse of sin. Thus the Christian, now frustrated because he, a regenerated personality with a regenerated intellect, will and emotion, must live in a depraved body (Rom.7:14-24) will finally have a body with the same God honoring propensities that now characterized his mind and will.

Since even the depraved human body of the believer is to be rescued from its curse, this fact has ethical implications for us now. We expect Paul to infer a demand for holy living.

*Verse 12 - "Therefore, brethren, we are debtors, not to the flesh, to live after the flesh."*

Ἄρα οὖν, ἀδελφοί, ὀφειλέται ἐσμέν, οὐ τῇ σαρκὶ τοῦ κατὰ σάρκα ζῆν.

*"So then, brethren, we are debtors, not to the flesh, to live according to the flesh —"* . . . RSV

Ἄρα (illative particle with οὖν) 995.
οὖν (inferential conjunction) 68.
ἀδελφοί (voc.pl.masc.of ἀδελφός, address) 15.
ὀφειλέται (nom.pl.masc.of ὀφειλέτης, predicate nominative) 581.
ἐσμέν (1st.per.pl.pres.ind.of εἰμί, aoristic) 86.
οὐ (negative conjunction with the indicative) 130.
τῇ (dat.sing.fem.of the article in agreement with σαρκὶ) 9.
σαρκὶ (dat.sing.fem.of σάρξ, personal advantage) 1202.
τοῦ (gen.sing.neut.of the article in agreement with ζῆν) 9.
κατὰ (preposition with the accusative, standard) 98.
σάρκα (acc.sing.fem.of σάρξ, standard) 1202.
ζῆν (pres.act.inf.of ζάω, epexegetical) 340.

*Translation - "Accordingly, brethren, we are debtors, not to the flesh, to live by its standards . . ."*

**Comment:** Paul is fond of ἄρα οὖν - "accordingly." The combination is a heightened form of the inference. The Christian is under a great obligation to God, not only for what He has already done in redeeming the soul and imputing to our account the righteousness of Christ, but also for what He is going to do in redeeming the body as well. But we have no obligation to the flesh as it is presently constituted. Why should we serve it? What has it ever done for us except embarrass us, degrade us, get us killed and do its worst to get us damned? The articular infinitive τοῦ κατὰ σάρκα ζῆν is epexegetical, serving to explain ὀφειλέται ἐσμέν, οὐ τῇ σαρκὶ. We are debtors, but not to the flesh, that we should behave in keeping with its evil demands. If we did, and when we do, we become its victims to manifest its works, listed in Gal.5:17-19. But it was precisely these sins, along with all others, which drove Christ to the cross. For them He was condemned and from their penalty we have been rescued. To pamper the flesh and subject ourselves to its hellish propensities is to vote for its perpetuation. But God has already decreed its glorification (Rom.8:30). Should the child of God insist upon giving the flesh its anti-God expression, God might find it necessary to terminate its physical existence prematurely. This is the thought of verse 13.

The contempt which the Spirit-filled Christian must feel for his fleshly nature will be supreme. But we express this contempt, not by torturing it as the ascetics do in terms of starvation and other forms of physical neglect. Our attack upon the flesh should be in terms of our steadfast refusal to follow its dictates. This we will be able to do only as we yield ourselves on a moment by moment basis to the indwelling Holy Spirit (1 Cor.6:19). It is the Holy Spirit, Who has indwelt us, since He baptized us into the body of Christ (1 Cor.12:13; Gal.3:27), even though we grieve Him (Eph.4:30) Who is the seal of God's ownership of all that Jesus purchased at Calvary. And that includes our bodies. Thus they are His temple. This gives dignity to the physical body of the child of God and he will do all within his power to keep it clean and healthy, in order that he may devote its energies to the completion of the "good works which He hath ordained that we should walk in them" (Eph.2:10). God is not glorified if we neglect our bodies because we know that if we listen to their demands, we will dishonor God and grieve the Holy Spirit.

*Verse 13 - "For if ye live after the flesh ye shall die: but if ye through the Spirit do mortify the deeds of the body, ye shall live."*

εἰ γὰρ κατὰ σάρκα ζῆτε μέλλετε ἀποθνῄσκειν, εἰ δὲ πνεύματι τὰς πράξεις τοῦ σώματος θανατοῦτε ζήσεσθε.

*". . . for if you live according to the flesh you will die, but if by the Spirit you put to death the deeds of the body you will live." . . . RSV*

εἰ (conditional particle in a first-class condition) 337.

γὰρ (inferential conjunction) 105.

κατὰ (preposition with the accusative, standard) 98.

σάρκα (acc.sing.fem.of σάρξ, standard) 1202.

ζῆτε (2d.per.pl.pres.act.ind.of ζάω, first-class condition) 340.
μέλλετε (2d.per.pl.pres.act.ind.of μέλλω, predictive) 206.
ἀποθνήσκειν (pres.act.inf.of ἀποθνήσκω, complementary) 774.
εἰ (conditional particle in a first-class condition) 337.
δὲ (adversative conjunction) 11.
πνεύματι (instru.sing.neut.of πνεῦμα, means) 83.
τὰς (acc.pl.fem.of the article in agreement with πράξεις) 9.
πράξεις (acc.pl.fem.of πρᾶξις, direct object of θανατοῦτε) 1218.
τοῦ (gen.sing.neut.of the article in agreement with σώματος) 9.
σώματος (gen.sing.neut.of σῶμα, description) 507.
θανατοῦτε (2d.per.pl.pres.act.ind.of θανατόω, first-class condition) 879.
ζήσεσθε (2d.per.pl.fut.mid.ind.of ζάω, predictive) 340.

*Translation - "Therefore if you persist in living according to the flesh you are going to die; but if, by the Spirit, you keep on putting to death the deeds of the body, you shall go on living."*

**Comment:** *Cf.* 2 Cor.6:9 and Rom.7:4. The idea of the physical death of the believer who, despite his salvation, insists upon pampering the flesh, may be in view here. *Cf.* Acts 5:1-11; 1 Cor.5:1-5; 1 John 5:16,17; 1 Cor.3:16,17. If a Christian presumes upon God's grace and decides to have the cake of salvation while he eats the sinful cake of his own lusts, thus to "enjoy" sin for a season, presuming upon his standing in Christ, there may be no further reason why God should allow that man to live. We are saved for God's glory (Eph.2:7-9), but we are also saved "unto good works" (Eph.2:10). When we frustrate God's purpose (Phil.1:6) we may force God to act to protect Christ's investment.

There is another possible interpretation of this passage. The sinning Christian dies in the sense that he loses all of the practical spiritual benefits in this life and becomes useless to God. (Heb.6:8; 1 Cor.9:27; 1 Tim.5:6). The two εἰ clauses are conditional and serve to show the antagonism of the flesh in its present unglorified condition to God's purpose. To follow its dictates is to die in terms of spiritual influence and perhaps even physically. On the other hand, to crucify it by yielding to the Holy Spirit (Gal.5:16), to reckon it to be dead (Rom.6:11) is to live the abundant life (John 10:10) and to become one of the choice saints. *Cf.* Romans 6:21,22.

All who have been "born from above" (John 3:3,7; 1 Pet.1:23) are "born ones" (τέκνα) of God (John 1:12) even though they live lives of defeat in bondage to the flesh. But there is a better way. It is possible also to be full grown sons (υἱοί) of God. The formula is in

*Verse 14 - "For as many as are led by the spirit of God, they are the sons of God."*

ὅσοι γὰρ πνεύματι θεοῦ ἄγονται, οὗτοι υἱοὶ θεοῦ εἰσιν.

*"For all who are led by the Spirit of God are sons of God."* . . . *RSV*

ὅσοι (nom.pl.masc.of ὅσος, relative pronoun, subject of ἄγονται) 660.
γὰρ (causal conjunction) 105.
πνεύματι (instru.sing.neut.of πνεῦμα, means) 83.

ϑεοῦ (gen.sing.masc.of ϑεός, description) 124.

ἄγονται (3d.per.pl.pres.pass.ind.of ἄγω, present progressive) 876.

οὗτοι (nom.pl.masc.of οὗτος, anaphoric, subject of εἰσιν) 93.

υἱοὶ (nom.pl.masc.of υἱός, predicate nominative) 5.

ϑεοῦ (gen.sing.masc.of ϑεός, relationship) 124.

εἰσιν (3d.per.pl.pres.ind.of εἰμί, aoristic) 86.

*Translation - "Because as many as are being led by the Spirit of God, these are the sons of God."*

**Comment:** γὰρ is causal as Paul supports his thought of verse 12 (where we have a moral obligation mentioned) and verse 13 with its warning and promise. Why should these things be so? Because (γὰρ) it was through the work of the Holy Spirit that we became sons of God in the first place. He brought us to Christ (John 16:7-11). He fathered our new nature (John 3:5; 1 Cor.12:13; 1 Pet.1:23). He enriched us with the Father's gifts (1 Cor.12:7). He produces His fruit in us, thus to enrich our lives (Gal.5:22,23) and He will raise our vile (Phil.3:21), natural (1 Cor.15:44) and corruptible (1 Cor.15:42) "bodies of death" (Rom.7:24) in glorification (Rom.8:11).

*Cf.*#876 for other uses of ἄγω in terms of spiritual guidance, *e.g.* John 10:16; Heb.2:10; Rom.2:4; Gal.5:18 (He rescues us from the toils of the law). The Holy Spirit will bring the saints who have gone before at the rapture (1 Thess.4:14). We were not always so wisely led (1 Cor.12:2). Thus God, the Holy Spirit, has guided us and He continues to guide us. And thus He puts us under obligation to reject the call of the flesh and, by His help, to consider our flesh as already dead.

Not only are we God's υἱοί by the Spirit's guidance (Rom.8:14) but also His τέκνα ("born ones" "partakers of His nature") by spiritual new birth (John 1:12,13; 2 Pet.1:4).

Some commentators point out that all who believe in Christ (John 1:12) are thus saved by new birth and are thus God's "born ones" (τέκνα), but that only those of that large number who submit to the leadership of the Holy Spirit at all times, after their initial encounter with Him (durative present tense action in ἄγονται) are His "grown up" or "mature" sons (υἱοί). *Cf.* our comment on verse 16. It seems to me that whatever we may say on this point, it is abundantly clear that not all children of God succeed in yielding equal obedience to the Holy Spirit after they are saved and that there are degrees of reward and degrees of capacity for appreciation of the culture of heaven. Otherwise passages like 1 Cor.3:10-17 and 2 Cor.5:10,11 are without point.

*Verse 15 - "For ye have not received the spirit of bondage again to fear, but ye have received the spirit of adoption, whereby we cry, Abba, Father."*

οὐ γὰρ ἐλάβετε πνεῦμα δουλείας πάλιν εἰς φόβον, ἀλλὰ ἐλάβετε πνεῦμα υἱοθεσίας, ἐν ᾧ κράζομεν, Αββα ὁ πατήρ.

*"For you did not receive the spirit of slavery to fall back into fear, but you have received the spirit of sonship. When we cry, 'Abba! Father!'"* . . . RSV

οὐ (negative conjunction with the indicative) 130.
γὰρ (inferential conjunction) 105.
ἐλάβετε (2d.per.pl.aor.act.ind.of λαμβάνω, culminative) 533.
πνεῦμα (nom.sing.neut.of πνεῦμα, direct object of ἐλάβετε) 83.

#3933 δουλείας (gen.sing.fem.of δουλεία, description).

King James Version

bondage - Rom.8:15,21; Gal.4:24; 5:1; Heb.2:15.

Revised Standard Version

slavery - Rom.8:15; Gal.4:24; 5:1.
bondage - Rom.8:21; Heb.2:15.

*Meaning:* Cf.δουλεύω (#604); δουλόω (#3103); δοῦλος (#725). Hence, slavery, bondage, servitude. Joined to the accusative - εἰς φόβον - Rom.8:15; εἰς δουλείαν γεννῶσα in Gal.4:24; followed by a genitive of description, τῆς φθορᾶς - Rom.8:21; as a gen.of description with ζυγῷ in Gal.5:1. Heb.2:15 like Rom.8:15; Gal.4:24.

πάλιν (adverbial) 355.
εἰς (preposition with the accusative, result) 140.
φόβον (acc.sing.masc.of φόβος, result) 1131.
ἀλλὰ (alternative conjunction) 342.
ἐλάβετε (2d.per.pl.aor.act.ind.of λαμβάνω, culminative) 533.
πνεῦμα (acc.sing.neut.of πνεῦμα, direct object of ἐλάβετε) 83.

#3934 υἱοθεσίας (gen.sing.fem.of υἱοθεσία, description).

King James Version

adoption - Rom.8:15,23; 9:4; Gal.4:5.
adoption of sons - Eph.1:5.

Revised Standard Version

sonship - Rom.8:15; 9:4.
adoption as sons - Rom.8:23; Gal.4:5.
to be sons - Eph.1:5.

*Meaning:* A combination of υἱός (#5) and θέσις, from τίθημι (#455). cf. ὁροθεσία - "right standing" and νομοθεσία - "legal standing." υἱοθεσία - "standing as a son." With reference to Israel as a nation - Rom.9:4. Believers are God's sons by birth (John 1:12,13) and also by legal adoption (Rom.8:15,23; Gal.4:5; Eph.1:5). In Romans 8:23 the word has special reference to the resurrection of the body.

ἐν (preposition with the locative, instrumental use) 80.

ᾧ (loc.sing.neut.of ὅς, instrumental use, means) 65.

κράζομεν (1st.per.pl.pres.act.ind.of κράζω, present progressive) 765.

Αββα (interjection) 2789.

ὁ (nom.sing.masc.of the article in agreement with πατήρ) 9.

πατήρ (nom.sing.masc.of πατήρ, nominative of interjection) 238.

*Translation - "So you did not receive a spirit of slavery again resulting in fear but you received a spirit of adoption by Whom we cry out, 'Abba! Father!' "*

**Comment:** It is possible to take ἐν ᾧ as a locative of time point. This means that the previous sentence ends with υἱοσθεσίας and the sentence goes on after ὁ πατήρ. Thus the Revised Standard Version which joins the last clause of verse 15 to verse 16 - "When we cry 'Abba! Father!' the same spirit. . . κ.τ.λ." It is a matter of editing. The United Bible Societies' Committee has chosen to end the sentence after ὁ πατήρ. Both ideas are true. Through the motivation of the Holy Spirit of adoption we call God our Father. And when we call God our Father, the Holy Spirit bears witness with our spirit that we are the children of God.

γὰρ is inferential as Paul pursues his thought of verse 14. Since to be led by the Spirit of God is to become a son of God, it follows that when we received the Holy Spirit, He was not a spirit of slavery with the result that we are again seized with the terror which, as unsaved sinners, we felt when we thought about our lost condition. In connection with fear and slavery see Heb.2:15. Christ in His death destroyed Satan (Heb.2:14) and rescued us who, before we were saved, because of our fear of death and judgment, were in bondage. We shall never fear again. This comports with 2 Tim.1:7a and Psalm 27:1, as well as with all other passages which state that children of God have nothing to fear. On the contrary the Holy Spirit assures us of sonship in the legal as well as in the spiritually genetic sense, and, as a result, by means of His inspiration we exult with the glad cry "Abba! Oh Father!" Hebrew scholars tell us that "Abba" (which is accented on the *ba* not on the *Ab*) is the informal endearing term, like the English "Daddy." εἰς φόβον is result. *Cf.* 2 Cor.2:12; 1 Cor.11:24; Mt.8:4; Phil.1:11; Rom.3:25; John 6:27; Mt.26:28. These result and purpose uses of εἰς and the accusative are rare but they occur in the New Testament. *Cf.* comment on verse 17.

Is Paul making a distinction between υἱοὶ τοῦ θεοῦ and τέκνα τοῦ θεοῦ? Not all τέκνα submit to continuous leadership by the Holy Spirit. To do so would be to live a sinless life, since the Holy Spirit could never lead us to sin. Verse 15 says that υἱοί have the assurance of salvation. Verse 16 says the same thing about τέκνα and verse 17 says that τέκνα are also κληρονόμοι (heirs). *Cf.* comment, *en loc.* All υἱοὶ τοῦ θεοῦ are also τέκνα τοῦ θεοῦ for the new birth is the initiative experience. Although this context does not say so it is clear from other passages (Heb.5:11-14, *e.g.*) that some τέκνα τοῦ θεοῦ are "babes in Christ" who resist the leadership of the Holy Spirit.

*Verse 16 - "The Spirit itself beareth witness with our spirit, that we are the children of God."*

αὐτὸ τὸ πνεῦμα συμμαρτυρεῖ τῷ πνεύματι ἡμῶν ὅτι ἐσμὲν τέκνα θεοῦ.

*". . . it is the Spirit himself bearing witness with our spirit that we are children of God, . . . "    RSV*

αὐτὸ (nom.sing.neut.of αὐτός, intensive) 16.

τὸ (nom.sing.neut.of the article in agreement with πνεῦμα) 9.

πνεῦμα (nom.sing.neut.of πνεῦμα, subject of συμμαρτυρεῖ) 83.

συμμαρτυρεῖ (3d.per.sing.pres.act.ind.of συμμαρτυρέω, aoristic) 3844.

τῷ (instru.sing.neut.of the article in agreement with πνεύματι) 9.

πνεύματι (instru.sing.neut.of πνεῦμα, association) 83.

ἡμῶν (gen.pl.masc.of ἐγώ, possession) 123.

ὅτι (conjunction introducing an object clause in indirect discourse) 211.

ἐσμὲν (1st.per.pl.pres.ind.of εἰμί, static) 86.

τέκνα (nom.pl.neut.of τέκνον, predicate nominative) 229.

θεοῦ (gen.sing.masc.of θεός, relationship) 124.

*Translation - "The Spirit Himself concurs with our spirit that we are born ones of God."*

**Comment:** αὐτὸ in the predicate position is intensive. The Holy Spirit Himself, in association with our human intellects concurs with us in assuring us that we are God's children by birth.

The KJV, in slavish conformity to the neuter gender of πνεῦμα and in direct violation of other passages which teach that the Holy Spirit is a person, not a thing or an influence, has translated the intensive αὐτὸ by "itself." The fact that the Greek has always written πνεῦμα as a neuter noun does not mean that the Holy Spirit is not a person. It would not be wise for one who is asking for a raise in salary to refer to his boss as "It." It is not likely that the KJV translators meant any disrespect for the Holy Spirit. Since He is God we will refer to Him in the masculine gender, despite the neuter form of the noun, and ask those in the Women's Liberation movement to forgive us! It is better to refer to the Holy Spirit as "Her" if you must, than to refer to Him/Her as "It." The Holy Spirit is not a thing or an influence, although as a person He has an influence which is sovereign.

ὅτι introduces indirect discourse. Even though the carnal Christian may not be wholly led by Him at all times, thus to become full-fledged υἱοὶ τοῦ θεοῦ, in complete victorious life, He Himself personally reinforces our own assurance that we are truly born from above. This verse demands the view that even when a Christian is in a backslidden state, he does not lack the assurance of salvation. Recently I talked with a man who told of his regeneration experience which had occurred several years ago. He then said that he was backslidden and that he was a member of a congregation that rejects the view that born again believers are nevertheless saved. He added that his head told him that he was lost because of his backslidings but his heart told him that he was still God's child.

*Verse 17 - "And if children, then heirs; heirs of God, and joint-heirs with Christ; if so be that we suffer with him, that we may be also glorified together."*

εἰ δὲ τέκνα, καὶ κληρονόμοι, κληρονόμοι μὲν θεοῦ, συγκληρονόμοι δὲ Χριστοῦ, εἴπερ συμπάσχομεν ἵνα καὶ συνδοξασθῶμεν.

". . . and if children, then heirs, heirs of God and fellow heirs with Christ, provided we suffer with him in order that we may also be glorified with him." . .
*RSV*

εἰ (conditional particle in a first-class condition) 337.

δὲ (continuative conjunction) 11.

τέκνα (nom.pl.neut.of τέκνον, subject of ἐσμέν) 229.

καὶ (adjunctive conjunction joining nouns) 14.

κληρονόμοι (nom.pl.masc.of κληρονόμος, predicate nominative) 1386.

κληρονόμοι (nom.pl.masc.of κληρονόμος, subject of ἐσμέν, understood) 1386.

μὲν (correlative conjunction of affirmation) 300.

θεοῦ (gen.sing.masc.of θεός, relationship) 124.

#3935 συγκληρονόμοι (nom.pl.masc.of συγκληρονόμος, apposition).

King James Version

fellow heir - Eph.3:6.
heir together - 1 Pet.3:7.
heir with - Heb.11:9.
joint heir - Rom.8:17.

Revised Standard Version

fellow heir - Rom.8:17; Eph.3:6.
heirs with - Heb.11:9.
joint heirs - 1 Pet.3:7.

*Meaning:* A combination of σύν (#1542) and κληρονόμος (#1386); hence, a joint heir; one who shares a legal bequest with another. The believer shares God's bequest with Christ - Rom.8:17; believers share the bequest with each other - 1 Pet.3:7; Gentiles and Jews - Eph.3:6; Isaac, Jacob and Abraham - Heb.11:9.

δὲ (continuative conjunction) 11.

Χριστοῦ (gen.sing.masc.of Χριστός, relationship) 4.

εἴπερ (intensive conditional particle in a first-class condition) 3879.

#3936 συμπάσχομεν (1st.per.pl.pres.act.ind.of συμπάσχω, first-class condition).

King James Version

suffer with - Rom.8:17; 1 Cor.12:26.

Revised Standard Version

suffer with - Rom.8:17.
suffer together - 1 Cor.12:26.

*Meaning:* A combination of σύν (#1542) and πάσχω (#1208). Hence, to suffer pain or disgrace, or both, together with other sufferers. To suffer with Christ - Rom.8:17; all members of the body, in the analogy of 1 Cor.12, suffer as any part suffers - 1 Cor.12:26.

ἵνα (conjunction with the subjunctive in a sub-final clause) 114.

καὶ (adjunctive conjunction joining verbs) 14.

#3937 συνδοξασϑῶμεν (1st.per.pl.aor.pass.subj.of συνδοξάζω, sub-final).

King James Version

glorify together - Rom.8:17.

Revised Standard Version

be glorified with him - Rom.8:17.

*Meaning:* A combination of σύν (#1542) and δοξάζω (#461); to be glorified at the same time and under the same circumstances. With reference to Christ and the victorious believer - Rom.8:17.

*Translation - "And since born ones are also heirs - heirs in fact of God and fellow-heirs with Christ, if, in fact, we are suffering together in order also (and with the result) that we will be glorified together."*

**Comment:** There is no doubt that believers are τέκνα (John 1:12,13; Rom.8:16). Hence εἰ introduces a protasis the assumption of which is not in doubt. *Since* we are τέκνα we are also heirs ( κληρονόμοι). We are heirs, both of God and of Christ, but only if we suffer with Him. In other words τέκνα τοῦ ϑεοῦ are permitted, by virtue of their position as children of God to qualify also as heirs, if they meet the conditions. The qualifying phrase is εἴπερ συμπάσχομεν ἵνα καὶ συνδοξασϑῶμεν. Note that εἴπερ (#3879) is the intensified form of εἰ, impossible to overlook in the exegesis. What is certain is that all children of God have the privilege of trying to qualify as heirs of God and co-heirs with Christ. Fellow suffering with Christ is prerequisite to fellow glorification with Christ. The implication here seems inescapable that those backslidden children of God, who, by compromising their morals with the world, who make peace with it in order to escape its censure, will not be heirs with Christ with the reward of a share in His glory. They will be save but only "so as by fire" (1 Cor.3:15). *Cf.* Phil.3:10-14. End-time saints are sure to qualify since refusal to take the mark of the Beast (Rev.13:16-18) will bring down his wrath upon them. But it would appear that some true Christians (τέκνα) have lived defeated lives and died without having suffered the offence of the cross (Gal.5:11; 1 Pet.5:1). In order to encourage the Roman saints not to avoid persecution, Paul describes in verse 18

# The Glory That is to be

*(Romans 8:18-30)*

*Verse 18 - "For I reckon that the sufferings of this present time are not worthy to be compared with the glory which shall be revealed in us."*

Λογίζομαι γὰρ ὅτι οὐκ ἄξια τὰ παθήματα τοῦ νῦν καιροῦ πρὸς τὴν μέλλουσαν δόξαν ἀποκαλυφθῆναι εἰς ἡμᾶς.

*"I consider that the sufferings of this present time are not worth comparing with the glory that is to be revealed in us." . . . RSV*

Λογίζομαι (1st.per.sing.pres.mid.ind.of λογίζομαι, aoristic) 2611.

γὰρ (explanatory conjunction) 105.

ὅτι (conjunction introducing an object clause in indirect discourse) 211.

οὐκ (negative conjunction with the indicative) 130.

ἄξια (nom.pl.neut.of ἄξιος, predicate adjective) 285.

τὰ (nom.pl.neut.of the article in agreement with παθήματα) 9.

παθήματα (nom.pl.neut.of πάθημα, subject of εἰσίν understood) 3919.

τοῦ (gen.sing.masc.of the article in agreement with καιροῦ) 9.

νῦν (temporal conjunction) 1497.

καιροῦ (gen.sing.masc.of καιρός, time description) 767.

πρὸς (preposition with the accusative, comparison) 197.

τὴν (acc.sing.fem.of the article in agreement with δόξαν) 9.

μέλλουσαν (pres.act.part.acc.sing.fem.of μέλλω, adjectival, ascriptive, in agreement with δόξαν) 206.

δόξαν (acc.sing.fem.of δόξα, comparison) 361.

ἀποκαλυφθῆναι (1st.aor.pass.inf.of ἀποκαλύπτω, completes μέλλουσαν) 886.

εἰς (preposition with the accusative, original static locative usage) 140.

ἡμᾶς (acc.pl.masc.of ἐγώ, locative usage) 123.

*Translation - "Now I have concluded that the sufferings of this present time are not to be compared with the coming glory which will be revealed in us."*

**Comment:** I see no real reason to interpret γὰρ inferentially here. He has just stated that glorification with Christ is contingent upon suffering with Him. Now, in an attempt to bolster the believer's determination to be always led by the Spirit of God (verse 14), even though such obedience will alienate the hostile world and result in suffering for the Christian, he indulges in a cost-benefit analysis and concludes that the cost of present suffering is less than the benefit of future glory. Thus present suffering is worth it, while a craven compromise with the world to avoid suffering is not a profitable deal. To escape the offence of the cross now is to forego much greater glory then. Just as the pain of saving money for those who suffer from a compelling positive time preference is rewarded by compounded interest on savings in the future, so the pain we invite by resisting worldly temptations is rewarded in quantum proportions in the future glory. *Cf.* comment on 2 Cor.4:16-18; 1 Pet.5:1; Mt.5:10-12. *Cf.*#767 for other instances of τοῦ νῦν καιροῦ. πρός with the accusative in comparison is also found in Luke 12:47; Gal.2:14 and adverbially in James 4:5. The victorious saints vill indeed share His glory - 2 Thess. 1:7-10. *Cf.* #361, VIII for the glory for the overcomers.

The glory to which Paul alludes in this passage refers to that in which all believers will share after the rapture and resurrection, which is also called glorification in Romans 8:30. This exchange of the natural for the spiritual body to be enjoyed by both living raptured and dead resurrected saints is to be had by all those who are justified. In this sense all of the children of God will share in His glory. The degree to which we are permitted to share in His eternal glory after the resurrection depends upon how much we suffer for Him now.

*Verse 19 - "For the earnest expectation of the creature waiteth for the manifestation of the sons of God."*

ἡ γὰρ ἀποκαραδοκία τῆς κτίσεως τὴν ἀποκάλυψιν τῶν υἱῶν τοῦ θεοῦ ἀπεκδέκεται.

*"For the creation waits with eager longer for the revealing of the sons of God;"*
RSV

ἡ (nom.sing.fem.of the article in agreement with ἀποκαραδοκία) 9.
γὰρ (explanatory conjunction) 105.

#3938 ἀποκαραδοκία (nom.sing.fem.of ἀποκαραδοκία, subject of ἀπεκδέκεται).

King James Version

earnest expectation - Rom.8:19; Phil.1:20.

Revised Standard Version

eager longing - Rom.8:19.
eager expectation - Phil.1:20.

*Meaning:* A combination of ἀπό (#70), καρά or κάρη (Ep. and Ionic for κεφαλή) - head and δοκέω (#287). Hence, an expectation; the anticipation of a coming event. The creation awaits the glorification of the children of God - Rom.8:19; with reference to Paul's anticipation of the progress of the gospel in Philippi - Phil.1:20.

τῆς (gen.sing.fem.of the article in agreement with κτίσεως) 9.
κτίσεως (gen.sing.fem.of κτίσις, description) 2633.
τὴν (acc.sing.fem.of the article in agreement with ἀποκάλυψιν) 9.
ἀποκάλυψιν (acc.sing.fem.of ἀποκάλυψις, direct object of ἀπεκδέχεται) 1902.
τῶν (gen.pl.masc.of the article in agreement with υἱῶν) 9.
υἱῶν (gen.pl.masc.of υἱός, possession) 5.
τοῦ (gen.sing.masc.of the article in agreement with θεοῦ) 9.
θεοῦ (gen.sing.masc.of θεός, relationship) 124.

#3939 ἀπεκδέκεται (3d.per.sing.pres.mid.ind.of ἀπεκδέχομαι, present progressive retroactive).

King James Version

look for - Phil.3:20; Heb.9:28.
wait for - Rom.8:19,23,25; 1 Cor.1:7; Gal.5:5.
wait - 1 Pet.3:20.

Revised Standard Version

wait for - Rom.8:19,23,25; 1 Cor.1:7; Gal.5:5; Heb.9:28.
await - Phil.3:20.
wait - 1 Pet.3:20.

*Meaning:* A combination of ἀπό (#70), ἐκ (#19) and δέχομαι (#867). To wait for assiduously; to look for; to expect; to anticipate with longing. The material creation awaits the second coming of Christ - Rom.8:19; the believer awaits the second coming as the time when his body will be glorified - Rom.8:23,25; Heb.9:28; Phil.3:20; 1 Cor.1:7. With reference to the hope of salvation - Gal.5:5; with reference to God's patience before the flood - 1 Pet.3:20.

*Translation - "Now the creation is waiting with eager anticipation for the unveiling of the sons of God."*

**Comment:** The distinction between τέκνα τοῦ θεοῦ and υἱοὶ τοῦ θεοῦ seems to be ignored in this verse, for all of the children of God are to be disclosed as the dead in Christ arise from the grave to meet Him when He comes (1 Thess.4:13-18). The difference between τέκνον and υἱός in terms of maturity is one of degree. There is no child of God (τέκνον) who has had no growth in grace. The indwelling Holy Spirit has succeeded in every case in implementing the will of God for the believer to some extent (Eph.2:10). There is no superstructure of Christian development upon the foundation, which is Jesus Christ, which is totally devoid of "gold, silver and precious stones" (1 Cor.3:11-15). Thus there is no comfort here for a partial rapture and resurrection view. All are to appear before the judgment seat of Christ (2 Cor.5:10). The degree to which each is to participate in the eternal glory of the New Jerusalem after the second coming will depend upon the decision of our Lord at that time.

Here Paul is saying that the glory which is to be revealed is an outstanding event toward which even the physical creation is looking for reasons that become clear in verses 20-23. Note that in the New Testament, with the exceptions of Gal.5:5 and 1 Pet.3:20 ἀπεκδέχομαι refers to the anticipation of the Second Coming of Christ.

That the physical creation has suffered under the curse and now needs divine rescue is clear in

*Verse 20 - "For the creature was made subject to vanity, not willingly, but by reason of him who hath subjected the same in hope."*

τῇ γὰρ ματαιότητι ἡ κτίσις ὑπετάγη, οὐχ ἑκοῦσα ἀλλὰ διὰ τὸν ὑποτάξαντα, ἐφ᾽ ἐλπίδι

"... *for the creation was subjected to futility, not of its own will but by the will of him who subjected it in hope;"* ... RSV

τῇ (dat.sing.fem.of the article in agreement with ματαιότητι) 9.
γὰρ (causal conjunction) 105.

#3940 ματαιότητι (dat.sing.fem.of ματαιότης, reference).

King James Version

vanity - Rom.8:20; Eph.4:17; 2 Pet.2:18.

Revised Standard Version

futility - Rom.8:20; Eph.4:17.
folly - 2 Pet.2:18.

*Meaning: Cf.* μάταιος (#3321), ματαιόω (#3801), μάτην (#1148). Folly, foolishness, absence of truth and order, that which is inappropriate, futility, frustration. Of the deterioration of the physical world - Rom.8:20; of the unregenerate mind - Eph.4:17; 2 Pet.2:18.

ἡ (nom.sing.fem.of the article in agreement with κτίσις) 9.
κτίσις (nom.sing.fem.of κτίσις, subject of ὑπετάγη) 2633.
ὑπετάγη (3d.per.sing.2d.aor.pass.ind.of ὑποτάσσω, culminative) 1921.
οὐκ (negative conjunction with the indicative) 130.

#3941 ἑκοῦσα (nom.sing.fem.of ἑκών in agreement with κτίσις).

King James Version

willingly - Rom.8:20; 1 Cor.9:17.

Revised Standard Version

of its own will - Rom.8:20; 1 Cor.9:17.

*Meaning:* voluntarily, willingly, of one's own will, with no coercion. With οὐχ in Rom.8:20; 1 Cor.9:17.

ἀλλὰ (alternative conjunction) 342.
διὰ (preposition with the accusative, cause) 118.
τὸν (acc.sing.masc.of the article in agreement with ὑποτάξαντα) 9.
ὑποτάξαντα (aor.act.part.acc.sing.masc.of ὑποτάσσω, substantival, cause) 1921.
ἐφ' (preposition with the instrumental of cause) 47.
ἐλπίδι (instru.sing.fem.of ἐλπίς, cause) 2994.

*Translation -* "*Because the creation was condemned to frustration, not by its own choice, but because of the one who placed it under the curse, in hope.*"

**Comment:** The idea that the physical creation anticipates the second coming, at which time the sons of God will be revealed in glory, needs explanation. Why should the physical universe do this? Because (causal $\gamma\grave{\alpha}\rho$) it also is cursed. It was subjected to frustration and futility (Gen.3:17). The earth, originally subject to man as a fruitful and efficient source of raw materials and energy, is under a curse. Vast areas of the earth are too high, too low, too cold, too hot, too dry or too wet or are inaccessible to man and hence useless. The law of nature is the law of the jungle with survival available only to the fittest. The animal and plant world is a world in which demand for subsistence exceeds supply. It is therefore a world of suffering and death. The sounds of nature are minor. Nature itself, as it supports human life, operates on a thin film of air, water and decomposed rock which lies between the uninhabitable core of earth and the equally uninhabitable void of space. Now this thin layer of resource, no more than twenty miles thick, is on the verge of irremediable deterioration. The soil is poisoned with DDT, a chemical that is nonbiodegradable; the air is polluted with pollutants lighter than air which cannot be drawn back to the earth's gravitational field. The waters of earth, even those of the oceans are becoming increasingly corrupt and bid fair to poison the race. The elements rage - tornados, floods, earthquakes, droughts, volcanic eruptions as a result of diastrophism - these all contribute to the peril of viable life upon the earth. The agonies of wild life, the dead deserts, impenetrable swamps, barren mountain sides - all of these because man sinned and God's curse fell upon the entire creation.

It was not until Hermann Ludwig Ferdinand von Helmholtz (1821-1894) introduced the world to the three laws of thermodynamics that it became clear that the eternal state, which the Bible calls heaven can be enjoyed only after there has been a creation of a "new heaven and a new earth" to replace "the first heaven and the first earth" which are to pass away (Rev.21:1).

Helmholtz formulated the first law of thermodynamics which states that energy, which equals matter, is neither created nor destroyed. There is exactly the same amount of energy (matter) in the universe now as there was in the creation.

But the second principle of thermodynamics, which we call entropy, says that although the total of energy within a closed system is constant, the amount of *available* energy, which we can command for useful work is constantly decreasing. The measure of this energy, formerly useful, but now forever unavailable, which we call entropy, is a basic term in physics. Entropy is always increasing. In other words the universe is running down.

The third law of thermodynamics states that the entropy of a crystal is equal to zero when the temperature approaches absolute zero. Thus when the minimal temperature is minus 273 degrees centigrade maximal order reigns.

It is clear then that analysis increases entropy while synthesis decreases it. Order is giving way to disorder. We move from the complex to the simple. This is in direct contradiction to the hypothesis of evolution which teaches that life has developed from the simple to the complex. But this is work and requires energy which decreases entropy.

> "Change and decay in all around I see.
> O Thou Who changes not, abide with me."

The objection to the application of the principles of thermodynamics to life upon this earth on the ground that the earth is not a closed system, but only a tiny portion of a larger universe and that earth's positive entropy can be countered by energy inputs from without disregards the fact the total amount of energy in the universe is constant. Thus there can be no energy recharge for the earth without a consequent energy loss elsewhere. Thus when a star falls into the black hole and is captured by some greater *e* it loses *m* and kinetic energy becomes potential. Some day, in God's own time, all of *m* will become *e* and God will then create a new heaven and a new earth wherein dwelleth righteousness.

The plight of the universe was not the result of the deliberate transgression of the universe. God did it. It was done διὰ τὸν ὑποτάξαντα ἐφ' ἐλπίδι - "because of the One who subjected it in hope. . . " What hope? The hope that when the curse of sin is lifted, and the bodies of the children of God are raptured/resurrected, the universe will also be delivered from its present pains. This is the promise of

*Verse 21 - "Because the creature itself also shall be delivered from the bondage of corruption into the glorious liberty of the children of God."*

ὅτι καὶ αὐτὴ ἡ κτίσις ἐλευθερωθήσεται ἀπὸ τῆς δουλείας τῆς φθορᾶς εἰς τὴν ἐλευθερίαν τῆς δόξης τῶν τέκνων τοῦ θεοῦ.

". . . *because the creation itself will be set free from its bondage to decay and obtain the glorious liberty of the children of God."* . . . RSV

ὅτι (conjunction introducing a causal clause) 211.
καὶ (adjunctive conjunction joining substantives) 14.
αὐτὴ (nom.sing.fem.of αὐτός, intensive, in agreement with κτίσις) 16.
ἡ (nom.sing.fem.of the article in agreement with κτίσις) 9.
κτίσις (nom.sing.fem.of κτίσις, subject of ἐλευθερωθήσεται) 2633.
ἐλευθερωθήσεται (3d.per.sing.fut.pass.ind.of ἐλευθερόω, predictive) 2385.
ἀπὸ (preposition with the ablative of separation) 70.
τῆς (abl.sing.fem.of the article in agreement with δουλείας) 9.
δουλείας (abl.sing.fem.of δουλεία, separation) 3933.
τῆς (abl.sing.fem.of the article in agreement with φθορᾶς) 9.

#3942 φθορᾶς (abl.sing.fem.of φθορά, source).

King James Version

corruption - Rom.8:21; 1 Cor.15:42,50; Gal.6:8; 2 Pet.1:4; 2:12,19.
to perish - Col.2:22.
to be destroyed - 2 Pet.2:12.

Revised Standard Version

decay - Rom.8:21.
perishable - 1 Cor.15:42,50.
corruption - Gal.6:8; 2 Pet.1:4; 2:19.

destruction - 2 Pet.2:12b.
be destroyed - 2 Pet.2:12a.

*Meaning: Cf.* φθείρω (#4119). Destruction, disintegration. The opposite of γένεσις. Corruption, decay, decomposition. Entropy is the concept in physics that matter, which is potential energy, can perform work only by becoming kinetic energy. As *m* becomes *e* it surrenders complexity for simplicity. The work thus produced synthesizes whatever is produced into a complex system, such as a watermelon, a computer or an automobile. The new production is synthesized (built into a complex system) at the expense of matter which was analyzed (reduced to simplicity). Thus analysis must come before synthesis because only as *m* is analyzed can *e* become available to do the work. And as long as the product (the watermelon, computer, auto) exists, the *e* which produced it is unavailable for other work. If all *m* were analyzed and all *e* thus produced were used in the synthetic production of complex systems, entropy would be maximized, and no more work could be done until some complex system decayed. In the decomposition *m* would become *e* and only then could more work be done. Thus plant and animal life disintegrates under pressure and thermal conditions in the earth to form peat, lignite, bituminous coal, anthracite coal and finally diamond. A ton of coal is the synthetic product of what was once the energy which caused an animal or a plant to live. The coal is *m* and potential *e*, but it becomes kinetic *e* only in analysis. We must break it down. It must be analyzed. When we burn it we get *e* in the form of heat which boils water to create steam to produce kinetic energy to turn a factory wheel to make a computer. But the synthetic process which turns plant and animal matter, through the stages of peat and lignite into coal requires thousands of years, while it takes only a moment to burn a ton of coal. Thus man on this earth with his bright ideas which some call civilization is using up *e* faster than it is being replaced, and can only look to *e* sources outside the earth. But the entire universe is a closed system which is as subject to the principles of thermodynamics as the earth itself. Thus *m* moves from complexity to simplicity until all *avilable* energy (*e*) is equally distributed at which time all motion will cease and universal death will result. This process is going on constantly in the black hole as excess *e* pulls stars and planets into its maelstrom. Since *e* equals *m* it follows that falling bodies, which in the process of falling are performing work (*erg*), lose weight because *m* is being transformed into *e*.

Thus thermodynamics opposes the evolution hypothesis which the Neodarwinians struggle with such amazing futility to demonstrate. Unable to demonstrate it they *believe* it with a religious zeal and credulity that "blows the mind" of the thoughtful skeptic. We are not moving from simplicity to complexity. We are moving in precisely the opposite direction.

Our text declares that the creation is now held in the toils of the "bondage which has its source in φθορᾶς (decay, analysis, inevitable simplicity)" - a bondage from which it will be set free at some future time when it will enjoy the same liberty which will be given to the children of God. φθορᾶς is now moving toward entropy and its simplicity. Why have we not disintegrated already? How is it that entropy is not already maximized and that universal death has not resulted? We might answer by pointing to finite time. The universe indeed is slowing down and available energy is decreasing constantly, but ultimate simplicity and death will come only in the indeterminate future. Thus atheists, with their nihilistic, materialistic determinism must admit that the universe is moving toward nothing and that life in the meantime is therefore without meaning. Some indeed have been courageous enough to say this already, though most, like a diplomatic politician, have compartmentalized their minds, and manage still to talk like Christians!

But the Christian must have an answer to the entropy problem that transcends the limits of finite time. We believe in an eternity. It does not help us to say that although universal death must come *eventually*, there is still enough available energy around to keep us going for another one hundred million (billion, trillion - it is a matter of taste!) years. How is heaven's society to be made viable forever? The answer is that "by Him (Jesus Christ) all things consist" (Col.1:17). The verb in Col.1:17 (συνίστημι - #2328) yields the opposite concept to φθορᾶς. *Cf.* ἀπωλεία (#666) and ἀπόλλυμι (#208). Thermodynamics generates simplicity as entropy approaches the maximum, but Christ generates synthesis, which is life and the complex systems of technology. Natural law tears everything down, but supernatural law in the person of our Lord holds them together. Thus things consist. The curse of God upon the universe results in disintegration. This is the bondage expressed in ἡ δουλεία τῆς φθορᾶς - "the slavery that has its source in decay." The universe will continue to suffer from this slavery until it will be set free by the same liberating power that will set the children of God free from what Paul called "the body of this death" (σώματος τοῦ θανάτου τούτου) - (Rom.7:24). φθορά means the decomposition of a dead body in 1 Cor.15:42,50; in Gal.6:8 it refers to the moral as well as the physical and societal disintegration. It is used of the abnormal condition of the condemned world in 2 Pet.1:4; of moral and chemical corruption in 2 Pet.2:12,12,19. Note that men as well as the physical world are δοῦλοι τῆς φθορᾶς in 2 Pet.2:19. With reference to the chemical breakdown to simplicity by the digestive process - Col.2:22.

εἰς (preposition with the accusative, result) 140.

τὴν (acc.sing.fem.of the article in agreement with ἐλευθερίαν) 9.

**#3943** ἐλευθερίαν (acc.sing.fem.of ἐλευθερία, result).

King James Version

liberty - Rom.8:21; 1 Cor.10:29; 2 Cor.3:17; Gal.2:4; 5:1,13,13; James 1:25; 2:12; 1 Pet.2:16; 2 Pet.2:19.

Revised Standard Version

liberty - Rom.8:21; 1 Cor.10:29; James 1:25; 2:12.
freedom - 2 Cor.3:17; Gal.2:4; 5:1,13a,b; 1 Pet.2:16; 2 Pet.2:19.

*Meaning: Cf.*ἐλευθερόω (#2385); ἐλεύθερος (#1245). Freedom, liberty, absence of external restraint. Freedom from the bondage of a cursed earth, such as will be enjoyed by the saints in glory, *i.e.* the universe will be operating under viable scientific principles after the curse is lifted. The liberty of total compliance with God's eternal principles - Rom.8:21; 1 Pet.2:16; the liberty to do everything that one wishes to do since his decisions are consistent with God's holy law - James 1:25; 2:12; 1 Cor.10:29; 2 Cor.3:7; Gal.2:4; 5:1,13a,b (but not a freedom to sin). See also liberty in the sense of license to sin - 2 Pet.2:19.

τῆς (gen.sing.fem.of the article in agreement with δόξης) 9.

δόξης (gen.sing.fem.of δόξα, description) 361.

τῶν (gen.pl.neut.of the article in agreement with τέκνων) 9.

τέκνων (gen.pl.neut.of τέκνον, possession) 229.

τοῦ (gen.sing.masc.of the article in agreement with θεοῦ) 9.

θεοῦ (gen.sing.masc.of θεός, relationship) 124.

*Translation - ("In hope, vs.20) that the creation itself also shall be set free from the bondage of disintegration into the liberty of the glory of the born ones of God."*

**Comment:** The clause begins with ἐφ' ἐλπίδι of verse 20, which in turn is adverbial, modifying ἀπεκδέκεται of verse 19.

The creation awaits the rapture/resurrection (when the sons of God will be revealed) in the hope (ἐφ' ἐλπίδι, verse 20) that (ὅτι and the object clause of verse 21). What hope? That the creation itself (intensive αὐτή) also (adjunctive καί) will share in the liberation which the children of God will then enjoy. The universe now suffers under the bondage of chemical disintegration known in physics as entropy, the second law of thermodynamics. It is to be set free from that rule and be given the liberty that will characterize the children of God in glory.

I have discussed before the implication that, although all who believe on Christ as Saviour are "born ones of God" (τέκνα), only those who are led by the indwelling Holy Spirit enough to become objects of persecution and suffering, are also designated as υἱοί, and that only these are to be glorified with Him. If the "glory of the born ones of God" - τῆς δόξης τῶν τέκνων τοῦ θεοῦ - means the same as the "glorification" of Romans 8:30, then all of the children of God will participate in the rapture and resurrection at the second coming of our Lord, and there is no partial rapture.

At the risk of unnecessary repetition, and in order to invite the reader to study the question with care and submit any input to the discussion which he deems enlightening, let us go over the ground again.

Note that Paul in verse 21 says τῶν τέκνων τοῦ θεοῦ. The student will note Paul's use of υἱός (#5) and τέκνον (#229).

Verse 14 - Christians led by the Spirit of God are υἱοί.

Verse 16 - The Holy Spirit concurs with us that we are τέκνα.

Verse 17 - The Holy Spirit also agrees with us that since we are τέκνα ("born ones") we are also κληρονόμοι ("heirs") of God and συγκληρονόμοι ("joint heirs") of Christ.

Verse 17 - But Paul adds that our mutual glorification is contingent upon our mutual suffering with Christ.

Verse 19 - The glorification of the creation awaits the disclosure of τῶν υἱῶν τοῦ θεοῦ - "the sons of God."

Verse 21 - The creation awaits the moment of its liberation from bondage and this moment is the same as the liberation of the "born ones of God" (τῶν τέκνων τοῦ θεοῦ).

Since υἱοί are also κληρονόμοι and both υἱοί and κληρονόμοι began their spiritual experience at the new birth when they became τέκνα, it seems correct to say that all sons (υἱοί) are heirs (κληρονόμοι) and all such will be raptured, resurrected and glorified. Since all Christians are τέκνα and since no Christian is led by the Spirit of God with such total consistency as to have established a record of sinlessness (1 John 1:8), it would seem that only the Judge (John 5:22) can determine whether the τέκνον has also qualified to be called υἱός. Paul does not say that all τέκνα will be glorified. Indeed he implies that none will unless he also suffers for Christ. But Paul does not say that it is possible for a Christian to live out his life without once suffering for the cause of Christ. There is some "fruit" of the Holy Spirit in every Christian life, and there is no Christian life in which the Holy Spirit has been totally defeated in His attempt to lead the child of God, in whom He dwells (1 Cor.6:19) to implement the will of God as set forth in Eph.2:10. The superstructure which the Christian builds upon the foundation, Christ Jesus, (1 Cor.3:11-15) will contain much that is "wood, hay and stubble" but it will also contain some "gold, silver and precious stones."

Does Paul say that the rapture of the saints at the second coming of our Lord is only for those whose lives have been lived with such conformity to the will of God that they also qualify as "mature sons" (υἱοί). Are all other τέκνα to lie undisturbed in their graves until the end of the millenium, thus to be deprived of participation in the kingdom of millenial glory?

The text does not identify rapture with glorification. Perhaps "partial rapture" theorists should teach instead "total rapture but partial glorification."

To display the problem for holistic study in an effort to arrive at an objective conclusion, shall we consider the following propositions as true?

All who receive Christ as Saviour are τέκνα τοῦ θεοῦ and will ultimately be admitted to heaven (John 1:12,13). This seems clear.

Romans 8:14 does not say that all Christians are *always* led by the Spirit of God, but the relative pronoun ὅσοι, which is conditional, indicates that "all who are always led by the Spirit of God are the υἱοί θεοῦ. True.

But 1 John 1:8 denies that any Christian is always led by the Spirit of God. To be always led by the Holy Spirit is to be without sin, but John insists that the Christian who says this deceives himself. Thus Paul cannot be pointing to anything except a hypothetical case. Otherwise he is contradicting both scripture (1 Cor.3:15,16; Heb.6:8) and experience, including his own (Rom.7:15-25).

But Rom.8:14 implies that some Christians live lives of total obedence to the leading of the Holy Spirit and that these only are called υἱοί θεοῦ. Or are we pushing the present tense in ἄγονται in Romans 8:14 too far. Perhaps it is a customary present.

The Christians of Romans 8:14 are also called κληρονόμοι in Romans 8:17. And they will be glorified with Christ (Romans 8:17).

Since υἱοί and κληρονόμοι are also τέκνα, it can be said that the creation awaits the glorification of some τέκνα who are also υἱοί (Rom.8:21). Are they also κληρονόμοι and συγκληρονόμοι? If they have not suffered with Christ will they be glorified with Him? Is it possible that one can be raptured but not glorified with Christ? To affirm this is to distinguish between the rapture/resurrection glory, as the natural body becomes a spiritual body (1 Cor.15:44; Phil.3:21) and the later glory as we participate in His heavenly kingdom.

What was Paul seeking in Phil.3:10-14? And what does 2 Tim.2:12 mean? Is reigning with Christ the same as being glorified with Him? How shall we interpret 1 Pet.4:13? 1 Peter 5:1?

The exegete must always struggle with the problem as to the amount of force to give to an implication in the absence of a clear-cut statement. These questions at present are unresolved, but one thing is clear. If there is a distinction between τέκνον and υἱός and if that distinction is that the latter is a more mature child of God than the former, then every τέκνον should obey Gal.5:16, submit to the leadership of the Holy Spirit at all times and qualify as a υἱός (Rom.8:14) and, by suffering with Christ, also as a κληρονόμος (Rom.8:17). Then there is no question about his reward. In the meantime exegetes should exercise Christian tolerance toward each other and "let brotherly love continue" (Heb.13:1).

φθορά produces δουλεία because the purpose of God's creation (κτίσις) is to sustain life for man, God's crowning achievement in creation. Since φθορά (#3942) operates to randomize the elements in the universe until all available energy disappears and all motion ceases, the extent to which it works is the extent to which the universe is able still to perform its intended function. The "heat-death theory" of the universe says that the entire universal system is approaching a heat equilibrium, by which they mean that every body in the system will have the same temperature as every other body, at which time all motion and hence all life will cease. The κτίσις must be liberated from the slavery of this circumstance and indeed it will be when the sons of God are revealed. Thus Paul magnifies the importance of the event, not only for the saints, but for the universe itself, and thus also he encourages Christians to live such lives as will qualify them to participate in the event.

Historians, geologists, astronomers and now that we have achieved atomic fission, nuclear physicists, have advanced various catastrophic theories, with reference to the origin and destiny of our earth, the solar system and the galaxies of the entire universe. Christians can be assured that life in the universe is under the sovereign control of Him Who created it and Who now holds it together (Col.1:17). The Christian *weltanschauung* (view of the world; philosophy of history) assures us that nothing accidental is going to happen and that no plan of man is going to frustrate the purpose of God Who is busily engaged in visiting the Gentiles to take out of them a people for His name (Acts 15:14). When that is finished (Rev.10:7) we can expect some heavenly pyrotechnics.

*Verse 22 - "For we know that the whole creation groaneth and travaileth in pain together until now."*

οἴδαμεν γὰρ ὅτι πᾶσα ἡ κτίσις συστενάζει καὶ συνωδίνει ἄχρι τοῦ νῦν.

*"We know that the whole creation has been groaning in travail together until now." . . . RSV*

οἴδαμεν (1st.per.pl.perf.ind.of ὁράω, intensive) 144b.
γὰρ (causal conjunction) 105.
ὅτι (conjunction introducing an object clause in indirect discourse) 211.
πᾶσα (nom.sing.fem.of πᾶς, in agreement with κτίσις) 67.
ἡ (nom.sing.fem.of the article in agreement with κτίσις) 9.
κτίσις (nom.sing.fem.of κτίσις, subject of συντενάζει and συνωδίνει) 2633.

#3944 συστενάζει (3d.per.sing.pres.act.ind.of συστενάζω, present progressive retroactive).

King James Version

groan together - Rom.8:22.

Revised Standard Version

groaning - Rom.8:22.

*Meaning:* A combination of σύν (#1542) and στενάζω (#2310). Hence, to groan together; to sigh in concert. With reference to the dissatisfaction of the creation under the curse - Rom.8:22.

καὶ (adjunctive conjunction joining verbs) 14.

#3945 συνωδίνει (3d.per.sing.pres.act.ind.of συνωδίνω, present progressive retroactive).

King James Version

travail in pain together - Rom.8:22.

Revised Standard Version

travail together - Rom.8:22.

*Meaning:* A combination of σύν (#1542) and ωδίνω (#4444). Hence, to feel birth pangs. σύν indicates that one part of the creation travails together with another part. The pain indicated by this verb intensifies with time. To suffer pain of increasing intensity - Rom.8:22.

ἄχρι (improper preposition with the genitive of time description) 1517.
τοῦ (gen.sing.neut.of the article, time description) 9.
νῦν (temporal adverb) 1497.

*Translation - "Because we know that the entire creation has been sighing together and suffering with increasing intensity until this present moment."*

**Comment:** γὰρ is causal as Paul explains verse 21. οἴδαμεν, the constative perfect, with emphasis upon the present durative result, is followed by ὅτι and indirect discourse. The direct statement is "The entire creation is becoming more and more weary and suffering with increasing intensity." Each part of the whole suffers with all of the other parts and because of all other parts. Here is Spinoza's "block universe" but without his pantheism. Our Lord, the Creator of the universe and the divine Promulgator of the scientific principles which govern it is not interfering with its operation. It is getting sicker and sicker all of the time, though we may be sure that it will hold together until the divine purpose is accomplished. When the balance of nature is destroyed, the ills of every part create ills in every other part. Thus nature's law of cause and effect operates. The wages of sin is death in the physical as well as in the spiritual realm, and one cannot eat onions and keep it a secret. Ecologists are increasingly aware of this fact. There is a general equilibrium for suffering that affects the whole.

*Cf.* Phil.1:5 for ἄχρι τοῦ νῦν. *Cf.*#1517 for a complete list.

Note our comment about entropy in the remark about δουλείας τῆς φθορᾶς in verse 21. The entropy disintegration always increases randomness and destroys organization. This tendency is never reversed. It takes kinetic energy to achieve synthesis and man, the inventor is a great synthesizer. We love to put things together and we pursue the game apparently without regard for the fact that the energy we use is forever lost to us. Analysis is asymptotic. The quantity of available energy approaches but never touches absolute zero, but it could and would if God did not intervene. Without His intervention matter would reach a point of randomness that would destroy all life. This will not happen because our Lord has other plans for His Story (history).

An industrial society, which is destined to become even more highly industrialized, until it reaches the scenario of Revelation 18, experiences greater and greater dependence upon power resources. In the past man has used human and animal power, wind and water power, fossil fuels, electricity, geothermal, solar and nuclear power. The burning of fossil fuels contributes to environmental pollution with its spate of disastrous spinoffs. Thus, as power resources become more and more scarce, in relation to demand for power in a growing industrial society, power costs increase to force up retail price of the finished product. It is not likely that we shall succeed in bringing down prices, since power is an essential input of the production process. Twenty years ago some scientists were promising that with the coming of nuclear power to generate electricity, electric utility companies would supply unlimited electric power at prices approaching that of a free good. Such a development has not taken place, nor will it, as the history of the development of nuclear power since then attests. Even if the power to produce goods became a free good, the raw materials from which goods are made are also increasingly scarce. High prices which are necessary to cover high costs reduce the spending power of money and create poverty, which in turn creates bad housing, slums, drug addiction, prostitution and violent crime. Thus the whole creation groans and travails. This was true in Paul's day. It is even more true now, 1900 years later.

*Verse 23 - "And not only they, but ourselves also, which have the firstfruits of the*

*Spirit, even we ourselves groan within ourselves, waiting for the adoption, to
wit, the redemption of our body."*

οὐ μόνον δέ, ἀλλὰ καὶ αὐτοὶ τὴν ἀπαρχὴν τοῦ πνεύματος ἔχοντες ἡμεῖς καὶ
αὐτοὶ ἐν ἑαυτοῖς στενάζομεν υἱοθεσίαν ἀπεκδεχόμενοι, τὴν ἀπολύτρωσιν τοῦ
σώματος ἡμῶν.

*"... and not only the creation, but we ourselves, who have the first fruits of the
Spirit, groan inwardly as we wait for adoption as sons, the redemption of our
bodies."* ... RSV

οὐ (negative conjunction with the indicative) 130.
μόνον (acc.sing.neut.of μόνος, adverbial) 339.
δὲ (continuative conjunction) 11.
ἀλλὰ (adversative conjunction) 342.
καὶ (adjunctive conjunction joining substantives) 14.
αὐτοὶ (nom.pl.masc.of αὐτός, intensive, in agreement with ἔχοντες) 16.
τὴν (acc.sing.fem.of the article in agreement with ἀπαρχὴν) 9.

#3946 ἀπαρχὴν (acc.sing.fem.of ἀπαρχή, direct object of ἔχοντες).

King James Version

first fruit - Rom.8:23; 11:16; 16:5; 1 Cor.15:20,23; 16:15; James 1:18; Rev.14:4.
from the beginning - 2 Thess.2:13.

Revised Standard Version

first fruits - Rom.8:23; 11:16; 1 Cor.15:20,23; James 1:18; Rev.14:4.
first convert - Rom.16:5; 1 Cor.16:15.
from the beginning - 2 Thess.2:13.

*Meaning:* A combination of ἀπό (#70) and ἀρχή (#1285). *Cf.* ἀπάρχομαι - "to
take away the choicest or best part first." First fruits therefore are the most
important of many functions. Prime priority. The first fruit of the Holy Spirit is
the regeneration of lost sinners, a priority over all other redemptive work of God
- Rom.8:23; James 1:18. The Gentile church - Rom.11:16. The Jewish remnant
of the 144,000 at the second coming of Messiah - Rev.14:4. Christ, in His
resurrection was the first in order of importance - 1 Cor.15:20,23. With reference
to the first convert in a given region - Epaenatus in Asis - Rom.16:5; the
household of Stephanas, one of the first in Achaia - 1 Cor.16:15. In Thessalonica
- 2 Thess.2:13.

τοῦ (abl.sing.neut.of the article in agreement with πνεύματος) 9.
πνεύματος (abl.sing.neut.of πνεῦμα, source) 83.
ἔχοντες (pres.act.part.nom.pl.masc.of ἔχω, substantival, apposition) 82.
ἡμεῖς (nom.pl.masc.of ἐγώ, subject of στενάζομεν) 123.
καὶ (ascensive conjunction) 14.
αὐτοὶ (nom.pl.masc.of αὐτός, intensive) 16.

ἐν (preposition with the locative of place) 80.

ἑαυτοῖς (loc.pl.masc.of ἑαυτοῦ, place) 288.

στενάζομεν (1st.per.pl.pres.act.ind.of στενάζω, present progressive retroactive) 2310.

υἱοθεσίαν (acc.sing.fem.of υἱοθεσία, direct object of ἀπεκδεχόμενοι) 3934.

ἀπεκδεχόμενοι (pres.mid.part.nom.pl.masc.of ἀπεκδέχομαι, adverbial, temporal) 3939.

τὴν (acc.sing.fem.of the article in agreement with ἀπολύτρωσιν) 9.

ἀπολύτρωσιν (acc.sing.fem.of ἀπολύτρωσις, apposition with υἱοθεσίαν) 2732.

τοῦ (gen.sing.neut.of the article in agreement with σώματος) 9.

σώματος (gen.sing.neut.of σῶμα, description) 507.

ἡμῶν (gen.pl.masc.of ἐγώ, possession) 123.

*Translation - "And not only that, but also we ourselves, who have the first fruit of the Spirit, even we ourselves are sighing within ourselves as we await the adoption, namely the redemption of our bodies."*

**Comment:** The creation is not alone as its groans and frets impatiently to be released from the bondage which now enslaves it. The saints do also. We are the ones who have the first fruit of the Holy Spirit's activity in redemption. The salvation of the elect is the first priority for the Holy Spirit. We have his first fruit as a result of our birth from above, of which He is the source (John 3:3,5,7,8; 1 Pet.1:23). Our bodies are His temple (1 Cor.6:19). He has sealed us as God's property until the day of redemption (Eph.4:30). Meanwhile He has given us His gifts (1 Cor.12:1-12) and baptized us into the body of Christ (1 Cor.12:13). He has also enriched our lives with His fruits (Gal.5:22,23). Since He dwells in us He will make our natural bodies which have died alive as spiritual bodies (Rom.8:11).

As we wait for resurrection, we groan because our bodies are now "bodies of death" (Rom.7:24). ἀπεκδεχόμενοι is a temporal adverbial participle. *Cf.* 1 Cor.5:2,4. God's first concern in redemption is man, His crowning creation achievement. The Holy Spirit chose to save us first. But He will also save the heavens and the earth (Rev.21:1,2).

The redemption of our body is in apposition with υἱοθεσίαν. This adoption involves sonship and rapture/resurrection. *Cf.* Eph.1:14; 4:20; Lk.21:28. Thus the second coming of our Lord is the one great divine event toward which the whole creation moves with eager anticipation. It is the moment when not only the saints but the physical creation as well, will be forever freed from the curse of sin.

Our bodies will never again know pain. Nor will we ever again feel the inducement to sin and thus experience the wretchedness of which Paul complained (Rom.7:24). As for the creation, the desert will blossom as a rose and they will not hurt nor destroy in all of God's holy kingdom for the earth will be full of the knowledge of the Lord as the waters cover the sea (Isa.11:9).

*Verse 24 - "For we are saved by hope: but hope that is seen is not hope: for what a* man seeth, why doth he yet hope for?"

τῇ γὰρ ἐλπίδι ἐσώθημεν, ἐλπὶς δὲ βλεπομένη οὐκ ἔστιν ἐλπίς. ὃ γὰρ βλέπει τίς ἐλπίζει;

"For in this hope we are saved. Now hope that is seen is not hope. For who hopes for what he sees?" . . . RSV

τῇ (instru.sing.fem.of the article in agreement with ἐλπίδι) 9.
γὰρ (explanatory conjunction) 105.
ἐλπίδι (instru.sing.fem.of ἐλπίς, means) 2994.
ἐσώθημεν (1st.per.pl.1st.aor.pass.ind.of σώζω, culminative) 109.
ἐλπὶς (nom.sing.fem.of ἐλπίσ, subject of ἔστιν) 2994.
δὲ (adversative conjunction) 11.
βλεπομένη (pres.pass.part.nom.sing.fem.of βλέπω, adjectival, ascriptive, in agreement with ἐλπίς) 499.
οὐκ (negative conjunction with the indicative) 130.
ἔστιν (3d.per.sing.pres.ind.of εἰμί, static) 86.
ἐλπὶς (nom.sing.fem.of ἐλπίς, predicate nominative) 2994.
ὃ (acc.sing.neut.of ὅς, relative pronoun, direct object of ἐλπίζει) 65.
γὰρ (causal conjunction) 105.
βλέπει (3d.per.sing.pres.act.ind.of βλέπω, aoristic) 499.
τίς (nom.sing.masc.of τίς, interrogative pronoun, subject of ἐλπίζει) 281.
ἐλπίζει (3d.per.sing.pres.act.ind.of ἐλπίζω, customary) 991.

Translation - "Now we have been saved by hope. But hope that is seen is not hope, because who hopes for what he sees?"

Comment: This statement does not deny that we have been saved by grace through faith. Faith provides a confident expectation of things to come for which we hope until the time when we see them, after which faith and hope are no longer needed. *Cf.* 1 Cor.13:13. The statement becomes clear in the light of

Verse 25 - "But if we hope for that we see not, then do we with patience wait for it."

εἰ δὲ ὃ βλέπομεν ἐλπίζομεν, δι' ὑπομονῆς ἀπεκδεχόμεθα.

"But if we hope for what we do not see, we wait for it with patience." . . . RSV

εἰ (conditional particle in a first-class condition) 337.
δὲ (adversative conjunction) 11.
ὃ (acc.sing.neut.of ὅς, relative pronoun, direct object of ἐλπίζομεν) 65.
οὐ (negative conjunction with the indicative) 130.
βλέπομεν (1st.per.pl.pres.act.ind.of βλέπω, customary) 499.
ἐλπίζομεν (1st.per.pl.pres.act.ind.of ἐλπίζω, first-class condition) 991.
δι' (preposition with the ablative of manner) 118.
ὑπομονῆς (abl.sing.fem.of ὑπομονή, manner) 2204.
ἀπεκδεχόμεθα (1st.per.pl.pres.mid.ind.of ἀπεκδέχομαι, aoristic) 3939.

*Translation - "But if we do not see that for which we are hoping we wait for it with patience."*

**Comment:** *Cf.* Rom.5:1-5. We see or even groan, as did Paul (Rom.7:24,25) and as does the entire universe, but ours is not a hopeless misery. Patiently we look forward to rescue and relief at the second coming. *Cf.* Heb.10:35-37. It is not a time for the Christian to lose his confidence. Faith in the divine revelation gives certitude, although it is not the certitude that the scientific method speaks of. Their certitude comes from sense perception. For them there is no certitude without experience, but the Christian epistemology is based upon the *a priori* stance that God's word can be trusted. Thus the words ἐλπίς and ἐλπίζω - the noun and the verb for "hope" in the context of Romans 8:25 do not admit of any doubt. We know that redemption, both of our sin-infested, pain-wracked and disease-ridden bodies and of the rest of creation - galaxies, stars, planets, moons, plants, fish, birds, animals and insects will be redeemed from the curse. There is no doubt about it. We are sure that we are going to see what we can only anticipate. Thus we wait with patience - "he that shall come will come and will not tarry." "Hope deferred maketh the heart sick" (Proverbs 13:12) in the unregenerate experience, but deferred hope sheds God's love abroad in the Christian heart and supports his patience.

Furthermore, as we are to learn in verse 26, we have the help of the Holy Spirit as we wait patiently for the second coming.

*Verse 26 - "Likewise the Spirit also helpeth our infirmities: for we know not what we should pray for as we ought; but the Spirit itself maketh intercession for us with groanings which cannot be uttered."*

Ὡσαύτως δὲ καὶ τὸ πνεῦμα συναντιλαμβάνεται τῇ ἀσθενείᾳ ἡμῶν, τὸ γὰρ τί προσευξώμεθα καθὸ δεῖ οὐκ οἴδαμεν, ἀλλὰ αὐτὸ τὸ πνεῦμα ὑπερεντυγχάνει στεναγμοῖς ἀλαλήτοις.

*"Likewise the Spirit helps us in our weakness; for we do not know how to pray as we ought, but the Spirit himself intercedes for us with sighs too deep for words."* . . . *RSV*

Ὡσαύτως (compound particle in a comparative clause) 1319.

δὲ (continuative conjunction) 11.

καὶ (adjunctive conjunction joining nouns) 14.

τὸ (nom.sing.neut.of the article in agreement with πνεῦμα) 9.

πνεῦμα (nom.sing.neut.of πνεῦμα, subject of συναντιλαμβάνεται) 83.

συναντιλαμβάνεται (3d.per.sing.pres.mid.ind.of συναντιλαμβάνω, present progressive retroactive) 2443.

τῇ (instrumental sing.fem.of the article in agreement with ἀσθενείᾳ) 9.

ἀσθενείᾳ (instru.sing.fem.of ἀσθένεια, association, after σύν in composition) 740.

ἡμῶν (gen.pl.masc.of ἐγώ, possession) 123.

τὸ (acc.sing.neut.of the article in agreement with τί) 9.

γὰρ (causal conjunction) 105.

τί (acc.sing.neut.of τίς, interrogative pronoun, in indirect question, direct object of οἴδαμεν) 281.

προσευξώμεθα (1st.per.pl.pres.mid.subj.of προσεύχομαι, deliberative in indirect question) 544.

**#3947** καθὸ (compound particle in a comparative clause).

King James Version

as - Rom.8:26.
inasmuch as - 1 Pet.4:13.
according to that - 2 Cor.8:12,12.

Revised Standard Version

as - Rom.8:26.
according to what - 2 Cor.8:12,12.
in so far as - 1 Pet.4:13.

*Meaning:* A combination of κατά (#98) and ὅς (#65). A particle in a comparative clause. As - Rom.8:26; according as - 2 Cor.8:12,12; to the extent that - 1 Pet.4:13.

δεῖ (present indicative impersonal) 1207.
οὐκ (negative conjunction with the indicative) 130.
οἴδαμεν (1st.per.pl.perf.ind.of ὁράω, intensive) 144b.
ἀλλὰ (adversative conjunction) 342.
αὐτὸ (nom.sing.neut.of αὐτός, in agreement with πνεῦμα, intensive) 16.
τὸ (nom.sing.neut.of the article in agreement with πνεῦμα) 9.
πνεῦμα (nom.sing.neut.of πνεῦμα, subject of ὑπερεντυγχάνει) 83.

**#3948** ὑπερεντυγχάνει (3d.per.sing.pres.act.ind.of ὑπερεντυγχάνω, present progressive retroactive).

King James Version

make intercession - Rom.8:26.

Revised Standard Version

intercedes - Rom.8:26.

*Meaning:* A combination of ὑπέρ (#545), ἐν (#80) and τυγχάνω (#2699). Hence, to hit the mark for us; to achieve for us what needs to be achieved; hence, to intercede; to pray for us. With reference to the ministry in prayer of the Holy Spirit for the believer - Rom.8:26.

στεναγμοῖς (instru.pl.masc.of στεναγμός, manner) 3132.

**#3949** ἀλαλήτοις (instru.pl.masc.of ἀλάλητος, in agreement with στεναγμοῖς).

King James Version

which cannot be uttered - Rom.8:26.

Revised Standard Version

too deep for words - Rom.8:26.

*Meaning:* α privative plus λαλητός, from λαλέω (#815). Inexpressible in words; too deep for words. Inaudible communication - Rom.8:26.

*Translation - "Likewise the Spirit also helps us bear the burden of our frailty, because we have never known how to pray properly, but the Spirit Himself, with inexpressible earnestness has always hit the bull's'eye for us."*

**Comment:** *Cf.*#2443 - "to take" (λαμβάνω) "the opposite end" (ἀντί) "with" (σύν) us. Hence, to help us carry a burden. The passage does not say that the Holy Spirit does all of the praying. He prays through and in us as we try, in our weakness, to pray for ourselves. But we miss the mark despite our sincerity and concern. We do not know (having not yet learned - perfect tense in οἴδαμεν) how we should pray. Note the deliberative subjunctive indicating doubt in the indirect question. For τὸ . . . τί, the article with the interrogative pronoun in indirect question *cf.* Rom.8:27; Luke 22:23,24; Acts 22:30. - "We do not know (the) what . . . ?" In Acts 4:21 we have indirect question with τὸ πῶς - "not finding (the) how . . .?"

ἀλλὰ is strongly adversative. αὐτὸ in the predicate position is intensive. Though τὸ πνεῦμα is neuter grammatically, He is masculine personally - thus the translation, in deference to our theology - "the Spirit Himself." #3948 is interesting! He prays properly because He is God. He asks for what God has already determined to do. He "zeros in on the target." He "hits the bull's-eye." When we pray the ignorance, which makes us ineffective (τῇ ἀσθενείᾳ), causes us to miss the mark. Thus we pray "amiss" (James 4:3), and ask for what would result in our own personal tragedy if God gave it to us. But the Holy Spirit has always carried the load with us (present progressive retroactive in ὑπερεντυγχάνει). A practical application of this great truth will lead the Christian, when he tries to pray, to allow the Holy Spirit to do the asking. The only prayer that is truly effective is the Spirit indited prayer. *Cf.*Rom.6:19 for the source of our infirmity. We are still controlled to some extent by the flesh. We have only an earth-bound and temporal viewpoint. We cannot see into the future as He can. Proper therapeutics always depends upon proper diagnosis. Since our flesh prevents the latter it precludes the former. But the Holy Spirit is the perfect diagnostician. Thus He knows exactly what we need. He knows exactly what to pray for, and His concern for us knows no bounds, since our body is His temple (1 Cor.6:19). He will abide with us forever (John 14:16) and He is charged with the responsibility of guiding us into all the truth (John 16:13).

There is a current charismatic view that, although the restrictions of 1 Corinthians 12-14 forbid the exercise of "tongues" in a public service, except on very rare occasions, the "gift" can be exercised in private prayer. This view is alleged to find support in Romans 8:26. But we should note that the prayer of the

Holy Spirit is offered inaudibly (στεναγμοῖς ἀλαλήτοις). Those who claim the gift of "tongues" when they pray should be asked this question: "Do you hear anything when you pray?" If the answer is "Yes" then the Holy Spirit is not the source of what is heard. *Cf.* our discussion of γλῶσσα (#1846). The word means "language," not gibberish. Let those who speak English pray in English. Let the French pray in French. God will understand. But it is always better for us to allow the Holy Spirit to transmit His requests in our behalf with His own *inaudible* communication to the Father.

The thought is pursued further in

*Verse 27 - "And he that searcheth the hearts knoweth what is the mind of the Spirit, because He maketh intercession for the saints according to the will of God."*

ὁ δὲ ἐραυνῶν τὰς καρδίας οἶδεν τί τὸ φρόνημα τοῦ πνεύματος, ὅτι κατὰ θεὸν ἐντυγχάνει ὑπὲρ ἁγίων.

*"And he who searches the hearts of men knows what is the mind of the Spirit, because the Spirit intercedes for the saints according to the will of God."* ... RSV

ὁ (nom.sing.masc.of the article in agreement with ἐραυνῶν) 9.

δὲ (continuative conjunction) 11.

ἐραυνῶν (pres.act.part.nom.sing.masc.of ἐρευνάω, substantival, subject of οἶδεν) 2099.

τὰς (acc.pl.fem.of the article in agreement with καρδίας) 9.

καρδίας (acc.pl.fem.of καρδία, direct object of ἐραυνῶν) 432.

οἶδεν (3d.per.sing.perf.act.ind.of οἶδα, intensive) 144b.

τί (acc.sing.neut.of τίς, interrogative pronoun, in indirect question, direct object of οἶδεν) 281.

τὸ (acc.sing.neut.of the article in agreement with φρόνημα) 9.

φρόνημα (acc.sing.neut.of φρόνημα, predicate accusative) 3931.

τοῦ (gen.sing.neut.of the article in agreement with πνεύματος) 9.

πνεύματος (gen.sing.neut.of πνεῦμα, possession) 83.

ὅτι (conjunction introducing a causal clause) 211.

κατὰ (preposition with the accusative, standard) 98.

θεὸν (acc.sing.masc.of θεός, standard) 124.

ἐντυγχάνει (3d.per.sing.pres.act.ind.of ἐντυγχάνω, present progressive retroactive) 3649.

ὑπὲρ (preposition with the ablative, "in behalf of") 545.

ἁγίων (abl.pl.masc.of ἅγιος, "in behalf of") 84.

*Translation - "And He who has always known the hearts has always known what the Spirit is thinking, because He has always prayed for the saints in keeping with God's will."*

**Comment:** ὁ ἐραυνῶν refers to God the Father. *Cf.* Rev.2:23. Since the subject of οἶδεν is God, the force of the perfect is intensive. To emphasize the preterite punctiliar force would mean that in the past God learned about the human heart

— a concept totally inconsistent with that of an eternal and omniscient God. God, having always known the human heart, still does. The Holy Spirit also knows what we are thinking and He reacts to our foolishness and ineptitude in the same way as does the Father and the Son. Thus God the Father knows what the Holy Spirit is thinking. The Holy Spirit has researched into everything (1 Cor.2:10).

The ὅτι clause is causal. The Father knows what the Holy Spirit is asking because He has always asked (present progressive retroactive in ἐντυγχάνει) what the Father has always wished. His thoughts and prayers are in keeping with the divine standard (κατὰ θεόν). Hence the Father's will is always the will of the Holy Spirit. The divine omniscience of the Holy Spirit is the safeguard that stands between the Christian and the tragic results of his own errant prayers.

A recapitulation of Paul's thought in context is in order if we are to understand what he says in verse 28. He urges us to follow the leadership of the Holy Spirit, thus to be sons and heirs (Rom.8:14-16), even though to do so will invite persecution (verse 17), but insure glorification (verse 18). He encourages us to embark upon this course, despite the sufferings which our decision entails, because they are nothing when compared with the reward that awaits us in glory (verse 18). The coming glorification is most important since not only the saints, but the entire universe anticipates it, as the time when both saints and the physical universe will be freed from the curse of sin (verses 19-23). We know that what is now the object of faith will some day be the object of sight. So we wait in hope and with patience for the great day ahead (verses 24,25). Our waiting period, fraught as it is with suffering and confusion, is safeguarded by the Holy Spirit Whose prayers for us are always in accord with God's will. Thus the Father listens to Him and disregards our misguided requests (verses 26-27). This is why Paul can conclude the chapter with the classic statement of total Christian optimism that is based upon total victory of God's love, grace and power over evil. Christ also intercedes for the saints (Rom.8:34; Heb.7:25).

*Verse 28 - "And we know that all things work together for good to them that love God, to them who are the called according to his purpose."*

οἴδαμεν δὲ ὅτι τοῖς ἀγαπῶσιν τὸν θεὸν πάντα συνεργεῖ εἰς ἀγαθόν, τοῖς κατὰ πρόθεσιν κλητοῖς οὖσιν.

*"We know that in everything God works for good with those who love him, who are called according to his purpose." . . . RSV*

οἴδαμεν (1st.per.pl.perf.act.ind.of ὁράω, consummative) 144b.

δὲ (explanatory conjunction) 11.

ὅτι (conjunction introducing an object clause in indirect discourse) 211.

τοῖς (dat.pl.masc.of the article in agreement with ἀγαπῶσιν) 9.

ἀγαπῶσιν (pres.act.part.dat.pl.masc.of ἀγαπάω,substantival, personal advantage) 540.

τὸν (acc.sing.masc.of the article in agreement with θεὸν) 9.

θεὸν (acc.sing.masc.of θεός, direct object of ἀγαπῶσιν) 124.

πάντα (nom.pl.neut.of πᾶς, subject of συνεργεῖ) 67.

συνεργεῖ (3d.per.sing.pres.act.ind.of συνεργέω, present progressive retroactive) 2931.

εἰς (preposition with the accusative, purpose/result) 140.

ἀγαθόν (acc.sing.neut.of ἀγαθός, purpose/result) 547.

τοῖς (dat.pl.masc.of the article in agreement with οὖσιν) 9.

κατὰ (preposition with the accusative, standard) 98.

πρόθεσιν (acc.sing.fem.of πρόθεσις, standard) 968.

κλητοῖς (dat.pl.masc.of κλητός, predicate adjective) 1411.

οὖσιν (pres.part.dat.pl.masc.of εἰμί, substantival, personal advantage) 86.

*Translation - "Thus, we conclude that for those who are loving God, all things have always worked together for good, to whose who, in accord with His purpose, are being called."*

**Comment:** The textual authorities are not certain whether the text as presented is correct or whether, with p46 A B 81 copsa (eth) Origengr 2/5 we ought to read συνεργεῖ ὁ θεός. The United Bible Societies' Committee opt for the text *supra*, with a C degree of certitude. If συνεργεῖς ὁ θεός is correct then συνεργεῖ is transitive and Goodspeed's translation is correct - "We know that in everything God works with those who love him, whom he has called in accordance with his purpose, to bring about what is good." This only means that God's purpose is to cooperate with the believer so that the desired result may be achieved, and that the result is contingent upon the believer's cooperation. This interpretation is no safeguard against eternal loss (though not the loss of salvation) to the disobedient believer. The passage as translated above (my translation) can be used to support antinomianism, if we argue that πάντα even includes the believer's sin, and that sin, cooperating with more sin and/or good adds up to good. This was the argument of the antinomians in Romans 6:1. Or does εἰς ἀγαθόν refer to good for God and not necessarily good for the believer? If so τοῖς ἀγαπῶσιν τὸν θεόν and τοῖς κατὰ πρόθεσιν κλητοῖς οὖσιν are not datives of personal advantage, as we have indicated, but instrumentals of means. Grammatically they can be either since the dative and instrumental forms are identical. If this be true it means that God is manipulating everything by means of the believer so that His own glory (εἰς ἀγαθόν) will be achieved. Thus God is glorified as His law in vindicated in the punishment of the sinning saint (1 Cor.3:15,16; Heb.6:8; 1 Cor.9:27 *et al*). If we reject ὁ θεός as the substantive joined to συνεργεῖ (Robertson doubts very much that it belongs, *Grammar*, 477), then the promise is taken at face value, but qualified as applying only to a select group - τοῖς ἀγαπῶσιν τὸν θεόν, within the large all-inclusive group τοῖς κατὰ πρόθεσιν κλητοῖς οὖσιν. In other words, not all who are called and therefore saved, in keeping with God's purpose, are in love with Him, and that only those who are, are in view here.

The Holy Spirit helps those Christians described in Romans 8:14-25, whose characteristics include obedience to His leadership (verse 14), sonship, heirship, suffering, prospect of glorification, dissatisfaction with our carnal bodies, anticipation, hope and our pitiable attempts to pray for help, despite the fact that we do not have sufficient knowledge to be able to pray properly. What about the Christians who, though having once been called and saved, have not allowed the Holy Spirit to lead them and hence are not in view in the language following Romans 8:14? It is clear that some saints will be saved even though they will suffer the loss of rewards. Salvation is not forfeited by the Christian's record of disobedience (1 Cor.3:15; Heb.6:4; 1 Cor.9:27; Acts 5:1-11; 1 Cor.5:1-5). Indeed there is no Christian with a record of sinlessness (1 John 1:8). Hence we conclude that πάντα in Romans 8:28 refers only to all the events, situations, and circumstances in the believer's life except his lapses into sin. His aches, pains, diseases, social misfortunes, financial reverses, persecutions, driving temptations to sin to which he does not yield, loss of friends and loved ones, personal tragedies which are a part of life in the flesh - in short, those events and situations that cause him to groan and long for release in glory - all of these things fit together into a divine plan for his life to bring about his eternal good and God's eternal glory. Thus Paul could write elsewhere to "Rejoice always" (Phil.4:4) and to give thanks for everything (1 Thess.5:16-18) and James could call us to rejoice even in trials (James 1:2).

It seems hardly coincidental that Paul's language in Romans 8:28 should parallel so closely Plato's observation in *The Republic,* Book X, 613, A,B,C.

Then this must be our notion of the just man, that even when he is in poverty or sickness, or any other seeming misfortune, all things will in the end work together for good to him in life and death: for the gods have a care of any one whose desire is to become just and to be like God, as far as man can attain the divine likeness, by the pursuit of virtue?

Yes, he said; if he is like God he will surely not be neglected by Him.

And of the unjust may not the opposite be supposed?

Certainly.

Such, then, are the palms of victory which the gods give the just?

That is my conviction.

And what do they receive of men? Look at things as they really are, and you will see that the clever unjust are in the case of runners, who run well from the starting-place to the goal but not back again from the goal: they go off at a great pace, but in the end only look foolish, slinking away with their ears draggling on their shoulders, and without a crown; but the true runner comes to the finish and receives the prize and is crowned. And this is the way with the just; he who endures to the end of every action and occasion of his entire life has a good report and carries off the prize which men have to bestow.

True.

This does not prove that Plato shared with Paul the gift of divine inspiration. It does tend to demonstrate that Paul had read Plato; indeed that he was so familiar with his work that unconsciously perhaps, under the Holy Spirit's guidance, he made Plato's formulations his own. Jesus' words in Mt.10:22 and Paul's in 1 Cor.9:24 and Phil.3:14 are also suggested in the passage from Plato.

*Verse 29 - "For whom he did foreknow, he also did predestinate to be conformed to the image of His Son, that he might be the firstborn among many brethren."*

ὅτι οὓς προέγνω, καὶ προώρισεν συμμόρφους τῆς εἰκόνος τοῦ υἱοῦ αὐτοῦ, εἰς τὸ εἶναι αὐτὸν πρωτότοκον ἐν πολλοῖς ἀδελφοῖς.

*"For those whom he foreknew he also predestined to be conformed to the image of his Son, in order that he might be the first-born among many brethren."*
RSV

ὅτι (conjunction introducing a causal clause) 211.
οὓς (acc.pl.masc.of ὅς, relative pronoun, direct object of προώρισεν) 65.
προέγνω (3d.per.sing.1st.aor.act.ind.of προγινώσκω, constative) 3655.
καὶ (adjunctive conjunction joining verbs) 14.
προώρισεν (3d.per.sing.aor.act.ind.of προορίζω, constative) 3042.

#3950 συμμόρφους (acc.pl.masc.of σύμμρφος, in agreement with οὓς).

King James Version

conformed to - Rom.8:29.
fashioned like unto - Phil.3:21.

Revised Standard Version

conformed to - Rom.8:29.
to be like - Phil.3:21.

*Meaning:* A combination of σύν (#1542) and μορφή (#2896). Hence, having the same form. Followed by τῆς εἰκόνος τοῦ υἱοῦ αὐτοῦ in Rom.8:29; followed by τῷ σώματι τῆς δόξης αὐτοῦ in Phil.3:21.

τῆς (abl.sing.fem.of the article in agreement with εἰκόνος) 9.
εἰκόνος (abl.sing.fem.of εἰκών, comparison) 1421.
τοῦ (gen.sing.masc.of the article in agreement with υἱοῦ) 9.
υἱοῦ (gen.sing.masc.of υἱός, description) 5.
αὐτοῦ (gen.sing.masc.of αὐτός, relationship) 16.
εἰς (preposition with the accusative of purpose/result) 140.
τὸ (acc.sing.neut.of the article with the infinitive in a sub-final clause) 9.
εἶναι (pres.inf.of εἰμί, accusative case, in a sub-final clause) 86.
αὐτὸν (acc.sing.masc.of αὐτός, general reference) 16.
πρωτότοκον (masc.sing.masc.of πρωτότοκος, predicate accusative) 1872.
ἐν (preposition with the locative, with plural substantives) 80.
πολλοῖς (loc.pl.masc.of πολύς, in agreement with ἀδελφοῖς) 228.
ἀδελφοῖς (loc.pl.masc.of ἀδελφός, place) 15.

*Translation -* *"Because He decreed that whom He foreknew should also be conformed to the image of His Son, in order (and with the result) that He might be the first-born among many brothers."*

**Comment:** ὅτι is causal as Paul moves to prove with a description of a chain reaction of God's sovereign decrees that the happy statement of verse 28 is true. How could such a triumphant philosophy find its implementation with sinful men in a time/space set of relationships? Because God foreknew some people. *Cf.*#3655 for other uses. There is no determinism in foreknowledge, though God, Who sees the end from the beginning and is omniscient, has never foreknown an event which did not after all take place. He has infinite awareness, understanding and insight. God can learn nothing. Others are like that but for a different reason? God can learn nothing because there is nothing for Him to learn that He has not always known. To say that God knows that something will happen is only to say that there is no doubt that it will in fact occur. The reason that it is certain to occur is either that He makes it occur, or that its occurrence is the result of the operation of natural law which God ordained in creation. God is not active in a chemistry laboratory when sodium and chloride unite to form common table salt, but He once decreed the principles of chemistry that such should be the result when the proper conditions were met. If God has not already decrees that certain results should follow certain specified causes, as in the case of table salt, He intervenes in history to bring about that which He desires. God has always known that on one occasion an axe head would float, and when the time came for the miracle He performed it, much to the amazement of the sons of the prophets (2 Kings 6:1-7). These overt acts, intruded into human history, which otherwise would not have taken place is what is meant by προώρισεν (#3042). This indeed is divinely deterministic. Foreknowledge is a passive state of perfectly accurate prior awareness of what is going to happen. It is available only to God. Predestination is an active decree by which a sovereign God orders that something shall be done.

Our verse says that God ordered that certain ones whom He foreknew should be conformed to Christ's image. This conformation to Christ's image takes place in time in two stages. The first is regeneration. The second is glorification, when the body of the believer is made like Christ's resurrection body (Phil.3:21). Note that the word σύμμρφος in Phil.3:21, with reference to glorification of the body is the same as in Romans 8:29.

Christ is εἰκὼν τοῦ θεοῦ τοῦ ἀοράτου - "the image of the invisible God." Thus, by looking at Him we can tell what God is like, even though we have never seen Him. (Col.1:15; 2 Cor.4:4b; John 14:9). God has ordered that the elect be made like the image of Christ, Who is the image of God. Since things equal to the same things are equal to each other, it follows that God has ordered the elect conformed to His own image. This shall be done. *Cf.* 1 Cor.15:49b; 2 Cor.3:18; Col.3:10; Rom.8:29. This conformation is physical (1 Cor.15:49b), ethical (2 Cor.3:18) and intellectual (Col.3:10). It should quickly be added that there are incommunicable attributes which only God possesses, which are not included in this miracle of conformation by which He takes the condemned universal felon and by His grace makes Him like Christ. Thus there is no comfort here for the Mormon doctrine that "what man is God once was and what God is man may become." That is a bit of arrant nonesense that should be interred in the same hole in the ground where Joseph Smith found it. God was never a sinner and men, though saved by God's grace and made like His Son will never be God.

There is another sense in which the elect are conformed to Christ's image. Our Lord, the divine personality with a divine nature took upon Himself in incarnation a human nature, thus to become a dual-natured personality. Always God (John 1:1,2) He became and shall forever remain a man, without ever relinquishing His divine nature (1 Tim.2:5). The elect, human persons with human natures, are given in regeneration a divine nature. Thus they also become dual-natured personalities. First men, we become and shall always remain possessed of our divine nature (2 Pet.1:4) without ever relinquishing our human nature, though, thank God (Rom.7:25) seeing it totally conformed to Him (Phil.3:21). Thus Christ's image is that of a God-Son of Man (Phil.2:5-8). Our image is that of a Man-Son of God.

This decree of God was for a specific purpose, expressed with εἰς and the articular infinitive τὸ εἶναι in the accusative case - "In order (and with the result) that Christ might become the first-born in association with many of whom He shall not be ashamed, when He calls them brethren. *Cf.* Heb.2:11; John 17:21. In the incarnation the Father made His eternal Son also a man and announced that He, the God-Man (1 Tim.2:5) was only the model - the pilot product, the first of many who would be made like him. *Cf.* Heb.1:6; Col.1:15, 18; Heb.12:23; Rev.1:5. Thus we have revealed (1) what God knew from eternity, (2) what He did about what He knew, and (3) why He did it. He foreknew the elect; He predestined that they should be conformed to His Son; and in doing so, He made Jesus Christ the first-born among many others who would follow and be like Him.

How does God move to conform the elect to His Son? It requires three definite steps.

*Verse 30 - "Moreover whom he did predestinate, them he also called: and whom he called, them he also justified: and whom he justified, them he also glorified."*

οὓς δὲ προώρισεν, τούτους καὶ ἐκάλεσεν, καὶ οὓς ἐκάλεσεν, τούτους καὶ ἐδικαίωσεν, οὓς δὲ ἐδικαίωσεν, τούτους καὶ ἐδόξασεν.

*"And those whom he predestined he also called; and those whom he called he also justified; and those whom he justified he also glorified."* . . . *RSV*

οὓς (acc.pl.masc.of ὅς, relative pronoun, direct object of προώρισεν) 65.
δὲ (continuative conjunction) 11.
προώρισεν (3d.per.sing.aor.act.ind.of προορίζω, gnomic) 3042.
τούτους (acc.pl.masc.of οὗτος, direct object of ἐκάλεσεν, deictic) 93.
καὶ (adjunctive conjunction joining verbs) 14.
ἐκάλεσεν (3d.per.sing.aor.act.ind.of καλέω, gnomic) 107.
καὶ (continuative conjunction) 14.
οὓς (acc.pl.masc.of ὅς, relative pronoun, direct object of ἐκάλεσεν) 65.
ἐκάλεσεν (3d.per.sing.aor.act.ind.of καλέω, constative) 107.
τούτους (acc.pl.masc.of οὗτος, deictic, direct object of ἐδικαίωσεν) 93.
καὶ (adjunctive conjunction joining verbs) 14.
ἐδικαίωσεν (3d.per.sing.aor.act.ind.of δικαιόω, gnomic) 933.

οὖς (acc.pl.masc.of ὅς, relative pronoun, direct object of ἐδικαίωσεν) 65.

δὲ (continuative conjunction) 11.

ἐδικαίωσεν (3d.per.sing.aor.act.ind.of δικαιόω, gnomic) 933.

τούτους (acc.pl.masc.of οὗτος, deictic, direct object of ἐδόξασεν) 93.

καὶ (adjunctive conjunction joining verbs) 14.

ἐδόξασεν (3d.per.sing.aor.act.ind.of δοξάζω, gnomic) 461.

*Translation - "And whom He predestined them He also called; and whom He called them He also declared righteous; and whom He declared righteous them He also glorified."*

**Comment:** The aorists are all gnomic (tenseless) since God is timeless and these are all relating to His actions and decrees. Glorification is contingent upon justification, which is contingent upon calling, and all three are contingent upon God's timeless decree to have it so. Obviously also He has always known about it. This is what the language says and it says nothing less. All of the gainsaying of Pelagius, Arminius and Thomas Aquinas cannot change it. The Calvinists are not obligated to explain it, since we do not profess to be Gnostics. There is much that God knows that we may never know. We have not forgotten Isaiah 55:8,9. We shall see in Romans 9 that Paul could not explain why God chose Jacob over Esau; nor could he explain why God treated Pharaoh as He did.

Glorification is still in the future for the body of Christ. Our calling and justification are in the past. There remain other members of the body of Christ, "elect according to the foreknowledge of God" (1 Pet.1:2) who have not yet been called and justified. The roster will become complete in the days when the seventh trumpet angel prepares to blow his horn (Rev.10:7). Then our Lord will return (1 Cor.15:52 - "at the last trump") and all who were foreknown, predestined, called and justified will be glorified "in a moment, in the twinkling of an eye."

We cloud the issue when we try to use past, present and future tenses as they relate to God. For God is eternal. He knows nothing of time, which is only a category, like space, which mortals must use in order to derive perception from sensation. from which perception we then derive concept, science and life. Noumena can be derived from phenomena only with the categories of time and space. But God is infinite. He knows what will happen *after* the end of time (!) in a spot *beyond* the end of space(!). Mortals cannot play philosophical games with God.

Note that τούτους, which occurs three times in our verse is deictic. In each case it points to the relative pronoun οὖς. Those predestined are called; those called are justified; those justified are glorified. There is no break in the chain which, including foreknowledge, is composed of five links. The chain cannot be broken without denying the sovereignty of God. Who in the universe is strong enough to stop God from doing what He wants to do?

None of these acts are contingent upon human merit. There are no if clauses in the passage. These statements are unconditional. They all use the indicative mode. We need not ask why? If you do, I will ask, "Why not?" What God does is consistent with what He wishes to do and what He chooses to do. To apply the criterion of human wisdom and thus to charge Him with folly is to join the ancient Greeks who accused Zeus of many follies. Christians do not make God in our image, as did the pagans described in Romans 1:18-32.

The Christian who has some appreciation of the depths of his own depravity will not ask why God has not chosen all. He is overwhelmed with the question, "Why me?"

Please note, pursuant to our discussion of Romans 8:17*ff* that all believers are to be glorified. Is the glorification of Romans 8:30 a different glorification from that of Romans 8:17. Or are all believers destined to suffer with Christ to a sufficient degree so as to merit sonship, heirship and glorification with Christ? When Jesus said, "In the world ye shall have tribulation" (John 16:33) did He refer only to the eleven Apostles who were present, or did He mean all Christians? If John 15:18,19 and Matthew 5:10-12 apply to all the elect, then the rapture is not selective.

## God's Love

*(Romans 8:31-39)*

*Verse 31 - "What shall we then say to these things? If God be for us, who can be against us?"*

Τί οὖν ἐροῦμεν πρὸς ταῦτα; εἰ ὁ θεὸς ὑπὲρ ἡμῶν, τίς καθ' ἡμῶν;

*"What then shall we say to this? If God is for us, who is against us?"* . . . *RSV*

Τί (acc.sing.neut.of τίς, interrogative pronoun, in direct question, direct object of ἐροῦμεν) 281.

οὖν (inferential conjunction) 68.

ἐροῦμεν (1st.per.pl.fut.act.ind.of εἴρω, deliberative) 155.

πρὸς (preposition with the accusative of reference) 197.

ταῦτα (acc.pl.neut.of οὗτος, reference) 93.

εἰ (conditional particle in a first-class condition) 337.

ὁ (nom.sing.masc.of the article in agreement with θεὸς) 9.

θεὸς (nom.sing.masc.of θεός, subject of ἔστιν understood) 124.

ὑπὲρ (preposition with the ablative "in behalf of") 545.

ἡμῶν (abl.pl.masc.of ἐγώ, "in behalf of") 123.

τίς (nom.sing.masc.of τίς, interrogative pronoun, in direct question, subject of ἔστιν understood) 281.

καθ' (preposition with the genitive, opposition) 98.

ἡμῶν (gen.pl.masc.of ἐγώ, opposition) 123.

*Translation - "What then are we going to say about these matters? Since God is for us who is against us?"*

**Comment:** The question is direct but it has the distinct flavor of the rhetorical. One wishes immediately to respond by saying "Nothing" to the first question and

"No one" to the second.

What is to be said in response to what things? The antecedent of ταῦτα may be considered the entire eighth chapter through verse 30. It is full of evidence that God has determined to justify the elect and place all of heaven's sovereign resources at our disposal. Now, who would want to speak against that?

One's soul is filled with merriment to recall the hilarious misquotation of the passage by the little girl who, when asked by her grandfather what the memory verse in Sunday School was, said, "If God be for us you are up against it!" With that kind of insight it is time for the benediction. The little girl understood the verse better than some who complain because apparently they want a universe governed, if not by Satan, then by chance. The Christian *weltanschauung* is optimistic because of Romans 8:28-30 as interpreted in the light of 1 John 4:4; Mt.28:18; Eph.1:19-23.

*Verse 32 - "He that spared not his own son, but delivered him up for us all, how shall he not with him also freely give us all things?"*

ὅς γε τοῦ ἰδίου υἱοῦ οὐκ ἐφείσατο, ἀλλὰ ὑπὲρ ἡμῶν πάντων παρέδωκεν αὐτόν, πῶς οὐχὶ καὶ σὺν αὐτῷ τὰ πάντα ἡμῖν χαρίσεται;

*"He who did not spare his own Son but gave him up for us all, will he not also give us all things with him?"* . . . RSV

ὅς (nom.sing.masc.of ὅς, relative pronoun, subject of ἐφείσατο and παρέδωκεν) 65.

γε (emphatic particle) 2449.

τοῦ (gen.sing.masc.of the article in agreement with υἱοῦ) 9.

ἰδίου (gen.sing.masc.of ἴδιος, in agreement with υἱοῦ) 778.

υἱοῦ (gen.sing.masc.of υἱός, objective genitive) 5.

οὐκ (negative conjunction with the indicative) 130.

ἐφείσατο (3d.per.sing.aor.mid.ind.of φείδομαι, culminative) 3533.

ἀλλὰ (alternative conjunction) 342.

ὑπὲρ (preposition with the ablative "in behalf of") 545.

ἡμῶν (abl.pl.masc.of ἐγώ, "in behalf of") 123.

πάντων (abl.pl.masc.of πᾶς, in agreement with ἡμῶν) 67.

παρέδωκεν (3d.per.sing.aor.act.ind.of παραδίδωμι, culminative) 368.

αὐτόν (acc.sing.masc.of αὐτός, direct object of παρέδωκεν) 16.

πῶς (interrogative adverb) 627.

οὐχὶ (negative conjunction with the indicative) 130.

καὶ (adjunctive conjunction joining verbs) 14.

σὺν (preposition with the instrumental, association) 1542.

αὐτῷ (instru.sing.masc.of αὐτός, association) 16.

τὰ (acc.pl.neut.of the article in agreement with πάντα) 9.

πάντα (acc.pl.neut.of πᾶς, direct object of χαρίσεται) 67.

ἡμῖν (dat.pl.masc.of ἐγώ, indirect object of χαρίσεται) 123.

χαρίσεται (3d.per.sing.fut.mid.ind.of χαρίζομαι, deliberative) 2158.

*Translation* - *"In view of the fact that He did not even spare His own Son, but in behalf of all of us delivered Him to death, why should He not also by Him freely give us everything?"*

**Comment:** The relative clause ὅς . . . αὐτόν is causal. The antecedent of ὅς is omitted, because it is made clear by the context. *Cf.* John 4:18; Luke 9:36 and Heb.5:7 for other examples. "Sometimes an antecedent is introduced which from the viewpoint of the English idiom seems superfluous (Mk.1:7). It is, however, perfectly good Greek, as may be seen from the history of the matter presented by R.722. While 'in ancient Greek it was a very rare "usage" (*ibid.*), yet it was used there, and all the way down through all the periods of the Greek language, and has "in modern Greek become very common" (R.723). So, this *pleaonastic antecedent* is perfectly normal Greek, though awkard to English eyes (cf. further Rev.7:2). (Mantey, *Manual,* 126,127). In our verse the ὅς clause "denotes the grounds for the assertion in the main clause" (*Ibid.,* 272). Paul's reason for insisting that God is going to give us everything through Jesus is that He had already sacrificed His own Son in our behalf. The price which the Trinity paid for our redemption was so great, as the Father turned His back upon His Son, Who suffered the agonies of the damned on the cross, that the sovereign God would not have entered into the covenant of redemption and He would not have gone through with it, if there had been any doubt that the result which He planned was not forthcoming. "If righteousness come by the law" (or in any other way) "then Christ is dead in vain" (Gal.2:21). *Cf.* Rom.5:6-11.

*Verse 33* - *"Who shall lay anything to the charge of God's elect? It is God that justifieth."*

τίς ἐγκαλέσει κατὰ ἐκλεκτῶν θεοῦ; θεὸς ὁ δικαιῶν.

*"Who shall bring any charge against God's elect? It is God who justifies;"* . . .
                                                                            RSV

τίς (nom.sing.masc.of τίς, interrogative pronoun, subject of ἐγκαλέσει) 281.
ἐγκαλέσει (3d.per.sing.fut.act.ind.of ἐγκαλέω, deliberative) 3495.
κατὰ (preposition with the genitive, opposition) 98.
ἐκλεκτῶν (gen.pl.masc.of ἐκλεκτός, opposition) 1412.
θεοῦ (gen.sing.masc.of θεός, relationship) 124.
θεὸς (nom.sing.masc.of θεός, predicate nominative, emphatic) 124.
ὁ (nom.sing.masc.of the article in agreement with δικαιῶν) 9.
δικαιῶν (pres.act.part.nom.sing.masc.of δικαιόω, substantival, subject of ἔστιν understood) 933.

*Translation* - *"Who is going to indict God's elect? The Justifier is God."*

**Comment:** It is stupid to bring one of God's elect into God's court, where God the Judge (John 5:22) sits to hear the case, since the Judge has already declared the defendant not guilty. The double jeopardy principle forbids any further condemnation. Romans 8:1.

*Verse 34* - *"Who is he that condemneth? It is Christ that died, yea, rather that is* risen again, who is even at the right hand of God, who also maketh intercession for us."

τίς ὁ κατακρινῶν; Χριστὸς (Ἰησοῦς) ὁ ἀποθανών, μᾶλλον δὲ ἐγερθείς, ὅς καὶ ἐστιν ἐν δεξιᾷ τοῦ θεοῦ, ὅς καὶ ἐντυγχάνει ὑπὲρ ἡμῶν.

"*Who is he to condemn? Is it Christ Jesus, who died, yes, who was raised from the dead, who is at the right hand of God, who indeed intercedes for us?*" ... RSV

τίς (nom.sing.masc.of τίς, interrogative pronoun, predicate nominative) 281.

ὁ (nom.sing.masc.of the article in agreement with κατακρινῶν) 9.

κατακρινῶν (fut.act.part.nom.sing.masc.of κατακρίνω, subject of verb understood, deliberative) 1012.

Χριστὸς (nom.sing.masc.of Χριστός, predicate nominative) 4.

(Ἰησοῦς) (nom.sing.masc.of Ἰησοῦς, apposition) 3.

ὁ (nom.sing.masc.of the article in agreement with ἀποθανών) 9.

ἀποθανών (aor.act.part.nom.sing.masc.of ἀποθνήσκω, substantival, subject of ἐστιν understood) 774.

μᾶλλον (adverbial) 619.

δὲ (emphatic conjunction) 11.

ἐγερθείς (aor.pass.part.nom.sing.masc.of ἐγείρω, substantival, subject of ἐστιν understood) 125.

ὅς (nom.sing.masc.of ὅς, relative pronoun, subject of ἐστιν, adjectival relative clause) 65.

καὶ (ascensive conjunction) 14.

ἐστιν (3d.per.sing.pres.ind.of εἰμί, aoristic) 86.

ἐν (preposition with the locative of place) 80.

δεξιᾷ (loc.sing.fem.of δεξιός, place) 502.

τοῦ (gen.sing.masc.of the article in agreement with θεοῦ) 9.

θεοῦ (gen.sing.masc.of θεός, place description) 124.

ὅς (nom.sing.masc.of ὅς, relative pronoun, adjectival, subject of ἐντυγχάνει) 65.

καὶ (adjunctive conjunction joining verbs) 14.

ἐντυγχάνει (3d.per.sing.pres.act.ind.of ἐντυγχάνω, present progressive retroactive) 3649.

ὑπὲρ (preposition with the ablative, "in behalf of") 545.

ἡμῶν (abl.pl.masc.of ἐγώ, "in behalf of") 123.

*Translation* - "*Who is the one who will condemn? The One Who has died is Christ Jesus, rather the One Who was raised from the dead, Who is even at God's right hand, Who also has been interceding for us.*"

**Comment:** There is growing asperity in Paul's argument. The rhetoricians call it *epidiorthosis*. The challenge is - "Who will rise in the court of heaven to condemn?" The future in κατακρινῶν is futuristic, not volitional. Not Christ Jesus, because He is the one who died. Note that Χριστὸς Ἰησοῦς, the predicate nominative is in emphasis, by virtue of its position ahead of the subject, ὁ ἀποθανών. The substantive with the article is the subject; the substantive without the article is the predicate nominative. In oral translation we bring out the emphasis with the voice stress - in this case on Χριστὸς Ἰησοῦς. We have the same principle in John 1:1 - καὶ θεὸς ἦν ὁ λόγος, which translates "and the Word was *GOD*" not "the Word was *a* God." There John is emphasizing the essential deity of the Word. In Romans 8:34, Paul is emphasizing that the One who died was CHRIST JESUS.

But that is not all we can say about Him. He was raised from the dead and He is even (ascensive καὶ) sitting at the right hand of God where He has been interceding for us (present progressive retroactive in ἐντυγχάνει). Here the text provides the antecedent for the relative pronouns. Who was raised from the dead? Who sits at the Father's right hand? Who intercedes for us? It is Christ Jesus. So how can He condemn us? He has already declared that we are righteous by virtue of the imputation of His righteousness (verse 33). To condemn us now would be to repudiate everything He has ever done for us - His death, His resurrection, His ascension, His intercession at the Father's right hand. Would a crucified, dead, buried, risen, and ascended substitute who has since His arrival back at the right hand of God, been pleading the efficacy of His shed blood, condemn the very people for whom all of this redemptive work was done? *Cf.* Heb.7:25 and Rom.8:27. With both Christ, the Son of God and the Holy Spirit interceding with the Father in behalf of, not against, the believer, who would dare to condemn? These are hard questions for the Arminians.

Paul has not said anything recently about the fact that God loves us. He mentioned that some believers love God (Rom.8:28). God has exercised His sovereign power in decrees of predestination, calling, justification and glorification. The objective side of the picture has been made clear. There is no condemnation before the Judge for the believer because the legal problem has been solved in His death. God the Father concurred in what happened when Jesus died, as He raised Him from the dead (Rom.4:25).

Now Paul speaks of the love of God and declares that it is so steadfast that nothing can separate the believer from it. This is the thought in the remainder of the chapter.

*Verse 35 - "Who shall separate us from the love of God? Shall tribulation, or distress, or persecution, or famine, or nakedness, or peril, or sword?"*

τίς ἡμᾶς χωρίσει ἀπὸ τῆς ἀγάπης τοῦ Χριστοῦ; θλῖψις ἢ στενοχωρία ἢ διωγμὸς ἢ λιμὸς ἢ γυμνότης ἢ κίνδυνος ἢ μάχαιρα;

*"Who shall separate us from the love of Christ? Shall tribulation, or distress, or persecution, or famine, or nakedness, or peril, or sword?"* . . . *RSV*

τίς (nom.sing.masc.of τίς, interrogative pronoun, subject of χωρίσει, deliberative) 281.

ἡμᾶς (acc.pl.masc.of ἐγώ, direct object of χωρίσει) 123.

χωρίσει (3d.per.sing.fut.act.ind.of χωρίζω, deliberative) 1291.

ἀπὸ (preposition with the ablative of separation) 70.

τῆς (abl.sing.fem.of the article in agreement with ἀγάπης) 9.
ἀγάπης (abl.sing.fem.of ἀγάπη, separation) 1490.
τοῦ (gen.sing.masc.of the article in agreement with Χριστοῦ) 9.
Χριστοῦ (gen.sing.masc.of Χριστός, possession) 4.
θλῖφις (nom.sing.fem.of θλῖφσις, subject of χωρίσει, as are all of the nouns which follow in the sentence) 1046.
ἤ (disjunctive) 465.
στενοχωρία (nom.sing.fem.of στενοχωρία) 3838.
ἤ (disjunctivie) 465.
διωγμὸς (nom.sing.masc.of διωγμός) 1047.
ἤ (disjunctive) 465.
λιμὸς (nom.sing.masc.of λιμός) 1485.
ἤ (disjunctive) 465.

#3951 γυμνότης (nom.sing.masc.of γυμνότης).

King James Version

nakedness - Rom.8:35; 2 Cor.11:27; Rev.3:18.

Revised Standard Version

nakedness - Rom.8:35; Rev.3:18.
exposure - 2 Cor.11:27.

*Meaning: Cf.γυμνός* (#1548). Lack of clothing; nakedness - Rom.8:35; 2 Cor.11:27. In a figurative sense, a lack of the righteousness of Christ, hence, spiritual nakedness - Rev.3:18.

ἤ (disjunctive) 465.

#3952 κίνδυνος (nom.sing.masc.of κίνδυνος).

King James Version

peril - Rom.8:35; 2 Cor.11:26,26,26,26,26,26,26,26.

Revised Standard Version

peril - Rom.8:35.
danger - 2 Cor.11:26,26,26,26,26,26,26,26.

*Meaning:* danger; peril. Generally in a physical sense - Rom.8:35 (absolutely); followed by an  ablative of source in 2 Cor.11:26 (8 times).

ἤ (disjunctive) 465.
μάχαιρα (nom.sing.fem.of μάχαιρα) 896.

*Translation - "Who shall separate us from the love of Christ? Tribulation or distress or persecution or famine or nakedness or peril or sword?"*

**Comment:** χωρίσει is futuristic, not volitive. Paul is looking into the future for something influential enough to separate the believer's from Christ's love. It is a rhetorical question. The list in intended to be all inclusive.

At all times, regardless of the circumstances that surround the believer upon the earth, he is the object of the advocacy of Christ, our High Priest, Who can be touched with the feelings of our infirmities (Heb.4:15). He also is the object of the prayers of the Holy Spirit (Rom.8:26). Thus when the rain descends, the floods come and the winds blow and fall near unto the house it does not fall because it is founded upon a rock (Mt.7:25). *Cf.* our comment on Mt.7:24-27 with special attention to the difference between προσπίπτω (#699) and προσκόπτω (#352). The Christian is only a sojourner upon earth where the tribulations are. His real life if "hid with Christ in God" (Col.3:3) Who is "far above all principality, and power, and might, and dominion, and every name that is named . . . " (Eph.1:21). How, then could earthly tribulations separate us from the love of Christ?

*Verse 36 - "As it is written, For thy sake we are killed all the day long; we are accounted as sheep for the slaughter."*

καθὼς γέγραπται ὅτι Ἕνεκεν σοῦ θανατούμεθα ὅλην τὴν ἡμέραν, ἐλογίσθημεν ὡς πρόβατα σφαγῆς.

*"As it is written, 'For thy sake we are being killed all the day long; we are regarded as sheep to be slaughtered.'" . . . RSV*

καθὼς (particle introducing a comparative clause) 1348.
γέγραπται (3d.per.sing.perf.pass.ind.of γράφω, intensive) 156.
ὅτι (recitative) 211.
Ἕνεκεν (improper preposition with the genitive) 435.
σοῦ (gen.sing.masc.of σύ, reference) 104.
θανατούμεθα (1st.per.pl.pres.pass.ind.of θανατόω, present progressive retroactive) 879.
ὅλην (acc.sing.fem.of ὅλος, in agreement with ἡμέραν) 112.
τὴν (acc.sing.fem.of the article in agreement with ἡμέραν) 9.
ἡμέραν (acc.sing.fem.of ἡμέρα, time extent) 135.
ἐλογίσθημεν (1st.per.pl.1st.aor.pass.ind.of λογίζομαι, culminative) 2611.
ὡς (particle introducing a comparative clause) 128.
πρόβατα (nom.pl.neut.of πρόβατον, predicate nominative) 671.
σφαγῆς (gen.sing.fem.of σφαγή, description) 3175.

*Translation - "According to what has been written, 'For your sake we have been made subject to death throughout the entire day; we have been considered to be slaughter sheep."*

**Comment:** The quotation is from Psalm 44:22. Note #1348 for καθώς when joined to γέγραπται and followed by recitative ὅτι. ἕνεκεν, the improper preposition with the genitive. θανατούμεθα describes the condition of the Christian at all times. ἐλογίσθημεν ὡς πρόβατα σφαγῆς is epexegetic. Paul means that the world has already mind up its evil mind about Christians and has assigned them to a fitting category as (ὡς and the comparative clause) though we were sheep to be slaughtered - very much as an army general might regard a company of infantry as expendable or a football coach who uses his least capable players as scrimmage fodder. Paul's argument is that since Christians are already marked for death at the hands of the unsaved world, what can the misfortunes listed in verse 35 do more?

On the contrary, they are blessings in disguise.

*Verse 37 - "Nay, in all these things we are more than conquerors through him that loved us."*

ἀλλ' ἐν τούτοις πᾶσιν ὑπερνικῶμεν διὰ τοῦ ἀγαπήσαντος ἡμᾶς.

*"No, in all these things we are more than conquerors through him who loved us." . . . RSV*

ἀλλ' (alternative conjunction) 342.
ἐν (preposition with the locative of sphere) 80.
τούτοις (loc.pl.neut.of οὗτος, sphere) 93.
πᾶσιν (loc.pl.neut.of πᾶς, in agreement with τούτοις) 67.

#3953 ὑπερνικῶμεν (1st.per.pl.pres.act.ind.of ὑπερνικάω, present progressive retroactive).

King James Version

be more than conquerors - Rom.8:37.

Revised Standard Version

more than conquerors - Rom.8:37.

*Meaning:* A combination of ὑπέρ (#545) and νικάω (#2454). To gain a victory as a result of which the final status is better than before the conflict. The army is more than a conqueror if, after being attacked and driven from previously held territory, it counterattacks, regains the lost territory, drives the aggressor from the field, invades his territory and forces a peace settlement on the basis of *uti possidetis*. This means that the new political boundaries are the same as the battle lines at the close of conflict. If the victorious army settled for *status quo ante bellum*, it would be a conqueror, but a *uti possidetis* peace treaty makes the winner "more than conqueror." So the Christian, subjected to the "misfortunes" of verse 36 finds, in keeping with Romans 8:28 that these trials are really blessings in disguise, since as a result he is ὁ ὑπερνικωμῶν - Thus 1 Thess.5:16-18; Phil.4:4; James 1:2; Rom.5:1-5.

διὰ (preposition with the ablative of agent) 118.
τοῦ (abl.sing.masc.of the article in agreement with ἀγαπήσαντος) 9.
ἀγαπήσαντος (aor.act.part.abl.sing.masc.of ἀγαπάω, substantival, agent) 540.

ἡμᾶς (acc.pl.masc.of ἐγώ, direct object of ἀγαπήσαντος) 123.

*Translation - "On the contrary, in the midst of all these things we are super-victorious through Him Who has loved us."*

**Comment:** One of Christ's functions in intercession (Rom.8:34) is to answer the Holy Spirit's prayer for us (Rom.8:26), when we groan as we try to be patient (Rom.8:23-25). Thus we go through the sequences of Romans 5:3-5 and, as a result, we are the better for the experience. It is in these times that the love of God is shed abroad in our hearts. It is tribulation that begins the sequence of Romans 5:1-5. Thus 2 Cor.2:14.

If the unsaved world could only understand this great principle it would serve its hellish purpose better by leaving the Christian alone, or even perhaps, making his path a little smoother. By making the Christian comfortable, prosperous and honored, his spiritual downfall might be accomplished. As it is, every injury inflicted upon the child of God is a highway to greater Christian victory. The supreme insult comes when the Christian is martyred. He then achieves his greatst honor (Rev.12:11).

*Verse 38 - "For I am persuaded, that neither death, nor life, nor angels, nor principalities, nor powers, nor things present, nor things to come . . . "*

πέπεισμαι γὰρ ὅτι οὔτε θάνατος οὔτε ζωὴ οὔτε ἄγγελοι οὔτε ἀρχαὶ οὔτε ἐνεστῶτα οὔτε μέλλοντα οὔτε δυνάμεις . . .

*"For I am sure that neither death, nor life, nor angels, nor principalities, nor things present, nor things to come, nor powers, . . . " RSV*

πέπεισμαι (1st.per.sing.perf.pass.ind.of πείθω, intensive) 1629.
γὰρ (inferential conjunction) 105.
ὅτι (conjunction introducing an object clause in indirect discourse) 211.
οὔτε (negative copulative conjunction) 598.
θάνατος (nom.sing.masc.of θάνατος - all nominative substantives in verses 38,39 are subjects of δυνήσεται in verse 39) 381.
οὔτε (negative copulative conjunction) 598.
ζωὴ (nom.sing.fem.of ζωή) 668.
οὔτε (negative copulative conjunction) 598.
ἄγγελοι (nom.pl.masc.of ἄγγελος) 96.
οὔτε (negative copulative conjunction) 598.
ἀρχαὶ (nom.pl.fem.of ἀρχή) 1285.
οὔτε (negative copulative conjunction) 598.

#3954 ἐνεστῶτα (perf.act.part.nom.pl.neut.of ἐνίστημι, substantival).

    King James Version

be at hand - 2 Thess.2:2.
come - 2 Tim.3:1.
present - 1 Cor.7:26; Gal.1:4; Heb.9:9.
things present - Rom.8:38; 1 Cor.3:22.

Revised Standard Version

things present - Rom.8:38.
present - 1 Cor.3:22; Gal.1:4; Heb.9:9.
impending - 1 Cor.7:26.
will come - 2 Tim.3:1.
has come - 2 Thess.2:2.

*Meaning:* A combination of ἐν (#80) and ἵστημι (#180). Hence, to stand or be in and with. To be present, in a temporal sense, as opposed to μέλλοντα (future events) - Rom.8:38; 1 Cor.3:22; the current situation - 1 Cor.7:26; Gal.1:4; Heb.9:9; 2 Thess.2:2. In the future, certain events will be at that future time, present - 2 Tim.3:1.

οὔτε (negative copulative conjunction) 598.
μέλλοντα (pres.act.part.nom.pl.neut.of μέλλω, substantival) 206.
οὔτε (negative copulative conjunction) 598.
δυνάμεις (nom.pl.fem.of δύναμις) 687.

*Translation - "Therefore I have become convinced that neither death nor life nor angels nor dictators nor thing present nor things in the future nor powers ... "*

**Comment:** γὰρ is inferential. Paul is about to speak out of his own experiences, which explains the magnificent eloquence of verses 31-39. The perfect tense in πέπεισμαι points both to the past experiences of learning and to the present conviction to which they have led. Hence our translation takes note both of the preterite punctiliar fact and the present intensive force. "Having learned from past experience, I now am sure that . . . κ.τ.λ." The disjunctive οὔτε ties together all of the various unlike forces, none of which (verse 39) will be able to separate the believer from God's love. Note the opposites - θάνατος and ζωή -if it is not alive or dead, what is it? Note the various types of power and influence - ἄγγελοι, ἀρχαί and δυνάμεις. Chronological periods are mentioned - things which happened in the past which are still in existence (perf.participle in ἐνεστῶτα) and things in the future (μέλλοντα). We need not worry about what is past. If what is future cannot separate us from God's love, then there is no need for worry. If it is neither dead nor alive, neither a heavenly nor an earthly power, neither spiritual nor earthly, neither past, present nor future, then what is it? We still might be concerned about that which is high or low or about the devil himself. Therefore Paul takes care of these in

*Verse 39 - "Nor height, nor depth, nor any other creature, shall be able to separate us from the love of God, which is in Christ Jesus our Lord."*

οὔτε ὕφωμα οὔτε βάθος οὔτε τις κρίσις ἑτέρα δυνήσεται ἡμᾶς χωρίσαι ἀπὸ τῆς ἀγάπης τοῦ θεοῦ τῆς ἐν Χριστῷ Ἰησοῦ τῷ κυρίῳ ὑμῶν.

" . . . *nor height, nor depth, nor anything else in all creation, will be able to separate us from the love of God in Christ Jesus our Lord."* . . . RSV

οὔτε (negative copulative conjunction) 598.

#3955 ὕφωμα (nom.sing.neut.of ὕφωμα).

King James Version

height - Rom.8:39.
high thing - 2 Cor.10:5.

Revised Standard Version

height - Rom.8:39.
proud obstacle - 2 Cor.10:5.

*Meaning: Cf.* ὑφόω (#946) plus μα the result suffix. Hence high thing. Generally as opposed to βάθος (Rom.8:39). Figuratively, in comparison to a high battlement used in military attack, with reference to academic sophistication, falsely so-called that prates about its atheism - 2 Cor.10:5.

οὔτε (negative copulative conjunction) 598.
βάθος (nom.sing.neut.of βάθος) 1031.
οὔτε (negative copulative conjunction) 598.
τις (nom.sing.fem.of τις, indefinite pronoun, in agreement with κτίσις) 486.
κτίσις (nom.sing.fem.of κτίσις) 2633.
ἑτέρα (nom.sing.fem.of ἕτερος, in agreement with κτίσις) 605.
δυνήσεται (3d.per.sing.fut.mid.ind.of δύναμαι, predictive) 289.
ἡμᾶς (acc.pl.masc.of ἐγώ, direct object of χωρίσαι) 123.
χωρίσαι (aor.act.inf.of χωρίζω, complementary) 1291.
ἀπό (preposition with the ablative of separation) 70.
τῆς (abl.sing.fem.of the article in agreement with ἀγάπης) 9.
ἀγάπης (abl.sing.fem.of ἀγάπη, separation) 1490.
τοῦ (gen.sing.masc.of the article in agreement with θεοῦ) 9.
θεοῦ (gen.sing.masc.of θεός, possession) 124.
τῆς (abl.sing.fem.of the article in agreement with ἀγάπης) 9.
ἐν (preposition with the locative of place) 80.
Χριστῷ (loc.sing.masc.of Χριστός, place) 4.
Ἰησοῦ (loc.sing.masc.of Ἰησοῦς, apposition) 3.
τῷ (loc.sing.masc.of the article in agreement with κυρίῳ) 9.
κυρίῳ (loc.sing.masc.of κύριος, place) 97.
ἡμῶν (gen.pl.masc.of ἐγώ, relationship) 123.

*Translation - ". . . nor height nor depth nor any other created thing will be able to separate us from the love of God which is in Christ Jesus our Lord."*

**Comment:** The sentence begun in verse 38 concludes in verse 39. If it is neither high nor low, what is it? And then, rather than to continue listing things which are opposite, Paul makes the all-inclusive statement - "any other created thing." It is is not a creature then it must be the Creator Himself, and He is the One Who loves us. Some may argue that Paul left Satan out of the list of things or persons capable to separating us from God's love. Not so. Satan is one of God's creatures

(Ezekial 28:15). Thus neither Satan nor anyone else will be able to separate us from God's love which we have in Christ Jesus (John 15:13; Rom.5:8; Gal.2:20; Rev.1:5).

Thus Paul's triumphant statement of total Christian victory in Christ, despite human trials, closes this most scientific statement of the plan of salvation in the New Testament (Romans 1:18-8:39).

The Apostle turns now, in chapters 9-11 to the relationship of Israel to God's eternal plan of the ages.

# INDEX